THE
ESOTERIC
TRADITION

VOLUME I

THE
ESOTERIC
TRADITION

G. de Purucker

VOLUME I

THEOSOPHICAL UNIVERSITY PRESS
PASADENA, CALIFORNIA

THEOSOPHICAL UNIVERSITY PRESS
PASADENA, CALIFORNIA

Copyright by G. de Purucker, 1935
Second Edition, 1940
Reprinted from the Second Edition, 1973

Library of Congress Catalog Card Number 73-81738

PRINTED IN THE UNITED STATES

To those who have bestowed the Priceless,
who have given immeasurably,
and to their Sublime Cause,
these volumes are offered with measureless
reverence and devotion.

TO THE READER*

THE writing of these volumes has not been an easy task, and this for a number of reasons, first and foremost among which has been the lack of leisure-hours to devote to it. Dictation proceeded from the first page to the last in a hurry and often at high speed, for it was the only way of producing this work within a reasonable time after its forthcoming publication had first been mentioned by the author in the summer of 1934. Had time been taken to prepare the manuscript in a manner pleasing to the author himself and his co-workers, its appearance might have been delayed for a year or two, or possibly longer. In that event the author would have been able to follow the most excellent advice offered by the genial Horace, the Latin poet, in his *Satires*, I, x, 73: *Saepe stilum vertas, iterum quae digna legi sint scripturus.* However, here has been no time to "reverse the pencil" for the purpose of erasing, nor has there been any leisure for revision and for the polishing of phrases.

It is due in large part to the devotion and enthusiasm of a number of friends and students attached to the different departments at the International Theosophical Headquarters at Point Loma, that THE ESOTERIC TRADITION now at last is given to its readers. To Dr. Joseph H. Fussell, who read the proof-sheets and offered valuable suggestions; Miss Helen Savage, who did the secretarial work; Mrs. Hazel Minot, responsible for checking and verifying of quotations; Mrs. Guy Ponsonby and Mr. S. Hecht, who prepared the copious index; Miss Elizabeth Schenck, Miss Grace Knoche, and Mr. W. E. Small, who read proof: to these and to all others who have helped in any way whatsoever to forward the publication of this book, the author gives his grateful thanks.

Special mention should be made of the Theosophical University Press, where everyone, the Manager and the Assistant Manager and all others composing the staff, co-operated to devote what time could be set aside from the regular issuing of our various magazines and other routine press-work, to the composition and later printing of these volumes.

As regards a number of citations appearing in this work and taken from books written in languages other than English, mostly

---

*Reprinted from the First Edition.

in ancient tongues, it may be as well to say that wherever possible the author has used standard or popular translations, but in certain cases where he felt better satisfied with his own renderings, he has done the work of translation himself.

One cannot too often repeat what H. P. Blavatsky pointed out in her 'Introductory' to *The Secret Doctrine,* Vol. I, p. xix:

It is above everything important to keep in mind that no theosophical book acquires the least additional value from pretended authority.

Every Theosophical book must stand on its own ground of merit, and if it have demerit greater than its merit, by that demerit it will fall — and the sooner it falls the better for all concerned. The present writer feels this fact very strongly in connexion with these volumes, his own latest contribution to Theosophical literature; and, although they are for him and his co-workers a labor of pure theosophical devotion and love, he not only expects but desires that these volumes shall speak solely for themselves, and shall stand upon their own grounds of appeal. What is good in them will endure: if there is anything that is not good, let it perish and perish rapidly.

Works like this present literary venture are badly needed in the world today. The dissemination of Theosophical thought among men can be aided greatly by new presentations of the age-old verities preserved by the Masters of Wisdom and of Compassion from immemorial ages in the past.

One is reminded in this connexion of an important letter written by the Master Kuthumi, dated December 10, 1880, and found in the memorable volume entitled *The Mahatma Letters to A. P. Sinnett,* transcribed and compiled by A. T. Barker. The following extract from this letter is found on pages 23 and 24, as changed, however, by the exalted writer's own corrections to be found on pages 425 and 426 of the same book:

The truths and mysteries of occultism constitute, indeed, a body of the highest spiritual importance, at once profound and practical for the world at large. Yet, it is not as a mere addition to the tangled mass of theory or speculation in the world of science that they are being given to you, but for their practical bearing on the interests of mankind. The terms "unscientific," "impossible," "hallucination," "impostor," have hitherto been used in a very loose, careless way, as implying in the occult phenomena something either mysterious and abnormal, or a premeditated imposture. And this is why our chiefs have determined to shed upon a few recipient minds more light upon the subject, ...

The wiseacres say: "The age of miracles is past," but we answer, "it never existed!" . . . [These truths] *have* to prove both destructive and constructive — *destructive* in the pernicious errors of the past, in the old creeds and superstitions which suffocate in their poisonous embrace like the Mexican weed nigh all mankind; but *constructive* of new institutions of a genuine, practical Brotherhood of Humanity where all will become co-workers of nature, will work for the good of mankind *with* and *through* the higher *planetary Spirits* — the only "Spirits" we believe in.* Phenomenal elements previously unthought of, . . . will disclose at last the secrets of their mysterious workings. Plato was right *to readmit every element of speculation which Socrates had discarded. The problems of universal being are not unattainable or worthless if attained.* . . . "Ideas rule the world"; and as men's minds receive new ideas, laying aside the old and effete the world (*will*) advance; mighty revolutions (*will*) spring from them; *institutions* (*aye, and even* creeds and powers, *they may add*) — WILL crumble before their onward march. . . . It will be just as impossible to resist their influence when the time comes as to stay the progress of the tide. . . . *all this* will come gradually on; and . . . before it comes *they as well as ourselves,* have all a duty *to perform, a task* set before us: that of sweeping away as much as possible the dross left to us by our pious forefathers. New ideas have to be planted on clean places, for these ideas touch upon the most momentous subjects. It is not physical phenomena . . . but these universal ideas that we *have precisely to* study: *the noumenon not the phenomenon,* for, to comprehend the LATTER we have first to understand the FORMER. They *do* touch man's true position in the Universe, . . . *It is not physical phenomena however wonderful that can ever explain to man* his origin *let alone* his ultimate destiny, . . . — the relation of the mortal to the immortal, of the temporary to the eternal, of the finite to the Infinite, *etc., etc.*

Verily, it is these "universal ideas" that all should study, and which by their influence over human minds will bring about the change in human consciousness that all true Theosophists work for and aspire towards, thus helping in the bringing about of that which the Theosophical Society was originally founded in 1875 to introduce.

Let it be remembered that there exists a universal and really infallible test or touchstone by which any new increments of Theosophical teaching may be tried, and this test or touchstone is UNIVERSALITY. Universality here is equivalent to spirituality; and any teaching which can be proved to be universal, in the sense of being accordant with and in concord with all other great teachings of the past — or of the present — has high probability of being a true Theosophical verity; and contrariwise, any teaching which cannot be proved to be inherent in and a part of the great deliveries of Theo-

---

*From here on the italics represent the 'corrections' above referred to.

sophical truths in the past, may by the same token be safely rejected as being new in the sense of different and more or less spurious, because failing to withstand successfully the test just mentioned.

In the future, it is the present writer's hope, if he can find the time and strength so to do, to publish another volume or two containing Theosophical teaching which up to the present time has been kept strictly private. The reason for this decision is the great, indeed enormous, advance in thought that has taken place since the days when H. P. Blavatsky labored in her Herculean fashion to break what she called the "molds of mind." What then was esoteric, at least in certain measure — esoteric simply because it was truly impossible then to state it openly, for it infallibly would have been misunderstood and misused — would in moderate degree be understood today by the more awakened intelligence of modern men; and the consequent larger measure of generous receptivity to new ideas has created an entirely different and indeed fallow field of consciousness, in which it has become the duty of Theosophists to plant seeds of truth. We shall see.

Meanwhile, the two volumes of the present work go to the reading public, whose verdict upon them the author will await with feelings composite of a sense of humor and a great deal of human interest. Nothing in either volume is the offspring of his own brain. His position in this respect is precisely identical with that of every Theosophical writer who is a true Theosophist at heart and who knows what he writes about: *Iti mayâ śrutam* — "Thus have I heard." "I pass on what has been given to me and in the manner in which I have received it. Not otherwise." Hence the author refuses to clothe himself in the skin of an ass, or — in that of a lion!

G. DE P.

CONTENTS OF VOLUME I

Globe-bodies and planes. 'Conservation of energy.' Who are the Kosmo-kratores? The Moon and moons. Reimbodiment of globe-chain. Entire Solar System interblended and interactive. Modern astrology and the ancient Wisdom-Astrology. Captures, galactic and electronic. Classes of Monadic Life-Waves. Kosmic Space, Hierarchs, and Wondrous Beings. Archaic Pantheism. Christian God and the Unknowable Principle. Space a container of Divine Atoms.

CHAPTER VII

Evolution and Revolution. No absolute endings in evolution. 'Soul' and souls explained. Evolution and emanation: an analysis. Infinite hosts of souls: numerous illustrations. What are 'group-souls' and what constitutes 'grouping'? Enduring Consciousness and fugitive 'events.' The eternal and the evanescent in all beings. What is immortality? The 'losing' of the self in the SELF. 'As a man thinks, so is he.' The difference between man and beast. Solomon and *Ecclesiastes*. Man, a microcosm in the Macrocosm is yet One with the All.

CHAPTER VIII

The four planes of Universal Being. Nature and evolution of elementals defined. Man his own architect. Our source and the origin of our life-atoms. Dual aspect of life-atoms. One Law but countless ramifications of detail and repetition. The heresy of Separateness. The rûpa-planes and the Sephîrôth of the Qabbâlâh. Every being a well-spring of 'creative' activity. What part of an ever-changing entity endures? Monadic generation of elementals continuous. Climbing the Ladder of Life.

CHAPTER IX

Monadism and Atomism: the essential carpentry of the manifested Universe. Druidic and other ancient teachings. Self-expression eternal and universal. Evolution and involution. Possibility of understanding states of consciousness during pralaya of a planetary chain or solar system. The Garden of Eden, and Man a 'fallen angel,' theosophically explained. The War in Heaven. Teleologic element in evolution and the evils of Darwinism. The great evolutionary Drama of Life. The Rivers of Lives and geologic Ages in the light of Theosophy. Evolution entirely a spiritual process.

CHAPTER X

H. P. Blavatsky, *The Secret Doctrine,* and Esoteric Evolution. Teachings of modern science, and the difficulties of expounding the Wisdom-teachings. Human development during past ages. Whence came the beasts and reptiles? Man, his physical structure during the First and Second Races, and physical modes of propagation. The human embryo and its prenatal development in relation to physical structure of early Man. Androgyne and uni-sexual development. Evolution and involution and the 'closing of the door' into the Human Kingdom. What are the anthropoid apes? Destiny of the beasts. Emanation of Mammalia from the human stock. What is a 'type'? Time periods, geologic ages, and radioactivity. Specialization. Spiritual, intellectual, and psycho-mental evolution. Consolidation and size of early root-race types. Man, a vast treasury. Embryology, the touchstone. Geological remains.

CHAPTER XI

Civilization and civilizations. Periods of transition illustrated by time of downfall of the Roman Empire. Divination, soothsayers, etc., then and now. Oracles and the Wisdom of the Ages. The closing of the Mystery-Schools and the age of spiritual barrenness in the Occident. Astronomical teachings of early Mesopotamia. Claudius Ptolemy and his legacy to the Dark Ages. Graeco-Roman world the alembic of religions and philosophies two thousand years ago. Pioneers of the Renaissance: their interpretations of Truth and the reception they received. The significance of the founding of the Theosophical Society. Mutability of Science and permanence of the Ancient Wisdom. The scientific attitude fifty years ago and now.

Intellectual conditions of 1875. H. P. Blavatsky, her life-work, the Message she brought, and her Teachers. Responsibility of the Sages and Seers, and the 'law' of Karman. The quickening of Science, Philosophy, and Religion. The Atomistic School of the Greeks and its influence on Newton and Huxley. 'Modes of Motion,' 'absolute time,' and 'absolute space.' Einstein's 'space-time continuum.' Relativity and Mâyâ. Seven points wherein the modern relativity-theory approaches the Esoteric Tradition. Vision versus dogmatism in Science: some examples. Modern Science becoming metaphysical and mystical. The promise of the future.

INTRODUCTION

TRUTH may be defined as that which is Reality; and present human intelligence can make but approximate advances or approaches to this Cosmic REAL which is measureless in its profundity and in its infinite reaches, and therefore never fully comprehensible by any finite intellect. It was a wise declaration, in one way, that Pontius Pilate made, as alleged, when Jesus, the great Syrian Initiate, was brought before him: "What is Truth!"; for a man who knows Truth in fulness would have an active intelligence commensurate with the Universe: and whose intelligence is universe-wide?

There are, however, relative truths, and it is relative truth that the human mind can comprehend and therefore can understand. In and by this reflexion we immediately cut away the ground from any assertion that the Theosophical Philosophy teaches dogmas, meaning by the term 'dogma' an unreasoning, blind, and obedient assent to the mere voice of authority — which is something that is inadmissible in genuine Theosophical study.

The Theosophist does not, therefore, proclaim these essentially natural truths as dogmas which one must accept, willy-nilly, if he expect to have any hope of being 'saved'! The Theosophical Philosophy admits nothing of the sort. As Theosophists our sole duty in teaching our sublime Philosophy is to present this Ancient Wisdom of the Gods in such fashion that men will be interested in it and begin to study it for themselves, and will learn to abide by the results of their own careful examination and sifting of the evidence. To those to whom the Theosophist presents his Theosophical doctrines, he says: "Here is a truth which we have tested, and we have found in it all that the heart and mind crave for. Try it. You are the judge in this case, and you must take the consequences of what you shall choose. You may err in your judgment, but the principle of self-choice and unfettered free will in choice is so sacred to us that on this point our teachings definitely tell us that it is better to be honest and true to the best in us, even if that best be imperfectly manifest, than to accept offhand or without lengthy examination the teachings of any other human being as gospel-truth; for by doing this latter you cripple your own will, weaken your own discrimination in judgment, and thus undermine the fabric and fiber of your own character."

What, then, is dogma? Dogma is a Greek word. It was originally a Greek political term, which became, through its adoption by the Christian church, a religious word, Christianly religious, having a Christian atmosphere about it and Christian meanings and consequent Christian implications, which in its original sense and usage this word dogma never had.

The word itself comes from the Greek verb δοκεῖν (dokein), 'to seem to be,' 'to appear to be.' A dogma, therefore, was something which appeared to be, or which seemed to be, a truth: an opinion about truth, if you like; and hence this term 'dogma' was frequently employed in certain ones of the Greek states as signifying the decision, the considered opinion, and therefore the final vote, arrived at and taken in a state council or assembly. It was thus used as a public ordinance or decree passed by the constituted authority in the Greek state. In Athens, however, these considered votes were called ψηφίσματα (psephismata).

Ἔδοξε τῇ ἐκκλησίᾳ — 'it appeared to the council,' i. e., to the gathering, to the assembly,— was the usual form in which such votes were recorded and quoted.

From this word ἐκκλησία (ecclesia) we have the modern word, ecclesiastical, at present meaning churchly, with an altered meaning, however, running from and through mediaeval to modern times — an entirely different meaning from its original sense, for Ecclesia in Greece meant a political convention or assembly of all the voting citizens of a Greek state.

Thus this word 'dogma' changed from its original significance, meaning a vote or the considered opinion of an assembly of Greek citizens voting in formal council upon a measure brought before them; for it came, through its adoption by the Christian Church, to mean a certain religious doctrine, a certain dogmatic tenet, supposed to represent the mere opinion of the best minds in a Christian community. Nothing more.

Having thus this first significance in Christian history, especially in the Greek Christianity of the hither Orient, this word retained this significance for a number of centuries during the early part of the Christian era, and only in later and early mediaeval times did the word 'dogma' acquire the meaning which it now commonly has, as signifying a doctrine based upon the declaration of an oecumenical council or upon an authoritative popular pronouncement, or mayhap deriving from some other widely recognised churchly or religious authority; and such authority and dogmatic sense it was finally considered by faithful Christians to be pernicious and wicked even to question.

Now, there would emphatically seem to be no such authority or inspired religious significance connected with the word 'dogma' either in very early Christianity or certainly not in the original Greek political sense; and, as stated above, it was only later in mediaeval times that the word 'dogma' included the inherent idea of some religious tenet imposed by an ecclesiastical or religious authority, by divine mandate, upon communicants.

In this modern sense of the word, then, it is abundantly obvious that Theosophy is wholly non-dogmatic: it has, in this last signification of the word 'dogma,' no dogmas whatsoever: no teaching, no doctrine, imposed as divinely authoritative upon members of the Theosophical Movement, or derivative from some individual, or body of individuals, claiming authority to tell the members of the Theosophical Movement that such or such other teaching or dictum or doctrine is truth, and that it must be accepted and believed in by those who wish to be Theosophists. The Theosophist, however, claims that the Theosophical teachings, as delivered or handed on to us by the great Masters of Wisdom, the Great Seers and Sages of the present age, have been tested by Adepts and Great Initiates through unnumbered centuries of the past, this testing being a comparison with Reality — that is to say, Spiritual Nature herself, which is the ultimate tribunal of proof, the final tribunal: because Nature, in the true Theosophical sense, is the Grand Unity, the great incomprehensible aggregate, of THINGS AND BEINGS AS THEY ARE IN THEMSELVES — Truth.

On the other hand, if we take the original meaning of the word 'dogma' as signifying an interior opinion based upon facts or mental conviction, and use it in the sense in which the early so-called 'Pagan' philosophers used it, as implying the doctrines or tenets of their respective schools: then the Theosophist would have no objection to using this word 'dogma' (or *dogmata* in the plural) as signifying one of the body corporate of Theosophical teachings. But, unfortunately, the use of the word 'dogma' in that sense would be misleading.

Theosophy, as we see from the foregoing, is utterly non-dogmatic; it is not a collection of dogmas; it is based on nobody's say-so, because it is based on Divine-Spiritual-Physical Nature herself, as interpreted by this age-old Brotherhood or Association of the Great Sages and Seers referred to. Each new generation of these Seers, as these generations succeed each other in serial line of Successors through the centuries, tests the accumulated knowledge and consequently formulated system of its Predecessors, i. e., of those who came before: the Sages of each new generation test this accumulated Wisdom and thus prove it anew; so that as time goes on, there is a continual perfecting of details, as it were.

Seers means those who *see:* who have so refined their inner nature, who have so largely brought forth into activity the spiritual faculties and powers in themselves, that this their inner spiritual nature can at their will penetrate deep into the Arcana of the Universe, go behind the veils of the outer seeming, and see; and thus seeing, these Seers can and do interpret truly. Being thus able to interpret with exquisite accuracy and fidelity, their doctrines are consistent, coherent, all hanging together most beautifully. From time to time this Brotherhood or Association of Mahâtmans or evolved Men gives forth to the world in its spiritual need new-old vistas into Nature's greatest secrets, stimulating man's ethical instincts, arousing his latent intellectual powers, and thus, in short, bringing about the constant albeit silent evolutionary urge forwards to greater and nobler highths of human achievement.

The Theosophical student and scholar thus finds it within the compass of possibility to examine these archaic and wonderfully inspiring doctrines and to test them in his turn and with his own capacities, however limited these latter may be; and thus it is that time, magic time, in its unfolding of things out of the womb of destiny, brings forth to the faithful and intelligent student abundant proofs, checked and examined at each step by himself, that the Theosophical doctrines are truths based on Universal Nature herself.

It should be added here for clearer understanding, that when the Theosophist uses the phrase 'Universal Nature' he never limits the meaning to Nature's mere physical shell which our material apparatus of sense tells us somewhat of; 'Universal Nature' to him means Nature spiritual and material with all the countless hierarchical ranges between, including worlds visible and invisible, beings divine, spiritual, intellectual, ethereal, astral, and physical.

In Webster's English Dictionary, Theosophy is defined somewhat after this wise: "A method of knowing truth and of approaching divinity through physical processes." This wholly naïve and quaint definition makes a Theosophist smile in rather grim humor.

'Physical processes,' such as scientific investigations and experiments in the laboratory, can indeed tell us something valuable of the phenomena of outer or physical Nature, and of natural events which are results of the hid and secret and mystic noumenal operations working behind the veils of Nature; but to know Truth, or a truth, infallibly, it is necessary to cultivate within oneself the seeing Spiritual Eye. Every human being has this inner Spiritual Eye. None but a congenital idiot[1] may be said to be without it. In every normal human being the spiritual nature is waiting all the time — not to be developed or evolved, but simply to have the veils enshrouding it: the mental, and the astral, and the physical veils: rent asunder or destroyed, so that the formerly ingathered supernal treasures of wisdom concerning Nature's inner realities may be poured forth into the hitherto dull and non-understanding brain. When this inpouring or inspiration happens in large or small degree, as the case may be, we have the Great Men of the world, the really inspired thinkers, the illuminated guides, the seeing leaders of mankind — the Sages and Seers.

Some may say: "I have seen this or that and I know it to be truth, and you should accept my dictum." Why? This is but one phase of the dogmatic spirit so common in the world, and it is one which no Theosophist would ever either himself permit for himself, or allow to be imposed upon himself. Never. If there is one thing that the Theosophist bases his conviction of realities upon, it is his own strictly conscientious sense of Truth eternal abiding in his own breast, and which he rarely or never communicates to others, and certainly never does so in the form of dogmatic pronouncement or asseveration. One may object: "A following of this your rule to individual guidance and vision would open the door of men's minds wide to all kinds of folly, un-wisdom, and erratic notions and beliefs sincere or insincere. An evil man might say: 'Lo, behold me a prophet. I see truth!' "

But, indeed, that is not the Theosophical idea. It runs directly counter to our idea. The man who truly KNOWS is always reticent, if not invariably silent. He never in any situation calls attention to himself as a prophet or a seer. He says to those around him: "You have within yourselves the divine touchstone, by which you may test reality. Use this; in fact, develop your own powers; and then you will see that what the Great Brotherhood tells you is indeed Truth: is indeed Reality."

---

1. Such a birth is that of one born a man indeed, yet not a complete man.

Probably not in historical times has there been such a widespread awakening in religious feeling and in general religious interests as exists today; but no longer do men quibble and quarrel and fight over mere questions of form, theological or ecclesiastical, nor over mere hair-splitting definitions of words involving doctrines. No longer do they oppose each other with such acrimonious and unbrotherly harshness in these matters as they formerly did during the Middle Ages and after. Rather is the feeling today abroad in men's hearts that there is a concealed but not unsolvable Mystery behind the veil of the outward seeming of Nature which men's minds only belittle, only bemean, in any attempt at a humanly limited and personally arbitrary description of it; and that the only way by which to acquire this reality, this truth, existing as a mystery behind the veils of the outward seeming, is to penetrate into the temple of Truth oneself — into the very heart of the Invisible. There is nothing so chastening to the aggressive, self-asserting mind, as this theosophical feeling of reverential aspiration: nothing that wipes away so quickly from men's brain-minds the feelings of egoism and of ignorant and foolish self-sufficiency of judgment. All men are able to see if they will but fit themselves for the seeing, and no man with this conviction in his heart will ever declare dogmatically: "I am the prophet of truth!"

We repeat that thus it can be seen that Theosophy is in no wise dogmatic. It teaches no dogmas at all in the modern sense of the word. Yet this does not mean that the Theosophical doctrines have no precision, have no definiteness in outline, that they are vague, mere intellectual nebulosities. Very much the contrary to this is the fact. These doctrines have been tested by every generation of great Seers and Sages, as already stated, and again tested and tested still again through unnumbered ages of past times; and as we now possess them they have all the precision of mathematics, albeit possessing a far sharper outline of definition than the latter does; and we are told clearly and with no uncertain voice that all the great Seers and Sages have come back from passing during initiation behind and beyond the veils of Universal Nature, all bringing back the same identic story, marvelous, amazing, and with the same proofs evident in their own being of what they have met with on that most glorious of Adventures comprised in the initiatory cycle.

How about proof? The Pontius Pilates of modern life are almost as numerous as are educated men; and each one, in the self-sufficiency of his own intellectual penetration and tacit belief in his own infallibility of judgment, listens to the recitation of any new natural fact or of any apparently incredible story with a final exclamation by which he thinks to prove his wisdom: "Where are your proofs?" It sounds so reasonable; but the slightest knowledge of the processes of human understanding, were that only exercised, would show to these self-wise skeptics that there is no proof outside of man himself.

As a matter of fact, what is 'proof'? Is proof something that exists outside of one? If so, how could it be understood? No; all proof lies within one's own self. When the mind is so swayed by the preponderance of evidence and testimony that it automatically assents to a proposition, then the case for that mind is proved. Another stronger mind may require stronger proof based on a larger field of more cleverly presented evidence and testimony; yet in all cases, proof is the bringing of conviction to the mind; and hence a man who cannot see the force, both internal and external, of evidence or testimony, or who sees it but feebly, will say that the proposition is not proved or insufficiently proved; and so forth. But this skeptical attitude does not disprove the proof, so to say, but merely shows that the mind in question here is incapable of receiving what to another and perhaps quicker and brighter intellect is clear enough to establish the case, and hence, to that intellect the proof is amply sufficient.

Is proof therefore infallible? Pray pause a moment over this question which so infrequently occurs even to thinking men. The answer is obvious. No. If it were then he who offers and he who accepts proof would likewise and equally be infallible. How many men have died innocent of the crime for which they were convicted in courts of law, because the evidence was apparently conclusive against them, 'proved' to the minds of the judge and jurors who tried the cases! They were condemned and the sentence duly carried out. These are cases in which the crimes were proved against innocent men; because the evidence was there and was duly submitted; there were, apparently, no missing links or lacunae in the chain of evidence, and therefore to the jurors the crimes were proved. The minds of the jurors were swayed and completely controlled by the evidence; yet in the cases alluded to, showing the fallibility of established proof, these jurors sent innocent fellow human beings to an infamous death.

Here we refer to courts of law alone because the argument there becomes clear and obvious enough; and while conviction of the innocent does indeed occur there, how much more often do the innocent suffer in the affairs of daily life! These latter cases occur with appalling frequency, even daily one might say. From what we see, from what we hear, from what we know or believe, by the working of our prejudices and in other ways, our minds are swayed, our judgment is over-ruled, our discrimination is warped, our instincts of compassion have no longer room in which to work freely, and we condemn. We feel that the case is proved; and it may be years afterwards before we finally learn that we have wrongly judged despite our sincerity and earnestness of desire to abstain from hasty and unfair conclusions. To us those cases were proved, proved to the hilt, as the saying goes, and yet we later find we were all wrong.

Let us then beware not merely of an uncharitable heart and of a biased mind, but likewise of mere 'proof' which so strongly sways both mind and heart. There is only one true guide in life, and that guide is the inner voice which grows stronger and ever more emphatic with cultivation and exercise of it, telling us: "This is true; that is false." In the beginning we hear this silent voice and recognise its clear clarion tones but faintly, and call it a 'hunch' or an intuition, which indeed it is. There is nothing except our own stupidity and the overweening consciousness we have in the righteousness of our own set opinions, which prevents us from cultivating this noblest of inner monitors more perfectly than we do. Egoism and vanity are two of the most formidable stumbling-blocks in the cultivation of these marvelous inner springs of the spirit-soul, whence streams the flow of intuition. Those springs belong to the impersonal and therefore purely unselfish part of us. Their flow which is like the quick and silent coming of light, will appear to us at first like the intimations or intuitions of the coming of a messenger, whose footsteps over the distant hilltops we may not hear at first, though inwardly we know that he is coming, coming, coming; and then finally we see the presence and recognise the intimations of the approaching truth which our inner nature gives forth to us in unceasing streams.

This is what is really meant by 'true faith.' As Paul of the Christians says: "Faith [or instinctive knowledge] is the reality of things hoped for [intuitively discerned], the evidence of things invisible."[2]

This is not blind faith. Blind faith is mere credulity, believing what one is told only because someone tells it, someone who is trusted perhaps, or perhaps because it happen to please at the moment. There is a very famous example of the working of blind

---

2. In his supposed *Epistle to the Hebrews*, chapter xi, verse 1.

faith in the writings of the fiery Church-Father, Tertullian. Inveighing against Marcion, who was a very eminent Gnostic teacher, he speaks as follows:

The only possible means that I have to prove myself impudent successfully, and a fool happily, is by my contempt of shame. For instance, I maintain that the very Son of God died; now this is a thing to be accepted, because it is a monstrous absurdity; further, I maintain that after he was buried, he rose again; and this I believe to be absolutely true because it is absolutely impossible.[3]

Declarations of this kind would have indeed no effect whatsoever on any well-balanced mind, were it not for the fact that there is in them a tacit or unspoken appeal to the contrarieties and contradictions and amazing surprises in life, all which arise merely because we are not under the beneficent and benign influence of our higher nature. Were we so, these contrarieties and contradictions which make us doubt our own reason and sanity sometimes, and all the rest of the panoply of the lower self, would never manifest at all, and such wildly illogical contradictions as those Tertullian allowed his mind to be swayed by, would have no such easy sway over credulous minds. A man who will say that because a thing is absolutely impossible, which is the same as saying absolutely untrue, it is therefore absolutely true, is simply playing ducks and drakes with his own reason and with the springs of inner consciousness; the boldness of the absurd declaration is its only force.

When an honest man will allow his judgment to be so biased and swayed that his mind thereby becomes a battlefield of conflicting theories and emotions, which he nevertheless manages to hold together by opinionative will-power, he is indeed, intellectually speaking, in a pitiful state; and this is the invariable result of mere blind faith. True faith, contrariwise, is the intuitive and clear discernment of reality, the inner recognition of things that are invisible to the physical eye.

The time will inevitably come — we cannot escape its coming — when the entire human race will know this sublime truth; and in those days the men and women who have run the race of evolution faster than their fellows have done, will then stand as Masters of Life, with a conscious knowledge of the truths of being, working henceforward as actual conscious agents in the Cosmic Labor, and no longer the mere tide-driven flotsam on the ocean of life, as most human beings today actually are. No wonder that Pythagoras spoke of the latter as 'the living dead,' living indeed in the lower

---

3. *De carne Christi* (Treatise 'On the Flesh of Christ'), ch. v.

principles of their constitution, but dead to the Divinity within themselves.

Another example of human credulity leading to what one may probably call mis-information of others on the very shaky basis that the end justifies the means, which will likewise show the tricks, moral or mental, that our minds do play upon us, is the following, taken from the writings of another and this time supposedly great Father of the Christian Church, possibly one of the greatest in that company, a saint likewise, Augustine, who was at one time Bishop of Hippo Regius in North Africa. In his thirty-third Sermon, he delivers himself unconcernedly of the following amazing statement:

> I was already Bishop of Hippo when I went into Ethiopia, with a number of servants of Christ, in order to preach the Gospel there. In that country we saw numbers of men and women who had no heads, but had two large eyes in the breast; and in countries still more to the south, we found a people who had but one eye, and that placed in the middle of the forehead.[4]

It is unfortunate that our geologists and anthropologists have found no traces of the acephalous races and cyclopean peoples. Suppose we say that Augustine dreamed a dream and saw a vision. He was at one time a rather fervid Pagan philosopher, but his later writings also show that he was more than credulous; which seems to be proved by the citation just given — although he says he 'saw' these amazing but utterly unknown races himself. As a former believer in the mystical and mythological teachings of his own and of preceding ages, he must have known well of the old Pagan allegories and legends, as for instance that of the Cyclops-race, who had but one eye, and that in the center of the forehead. Odysseus, in Homer's Odyssey, it will be remembered, escaped with his companions from out the cave near Mt. Aetna where the Cyclops, Polyphemus, cannibal as he was alleged to be, was holding them for his future meals, by clinging to and under the belly of rams and sheep, the herds of the giant. Polyphemus, according to the mythological story, was the son of Poseidon, and of the nymph Thoosa. He was representative, according to the esoteric story, of a former titanic race, which preceded our human kind, and he is usually represented in story as a gigantic quasi-human monster having more or less human shape, with one eye situate in the center of his forehead, defiant of the gods, and, as the legend of the ancients runs, of cannibalistic propensities.

---

4. *Sermones,* xxxiii.

I suppose that Shakespeare, having this report of Augustine in mind, probably referred to it when he makes Othello speak as follows, when the latter is explaining how he won the hand and heart of the fair Desdemona:

> Wherein of antres vast and deserts idle,
>
> . . . . . .
>
> And of the cannibals that each other eat,
> The Anthropophagi and men whose heads
> Do grow beneath their shoulders. This to hear
> Would Desdemona seriously incline:[5]

There seems to be little question that the sole foundation for this yarn of Augustine's was the various legends and stories current in the Roman Empire and commonly accepted in the intellectually degenerate days when Augustine lived. Among other sources of possible information whence Augustine probably drew the material for his alleged anthropophagi and cyclopean peoples, we may perhaps cite the *Historia Naturalis* of the great Pliny, often called Pliny the Elder, who in his very interesting if rambling History has a number of allusions to wonders in the various countries which he describes.[6]

These two illustrations of human credulity and of love of the marvelous, to wit, the examples just drawn from Tertullian and Augustine, show that mere belief or faith, whether honest and sincere or dishonest and insincere, is not enough as a sure guide in life, be it either in conduct or in knowing, for such blind credulity is virtually identic with blind faith. A belief, on the other hand, may be very honest, held with sincerity and fervor, and yet be untrue. Of this stuff are fanatics partly made. Of this latter kind were the beliefs and convictions which sent Mohhammed and his cavalry over the plains and deserts of the Hither East, with the Qûr'ân in the one hand and the sword in the other, giving to all whom they met the choice of three things: Tribute, the Qûr'ân, or death! Such likewise was the nature of the pathetically blind convictions and beliefs of various kinds and held by various religious groups which sent so many noble-minded men and women to a horrible and untimely death throughout the long centuries of mediaeval European religious history.

The entire course of modern education — to say nothing of mod-

---

5. *Othello,* Act I, Scene iii.
6. *Historia Naturalis,* Bk. VI, ch. xxxv, and elsewhere.

ern instruction — is against accepting the idea that man has within himself unused and usually unawakened faculties by the training and employment of which he may know truths of Nature, visible and invisible, with a depth of intellectual penetration and keen accuracy of instinctive feeling obtainable in no other manner whatsoever. Differing in this from our modern selves, the ancient peoples without exception knew this now forgotten verity; they knew that all proof lies ultimately in the man himself; they knew that judgment and cognition of truth lie within him and not without; and for these reasons they were more largely introspective than we are, who pride ourselves upon, yes, actually boast of, the modern idea that extraspection, or looking without, is the sole highway to truth. This modern conception is all wrong because it is entirely one-sided. The attaining of truth by the individual runs in both directions, in the sense that while we should cultivate the faculty of looking outwards in order to discern the facts of Nature, we can only understand those facts by using the power of understanding, of discrimination, of judgment, of intellectual analysis; and that power of understanding and comprehension is not outside of but within us, as seems obvious enough.

It is with a recognition of this inner power of understanding that the Theosophical teachings should be approached. It is indeed a maxim with Theosophists: "Believe nothing that your conscience tells you is wrong, no matter whence it come. If the very divinities came to earth and taught in splendor on the mountain-tops, believe naught that they tell you, if your own spirit-soul tells you that it is a lie."

Yet while we teach this rule as an absolute necessity of prudence for inner growth and as an invaluable exercise of the spirit and of the intellect, which by that exercise of attempting to understand have the means thereby to manifest themselves with ever increasing power: nevertheless others of our teachings tell us, and we try to follow these injunctions with equal fidelity because we have proved their merit: "Be of open mind. Be careful lest you reject a truth and turn away from something that would be of inestimable benefit and help, not only to you but to those whom you love and therefore to your fellow-men." For these two rules not only complement each other but balance each other in their functioning, the one avoiding and preventing credulity, the other forestalling and uprooting intellectual egoisms.

There is no contradiction or contrariety in sense or of feeling between these two attitudes or intellectual positions. It is the most logical and natural thing in the world for an honest, truth-seeking man or woman to follow both these rules for obtaining knowledge of verity. How can a man honorably teach that which he believes to be false? How can he accept it? How can a man refuse to believe that which he inwardly knows to be true?

With these inner faculties awakening within him, should the Ancient Wisdom be approached by every honest man. That sublime System of thought is not based upon blind faith, nor on anyone's 'say-so,' nor again is it based upon the equally blind assurance of our own intellectual self-sufficiency. The Ancient Wisdom of the Gods is kept in the most sacred guardianship of Great Adepts, of Initiates or Masters of Life. It is astonishing that European and American scholars, who are more or less conversant with the various world-literatures, have not themselves discovered, at least intuitively, that this Ancient Wisdom exists as a coherent body of teaching based on inner and outer Nature's structure and operations. The explanation of their cecity in these matters is simple indeed: they have never believed that such a systematic formulation of the Ancient Wisdom of the Gods exists or indeed ever has existed; they do not see the wood, as the old saying goes, on account of the trees. They see so many individual instances of high thinking and noble thought in those old literatures that they have failed to realize that behind these diversities in the various religions and philosophies, as we find them in the literatures, there is likewise a universal system, common to them all and veiled from merely superficial observation by the forms and methods of presentation that each one of these ancient systems is imbodied in.

How can these diversities, with their common background of an identic Universal Doctrine, be otherwise explained than as above stated, remembering that all systems of human thinking, religious, philosophical, and scientific, are the productions of the human soul and mind? Take any truth, any fact of Nature, and put ten men to giving an explanation of this truth or of this fact: while they all will base their thoughts on the same background of substantiated facts, each one of the ten men will give a different version of the truth that he observes; and thus it is that the framework, the format, in which this essentially coherent and synthetic Ancient Wisdom lies, this Archaic System in fact, is expressed in the divergent manners that exist in the various great World-Religions and World-Philosophies.

Our learned Occidental scholars and researchers into the ancient religions and philosophies, have, as above stated, not seen the wood on account of the trees. They are in the wood, and they see only the trees immediately surrounding their own field of thought, their own field of research. But they have no general view over the whole; and having no such general view, of necessity they cannot see the undivided whole, of which these various portions or mere fragments are only parts. Yet once that the student has the wonderful key to interpretation that the Ancient Wisdom, in other words that Theosophy, gives, then he himself will be able to prove for himself the statement hereinbefore made: that there is a systematic formulation of spiritual and natural law and of spiritual and natural verities existent in the world, which today is called Theosophy, and which Theosophists love to call by other names: the Ancient Wisdom, the Wisdom of the Gods, or the Wisdom-Religion of the archaic ages; and which has given its title to this present work — THE ESOTERIC TRADITION.

From this Ancient Wisdom or Esoteric Tradition have sprung forth at various times in the history of the world the great world-religions or world-philosophies which either have existed and have disappeared, or which still exist in more or less degenerate and incomplete form. Understanding somewhat at least of this Esoteric Tradition or Ancient Wisdom, the student has thereby the master-key which will unlock those mysterious and tightly closed portals opening into the archaic thought of the human race, and which portals intuitive scholars now and then dimly perceive as they study, but whose existence is almost reluctantly acknowledged.

That original Truth, from which all great religions and all great philosophies sprang in their origin, the earnest Theosophical student may discover for himself, if he will; and he shall then know that Truth is ageless and deathless, but yet takes up its abode in every earnest human heart, where it awaits recognition in order to pour its flood of light into the waiting mind. In each age a new revelation of this deathless Truth is given forth to the peoples of the Earth from and by the Guardians of this Ancient Wisdom; and each such 'revelation,' if we may call it by that much abused word, contains the same old Message that previous revealings had brought to the world, albeit the 'new' instalment may be couched in a later and different tongue and in newer and differing expressions from those employed in its last revealing. Therefore, behind all the various religions and philosophies, there is, the Theosophist emphatically declares, a secret or esoteric Wisdom, common to all mankind, existent in all ages, and revealed in one form or another as the cycling centuries slowly pass and drop into the ocean of bygone time. This

Wisdom is Religion, *per se,* and unadulterate Philosophy of Nature, and impersonal Science, explaining the structure and habits of the Universe: this Wisdom is universal and impersonal, and its human proponents, however grand, are merely the Voice announcing it to mankind from age to age.

It is therefore obvious that the Theosophist makes a distinction of importance between Religion and Philosophy and Science on the one hand, and on the other hand religions, philosophies, and sciences. It has been for the last hundred or hundred and fifty years quite common in the Occident to talk of the 'conflict between religion and science.' This supposed antinomy between two things which are, in truth, radically identical, is both unfortunate and untrue; for in point of fact there can be no such natural conflict or disagreement between any two or more of these three: Religion, Philosophy, and Science. But, unfortunately, there can be conflicts between the brain-mind ideas of this man and the brain-mind ideas of another man, because the brain-mind is essentially a material organ, however useful it certainly is when properly disciplined and trained to the uses of the intuitive spirit. Between religions and sciences, or between either of these two and philosophies, yes, it is quite possible that there may be many conflicts; and this for the reason already set forth: that the great religions and philosophies have degenerated from their pristine purity and have been in consequence misunderstood, and of them there remain at present naught but psychological mounds and tombs, and speculations about them, and no certain knowledge among scholars of the inner meaning of any one of them. So that now, religion, philosophy, and science, in the common understanding of us modern men are supposed to be intrinsically separate things, and to be often in irreconcilable natural conflict. They are considered as being more or less artificial systems outside of the intrinsic operations of human spiritual and psychological economy, instead of being, as they obviously are, expressions of three different operations of the human soul and mentality.

This popular conception of these three fundamental activities of the human soul is entirely false; to the Theosophist, Religion and Philosophy and Science are fundamentally but one thing manifesting in three different manners. They are not three things outside of man, foreign to him, which he has to learn much in the way in which he learns that square things are not round. On the contrary, they are themselves activities of the human psychological and spiritual natures; and while they can be considered as three different ways of arriving at Truth, or Reality, or the Heart of Things, this is merely for convenience of expression. They are like the three sides of a triangle: if any one side or any two sides were lacking, the figure obviously would be *de facto* one-third or two-thirds imperfect. Religion, Philosophy, and Science, must unite and all at the same time, if we wish to attain to the actual truths of Nature, because our mind conceives those truths through these, its three main activities, which are essentially one because springing from the unitary faculty of understanding which man, their creator, has. They are but the three aspects, or the three operations, of the human mind in its transmitting, and in its setting forth, of the inspirations flowing into it from the spiritual inner sun which every man is in the arcanum of his being, and of which spiritual sun itself, more accurately speaking, he himself actually is the offspring, or imperfectly evolved ray.

Some say that the religion of the future is to be a scientific religion; others, knowing well the strong appeal of religious emotional feelings to the human heart, say "Nay, Science will have its day; it will be some new form of religious thought, perhaps not based on the old forms of the past, or perhaps so based, but in any case it will be a new religious feeling." Others again think that the religion of the future will be rather philosophical in character. Emerson, for instance, glimpses only half a truth when he says:

> The religion which is to guide and fulfil the present and coming ages, whatever else it be, must be intellectual. The scientific mind must have a faith which is science. . . .
> There will be a new church founded on moral science, at first cold and naked, a babe in a manger again, the algebra and mathematics of ethical law, the church of men to come, without shawms, or psaltery, or sackbut; but it will have heaven and earth for its beams and rafters; science for symbol and illustration; it will fast enough gather beauty, music, picture, poetry.[7]

Beautiful thoughts, beautiful words are these, and doubtless in large part true; but yet one may well ask, why make of religion something that grows like a weed in the fields of human thought and that has to gather unto itself as time passes, and more or less at haphazard, the noblest aspects of human thinking? Indeed, religion is truly but a human weed, if that be all it is. Nay, the workings of the human spirit are sublime in themselves; it knows truth instantly; and all is in it, and true religion springs from it like Athene from the brain of Zeus; while a religion which grows merely by accretion of things to be preferred is destined to degenerate in turn by loss and decay. That indeed has been the history of degenerate religions

---

7. *The Conduct of Life,* VI, 'Worship.'

in the past, because of the accretions which foolish and ambitious men have added to the spiritual core which the great founders of religions gave to their spiritual children; but it need not have been so.

The fact is that our Western peoples really do not understand what Religion *per se* is. They took over a certain body of religious tradition from the old Roman Empire, and distorted that body of tradition greatly, for they did not understand it, and indeed feared a great part of it. For the old religions of the Greeks and the Romans had degenerated into a system of ceremonial ritualisms and of so-called 'prayers' addressed to the gods; but RELIGION in itself is perhaps the noblest, the highest, instinct of the human spiritual soul. It is something apart from all forms, from all ceremonies, from all ritualisms; it is in fact truly innate and intuitive consciousness of the nature of Being; it is a visioning of Reality; indeed, it is a growing Wisdom; it is therefore likewise knowledge, because it is intuitive wisdom.

It was through the crystallization of ideas around a sublime core that the dogmatic religions were born. Some great primal truth, or body of verities, coming from the sublime Brotherhood of the great Seers and Sages of the ages is given forth at cyclical times in human history, and a new religion is then and there begun; and as long as the original promulgator with his magnificent mind and high intuitional faculty is there to direct and to guide the works and channels of the movement, it prospers well; but when he passes on, vanishes from the sight of men, then come smaller men on the scene: less intuitive, less profound in their views, less piercing in their vision, and often ambitious and it may be self-seeking; and they also teach, and add accretions of their own imaginings to the primal spiritual verities; and their teachings are not grand and inspiring as were those of the original Promulgator. The consequence is ecclesiastic or religious dogma in the modern sense; and therefore ultimate disappointment and heart-breaking sorrow ensue to the faithful; for man clings very closely to his religious ideas, because fundamentally he is a religious being, since his own inmost nature is not only linked by unbreakable bonds with the Cosmic Spirit, but is a ray of that Cosmic Spirit itself. It is man's instinct to be impersonally religious; but it is not instinctual in him to be religious in a dogmatic sense. All ecclesiastical dogmas are the offsprings of the minds of men far inferior to the Great Seer who inaugurated such or such other of the great World-Philosophies or World-Religions.

The Theosophist has, in consequence, little patience with the

divisions of the workings of the constitution of man into three supposedly intrinsically separate and essentially distinct things; for
man cannot be divided against himself; man in his essence is an
inner harmony; and unless heart, and mind, and spirit work in harmony, he has neither inner rest nor peace. Origins, fundamentals
(not in the absurd modern religious sense, but in the etymological
sense), basic things, these are in the spirit of man, whence they come
forth; for the spirit of man is the father of all human works.

Hence, Religion, Philosophy, and Science, *per se,* that is to say,
the things in themselves, do really represent truth, in proportion as
these three operations or functionings of the human spirit are un-
inhibited by mental or emotional obstacle or veil; for Truth in itself,
as man can understand it, is but a formulation in systematic form
of Nature's own operations and functions — Nature here signifying
not merely the physical nature which our optics enable us to sense,
or our auditory apparatus gives us some information of, or our
senses of touch or of taste or of smell give us still further ideas about:
but meaning rather, the vast realms of the inner worlds, our native
habitat as spiritual beings and as thinkers, having aspirations, and
hope, and enthusiasm, and intellectual penetration, and other similar
faculties, all which are human interpretative transmissions of the
forces at the heart of being.

Few sane men believe today the old materialistic and now moribund notion that the noblest activities of the human spirit, or indeed
any others of the energies of the human constitution be they intellectual, psychical, or emotional, are the mere products of fortuitous
or chance movements among the atoms of the physical brain, in
other words, that all feeling, and ethical sense and consciousness, are
derivatives of molecular changes in the brain-cortex. That extravagant notion, thanks be to the immortal gods, is now seen to be an
outworn fad of a defunct materialism; for indeed it never was anything else than an entirely unsupported theory. It never had a
shred of real proof to support it, but was a theory evolved only in
a desperate attempt to answer searching questions which would be
inevitably asked by thinking men; and because the theory never did
answer these questions satisfactorily, it lived its little life of folly
and turned up its toes and died.

How did this theory arise? Thinking men revolted, some one
hundred and fifty years ago, against all dogmatic and crystallized
thought in both religion and philosophy, and sought out truth blindly
along what seemed to be the new avenues of research and experiment that inquisitive European science was so rapidly opening. That

revolt in many ways was in itself, at least in its beginnings, a fine and noble effort for intellectual freedom. But, like all one-sided albeit enthusiastic movements of the human soul and mind, the rebuilders who later became destroyers, in their work went too far beyond the point of reason and ascertained fact; and in the fervor of destroying what they honestly believed to be false idols, falsehoods and falsities, they did away even with much that was ethical and good. Men today have learned better, and are more moderate in their judgment. Time has brought wisdom to them, and a chastened mind and a high toleration, and a far wider field of vision.

Yet men of the Occidental world today, despite the great and highly praiseworthy achievements of physical science, have no fully comprehensive and therefore satisfying system of intellectual and spiritual standards by which they may test, with confidence of arriving at the truth, any new discovery that may be made in the Nature that surrounds us, whether in its invisible, or visible physical parts. Now the ancients had such a comprehensive system of standards, and it was composite of the three activities of the human soul which have just been referred to. This system was at once religious, philosophical, and scientific, and for that reason provided a satisfactory test and explanation of the discoveries made in the search for Truth, because it comprised the three essential activities or faculties of the human understanding.

Most people in our Occidental world seem to think that religion is something which exists only for one part or range of life; that philosophy is another branch of human thinking which exists merely for a more or less noble intellectual pastime, consisting of a more or less successful effort, intellectually to penetrate into the causal and effectual structure and relations of the universe around us; and again most people seem to think that science is but an investigation into the physical nature in which we live as physical human beings, and the ensuing classification and recording of the various results of that investigation. The point of objection here to this manner of viewing these three functions of the human mind, is the underlying supposition that religion and philosophy and science are three things inherently distinct from each other and having no inherently natural and co-ordinating relations or points of inseparable union.

The Theosophical philosophy says: These three are fundamentally derivatives of human consciousness and, therefore, fundamentally one. They all spring from the human understanding. They are the children of the human spirit. They are, as it were, but three methods or ways in which the Self, the thinking self, the conscious self, the root of our being, endeavors to express what it cognises and recognises as truth. Science, Philosophy, Religion, are the offsprings of man himself; and more definitely they are spiritual and mental children of Great Men: the founders of the various religions and philosophical systems of the ancient world, and historically of our modern world as well. These Great Sages laid down basic or fundamental principles, based on Nature, on natural law — not physical nature alone, but on inner Nature more especially — that is to say on the roots or radicals of things; inner and invisible and to us intangible substances and energies and laws, potencies, powers, dominions, and virtues, which rule the world by action from within outwards, and thus among other things keep the stars in their courses.

Thus, religion, philosophy, and science compose one triform method of understanding — what? The nature of Nature, of Universal Nature, and its multiform and multifold workings; and not one of these three activities of the human spirit can be separated from the other two if we wish to gain a true picture of things AS THEY ARE IN THEMSELVES. For Science is an operation of the human spirit-mind in its endeavor to understand the *How* of things — not any particular science whatsoever, but the thing in itself, science *per se* — ordered and classified knowledge, based on research and experimentation. Philosophy is that same striving of the human spirit to understand not merely the *How* of things, but the *Why* of things — why things are as they are. And, lastly, Religion is that same striving of the human spirit towards union with the COSMIC ALL, involving an endlessly growing self-conscious identification with the Cosmic Realities therein — commonly and so feebly called by men, 'God' or gods.

These three children — functions and activities — of man's spirit-soul all have one tendency, one trend, because all working towards one objective. This is to reach the Heart of Things, Truth, Reality, and to become united therewith. The scientist seeks truth; the philosopher searches for reality; the religionist yearns for union with the Divine; but are these three not essentially one? Is there any essential difference as among Truth, Reality, and union with Divine Wisdom and Love? It is only in the methods of attainment by which the three differ. Their object is but one. Moreover, as becomes abundantly obvious, Science should be as spiritual and as philosophical as Philosophy should be religious and scientific and as Religion should be scientific and philosophical.

What is the origin of the word 'religion'? — because the search for etymological roots often casts a brilliant light upon the functioning of human consciousness. It is usual among modern Europeans to derive the word 'religion' from the Latin verb meaning 'to bind back,' or 'to fasten' — *religare*. But there is another and perhaps a better derivation, which is the one that Cicero, the great Roman statesman, poet, and philosopher chooses; and, a Roman himself and a scholar, he unquestionably had a deeper knowledge of his own native tongue and its subtilties of meaning than even the ablest scholar has today. This other derivation comes from a Latin root meaning to select, to choose, from which likewise, by the way, comes the word *lex* — 'law,' that course of conduct or rule of action which is chosen as the best, and is therefore followed: in other words, that rule of action which is the best of its kind, as ascertained by selection, by trial, and by proof. Typically scientific is this in idea, even in our day.

In his book *On the Nature of the Gods,* speaking through the mouth of the eminent philosopher Quintus Lucilius Balbus, of the Stoic school, during the course of a discussion on philosophy and religion at the home of Cicero's friend, Cotta, Cicero writes as follows:

Do you not see, therefore, how from the productions of Nature and the beneficial inventions of men, imaginary and false deities have come into view; and that those have become the basis of wrong opinions, pernicious errors, and miserable superstitions? We know, as regards the gods, how their different alleged forms, their ages, clothing, ornaments, families, marriages, connexions, and all appertaining to them, follow examples of human weakness and are represented with human passions. According to the history of fables, the gods have had wars and fightings, governed by grief, lust, and anger, and this not only, as Homer says, when they interested themselves in different armies, but also when they battled in their own defense against the Titans and the Giants. Such tales, of the greatest folly and levity, are told and believed with implicit stupidity.

However, repudiating such fables with contempt, Divinity is diffused throughout all parts of Nature: in solids under the name of Ceres; in liquids under the name of Neptune; elsewhere under different names. But whatever the gods may be, whatever characters and dispositions they may have, and whatever the names given to them by custom, we ought to revere and worship them.

The noblest, the chastest, the most pious and holy worship of the gods is to revere them always with a pure, wholehearted, and stainless mind and voice; our ancestors as well as the philosophers have all separated superstition from religion. Those who prayed entire days and sacrificed so that their children should survive them, were called superstitious, a word which later became more general; but those who diligently followed and, so to say, read and practised continually, all duties belonging to the worthship of the gods were called *religiosi,* religious, from the word *relegendo,* reading over again or practising; [a derivation] like *elegantes,* elegant, meaning choosing, selecting a good choice, or like *diligentes,* diligent, carefully following our selection; or like *intelligentes,* intelligent, from understanding: for all these meanings are derived from the same root-word. Thus are the words superstition and religion understood: the former being a term of opprobrium, the latter of honor. . . .

I declare then that the Universe in all its parts was in its origin builded, and has ever since, without any interruption, been directed, by the providence of the gods.[8]

Never has a Christian monotheistic critic of the errors of a degenerate polytheism spoken in stronger terms than does this ancient Roman philosopher-polytheist, against the mistake and impiety of looking upon the divine, spiritual, and ethereal beings who inspire, oversee, and by their inherent presence control the universe, as being but little better than, or superior to, merely enlarged men and women. No Church-Father ever used more emphatic or stronger language against superstitious and ignoble ways of looking upon these divine and spiritual and ethereal beings than does the great Roman philosopher-statesman here, and than did Varro and Empedocles and Epicurus and Democritus and Plato and many another great man of the Greek and Roman worlds.

One has but to read the scathing and caustic words of Lucian, the Greek satirist, to realize how the revolt against superstition and degenerate religion was as widely diffused and ran with as strong a current in ancient times as it may have done in any later period, including our own period.

Thus then, the meaning of the word 'religion' from the Latin *religio,* and following Cicero's etymological derivation, means a careful *selection* of fundamental beliefs and motives by the higher or spiritual intellect, the faculty of judgment and understanding, and a consequent joyful abiding by that selection, the whole resulting in a course of life and conduct in all respects following the convictions that had been reached. This is the religious spirit.

Philosophy is another part of the activity of the human consciousness. As religion represents the mystical and intuitional and devotional part of our inner human constitution, so does philosophy represent the co-ordinating and correlating and the examining portion of our intellectual-psychological apparatus; and it would seem to be instantly obvious to the reflective mind that the same faculty of discrimination, or what has been called selection in the preceding paragraph when dealing with religion, is as strongly operative in this field of thought as it is in the other, but with and by means of a different internal organ of the human constitution — that of the mentality. Just as religion divorced from the intellectual faculty

---

8. *De natura deorum,* Bk. II, sec. xxviii.

becomes superstition or a showy emotionalism, just so does philosophy divorced from the intuitional or discriminating portion of us become empty verbiage, logical in its processes mayhap, but neither profound nor inspired. If philosophy mean, as it is said that Pythagoras stated it to mean, the love of wisdom or σοφία (*sophia*), so indeed may one truthfully offer that equally with religion, but in a different field of human understanding, philosophy contains likewise the elements which we may qualify as the wisdom of love — one of the intrinsic or inherent attributes or qualities of the instinctive religion of the human spirit.

Likewise, and in a virtually identic manner, when the inner faculties of our constitution operate in such fashion as to classify and record the knowledge that they have gathered from instinctive love for investigation and research into Nature, and subject to measurement and category the facts and processes which Nature thereupon presents to the human intellect — that indeed is Science. Here again we see that Science like Philosophy and Religion, is universal and impersonal, and of equal spiritual and intellectual dignity with the two former; all three are but 'joint and several' interpretations in formal system of the relations — inherent, compelling, and ineluctable — of man with the Universe of which he is not only a child but an integral and inseparable part. Does not the meaning by which this branch of human understanding is known, Science, signifying Knowledge, clearly set forth its origin in human understanding, an intrinsic part of the human constitution?

How obvious it is then that precisely because man is integral with the Universe in which he lives, and moves, and has his being, all and everything in that universe is represented both energically and substantially in himself; so that by obeying the mandate of the Delphic Oracle, "Man, know thyself!", man learns not only the nature and characteristics and structures and functions of his own constitution, but by an expansion of his own perceptive consciousness derived from training and thought can enter into and understand the identic energies and substances in the Great Mother, Universal Nature. Man, therefore, because he is the microcosm of the macrocosm, an integral and inseparable part of the Cosmic Whole, can, by entering into the mysterious realms and structure of his own inner constitution, enter by that fact with increasing cognition, as his own inner constitution is awakened, into the realms visible and invisible of the Cosmic Whole; and when this is done by highly evolved Men, Initiates, and Great Adepts, what is then and there learned in this most wonderful of Adventures, is brought back from these Adventures of exploration and wrought into systematic formulations of human thinking, which the Theosophist calls in their aggregate, *Theosophia* — the Wisdom of the Gods. It is this Wisdom, this Esoteric Philosophy, which it is the intention in this present work to study, and which, considering its transmission from generation to generation of the Great Seers and Sages through the ages, and from immemorial time in the past, can with justice and truth be called the Esoteric Tradition.

Thus then, if we understand the nature and working of our own spiritual-intellectual consciousness, we have an infallible test or touchstone by which we may subject to trial and experiment all that comes before our attention. Theosophy indeed is the 'touchstone' most wonderfully formulated into a comprehensible human system. With its help and from its conscientious study, we are enabled to sift with certainty the false from the true, facts of Nature from mere human phantasy, and the merely imaginary from those enunciations of everlasting natural and spiritual truth which are the results of the working of man's spiritual consciousness, cast by the Great Sages aforesaid into philosophic, religious, and scientific systems.

Let men once realize and feel the force of the verity that true religion and philosophy and science all spring from within, all spring from the higher nature of man, and are therefore different but closely similar pathways in man's intellectual journey towards Truth, and instinctively man will then search for larger knowledge of the unifying spiritual-intellectual power behind and within and beyond these three functionings of his consciousness. He will not rest until he has acquired a larger acquaintance with that god-like System demonstrating the essential unity of these three as being derivatives from one common source — Universal Nature in both her invisible and visible hierarchies of spheres. It is to aid in this search that the present work has been written, pointing to the existence in the world of that formulated Wisdom of the ancients which is here called The Esoteric Tradition.

———————————

IN opening the study to which the present work is devoted, mention should be made of two Theosophical books of outstanding esoteric value and of pre-eminent importance because of the fact that both were literary pioneers in the same field. These two books are, in the order of their writing, *The Mahatma Letters to A. P. Sinnett,*[9]

———————————

9. These letters, written between the years 1880-4, did not appear in book-form until 1923, in which year they were first edited and published by A. Trevor Barker.

and *The Secret Doctrine*[10] by H. P. Blavatsky, the true foundress of the modern Theosophical Society, and during her lifetime, the spiritual and intellectual inspiration of the Theosophical Movement. The value of these two works in logically establishing and aiding in proving the existence of the Esoteric Tradition has to this day not yet been fully recognised, although students of a more intuitive mind, and with more than the average capacity for weighing evidence, are beginning to understand, first, the purposes for which the material in these two books was gathered together, and second, the foundation which they furnish for future efforts in the same direction. The literary material in each was chosen as appropriate for publication for the time in which it appeared — an observation which applies perhaps with particular point to the letters written by the two Masters to Mr. A. P. Sinnett, and out of which this gentleman drew the substance of fact and idea incorporated by him in *The Occult World* and *Esoteric Buddhism*. Mr. Sinnett's two books still have value of a kind, despite the fact that, due to the limitations of his understanding of the noble letters that he received, and due likewise to the very definite materialistic bias inherent in himself, he distinctly failed to convey to his readers the lofty spirituality and long line of esoteric or occult suggestions which the letters from the two Mahâtmans to himself contained.

As between *The Mahatma Letters to A. P. Sinnett* and H. P. Blavatsky's *The Secret Doctrine* there is after all but little to choose as being preferential material, for, in the last analysis, *The Secret Doctrine* was in very large part directly inspired by, if not indeed the actual compilation of, the same lofty mahâtmic minds[11] which in-

---

10. Published in 1888.

11. With regard to the very substantial aid that the Masters gave to the writing of *The Secret Doctrine* by H. P. Blavatsky, it may be as well to reproduce here, in this footnote, some statements from the Masters themselves as regards this matter, which were published by Mr. W. Q. Judge in *The Path* of April, 1893, Vol. VIII, No. 1. These statements appear in the form of what the writer of *The Path* article calls "a certificate signed by the Masters"; and in order that the reader may have before him the pertinent points of the "certificate," the latter part of *The Path* article is here reproduced in entirety:

" 'I wonder if this note of mine is worthy of occupying a select spot with the documents reproduced, and which of the peculiarities of the "Blavatskian" style of writing it will be found to most resemble? The present is simply to satisfy the Doctor that "the more proof given the less believed." Let him take my advice and not make these two documents public. It is

dited through their chela-amanuenses the letters printed in the book published by A. Trevor Barker.

Both books were what it was at one time customary among a certain class of English writers to call 'broadsides,' having as their objective to prove the existence of the Esoteric Tradition in all past archaic ages, and that this Esoteric Tradition has from immemorial time been the Mother-Source giving birth to, in cyclical times, the great Philosophies and Religions of former ages.

The Secret Doctrine alone contains an almost untouched mine of esoteric wisdom and teaching, untouched because its most devoted students apparently have done little more than scratch the surface of this genuine treasury of the Ancient Wisdom-Teaching. One might include in this work of resuscitation in public consciousness of the existence of the Esoteric Tradition, H. P. Blavatsky's *Isis*

---

for his own satisfaction the undersigned is happy to assure him that the *Secret Doctrine,* when ready, will be the triple production of [here are the names of one of the Masters and of H. P. B.] and — most humble servant, [signed by the other.] '

"On the back of this was the following, signed by the Master who is mentioned in the above:

" 'If this can be of any use or help to ——, though I doubt it, I, the humble undersigned Faquir, certify that the *Secret Doctrine* is dictated to [name of H. P. B.], partly by myself and partly by my brother ——.'

"A year after this, certain doubts having arisen in the minds of individuals, another letter from one of the signers of the foregoing was sent and reads as follows. As the prophecy in it has come true, it is now the time to publish it for the benefit of those who know something of how to take and understand such letters. For the outside it will all be so much nonsense.

" 'The certificate given last year saying that the *Secret Doctrine* would be when finished the triple production of [H. P. B.'s name], ——, and myself was and is correct, although some have doubted not only the facts given in it but also the authenticity of the message in which it was contained. Copy this and also keep the copy of the aforesaid certificate. You will find them both of use on the day when you shall, as will happen without your asking, receive from the hands of the very person to whom the certificate was given, the original for the purpose of allowing you to copy it; and then you can verify the correctness of this presently forwarded copy. And it may then be well to indicate to those wishing to know what portions in the *Secret Doctrine* have been copied by the pen of [H. P. B.'s name] into its pages, though without quotation marks, from my own manuscript and perhaps from ——, though the last is more difficult from the rarity of his known writing and greater ignorance of his style. All this and more will be found necessary as time goes on, but for which you are well qualified to wait.' "

Unveiled and also her minor works and her scores of different articles printed at various times in the magazines which she herself edited or to which she was a more or less continual contributor.

It is imperative for a proper understanding of these two noble books, *The Mahatma Letters to A. P. Sinnett* and *The Secret Doctrine,* that the reader and student of them should invoke for their perusal not merely the ordinary ratiocinative faculty, but should strive to read them in the light of his intuition — a faculty which when successfully invoked and evoked becomes a virtually infallible guide in understanding, and in all intellectual activity.

The purpose of this present book is to aid in the research for a greater truth for men; and however small this contribution may be to that really sublime objective, the reader is asked to remember the will while he is studying the deed.

Like the other books, or at least most of them, of which the present writer is the author, the work now before the reader is constructed upon the same general principle which has governed the making of the author's former literary contributions to the same purpose: that is to say, the study proceeds from the more simple to the less, from the easier to the more difficult themes of thought; and the reader is requested to remember this as he follows the author into those fascinating fields of research and inquiry which the Esoteric Tradition so lavishly opens to honest and thoughtful investigation.

CHAPTER I

THEOSOPHY: THE MOTHER OF RELIGIONS, PHILO-SOPHIES, AND ESOTERIC SCIENCES

FROM immemorial time, and in all races of men — whether civilized, barbarian, or savage — there has been current, especially among minds more receptive and thoughtful than the average run, an intuition, an intimation, persistent and ever-enduring, that there exists somewhere a body of sublime Teaching or Doctrine which can be had by those who qualify to receive it, by becoming worthy depositaries of it. Like those vague yet undying rumors, found in all religious and philosophic literatures, of the existence of mysterious Personages, who seem to come for a while and then to vanish, and whose names flash out into dimly seen lineaments of individuality in the annals of history and then fade away into indistinguishable traces in the mists of time, just so have these intuitions, these intimations, of the existence of a sublime Wisdom-Teaching appeared at frequent intervals in the annals of both history and story, but, and in this being somewhat different from the mysterious Personages just mentioned, these intuitions, intimations, instead of vanishing, have frequently found lodgment in legend and myth, so called, and thus have become enshrined or crystallized in the different religious and philosophical records of the human race.

There is probably no single group of religious and philosophical works which does not contain some more or less clear record, given either in open statement or by vague hint, of the existence of this Wisdom-Teaching; and it is one of the most interesting of literary pursuits to trace out and to assemble together these scattered and usually imperfect records, found everywhere; and by juxtaposition to discover in them distinct and easily verifiable proof that they are indeed but fragments of an archaic Wisdom common to the human race. The literary historian, the mythologer, the anthropologist, all know of the existence of these scattered fragments or *disjecta membra* of archaic thought, but being utterly unable to make anything coherently sensible of them, they are usually ascribed — and utterly falsely ascribed — to the inventive genius of so-called 'primitive' man weaving myths and legendary tales about natural phenomena which had occurred, and which, because of the fear and awe their appearance had aroused in the mind of primitive man, were thought to be the workings of gods and genii, godlings and demons, some friendly and some inimical to man himself. This is the usually inexpressibly trite and unimaginative explanation given of these universally found but disconnected relics of ancient human thought.

Running in a directly contrary direction is the teaching brought again to the Western World by H. P. Blavatsky, who showed in her marvelous books and proved in them the real existence, and continuing existence in the world, of such a body of Wisdom-Teaching, full and complete, coherent throughout and throughout logically satisfying, and comprising in its totality a marvelous System of very difficult teaching, of information dealing not only with cosmogonic matters embracing the noumena and the phenomena of the Universe, but, because naturally included in this totality, likewise a complete historical story of the origin, nature, and destiny of Man himself.

This great System of Teaching is commonly called by its students — and has been so called in different ages — the Esoteric Philosophy, or the Wisdom-Religion, or the Secret Doctrine, or the Ancient Wisdom, or again, the Esoteric Tradition — the title of this present work — or by other more or less descriptive names.

As stated by H. P. Blavatsky herself in the 'Introductory' to her *The Secret Doctrine:*

The "Wisdom Religion" is the inheritance of all the nations, the world over. . . .

. . . the Esoteric philosophy is alone calculated to withstand, in this age of crass and illogical materialism, the repeated attacks on all and everything man holds most dear and sacred, in his inner spiritual life. . . . Moreover, Esoteric philosophy reconciles all religions, strips every one of its outward, human garments, and shows the root of each to be identical with that of every other great religion. It proves the necessity of an absolute Divine Principle in nature. . . .

Time and human imagination made short work of the purity and philosophy of these teachings, once that they were transplanted from the secret and sacred circle. . . .

That doctrine was preserved secretly — too secretly, perhaps — within the sanctuary. . . .

This is the true reason, perhaps, why the outline of a few fundamental truths from the Secret Doctrine of the Archaic ages is now permitted to see the light, after long millenniums of the most profound silence and secrecy. I say "a *few* truths," advisedly, because that which must remain unsaid could not be contained in a hundred . . . volumes, nor could it be imparted to the present generation of Sadducees. But, even the little that is now given is better than complete silence upon those vital truths. The world of to-day, in its mad career towards the unknown . . . is rapidly progressing on the reverse, material plane of spirituality. It has now become a vast arena — a true valley of discord and of eternal strife — a necropolis, wherein lie buried the highest and the most holy aspirations of our Spirit-Soul. That soul becomes with every new generation more paralyzed and atrophied. . . . there is a fair minority of earnest students who are entitled to learn the few truths that may be given to them now; . . .

. . . The main body of the Doctrines given is found scattered throughout hundreds and thousands of Sanskrit MSS., some already translated — disfigured in their interpretations, as usual,— others still awaiting their turn. . . .

. . . The members of several esoteric schools — the seat of which is beyond the Himalayas, and whose ramifications may be found in China, Japan, India, Tibet, and even in Syria, besides South America — claim to have in their possession the *sum total* of sacred and philosophical works in MSS. and type: all the works, in fact, that have ever been written, in whatever language or characters, since the art of writing began; from the ideographic hieroglyphs down to the alphabet of Cadmus and the Devanagari. . . .

. . . The Secret Doctrine was the universally diffused religion of the ancient and prehistoric world. Proofs of its diffusion, authentic records of its history, a complete chain of documents, showing its character and presence in every land, together with the teaching of all its great adepts, exist to this day in the secret crypts of libraries belonging to the Occult Fraternity. . . .

. . . it is not a *religion*, nor is its philosophy *new;* for, as already stated, it is as old as thinking man. Its tenets are not now published for the first time, but have been cautiously given out to, and taught by, more than one European Initiate. . . .

. . . Yet there remains enough, even among such mutilated records, to warrant us in saying that there is in them every possible evidence of the actual existence of a Parent Doctrine. Fragments have survived geological and political cataclysms to tell the story; and every survival shows evidence that the now *Secret* Wisdom was once the one fountain head, the ever-flowing perennial source, at which were fed all its streamlets — the later religions of all nations — from the first down to the last.[12]

It would be impossible to express in more striking language than the above citations from H. P. Blavatsky, just what the character and nature of the Esoteric Tradition is. An exhaustive and genuinely critical examination, conducted in a wholly impersonal and impartial spirit, of even the remains of the religious and literary relics

---

12. *The Secret Doctrine,* I, pp. xviii-xlv.

of ancient times, will convince one that the statements made in the preceding paragraphs are founded on truth and fact; and the conviction grows upon the impartial student that it is a marvel that scholars could have been so blind as to allow the actual existence of the Esoteric Tradition to escape observation and discovery for so long. What is needed, very evidently, is more intuition and less merely brain-mind analysis of dates and grammar and names and spellings; for these, howsoever important they may be and often truly are, all too frequently distract the searching mind from the underlying mine of truth to the overlying details of literary rubble and historical literary detritus. It is intuition that is needed indeed!

I

Intuition, be it active or relatively inactive, is the source of all human understanding of truth. It lives in the heart of man, i. e., in the core of his being; and it is the working of this intuition which gives to him all his highest and best ideas regarding the nature of man and the universe. Doubtless every one has at some time thought: In the name of all that is holy, is there no truth in the universe that a thinking man can find and understand? Is there in fact nothing but uncertainty, and vague surmises, and speculations without number, all based upon a mere researching, albeit faithful enough, among natural facts? The answer comes like the 'still small voice' saying: There must be, in a Cosmos of order, in a Universe regulated and ruled by 'law' and consequence, some means of arriving at a fully satisfying explanation of that Universe, because it is One, and therefore wholly and throughout consistent with itself. Where then may be found the truth about the Universe — in other words some satisfactory explanation of THINGS AS THEY ARE?

There can be but one Truth, and if we can find a formulation of that truth in logical, coherent, and consistent form, obviously we then can understand it, or at any rate comprehend portions of it equal to our capacity of comprehension. It is the Esoteric Tradition, today called Theosophy, which may be proved to be this formulation of truth — formulated in our present age according to the spiritual-intellectual fashions and manners of the time, it is true, but nevertheless conveying the age-old Message of Wisdom and cosmic Reality.

The subjects of which it treats deal with the Universe, and, *de facto*, with man collectively as an offspring of that Universe. It tells us what man is, what his inner constitution is, how the latter is

held together in a coherent unity, whence it comes, what becomes
of its various principles and elements when the great liberator, Death,
frees the imprisoned spirit-soul; and, telling us all this, it teaches
us likewise how properly to understand men: and, understanding
them, this comprehension enables us to go behind the veil of outer
appearances and under the surface of the seeming into the realms
of reality. It teaches us likewise of the nature of civilizations, the
productions of man, and how they arise, and what they are based
on, and of the working of the energies springing from human hearts
and minds which form civilization. It offers, moreover, an explanation of what to the materialist are the unsolved or unsolvable riddles
of life, an explanation which is entirely based upon that Mother-
Nature which is the source and background of all our being.

Theosophy is not an invention; it was not discovered; it was
not composed or formed by some finely intellectual and spiritual
mind. Nor is it a mere syncretistic aggregate of philosophical and
religious doctrines, taken piecemeal from the various religions and
philosophies of the world. This last absurdity — for such it really
is — has been put forth as a theory in an attempt to explain its appearance in the modern world, by one or two mild lunatics, whose
intellectual powers of penetration were far weaker than their wish
to denigrate, and probably arose because they saw in Theosophy
doctrines parallel with, similar to, and in cases identical with, other
doctrines in the various ancient religions and philosophies. They
took, or pretended to take, this well-known fact as an explanation
of the entire Theosophic system. They did not see that the alter-
native explanation, to wit: that these religions and philosophies were
originally derived from the mystical archaic Theosophical system,
the Esoteric Tradition of antiquity, is equally and indeed far more
reasonable, and that upon examination it is found to be the only
possible explanation. They did not see that Theosophy is that original formulation of truth, that Mother-System, from which all the
great religions and philosophies of antiquity sprang in their origin.

The average reader may ask: "What is this Theosophy which
pretends to be the fountain-head and source of the world's philosophies and religions? These claims seem to us to be greater, more
inclusive by far, than the most ambitious claims ever made by any
religionist or philosopher."

So far as the truly illimitable field of thought covered by archaic
divine Theosophy is concerned, its 'claims,' which nevertheless rest
upon demonstrable facts, are indeed greater than any that have
ever been made by any exoteric religionist or philosopher; but they

are not unsupported claims unduly made for a merely syncretistic philosophy-religion-science: that is to say, for an invented system; they are not claims made for a system of thought or belief which has been put together piecemeal from parts or portions taken by some great mind, or by a number of great minds, from either various religions or philosophies which preceded it in time. Never would a true Theosophist explain his sublime philosophy in such a manner, for the simple reason that it would not be true.

We aver, and base our averments upon demonstrable facts, that this majestic Wisdom-Religion, indifferently today called Theosophy or the Esoteric Tradition, is as old as thinking man, far older than the so-called enduring hills; because races of thinking men have existed in times so far past that continents have been submerged under the water of the oceans and new lands have arisen to take the places of those which disappeared, and these geologic convulsions were long posterior to the first appearance of *homo sapiens* on this globe. As every educated man today knows, Geology tells us somewhat of the wondrous story of the rocks and of the seas; how continents replaced seas and oceans which in their turn now again roll their waters over what was once vast stretches of plain and mountain — and, Theosophy adds, lands which were the habitats of highly civilized races of men.

Indeed, this Wisdom-Religion, this Ancient Doctrine, this Esoteric System, this Esoteric Tradition, was delivered to the first human protoplasts, the first thinking human beings on this earth, by highly intelligent spiritual entities from superior spheres; and it has been passed down from Guardians to Guardians to Guardians thereof, until our own time. Furthermore, portions of this original and majestic System have been given out at various periods of time to various races in various parts of the world by those Guardians when humanity stood in need of some new extension and cyclical renewal of spiritual verities.

Who are these Guardians of the Wisdom-Religion? They are those whom we call 'the Elder Brothers' of the human race, and by other names, and are men in all senses of the word and not excarnate spirits; but they are, relatively speaking, fully evolved or perfected men — men who have, more successfully than we as yet have, run the evolutionary race and are therefore now in point of spiritual and intellectual grandeur, where we shall be many ages hence.

To put it briefly: there has existed in the world for almost innumerable ages, a completely coherent and fully comprehensive system of religious philosophy, or of philosophical, scientific religion, which from time to time has been given out to man when the world needed a fuller revealing of spiritual truth than it then at such time had. Further, this wonderful system has been for all those past ages in the safe guardianship of the relatively perfected men mentioned above; and, still further, the present Theosophical Movement is, in our age, one of such fuller revelations or renewals of that wonderful System, because the conditions in the world warranted its appearance in our age; and H. P. Blavatsky was the Messenger who brought this new revealing of the age-old Truth to the world from the secret Brotherhood of these Masters or Guardians or Elder Brothers, who are likewise commonly called by the Sanskrit word Mahâtmans, signifying Great Selves or Great Souls.

This likewise means that every one of the great world-religions and every one of the great world-philosophies of antiquity issued originally from this Brotherhood of Sages or Guardians, and that all such religions and philosophies in consequence, have, each one at its core, the Theosophical System of thought, a statement that any earnest and determined student can prove for himself and as fully as he may wish, by adequate study and reflexion, as has already been stated elsewhere.

Thus then, it may be said that there are three sources from which the Truth about Life and hence about Man, flows forth into the world; or, preferably, one single Source which may be divided into three branches:

1. The primeval 'Revelation,' if we may use that much-abused word, delivered to primordial humanity by Beings from higher spheres, of glorious spiritual and intellectual capacities and power, who inspired and taught the then youthful mankind, and who finally withdrew to their own spheres, leaving behind them the highest and best of their pupils, chosen from among selected individuals of the youthful humanity.

2. The Elder Brothers, Teachers, Masters, who are the particular and especial Guardians and Deliverers of this Primeval Wisdom to men, whenever the times permit a new impulse of spiritual and intellectual teaching to be given to the world.

3. The esoteric or hid meanings of the fundamental tenets of the great world-religions, all of which contain various aspects of the Truth about the Universe and Man, but which inner meanings are virtually unattainable unless the student have the esoteric, Theosophical key enabling him to read these esoteric tenets correctly.

II

Theosophy is not infrequently spoken of by its students as Esotericism or the Esoteric Philosophy, when reference is made to its deeper, more recondite, more hid, and more difficult doctrines; and this manner of qualifying it is done with the intent of distinguishing those parts from the exoteric or outer forms of religious or philosophic or scientific belief, or it may be faith, that have existed in the world at various times, and exist today. Esotericism, therefore, *reveals* the truth; exotericism — that is to say, the outward and popular formulation of religious and philosophic doctrines — *re-veils* the truth; the self-assurance of ignorance, alas, whether it be learned ignorance or mere folly, always *reviles* the truth. All pioneers of thought in every age have experienced this; many a human heart has broken under the cruel revilings of the ignorant; but the greater ones of mankind, the Seers, have marched steadily onwards through time and have transmitted the torchlight of truth from race to race. Thus has it come down to our own time as 'Theosophy' in the guardianship and charge of these Great Seers who today even, yea, even in our own time, compose what it is customary among Theosophists to call, with somewhat affectionate familiarity, the 'Great White Lodge.'

Lest there be some misunderstanding of the above, a misunderstanding running to the idea that the entirety of the Theosophical Doctrines is now given out publicly to the world, let it be stated here, once for all, that this supposition wanders far and wide from the truth. The complete unveiling or delivery of the Esoteric Tradition simply could not be made — because of its magnitude, quite outside of other reasons; and therefore is it, that following of necessity the ancient custom or tradition of reticence, a certain most holy portion of this Doctrine is reserved, retained, kept back, withheld, for those who have proved themselves, by their lives and unselfish work for humanity, capable of understanding it at least in part, and incapable of misusing it for personal advancement or individual profit.

This reticence is not motivated by any spirit of selfishness, but merely by the necessities of the situation. No conscientious chemist, for a simple instance by way of illustration, would publish dangerous secrets concerning explosives to all and sundry; the situation is bad enough as it is where some of the latest discoveries in that noble branch of science are misused, in war and otherwise, for destruction of life and property. It is only to those who have proved themselves worthy, spiritually and intellectually capable of grasping these more recondite and difficult teachings, that they are entrusted by their

Guardians, because such selected men and women — selected not by favor, but because of intrinsic merit — have proved themselves, by their lives and impersonal work for their fellow human beings, to be worthy depositaries of that holy trust. Knowledge itself is not wrong; it is the abuse of knowledge that works widespread mischief in the world. All knowledge of itself is holy, but it can be made a very instrument of demons of hell when employed for selfish purposes by conscienceless men and women.

To those who are worthy receptacles of it, such holy knowledge would not be abused when given to them, nor misused. Money would not be made out of it, nor would it be employed as an instrument for gaining evil or malevolent influence for selfish purposes over the minds of their fellow-men.

Alas! such misuse and abuse of knowledge have only too often occurred, despite all the safeguards that the Guardians of this Wisdom have thrown around it. History records many cases where even simple religious teaching has been abused, as in the lamentable history made by periods of religious persecution, and power and influence of vast extent gained over the minds of those who had it not, who thus suffered pitiably and helplessly because they thought that others had religious wisdom in greater degree than themselves.

The fact is that as the ages passed, every religion or philosophy fell from its state of pristine purity and suffered more or less complete degeneration, each one of them in later times needing re-interpretation by men less great than the original Founders of such religions and philosophies; and the result has been what we see around us today — religions from which the life and inner meaning have fled, more or less, and philosophies whose appeal to the human intellect and heart no longer is imperatively strong as once it was.

Yet despite this universal degeneration, if we search the records enshrined in the literatures belonging to these various religions and philosophies, we shall find underneath the words and technical phrases in which they are couched, behind the expressions which once conveyed their full and luminous meaning, the same fundamental truths everywhere over the earth's surface and in all races of men — we shall find the same Message, indeed the same identic Messages, given to the men of this or of that or of another historical period for their inspiration and guidance and for mental comfort and peace, and for the consolation and inspiration of the heart in all lines of higher human endeavor that it may at any time follow.

The words varied indeed, the expressions varied, in which the inner sense lay, according to the age and the characteristic intellects of the men who promulgated the primal truths, but the Message behind the words and the expressions was essentially the same in them all: a religious, philosophic, and scientific Doctrine; fundamentally the same moral system everywhere; hence fundamentally the same truths based on the structure and operations of visible and invisible Nature, which had been investigated and tested by generations of Seers.

Moreover, if one examine the religions and philosophies of all past time, as far as we know them from the literatures of them that have survived to our day, it will invariably be found that they all tell of a Secret Doctrine, give hints of an Esoteric System, containing a wonderful and sacred body of teachings delivered by great human individuals who were the respective founders of those religions and philosophies; and that this Wisdom was handed down from generation to generation of men in each particular race as the most holy and precious possession that they had.

In ancient Greece and in the countries under the sway of Rome, for instance, one finds that the greatest men during many centuries have left it on record in unequivocal and direct language, and in phrasing that never varies from the one line of thought, that there is indeed such an Esoteric System; in the Greek and Latin countries that Esoteric System went under the name of 'the Mysteries' — most carefully guarded, considered most holy, restricted to those men and in certain cases to those women (because in Greece and in the Roman Empire the women had esoteric mysteries of their own and for their own sex in particular) who had proved themselves worthy depositaries of that holy trust, worthy to be the receptacles of that original and most majestical System which the earth has ever known, and which, because it was universal, was as much the spiritual heirloom of Initiates in the Mediterranean countries as it was in other parts of the globe.

In India, 'the mother-land of religions and philosophies,' as it has been so often called, is found the same tradition, the same body of teachings — a wonderful Doctrine kept holy, secret, esoteric; therefore, as in Greece and Rome, called 'a Mystery,' *rahasya* — not in the sense of something non-understandable or that no one actually understood, as the word 'mystery' is commonly used or misused today in the European tongues, but in the original ancient sense which the Greek word μυστήριον (*mysterion*) had: something kept for the mystai or mystics, those initiated in the Mystery-Schools, to study and to follow as the supreme ethical guidance in life.

For in Hindûsthân, all religious and philosophical teaching from time immemorial has been divided into two parts: that for the multitude and that for the Dwijas, i. e., the 'twice-born,' the initiated. This inner, secret, sacred, holy teaching, properly withheld from the thoughtless multitude, given only to worthy depositaries selected for merit from amongst the multitude — this holy teaching was called in India, as above stated, रहस्य (*rahasya*), a Sanskrit word meaning esoteric doctrine or mystery. Examples of literary works in which such teachings were imbodied are the Hindû Upanishads, *upanishad* being a Sanskrit compound word meaning verbally 'according to the sitting down,' or 'following upon the sitting down.' The figure is that of pupils who sat in the Oriental style at the feet of the Teacher, who taught them in secret and in strict privacy, and in forms and manners of expression that later were reduced to writings and promulgated for private reading in the manner still rendered customary by universal tradition.

If the Sanskrit compound उपनिषद् (*upanishad*) be analysed, it is found to be composed of the prepositional particle उप (*upa*), 'according to,' the prepositional particle नि (*ni*), 'down,' and the verbal root सद् (*sad*), 'to sit,' which becomes षद् (*shad*), by the rules of Sanskrit grammar when preceded by the particle *ni:* the entire compound thus signifying 'following upon or according to the teachings which were received when we were sitting down at the feet of the teacher.'

Every great Teacher or Seer who has publicly come into the outer world of men from the Brotherhood of the Sages has founded an inner circle, an inner school, if you will: i. e., gathered together a select company of worthy disciples, and taught to these disciples of the inner school, in more open form than was given to the outer world, the solution of the riddles of the universe and of human life.

As the Christian New Testament has it in substance, quoting a saying of Jesus the Avatâra, the Initiate Syrian: "Unto you it is given to know the mysteries of the kingdom of God: but to others in parables: that seeing they might not see, and though hearing they might not understand."[13]

How cruel the latter part of this quotation sounds to the careless ear — 'that seeing they might not see, and though hearing they might not understand'! Yet if the meaning be understood it is readily seen that there is nothing cruel or selfishly restrictive in these words. One understands clearly that the phrasing is merely veiled language expressing some recondite truth. The idea was that certain doctrines might be and could be and should be taken from the Mysteries and given at appropriate time-periods to the mass of the people

13. *Luke,* viii, 10.

for their great help and inspiration; but even then in veiled language only; for an unveiled exposition of the full meaning would have amounted to a betrayal of the Mystery-teaching to those who had not been educated to understand it, and thus would have led on step by step to thoughts and acts and practices detrimental not alone to themselves but to those with whom they were in daily association.

To the disciples of Jesus, who had been secretly taught by him, were given the Mysteries 'of the Kingdom of God,' as Jesus is alleged to have expressed it, but the same truth was given to the others in parables or metaphors, because they had not been educated to understand; and it is thus that though they saw, they did not see with the inner vision and understand, and although they heard the words and obtained some help therefrom, their relative lack of training in the mystical language brought them no esoteric understanding of the Secret Doctrine behind the words. It was inevitable, based on immemorial tradition, and could not safely be otherwise. "To you, 'little ones,' 'my children,' " said Jesus in substance, "I tell you plainly the mysteries of the Kingdom of the Heavens."

It must be understood that this symbolic language is the speech even of the Greek Mysteries; such words as 'little ones,' or 'children,' were technical terms in and of the Mysteries, and referred to those who were newly born in, or who had begun to tread the pathway of, the secret teachings. This very word 'mysteries,' is taken directly from the Greek esoteric rites and doctrines; and in the original Greek, as found in *Luke* in the Christian New Testament, the word 'mysteries' is there used as having been employed by Jesus, while the expression 'the Kingdom of the Heavens' is a phrase belonging to the esoteric system of the Hither East. All these are words and phrases, which, among others, were religious and philosophical commonplaces in the time and to the people to whom this great Sage, Jesus, was then speaking, or to whom he was alleged in the New Testament to have so spoken. All of which proves that even Christianity had such an inner or esoteric doctrine, but no longer has, nor has it had for centuries, at least as a recognised branch or department of Christian study.

III

Now, although it is not generally recognised, it is yet true that the early doctrines that the Christian scheme during the first centuries of its existence promulgated in the world, were not so very far removed from the Neo-Platonic and Neo-Pythagorean teachings so generally current among the Greeks and Romans of that period. But as the years went by and dropped one by one into the ocean of the past, the real meaning of these Neo-Pythagorean and Neo-Platonic doctrines became deeply obscured in the Christian system, in which literalism and blind faith with increasing rapidity took the place of the original religious idealism. Mere metaphor and literal interpretation finally supplanted the intuitive feeling, and in many cases the knowledge, among those early Christians, that there was indeed a secret truth behind the writings which passed current as canonical — or indeed apocryphal — in the Christian Church.

There were during the earliest centuries a number of remarkable men in their respective ways, who sought to stem this tide of the growing crystallization of religious thought: to effect, in so far as they could, a spiritual, that is to say, a doctrinal-spiritual reconciliation between the highest teachings of the philosophies and religions of the peoples surrounding the Mediterranean Sea, with the new religious scheme which had come to parts of those peoples and which in later time was called Christianity. Such men were, for instance, Clement of Alexandria, who lived in the second century of the Christian era. Another was the very famous Origen, likewise of the Alexandrian school, who lived in the second and third centuries of the same era. A third was the Neo-Platonist Christian bishop, Synesius, who lived in the fourth and fifth centuries of Christian times.

In what manner Synesius managed to reconcile his strong Neo-Platonic convictions with the new Christian scheme and the duties of his episcopal position, is something which offers to the student of history an interesting example of mental and psychological gymnastics; but he did so, and apparently managed to retain for all that the respect of all sides, for he seems to have been at heart a good and sincere man, as these terms go. Synesius remained a Neo-Platonist until the day of his death. He was and always continued the warm friend of the noble woman-philosopher, Hypatia, whose misfortunate and tragic end Charles Kingsley, the English novelist, has made so well known to the general reader in English-speaking countries. Hypatia in fact was Synesius' early teacher in philosophy.

The Alexandrian scholar and Church-Father, Origen, who preceded Synesius by two centuries, taught many things so curiously alike in certain respects to the Theosophical doctrines, that were one to change names and manner of phrasing, one could probably find in these particular Origenistic teachings a good deal of the esoteric philosophy.

What was it that then happened to the new Christian religion, as time passed, which brought about the deterioration or decrement in mystical and esoteric thought, which, as far as it went, prevailed so strongly in the very earliest Christian writers, as for instance in Justin Martyr and others? It was the loss of the key to the esoteric meaning of the Christian scriptures, this esoteric or secret or mystical portion being their best and holiest part. Origen fought all his life in order to keep some at least of these esoteric keys imbodied in the doctrines of his church and in their interpretation, to work as a living spiritual power in the hearts and minds of Christians; and as long as he lived and could personally direct the movement of which he was the brilliant head, there were always in the Christian Church some numbers of men and women who followed these inner teachings devoutly, for this inner sense they felt to answer the inward call of their souls for a larger and greater revealing of truth than was usually expressed in the outward or literal word.

But in the year 538 — it may have been in 540, it may have been in 542, for there are differences of opinion as regards this particular date — some two hundred years or more after the death of Origen, there was held in Constantinople what has been called the Home-Synod, convened under the Patriarch Mennas, in obedience to an imperial Rescript issued by the Emperor Justinian setting forth in official statement the complaints that had reached the imperial palace alleging that certain doctrines ascribed to the Alexandrian Origen were 'heretical,' and that, if the Council then convoked by him should in fact find them to be such, these doctrines were by the said Synod to be placed under the ban and prohibition of the ecclesiastical anathema.

The doctrines complained of were duly set forth and hotly discussed in this Home-Synod held under Mennas in Constantinople in, let us say, 538, and after long and envenomed dispute, the result of the deliberations was that the specified teachings of Origen, so strongly objected to, were finally and formally condemned and anathematized.

It is noteworthy that even during the time when this controversy over the alleged Origenistic heresies was taking place, and from a day preceding the above-mentioned synod, a new line of spiritual teachings of closely similar type with the Origenistic doctrines pronounced heretical by this Home-Synod, was attempting to find an entrance into the growing crystallization of Christian dogma, and in fact in time did so find a successful entrance therein. These new doctrines, which then came into popular ecclesiastical and theological acceptance, were imbodied in the writings of the individual whom scholars today call the pseudo-Dionysius the Areopagite.

These Dionysian teachings, as has just been set forth, did succeed in gaining a firm foothold in the minds and hearts of the Christians of succeeding centuries, and became indeed so respected and
theologically popular that in due time they were accepted universally
as at least quasi-canonical and orthodox and became the source,
at least the most important source, whence the greatest of later
Christian theologians drew their material for religious thought and
exegesis.

It is said by many scholars that Origen was likewise condemned
and anathematized at the Fifth Oecumenical or General Council of
the Christian Church, held in 553, likewise convoked in obedience
to a Rescript of the Emperor Justinian. This second anathematiza-
tion and condemnation at this Fifth General Council of the Christian
Church, probably did actually take place. Certain it is that Origen's
name in connexion with his alleged heretical teachings is mentioned
also in the Reports of the Acts of that Fifth General Council; but
he was in fact first formally condemned for these certain specified
so-called heresies in 538 or thereabouts at the Home-Synod, as before stated.

The first anathema was pronounced against Origen's doctrine
running to the following effect:

1. The pre-existence of the soul before its present earth-life; and its ultimate
restoration to its original spiritual nature and condition.

The second anathema was directed against the following:

2. The derivation of all rational entities from high spiritual beings, which
latter at first were incorporeal and non-material, but are now existing in the
universe in descending degrees of substantiality and which are differentiated
into various orders called Thrones, Principalities, Powers, and in other grades
or orders called by other names.

The third anathema was directed against this doctrine of Origen:

3. That the Sun, the Moon, the Stars, and the other heavenly bodies, are
the visible encasements of spirits now more or less degenerated from their
former high condition and state.

The fourth anathema was directed against the following:

4. That man now has a material or physical body as a retributive or punitive
result of wrong-doing, following upon the soul's sinking into matter.

The fifth anathema was directed against the following:

5. That even as these spiritual beings formerly fell into matter, so may and
will they ultimately rise again to their former spiritual status.

The tenth anathema was directed against this doctrine of Origen:

10. The body of Christ in the resurrection was globular or spherical; and so will our bodies likewise finally be.

The eleventh anathema was directed against this:

11. The Judgment to come is the vanishing of the material body; and there will be no material resurrection.

The twelfth anathema was directed against this doctrine:

12. All inferior orders of entities in the vast hierarchy of Being are united to the divine Logos (whether such beings be of Heaven or Earth) as closely as is the Divine Mind; and the Kingdom of Christ shall have an end when all things are resolved back into the Divinity.

The thirteenth anathema was directed against this:

13. That the soul of Christ pre-existed like the souls of all men; and that Christ is similar in type to all men in power and substance.

The fourteenth anathema was directed against the following:

14. All intelligent beings wheresoever they be, ultimately will merge into the Divine Unity, and material existence will then vanish.

The fifteenth and last anathema was directed against this:

15. That the future life of all spiritual beings will be similar to their original existence; and hence the end of all things will be similar to the original state or condition of all things.[14]

All these doctrines of Origen find a perfect and satisfactory explanation in the wonderful Theosophical Teachings, where they are, of course, far more fully elaborated and unfolded, thus illustrating the perfect universality and philosophical and religious applicability of the Theosophical System. This System is a true spiritual touchstone by which, if we be skilled enough so to do, we may test the reality and truth of the doctrines of any religious or philosophical system that the minds of men, however great and grand, have formulated on this earth.

IV

In the religion which is commonly supposed — and wrongly supposed — to be the main fountain-head of Christianity, i. e., in the doctrines of the Jews, can be found clear traces of the same esoteric teaching that exists everywhere else; yet in the case of Judaism it is mainly imbodied in what the Jewish initiates in it called 'the Tradi-

---

14. These anathemas are here summarized by the author of the present book.

tion,' or 'the Secret Doctrine'; the Hebrew word for tradition being Qabbâlâh,[15] meaning something which is handed down or passed down from generation to generation by traditional transmission.

In this connexion, a short extract from what may be called the principal book of the Qabbâlâh may be pertinent and useful. This book is called *Zôhar*, a Hebrew word meaning 'Splendor.' The following is the extract:

> Woe unto the son of man who says that the Tôrâh [comprising the first five Books of the Hebrew Bible] contains common sayings and ordinary tales. If this were so, we could even today compose a body of doctrines from profane literature which would arouse greater reverence. If the Law contains only ordinary matter, then there are far nobler sentiments in the profane literatures; and if we went and compiled a selection from them, we could compile a much superior code of doctrine. No. Each word of the Law contains a sublime meaning and a truly heavenly mystery. . . . As the spiritual angels were obliged to clothe themselves in earthly garments when they descended upon earth, and as they could not have remained nor have been understood on earth, without putting on such garments: so is it with the Law. When the Law came to us, it had to be clothed in earthly fashion in order to be understood by us; and such clothing is its mere narratives. . . . Hence, those who understand, look not at such garments [the mere narratives] but to the body under them, [that is, at the inner meaning] whilst the wise, the servants of the heavenly One . . . look only at the soul.[16]

Now, unquestionably, and despite plausible arguments to the contrary, the Jewish Qabbâlâh existed as a traditional system of doctrine long before the present manuscripts of it and their literary ancestors were written, for these are of comparatively late production and probably date from the European Middle Ages, and one proof of this statement is found in the fact that in the earliest centuries of the Christian era, several of the Church-Fathers of the new Christian religion are found using language which could have been taken only from the Hebrew Theosophy, that is, the Hebrew Qabbâlâh. The expressions are in some cases identic, and the thought is in all cases the same.

Each and every people in ancient times, such as the Greeks, Hindûs, Persians, Egyptians, Babylonians, used differing tongues, used different phrases for expression: used in many cases differing symbols of speech; but in all cases the esoteric Messages were iden-

---

15. From the Hebrew verbal root קָבַל (qâbal), which means 'to receive,' 'to take,' 'to hand down.'

16. Chapter iii, Paragraph 152 b.

tic; and this esoteric system behind the outward garments is Theosophy, the Esoteric Tradition, the Mother of the world's great religions and philosophies.

In each age which needs it — and these needs recur cyclically due to the revolving wheel of life — there comes a new 'revelation,' a new revealing or unveiling with an accompanying spiritual and mental revolution in the minds and hearts of men, from this great Brotherhood composed of these Sages whom Theosophists call 'Masters' because they truly are Masters of life and wisdom — a mastery gained through the unfolding in the individual of the spiritual and intellectual powers and faculties which are innate and native to all men, but which require 'evolving' or bringing forth or unfolding, partly by self-induced efforts in training, and partly by teaching given in the initiation-chambers.

Human mentality, while differing greatly in individuals, due to differences in individual evolution and because each one follows his own individual path, nevertheless pursues one common type of activity or course of action, because we are all intimately related as human beings: and on account of this fact, our minds do tend, through the natural operations of thinking itself, which make us men, towards one common end; so that the common assent, the universal consent, of men everywhere to certain fundamental principles of doctrine, based on Nature's workings in the human constitution, is a *de facto* proof, as far as it goes, that any system of thought comprising fundamental truths, acknowledged by all men, must be a truthful presentation of the elementary workings of Nature, so far as the human intellect can understand and transmit these workings into human mental systematization; and those elementary, or indeed more complicated and developed, workings of Nature: or what comes to the same thing, those natural principles of Universal Being: are what we call Truth — in other words, things and beings AS THEY ARE IN THEMSELVES.

Man's mind is a mirror, when it is clean, pellucid, limpid, and therefore capable of accurately reflecting the thoughts, the impulses, the inspirations, the intuitions, which spring up in the human spirit and flow thence through that mind in order to take shape as innate ideas, intuitive recognitions of verities, finally manifesting as doctrines or teachings of truth. On the other hand, man's mind may likewise be the distorter of such inspirations and intuitions when that mind is imperfectly developed or so filled with mental and passional images that it cannot translate and transmit with fidelity, accuracy, and perfect verisimilitude. There is no Truth which is not based on Universal Nature; and by Nature we mean not alone the shell of things which is the physical universe: we mean rather the vast range of the inner spheres of being, of which the outer physical cosmos or universe is but the living, quivering, and more or less faithful garment or copy.

This Esoteric Doctrine, this Esoteric Tradition, this body of teachings, kept and withheld and reserved for worthy depositaries, yet divulged at cyclical intervals for the common human weal, existing all over the world and in all ages, is the common property of mankind, and from what has preceded is seen always to have been so. Consequently, in all the various great religions and philosophies are to be found fundamental principles which, when placed in juxtaposition and subjected to meticulous examination and analysis, are easily discovered to be identic in substance. This substance is the Esoteric Tradition, the Mother of Religions and Philosophies and Sciences. Every one of such fundamental principles of essential religion or essential philosophy being in each such world-religion or world-philosophy, albeit disguised and screened in doubtful formulation: it becomes clear why all such world-religions or world-philosophies contain the entirety of such fundamental principles, in each and every case more or less clearly expressed or developed as an integral part of the respective systems.

However, all such world-religions or world-philosophies, as we may call them, did not in any one case give out in fulness and in clear and explicit shape or form, the entirety of the body of teachings which are at its heart; one religion emphasizes one or more of such fundamental principles; another religion or philosophy will emphasize other such principles, the remaining principles lying in the background thereof and relatively veiled in formulation. This readily accounts for the reason that the various world-religions and world-philosophies vary in type and characteristics and often, to the unreflecting mind, seem to have little in common, and perhaps to be contradictory the one of others. Another cause of this variety in shape and appearance is the varying manner in which each such religion or philosophy was originally given or promulgated to the world, the form that each took being best for the period in which it was propagated. Each such religion or philosophy, having its own place and period in time, represents, in its later forms, the various human minds who have developed its doctrines, or who, so to say, have translated it to the world in this or that particular form.

These manners or mannerisms of thinking we may discard if we wish, but it is the fundamental principles behind every great religion or great philosophy, the Universal Doctrine, the Esoteric Tradition, which are pointed to here. In this Universal Doctrine lies the mystery-field of each great religion or philosophy, in the sense that has already been set forth thus far in these pages.

v

Complete ignorance, outside of all possible intuition of the existence of this mystic background or mystery-field of Esoteric Wisdom as being the heart of the great religious and philosophic systems of the world, has led some people to say that Theosophy is nothing but old and outworn theories of religion and philosophy, popular five hundred, a thousand, two thousand, five thousand years or more ago. Such would-be critics as these say: "It is useless and foolish to go back to the ancients in our search for truth: only the new has value for our age." Or they say: "Let us turn our faces to the future, and leave the dead past to bury its own decay and its moldering bones!" What a wonderful and soul-stirring declaration is this — perhaps for people who do no real thinking for themselves! Such people are fully under the influence of the now rapidly passing notion of our immediate forefathers that all the past there is to know, which is worth while, is the dying past of the European countries, and that all future knowledge worth while is to be had in investigating physical nature, only the clothing of Reality, in order to discover still other hid forces for practical utilitarian use by man; and, secondly, their minds are enchained by the scientific myth — for such it really is — that man has only very recently, comparatively speaking, evolved from an ape-ancestor, or from a semi-animal ancestor common to both man and the apes, which passed the halcyon times of its freedom from any moral or intellectual responsibility in chewing fruit and insects in its intervals of swinging from branch to branch in some tropical forest-tree; that, therefore, all our future is in what is to come, and that the past holds nothing of worth, and that hence it is a huge waste of time to study it otherwise than in the more or less academic manner of the archaeologist.

What egregious folly! What a perverse and obstinate running counter to all the facts not only of history but also of the most recent scientific discoveries themselves which point with increase of emphasis, as fresh discoveries are accumulated, to the now well recognised fact that the origins of the human race run far back into the night of past time, and that, for all we of the present know to the contrary, these dark corridors and chambers of the now forgotten past, buried in oblivion, may actually, should they ever be opened again, reveal to us what Theosophy teaches to be the fact: that that long past of distant time saw grand and mighty civilizations covering the earth on continents formerly existing where now the turbulent waters of the present oceans roll their melancholy waves.

In architecture, in engineering, in art, in philosophy, in religion, in ethics, in abstract science, and often in technical science also — in other words, in all the things that make life valuable and that refine it: in all the things that form the basis of civilization: in all these various subjects that we still cultivate so ardently, improving upon them it is true, with our own native genius — in them all we find ancient thought and ancient work lying there, the foundation of our own civilization and thinking, and the as yet unrecognised inspiration by heritage and transmission of the best that we have.

Where have we built anything which in magnitude of fine, technical engineering, in grandeur of conception and in wonder of execution, is comparable with the Great Pyramid of Egypt: so stupendous in its colossal pile, so finely orientated to astronomical points, so accurate in the laying of its masonry, so magnificent in the ideal conception which gave it birth, that our modern engineers, technicians, and scholars, stand before it in amazement proportional with their own ability, and wonder, and frankly say that were the utmost resources of modern engineering knowledge and skill brought to bear upon a similar work, doubtless we could not improve upon it, possibly even barely equal it?

How about the Nagkon Wat in Cambodia, of which much the same might be said, albeit in minor degree; and the gigantic and astonishing megalithic monuments in Peru and Central America — yes, even the remarkable archaic structures that still exist in Yucatan and in parts of Mexico, and in other parts of the world? How about the beautiful temple of Boro-Budur in Java — a relatively recent mass, however, of apparently solid masonry, standing in wondrous beauty even yet, after the lapse of centuries and centuries of time and despite the destructive and corroding influences of earthquakes and weathering — literally covered with a wealth of carving which in places is so delicately done that it looks as if the work had been picked out with a needle? It is in places like lace-work in stone.

How about the marvelous temple of Karnak in Thebes, Egypt, quite recent from an archaeological standpoint, of which today but portals and columns and pylons in a more or less ruined state remain, but the ensemble of which still strikes the observer with awe and amazement? As a modern author once graphically said: "They built, these ancients, like giants, and they finished like jewelers!"

We are proud of our own glass; but the Romans had glass which could be molded, so Roman writers have reported, into any desired shape with the hammer or mallet. Just think what such glass would mean to us in the technical arts of our modern industries! The Mediterranean nations of southern Europe likewise had in ancient times a method of hardening copper so that, if we may trust ancient reports, it had the temper and took the edge of our good steel. We know today neither of these two technological secrets.

We heat our houses by means of hot water, among other methods of doing it, and by hot air; but so did the Romans heat their houses in the days of Cicero. We use the microscope and the telescope and are justly proud of our skill in employing them; but we also know that the ancients, the Babylonians, for instance, carved gems with lines and designs so fine and small that the naked eye cannot discern these with any clearness whatsoever, and we must use a microscope or magnifying-glass in order to see clearly the design and line-work. How did they do this, if they had no magnifying facilities? Were their eyes so much more powerful than ours are? That supposition is absurd, and there is no proof whatsoever of it. What then can we conclude but that they did have some kind of magnifying apparatus, of glass or other material? How is it that the ancient astronomers are said to have known not merely of other planets, which indeed the naked eye could see in most cases, but also are stated by certain scholars to have known of their moons, which latter fact we with our improved astronomical instruments have known only for a few score of years? We read in ancient works that the Roman Emperor Nero used a magnifying-glass of some kind — indeed, what we would call an opera-glass — in order to watch the spectacles in the Roman theaters; and legend states that he used this magnifying-glass of his in order to watch the dread spectacle of the burning of the capital of the Roman Empire.

How about shorthand — tachygraphy? The speeches of Cicero and of others also, given in the Roman Forum and elsewhere, were, we well know, taken down in the former case in shorthand or tachygraphical writing by his freedman and beloved Tiro, who later also became the great Roman's biographer. How long have we Europeans employed this most useful means of perpetuating the exact words of human discourse?

We are also told that lightning-rods were placed on the Temple of Janus in Rome by Numa, one of the earliest and according to report greatest and wisest of the Roman kings, who lived in the first ages of Rome according to tradition, centuries before the formation of the Republic.

How about the canon of proportion in art as used by the ancient Greeks? Compare their exquisite and inspired art with our own best, its child and inspired by it, and then turn to our modern artistic vagaries, such as cubism and futurism, and other things that make one think that he is crazily seeing into the Astral Light, when he tries to observe and in observing to understand, what his eye is plagued with. What is, indeed, the fundamental canon that the majority of our artists and technicians follow today, not merely in architecture, but in sculpture also? The Greek canon as we understand it. Where did the best in modern European religion originally come from; where did it take its rise? From the Greek and Latin ancients — modified more or less by us, it is perfectly true, but ultimately from them. They gave to us all the fundamental ideas, greatly modified in recent times by still nobler ideas and far grander principles derived from the Far Orient, mostly from the records of ancient religious and philosophical India. From this same source we moderns derive our universally recognised principles of ethics and morals and their applications to human thinking and conduct.

Thucydides, the Greek historian, taught modern Europeans how to write history: that is, the general style and type of historical writing that Thucydides himself followed has served for ages since his day as the exemplar and copy for all later historians. It is true that a number of historical writers and critics object, and object with a good deal of force, to the manner of writing history that Thucydides pursued: mere records of battles and their military consequences, etc.; and claim that history concerns rather the achievements of the human mind and heart as expressed in civilization, more especially the social, religious, philosophic, moral, and artistic, elements. One such critic, eminent in his own day, although necessarily limited in his vision from lack of wider knowledge, was Count Leo Tolstoi. With a good deal of truth, this eminent Russian said that history should be not merely a record of the dates of battles, and of the reigns of men, many of whom were far from wise; but should be rather a description of the workings of human genius expressed in civilization. One fully agrees with him thus far; but many and perhaps most people as yet do not; they still cling to the old Greek idea of what historical writing should be. At any rate, Thucydides taught Europeans how to write history; and Plato and Aristotle respectively how to write philosophy and how to be scientific.

How about the heliocentric system of our own sun and its planets;

the astronomical system which tells us that the sun is at the center of his realms, that the planets circle around the sun, each in its own orbit, and that the earth is a sphere poised in space as a planetary body? It took European thinkers and discoverers a long time, in the face of great persecution and at the cost of the lives of not a few great men, to bring their less intuitive and more unthinking fellows to a recognition of this fact of Nature; but the greatest among the ancient Greeks taught it all — Pythagoras, Philolaus, Ekphantos, Hiketas, Heraklides, Aristarchos, and many more. Others, of equal greatness at least, would have taught it openly had it not been for the fact that the heliocentric system of our solar world was a teaching confined to the Mysteries, and that only a few dared to do more than hint at it.

What again about Archimedes of Syracuse, one of the greatest of physical scientists and discoverers who lived between his time and our own? Again, 'Vimânas,' or flying machines, are found mentioned in very ancient Sanskrit writings of the archaic Hindûs as in the *Mahâbhârata* and the *Râmâyaṇa*, the two greatest epic poems of India; although it is true that these airy vehicles are also spoken of as being the 'vehicles of the gods' when they flew through the air — a statement which should not be considered literally but as referring to men who were god-like in their intellectual and therefore scientific accomplishments; for such allocation of divinity to human beings is well-known as one of the commonest facts in archaic Hindû literature.

So that when it comes to boasting of our prowess in science, discovery, invention, it is well not to forget that modesty is a virtue.

There are other critics, of quite different mental caliber and outlook on life, who, swayed by an equally aggressive and foolish animus, imagine Theosophy to be an outlandish and new-fangled religion: that those who teach it do not hold to the 'good old things' of bygone times — a perfectly preposterous asseveration — those more or less recent bygone times which are alleged to have proved their superior worth and permanent value by lasting for a certain number of centuries only: and that the propagandists of this outlandish and new-fangled religion are audacious enough to go forth and hunt up new and strange and barbaric words and terms, in which are imbodied the foreign notions which they attempt to promulgate in Occidental lands.

But the truth is that Theosophists are neither moss-covered conservatives on the one hand, nor howling innovators of fantastic theories on the other. For Theosophy is the true and authentic

Mother of Religions and Philosophies and Sciences: the great central systemic Source whence all the latter originally derived in past times, and therefore is their Interpreter: it interprets the hid meaning and secret symbology of all these ancient systems.

Yea, verily, the mystery-teaching hid beneath the outward and often varying forms was reserved for the Initiates — that is to say for those who could understand it and who were fit to receive it *because* they could understand; and who would never prostitute it to base and ignoble uses. It was held as the most sacred thing that men could transmit to their descendants, for it was found that the revelation of this Mystery-Doctrine under proper conditions to worthy depositaries, worked marvelous changes in their lives. It made men better and different from what they were before they received this spiritual and intellectual treasure. Why? The answer can be found in all the old religions and philosophies — if one study these honestly — under the same metaphor, the same trope, the same figure of speech: the figure of a new birth, a birth into truth, for, indeed, it was a spiritual and intellectual awakening of the powers of the human spirit, and could therefore be called in truth a *re-birth* of the soul into spiritual self-consciousness. When this happens, such men were called Initiates or the Reborn. In India, as before said, such 'reborn' men were called Dwijas, a Sanskrit word meaning 'twice-born.' In Egypt such Initiates or reborn men were called 'sons of the Sun.' In other countries they were called by other names.

H. P. Blavatsky wrote as follows in her capacity as the Messenger of the Great Brotherhood of Seers, proclaiming anew the ancient Wisdom-Religion to the modern world:

The Gnosis [or wisdom] supplanted by the Christian scheme was universal. It was the echo of the primordial wisdom-religion [or Theosophy] which had once been the heirloom of the whole of mankind; and, therefore, one may truly say that, in its purely metaphysical aspect, the Spirit of Christ (the divine *logos*) was present in humanity from the beginning of it. The author of the Clementine Homilies is right; the mystery of Christos — now supposed to have been taught by Jesus of Nazareth — "was identical" with that which *from the first* had been communicated *"to those who were worthy,"* . . . We may learn from the Gospel *according* to Luke, that the "worthy" were those who had been initiated into the mysteries of the Gnosis [or Wisdom], and who were "accounted worthy" to attain that "resurrection from the dead" [initiation] *in this life* . . . "those who knew that they could die no more, being equal to the angels as sons of God and sons of the Resurrection."[17]   In other words, they were the

17. H. P. Blavatsky is here making a series of quotations from the early Christian work, the *Clementine Homilies,* and these quotations are here printed between inverted commas.

great adepts *of whatever religion;* and the words apply to all those who, without being Initiates, strive and succeed, through personal efforts to *live the life* and to attain the naturally ensuing spiritual illumination in blending their personality — the ("Son") with (the "Father,") their individual divine Spirit, *the God within* them. This "resurrection" can never be monopolized by the Christians, but is the spiritual birth-right of every human being endowed with soul and spirit, whatever his religion may be. Such individual is a *Christ-man.*[18]

---

18. *Lucifer,* 'The Esoteric Character of the Gospels,' Vol. I, p. 180, Nov. 1887.

CHAPTER II

ALLEGORY AND MYSTICAL SYMBOLISM

T HE matter for reflexion and study which the present chapter contains is in continuation of the general theme dealt with in the preceding chapter. It is of paramount importance that the student, or the interested reader, understand that behind and within the outer or exoteric literatures of each and every great religion and philosophy, there is a heart or core of more mystical teaching, which, indeed, is the real substance, clothed and all too frequently hid by the outer exoteric literary garment or veil. This is, in fact, the body of esoteric teaching which is never promulgated publicly — a reticence or a reserve not inspired by motives arising in spiritual or intellectual selfishness, nor because the part withheld differs in the slightest degree from the parts given out publicly as regards authenticity or actuality, but simply because, without some adequately prolonged study, no one could properly understand this secret portion, which is from this fact of necessity held for the use of students who are willing to devote, and do devote, the necessary time and sacrifice of personal interests to understand it.

Yet any honest man or woman, especially one who is a member of the Theosophical Society and who thereby has at his hand the keys for understanding this Secret Doctrine, may unveil it by due and proper intellectual application, especially if such student lead the life necessary for the clarifying or thinning of the inner veils of consciousness, thus exemplifying the old adage: "It is necessary to live the life if ye will know the Doctrine."

The fact of a body of esoteric teaching which is held private for the study and use of those who prove themselves to be worthy and well qualified, is nothing new in the history of religion and philosophy. It is, in fact, one of the commonplaces of knowledge that the great ancient religions and philosophies had and in some cases still have an esoteric side — that is to say, a system of secret teachings given only to those who have proved themselves worthy and fit to receive and to understand. Even the Syrian Sage, Jesus the Avatâra, according to the allegation found in the Christian New Testament, is said to have taught certain things to his disciples in private, whereas to the multitude the same truths, or at least parts of them as the case may have been, were taught not openly, that is to say, in an unveiled manner, but in parable and mystical symbol. This procedure is a matter of actual necessity, as a few moments of reflexion will show to anyone, for it is not possible to teach one unacquainted with the elements of a study the deeper reaches thereof until he has fitted himself by at least a modicum of moral and intellectual training to understand them.

Particularly is this the case when the doctrines to be communicated in private, deal with the profoundest religious, scientific, and philosophical truths. These doctrines are not withheld from public knowledge merely because they are in themselves perilous either to intellectual sanity or to moral stability. On the contrary, they are most wonderfully helpful, in every respect illuminating and inspiring; but to those who are not fit to receive them, and who in turn would give them out indiscriminately to all and sundry at any time and in any place and without due preparation, it is only right to state that they could indeed possibly work a very real mischief, because of the unprepared state of such minds into which these teachings would be received.

Who has not heard of religious fanatics, and the mischiefs and wrongs that they have wrought upon their fellow-men? This single instance, as an example in point, demonstrates what ill-digested and often misunderstood religious and indeed philosophical thought can and usually does do in and upon weak or unprepared minds. If a man do not understand a noble teaching properly and with relative fulness, its very beauty, its very profundity, may so fascinate and distort his unprepared judgment, that he may be swept from his normal mental moorings in ordinary principles of ethics, so to say. The stream of such an unprepared man's emotions, sympathetically and automatically following the lead and urge that these teachings give to him, might readily at some moment of mental or moral weakness cause him to do a psychological injury to another, quite apart from more common mischief, thereby readily becoming the cause to such man of intellectual ethical damage of no small magnitude, as the history of religious fanaticism shows us clearly; and such a condition of affairs all students of the Esoteric Tradition are strictly enjoined to avoid becoming participators in.

Yet some of the religious and philosophical teachings given out publicly in our own age, were esoteric in past times, and were then taught under the veil of allegory and mystical symbol. It is not easy for men and women of our pragmatical and matter-of-fact age

to understand why such reticence should be had in religious, philosophical, and scientific matters, because today a common saying is
that truth is a sacred thing and at all times and in all places can
do only good; or again, that facts of Nature are the common property
of mankind, and that there is no possible danger in the communication of knowledge by one who has it to others who have it not; yet
surely a more fantastic fallacy, or a greater untruth, does not exist.
Who does not know that knowledge can be and often is most abomin-
ably abused and misused by selfish or self-seeking individuals? Even
our scientists today are beginning to see that the communication of
all the truths of Nature to everybody, without certain preparatory
safeguards erected in the first instance, is a course of proceeding
which is fraught with perilous and hid dangers of its own not only
to individuals but to the masses of mankind.

Two of the teachings now promulgated publicly by the Theosophical Movement, but which were esoteric or secret in certain eras
of past time, are the doctrines of Karman and Reimbodiment. Karman is a word used briefly to describe those majestic and quasi-
automatic operations of Nature, the so-called 'laws of Nature,' which
are briefly set forth in the famous saying of Paul, the Christian
Apostle: "Whatsoever a man soweth, that shall he also reap."[19] It
is, as modern Theosophists phrase it, the doctrine of consequences,
of results following thought and action inevitably, ineluctably, and
with absolute justice, whether such consequences or results be immediately forthcoming in time or be postponed to a later period.[20]

19. *Galatians*, vi, 7.

20. KARMAN — all that *total* of a soul, which is itself, brought into present
being by its own willing and thinking and feeling, working upon the fabric
and the substance of itself, and thus preparing its future destiny, as its present
existence was the destiny prepared for itself by its own past lives. The basis,
or root, or essence, or, may we not say the law of itself — KARMAN — rises in
the 'heart' of the Universe which is immortal, impersonal, infinite, LIFE itself,
Divine Harmony, whence spring into active operation all the so-called 'Laws'
of Nature that make the Mighty Mother what she is in all her septenary or
denary constitution. As H. P. Blavatsky says in her *The Voice of the Silence*,
Section 'The Two Paths,' pp. 34-5 (orig. ed.):

"Learn that no efforts, not the smallest — whether in right or wrong
direction — can vanish from the world of causes. E'en wasted smoke remains
not traceless. 'A harsh word uttered in past lives, is not destroyed but ever
comes again.' (Precepts of the Prasanga School.) The pepper plant will
not give birth to roses, nor the sweet jessamine's silver star to thorn or
thistle turn.

Reincarnation, as the next example of an esoteric doctrine now become public in its more or less adequate explanation, really comes under the more general doctrine of Reimbodiment of which it is a 'special case' as the mathematicians say. It is the teaching that

"Thou canst create this 'day' thy chances for thy 'morrow.' In the 'Great Journey' ('Great Journey' or the whole complete cycle of existences, in one 'Round'), causes sown each hour bear each its harvest of effects, for rigid Justice rules the World. With mighty sweep of never erring action, it brings to mortals lives of weal or woe, the Karmic progeny of all our former thoughts and deeds.

"Take then as much as merit hath in store for thee, O thou of patient heart. Be of good cheer and rest content with fate. Such is thy Karma, the Karma of the cycle of thy births, the destiny of those, who, in their pain and sorrow, are born along with thee, rejoice and weep from life to life, chained to thy previous actions. . . .

"Act thou for them to 'day,' and they will act for thee, 'to morrow.' "

Or again as H. P. Blavatsky describes this ineffably just Principle of Universal Nature, guided by Infinite Compassion, but inflexibly just in all its operations, whether upon star or glow-worm or man, which the Esoteric Tradition calls Karman — in her *The Secret Doctrine,* Vol. I, pp. 642-644:

"In the West, since Pagan Wisdom has been repudiated as having grown from and been developed by the dark powers supposed to be at constant war and in opposition to the little tribal Jehovah — the full and awful significance of the Greek NEMESIS (or Karma) has been entirely forgotten. . . . Nemesis is without attributes; that while the dreaded goddess is absolute and immutable as a Principle, it is we ourselves — nations and individuals — who propel her to action and give the impulse to its direction. KARMA-NEMESIS is the creator of nations and mortals, but once created, it is they who make of her either a fury or a rewarding Angel. . . . unwise they, who believe that the goddess may be propitiated by whatever sacrifices and prayers, or have her wheel diverted from the path it has once taken . . . begotten by ourselves. There is no return from the paths she cycles over; yet those paths are of our own making, for it is we, collectively or individually, who prepare them. Karma-Nemesis is the synonym of PROVIDENCE, minus *design,* goodness, and every other *finite* attribute and qualification, so unphilosophically attributed to the latter. An Occultist or a philosopher will not speak of the goodness or cruelty of Providence; but, identifying it with Karma-Nemesis, he will teach that nevertheless it guards the good and watches over them in this, as in future lives; and that it punishes the evildoer — aye, even to his seventh rebirth. So long, in short, as the effect of his having thrown into perturbation even the smallest atom in the Infinite World of harmony, has not been finally readjusted. For the only decree of Karma — an eternal and immutable decree — is absolute Harmony in the world of matter as it is in the world of Spirit. It is not, therefore, Karma that rewards

the human ego returns to earth at some future time after the change men call death, and also after a more or less long period of rest in the invisible realms, in what the Theosophical teachings call the Devachan; such reincarnation taking place in order that the ego

---

or punishes, but it is we, who reward or punish ourselves according to whether we work with, through and along with nature, abiding by the laws on which that Harmony depends, or — break them.

"Nor would the ways of Karma be inscrutable were men to work in union and harmony, instead of disunion and strife. For our ignorance of those ways — which one portion of mankind calls the ways of Providence, dark and intricate; while another sees in them the action of blind Fatalism; and a third, simple chance, with neither gods nor devils to guide them — would surely disappear, if we would but attribute all these to their correct cause. . . . Were no man to hurt his brother, Karma-Nemesis would have neither cause to work for, nor weapons to act through. . . . We stand bewildered before the mystery of our own making, and the riddles of life that *we will not* solve, and then accuse the great Sphinx of devouring us. But verily there is not an accident in our lives, not a misshapen day, or a misfortune, that could not be traced back to our own doings in this or in another life. If one breaks the laws of Harmony, . . . one must be prepared to fall into the chaos one has oneself produced. . . .

". . . Karma-Nemesis is no more than the (spiritual) dynamical effect of causes produced and forces awakened into activity by our own actions."

In the above flowing and majestic paragraphs from the Great Theosophist, H. P. Blavatsky, one finds the best and most comprehensive definition of that never-erring, universal, and never-resting Principle, or 'Law,' of Cosmic Being, which is briefly and technically expressed by the Esoteric Tradition in the one word KARMAN. It is an utterly erroneous notion to suppose on the one hand that Karman is fatalism, and that human beings are under its blind and fortuitous action, the victims of an inscrutable, unmoral, destiny of blind chance; and equally erroneous on the other hand to suppose that Karman is the creation or created law of action of some Cosmic Entity, different from and apart from the Universe itself, and therefore extra-Cosmic. It is equally erroneous to suppose that whatever happens to a man in his endless series of lives in time and space, in the worlds visible and invisible, during the aeons-long course of his peregrinations, is in strict accuracy 'unmerited,' or that events in any particular, or in general, happen unto him apart from his own original causative action. It is necessary to emphasize this because one or two otherwise excellent Theosophists are under the impression derived from certain passages of H. P. Blavatsky's that there is such a thing as 'unmerited Karman'; forgetting that in order properly to understand the Great Theosophist's teaching, one must include every statement by her on this topic, ignoring none. There is, indeed, relative injustice, or relative 'unmerited suffering' in the world, brought about by the interaction of the various parts of man's complex constitution, the higher

may learn new lessons on our Earth, in new times, in new environments; and taking up again on this plane, and on this Earth, the old links of sympathy and of friendship, of hatred and dislike, as the case may be, which were apparently ruptured by the hand of death when the ego-soul left our spheres.

The foregoing two very brief statements of two teachings once held secret, or which were openly promulgated in a more or less imperfect or emasculated form, are two examples of the manner in which from age to age and for good and sufficient reasons, and when the need arises for so doing, esoteric teachings are openly developed with far more adequate explanation of their inner significance by the Brotherhood of Sages and Seers, whom the modern Theosophists more commonly call the Mahâtmans. There are many such doctrines which at one time it was considered improper openly to promulgate; with changing times the need for reticence or reserve in this or that instance, or with regard to this or that particular teaching, vanishes; and then some teachings taught anew to a bewildered and perhaps hopeless generation, breathe their refining and inspiring influence into the minds and hearts of men. Such

---

principles of his constitution, such as the Reincarnating Ego, frequently in the course of karmic destiny bringing upon the merely *personal man* events which that *personal* man in any one life is not himself directly and absolutely responsible for. But the Reincarnating Ego *was* fully responsible, although its lower vehicle, the astral or personal man, through which the Reincarnating Ego works, does not recognise the justice of the misfortunes and sufferings and karmic destiny caused in other lives — and therefore to this astral or personal man these blows of destiny seem to be both unmerited and unjust. Yet, in very truth, as H. P. Blavatsky so nobly says in the above paragraphs, "there is not an accident in our lives, not a misshapen day, or a misfortune, that could not be traced back to our own doings in this or in another life."

This, with her other statements, is conclusive; and it is but insufficient study and lack of intellectual realization of the subtil logic of the teaching which could ever bring any man to suppose that what he undergoes in suffering or sorrow or pain in any one life, he himself is not responsible for. He himself in former lives set in action the causes which later, by rigid karmic justice, bring about the effects which he in the present life complains of and calls 'unmerited.' This same mistake in misunderstanding the rigid logic and the delicate and subtil reasoning of the teaching, caused, in early Christianity, that first fatal departure from the recognition of infinite and automatic Justice in the world, to the idea, that because man's sufferings seemed inexplicable, they were therefore unmerited and were due to the inscrutable wisdom of Almighty God, whose decrees man should accept in humility without questioning the wisdom of the Providence thus erected in explanation.

teachings profoundly modify civilization because they profoundly change human psychology and the spiritual and intellectual vision of mankind. Few people realize, it would seem, the enormous but always invisible and quiet psychological leverage that new ideas have upon human consciousness; and this is especially so with regard to teachings of a spiritual or intellectual type or character and which are part of the treasury of Wisdom of the Esoteric Tradition. All these teachings are replete with the divine conceptions of the gods who first gave Truth to men; and this is the secret of the immense sway that Religion *per se* — apart from mere degenerate religions — has upon human intellect.

I

It was the archaic imbodying of these divine conceptions of the gods in ancient mystery-rites and stories that brought about the formal institution on earth and among ancient peoples of various kinds of ceremonial initiations, of which men in the world have heard a great deal and concerning which they *know* naught. Every nation, every people, every race, had its own variety or exemplification of the same body of fundamental verities, which after all, is but another way or manner of saying 'the divine conceptions of the gods who first gave truth to men.' The Greeks had their own Mysteries, which from earliest times were functions of the State, and carried on under the sanctions of law, such as the initiatory institutions of Eleusis and Samothrace and of other places in the various Greek Republics.

The Jews likewise had their own particular variety of a system of mystical research and investigation, which in a more or less complete degree is imbodied in the Qabbâlâh, a Hebrew word meaning 'tradition' — the traditional teaching handed down from teacher to pupil, who in his turn graduated and became a teacher, then handing it to *his* pupils as a sacred, secret charge communicated from the 'Fathers'; and so forth. Even among the Christians there remain rumors which have reached our own age of the former existence in primitive Christian communities of a body of secret doctrine or teaching. Jerome, for instance, one of the most respected of the Church-Fathers, mentions the fact, although indeed with his sense of strong orthodox loyalty, he speaks of it with contempt — a proof, if nothing else existed, of his ignorance of the heart of the teaching of his Master Jesus.

It is also common knowledge that the great religions of Hindûsthân all had their respective secret schools or esoteric bodies, in which the fitter, abler, and more trustworthy students of these different religions received and later passed on the Noble Wisdom.

Even so-called savage or barbarous tribes, as our European anthropologists have shown us, have each one its peculiar and secret tribal mysteries — fearfully degenerated memories in most cases from the days when their forefathers formed the leading and most civilized races of the globe.

This necessity for keeping secret a certain amount of the Esoteric Tradition, accounts for the symbolic imagery, often beautiful, but in some cases almost repulsive, in which all the old literatures have been cast. The same natural difficulty of delivery to untrained ears and minds, was as operative in the early days of the Christian Church, for instance, as it has been to other races and in all other times. One may find many of the early Church-Fathers writing about the so-called Kingdom of Christ, which was to come. They evidently enough did not tell all that they believed about this, doubtless for very good reasons of their own. Many books have been written about this matter in later times also, in which a good deal of guessing occurs as to the meaning of the early Patristic writings; and it has occupied the thought of many people in Christendom, because there is an instinct in the human heart which tells us that the world is not perfect in its present state, and that it might be very much better, a far nobler place to live in than it is. Dare anyone say that man is a perfect being, or that the universe in which he lives could not be better: that there is nothing superior in the infinite spaces that surround us than this globe of stone and mud upon which we pass our lives?

A Christian witness to the existence of an esoteric teaching in primitive Christian communities, was Origen, one of the broadest-minded Fathers of the Christian Church, the condemnation of a portion of whose doctrines at Constantinople in the early part of the sixth century has already been alluded to.[21] Origen, who in his way was really a great man, wrote as follows, on the subject of an esoteric doctrine as existent in the non-Christian religions even of his own time:

In Egypt, the philosophers have a most noble and secret Wisdom concern-

---

21. Origen mentions this really esoteric teaching especially in his book, *Contra Celsum* ('Against Celsus'). Celsus was a Greek philosopher who disputed the claims of the Christian teachers of his day to have pretty nearly all the truth that the world contained.

ing the nature of the Divine, which Wisdom is disclosed to the people only under the garment of allegories and fables. . . . All the Eastern nations — the Persians, the Indians, the Syrians — conceal secret mysteries under the cover of religious fables and allegories; the truly wise [the initiated] of all nations understand the meaning of these; but the uninstructed multitudes see the symbols only and the covering garment.[22]

The wording here reminds one strongly of a similar statement contained in the *Zôhar* of the Qabbâlâh.[23]

This was said by Origen in his attempt at rebuttal of the attack made against the Christian system by many 'Pagans' to the effect that Christianity was but a compost or a rehash of misunderstood Pagan mythological fables. Origen claimed that in Christianity there was, as there was indeed in all other religions, a similar, indeed an identic, esoteric system; and he was right, so far as that one argument goes; but while he was right in the argument, one fails to see that it was a successful plea in extenuation of the charge that the Christians of the day claimed the only real knowledge of things in religious matters that there was then to be had by inquisitive, thinking, and earnest minds.

Turning to the Jews, one may find in the *Zôhar* — a Hebrew word meaning 'splendor,' which is perhaps the greatest text-book of the Jewish Qabbâlâh, and which has been mentioned before — a statement to the effect that the man who understands the Hebrew Bible in its literal meaning is a fool. "Every word of it," says the *Zôhar* in this connexion, "has a secret and sublime sense, which the wise [that is, the initiated] know."

One of the greatest of the Jewish Rabbis of the Middle Ages, Maimonides, who died in 1204, writes:

We should never take literally what is written in the Book of the Creation, nor hold the same ideas about it that the people hold. If it were otherwise, our learned ancient sages would not have been to so great labor in order to conceal the real sense, and to hold before the vision of the uninstructed people the veil of allegory which conceals the truths that it contains. Taken literally, that work contains the most absurd and far-fetched ideas of the Divine. Whoever can guess the real sense, ought to guard carefully his knowledge not to divulge it. This is a rule taught by our wise men, especially in connexion with the work of the six days. . . .[24]

It is quite possible that many things will be met with that at

---

22. Origen: *Contra Celsum*, Bk. I, chap. xii.
23. See *supra* page 44.
24. *Môre Nevôchîm*, (Guide of the Perplexed), part II, chapter xxix.

first sight may not please the inquirer in searching these old literatures of by-gone times. Whose is the fault? That of the literatures, which is equivalent to saying that of the great men who cast
them into that form, belonging to and appropriate to the day in
which they taught; or is it our own fault, who do not know how to
read correctly the meaning of what these great men wrote?

Hence, before forming final conclusions adverse to what we do
not understand, is it not wiser to withhold judgment, and instead of
saying that the ancients were a pack of ignorant, or silly, or sensuous
dolts in writing as they did sometimes write, to say instead: "Perhaps it is I who do not understand what they meant to say; or I
understand it perhaps only in part." The present writer in his own
studies has found that in ordinary fairness and in order to reach the
inner sense of these old literatures it is necessary to take this
mental attitude, and to withhold judgment; and he has been well
repaid for nearly a lifetime passed in this most wonderful and indeed
sublime study of ancient esoteric mystical wisdom.

Let us not, therefore, mistake the garment in which these old
teachings are clothed for the sublimity of the meanings which form
their core, and the substance of sense around which the clothing
is thrown.

Some of the veils and garments in which the old teachings are
inwrapped may seem at times ludicrous to us of our sophisticated
modern era; yet some of these garments themselves often are really
sublime in their significant harmony and symmetrical outline, while
on the other hand, some, to our modern eye, are actually gross in
expression and offensive in suggestion. But the fault perhaps —
and the writer affirms that this is actually the case from his own
experience — is as much in us as it may be to some extent in the
method of setting forth what those great men of ancient times needed
to set forth, because we neither grasp the spirit which dictated those
particular forms of expression, nor understand clearly the conditions under which they were enunciated — the circumstances which
those great men had to take into consideration when they taught
after that manner.

For instance, turn to the Christian New Testament. Therein
one finds a statement to the effect that Jesus, the Syrian Initiate and
Avatâra, said: "I come not to bring peace but a sword."[25] An amazing speech for the 'Prince of Peace,' is it not — if taken literally!
Shall we then accept it at its face-value? Or does not our instinct,

---

25. *Matt.*, x, 34.

does not our intuition, do not all the faculties which we have within us, tell us, whisper to us, that there is a meaning behind the verbal framework, behind and within the mere words, which has not yet been clearly seen?

II

The Church-Father, St. Clement, said that Jesus, once having been asked when his 'kingdom' would come, replied: "It will come when two and two make one; when the outside is like the inside; and when there is neither male nor female."[26] Many people have exercised their minds over this enigma, and no Christian, as far as the writer knows, has found an explanation of Clement's meaning. A Theosophical student will turn to Theosophy, to the 'Interpreter' as many love to call it, for an explanation of this exceedingly interesting parable, if we may give to it that name; and in applying this wonderful Theosophical touchstone, we obtain the following result: that this parable sets forth in actual prophetic strain what Theosophy says will some time in the future come to be.

Taking it clause by clause: 'When two and two make one.' The human being is divided into seven principles, seven elements if you like, which we may distribute as follows: an uppermost duad, which we call the spiritual Monad, because its parts are really inseparable, and dual only in manifestation; and an intermediate or psychological duad; and a lower ternary; this lower ternary is the purely physical human being, composed of his body, his vital essence, and of what is called the model-body, or astral body, the Linga-śarîra, around which the physical body is built or framed from conception till death. This ternary, or these three principles last enumerated, all undergo complete dissolution at death, pass away, leaving the inner two duads, which may be looked upon, for more easy understanding, each one as a unit — the spiritual nature and the psychological nature. Now in time to come, in the far distant future, these two duads, through the processes of evolutionary growth, will become one entity: that is to say, the psychological or intermediate nature will be so improved, so developed, will become so perfect and fit a vehicle for the manifestation of the upper duad or the inner spiritual god within, that it will coalesce with the latter and thus become one intrinsic unitary being.

Men who in our own and in past times have succeeded in accom-

---

26. 'The Second Epistle of Clement,' chap. xii.

plishing this unification of the two duads — 'when the two and two make one' — are what may be called Christs, adopting a term from the Christian system. The Buddhists call such a human being a Buddha, 'an awakened one,' 'an enlightened one'; and other religions have appropriate names for the same exalted human beings. This then, very briefly explained, is the substantial meaning of this first clause: 'When two and two make one.'

We pass on to the next clause: 'When the outside is like the inside.' The human body was not always as it now is — an opaque, hard, coarse, physical instrument, through which the most delicate forces of the soul and of the spirit must play, if they are to express themselves at all; and, as our teachings tell us, this difficulty in expression of the inner faculties and powers will not be so great in the distant future as it now is; because as the inner man evolves, so also does his physical encasement evolve: the latter becomes more refined, more delicately balanced, a more sensitive and more quickly responsive instrument upon which the god within him plays the divine melodies of the spirit. This increase in responsiveness and subtilty of the lower parts of man is very largely achieved through evolution, which also works constantly towards thinning out the gross compactness of the material, and thus causing it to approximate ever more closely to the substantial fabric of the sheaths of consciousness of the inner man.

Thus it is that the outer in evolutionary time will become like the inner, because the outer continuously, albeit slowly, evolves nobler and higher attributes and qualities. 'When the outside is like the inside,' therefore simply means when the living, conscious, exterior instrument or encasement becomes more and more like unto its inner god which it inshrines; becomes fitter to express more and more easily the divine and spiritual faculties of that inner luminary.

Yes, the time is coming in the far distant future, the new condition is coming as surely as that future itself, so our teachings say, when the physical human encasement, the 'outside,' will no longer be the opaque, dense, compact physical vehicle that it now is, but will be relatively transparent or diaphanous and luminous — an ethereal body of actually condensed light. 'The inner then shall be like the outer,' because the outer shall have become the inner, coalescing with it almost entirely, thus becoming the relatively perfect and adequate transmitter of the god-like Powers within.

Now for the third clause: 'When there is neither male nor female.' It is one of the Theosophical teachings that the present state of the human race as divided into men and women, into beings of opposite sexes, was not always thus in the past, nor will it be thus in the far distant aeons of the future. The time is coming when both 'men' and 'women' as such shall have disappeared; and there then will be neither 'men' nor 'women,' but human beings only, in those distant aeons of the future; for sex, like many other attributes of the human entity, is a transitory evolutionary stage through which the race is now passing; once sex did not exist; at present the sexual state exists; in the future it will again not exist, for the human race shall then have evolved out of this manner of expressing the positive and negative qualities of the psychological economy of the human being. When this shall have taken place — when sex shall have disappeared, when there shall no longer be either male or female, but simply human beings dwelling in bodies of luminous light — then the inner god, the inner Christos, the Christ Immanent, or as the Oriental mystics of High Asia express it, the Dhyâni-Bodhisattva, will be able to express itself and its powers and faculties with relative perfection; and when all human beings shall thus be 'Christs' in greater or less degree, then the 'Kingdom of Christ,' of which the early Christian Mystics spoke and wrote so much, shall have arrived.

A study of the Theosophical teachings will prove the existence of a great wisdom lying behind these mystical parables, and not only in the Christian system, but likewise in all the great philosophical and religious literatures of whatever race of the globe. These parables and mystical teachings given under the veil of metaphor and allegory are in no sense merely invented mystical imaginings, but actually symbolic or pictorial representations of events which have occurred in the past history of the human race, or, mayhap, they are prophetic visionings of events which will arrive in the future history of the human race. The rapidly advancing knowledge of physical science gives us today a great many hints of what is to be, if we are only alert enough and sufficiently intuitive to understand these hints, and it tells us a good deal by way of suggestion along the same line as to what the human race shall one day become; but naturally these scientific hints and suggestions are couched in the pragmatic and matter-of-fact style so dear to the scientific heart, and in this differ radically from the always mystical, invariably metaphorical, and often mythological style of these ancient allegorical parables.

Another example of the mystical method of teaching with which this chapter specifically deals, is taken from the writings of the early Church-Father, Irenaeus, born in Gaul. He wrote a book called 'Against Heresies.' These early Church-Fathers, by the way, were very fond of writing against the notions or ideas of people who did not hold the particular religious views favored in the Patristic literature, and whom these Church-Fathers very consistently and always unkindly called 'heretics'; and the Gallic Irenaeus was no exception to this amiable and then universally common Christian custom.

In this work he says that Papias, a disciple, as alleged, of John the Apostle and Evangelist, heard the following parable or allegory from John's own lips, to wit:

The Lord taught and said that the time will come when vines shall grow, each having ten thousand branches, and each branch shall have ten thousand branchlets, and each branchlet of a branch shall have ten thousand tendrils, and each tendril will have ten thousand bunches of grapes, and each bunch shall contain ten thousand grapes, and each grape, when pressed, will yield twenty-five gallons of wine; and when any one of the saints shall take hold of any bunch, another bunch will exclaim, 'I am a better bunch; take me; and bless the Lord by me!' [27]

We prosaic Occidentals find it more than difficult to forgo a certain sense of conscious amusement when we hear tales or allegories so quaintly simple in their blind trust; but, doubtless, large numbers in those early Christian times believed these tales as true prophetic forecasts of future events, and, doubtless, likewise believed that they contained a great truth under a mystical garment. Any such allegory or parable proffered to them, with an accompanying statement that it was handed down as one of the sayings of the great Syrian Sage, their Lord Jesus, was accepted by them either at face-value, or as containing some deeply hid mystic verity; and, indeed, the latter belief was very often valid, and was a true intuition. It was the custom in those days, even as it was the custom in many other countries, to clothe difficult scientific, religious, or philosophical doctrines under the guise of allegories or parables, or even to cast such doctrines into the form of what is modernly called fairytales.

It is perhaps interesting to venture upon a brief interpretation of this remarkable 'History of the Vine and the Grapes,' with the help of Theosophy, the Interpreter. Jesus in *The Gospel according to John*, who is this same Apostle, is alleged to have said:

I am the true vine, and my Father is the husbandman. . . . I am the vine, ye are the branches. He that remaineth in me and I in him, he bringeth forth much fruit, but cut off from me [the Vine] ye produce nothing. If a man remain not in me, he as a branch is cut off, and withers; and men gather such and throw

27. *Contra Haereses*, Bk. V, chap. xxxiii.

them into the fire and they are burned [destroyed]. Remain in me and I will remain in you. As the branch produceth no fruits unless it remain in the vine, so ye cannot unless ye remain in me.[28]

This is the beautiful Christian New Testament parable of the 'Vine and the Branches.' In it is the direct statement that the Vine is the spiritual nature of man; and in the allegory from Irenaeus these various branches and branchlets and tendrils and individual grapes are evidently intended to represent the disciples, great and small, of the Teachers of men, such as Jesus was. These brief comments, therefore, summarize the essential meaning of this quaint and instructive and truly esoteric parable or allegory. With the Theosophical key, it is as easy as can be to understand the meaning of it. It no longer is a yarn exciting merely amusement, but is seen to contain a substantial meaning which is at once profound and beautiful.

The early Christians, as has already been stated, were not the only ones who used this mystical or metaphorical method of teaching secret verities in their literature. On the contrary, the method was common to all nations, and the Christians in this case were the copyists and very wisely adopted the universal custom. The Jews, for instance — and in this case reference is more particularly made to the Talmudic writings of the Jewish Rabbis in their mediaeval artlessness — are well known for what modern ecclesiastical scholars of matter-of-fact minds, who do not understand what was meant, call 'a love of exaggeration.' But it is to be remembered that perhaps it is we ourselves who are exercising our imagination and giving play to our phantasy in seeing things which do not really exist. It is a quite common failing of human nature to think itself very wise; albeit this is almost invariably a mark of ignorance; and that our own understanding is the infallible touchstone of truth; and because we do not understand a thing, this common failing drives us to say: "The thing is but foolish imagination, extravagant exaggeration, mere play of fancy." The man who says this and applies it universally without discrimination, is unwise; other men have lived in past time, possessing an understanding in no respects inferior to the critic — perhaps having much more understanding than he has. Criticism is by no means the mark of superiority. Indeed, one is inclined to think that the quick and ready critic is precisely the one who speaks from ignorance and understands often the least. The truly wise man knows too much to allow himself easily to criticize.

There is one thing that every scholar knows and none dare deny,

28. *John*, xv, 1-6.

and it is this: that all ancient religious, and indeed, philosophical teaching also, was given under the guise or garment of symbol and allegory, of veil and parable, of metaphor and other figures of speech. It was so in all nations of the world; and the man who, knowing this, deliberately turns his back on what he knows to be a fact, and proceeds to embark upon a critical argument destined to illustrate his own supposititious wisdom at the expense of far greater men than he, is, probably, simply a fool. It is one of the commonest bits of knowledge today, recognised by really great scholars, that mystical writings inshrine secret or hid truths; and that all the great World-Teachers, probably without one exception that is known, taught their more esoteric doctrines after that fashion.

The Buddha, the Christ, Plato, Apollonius of Tyana, Pythagoras, Empedocles, Zoroaster of Persia, all thus taught. One could continue citing names and making a long list of the great men who have set forth truly wonderful thoughts in allegory, in parable, in symbol, in mystical allusion, but all conveying profound truths based on the structure and operations of Nature — not physical nature alone, but Universal Nature, which is Nature all inclusive and both visible and invisible.

Yes, even the racially pragmatical-minded Jewish Rabbis write in the same allegorical and veiled strain. They inform us, for instance, that there will be 60,000 towns in the hills of Judaea, and that each of these towns will contain 60,000 inhabitants; likewise they say that when their Messiah shall come, Jerusalem will be a city of immense extent: that it will then have 10,000 towns within its purlieus and 10,000 palaces; while Rabbi Simeon ben Yachia declares that there will be in the city 180,000 shops where nothing but perfumes will be sold, and that each grape in the Judaean vineyards will yield thirty casks of wine!

This example of Jewish mystical allegory is taken from Bartolocci's *Bibliotheca Rabbinica*. So it is evident that among the Jews there was the same use of allegorical symbolism, and that in the particular instance cited, the allegory employs the same images that the Christian allegory does, of the vine and the grape and the wine, with, doubtless, the same essential or secret meaning.

III

Without the Key to interpretation, much in the various ancient world-systems remains not only paradoxical to modern scholarship, but usually inexplicable. To illustrate the point further let us turn to two very interesting passages in the New Testament referring to

Jesus, the Syrian Sage and Avatâra, and consider them as Theosophy teaches us the inner meaning of them. In *The Gospel 'according to' Matthew*[29] occurs the following:

And about the ninth hour Jesus cried out with a great voice, saying: 'Eli! Eli! lama shabahhthanei!' which is: 'God of me! God of me! Why hast thou forsaken me?' And certain of those standing there, having heard, said that 'This man calls upon Elias.' [30]

In *The Gospel 'according to' Mark* occurs the following:

And in the ninth hour Jesus cried out in a great voice: 'Eloi! Eloi! lama shabahhthanei!' which, interpreted, is: 'The God of me, unto what hast thou forsaken me?' And certain of those standing, having heard, said: 'See, he calls upon Elias.' [31]

---

29. Here the significant phrase *according to* obviously signifies that the writer is not Matthew, but someone who wrote or who claimed to write 'according to' Matthew's teachings.

30. *Matt.*, xxvii, 46-7.

31. *Mark*, xv, 34-5. The reader is requested to note that in the two extracts from the Christian New Testament, respectively from *Matthew* and *Mark*, the author of the present work has himself made the translation into English from the original Greek, and consequently the Hebrew sentence which appears in both these extracts is transliterated into English characters in such fashion as to give as closely as possible the phonetic pronunciation of the original Hebrew. The Greek manuscripts vary among themselves as to the spelling of this Hebrew sentence, and this is the fact not only in the different Greek manuscripts of *Matthew*, but likewise in the different Greek manuscripts of *Mark*. Yet in no case are the variations more than different attempts by the Greek writers to spell in Greek characters the Hebrew words of this sentence. Hebrew has certain sounds which Greek has not, and consequently the Greek writers had to choose such Greek alphabetic characters as seemed to be closest in sound to the Hebrew.

On precisely the same grounds the present writer has chosen such English alphabetic characters as would give the original Hebrew sounds as closely as possible. This explanation is made in order to forestall the entirely wrong objection that any liberty has been taken with these Hebrew words.

The really important point is, that these are unmistakable Hebrew words which anyone knowing both Greek and Hebrew will easily understand the need of properly transliterating in order to approximate to the sounds of the original Hebrew vocables. Whatever the transliteration of the Hebrew may be, the meaning is perfectly clear, and both *Matthew* and *Mark* have mistranslated the Hebrew to mean something that the Hebrew words do not contain. Such mistranslation arose either from ignorance or from deliberation; and the reason for this the present writer has attempted to explain in the paragraphs of the text which follow the New Testament extracts given above.

These two writers obviously suggest that the witnesses standing around the cross, according to the legend, thought that the cry was made to Elias: in other words, that the witnesses misunderstood the Hebrew, Eli, Eli, meaning 'God of me, God of me,' to be the name 'Elias.' This gives a curious idea with regard to these two Gospel-writers, for the witnesses of the crucifixion, apart from the Roman guard alleged to have been there, must have spoken Aramaic as their mother-tongue, which is one of the Shemitic dialects, even as Hebrew is, and therefore ought to have understood the Shemitic root *'el* of such wide and common currency in the Shemitic dialects. This strongly suggests that the two Gospel-writers themselves either lacked reflexion or did not understand the proper meaning of the quoted Hebrew cry, which indeed both of them mistranslate.

However this may be, there are some other curious things in this jumbled matter, besides the very awkward and actual mistranslation by the writers of the Gospels 'according to' Matthew and 'according to' Mark.

It should be stated in passing that of course Theosophists do not accept the mediaeval idea of a word-for-word divine inspiration controlling the original writers of the Christian New Testament, nor again the inspiration, divine or otherwise, of the translators of the so-called 'English authorized version' of King James of England; Theosophists look upon the mystical story of Jesus as it exists in the Christian New Testament as a vaguely symbolic history of initiation, in which Jesus, later called the Christ, is figurated as the exemplar or type of any Great Man undergoing the various trials of the initiatory cycle: in other words he, Jesus, therein is a type-figure. This does not mean that such a Sage as Jesus did not exist. It is true that such a great Sage did exist in a period somewhat earlier than the supposed beginning of the Christian Era. The idea therefore is that the Christian New Testament sets forth a symbolic picture, a symbolic history, of the initiation of a sage therein bearing the name of Jesus; but this particular symbolic picture, or symbolic history, was written according to the type or method of initiation followed in that part of the world, and in form and in method differed from the form and type of initiation followed in other parts of the world, such as in Greece or in Egypt or in India, or elsewhere. The fundamentals of the idea, however, were the same all over the world.

Now, these words *'Eloi! Eloi! lama shabahhthanei!'* are Hellenized Hebrew so far as the New Testament spelling goes. It is usually said by biblical apologists that they are Aramaic words, and therefore that the alleged mistranslation of the Gospel-writers is probably imaginary; but this explanation is no explanation at all, and seems to the Theosophist to be itself purely imaginary and a forced attempt to explain the otherwise inexplicable; for the words are good Hebrew and also virtually good Chaldaic, and contain a sense violently different from the translation as given in these two extracts, as will be shown. It is interesting to note here also that Aramaic is a common name for the various kindred dialects spoken in Syria, and, therefore of course spoken in Palestine during the times when Jesus is alleged to have lived. The apologetic suggestion that these are Aramaic words seems to rest on no foundation of any fact whatsoever, and as far as the present writer knows, the suggestion has never been substantiated. The apology seems to arise out of a wish to 'save the face' of these two scriptural writers by the device of alleging an Aramaic origin of these words without producing the Aramaic words in proof thereof.

The meaning of this Hebrew sentence is not 'God of me! God of me! Why hast thou forsaken me?' but 'God of me! God of me! Why *givest thou me such peace?*' or also, as the Hebrew verb שבח could be translated: 'Why glorifiest thou me so greatly!' The Hebrew word *shâbahh* means to 'praise,' to 'glorify,' also to 'give peace to.' Surely this correct translation, outside of the original words being good and true Hebrew, is more concordant with the story of the Gospel itself according to the Christians' own interpretation, in other words, nearer to the story of Jesus as the Christians themselves give it to us! What earthly reason could have made these two Gospel-writers mistranslate something, which mistranslation, on the face of it, stood against themselves, and imparted into the sense an apparently inexplicable enigma? Why should the 'Son of God,' according to the Christian teachings (but not the Theosophical), who was likewise the human vehicle of one of the three inseparable persons of their Trinity, therefore an inseparable part of the Godhead itself according to the Christian teachings, exclaim in his passion in words of agony from the Cross, according to the legend, 'My God! My God! Why hast thou *forsaken* me?'

To turn to the Old Testament: in one of the *Psalms* occurs this: "My God! My God! Why hast thou forsaken me? Why art thou so far from helping me, and from the words of my roaring?"[32] The first Hebrew words here are: אלי אלי למה עזבתני "Êlî Êlî Lâmâh 'azabtânî!" and are correctly translated. The Hebrew word

---

32. *Psalm* xxii, 1.

'*âzab* as used in this Psalm means 'to forsake,' 'to leave,' 'to abandon,' and is a very natural exclamation for David, or whoever was the writer of the *Psalms*, to make in view of the situation that then supposedly existed with him, and in view of the thoughts supposedly in his mind, and is a very human cry, a cry uttered in despair, which any man might have made under stress of great spiritual and intellectual trial. All this is reasonable and true enough.

But here in the New Testament we have the 'Son of God,' the second person of the Trinity itself, according to the Christian teachings, saying: 'My God! My God! Why hast thou *abandoned* me?' And when we look at the words which the two New Testament writers themselves give, we find that they mean nothing of the sort, but mean, on the contrary, an exclamation of ecstasy: 'My God! O God within me! How thou dost glorify me!' Or, if you like: 'How thou dost give me peace!'

The suggestiveness involved in the hints of an esoteric significance contained in this tangled New Testament episode is so important in a way that it would seem to merit here a little more elaboration in the light that Theosophy casts upon ancient thought whether of a religious or philosophical character. A short attempt, therefore, briefly to explicate the meaning of this extraordinary enigma found in the New Testament, follows: If, as some have suggested, the writers 'according to' Matthew and 'according to' Mark, had this first verse of *Psalm* xxii in their minds when they made this mistranslation, we only ask why they did it, since they were supposedly two men who understood Aramaic and Hebrew better than modern scholars do, for Aramaic, *ex hypothesi*, was their mother-tongue; and, on the other hand, if these two Gospels were written in Alexandria, as is indeed probable, the situation remains the same because Alexandria then had a very large and learned Hebrew colony. It would seem that any such attempt to explain the enigma is entirely impermissible, because the Hebrew word '*âzab* used in *Psalm* xxii, verse 1, and meaning 'to abandon' or 'to forsake,' is not the Hebrew word used by these two Gospel-writers in their respective Gospels, for this word so used is *shâbahh*, which means 'to praise,' 'to glorify,' 'to give peace to.'

But — and just here is the point that it is attempted now to explain — the writer 'according to' Matthew and the writer 'according to' Mark, actually writing as they did of this 'suffering'— to use this ancient term for the initiation of one undergoing his glorification, his raising into temporary divinity in other words — used exactly the proper word therefor; for there comes a moment, we are told, in this initiation-cycle, a moment which approaches the supreme test, the supreme trial, when the initiant has to face the worst that in himself is, and the worst that the world of matter can bring against him, and pass through this severest of trials successfully; and in that solemn moment, when no inner light seems present to strengthen, to assist, and to illuminate: when, according to the pre-arranged mechanism itself of the initiatory rite, which was both spiritual and psychologic, working on the suffering man, he was temporarily divorced from all the help that his own spiritual-divine nature could give him: he was then obliged to stand alone as a *man* in his sole but nevertheless highly trained human nature, and, facing the worst, to come through the test successfully as a man, and to achieve the self-conscious *reunion* with his inner god, then and there. Success spelt glory such as human consciousness can never experience greater. It was at this supreme moment of reunion with the glory of the living god within that the *man,* thus successful and surmounting in his sole manhood the fearful trial before him, cried in both ecstasy and inexpressible spiritual relief: 'O my God! O my God within me! How thou dost glorify me!'

How many times in that solemn hour must not the cry of agony also have gone forth from that human heart: 'O my Inner God! Why hast thou forsaken me?' for to the sole manhood of the man the temporary separation from the guiding inspiration of the divinity within seems like being forsaken by the inner divinity. Yet these two Gospel-writers used a wrong translation or term for the Hebrew *word* which they gave: they used the term signifying glorification and not the Hebrew word meaning *forsaking,* thereby achieving a contradiction in terms which nevertheless gives the key to the initi-atory mystery — the mystical key showing that in this temporary divorce of the man's inner constitution, i. e., of the higher from the lower, during the trial of the human being thus temporarily separated from his inner God, there lie the seeds of the glorification in reunion which is to come afterwards, if the aspirant in his humanhood be successful in the test.

It is quite possible, indeed it is almost certain, that these two writers, respectively 'according to' Matthew and Mark, may have themselves been copying from an older and still more mystical doc-trine, imbodied or written in some earlier document then under their hands, and, either from deliberation or from error may have omitted words or passages which were intermediate between the Hebrew sentence they gave and the mistranslation of it which they either themselves made or quoted. What was this older and now lost source?

However, it is also true that in this complex and tangled manner, as thus exemplified in this New Testament enigma, was all or most of mystical literature written in ancient times; and it is precisely this complication of ideas and mingling of mystical thoughts cheek by jowl, so to say, that has made the ancient mystical literatures dealing with the initiation-cycle so difficult — if not utterly incomprehensible — for moderns to understand. But just here is it that the wondrous Theosophical teachings give to the thoughtful and persevering student the keys to it all and enable him to interpret, so to say, to wrench from the whirlpool of ideas, the real meaning; enable him to point out the apparent contradictions or faults and the *why* of these apparent verbal contrarieties and tangles. In the present instance taken from the New Testament and now here in discussion, we find a deliberate mixing in explanatory terms and in a highly mystical sense, of the facts contained in the most sublime moment that can come to a disciple. Later, when the test has been successfully passed, when the victory has been won 'on the cross' —for the cross is not a Christian symbol alone, but belongs to ancient so-called pagan symbolology, as every scholar knows: later, when the 'suffering' on the cruciform couch of initiation is ended, when the victory finally has been won, and the inner Light has come: in other words when the reunion with the inner god has been made again, then the victor can cry in ecstasy: 'O God of me! O God of me! How thou dost give me peace and glorify me!'

The average man whose mind and whose thinking apparatus have been uninjured and unspoiled by some predominating mental or other vice may discover these supernal truths for himself, and then there will be no need to take any other man's word for it, because he from his own experience will know the truth; but to do so of course he will need the training imperatively necessary for the bringing of understanding.

For this training, the teaching of a competent instructor is extremely helpful to and perhaps needed by every man whose mind is not so warped by egoism as to prevent him from accepting a verity when he hears it. Nevertheless, and although the aid of a true spiritual teacher is for a time a necessity which cannot be obviated, any man or woman may reach truth for himself or for herself, although when working alone and unaided the attainment is minor and the revelation is less great; and the method of so doing is cleanliness of mind and of heart, impersonal sincerity in service to the world, combined with study and honest abiding by the results of the convictions which follow upon that study and bear upon life.

IV

The grossness, at least verbal, of some of the imagery of the ancient allegories or symbols in religious and philosophical matters has already been pointed out. In one sense one may fully agree with the fastidious and difficult to please, and admit that this form of imbodying a great truth is unfortunate, but assuredly no such offense was in the intention of the formulators. The Persian Sûfî mystics, for instance, who were adherents of what may be called the Theosophy of Persian Mohhammedanism, wrote of the flowing wine-cup and of the pleasures of the tavern, and spoke of the unalloyed joy and the transcendent bliss that they experienced in company with their Beloved. These mystics employed all the amorous imagery of the love-song; and yet, most emphatically their writings were the precise opposite in meaning and intent of the sensuous imagery or suggestiveness of the lower human love. The Persian Mystic, Abû Yazîd who lived in the ninth century, wrote:

> I am the wine I drink, and the cup-bearer of it.

The wine-cup, for these mystical writers, symbolized in general the 'Grace of God' as Christians might say, the influences and work-ings of the spiritual powers infilling the Universe. The same Sûfî writer said also:

> I went from god to god until they cried from me, in me, "O! Thou, I!"

What graphic language is this! It is as though the soul of the poet were attempting to wash itself clean of all personality, and striving to say that his own Inmost was the Inmost of the All — which is the exact truth.

Anyone who reads carefully the profound poems of some at least of the Sûfî mystics, and is conscious of the delicate spirituality of many of these wonderful Sûfî poems, knows, unless he be insane or ren-dered foolish by prejudice, that the writing was wholly symbolic. Turn but to the quatrains of 'Omar Khayyâm, as an instance in point; or as another example, to an extract from the Dîwân of Jal-âlu'd-Din Rûmi, which an English scholar, Nicholson, has beautiful-ly translated as follows:

> Lo, for I to myself am unkown; now in God's name what must I do?
> I adore not the Cross nor the Crescent, I am not a Giaour or a Jew.
> East nor West, land nor sea is my home, I have kin nor with angel nor gnome,
> I am wrought not of fire nor of foam, I am shaped not of dust nor of dew.
> I was born not of China afar, not in Saqsîn and not in Bulghâr;

Not in India, where five rivers are, nor 'Irâq nor Khurâsân I grew.
Not in this world nor that world I dwell, not in Paradise neither in Hell;
Not from Eden and Riḍwân I fell, not from Adam my lineage I drew.
In a place beyond uttermost Place, in a tract without shadow or trace,
Soul and body transcending I live in the soul of my Loved One anew! [33]

Of what is this Sûfî poet singing here? What does his delicate spiritual sense tell him of, in the words in which he has tried to convey it to us? It is the Divine Source of which he sings, the Divine, the Source of us all, and the ultimate Home of us all, when we shall finally have run our evolutionary journey successfully.

The *Song of Solomon* in the Hebrew Bible contains the same suggestive sensual imagery as that employed by many Sûfî mystics, although these Sûfî mystics had the excuse for their language that under the then fear of the strong arm of the Moslem Government, they dared not write what this government would certainly have considered to be unorthodox teachings, and thus they were obliged to write under some other form and in consequence chose that of the love-song, which had the appearance of innocuousness — as if suggestively sensuous thoughts were not infinitely more harmful to the moral sense than any amount of theological speculation!

For grossness of physical imagery the *Song of Solomon* probably has few parallels. Apparently it describes naught but the physical charms of the most beloved of the Hebrew King; and yet anyone who has some knowledge of this figurative method of symbolic writing, easily reads beneath the lines and seizes the inner thought.

v

Let us leave the setting sun of the West and turn our faces to the rising sun, to the Far Orient; and here we shall come upon things so delicately beautiful, so spiritually fine, that it will take all our inner faculties of intuition to understand them even a little at our first reading. Then, as the student pursues his studies, the marvelous thoughts contained in the philosophical and theological systems of the Far East grow on him. They become in time life of his life, heart of his heart; they remain with him in the silences of the night-time as an inspiration and peace-bringing balm, and when awake they recur to his mind like a blessing. When they are once understood, at least in part, he will find his heart beating in sympathy with the *universal* human heart, of which these noble writings

---

33. Cited in E. G. Browne's *A Literary History of Persia.*

imbody so much that is noblest and best in philosophy and in religion.

To particularize. The Chinese, as a rule, are considered to be and probably rightly so, among the most matter-of-fact, pragmatic, common-sense, so-called 'sensible' people to be found anywhere on our globe. Yet, despite this well-known 'sensible' trait of the Chinese character, and when turning to the beautiful poesie that has been written by some of their great men, and likewise to the various religious and philosophical systems of thought that they have given birth to, one will be amazed at the revelations of the human spirit that are to be found there in the various branches of ancient Chinese literature, mystical, religious, and philosophic.

One of the greatest teachers of China was Lao-Tse, who was the founder or rejuvenator of Taoism, one of the noblest religions and philosophical systems of China, and, it may be said, of the entire world. According to the legends which have gathered about his personality, he was conceived before birth in a supernatural fashion, as so many others of the great World-Teachers are alleged to have been also. His mother, according to these legends, carried him for seventy-two years before he was born, so that when at last he saw physical light, his hair was white, as if with age — at least so the legend runs; and it is supposed that from this mythological or mystical fact, he was known in after times by the name 'the old son,' or 'the old boy.' His biographers tell us that when his life-work was done, he left China, traveling westwards towards Tibet, and finally disappeared on the western frontier of China; and, as his biographers rather pathetically say, it is not known where and when he died.

This great Chinese Sage is one of the least understood of all the great Brotherhood of Initiates or Adept-Teachers who from time to time appear among men, giving teachings or systems of doctrine which inspire and enlighten their age, and then — usually disappear. Following the few facts which seem to be authentic, and setting aside the mass of mythological material which has been woven around his name and personality, he would appear to have been one of those periodic incarnations of a ray of what in the Esoteric Tradition is mystically called Mahâ-Vishnu, or in other words an Avatâra. There seems to be no doubt whatsoever that he was one of the periodic Envoys or Messengers from the Holy Brotherhood who, as previously stated, send out representatives from among themselves in order to introduce an impulse or urge towards spirituality, and to bring about an intellectual awakening in the different parts of the world and in the respective races to which these Envoys are sent.

His great literary work is called the *Tao-Teh-Ching*, a Chinese title-phrase meaning 'The Book of the Doing of Tao.' *Tao* means the 'Way,' or the 'Path,' among other very mystical significances. *Teh* means 'virtue.' But *Tao*, while meaning the Way or the Path, also means the wayfarer, or he who travels on the Path. As Jesus is alleged to have said: "I am the Way and the Life." This truly great sage of China wrote as follows:

It is the Way of Tao not to act from any personal motive; to conduct affairs without feeling the trouble of them; to taste without being aware of the flavor; to account the great as small and the small as great; to repay injury with kindness.[34]

The last sentence of this really remarkable book is cast in the following strain:

It is the Tao [the Way] of Heaven, to benefit and not to injure; it is the Tao [the Way] of the Sage to do and not to strive.[35]

The meaning of these logical opposites is: Make no unnecessary ado about being and doing; fret not at all; worry not at all; but simply be and do! Here most graphically expressed is the difference between the undeveloped understanding of the ordinary man and the spiritual wisdom of the Sage. The latter knows that individual men, as units in a common humanity, contain within themselves, i. e., in their constitution, all that wherever is; everything the Universe contains is in man, because man is its inseparable offspring, an inseparable part of the Cosmic Whole; and a man stands in his own light, hinders his own progress, by contentious striving and striving and by constantly tensing his spiritual and intellectual and mental and physical muscles, as it were, and thus wearing out his strength in vain and futile notions. Lao-Tse said: "Be what is within you. Do what that which is within you tells you to do." This is the secret of Tao.

Thus far the mystical thought of ancient China as exemplified in the teachings regarding the *Tao* from the soul of the great Lao-Tse. It is to be regretted that lack of space forbids illustrating further strata of Chinese mystical thought by drawing examples from other Chinese sources such as are imbodied in the really wonderful Mahâyâna Buddhism as developed by native Chinese and foreign thinkers in the Flowery Kingdom. Chinese Buddhistic literature alone is a mine of profound mystical philosophy, and doubtless no part of it

---

34. *Tao-Teh-Ching*, section lxiii.
35. Section lxxxi.

lacks the same undercurrent of esoteric teaching which has been universal in all lands and among all peoples.

But it is to India, the so-called 'Motherland of religions and philosophies' — a title more or less based on fact — that one should turn to find probably the best and most open examples of the systems of that part of the archaic Esoteric Tradition which during the last three or four millennia has spread its pervasive influence not only throughout the Asia of these eras, but since the time of Anquetil Duperron has been affecting more strongly with each passing century the great peoples of the West. Yet even in India, as history shows to be the case in all other ancient lands, the modern representatives of the old religious philosophies or philosophical religions have degenerated from what one may with justice call their pristine purity and vigor of propaganda. If China and Tibet may be called mines of esoteric lore to be unearthed by the intuitive and inquisitive researcher, still more aptly may this qualification be given to the magnificent philosophical and religious literatures of ancient Hindûsthân. Possibly some of the noblest of archaic Indian mystical and esoteric thought is imbodied in those remarkable literary documents, relics of a now almost forgotten past, which are called the Upanishads, and which, with the remainder of the cycle of Vedic literature of which the Upanishads themselves are a portion, have been the fountain-head of the great systems of religion and philosophy which later times gave birth to in the peninsula. In the Upanishads, just as much as elsewhere, the inner or esoteric teaching is carefully hid from superficial scrutiny; for in these noble philosophical documents, gems of unparalleled beauty and of pure esoteric derivation are hid under the habiliments or garments of veil and allegory, parable and symbol, that cloak the teachings of the same Esoteric Tradition in other lands — albeit the lineaments or outlines of these veils and allegories differed and varied in each ancient race.

It would be a genuine pleasure to quote in these pages extensive passages conveying fragments of the Lost Word of antiquity, i. e., of the archaic Esoteric Tradition; but this delightful and profitable occupation may be freely left to the intuitive research of the reader himself. Let us content ourselves, therefore, with pointing to the Upanishads as being a veritable mine of ancient wisdom, and draw therefrom one single instance of mystical teaching which will likewise illustrate the method of imparting information in public works that the ancient Sages adopted.

Here we have the case, actual or imaginary, of an ancient teacher called Uddâlaka-Âruṇi, one of the great Brâhmaṇa-teachers of this portion of the cycle of the Vedic literature. Uddâlaka-Âruṇi is teaching his son, Śwetaketu, who asks him for knowledge:

"Fetch me from that spot a fruit of the Nyagrodha-tree."

"Here it is, Sir!"

"Break it open."

"It is now broken open, Sir!"

"What do you see there?"

"These seeds, exceeding small."

"Break open one of them."

"One is broken open, Sir."

"What do you see there?"

"Nothing at all, Sir!"

The father then said: "My child, that very subtil essence which you do not see there, of that very essence this huge Nyagrodha-tree exists. Believe it, my child. That which is this subtil essence — in it all that exists has its self. It is the Real; it is the Self; and you, O Śwetaketu are it!"

"Please, Sir, tell me yet more," said the child.

"Be it so, my son," the father answered. "Place this salt in water, and then come to me in the morning."

The child did as he was ordered to do. [In the morning] the father said to him: "Bring me the salt which you put in the water last night."

The child looked for it and found it not, for it was melted. The father then said: "Taste the water at the top. How is it?"

The son answered: "It is salty."

"Taste it from the middle layer. How is it?"

The son answered: "It is salty."

"Taste it from the bottom. How is it?"

The child answered: "It is salty."

The father then said: "You may throw it away, and then return to me." The boy did so; yet the salt remained always as before.

Then said the father: "Just so in this person you do not see the Real, my child; yet there in very truth It is. That which is this subtil essence — in it all that is has its Self. It is the Real; it is the Self; and you, O Śwetaketu, are It!

"If someone were to strike at the root of this great tree before us, it would bleed, but it would live. If he were to strike at its trunk, it would indeed bleed, yet it would live. If he were to strike at its top, it would indeed bleed, yet it would live. Permeated by the living Self the tree stands strong drinking in its food and rejoicing.

"But if the life [which is the living Self] depart from a branch of it, that branch dies; if it leave another branch, that also dies. If it abandon a third, that third dies also. If it leave the whole tree, the entire tree dies. After just this manner, O my child, know the following." Thus spoke the father again.

"This body indeed withers and dies when the living Self abandons it; but the living Self dies not.

"That which is its subtil essence — in it all that exists has its self. It is the Real. It is the Self, and you, O Śwetaketu, are it."

"Please, Sir, teach me yet more," said the child.

"Be it so, my son," the father answered.[36]

The different religious and philosophical systems of Hindûsthân all merit careful study by the student in search of philosophical proof of the existence of the Esoteric Tradition as the background of archaic Wisdom which has inspired the greatest literary works of the civilized world of past ages. Here it is necessary merely to point to the six *Darśanas* or 'Visions,' i. e., systems of philosophy which the metaphysical and philosophical genius of the Hindû mind has given birth to at different times in the past. Chief among these six systems of faith on account of its metaphysical esoteric profundity and also because of the fact that it is, chronologically speaking, one of the most recent to appear, although far older than the Christian era in the West, is the Vedânta in its three several schools; and chiefest and noblest of these three schools is the Adwaita-Vedânta. The three schools or divisions of the Vedânta are respectively: the *Adwaita* or non-Dualistic, of which the Avatâra, Śankarâchârya was the chiefest and loftiest exponent; the *Dwaita,* or Dualistic, the philosophical converse, so to speak, of the former; and the Viśishṭa-Adwaita, or modified non-Dualistic.

The word Vedânta, वेदान्त, itself means 'end of the Vedas,' not signifying the mechanical end of a unitary literary effort, nor the last in chronological sequence of a series of philosophical and religious documents; but meaning the philosophical completion in the sense of philosophical perfection of the cycle of the Upanishadic philosophic and religious thought that preceded it: its full completion or fullest and noblest elaboration. Yet with all the intrinsic majesty and deep philosophical and religious merit of these various 'Visions' of ancient India, not one of them, not even excepting the great Adwaita-Vedânta of Śankarâchârya, rises to higher levels of genuine esoteric teaching, than the amazingly subtil, profound and mystical thought imbodied in the system bearing the name of its great Founder, Buddhism. Probably no system known to the modern student is so wide in its sympathies, so appealing to the human heart, so cosmic in its philosophical range and so replete with esoteric doctrine — all when properly understood — as is the teaching of that greatest of

---

36. The example chosen is one which was likewise employed by the present writer in his volume *Fundamentals of the Esoteric Philosophy,* and is taken from the *Chhândogya-Upanishad,* vi, 11-13.

human Sages and Seers in recorded history, Siddhârtha-Śâkyamuni, Gautama the Buddha. Whether one search into the literature of the Southern School of Buddhism, commonly called the Hînayâna, or whether one turn to the more mystical elaboration of the Lord Buddha's teaching as found in Central and Northern Asia, and called the Mahâyâna, in either case the researcher discovers with each new spiritual and intellectual effort of his mind in research, new visions of Reality, and whatever Occidental Orientalists may have to say in denial of there having been, or of there now being, an esoteric Buddhism — or an esoteric and secret teaching in Buddhism — these objections are seen to be valueless and without substantial foundation by any careful student of the Esoteric Tradition who cares to pursue his researches into the deeper meaning underlying the outward form of the doctrines of the schools into which Buddhism is divided. The statement is made unqualifiedly that Buddhism, particularly in its northern Branch or School, has as strong and vital an inner meaning or recondite sense of an esoteric character imbodied in its various scriptural writings as has any other one of the great world-religions.

However this may be, and excluding for the moment the veils and allegories which inshrine and hide the Esoteric Tradition which is the living substance of any form of Buddhism or of Hindûism, the fact remains that so intuitive and urgent is the human mind in its higher strivings to attain Truth, that it makes contact, as it were, in such cases with underlying cosmic verities, and thus, through the minds of those outstanding examples of human philosophical and religious genius, their teachings converge often closely, thus again providing a proof of the statement that behind veil and within allegory, or symbol or parable, the fundamental ideas are identical in all the great systems of religious and philosophical thought.

As an example in illustration, one may point to the fact that the adherents of the Adwaita-Vedânta, mainly derivative from the teachings of the great Śankarâchârya, are called by their critical opponents Buddhists in disguise, Chhanna-Bauddhas; while in an exactly similar fashion, the adherents of the more metaphysical and mystical school of the Mahâyâna Buddhist systems are called by their Buddhist critics, Vedântists in disguise. Both these criticisms when taken from either side are fallacious when considered from the standpoint of their makers; but true, if the criticism merely means that at bottom the Adwaita-Vedântists and the mystical Mahâyâna Buddhists teach fundamentally doctrines which are identic and common to both systems. So strong, thus, is the influence of the

Esoteric Tradition, which is but another way of saying the natural intuitions and the workings of the human spirit in its visions of essential verities, that it expresses identic truths at all times and among all races of men, albeit often in widely differing structural frameworks of veil or allegory.

VI

From the substance of this chapter, therefore, the student should readily see that veil and allegory, parable and symbol, while enclosing and hiding still more sublime truths, nevertheless have their universal functions to perform in the delivery of philosophical and religious teaching. Some of these veils and allegories in expression or in form are often crude, possibly even repulsive to the Occidental eye, as has hereinbefore already been stated; but this feeling of strangeness or displeasing crudity arises, at least in a very large degree, in our automatic mental rejection of what is unfamiliar and therefore unpleasant to us in religious or philosophical thought.

What symbol or emblem or metaphor, after all, could be more displeasing to most Occidental minds than that of the serpent or the snake as so crudely if not coarsely set forth in the Hebrew *Genesis* for instance? Yet the Hebrew scriptures are not singular in their employment of the serpent as a symbol of a spiritual Teacher, because Hindû literature has instances almost without number where the snake or serpent called either Nâga, नाग, or Sarpa, सर्प, stands as a name or metaphorical appellation for Great Teachers, Wise Men, Spirits of Light as well as of Darkness. Indeed, the inhabitants of Pâtâla — which signifies both a 'hell' and also the regions which are the antipodes of the Hindû peninsula — are called *Nâgas* or 'snakes' alias 'serpents'; and Arjuna, the hero of the episode in the *Mahâbhârata* called the *Bhagavad-Gîtâ* is shown traveling to Pâtâla and there marrying Ulûpî, the daughter of Kauravya, King of the Nâgas in Pâtâla.[37]

Why should the serpent, or the snake, in both the Hebrew and Christian scriptures, have been called a 'liar,' 'deceiver,' and that pathetic mythical figure of early and late mediaeval theology, the Devil, be called by the name of 'the tempting serpent' and also the 'Father of Lies'? Why should it have been thought that the Serpent in the Garden of Eden which tempted the first human pair to evil-doing, according to the Hebrew mythology, was an imbodiment of

---

37. Âdiparva, ślokas 7788-9.

or the symbol of Satan? Why should the serpent have become the symbol of insinuating evil, of crafty evil-doing, or of deceitful craft? Or on the other hand, why should the silent, creeping serpent with its slow sinuous progress have been taken as the symbol of Wisdom as well as being used as an appellation for an Initiate, as in the expression attributed to a very lofty source, Jesus the Christos himself, in the Christian New Testament: "Be ye wise as serpents and harmless as doves"?[38]

The answer is simple enough. Just as the forces of Nature are neutral in themselves, and become what humans call 'good' or 'bad' because of their use or misuse by individuals, just exactly so a natural entity when employed as a figure or type-figure in symbology becomes usable in either a good or a bad sense. Such use as a symbol, or metaphorical appellation or title, always depends upon certain characteristics or qualities possessed by the natural entity and which the human mind by force of association of ideas, chooses or separates off from other characteristics or qualities, and employs in a symbololologic or metaphorical sense in order to depict either abstract or concrete ideas. This fact is shown for instance in the Sanskrit language, where Initiates of both kinds, i. e., of both the Right-Hand Path and of the Left-Hand Path, are referred to in words conveying serpentine ideas or characteristics. The former kind, otherwise called the Brothers of Light, are more properly designated in Sanskrit as Nâgas; whereas the Brothers of Darkness or of the Shadows are perhaps more properly designated as Sarpas, this latter word being derived from the Sanskrit verbal root सृप्, *srip*, meaning 'to crawl,' 'to creep,' in sly and stealthy manner, and hence metaphorically 'to deceive' by craft or insinuation.

We see here the main reason why the serpent or snake has, in probably all countries, and certainly in all times, been used as a symbol or emblem on the one hand of the Brothers of Light and their servants, and on the other hand of the Brothers of Darkness and their slaves. The reason is obvious, because both the Brothers of Light and the Sons of the Darkness are focuses of power, of subtil thought and action, of wisdom and energy, in the former case righteously and lawfully applied for sublime and compassionate ends, and therefore belonging to the 'right-hand'; and in the other case, of wisdom and energy wrongly or evilly applied to the uses of the 'left-hand.' The use applies to the cases of Initiates, because both the Initiates of the right-hand and of the left-hand are alike in one

---

38. *Matt.*, x, 16.

thing: they employ subtilty and the forces of Nature, and secret powerful wisdom, or rather secret knowledge combined with power. The same forces of Nature are employed by both — one class using these powers for impersonal and holy ends; the other class using these same powers and energies for unholy and evil ends. One class, as just said, we may perhaps call the Nâgas, i. e., the spiritual 'serpents' of Wisdom and Light, to whom Jesus alluded, who are very subtil, very benevolent, very wise, and endowed with the spiritual power to cast off the physical garment, i. e., the 'skin' or body, when the Initiate has grown old, and to assume another fresher, younger, and stronger human body at will. This noble class of Great Men are all infinitely kindly, perpetually engaged in works of human benevolence and beneficence, and yet are still and secret in their operations, among other reasons in order to avoid the plaudits and adoration of foolish men.

The other class are insinuating, worldly-wise, worldly-shrewd, deceitful, venomous in motive and action, therefore very dangerous; and yet using the same powers as the former class, but for evil ends.

Thus it is that on the one hand we find in all the greater of the old world-scriptures, 'serpents' spoken of as symbols of wisdom, as a metaphorical name for the Sons of Light, all possessing power, wisdom, knowledge, love, and splendor, as being Sons of the Sun; and, on the other hand, we see why other 'serpents,' 'snakes,' are spoken of as being symbols of the Dark, often called the Black, Brothers, who are essentially wrongdoers from Nature's own stand-point, and all too often succeeding in their diabolic work by means of lies and misrepresentations. Hence it is that Jesus said: "Be ye wise as serpents and harmless as doves."

In this usage of the displeasing figure and characteristics of the serpent or snake as the veil of a secret sense, and the elaboration of the serpentine characteristics in the form of allegory and story, the ancient habit or manner of disguising natural truths is clearly seen.

CHAPTER III

THE SECRET DOCTRINE OF GAUTAMA
THE BUDDHA — I

THE writer of the present study in the teachings and evidences of the Esoteric Tradition, is as well aware as any other one may or may not be of the fact that it is quite customary in Occidental countries strongly to question, if not to deny outright, the existence of a Universal or Esoteric Wisdom upon which repose as upon a foundation the various and different and differing great religions and great philosophies of the ancient world. It has always seemed that this opinion is more arbitrary than substantial; arising rather in Occidental prejudice and scientific skepticism than as the fruit of years of searching study of the evidences of the existence of such a fundamental Esoteric Wisdom — which latter, indeed, to the philosophically researching student seem to be as plainly apparent as are the various phenomena of the physical universe surrounding us, or, more accurately perhaps, as are the evidences of a kinship in human aspiration, thought, and mystical feeling, the world over.

This skepticism concerning the existence of a fundamental body of esoteric and mystical teaching as the religious and philosophical basis of each and every one of the great religions of the globe, seems to run particularly strong in the cases of the great schools of Buddhistic thought which Gautama-Śākyamuni was the founder of. There would seem off-hand to be as little proof that this skepticism is well based in this case as it is equally unfounded in the cases of Christianity, or Judaism, or the various branches of Hindûism; and it is to be supposed, in lieu of stronger support for this skepticism, that its sole foundation is the obvious fact that such esoteric background is not openly announced and elaborated in the exoteric literature of the two main forms or schools of Buddhism, respectively, the Hînayâna and the Mahâyâna — although even this statement must be qualified by the well-known fact that the various forms of the Mahâyâna, and probably not excepting a single instance, do indeed claim in their theological elaborations of the teachings found in the canonical Mahâyâna scriptures, that the Buddha-Gautama did in very truth teach a deeper or secret doctrine to the selected circle of his Arhats, who in their turn passed it on.

These claims, however, as is notoriously the case, are usually rejected bodily as well as singly and individually by virtually every Occidental scholar or Orientalist; but one searches in vain for any sufficient cause for this rejection, outside of the one which the student of ancient literatures has learned to expect, to wit, prejudice, pre-conception, insufficient understanding of the philosophical and religious import of the canonical Buddhist scriptures themselves.

In consequence, and because basis for such skepticism seems entirely lacking, outside of the very fallacious and shaky arguments based on prejudice, the present writer in common with most other students of the Esoteric Tradition takes the path of common sense and scholarly good taste by simply ignoring airy and unfounded charges which have not been proved, and, probably, are not susceptible of proof.

The present and the succeeding chapter will be an attempt to elaborate the thesis that essential Buddhism, in common with the essential or fundamental teaching of all the other great world-religions or indeed world-philosophies, contains as its substance or core the identic Esoteric Tradition that is found universally elsewhere. This chapter is no attempt at a complete and inclusive proof of the foregoing statement, because obviously the limits of this volume would be themselves too small to imbody a complete and formal statement of the facts. We shall here treat the matter more as a sketch, and as an outline, which, it is hoped, will point the way to others having more time at their disposal for this work than the present writer has.

The burthen of proof, the *onus probandi*, in this case rests wholly on the shoulders of the skeptics; for, when one remembers and weighs impartially the facts as they are: the notorious reluctance of the ancient Hindû and even of his modern descendant to uncover the deeper secrets of their religions and philosophies; when one remembers the jealous religious reserve for which India has in all ages been famous; when one considers and duly weighs the notorious inclination, both ancient and modern, to secret mystical thought, secret or esoteric religious schools, and the virtually innumerable references to initiations and hid doctrines with which all Hindû religious and philosophical literature is replete — remembering and properly considering these various facts, it is something that would require lengthy and positive proof to aver that Buddhism alone, itself an Indian Religion-Philosophy, is exempt from a universal custom, a

mundial habit, stronger in India than perhaps elsewhere. The burthen of proof finally, as stated, rests on those who deny rather than
on those who affirm a well-established, universal, and in India national, custom dating from immemorial antiquity.

It is important to remember in this connexion, that it is absurd
to assume that the titan intellects of the human race who are at the
same time great ethical and religious Teachers of men, fall into
either one or the other of two categories: first, that they are deliberate
deceivers of human hearts, instigated by human ambition, vaulting
or paltry as the case may be, and that the esoteric schools which
they invariably instituted, each one in his time and to his own race,
were products of an abominable desire for personal supremacy or
for the gaining of other advantage; or, second, that they were un-
balanced if not mentally deranged egoists who began these respective schools from motives arising in ignorant self-deception and
because of an unregulated fanatical desire to domineer over others
and to sway them. To allege either of these hypotheses, to wit,
either selfish ambition or fanatic ignorance, wanders so wide of the
facts and of the lofty spiritual and intellectual standard of teaching
and work which each such World-Teacher exemplified, and for which
posterity has invariably revered him, that it would seem sufficient
thus baldly to state facts, to uncover the entire lack of substantial
ground of reason on which the above-mentioned skeptics in virtually
every case have placed their structure of indefinable theory.

Then, again, neither of the foregoing hypotheses, to wit, either
fanatic ignorance, or selfish personal ambition, is capable of explaining what all students of the Esoteric Tradition know: the universality of the fundamental substantial identity of the background
of esoteric thought forming the body of Teaching which, as delivered
from time to time through these Great Teachers, has taken the form
of the Esoteric Tradition of which the present book treats.

I

There are two ways of reaching Truth, two methods of penetrating
into the arcana of the mysteries of the Universe, from its spiritual
parts down to its physical; and these two ways or methods are, first,
by means of Man's spiritual-intellectual nature itself which is rooted
in the very substance of the spiritual world, and indeed is an integral
part thereof. For any normal human being whose constitution has
not been undermined by vice, nor weakened by some wasting disease,
can, if he will lead the life proper thereto, come into sympathetic

unity or oneness with spiritual Nature through his own inner being's cognising its essential unity with the Universe, and thus becoming the recipient, as a channel or canal, through which the higher energies of the Universe may flow and become manifest as thoughts, intuitions, intimations of truth, in the chela's or disciple's mind.

The other way or method is that of training and initiation, which is not different from the former method, but is the former method elaborated into systematic procedures; because such initiatory training and final success are but a quickening of or hastening over the evolutionary progress that all human beings undergo through the cycling ages. In other words, initiation is but quickened evolution.

These Great World-Teachers combine both these ways or methods during a brief period of lives on earth. Beginning as chelas or disciples of some teacher selected by each individual of them, with which teacher such chela finds intuitive and instinctive links of sympathy and understanding, he undergoes training, i. e., quickened evolution, under the watchful eye of the teacher chosen by him; and bending every energy and all the faculties of his being towards success, he passes from life to life through this brief period of reincarnations, advancing steadily higher in each such life, until finally he himself blossoms out as a Master, a Mahâtman, in his turn now ready to carry his portion of the labor, pitiful, compassionate, of the Great Brotherhood. Then his turn comes to be sent forth among his fellow-men of less evolutionary degree of advancement, to become unto them a Teacher, a Guide, an Inspirer, delivering unto them in ideas and language appropriate to the age the new instalment of universal truth which it thus becomes his sublime destiny to give. Thus a new great Religion is founded, a new and possibly world-shaking Philosophy of Life is inaugurated; yet, mark it well, each and every one of this long line of Sages and Seers, each one of the World-Teachers, imbodies in his new instalment of teaching the same fundamental verities, the identic truths, albeit delivered in new garments, which all his Predecessors had given, each one in his turn. It is thus that the Esoteric Tradition is carried on and renewed from age to age, and given to man in those periods of spiritual and intellectual somnolence, which Plato called epochs of spiritual barrenness.

Such a one in the long line of Successors was Śâkyamuni, the Buddha-Gautama. It is true that in his case, and because of a certain Mystery which it would be improper openly to set forth even by sketch in a published work, he was of a spiritual and intellectual stature exceeding many, possibly most, of those who had preceded him in the same World-Order in recorded human history; but even in his case the rule of successorship was the same as in that of all his Predecessors, and he but exemplifies, more brilliantly than most, the natural Law of Periodicity which governs the cyclical unveiling or revealing of the Esoteric Tradition to the human species.

II

Let us now turn to the more particular topic of the present chapter:

बुद्धं शरणं गच्छामि
धर्मं शरणं गच्छामि
संघं शरणं गच्छामि ।

Buddham śaraṇam gachchhâmi;
dharmam śaraṇam gachchhâmi;
samgham śaraṇam gachchhâmi:

"I take my refuge in the Buddha; I take my refuge in the Light of his teachings (or Law); I take my refuge in the company of the Holy Ones." This slight paraphrase of the Sanskrit three-stanzaed 'Confession of Faith' so called, contains the substantial core of what the modern Buddhist, equally with the ancient Buddhist, considers to be the true Buddhist's outlook as a believer in the teachings of the Tathâgata, i. e., he who came as his forerunners came, as his Predecessors came, in order to bring salvation into the world — salvation to gods and men, salvation to the greatest and to the humblest; and this 'salvation,' as the Lord Buddha taught, was not salvation from any outside power, not something entering into human minds and hearts from outside, and thus 'saving' them, as is the vain belief of so many Occidentals: but was an interior change, a true reformation, in the very spiritual, intellectual, and psychical, structure of the man himself.[39] For, as the mystical Buddhism of the North taught,

---

39. This threefold Buddhist formula is likewise known under the title त्रिरत्न (Tri-ratna), or 'Three Gems'; or त्रिशरणं (Tri-śaraṇam), or 'Three Refuges.' As stated in the text of this chapter, this formula of devotion or allegiance, accepted by both the Northern and the Southern Schools of Buddhism, is universally taken, or nearly so, by the entire Buddhist world in a rather pragmatical or matter-of-fact manner, following the literal meaning of the words, to wit: 'I take refuge in the Buddha; I take refuge in the Dharma or Law; I take refuge in the Company or Congregation' — the 'Company' or 'Congregation' thus signifying the Buddhist priesthood, or in a still larger sense, the entire body of professing and faithful Buddhists.

Yet this literal meaning, in the opinion of the present writer, is but an exoteric

and still teaches with fervid devotion: There is in every entity, not only in man but in the gods and in the beings beneath man, a threefold essence — or perhaps more accurately three interblending essences, nevertheless having a common identic substance, which they describe as, (a) a Celestial or Dhyâni-Buddha; (b) a Bodhisattva,

form of what was originally intended by the esoteric Initiates who drew up this formula or composed it. In other words, the formula suffered the same deterioration in meaning that has happened in all similar cases in all great religions: the words originally having a highly mystical and philosophical significance finally lose it and are accepted or taken at their mere face-meaning.

The original sense of this formula was extremely profound and beautiful, and conveyed a threefold teaching — or a teaching referring to three aspects of the Esoteric Philosophy — somewhat as follows: The 'Buddha' has reference to *Âdi-Buddha,* which we may call the First or Unmanifest Logos, or Primeval Spirit in the Universe, manifesting throughout the Universe in a sublime Hierarchy of spiritual beings emanating from itself. These spiritual beings extend from the highest even to the human spheres, and frequently are called in the Esoteric Philosophy, the Hierarchy of Compassion, or sometimes the Sons of Light. It is the Hierarchy of Compassion, or the Sons of Light composing it, and ranging from the Dhyâni-Buddhas downwards through intermediate grades to the Mânushya-Buddhas, which form the *Saṃgha* or Company, or Congregation, this being the Third of the Refuges. The Wisdom that is taught by them on the different planes of the Universe and to the different ranges of world-spheres, and mystically and traditionally handed down from the highest Dhyâni-Buddhas to human disciples is the second Refuge, called in this formula, the *Dharma.*

We have thus, when this formula is properly understood, an outline, albeit briefly sketched, of the structural framework of all the teaching of the Wisdom of the Gods, today in its public delivery called Theosophy. In other words, and summarizing briefly, we have under the one term 'Buddha' the entire line of spiritual beings, reaching from the Cosmic Spirit through all intermediate ranges of the Universe down to the Mânushya-Buddhas or human Buddhas and their human disciples, who in their aggregate form the so-called 'Congregation'; and all teaching the Divine Wisdom sprung forth in its origin from the highest gods themselves, and of which every Buddha on earth is an exponent.

Corresponding to the same threefold division of the 'Buddhas,' their 'Law,' and their 'Hierarchy,' we have the three forms of Vestures or Appearances in which this Hierarchy of Beings express themselves, to wit: first and highest, the Dharmakâya, that of the highest cosmic spirits or Dhyâni-Buddhas; second, the Sambhogakâya, the vesture, thus summarized, of the intermediate grades of spiritual beings in this Hierarchy; and finally, the Nirmânakâya, the vesture of those spiritual beings and Great Adepts who are closest to and therefore, *de facto,* are the Guardians of, mankind and all beings on Earth.

Corresponding with these three Vestures again, we have the third general

'son' of the Celestial or Dhyâni-Buddha; and (c) a Mânushya-Buddha or human Buddha; and it was in order to awaken this living threefold Buddhic consciousness in the constitution of every human being, that the Buddha taught his noble Law, his majestic Philosophy, which perhaps has held, during the course of its existence, more human minds in fealty and devotion than any other religio-philosophic system known to the human race.

III

Buddhism has always been greatly misunderstood in the Occident, and this misunderstanding has arisen almost wholly because Occidental scholars themselves have misapprehended a large number of the most important teachings of the religio-philosophy of Gautama; and because these Occidental scholars imbodied their misapprehensions in their studies in and of Buddhism, and because such studies were printed and published, the reading Occidental public followed suit as was only to be expected; and thus it is that there is perhaps no single world-religion known today which has suffered so greatly in this respect as Buddhism has.

It has at times been called a religion of pessimism, simply because Occidentals have not understood its profound intellectual reaches nor its proper placing of the values of the material side of life. In the Occidental view, to teach that a man is an impermanent composite of elements of varying ethereality, and that when he dies this composite is dissolved, and that its component parts then enter into their respective realms or kingdoms or spheres of Nature: all this signifies to the Occidental mind that such a doctrine teaches utter annihilation of the compounded entity *as an entity;* for, consciously or unconsciously, such Occidental critics ignore the unifying and binding root of being of every such entity which brings at periodical intervals this compound together again out of the identic life-atoms that composed it in former existences.

---

division above alluded to: the Arûpa-dhâtu, or so-called 'Formless' World or Worlds, the mystical abode of the Dhyâni-Buddhas or Chohans, etc.; second, the Rûpa-dhâtu, or so-called Manifested or Form-World or Worlds, the abode of the beings living in the Sambhogakâya Vesture or condition; and third, the Kâma-dhâtu, or so-called 'World of Desire,' or Worlds wherein reside beings still heavily involved in the attractions and conditions of material existence.

The matter is so important in its immense bearing on the esoteric heart of the Buddha's teaching that it was felt both useful and needed to explain it, however briefly, in the present footnote, for those who can understand it.

Occidental scholars so think, or they think that they so think, because they do not understand that this very 'root,' or element, or subtil bond — call it what you like — i. e., the individualizing energy which brought these saṃskâras[40] or compounds or composites together, is, when all is said and done in argument, a unifying and therefore individualizing *force;* and that this unifying or individualizing force, no matter what we may call it, remains after the dissolution of the compound, and likewise has its own cosmic reservoir or kingdom or realm to which it returns; nor do they understand that this unifying or individualizing force the Lord Gautama in his great wisdom called the 'Buddha,' the inner originant, for which an equivalent term in the Mahâyâna of Northern Asia is Dhyâni-Buddha.

It is quite true that from certain Occidental philosophical standpoints, the teaching of Gautama the Buddha may formally be considered 'pessimistic'; but only so if one judge it by Occidental philosophical standards alone, and ignore the intrinsic meaning of the Buddha himself; and is this either wise or fair? Ignoring a factor in a problem is not solving the problem properly. Can it, one asks, then be rightly done? How can we judge something which arose in the Orient and became the Law of the more civilized Oriental world for its own time-period, and successfully passed the examination of the keenest minds and the most astute intellects of ages, by the changing and therefore biased standards of Occidental scientific speculations, with a vague background of European philosophy, which speculations themselves are only some three hundred or more years old in their origin, and probably not more than seventy-five years old, or less, in their present form?

There was a time, not so long ago, when one teaching of the Buddha, that of the Nirvâna, was considered by Occidental scholars to mean that the Lord Gautama taught that annihilation, utter, complete, was the end of every living conscious being, when that being had attained unto the stage of inner growth where it entered into this nirvânic state; and they pointed, naturally enough, to the Sanskrit meaning of this compound word: निर् (*nir*), 'out' or 'off,' and वान (*vâna*), the past participle passive of the root वा (*vâ*), 'to blow': hence 'to blow out.' As they sagely and logically enough said: "Nirvâna means 'blown out,' as a candle-flame is 'blown out' by the breath!" Ay, so it does. But what is it that is 'blown out'? What is it

---

40. Psycho-mental attributes forming a portion of the intermediate constitution of man.

that ceases to exist? Is it the unifying spiritual force which brings this compound entity into being anew in a serial line of succession which has no known beginning, and which the Buddhist teaching itself shows to be *something* which reproduces itself in this series of illusory, because compounded, vehicles? This is impossible, because if this individualizing or unifying energy were 'blown out,' i. e., annihilated, it obviously could not continue to reproduce itself as the inspiriting energy of newly compounded bodies due to its own working. Therefore obviously enough what is blown out is the samskâras, the compounds, resulting from, i.e., born or produced by, the *karman* of the individual. This karman, therefore, and speaking with strict logical sequence of thought, which the doctrine imbodies, is *the individual himself or itself;* because the Buddhist teaching is that what is reproduced is the karman of the preceding individual, i. e., that any composite entity changes from instant to instant, and that at each new instant, the change is the resultant or effect or consequence of the preceding instant of change. Thus, then, the individual is his own karman at any instant in time, because that karman is the totality of what he is himself. When a man's composite parts are 'blown out,' i. e., 'enter Nirvâna,' i. e., are 'extinguished,' rendered extinct, as the just previously existing compound, then all the rest of the being, that deathless center of unifying and individualizing spiritual force around which these composites or samskâras periodically gather — lives as a Buddha.

This is exactly and as far as it goes (because there is much more that might be said), the teaching of Esoteric Theosophy, of the Esoteric Tradition. All the evil and lower part of us must be wiped out, extinguished, 'annihilated' if you like; in other words the karman that produced these illusory composites must be caused to cease; and new composites, nobler ones — *the products or effects or resultants of the preceding composites* —those henceforth joined to the Buddhic essence of the being, that spiritual force which is the inner Buddha, will then continue and on its own high plane live, because no longer controlled by the veils of the world of Mâyâ, Illusion — the worlds of impermanent structural composites. The being thus become a Buddha because of its delivery from enshrouding veils, has now reached the state and condition of passing out of the impermanence of all manifested existence into the utter permanence of cosmic Reality.

The matter of the real meaning of the Nirvâna has thus been elaborated, albeit in somewhat sketchy fashion, in order to show that the supposition of many Westerners that the teaching of the

Nirvâna is a pessimistic doctrine because meaning utter extinction into the abyss of non-entity, is baseless. Hence, far from being pessimistic, the doctrine of the Nirvâna is one of extraordinary hope. The word 'optimism' is not here used, because it is as subject to adverse critical comment as is its antonym 'pessimism.'

Far from being a religion of pessimism, when properly understood the religion of the Buddha is a religion — not of optimism indeed, but of wisdom. These words are used advisedly, because it is certain that unthinking optimism is as foolish in its way as is un-thinking pessimism. Neither is wise, because each is an extreme. The teaching of the Buddha was so wisely given by that Great Sage that it showed to men a pathway which went neither to the right — to one extreme — nor to the left — to the other extreme; but chose the Middle Way, the way of Truth, avoiding the falling into the extremes of either side. All extremes are unreal, no matter what they may be, because unphilosophical; and it is the great subtilty of the Tathâgata's teaching which has rendered it so difficult for Occidentals to understand. One often reads essays printed in the Occident by Westerners who have become Buddhists; and one may admire them for the courage with which they work in their new field; but, with no wish to hurt anyone's feelings, it is difficult to avoid being grieved by their usual lack of understanding of what is after all the heart, the core, of the great Buddha's teaching. The letter indeed of the Buddhist scriptures has been grasped — more or less; but the spirit, i. e., the Buddha's 'heart,' is rarely or never under-stood. The Eye-Doctrine, in other words, is comprehended to a certain extent; but the Heart-Doctrine, the hid part, the esoteric part, is not seized, or only grasped intuitively and to a certain extent only at the rarest intervals.

IV

Ay, there *is* such a thing as esoteric Buddhism,[41] despite the

---

41. With regard to the statement in the text of this chapter, that the great Hindû Reformer and Initiate, known to the world as Gautama the Buddha, had indeed a Secret Doctrine, or Esoteric Tradition, which he himself had received from and in initiation, and which he kept for those worthy and qualified to receive it among his own chelas or disciples, and quite outside of a conviction to that effect born in the minds of students who have given the matter sufficient study to understand it, the reader is referred to certain statements made by H. P. Blavatsky, the Great Theosophist, in her *The Secret Doctrine* and else-where, pointing to the same fact. As an example, she writes in her *The Secret Doctrine,* 'Introductory,' Volume I, pages xx-xxi, as follows:

denials of this fact by very eminent Occidental Buddhist scholars. After all, what value is there in following the more or less unconsciously biased deductions of our Occidental scholars in Buddhistic lore, who, taking merely the letter of that great religious and philosophical Law, translate, and, in combination with their own more or less biased reflexions, thereby render, as they think, the truth of the doctrine?   What value, indeed, when studies with the background of illumination furnished by the teachings of the Esoteric Tradition show to the Theosophical student that there is verily an esoteric teaching or foundation of both a philosophical and a religious character which the Buddha evidently must have taught to his Arhats, or disciples most favored for their spiritual and intellectual abilities to understand his meaning.   When these skeptical Occidental scholars are asked: Did the Buddha have an Esoteric School, or does his Law contain an esoteric teaching? they almost invariably say Nay, and point with emphatic finger to a statement by the Buddha himself, which they believe proves their allegation that he himself denied it.   This statement is found in the teaching of the *Mahâ-Parinibbâna-Sutta,* or the teaching of the 'Great and Ultimate Nirvâna'; which title we may perhaps otherwise render as meaning the 'Great Passing.'   Before going on farther with the present argu-

---

"Indeed, the secret portions of the *'Dan'* or *'Jan-na'* (*'Dhyan'*) of Gautama's metaphysics — grand as they appear to one unacquainted with the tenets of the Wisdom Religion of antiquity — are but a very small portion of the whole.   The Hindu Reformer limited his public teachings to the purely moral and physiological aspect of the Wisdom-Religion, to Ethics and MAN alone.   Things 'unseen and incorporeal,' the mystery of Being outside our terrestrial sphere, the great Teacher left entirely untouched in his public lectures, reserving the hidden Truths for a select circle of his Arhats. The latter received their Initiation at the famous Saptaparna cave. . . .

"Thus the reader is asked to bear in mind the very important difference between *orthodox* Buddhism — *i. e.,* the public teachings of Gautama the Buddha, and his esoteric *Budhism.*   His Secret Doctrine, however, differed in no wise from that of the initiated Brahmins of his day. . . . His teachings, therefore, could not be different from their doctrines, for the whole Buddhist reform merely consisted in giving out a portion of that which had been kept secret from every man outside of the 'enchanted' circle of Temple-Initiates and ascetics.   Unable to teach *all* that had been imparted to him — owing to his pledges — though he taught a philosophy built upon the ground-work of the true esoteric knowledge, the Buddha gave to the world only its *outward* material body and kept its *soul* for his Elect. . . . Many Chinese scholars among Orientalists have heard of the 'Soul Doctrine.' None seem to have understood its real meaning and importance."

ment, it may be useful to examine just what this supposedly conclusive statement of the Lord Buddha really was:

Now very soon after the Blessed One began to recover; when he had quite
got rid of the sickness, he went out from the monastery, and sat down behind
the monastery on a seat spread out there. And the venerable Ânanda[41a] went to
the place where the Blessed One was, and saluted him, and took a seat respect-
fully on one side, and addressed the Blessed One, and said: 'I have beheld,
Lord, how the Blessed One was in health, and I have beheld how the Blessed
One had to suffer. And though at the sight of the sickness of the Blessed One
my body became weak as a creeper, and the horizon became dim to me, and
my faculties were no longer clear, yet notwithstanding I took some little comfort from the thought that the Blessed One would not pass away from existence
until at least he had left instructions as touching the order.'

'What, then, Ânanda? Does the order expect that of me? I have preached
the truth without making any distinction between exoteric and esoteric doctrine: for in respect of the truths, Ânanda, the Tathâgata has no such thing as
the closed fist of a teacher, who keeps some things back. Surely, Ânanda,
should there be any one who harbours the thought, "It is I who will lead the
brotherhood," or, "The order is dependent upon me," it is he who should lay
down instructions in any matter concerning the order. Now the Tathâgata,
Ânanda, thinks not that it is he who should lead the brotherhood, or that the order is dependent upon him. Why then should he leave instructions in any matter
concerning the order? I too, O Ânanda, am now grown old, and full of years,
my journey is drawing to its close, I have reached my sum of days, I am turning eighty years of age; and just as a worn-out cart, Ânanda, can only with
much additional care be made to move along, so, methinks, the body of the
Tathâgata can only be kept going with much additional care. . . .

'Therefore, O Ânanda, be ye lamps unto yourselves. Be ye a refuge to
yourselves. Betake yourselves to no external refuge. Hold fast to the truth as
a lamp. Hold fast as a refuge to the truth. . . .'[42]

— i. e., to the Celestial Buddha abiding in secret within every human
heart, in the core or spiritual center of every human being, 'the
inner god.'

Lest this citation be taken to mean that the Buddha taught no
need of any teachers following him in his Brotherhood or Association, it is well to look even at the pragmatical Buddhism of the South,
and more particularly to consider that of the mystical School of the
North, where there were during later ages millions of human beings

41a. Ânanda was the god-son of the Lord, and his favorite disciple, somewhat
it may be as legend says John was the favorite disciple of Jesus the Syrian Avatâra.

42. The *Mahâ-Parinibbâna-Sutta*, chapter ii, verses 31, 32, 33 as translated
by T. W. Rhys Davids, the well-known Pâli scholar. (*The Sacred Books of the
East* series, Vol. XI.)

who, without any exception whatsoever, as far as one recollects at the moment, followed the different schools, each one of them founded by a more or less great man whose rights to teach were scarcely ever challenged, simply because of the greatness of these individual teachers each in his own especial line of pragmatical or of mystical Buddhism. In all these cases, whether of the South or of the North, the existence of legitimate successors of the Buddha following each other in century after century was universally recognised, although obviously none was ever considered to be equal to the great Master himself. His unique standing as Teacher is indeed one of the fundamental teachings of Buddhism, which states that Buddhas appear only at long intervals and in periods governed by cyclic time, thus re-echoing the Brâhmanical teaching of a succession of Doctors of the Law which Krishṇa alludes to in the *Bhagavad-Gîtâ* in the words: 'Whenever there is a decline of righteousness in the world, etc., then I reproduce myself.'[43]

This succession or serial line of teachers is technically called the Guru-paramparâ in Brâhmanism. It is a good phrase or title for the Teachers coming in serial order, because it is both descriptive and exact. It has had of course varied and different meanings in different ages, but the substantial idea inherent in the thought is the same everywhere; and whether certain Buddhist scholars like to admit it or not, the fact remains that historical Buddhism shows to us teacher succeeding teacher in the annals of the great Buddhist faith: these teachers sometimes separated by fairly long periods of time, and in other cases of more mystical and restricted schools, teacher succeeding teacher when the predecessor dies and the successor assumes his office.

Even the simplest examination of the historical facts will show the student that minor sages and seers have sprung up from time to time in the Buddhism of history, such as Nâgârjuna and Âryasamgha, founding schools, or taking them over from their predecessors; teaching, if you like, each one a new version of the Ancient Buddhist Wisdom, yet all faithful followers of the Lord Buddha; and whatever their differences as individuals may have been, all these various schools look to the great Master as the fountain-head of their respective and more or less differing wisdoms.

It would be preposterous to attempt to aver that so enlightened a spirit, so profound an intellect, so wise and far-reaching a mind, as found in the Buddha, could have been ignorant of one of the

---

43. Ch. iv, śl. 7.

elementary facts of human psychology in religious matters, to wit, that it was a foregone conclusion, human nature being what it is, that teachers would arise in the Order after his death; nor can one for an instant agree with those who would attempt to show that most, if not all, of these later teachers in Buddhistic philosophy were more or less ambitious upstarts, craving personal prominence and seeking a personal following. This opinion, which seems to be so widespread in the Occident, as regards religious matters, discovers to public view what is really a deplorably pessimistic opinion of human nature. Indeed, the view of the present writer runs directly counter to this opinion, for he looks upon most, if not all, of the great men who succeeded the Buddha as heads of the different Buddhist Schools, as being genuine initiates, profound, thoughtful, and high-minded men, who, because of their own spiritual and intellectual and psychical degree of evolution, developed in their respective logical fields the teachings of the Buddha-Gautama dealing with different parts of the widely inclusive range of Buddhist philosophy.

To return to the quotation cited above: At first reading, it does indeed sound as if the Lord Buddha declared to his disciples that he had no esoteric doctrine, reserved of necessity for the more spiritually and intellectually advanced of his chelas or disciples. Is this, however, what he actually said? It most certainly is not. Ânanda's plea was: "Leave us instructions, Lord, as to the conduct of the Order, before thou passest on"; and the Buddha refused, saying: "I have told you all that is necessary for the conduct of the Order, and I have kept naught back. I am not like a teacher who tells you some things as to your own conduct and the conduct of the Brotherhood, and secretly hides other things in his 'closed fist.' I have told you all that is necessary for the conduct of the Order that will bring you success in the saving of man; but should there be anyone who arises in the Order and who points out what is required for its proper care and leading, then it is he who should lay down instructions in any such emergency concerning the Order. You will soon find out in such case whether he be a true teacher or a false; for the rules that I myself have given unto you are the fundamental rules for guidance and conduct both of yourselves and of the Order, and they are sufficient. I have spoken."

There is no small number of passages in the different Buddhist Scriptures of both the two great Schools, which, both by direct statement and by indirection in statement, declare plainly that the Buddha had not revealed, nor would he reveal, all the truths that he knew.

Two instances briefly designated should suffice in illustration, both of the Hînayâna School. The first states that Śâkyamuni took a handful of the leaves of the Śiṇśapâ, and pointing to them, explained that just as this bunch of leaves in his hand, so few in number, were not all the leaves of the tree from which they were taken, just so in exactly similar fashion the truths that he himself as Teacher had announced were not by any means all that he knew.[44] The figure is both graphic and strong, and highly significant.

The other instance, also in a Scripture belonging to the Hînayâna-system, is one in which the Great Teacher explains his refusal to describe whether a Buddha lives after death or not.[45] Both illustrations are declarations of the fact of the reserve in teaching, and reticence in delivery thereof, which are so universally characteristic of the transmitters of the Esoteric Tradition.

V

बुद्धं शरणं गच्छामि
धर्मं शरणं गच्छामि
संघं शरणं गच्छामि ।

Buddhaṃ śaraṇaṃ gachchhâmi;
dharmaṃ śaraṇaṃ gachchhâmi;
saṃghaṃ śaraṇaṃ gachchhâmi:

"I go to the Buddha as my refuge." "I go to the *Dharma* or the Law as my refuge." "I go to the Order of Holy Ones as my refuge."

This so-called 'Confession of Faith,' although undoubtedly accepted in the spirit as well as in the letter in Northern Asia, is perhaps especially the teaching comprising the substance of the scriptures of the Hînayâna. The compound word Hînayâna, descriptive of the spirit of Buddhism of Southern Asia, as contrasted with the Mahâyâna, descriptive of the Buddhism of the North of Asia, means the 'defective' vehicle, the 'inferior' or 'imperfect' vehicle, i. e., that part of the Lord Gautama's teaching which did not contain in explicit formulation the whole of the doctrine which he taught — a fact which itself declares the existence of another part not herein contained. The name itself declares the fact: हीन (*hîna*), i. e., defection, imperfection, incompleteness; and यान (*yâna*), vehicle.

Now this statement of incompleteness or imperfection does not signify, as might readily be supposed from these words, inaccuracy, falsity, or error; the meaning of the compound *Hînayâna* is that

---

44. *Samyutta-Nikâya*, vi, 31.
45. *Chula-Mâlunkyaputta-Sutta*, i, 426.

this system, virtually exclusively popular in Southern Asia, gives
the formal intellectual teaching of the Buddha — or what has been
called the 'Eye-Doctrine,' that which emanated from the Buddha's
mind as a categorical framework of his thought; the *Mahâyâna,*
contrariwise, is stated to contain the more secret — as well as the
outer or public — and therefore more difficult aspects of the Buddha-
Gautama's teaching, and consequently has often been called the
'Heart-Doctrine.'

The teaching of the Buddha's heart, i. e., the esoteric Wisdom
which he kept hid in his 'heart' and delivered solely to those ready
to receive it, is, as just stated, called the Mahâyâna; and it runs
back in its origin to a date at least equal in time to that of the
beginning of the Hînayâna, which, as stated above, is the body of
teaching which he delivered openly, visible to the eye so to speak.
Both systems, therefore, are truth, i. e., both the Hînayâna and the
Mahâyâna are true; but one must combine the teaching of the 'eye'
with the teaching of the 'heart': one must combine the exoteric teaching of the Hînayâna with the esoteric of the Mahâyâna — combine
the North and the South, so to speak — if one desire to receive the
full message of the Tathâgata as he delivered it in its relative fulness
to his chelas or disciples.

From which of these two systems have our Western Orientalists
drawn the far greater part of the Buddhist material which they have
subjected to the really conscientious and thorough examination and
study which one gladly recognises they have given? Mostly, if not
wholly, they have gathered this material out of the scriptures of
the Hînayâna, the 'defective' vehicle, a system held by some twenty
millions of human beings more or less. Of the teachings of the Mahâyâna of the North and Center of Asia, the esoteric teachings, the
'heart' of the Buddha, they have intimate knowledge as yet of only
a few scriptures. It is well known that a vast amount of Mahâyâna-
material still awaits examination and study, but all this material
is as yet more or less an unworked field of thought.

As examples of the Mahâyâna-material already studied, may be
mentioned the *Saddharma-Puṇḍarîka* as one; the *Lalita-Vistara* is
another Northern Buddhistic work which has received some small
attention from European Orientalists. There are a few other works
belonging to the Northern School which have received passing but
quite inadequate attention in Europe; and it is doubtful if more
than this can be truthfully claimed.

Consequently, it certainly would seem that the opinion of Occidental scholars as to whether there is or is not an esoteric teaching

which the Buddha taught or left behind him, is based almost solely upon their studies of the hitherto available scriptures of the Hînayâna of the South, the 'defective,' 'imperfect,' because, as said, incomplete, vehicle or system. It is a strange thing indeed to suppose that the Buddha-Gautama is the sole historical instance of a Sage and Seer who was at the same time a religious and philosophical Preceptor, who has left behind him no teachings of a more recondite or secret character than those which he openly proclaimed in his wanderings over Indian mountain and plain. The exception would be so remarkable that it would require particular explanation.

Let us turn now for a few moments to another one of the Sûtras[46] or religio-philosophical scriptures, held in utmost reverence by something like 400 millions of human beings, all followers, more or less, of the Mahâyâna-teaching, which, mark you, is as much Buddhism, and genuinely 'orthodox' as is the Hînayâna of the South; and the bulk of the testimony as to the value of the teaching certainly remains in the scriptures of the North. Remembering these 400 millions of the North as compared with the twenty millions more or less of the adherents of the Hînayâna of the South, this is what is found in the scripture to be quoted from; and it is beyond doubt that many more similar passages could be found, with adequate study, of an even more emphatic tenor.

You are astonished, Kâśyapa, that you cannot fathom the mystery expounded by the Tathâgata. It is, Kâśyapa, because the mystery expounded by the Tathâgatas, the Arhats, etc. is difficult to be understood.

And on that occasion, the more fully to explain the same subject, the Lord uttered the following stanzas:

1. I am the Dharmarâja, born in the world as the destroyer of existence.[47]

Now it is the philosophical teaching of Buddhism, when this teaching is properly understood, that the entire world around us is impermanent, illusory, *mâyâvi;* but that all existences are founded upon and builded around something inner, secret, esoteric, hid, fundamental, which the Northern Schools, collected under the great Mahâyâna-teaching, call the Śûnyatâ, i. e., the 'Void,' the Unmanifest as the Theosophist would say. To continue with this quotation from the *Saddharma-Puṇḍarîka:*

---

46. Reference is here made to the *Saddharma-Puṇḍarîka* mentioned above, to its chapter v, as translated by H. Kern, of the University of Leiden, Holland, as found in Volume XXI of the *Sacred Books of the East* series, pages 121-2.

47. *Ibid.*

I declare the law to all beings after discriminating [examining] their dispositions.

A selective teaching, mark you!

2. Superior men of wise understanding guard the word, guard the mystery, and do not reveal it to living beings.[48]

Yet obviously, the Lord Buddha taught it and revealed it to living beings, to all who were prepared to hear and to understand it. It is pertinent here to ask: What is the meaning of these phrases imbodying the expressions 'word,' 'guarding the mystery,' if the significance is not that of a teaching too difficult for the ordinary man to receive in its fulness, which is therefore kept only for those who, after discriminate examination, have been tested and found to be worthy and well qualified to receive it? Obviously, we have here a distinct reference to a restraint in the delivery of the Secret Doctrine or Esoteric Tradition, which is not revealed indiscriminately to all and sundry because it is a 'mystery' which must be guarded; and yet 'superior men of wise understanding' have received this mystery, for they are enjoined not to deliver it nor to reveal it to 'living beings' unless, indeed, such be fit for the reception.

3. That science is difficult to be understood; the simple, if hearing it on a sudden, would be perplexed; they would in their ignorance fall out of the way and go astray.[49]

Mark you, did the Buddha teach in order to lead people astray? Is such the declaration of the body of Buddhist teaching, and is such an absurdity the burthen of Buddhist belief? Cannot one see the immediate and necessary deduction as just cited? There is, clearly, an inner Teaching which is given only to those who have been examined and found fit to receive it, and examined in order that they may not be led astray by receiving a teaching too comprehensive for them to grasp, and therefore certain to be misunderstood by them. One is well aware of the fact that the *Saddharma-Puṇḍarîka* is alleged by Western scholars to be the product of a later date, one of the works of a mystical school which became very popular in the North of Asia some centuries after the Buddha had passed on. This may very well be the fact, and it was to be expected; but the fact does not invalidate the main point that such teaching of restriction or of withholding could not have arisen nor have been so widely accepted, had there not been current throughout the Nor-

---

48. *Ibid.*   49. *Ibid.*

thern Buddhism the strong flow of esoteric thought and suggestion which it therefore becomes only proper to trace back doubtless even to the days of the Buddha himself and to his Arhats. Otherwise, the high probability is that any mere later invention or mere mystical speculations of a later date would have been found highly unacceptable, and would have been peremptorily rejected, when the first attempts were made to promulgate them. The history of mystical thought in all other great systems shows clearly enough, and in every case that is remembered by the writer at the moment, that the estoericism of the respective founder of each of these great systems gradually faded out with the passage of time ensuing after his death, and its place was taken by mere orthodoxy, in which the traditional or written scriptures as received became sacrosanct, untouchable, and often clothed with an atmosphere of holiness which forbade any adding or substantial change. This is clearly shown, for instance, in the literature and mystical history of Christianity.

4. I speak according to their reach and faculty; by means of various meanings [i. e., by means of permutable meanings or parables] I accommodate my view (or the theory).[50]

Is this the supposititious 'closed fist' of the Great Teacher, Gautama the Buddha? When one recollects that the main or fundamental teachings of the Buddha were recognised in both the Northern and the Southern Schools, and that the very phrase 'closed fist' must have been current in both schools as one of the graphic expressions of the great Master himself, it is difficult to avoid the conclusion that the 'closed fist' argument, so often cited by European scholars as against the fact of an esoteric teaching in Buddhism, must be understood as it has been attempted in this present chapter to explain it, i. e., as referring solely to the government of the Order after the Buddha's passing; for indeed, the passage in which the 'closed fist' expression occurs, refers *solely* to matters of government in the Order after the Buddha's death. The words of this passage state this unequivocally, and it is merely distorting the scripture itself to read into it something that the scripture does not say.

All that the Lord Buddha taught was true in essentials, but he most certainly did not teach everything to all men. He taught all that was needed for the promulgation of the philosophic and religious doctrine which he delivered; identically so as concerns the government of the Order to prevail during his life-time and for its direction after his demise, and did not hold anything back in a 'closed

50. *Ibid.*

fist'; and the 'closed fist' passage says nothing but that. Hence, the deductions drawn by Westerners from the 'closed fist' phrase, that the Lord Buddha had no esoteric teaching to deliver and he delivered none, and that no esoteric School or Body of disciples existed during and after his life-time, seem to be simply a preposterous inversion of the historical record; and in addition one must submit the entire history of the life-drama of the Lord Buddha as strong witness, testimony, to the contrary. The whole system of the Mahâyâna of the North as existing in its different varieties in all its various schools, such as that of Nâgârjuna, of Âryasaṃgha, and of others, every one of them teaching an esoteric doctrine, every one of them hinting at a Wisdom which is not given to all and sundry, provides excellent and to every reasonable mind convincing proof that an esotericism or an Esoteric Doctrine, or Esoteric Tradition, existed in Buddhism from the earliest times, and by the logic of history and the well-known traits of human nature must be traced back to the great Founder himself.

If we are to take one Buddhist scripture of the South, the *Mahâ-Parinibbâna-Sutta*, hereinbefore quoted from, as being the words of the Lord Buddha — and this one is perfectly willing to do with certain natural and necessary reservations depending upon the difficulties of accurate transmission and delivery through the centuries, and having due regard also to the literary formulation of his teachings in scriptural structure — then here on the other side, we have a Northern scripture alleging to be the equally authentic words of the Master, which it seems unreasonable to set aside on grounds of theory or merely literary prejudice, this Northern work stating that the Doctrine is to be delivered with prudence and care, and not to all men, and that the Wise guard it and reveal it not, except, as the preceding śloka or verse says, with discriminating judgment to minds which differ in 'their disposition.' Indeed, and speaking generally, one knows not a single great religious philosophy or philosophical religion, which has not, or which has not had in its origins, an esoteric doctrine. The mere fact that such esoteric doctrine is not properly understood and perhaps even not recognised by all, and possibly again, forgotten in this or some other religion, argues nothing to the contrary, and is certainly not a proof that such esoteric School or Doctrine did not once exist therein.

The objections alleged against the existence, or possibility of the existence, of an esoteric School or body of doctrine in Buddhism, limp painfully because running directly counter to human psychology in such matters; and therefore objections of this character should be scrutinized with meticulous and jealous care. Nor should the religio-philosophical works presently existing in the world and alleging to give the teachings or doctrines of mystical or so-called esoteric or quasi-esoteric schools, be accepted at the face-value of their averments or statements; because virtually all such mystical works are written in veiled fashion, and when read, often repel by the unconscionable exaggerations and often apparently ridiculous distortions of natural fact which they occasionally if not frequently imbody. Such luxuriance in statement and pageantry of metaphor themselves prove that these scriptures are written in the common and usual esoteric cipher, and can be properly construed and understood only by those who possess the keys thereto. It is clear enough that if a doctrine is intended to be esoteric, of necessity, when delivered to the public, its teachings must be hid under veil and allegory; and it is absurd to take veils and allegories, parables or metaphors, tropes or figures of speech, as statements of plain, unvarnished, pragmatical fact. It seems indeed high time that our Western scholars should use ordinary sense in these matters, and if they do not understand and are repelled by the highly figurative language of Oriental or other mystical works, this is no reason for condemning these scriptures as not being what they are alleged to be, or themselves purport to be.

If our Occidental scholars, our European Orientalists — and the writer craves pardon if his language here seem a bit unkind — would use their human common sense and intuitions a little more, i. e., would allow them a freer play in their work and criticism, they would themselves see what the ordinary man who reads these scriptures easily sees for himself; and, furthermore, they would probably realize that taking one half of the scriptures of Buddhism, i. e., those of the Hînayâna only, or very nearly 'only,' and drawing deductions from this one half, is not only inadequate and therefore imperfect study, but is likewise distinctly reprehensible work in scholarship. It is, as it were, taking the teaching of the Roman Catholic Church, or of the Church of Martin Luther, or of the Church founded by Calvin, and thereupon saying: Here, this is Christianity; it teaches so-and-so; and thus-and-thus; and although other phases of Christian thought may be found in other branches of the Christian Church General, nevertheless the phase of it that we have been studying seems to contain the most ancient ideas and therefore probably the most accurate presentation of the thought and will of the great Founder.

Now, such one-sided study is more or less precisely what too many of our Occidental Orientalists have done — and continue to do. The present writer states, without fear of any consequences arising from contradiction, that there is and always has been as much esoteric teaching in Buddhism — i. e., that there is in fact an esoteric Buddhism, an Esoteric Tradition in it — as there was a very early esoteric or secret side under the Christian doctrinal scriptural tradition; there was as much esotericism in early Buddhism, and it still lives and flourishes in certain places, as there was esotericism in the religions and philosophies and the Mysteries of ancient Greece and of Rome and of Egypt and elsewhere; and that there is and always has been an equally esoteric or secret doctrine in Brâhmanism.

VI

In the succeeding chapter reference will be made in fuller explication to the frequent charge brought against the Buddhist system and the teachings of its great Founder by Western scholars and indeed by many Oriental Buddhists themselves, that when all is said and done Gautama the Buddha taught a species of philosophical nihilism as concerns the non-existence of any spiritual or continuous self-hood in the compound aggregate making the constitution of a man or of any other conscious entity. This idea is so far from the truth, indeed wanders so widely from the whole tenor or significance even of the various Buddhist scriptures themselves, that one can only wonder how this totally erroneous idea could have arisen both in the minds of Occidental students and in the consciousness of Buddhists themselves. It is to be explained, the present writer believes, solely on the ground that the key unlocking the inner meaning of the Buddha's teaching has been forgotten — has vanished out of the consciousness of Buddhists themselves even of a fairly early date; so that the mere words of the scriptures were taken and understood literally and their inner significance was not grasped.

It is, however, unquestionably true, that Sâkyamuni taught the non-reality, the non-existence of a static, continuous, 'soul' or minor self such as is taught in Christianity and in certain other religions or religious philosophies of similar type. This last fact, or rather averment, is true and admits of no contradiction; but instead of being, as it is so wrongly misunderstood to be, the mark of philosophical and religious imperfection, or as signifying a lack of penetrating sagacity into human psychology, it would be easy to show that precisely the contrary of this is the case; and that, indeed, this teaching of the Buddha, as more or less imbodied in the scriptures of the Mahâyâna and Hînayâna, and especially in the latter, is one of the greatest glories of the great Master's doctrine, and is, further-more, most curiously and suggestively parallel with the best in modern scientific and philosophical speculation in the West.

As above stated, these thoughts will be elaborated in the succeed-ing chapter. Here let it suffice to point to one or two highly signi-ficant and pregnant passages in ancient Buddhist scriptural lore, the importance of which is consistently passed over because mis-understood. In the *Dhammapada,* dealing in general with the matter of the Self or the intrinsic selfhood of beings and entities around which the 'compound aggregates' are builded as vehicles, we find the following very interesting and certainly highly suggestive thoughts:

The Self is the master of self — for who else could be its lord? With the self [the lower self, or 'compound aggregate'] thoroughly controlled, the man finds a Master [or Guide] such as cannot elsewhere be found.[51]

Here is a pointed and emphatic statement of the existence in the human constitution of the governing, controlling, Root-Self which lives and manifests its transcendent powers in and through the lower self or 'soul,' the latter being naught but the 'compound aggregate' of elements, which is the man in his ordinary being. When it is re-membered that the Dhammapada is one of the most authoritative and respected scriptures of the Hînayâna or Southern School, one can appreciate the force of this statement, the more so as it is found in the cycle of scriptures of the Hînayâna which far more than the Northern or Mahâyâna is always cited as the Buddhist School teach-ing the supposed, but wrongly supposed, nihilism so often brought against Buddhism in support of its being a pessimistic system without spiritual basis or import.

Here we have a direct reference to the emphatic existence of the essential *Âtman* or fundamental Self, or Self-hood, in the human constitution.

One more instance, drawn this time from the Mahâyâna, and due to one who in Buddhism itself has always been recognised as being a Bodhisattva — Nâgârjuna. This true mystic Sage and Initiate-Teacher, and one of the most devoted of the Buddha-Gautama's later followers who faithfully carried on the Esoteric Tradition, in his commentary on the Sûtra or scripture of the famous Buddhist work *Prajñâ-Pâramitâ,* states the following:

Sometimes the Tathâgata [the Buddha] taught that the Âtman verily ex-ists, and yet at other times he taught that the Âtman does not exist.[52]

---

51. *Dhammapada,* chapter xii, verse 160.
52. From the Chinese recension of Yuan Chuang.

Just so. Are we then to suppose that the Buddha-Gautama taught, and deliberately taught, contradictions in order to befuddle and to mystify his hearers? Hardly, for the idea is ludicrous. What has already been said, and will in this work later be said, about the compound constitution of man, through which the eternal Self or Âtman, i. e., in this case the Dhyâni-Buddha, works through its erring, wayward 'lower self' or vehicle, or 'soul,' should sufficiently explain that the various meanings of 'self' were as keenly recognised in ancient Buddhist thought and by the great Master himself as they are recognised today. The meaning of the Buddha was obvious enough, that the Âtman as the essential Self, or the Dhyâni-Buddha in the human constitution, exists and evolves perennially, is ever-enduring; but that the 'lower self' or inferior selfhood of a man is merely the feeble reflexion of it, and is what the Europeans call 'soul,' and hence does not 'exist' as an *enduring* entity. The same play, for this is what it really is, upon the word 'self' is distinctly perceptible in the citation from the *Dhammapada* just previously made where the Self as Master is the lord of the lower self as mere man. The present writer is well aware of the many passages in Buddhist scriptures concerning the non-existence of the Âtman as the *human self* or soul — the doctrine of *Anattâ,* in the Pâli writings — and fully concurs, for the truth is obvious enough; but these passages cannot be considered alone and apart from other teachings distinctly stating the Âtman is: constantly in the Mahâyâna, and in the Hînayâna as in the above citation from the *Dhammapada.* In any case, the Âtman is most certainly not the transitory and impermanent human 'soul'; and it is thus that the Buddha's true thought and doctrine should be construed. It reconciles all the difficulties.

[Selections from the material of this chapter and from the material of the succeeding one were extracted and formed into a brief essay for publication in the pages of *The London Forum* (*The Occult Review*). This essay, divided into three instalments, appeared in the above magazine in the first part of 1935. The first instalment was printed in the March, 1935, issue of that periodical.]

CHAPTER IV

THE SECRET DOCTRINE OF GAUTAMA
THE BUDDHA—II

PROBABLY the main reason for the widespread misunderstanding of the essential nature of Buddhistic teaching as first delivered to his Arhats or disciples by Gautama the Buddha, and leaving aside for the moment the later development of Buddhistic philosophy due to the labors of monkish philosophers and exegetes, or expounders, is the almost total lack on the part of Western scholars of the past to see that what the Buddha aimed at more than anything else was the bringing to men of a greater light, a larger hope, and a wider spiritual vision. The truth was that he threw open some of the hitherto fast-closed doors of Brâhman philosophy, and instantly gained the opposition and ill-will of the larger part of the Brâhmaṇas of his time. The objective of the great Teacher's Wisdom was the improving, or better still unfolding, of human intellectual faculty and spiritual power, as demonstrated by his insistence, emphatic, reiterated and unceasing, on what one may term the Doctrine of Becoming. In the eyes of the Buddha-Gautama, man is a Pilgrim, Child of the Universe, who at times is blinded by *Mahâmâyâ* or the Great Illusion of cosmic existence, and at such times therefore needs to be shown the Way or Law, called the *Dharma,* pointing to a realization of the fact that only by *becoming* rather than by mere being could man become the Greater Man which he is in his essential constitution.

It is with genuine pleasure that one may point to a wider and deeper view of the Buddhistic philosophy than has hitherto prevailed in Western countries; and that such wider and therefore wiser visioning of the essential meaning of Buddhism is now coming to the fore, is proved by the very recent appearance of books treating the Buddha and his life-work and religion-philosophy from a more sympathetic viewpoint than has hitherto been customary in the West. Such a work, just off the press (1935), is the booklet entitled *Indian Religion and Survival* by Mrs. Rhys Davids. In her extremely interesting little work, this brilliant Buddhist scholar, so well known for her labors in the Pâli scriptures and translations therefrom, writes as follows, in showing just what the Buddha had in mind in his work:

[The Buddha] sought to show each and every man a More which lay in his nature, his life, his destiny. This was, that to become, to grow spiritually was of the essence of his nature, as spirit or very-man; that to become 'in the right way' he had to exert will, choice; that in him moved and worked Deity in man's inner sense-of-right, of the 'ought,' known as *dharma*.[53]

Mrs. Rhys Davids is unquestionably right in the ascription to Buddhism of the substance of the great Teacher's message which she sees and briefly refers to in the extract just given. Yet the suggestion that the Buddha taught of a 'Deity' in the manner so commonly understood in the West, even by thus proclaiming the divine immanence, is to wander from what the entire testimony of the Buddhist thought so strongly avers; although indeed if Mrs. Rhys Davids means merely the implication that the 'Deity' here spoken of is the abstract or neuter *Divine* — as contrasted with the masculine *God* — this being slightly if at all different from the essential abstract divinity of the Upanishads, then one can only question the propriety of the usage of the word Deity, and agree.

The main thing to note in all this is that the substantial burthen of the Great Teacher's Message, outside of many other important matters, was the emphasis placed upon his doctrine of Becoming, i.e., evolving, growing, unfolding, unwrapping what is within, by all entities whatsoever, man included, through and by means of that ineluctable and wonderful operation of the Universe which the Buddha in common with his predecessors called *Karman:* the doctrine of inescapable consequences for every thought, act, emotion, or feeling, undergone passively, or initiated actively, by every individual being or entity. It was precisely this union of willing and doing on the part of every entity which brought about its Ever-Becoming, in other words, its constant growth, or, mayhap, in minor stages its periods of retrogression, likewise instances of 'becoming.'

In this really sublime teaching one finds the philosophical structure of Buddhism both exoteric and, as Theosophists claim, esoteric. By his 'becoming,' i. e., by his progress from stage to stage in evolutionary changes which are continuous and uninterrupted, a man, among other beings, may raise himself as high as the highest gods, or may debase himself through his willing and doing to the low and

---

53. *Indian Religion and Survival*, p. 8: by Mrs. Rhys Davids, D. LITT., M. A.; President of the Pali Text Society.

dread levels of the beings in the so-called hells of which so much is found in Buddhistic literature.

In this teaching of *Becoming,* just as the same is found in esoteric Theosophy, in the Esoteric Tradition, we find both the reason and the rationale of the many statements both in Buddhism and indeed elsewhere that every man has it within his power, by appropriate spiritual, intellectual, psychical, and ethical willing and doing, himself in the course of ages to become a Buddha — a doctrine which, as Mrs. Rhys Davids properly hints, is expressly taught in the Buddhism of Northern and Central Asia. As she truly says:

> That not this Bodhisattva only, [the Buddha-Gautama in a former existence] but every man has it in him eventually to realize Buddhahood: this was brought to the front by Mahâyâna Buddhism.[54]

This is admirable; but it is to be regretted that this able and conscientious Pâli scholar should labor under the impression that the Buddhism of Southern Asia should have "neglected to show it as equally applicable to every man."

The reason for Mrs. Rhys Davids' belief that this teaching is lacking in the Pâli Scriptures seems to lie in the fact that it is not expressly stated as a doctrine; and yet to the present writer the Hinayâna-system contains, both by numerous hints in the various scriptures which imbody its teachings, and in rarer instances by direct allusion, the same doctrine of becoming and the same pointing to the results of such becoming that the Mahâyâna does, albeit in the latter system the doctrine is explicit and fairly well elaborated.

I

It may be as well before passing on to the main subject of this chapter to refer once more to Mrs. Rhys Davids' clever and very readable little book if only in order to show that modern Western Buddhistic Scholarship is veering markedly away from the Occidental and quasi-Christian prejudices and pre-conceptions that so strongly and injuriously colored the work of virtually all former Occidental Buddhist studies. She speaks at length of the doctrine of 'survival,' around which so much useless controversy has raged in the past as to whether Buddhism does or does not, did or did not, teach the utter annihilation of the human compound at death. Most Western Buddhist scholars of former days, if not all of them, seem

---

54. *Op. cit.,* p. 42.

to have united in a common opinion to the effect that one proof of the so-called 'Pessimism' of Buddhism was the fact that it taught that with the dissolution of the human compound entity, i.e., at death, the entity vanished, disappeared utterly, was completely annihilated: this in the face of the iterated and reiterated statements of the Buddhist scriptures themselves, even of the Hînayâna, that what survived dissolution of the compound entity was its Karman, i. e., the results, consequences, of what the compound entity itself was at the moment of dissolution. It would seem evident to the merest tyro in philosophical thought that the word Karman thus used must have a technical substantial significance, because it is obvious that results or consequences cannot survive the death of their originator, for the reason that if results or consequences do not inhere in some thing or in some entity — i. e., if they are not parts or portions of an entity — they have no existence in themselves. An 'act' cannot survive, nor can a 'consequence' survive, except in the modern Western scientific sense of impressions made on surrounding material, and this is not the meaning of the Buddha's teaching because the scriptures of both the Mahâyâna and the Hînayâna are replete with instances of entities, 'compound aggregates,' which nevertheless after death and after a certain period of other existence in other worlds are reborn as men on earth.

The stories about the Buddha himself are both emphatic and luminous illustrations to the point, as exemplified in the famous Jâtaka-stories, meaning rebirth-stories. These 550 or more rebirth-stories describe the alleged repeated reincarnations or rebirths of the Buddha, and show him rising from lower stages to higher; and if the 'compound aggregate' is utterly annihilated at its death or dissolution, how, obviously, can such a non-existing entity be reborn in an unending series of reappearances of such entity's intrinsic karman? Is it not obvious that Western Scholars have failed to grasp the subtility and profound meaning of the Buddha's teaching? The riddle is solved — although indeed it is no riddle at all — by remembering the teaching of Theosophy, of the Esoteric Tradition, to the effect that man, equally with every other being or entity or thing, is his own karman: his karman is himself, for he himself is the results, the consequences, the fruitage, the production, of every preceding thought, feeling, emotion, or act in the virtually unending series of past rebirths, each such birth automatically reproducing itself as changed or modified by its own willing and doing — to wit, the consciousness acting upon the 'compound aggregate' thus producing karman, or modifications, or changes, in the substance of the man himself. Thus verily a man is his own karman; he is his own child, the offspring of what he formerly willed and made himself now to be; just as at present, in his actual compound constitution he is willing and making himself, through results or consequences produced upon his constitution, to be what in the future he will become.

Just here, again, we see the tremendous force and philosophical power of the Buddha's doctrine of *Becoming*.

Turning now to the promised citation from Mrs. Rhys Davids' booklet, we find:

That it was, in original Buddhism, a given man or woman who survives, who lives on, after death of the body, is always referred to as a truth to be accepted and understood.[55]

And again, wherein she culls a passage from one of the Jâtakas:

'Now it may seem to you, Ânanda, that at that time Jotipâla was a different person, but you should not look upon it like that. *I* at that time was Jotipâla.' Could emphasis further go? I say this, because later Buddhism came to deny the passing over of the identical person, came to deny there was any personal survivor.[56]

Now these citations from Mrs. Rhys Davids certainly prove that something survives the dissolution of the compound aggregate, following Buddhist thought, when death comes upon this aggregate; but it should be pointed out that this is wholly admitted and emphatically stated in the Buddhist writings themselves, which employ no small emphasis in this ascription of continuity to the x-factor in the compound aggregate which has repeated existences or reincarnations on earth as well as in other worlds. The Buddhist scriptures, as has been stated above, declare that this x-factor is the karman of the entity; Mrs. Rhys Davids seems to rebel at this abstract philosophical statement and believes that she finds in what she calls original Buddhism teaching to the effect that there is an actual person who survives physical dissolution or death. Just so, the present writer is wholly at one with her in this, but he is likewise wholly at one with the statement of the Buddhist scriptures themselves, for he has in preceding paragraphs shown with sufficient clarity although sketchily, he believes, that this surviving 'person' is the karmic entity or karman of the preceding entity which died and which thus survives.

What is a 'person,' after all, except a mask, a vehicle, a veil, composed of compounded or aggregate elements drawn from the

---

55. *Op. cit.,* p. 56.   56. *Op. cit.,* p. 57.

surrounding nature through which works and lives the spiritual force alluded to in preceding paragraphs, and which, traced to its source, is seen to be the inner Buddha, the Dhyâni-Buddha, the inner god? This, the Buddha himself taught, as so well outlined in the Mahâ-yâna-system, man could again *become* by so living and striving as to bring it into karmic relationship or existence even here on earth.

Mrs. Rhys Davids unfortunately seems to ascribe the teaching of the Pâli Buddhist scriptures of the survival of the karman as the entity itself, to the monkish elucubrations of Buddhist anchorites who sought to flee from the world, and who thus craved utter anni-hilation of their essence in preference to its continued existence in conscious rebirths. The present writer is positive that Mrs. Rhys Davids has here completely misunderstood the subtil philosophical sense of this entire matter; and he believes that Buddhist scholar-ship in the future will trace back the essential teaching on this matter of the Hînayâna Pâli scriptures to declarations of Buddha-Gautama himself. Time will show.

Yet one can only desire to render due meed of respect to this courageous student and scholar who, apparently alone, at the present time, is unafraid to face the current of misconception and prejudice which previous Western Buddhistic scholarship has so strongly set in movement.

II

Turning now to a more particular examination of metaphysical and religio-philosophical ideas imbodied in Buddhism, one would like to ask a very pertinent question: What indeed are the doctrines — some of the more important of them at least — that the Buddha-Gautama taught? Or again: What is the *fundamental* teaching of Buddhism? One will find this question constantly asked and an-swered by Occidental Orientalists; but the present writer has always wondered, in his study of Buddhism which has extended over some thirty years, why these really learned and scholarly men of the Occi-dent, so earnest and devoted in their studies, so industrious indeed, invariably seem to hunt for, and to insist that Buddhism must have, one fundamental doctrine. To tell the truth, the present writer does not know what this *one* fundamental doctrine is. It is easy to know what many if not most European scholars have to say about it; but yet the writer of these lines has searched for thirty years more or less to find the 'one fundamental doctrine' in Buddhism, and instead of one he has found a hundred or more.

What are some of these? The impermanence of all manifested

existence or existences; that in consequence of the impermanence and illusory nature of all manifested beings and things, pain, suffering, sorrow, are native to all beings who live in this illusion, or mâyâ; yet there is a Way leading to the cessation of all this sorrow, of all this pain, and of all individual illusions about them; and this Way is eightfold in character. It is commonly called in Europe 'the Noble Eightfold Path,' based upon Four Fundamental Truths or Verities. What are, first, these Four Noble Truths:

> The noble truth about sorrow and pain;
> The noble truth about the cause of sorrow and pain;
> The noble truth about the cessation of sorrow and pain;
> The noble truth about the path that leads to this cessation.

These four truths may be somewhat paraphrased as follows:

1. Suffering and sorrow exist in all manifested beings.
2. There is a cause for the suffering and the sorrow that exist.
3. There is a way to render extinct the causes of the suffering and sorrow that exist.
4. There is a path, by following which the causes of the suffering and sorrow that exist are rendered extinct. This path consists in a continuous changing to betterment of the factors or saṃskâras of our consciousness. These factors are eight and comprise the Noble Eightfold Path.

The Noble Eightfold Path

1. Recognition of the truth of the preceding four verities.
2. Holding the objective to be attained clearly in the mind, holding it firm, with discrimination.
3. Right words, or controlled and governed speech at all times and in all places.
4. Controlled and governed action at all times and in all places.
5. Appropriate and honorable means of livelihood.
6. An inflexible will to achieve the objective visioned.
7. An eager intellect, always open for a greater truth, and ready to learn; and the cultivation of a strong and retentive memory.
8. An unveiled spiritual perception, combined with great care in thinking, which is the keynote of all the preceding items, and which expressed in other words means right meditation with a tranquil mind into which wisdom thus enters.

In addition to this 'Noble Eightfold Path,' based on the Four Verities, which those especially who follow the Hînayâna love, and rightly love, there are the six, seven, or indeed ten, Pâramitâs or Sublime Virtues studied and followed, let us hope, by the disciples of the Schools of the North — they who believe that they have received and that they have developed the teaching of the Lord Buddha's heart, and who, likewise, accept at least in their principles the teachings of his brain, the 'Eye-Doctrine' of the Hînayâna.

What are these Pâramitâs? They are stated below, and given largely in the words of H. P. Blavatsky, as found in her noble little handbook *The Voice of the Silence*.[57] Although a Theosophist first and foremost, she was likewise a formal Buddhist, having at one time when in Ceylon taken Pansil or the Five exoteric Vows; thus she was well qualified to speak about the doctrines of him whom she loved because she understood him far better than the rather stiff-minded European Orientalists, governed to a large extent as they have been by the psychological atmosphere of a now moribund anthropological science, combined with a mind more or less swayed by equally moribund Christian theology. These, then, are the famous Pâramitâs, the first seven given more or less in the words of H. P. Blavatsky:

1. The key of charity and immortal love.

2. Harmony in word and act, thus cutting at the roots of the making of future evil karman.

3. Patience, that naught can ruffle.

4. Indifference to pleasure and pain, by which illusion is conquered and truth is perceived.

5. Dauntless energy or fortitude, that finds its way to the supernal truth out of the mire of lies.

6. Spiritual meditation, a golden gate which once opened leads the chela or neophyte to the realm of eternal verity and ceaseless contemplation of it.

7. Wisdom combined with discriminating intelligence, which makes of a man a god, creating him a Bodhisattva, a son of the Dhyânîs.

In addition to these Seven, the following three are also frequently mentioned in Buddhist literature; and they are of equal importance

---

57. Fragment III: 'The Seven Portals,' pp. 47-8 (original edition).

with the former, although they are here enumerated out of their usual order as they are commonly found in the exoteric books:

8. Proper method or discipline in following the Path.

9. The urgent wish to achieve success for the sake of being an impersonal beneficent energy in the world.

10. A continuous exercise of the intellect in study of self, of others, and incidentally of the great religious literatures and philosophies of the world.

Mind you, these ten are among the most widely accepted mystical teachings of the Northern School of Buddhism which is followed more or less faithfully by some 400 million human beings — at least let us hope so.

III

It has often been said by those who understand but little, one fears, of the essential teaching of the Tathâgata, of Gautama the Buddha, that he taught that when a man dies, then *finis*, complete and utter, is his fate or destiny. The man is; he dies; he now is not! This is a monstrous perversion of the Buddha's own teaching. It has often been said by those who have studied but have misunderstood the Buddha-Gautama's teachings, that his doctrine was that there is no reincarnating or reimbodying entity, as an entity; and yet the teachings of the Buddhist scriptures, both of South and of North, are filled with the stories of what it is popular to miscall the 'metempsychosis' of individuals.

Take the Jâtaka-Tales, already alluded to, the birth-tales supposed by the multitude of unthinking to be stories of the former imbodiments of Śâkyamuni himself, dealing with events that were said to have taken place in these past imbodiments of his on Earth — take these as instances; and one will find in these curiously interesting and sometimes profound tales, for they are largely mystical and metaphorical, that the existences of the Buddha began, as it were, in the very beginning of this present world-period, as one of the lowest and humblest of creatures, and that he slowly evolved through repetitive imbodiments developing and growing in each, until finally he attained Buddhahood as Śâkyamuni.

Question: If there be no surviving entity, what was it that passed from birth to birth in those numerous stories, which, whatever one may think of them, proclaim the common acceptance by the multitude of Buddhists of there being some kind of x-factor in the complex of skandhas forming the human being which passes from life to life? Or how about the many instances in canonical Buddhist scriptures themselves, which place in the mouth of the Great Teacher himself observations, remarks, parables, references, to the preceding births of such or such other individuals? If Buddhism taught no such continuity through repeated imbodiments of *something,* why all this allusion to reincarnating beings?

In the preceding chapter the matter has been treated at some length with due reference made to the theory of the man being his own karman or skandhic aggregate which as a compound is re-collected or gathered together anew in order to produce a new person or man for each successive imbodiment or reincarnation.

Buddhism teaches an evolution or development of this x-factor of consciousness and will slowly followed through many rebirths, through repeated imbodiments, bringing about constantly increasing faculty and power, until finally the entity whose evolving destiny is thus traced, becomes a man; and after becoming a man finally becomes a Bodhisattva — one filled with the spirit of the inner Buddha, or rather of the Buddhic principle, the Bodhi, the principle and fountain-head of utter wisdom. Furthermore, that taking the Bud-dha-Gautama as an example or illustration of such an evolving entity, in his last incarnation on earth, he was born the human Bodhisattva-Siddhârtha, later called Śâkyamuni, in the year 643 B. C., and that when he was eighty years of age, after having passed through manifold experiences and trials, and after he had gathered together and taught his disciples and had sent them abroad in order to proclaim the Good Law, he then entered the Nirvâna, with an entering which left naught behind save his Dharma — the Law, i. e., the Truth that he taught.

Now, let one ask: What is it that thus passes from the humblest of beings through the many and varied *gatis* or 'ways' of existence, through repeated and incessant rebirth, until that Something, that x-quantity, hereinbefore called the x-factor, becomes a Buddha? What is it, one asks? The scriptures of the South of Asia, of the Hînayâna, will say that it was results, consequences, i. e., *karman.* Precisely! What then is this karman? The word itself means action, signifying results, consequences, effects. But is it thinkable that the noblest Sage of historic times, the titan-intellect of the human race, perhaps the loftiest spiritual genius of his kind known to the human species for scores of thousands of years past, taught that bare consequences, naked composites, sheer effects, technically called *saṃ-skâras* or mere collections (one may properly ask, collections of what?) can and do pass in entitative fashion from life to life, re-collect themselves — re-collect themselves after being time after time dispersed as atomic aggregates into the various realms of Nature from which they were originally drawn? The answer depends entirely upon the meaning that we give to this term *samskâras*, and to the term *skandhas*. If these are mere aggregates of atoms existing on the psycho-emotional as well as on the physical plane, and without any internal bond of spiritual-psychological union, thus voicing the merely and completely materialistic idea: then we must infer that this titan-intellect taught an impossibility, which the merest tyro in philosophical and scientific thought would reject with impatience as being words without meaning, thoughts without content, ideas void of sense or foundation. Or if, on the other hand, we understand, as we should understand, *samskâras* to mean psycho-magnetic and material aggregates of life-atoms attracted to each other because of their intrinsic magnetic vital power, and unified and governed by the repetitive action of the same spiritual and intellectual forces, previously described, which formerly held them in union as an aggregated vehicle, then indeed we have a reasonable and logical teaching consistent with what we know ourselves of the intricate and unitary yet compounded character of our constitution, and likewise thoroughly consistent not only with all the teaching of the Hindû philosophy of the day, but with all the remainder of the Buddha's own sublimely comprehensive and profound philosophy.

The following observations, therefore, give the undoubted meaning and inner content of the Gautama-Buddha's Doctrine; and it is likewise precisely the meaning and content of the 'heart' of his teaching as found in the Mahâyâna-Schools of the North, and taught today by Theosophy. One may add that it is also the meaning and content of the Hînayâna-School, although in this last school the inner content is less easily uncovered, though seen to be as much a part of it when thus uncovered as it is an essential part of the great Mahâyâna-Systems.

While it is perfectly true that the lower parts, or inferior portions, of every entity, of a human being for instance, form a compound or 'complex,' and therefore are a compounded aggregate, and consequently because of this combination mortal and perishable as such compound, being what in Buddhism are called the *samskâras,* or the body of composites, nevertheless, there is *something* of a spiritual, intellectual, and psychological character, previously called the x-factor, around which this aggregated compound re-gathers or re-collects itself at each new rebirth; and it is this *something* by which the compound is re-assembled and during life is held together as an entity, thus forming a man — or indeed any similar being. There is here no such teaching as that of the imperishable, immortal soul in the Christian sense, static through eternity in unchanging essential characteristics, as is obvious enough; and this deduction of no such imperishable immortal soul in the human being as drawn from the teachings of the Buddha himself, and as found in the many and various scriptures, is perfectly correct, for such a soul, to be immortal, must not and cannot essentially change, which likewise would mean that it cannot evolve or grow, because if it did so grow, so evolve — which means changing to something different and better — it then no longer is what it was before. It is something different because it is changed; and therefore, not being what it formerly was, it obviously cannot be 'immortal' in the Christian sense. This is a subtil and profound thought which, once grasped, unveils the inner meaning of Śâkyamuni's teaching in this respect, and one's sense of logical consistency is aroused to admiration by it.

Consequently this x-quantity, call it what you like, call it karman if you will — and if you understand the proper meaning of the word karman as signifying consequences, or results, of whatever kind, spiritual, intellectual, psychical, physical or what not, it is as good a word as any — is that vital-psychological *something* which insures the re-collecting of the *saṃskâras* together for the new life, thus reproducing the new man, as the fruitage or results of his past life. It all is simply a continuance in existence of this x-quantity in life after life by means of the karmic consequences or results of the life and of all the lives which have preceded any new appearance or imbodiment or incarnation of the peregrinating entity.

Let us try to illustrate this very mystical doctrine, so difficult for Occidentals to understand. Consider a child. The child is born from an infinitesimal and invisible human life-germ, and yet in a few years it grows to be a six-foot man. Now then, in order to become a six-foot man from the little child that it was, it must pass through many and differing stages of growth, of *evolution* which means development, unfolding. First it is the microscopic germ, developing into the embryo, then born as an infant, then growing into the lad, the lad changing into the young man, the young man becoming the man in the maturity and plenitude of his powers, and finally, the man after the maturity and plenitude of his powers enters upon the phase of senescence, decay, decrepitude and death. Now every one of these phases is a change from the preceding one, and is based and founded upon the preceding one. Each such new phase is the karman of the next preceding phase and all preceding phases. Yet the man is the same through all the changes, although the man himself changes because growing likewise.

The boy of six is not the boy of ten; the boy of ten is not the lad of fifteen; and the young man of twenty-five is not the man of forty; and the man of forty is different from the man of fifty-five when he is at his prime — or should be; and the man of eighty, usually weak and tired, worn with toil and labor, soon going to his rest and peace for a while, is not the new-born child — yet the entity is the same from the beginning of the cyclic series unto its end; because there is an uninterrupted series of steps or stages of *change* signifying growth, which means development or evolution.

In this example, simple as it is, you have the key to the Buddhist thought. Precisely as it is with the birth and development and growth of a child into a human adult, so is it with the passage of the karman of an entity from body to body through the different life-stages of rebirth, through the different ages: the passing from low to high of that x-quantity which the Theosophists call 'the reincarnating ego,' and the mystical Buddhists speak of as the shining ray from the Buddha within, and which the Hînayâna of the South, the defective vehicle, the exoteric teaching of the Lord Buddha, spoke of as the 'karman' of the man growing continuously nobler, better, grander, greater, more evolved, until the man through these karmic changes or changings of karman finally becomes a Bodhisattva; the Bodhisattva then becomes a Buddha, finally entering the Nirvâna.

It may as well be said here that this 'something,' this x-factor, is what in Theosophy is called the Monad which, imperishable in essence, and the fountain-head of all consciousness and will, passes from age to age throughout the Manvantara and reproduces itself by means of rays from its essence in the various reimbodiments or reincarnations which it thus brings about. In mystical Buddhism, especially of the North, this Monad is identic with the Dhyâni-Buddha or inner spiritual 'Buddha of Meditation' which is the heart or core of every reimbodying being. Just as in Esoteric Theosophy or the Esoteric Tradition each and every monad is a droplet, or ray, to change the figure of speech, of and from the cosmic Mahâ-buddhi, just so in mystical Buddhism, every Dhyâni-Buddha is a ray from Amitâbha-Buddha, a form or manifestation of Alaya or the Cosmic Spirit.

When one hears that Buddhism teaches the final ending, signifying the thorough-going transmuting, wholly complete, of that intangible and vague entity which Christians miscall 'soul,' and which

the Buddhists of the South call the 'karman' of a man — the sum-
total of all that a man is, all his feelings, thoughts, yearnings, energies, forces (in short everything that the man is, for everything is
his karman), passing ever to greater and greater things — then it
should be remembered that while this statement is true when properly understood, nevertheless the Northern School of Buddhism
which is incomparably more mystical than that of the South, still
retains, however imperfectly, the more explicit and lucid teaching
emanating from the Buddha's 'heart,' to wit: That there is a ray
from the celestial Buddha within the composite entity called man
builded of the *saṃskâras,* and that it is the influence of this ray
which first brought the *saṃskâras* together, which ray persists
throughout the ages, and re-collects the same *saṃskâras* together
anew, thus reproducing through repetitive imbodiments on Earth
the same karmic entity who or which formerly existed. Try to
understand the essential meaning of this karman-doctrine as taught
by the great Master and as more or less faithfully imbodied in the
Buddhist scriptures, and the fact will be grasped that the karman
of the man *is the man himself;* and that just because the man himself
is continually changing because continually growing, thus the karman
of the man which is himself is obviously likewise continually changing for the better. The teaching of the South, of the Hînayâna, is
true, when it states that what remains of a man after his death
is his karman, because as just shown this karman is the man himself.

IV

With all that has been said in this and the preceding chapter,
the theme has been little more than sketched, yet with sufficient
outline, it is hoped, to develop forth its inner sense. He whom his
followers and whom the West know under various titles, such as
Gautama the Buddha, Śâkyamuni or the Śâkya-Sage, or by his personal name Siddhârtha — which means 'one who has achieved his objective' — was born in the Spring, at or about the time of the Spring-
Equinox, in the waxing moon, and in the year 643 B. C., reckoning
according to Christian chronology, in a North Indian town which is
now thought to have been in the foot-hills of the Himâlaya-moun-
tains. His father was Śuddhodana which our very pragmatical Occi-
dentalists say means 'pure rice,' or 'pure food,' apparently forgetting
that it is virtually impossible that this could be the translation because it would be a violation of Sanskrit grammar, and the original
of such translation would have to be spelled *Śuddhaudana* — which

it is not. The word means 'pure water' or 'pure flow,' and is obvious-ly in connexion with the fact that his mother was called Mâyâ or Mâyâdevî, meaning Illusion, or Illusion the goddess, a mystic name referring to the Buddhist teaching itself that his origin was divine, from the Celestial Buddha, from whom *flowed* a pure ray of the spirit which, passing through the realms of Illusion the mother, mystically gave birth to the Buddha. Remember also that the name of his wife was Yaśodharâ, which can be translated as 'holder of glory' or perhaps better 'possessor of glory,' pointing to the fact of his possession as the other 'half' of himself of spiritual qualities and powers through which and in connexion with which he lived and worked.

It is unnecessary here to relate anew the world-famed story of the Buddha's life, as it is so well known not only to scholars but to every student of the life of the great Master. Those who are even today so strangely and strongly fascinated by the various forms of the lower Indian Yoga, as this has been proclaimed abroad in Western lands by itinerant thinkers from the Indian Peninsula, and who imagine that the pathway to initiation and interior development is the mortification or, even worse, the mutilation of the physical frame, should take serious counsel of the fact the Buddha, so the story of his life runs, after trying these various means of interior develop-ment through yoga, cast them all aside, renounced them as virtually useless for his sublime purpose. Iconography and pictorial art gene-rally in Buddhism show the various phases of the different events in his life before he attained utter illumination or Buddhahood under the Bodhi-tree, so called in commemoration of this great Event; and the most informative of these representations are they which show the Buddha in one of the various postures of spiritual meditation, interior re-collection; but equally significant are those which repre-sent him in the pre-Buddha state as a veritable image of skin and bones, what the Germans call a *Hautskelet*. The pathway to the Temple of Wisdom and of interior illumination is not the pathway of mortification of the flesh, but the control of the will, the living of the life, combined with intellectual awakening — i. e., the path of interior development, and the becoming at one with the superior elements of the human constitution which are at one and the same time divine in their highest parts, spiritual in the next lower range, and intellectual in their third.

The term 'Buddha' itself means awakened, from the verbal root बुध् (*budh*), signifying 'to observe,' 'to recover consciousness,' and therefore, to 'awaken' — i. e., a Buddha is one who is fully awake

and active in all the parts or ranges of his septempartite constitution, and is therefore a full, complete, and relatively speaking a perfectly evolved human being.

The esoteric Theosophical teaching is here likewise passed over
in relative slightness, which teaching contains the statement that the
Buddha did indeed 'die' to all human affairs at the age of eighty
years, because then the higher parts of him entered the Nirvâṇa, and
no Nirvâṇî can be called a living man if he has attained the seventh
degree of this range of Nirvâṇa as the Buddha did; yet the esoteric
Theosophical teaching likewise states that in all the remainder of
his constitution, in those parts of him beneath the range of the
Dhyâni-Buddha within him, he remained alive on Earth for twenty
years more after this date, teaching his Arhats and chosen disciples
in secret, giving to them the nobler 'doctrines of the heart,' as
obviously he had publicly taught 'the doctrines of his brain,' i. e.,
the eye-doctrine; and that finally, in the hundredth year of his
physical age, Gautama-Śâkyamuni, the Buddha, cast his physical
body aside and thereafter has lived in the inner realms of being as
a Nirmâṇakâya.

v

This chapter relates briefly only and with extreme succinctness
what is indeed a fascinating theme of study, but it would make the
present portion of this book intolerably long were one to embark upon
a more extended analysis of the noble topic which hereinbefore is
briefly discussed. Yet one must say a little more about a phase of the
Buddha's teaching which exoteric Buddhism, whether of North or
South, does not openly tell of. There is a Wisdom, the Secret Wisdom of the Buddha-Gautama, his esoteric dharma — and the present
writer does not hesitate to state this openly, and he ventures to say
that it may be found, although more or less veiled, in the teaching
of the books of the great Mahâyâna-School of Northern and Central
Asia. Furthermore, this dharma, this Secret Wisdom, this Gupta-
Vidyâ, can verily be taught. Among its doctrines, likewise found
in the teaching of the Northern School, is the statement that every
man is a manifestation on this earth of a Buddhic principle belonging to his constitution and manifesting in three degrees or phases:
(a) as a Celestial or Dhyâni-Buddha, (b) as a Dhyâni-Bodhisattva,
(c) as a Mânushya-Buddha; and that all human faculties and powers
are, like rays from a spiritual sun, derivatives from this wondrous
interior compound Buddhic entity. It is the core of the core of all
our being. Union with this 'heart' of us is the aim of all initiation,

for it is the union, the becoming at one, with the Buddhi-principle within us, the seat of abstract Bodhi; and when this union is achieved, then a man becomes a Buddha.

This is the fundamental thought, in the writer's considered opinion, of all the teaching of the Buddha-Gautama; and even the very last words which popular legend ascribes to the Master on his death-bed, 'Seek out your own perfection,' imbody the same fundamental thought of the human being as an imperfect manifestation of the celestial or Dhyâni-Buddha within himself — the man ever striving, consciously or unconsciously, to attain union with this divinity within. This is the yoga of Buddhism, although one readily grants that we hear little of it; yet it is averred that it is likewise the real yoga, and the only yoga worth anything, in the various systems of Hindû yoga-teaching likewise.

We have in these thoughts, drawn from the recorded teachings of the Buddha himself, exactly the same sublime adhortation or injunction that all the great Sages and Seers of all the ages have taught, to wit, that the way to the unutterable Wisdom and Peace of the Divine is found within oneself. All the great spiritual and intellectual human Titans, whose vast minds have been the luminaries of the human race in all past times, were precisely they who had developed more or less of this Buddha-principle within themselves; and the value, philosophic, religious, and ethical, of this teaching lies in the fact that every human being may follow the same path that these great Masters have followed, because every human being has in his constitution the same identical cosmic elements that the Great Ones have.

Even the School of Southern Asia, the Hînayâna, gives as the unquestioned teaching of the Tathâgata that a man can attain union with Brahman, as is evidenced by a number of passages in the Pâli scriptures. Now, what is the path by which this union may be achieved? In answer, consider the following citation from one of the 'orthodox' scriptures of the Hînayâna-School, and thus the reader will have the Buddhist scriptures' own words before him. This teaching of the Buddha-Gautama concerning the gaining of union with Brahmâ will be familiar to him as likewise being the teaching of orthodox Brâhmanism. Thus, then, from the *Tevijja-Sutta:*

'That the Bhikkhu who is free . . . should after death, when the body is dissolved, become united with Brahmâ, who is the same — such a condition of things is every way possible!

'In sooth, . . . the Bhikkhu who is free from anger, free from malice, pure in mind, and master of himself should after death, when the body is dissolved, become united with Brahmâ, who is the same — such a condition of things is every way possible!' [58]

'For Brahmâ, I know, . . . and the world of Brahmâ, and the path which leadeth unto it. Yea, I know it even as one who has entered the Brahmâ world, and has been born within it!' [59]

'And he lets his mind pervade one quarter of the world with thoughts of Love, of pity, sympathy, and equanimity, and so the second, and so the third, and so the fourth. And thus the whole wide world, above, below, around, and everywhere, does he continue to pervade with heart of Love, with heart of pity, sympathy, and equanimity, far-reaching, grown great, and beyond measure. 'Verily this . . . is the way to a state of union with Brahmâ.' [60]

In what stronger words could a more emphatic and clear-cut statement be made than the above, of the fact that there is *something* of a spiritual-intellectual character which works through the compound aggregate of the skandhas that form the 'mere man,' and which spiritual substance or entity — called by the Theosophist the spiritual Monad — can and finally must attain union with the Cosmic Spirit here called Brahmâ, or, in other words, what the Esoteric Philosophy or the Esoteric Tradition frequently calls the Logos, in this instance the Third or so-called 'Creative' Logos. We have here the essence or substance, in almost identic formulation, of the teaching of the Vedânta of India, that the essence or the substantial root of all beings and things, man therefore included, is the cosmic Brahman or Cosmic Spirit, of which all beings and entities are the offsprings, and reunion with which is, in the long course of ages, finally inevitable; and that there exists a Way or Path by which such reunion may be attained, by which Way the aeons'-long evolutionary pilgrimage may be vastly shortened.

Now then, after the conclusive paragraphs just cited above from the *Tevijja-Sutta,* one of the standard scriptures of the Southern School of Buddhism, in which the x-quantity, that *Something,* is emphatically and plainly stated herein as being capable of attaining 'a state of union with Brahmâ,' it becomes necessary to point with emphatic finger to one of the most pregnant and important teachings of the Great Master which shows that the Buddha-Gautama by no means considered such a state of union with Brahman as the ultimate or ending of the existence of the fortunate Jîvanmukta or freed

---

58. From the *Tevijja-Sutta,* rendered from the Pâli into English by T. W. Rhys Davids, as found in Volume XI of the *Sacred Books of the East* series, chapter iii, verses 7, 8.

59. *Op. cit.,* chapter i, verse 43.

60. *Op. cit.,* chapter iii, verses 1, 3, 4, combined.

Monad. Indeed, his teaching ran directly contrary to such erroneous idea; for both implicitly and explicity, as may be found in the scriptures of both the North and the South, there is the reiterated statement that even beyond the 'world of Brahmâ,' i. e., beyond Brahman, there are realms of consciousness and being still higher than this 'world of Brahmâ,' in which reside the roots, so to speak, of the Cosmic Tree and therefore the Root of every human being, the offspring of such mystical Cosmic Tree. What is this Mystic Root, this that is higher even than Brahmâ? It is the individualized Âdi-Buddha, the Cosmic 'Creative' Logos of Âdi-Bodhi, or Alaya, the Cosmic Originant; for even a 'world of Brahmâ' is a manifested world; and, therefore, however high it may be by comparison with our material world, is yet a relatively imperfect sphere of life and lives. In consequence, the teaching runs that higher even than Brahmâ there is something Else, the rootless Root, reaching back and within, cosmically speaking, into Parabrahmic Infinitude. One who is a Buddha, i. e., one who has become allied in his inmost essence with the cosmic Bodhi, thus can enter not only the 'world of Brahmâ,' but pass out of it and above it and beyond it, yea, higher and higher still to those cosmic reaches of life-consciousness-substance towards which human imagination may aspire and indeed always does aspire, however feebly; but which, unless we are Buddhas in fact, i. e., more or less straitly in self-conscious union with the Dhyâni-Buddha, the spiritual Monad within us, we cannot understand otherwise than to be an adumbration of ineffable Nature.

These citations, and the more or less necessarily condensed arguments that have been drawn from them, and more especially and somewhat more widely from the general teaching of Esoteric Theosophy, the Esoteric Tradition, should prove to any really thoughtful and impartial mind that there was something more, and indeed vastly more, in the great Master's teaching than the sketchy scriptural records, and the all too often prejudiced and distorted outline of it drawn by the willing and sincere but unskilled hands of most European Orientalists. A Secret Doctrine, an Esoteric Wisdom, a prehistoric Esoteric Tradition, is seen to be a necessary component part — indeed the best part because the entire background — of the teaching of the Buddha; for towards such background every one of his public teachings points, and when considered collectively rather than distributively, when synthesized after analysis, the impartial student reaches the conclusion which seems to be irresistible, that such an Esoteric Doctrine or Tradition was in very truth the 'heart' and foundation of the great Master's teaching and life-work.

CHAPTER V

WORLDS VISIBLE AND INVISIBLE

ONE of the main tenets or teachings of the Esoteric Tradition which is of the very substance of esoteric Theosophy, i. e., of the Esoteric Philosophy, is the doctrine that the Universe is a septempartite — or indeed decempartite — Organism: that is to say, that it is a living Entity or Being of which the various component parts are some more and some less intelligent than others, some more and some less conscious than others, the relative fulness of such consciousness and intelligence diminishing with each step 'downwards' on the cosmic 'Ladder of Life.' So common is this teaching that it is found everywhere, in every ancient religious or philosophical system worthy of the name, although, indeed, the fact is not always immediately perceptible because not always explicitly stated in the outer or exoteric formulations which find imbodiment in the various old literatures of the globe.

Yet, whether such septempartite or decempartite structure of the world be openly proclaimed, or delivered only under the veil or guise of metaphor, it would seem perfectly safe to aver that the earnest student, curious to attain a larger measure of acquaintance with the substance of these ancient literatures, may find it in them all, provided he give to his studies the attentive examination which experience must have shown him is the only way of uncovering the 'body' underneath and enshrouded by the 'garment.'

The facts stated in the preceding paragraphs will be recognised quickly enough to be true, if the researching mind of the student remember that the commonest form in which this doctrine is stated, is that of 'heavens' and 'hells': that is to say, spheres of recompense for right living, and spheres of purgation or purgatorial punishment for evil living. To the best of the present writer's recollection, these realms or spheres were never located, by the most ancient literatures, in any part or parts of the material or physical world in which our bodies live, and of which we human beings are more or less conscious through the avenues of report of our five senses; these realms of felicity or suffering are invariably stated to be in invisible spheres or as being 'spiritual' or ethereal domains of the Universe.

Even such baldly exoteric and monastic ideas as that 'hell' is situated at the center of the earth, and that 'heaven' is located in the upper atmosphere, such as were popular in early and later mediaeval Christianity, and as they were so beautifully and gracefully set forth by Dante in his *Divina Commedia* — a distorted echoing of misunderstood Greek and Roman mythological stories about Olympus and Tartarus: even such wholly exoteric ideas invariably carried with them the usually unstated corollary that these realms were nevertheless more ethereal in either sense than our gross earth is; and, furthermore, these ideas were the latest despairing effort of man's mystical instincts to weave a structure of place and time whereto would finally pass the souls of men when their life on earth had run its course.

Similar to the foregoing ideas were the still later notions of some Christian theologians or half-baked mystics, that hell was in the sun, or, mayhap, was located on the arid surface of the moon, or in some other out-of-the-way and unreachable place; or, again, heaven was located beyond the clouds, beyond the sky, in some invisible far-distant region of the ethery blue. Nevertheless, all these quasi-physical localities for either heaven or hell respectively were of extremely late origin; and when the last whispering admonitions of the Esoteric Tradition had been forgotten, and the earliest teachings of invisible realms and spheres had passed out of the memory of the West, then came the new and mentally rejuvenating influence of the teachings of European scientific research and study, showing to the minds of the least reflective that there was no more reason to locate 'hell' in any portion of the physical universe than there was to locate 'heaven' therein.

Nevertheless, for thousands of years past, from a period long preceding the decline and fall of the Graeco-Roman civilization and of that of the other countries surrounding the Mediterranean Sea, and reaching throughout the various and often conflicting views just mentioned regarding invisible realms, and reaching even to our own days, and acting as one of the most widespread of human intuitions, often expressing itself in highly figurative and indeed in superstitious form, there has been the steady flow of a consciousness that the physical sphere around us is but the shell or garment of inner and invisible worlds. This intuition of this grand natural truth has been as widespread and powerful in its influence among civilized men as it has been among the barbarian and the savage peoples.

The science of anthropology, including its studies of the respective mythologies of the races of men, has proved to the hilt the fact that the human mind is far more prone to elaborate systems of thought dealing with invisible or unseen worlds, which are both the origin and final bourne of human souls, than it is to find or to suppose respective places of purgation or of reward in districts of our physical globe, as did the very exoteric mythology of Greece and Rome, and as did the mediaeval mythology of Christendom, the faithful copyist of the former.

The present writer would indeed that his tongue were free to tell the real reason, so logical and simple when once understood, of the translation of such spheres of retribution or punishment from the realms of the invisible to actual localities of the physical globe. But this he cannot do, for obvious reasons.

It would seem sufficient, therefore, to make the simple statement that the farther back in time the student goes in his researches, the more clearly and unmistakably will he discover that so-called 'primitive man' — who, indeed, has never existed as he has been picturated except in the minds of Western theorists — who, indeed, was a highly civilized and sophisticated human, was universally of the conviction that the fabric of the Universe is, as said above, of septempartite or indeed of decempartite character; and that the farther this cosmic structure is traced inwards, i. e., into what is to us men the invisible, the more ethereal and finally the more spiritual are these interior realms discovered to be.

It was the worlds invisible, the spheres unseen, because of their high ethereality or indeed spirituality, which were considered to be the causal realms, whence flowed into manifestation, by regular gradations or steps of increasing materiality, the various worlds or spheres of existence — actual entitative bodies — which in their aggregate form the living Organism of the Cosmos, and of which Cosmos our own gross physical World is the outer shell or garment.

I

All these archaic ideas were originally derivatives from the sublime teachings of that pre-historic Wisdom which modern Theosophists have called by divers and diverse names, such as the Ancient Wisdom, Esoteric Theosophy, the Esoteric Tradition, etc., and of which modern Theosophy, as brought in our times to the world by H. P. Blavatsky, is the latest historical formulation.

Now when a Theosophist speaks of 'invisible worlds,' he does not mean worlds which are merely worlds which are invisible in the sense of not being seen: he means worlds which are much more than that, although he means that also; he means worlds which are the background and cosmic foundation of the visible universe that we sense: indeed, he means even far more than a background, because, as stated above, these invisible worlds are the *causal* realms, the roots of things that are before and around us men.

When the Spiritist — the modern Occidental Spiritist — speaks of his 'Summerland,' or when the Christian speaks of his 'heaven' and 'hell,' the Theosophist feels instinctively that neither understands the reality behind the physical veil; but that they both have some vague and fleeting intuition that there is a truth back of what they say; and this intuition is true, although their respective methods of explaining their intimations are to him in each case wrong. Both the Spiritist and the Christian have a feeling that there exists something behind the physical veil. That feeling is undoubtedly correct. But it is more than *some thing,* it is a vast universe, a Cosmos, an Organic Cosmos of all-varied and manifold kinds of worlds and planes and spheres, interlocked, interrelated, interworking, interconnected, and interliving.

What is this visible physical world of ours, really? What is our globe, Earth, composed of, and how does it keep its place and composite movements in space? How, indeed, does it hang poised safely in the so-called 'void'? How do the other planets and the sun hang or exist in space, or find position in the vast realms of the outer infinitude — or indeed of the inner infinitude likewise? What are the stars, the nebulae, the comets, and all the other bodies that are scattered apparently at random in the spaces of physical Space — if one may use so quaint an expression? Is there nothing but the visible celestial bodies that our physical senses do take cognisance of: and back of them, behind them, around them, within them, is there nothing but nothingness? Such questions, seeming perhaps trivial and superficial at first asking, but recurring with imperative insistence to the truly reflective mind, require answers; and the superficiality of the answers that have hitherto been attempted by virtually every branch of established modern Western knowledge, make these answers wholly unsatisfactory.

One is reminded of the early Christian theological idea that the Lord God created the heavens and the earth out of 'nothing.' Nothing is *nothing,* and from nothing nothing can come, because it *is* nothing; it is a word, a phantasy, somewhat after the fashion of the phantasy of the imagination when we speak of a flat sphere or a triangle having four sides. These are words without sense and are therefore nonsense. They mean nothing substantial, and so far as the Christian theological explanation goes, one is driven to infer that the theological pre-cosmic 'nothing' must have contained at least the infinitely substantial body of the Divine Imagination, or thought plus will.

One may venture to state that even the most orthodox and most exoteric of theologians would hardly asseverate that the Divine Will and the Divine Imagination and the Divine Creative Power were nothing!

We see just here that, when properly analysed in the light of the Esoteric Tradition, even the Christian scheme, based on half-forgotten and misunderstood pagan philosophy, becomes singularly alike to and akin with the teaching of all historic and indeed of all prehistoric philosophy and religion, to the effect that in the last analysis, and running back to primal manvantaric origins, the universe and all its bewildering web of manifested being was woven out of the substance of the Divine Essence itself. One is fully aware that this conclusion will be, mayhap, extremely unwelcome to the later school of Christian exegetes, but if their biblical, theological scheme means anything, and is to be saved from the trash-heap, it will have to acknowledge its lofty origin, in the manner just hereinbefore outlined.

It should be obvious from mature consideration of the facts sketched in the preceding paragraphs, that it was the universal consensus of all antiquity that there is an invisible background, a vast cosmical web of beings and things which in their aggregate and in conjunction with the realms in which they live, form the causal realms of all the physical worlds which are scattered over the spaces of Space: the invisible, substantial structure of the cosmos in which these visible worlds find lodgment and position, and in which therefore they live, and from which they derive all the forces, substances, and causal laws of being which make them what they are. This indeed was ever the teaching of the archaic, pre-historic Wisdom-Religion of antiquity, otherwise in its religio-philosophical formulations, the Esoteric Tradition.

II

Before passing on to a further consideration of the theme of this chapter, it should be carefully noted that the observations of the preceding paragraphs having reference to the so-called 'heavens' and 'hells,' were chosen merely to illustrate one manner in which the human mind phrased its intuition of the existence of invisible worlds. The reader should not imagine that either the Wise Ones among the ancients, and still less the Esoteric Tradition, limited the extent of the invisible worlds and the various ranges of semi-conscious, and self-conscious, beings which infill them, to what we children of Earth have in our brain-mind when we indulge ourselves — or when our forefathers indulged themselves — in speculations concerning spheres of retributive justice whether of compensation for unhappiness here on earth or of 'punishment' for evil worked here on earth. The inhabitants of these invisible spheres are good, bad, and indifferent, judging in each case by the standards of the respective spheres in question; yet, it is true enough to say, from one standpoint, that all manifested spheres or worlds of a material or quasi-material character are, strictly speaking, what in the Esoteric Tradition are called 'hells.' This is because the existence of self-conscious beings in worlds of matter or semi-matter is so low, relatively speaking, and by comparison with superior spheres, that their sojourn therein is very properly considered to be, in a sense, retribution for failure to retain their more native position or status in higher realms. It is true enough that these 'descents' or 'falls' and 'ascents' are all involved in the wondrous aeons-long evolutionary pilgrimage that the peregrinating monads have to undergo or to follow in order to gain full self-conscious experience in every one of the manifold planes or spheres of cosmic life; nevertheless such 'descent' into the more material spheres from the higher is justly and properly considered to be a 'fall'; and hence such lower spheres are technically, as above stated, hells.

Many of the ancient scriptures look upon some of these hells or describe some of these hells to be quite the reverse of what the average Christian of mediaeval European times regarded as the theological 'Hell' of his religious guides. Some of the hells in the Brâhmanical or Buddhistic scriptures, are, judging by the mystical descriptions of them, quite pleasant places!

It should be noted, furthermore, that the general term or name or appellation for the vast multitudes or armies of beings, semi-conscious, conscious, and self-conscious, inhabiting the worlds or spheres superior in ethereality or spirituality to earth-life, is 'Devas' — to employ a name commonly used in Hindû writings; and the same term is properly given, therefore, to those classes of self-conscious beings, who, springing forth from the spiritual ranges of life as their fountain-head, under the evolutionary urge make the 'descent' into the lower spheres for the purpose of gaining experience. Such a family, in consequence of the foregoing, is the human family, which, strictly speaking, is therefore a hierarchy, or compact group, or aggregate of devas. Yet the human family is not the only hierarchy of devas.

The importance of this observation will be seen and felt immediately by every student of ancient lore who is acquainted with the usage of this word 'deva' in Buddhist and Brâhmanical literatures. Thus, for instance, when it is stated that there are four general divisions or great groups of devas, living in spheres or realms of ethereality or spirituality superior to that of earth-life, the reference here, as any student of the Esoteric Tradition can plainly see, is to the four cosmic planes just above the plane on which our planet Terra is, and therefore has direct and specific reference to the six globes of our Earth's planetary chain superior to this globe, Earth.[61] This fact, alone, sheds a brilliant meaning upon the inner significance of much in the ancient Hindû scriptures, for instance where the Devas are shown under certain conditions to be in strait union with, and in more or less close association with, the human subhierarchy or family.

III

This physical universe of ours, as before stated, is but the shell of inner things, the outer appearance, the manifestation, of inner and causal realities; within the shell are the forces that run it, that govern it, that control it: the inner substances and energies rooted in which it lives, from the life of which it lives, through inner perception with which it lives, without inner union with which it could not be. The inner worlds are its roots in other words, striking deep into the inner infinitude, which 'roots' collectively are that 'endless path' of which all the Great Seers, the World-Teachers, have spoken, and which, if followed faithfully, leads man with an ever-expanding consciousness direct to the Heart of the Universe — a Heart which has neither location nor dimension, neither position nor clearly defined material definition, because it is Infinitude itself.

True Seers with spiritual training and with the 'inner eye of vision' awakened in them, in the East mystically called the 'Eye of Śiva,' can and do have direct knowledge at will of these Worlds and Spheres outside of our own Hierarchy, because these Seers can throw themselves into what modern Westerners might colloquially call 'vibrational intercommunication' with these inner and higher spheres, energies and powers; and thus not merely enter them, but actually, self-consciously for the time being live in those inner planes and then

---

61. For a further elaboration of this matter of the invisible globes of the Earth-chain, and the doctrines deduced therefrom, see *infra* in the succeeding chapter.

and there gain knowledge of those inner and superior realms at first hand. Yet this 'opened eye,' this spiritual faculty of inner vision, all normal human beings can obtain by 'living the life' as the saying goes, which fits them for it, and, last but not least, by training under a proper teacher. Their own first move in the direction of such communion is for them by willing and doing to set their own feet upon the pathway — the pathway to Reality and Truth: the pathway leading direct to the Heart of the Universe just mentioned.

Thus it is that Nature in her realms both inner and outer is experienced by the only trustworthy testing-stone in human life — the consciousness of the individual. The inner consciousness comes into direct relation, without interfering secondaries, with the Heart of the Universe, and realization of Truth then comes to the sincere aspirant because he identifies himself in such manner with the inner and causal energies of which all outer Nature is but the effect, the result, the product, the fruit — the manifestation. Thus does the Adept learn the inner nature and secret workings of the Universe.

It becomes clear enough from the foregoing thoughts that there is really no other method of coming into touch with and of understanding the inner worlds, than by making one's own consciousness enter into union of substance therewith; for it is one of the first lessons taught to, and learned by, the disciple or chela, that the only way really to *understand* a being or thing is by becoming, temporarily at least, the being or thing itself. There is far more in this simple statement than appears on the surface of it, because founded upon it are all the rites and functions of genuine initiation.

Furthermore, an examination into the processes of human understanding and psychology shows us clearly that it is utterly impossible to grasp, to comprehend, to understand, anything unless the aspirant's own consciousness actually temporarily *becomes* the thing studied. As illustration: In so simple a matter as human love or sympathy, it is not possible for a man to understand love or to feel sympathy unless for the time being his own essence becomes love itself or becomes sympathy itself. Standing merely apart, and examining such functions of the human constitution, immediately creates a fatal duality of observer and observed, of subject and object, thus setting up a barrier of distinction. It is only by loving that one understands love, that is by being it; it is only by becoming sympathetic that one understands and comprehends sympathy; otherwise one merely talks about or speculates upon what love and sympathy are in themselves.

Or as another illustration in point: When one studies the form, the beauty, or senses the fragrance of some lovely flower, one senses enjoyment and a certain elevation of both thought and feeling; but we find ourselves *different* from the flower because we are the observer and the flower is the observed — thus recognising a difference between the twain; whereas if we can cast our consciousness, as it were, into the flower itself and temporarily become it, we can understand all that the flower means to itself and in itself.

Or again, when a man studies the frolicsome behavior and antics of his pet dog, he finds a certain amusement in so doing, he senses an affection for the creature growing in his heart, but he actually does not enter into the dog's thought or feeling because he stands apart from the beast and studies it as an object, thus creating a barrier of difference between himself and it; whereas if he have the power to throw himself into becoming, as it were, a portion of the dog's consciousness and thought, quaint as the illustration appears, he then enters into the dog's consciousness and understands it because for the time being he is to a certain extent that dog itself.

These are thoughts more or less strange to Occidental minds, but they contain the gist and substance of a great truth. Just as one cannot enter into the soul of a beloved human companion until one has become a portion of that companion's soul, at least temporarily, just so cannot even the greatest Adept enter into and fully understand, relatively speaking, the nature and secrets of the invisible worlds unless he throw his percipient consciousness into spiritual and psychic oneness with these inner and invisible worlds. When this is done, for the time being he is an integral portion of these interior worlds, or of the part or division thereof that he has chosen for his study. He thus has most intimate knowledge at first hand of what these invisible worlds are, what their nature, their respective characteristics and different energies and qualities.

One might add in conclusion to this brief excursus that it is only thus, by sympathetically *becoming* one with the subject or object of study that one can translate into human thought for others what one experiences. It is thus that the great geniuses of the world of whatever type or kind have enriched human life and have clarified it with what they have brought to their fellow-men. It is only thus that the true poets have brought to us their differing and respective messages of inner realities and of beautiful and unsuspected relations among things both seen and unseen. For the time being such men have themselves *become* what they were studying and thus have understood.

One is keenly cognisant of the truth of all this when one reads some of the mystical, or mystical and theological, poetry of all ancient lore, as for instance, in both Celtic and Scandinavian mythology, when one reads of the seer or bard hearing the growing of the grass or the singing of the celestial bodies in their orbits, or being able to understand the language of the bee or interpret the voices of the wind.

As a matter of fact it is not only possible, but feasible, indeed easy to one who knows how to do it, to pass self-consciously from one universe or hierarchical range of being into some other hierarchical sphere. As a matter of fact, it is one of the commonest human experiences, so common and ordinary indeed, that the experiences in so doing enter our consciousness as mere routine transitions of thought, and we do not see the forest in its beauty because of the trees; the details of familiar things are so numerous and so common-place that we fail to catch the messages that they are constantly telling to us.

Each and every one who sleeps enters into another plane or realm of consciousness. This is meant to be considered literally, not to be taken merely as suggesting a pictorial variation of the thoughts and emotions of the day just closed. Change the rates of vibration of any particular state and you then have, or enter into, different realms of the Universe, higher or lower than our own as the case may be. Every one who changes his emotional vibration of hatred to love, and does so at the command of his will, is exercising a part of his internal constitution which some day, when trained more fully along the same line, will enable him to pass behind the supposedly thick veil of appearances, because in so exercising his power he will have cultivated the proper faculty and its co-ordinate organ for doing so. Everyone who successfully resists temptation to do wrong, to do evil, to be less than he *is,* is exercising the faculty within him which one day will enable him to pass self-consciously behind the veil in the dread and even dreadful tests of initiation.

IV

We live in a wonderful universe, full of mysteries, mysteries which are on the one hand strange and beautiful, and on the other hand equally strange but on occasion involved in horror and dread; but they are mysteries only because we have not solved them, not mysteries in the sense of being unsolvable.

They are as yet hid and mysterious to us only because our physical senses are such poorly evolved instruments of report, imperfect tools which have not yet reached the plenitude of their powers. We thus get but extremely imperfect and often frightfully distorted reports of things *as they really are in themselves*. This aggregate sense-apparatus of ours, consisting of five senses, has not yet reached its full perfection by any means. It is still in a very imperfect state, so much so, that our organ of sight for instance, was declared as much as fifty or sixty years ago by one or two of the greatest optical physicists of that time — Helmholtz is here referred to particularly — to be so imperfect that as Helmholtz put it in substance, "If an optician constructed for me a physical apparatus so imperfect as the human eye is, I would send it back to him with a reprimand."[62]

Therefore, as our senses tell us of but a small part of the scale of forces, of the gamut of universal energies and substances, that infill, yea, that verily *are*, the Universe around us, there must obviously exist other worlds, other planes, other spheres, which are invisible to our sight, intangible to our touch, unknown or relatively unknown, and that we can cognise in no other manner than through the far more delicate apparatus of the mind — and even hesitatingly and imperfectly and haltingly, because here too we have not yet trained our mind to become, to make itself to become, *at one* in sympathetic vibrational union with what it investigates.

Our physical sense-apparatus is but a channel, or fivefold channel, through which we gain knowledge of the physical world alone, and imperfect knowledge at that; and it is the thinking entity within or behind — the receiving entity, call it what you like: the mind, the soul, the consciousness — possessing senses far finer and more subtil than those of our gross physical body, which is the real thinker and the cognising Knower; and no man, particularly in the Occident, has yet tested the vast powers of this psycho-spiritual receiver — what it can do, what it can know, what it can gain, by looking within or by throwing itself back upon itself. Indeed, our physical sense-apparatus, our five senses, actually distract our attention away from the very channels to wisdom and knowledge, outwards into the vast confusing welter of phenomenal things, instead of turning it into the causal realms within, whether of the Universe or of our own constitution, where we can know the causes of things by knowing ourselves.

Nor have we any adequate control even over our thoughts. They

---

62. The human eye: "A living optical instrument . . . as superior to one of glass as the works of the Creator are to those of man."— Darwin: *On the Origin of Species,* ch. vi, p. 146.

One is strongly inclined to believe that, whatever the imperfections of the human eye may be, Darwin was nearer the truth than was Helmholtz.

run helter-skelter and wild through our brains like the horde of elementals that they are, playing havoc often even with our morals.
We have little self-control, and even less capacity for continued
self-conscious and self-directed, one-pointed thought. We know
little indeed of our inner faculties — spiritual, intellectual, psychical
—and of the sense-apparatus corresponding to each category thereof
which in every case is far higher and more subtil than is the physical.
Were these our inner senses more fully recognised and exercised, what
the average man would call 'more fully developed,' one then could
and would be cognisant, at least in degree, of the inner and invisible
planes and worlds and their inhabitants, and one would have conscious intercourse with them — and in the higher realms actually
be able to confabulate with the gods. These remarks have no reference whatsoever, nor in any manner however remote, to intercourse
with spooks or the so-called 'spirits' of 'dead men.'

What we learn through our senses, therefore, is but a very small
part of what Nature must enclose within her myriad enshrouding
veils. Wonderful in their own way as our senses are, wonderful as
the fact is that we have been enabled to build them up through evolution to the point of sensitivity that they now possess, so that they
can and do respond to the impacts of the vibrational forces of the
universe as well as they do, nevertheless, we are obliged to say that
they are still but lamentably imperfect reporters of what even these
purblind senses of ours constantly receive as messages from surrounding energies and substances. Yet even what our senses tell
us about, limited though it is, nevertheless gives abundance of food
for serious thinking even if we did not have the far higher inner
apparatus of our understanding faculty, working in the field of our
consciousness, which latter in its highest reaches is divine and therefore godlike.

Indeed, we human beings live in a marvelous world, of which
we are beginning to know somewhat, but as yet know very little;
and our physical scientists are constantly telling us more about it.
The discoveries that they are making — some of them — are very
wonderful indeed, and so far have completely altered the outlook of
human beings on life. These scientists are showing us more and
more of the mysteries of the physical nature surrounding us; and
the manner in which the facts of the latest scientific discoveries are
explained by our most eminent scientific men, so closely follows
Theosophical ideas in some respects, that we can but pause and marvel at it all, having, withal, a sensation of pure delight that some at
least of the Theosophical teachings are beginning to be proved to

be based upon facts existent in Nature itself. These new discoveries, growing in volume with each passing lustrum, are leading our scientists, in fact, straight into the teachings of the Ancient Wisdom — those teachings about the inner as well as outer structure and functioning of the Universe which the Western world has known so little of for the past two thousand years.

Our scientists of these modern days are beginning to dream dreams of truth, and to see visions of reality, although indeed many are the strange and wondrous imaginings in which they indulge. Wonderful things they are beginning to think, and from these thoughts they are making deductions, sometimes equally wonderful, which are acting as it were not merely as an evolutionary influence in the minds of men, giving them broader outlooks, but these deductions are actually overthrowing the older ideas and so-called principles of science, as well as of Western religion and philosophy, which were considered at one time to be so stable, so settled, so proved, as the saying runs, that nothing might ever undermine the supposedly eternal bases on which they rest. The greatest minds in modern science are approaching a vaster conception of Universal Life and man's relations therewith. They are saying some amazing things, if we contrast them with the scientific ideas of even fifteen years agone.

The *Manchester Guardian* (England) quite recently published an article entitled 'New Vision of the Universe,' written by a well-known scientific author who spoke as follows:

Why should all the matter in the universe have divided itself up into millions of fairly uniformly sized and distributed systems of stars and gas and dust? Why should these systems be about a million and a half light-years apart, and why should each system be about five times as broad as it is thick, and contain some decades of millions of stars?[63] These astonishing uniformities in the universe imply that the laws of mechanics are being obeyed everywhere, under comparatively simple conditions. In the scale of magnitudes we have first the universe. The second order of objects are the great nebulae. These are approximately uniform in size and constitute the second scale of magnitude. In the great nebulae the chief unit is the star. Like the great nebulae themselves, the stars have extraordinary uniformity, in mass if not in brightness. The stars give the third scale of magnitude. From the stars we have to plunge down to the puny, dark and cold objects called planets. These are about one ten-thousandth the mass of the sun. Then there are the planets' satellites, which make a fifth scale of magnitude. . . . Smaller things than these nature has

---

63. The statements relative to mensuration of various kinds contained in this sentence would doubtless have to be considerably modified or changed in view of still more recent scientific speculations. *Eppur si muove!*

huddled together in a miscellany of oddities, until the uniformity of molecules and atoms is reached. Ourselves are in the miscellany, looking round proudly and feeling a little hurt. We regret our size but admire our intelligence.

Where did the primeval cloud come from? Possibly from the fifth dimension! Sir J. H. Jeans considers that the difficulty of explaining the shape of the spiral arms in the great nebulae may only be solved by the discovery that the centers of such nebulae are taps through which matter pours from some other universe into ours. . . .

Immortal gods! Here we have a modern scientist, at any rate a well-known scientific writer, talking in this extract from his most interesting article like a mystical theosophical seer!

To continue the quotation:

If this should be true, what of the fifth dimension? What is the hyper-universe of the fifth dimension like? What sort of entities populate it? Where did the fifth dimension itself come from?

Here we have a modern scientific writer speaking along the lines that might have been followed by an ancient seer. He talks of these other 'dimensions' as he calls them, and apparently draws the conclusion that it is from these other 'dimensions' that there pours into our own physical universe matter, which means energy, from a universe superior to our own, which is an old teaching of the archaic Theosophy of the pre-historic ages, and of the great religions and philosophies of subsequent times, which drew from that pre-historic Esoteric Tradition their own substantial contents.

Sir J. H. Jeans, whom this writer quotes, at that time brought forward certain ideas that the present writer frankly cannot alto-gether agree with; yet nevertheless Jeans expresses in most re-markably terse and brilliant phrasing a very wonderful Theosophical teaching, a truth of Nature. This old teaching, unconsciously by Jeans imbodied in the deduction which he has drawn from his scien-tific studies, is a true and intuitional statement of occult wisdom, to the effect that at the heart of the nebulae which bestrew the spaces of Space, there exist what he called 'singular points' or centers from which and through which matter streams into our own physical uni-verse, and, as he expressed it, this stream of substantial energy comes to us from a 'fifth dimension'; or to give his own words, these centers are points

at which matter is poured into our universe from some other, and entirely ex-traneous, spatial dimension, so that, to a denizen of our universe, they appear as points at which matter is being continually created.[64]

---

64. *Astronomy and Cosmogony*, p. 352. By permission of the Macmillan Company, publishers.

But this usage of the word 'dimension' the Theosophist strongly objects to, first because it is inadequate; second, because it is inexact; and third, because it is non-descriptive. 'Dimension' is a term of mensuration, of measurement. But, after all, what does it matter, if the essential idea that we are discussing be there? This 'fifth dimension,' of which this writer speaks, he calls 'fifth' because, according to modern science, following the lead of Dr. Albert Einstein of Relativity-fame, the 'fourth dimension' is time, apparently; and time in one sense can be rightly so called, because time is subject to mensuration or measurement; but otherwise these 'dimensions' of this very interesting scientific writer and of other modern scientists, the Theosophist would prefer to call 'worlds,' 'spheres,' 'planes,' according to each respective case; and we say that they form the causal background of all the universe we see, and that our own higher human principles, the superior parts of our constitution, live in these invisible realms, in these so-called, but mis-called 'other dimensions.' We are as much at home there, as our physical bodies are at home here on our physical earth.

For the Universe is one vast Organism, of which everything in it is an inseparable because inherent and component part; and therefore likewise man is an inseparable part thereof, and therefore again man has in himself everything that the Universe has, *because* he is an inseparable portion of the Cosmic Whole. He cannot have more, because the part cannot have more than the Whole. Further, because he is an inseparable part of the Universe, every energy, every substance, every form of consciousness, in the infinitudes of Boundless Space, is in him, latent or active, as the case may be. Therefore *he can know* by following the path leading inwards into himself and ever more within himself, ever more within, towards his Essential Self, the spirit of him which is a ray from the Universal. In this way is knowledge of reality obtained by him at first hand. Upon this fact is based all the cycle of initiation and the vast wisdom and knowledge that are gained therein and thereby.

The old Hermetic teaching of the Alexandrian Greeks, transmitted by them from still older sources, is a fine one. It is roundly expressed in their well-known aphorism: 'What is above is mirrored below; what is below is a reflexion from the superior worlds.' Or, more commonly phrased: 'What is below is the same as what is above; what is above is the same as what is below.'

This is one of the foundation-doctrines of the ancient Wisdom-Religion, of the Esoteric Tradition: upon it is based what is called the Law of Analogy; that is to say, that the Great is mirrored in the minute, in the infinitesimal; in other words, the infinitesimal reflects the kosmic. Why? Because the Universe is one vast Organism, as before stated, ensouled by one Universal Life, and one Law runs through all; therefore and consequently, what is active or latent on one plane or in one world or in one sphere must be active or latent in all, *mutatis mutandis* — making due and necessary allowances for differing degrees of ethereality or materiality of the substances of these respective worlds.

Therefore our world is as it is, with the things and beings that we can see and feel, with the humanity of our present time, with our types of civilization, bearing the humans, vegetation, beasts, and minerals, which live and are on it, because it is a reflexion, a mirroring, an effect, a manifestation in other words, of inner, hid, vital causes which reproduce themselves analogically around us and make our world what it is. These inner worlds so control the outer, that all that happens on this our physical plane is the resultant of the inner forces, energies, substances, powers, at work expressing themselves outwardly. A man's faculties work through his physical body in exactly the same manner; for man in the small is a copy of what the Universe is in the great.

Earthquakes, tidal waves, the belching volcanoes, the aurora borealis and the aurora australis, wind-storms, rain-storms, hailstorms, and electrical storms; the precession and recession of glacial periods; diseases endemic, epidemic, and pandemic; the quiet growing of the grass in the fields or the blossoming of the flowers; the development of a man from a microscopic cell into a six-foot human being, or the equivalent evolution of any other animate entity; the vast and titanic forces working in the bosom and on the surface of our Sun, and the regular and periodic pathways followed with unvarying precision and punctuality by the planets, as well as the phenomena of their own planetary evolution, are still other instances, and everywhere in physical Nature the same observation applies. These are all examples of how these inner causal forces work outwards from within, illustrations of the inward and driving and impelling forces locked up and at work in the inner worlds, and now self-expressing themselves outwards. In fact, and speaking in plainer language, all these physical phenomena which have just been enumerated, and all others which the reader's own knowledge and imagination will readily suggest, are but the effects in our outer physical sphere of what is taking place in the inner and invisible realms — the inner and invisible worlds and planes. Things are happening there within, and when the points of union or contact are sufficiently near us, then

our own physical sphere feels the effects as exemplified in the bewildering mass of phenomena which Nature produces.

As before said, scientists are saying some amazing things which,
on the whole, and making due allowances for the modern scientific
methods of guarded expression, corroborate some of the teachings
of the Ancient Wisdom, but as yet they have not accepted the existence of invisible and causal worlds — unless, indeed, many of our
scientists of outstanding merit and penetration have private opinions
of their own along the same line which they are either too canny
publicly to voice, or too uncertain in their own judgment openly
to declare.

One heard much a few years ago about 'the laws of probability,'
so-called, which, as one scientist puts it, is just another name for
chance or luck. The idea is that if a person take a certain set of
circumstances, whatever they may be, and perform a certain number
of operations with that set of circumstances, certain numerical factors
inherent in the group of circumstances will always reappear on
account of the quantitative relations which this set of factors has
to the aggregate. If, for example, he put a certain number of black
beans in a bag with a certain number of white beans and shake the
bag thoroughly and then withdraw the beans at random by ones
or twos or tens or by dozens — by machinery, if you will, in order
to eliminate the personal equation — then when he shall have withdrawn one hundred, followed by another hundred, succeeded by a
third, a fourth, and a fifth hundred, perhaps, and then compare the
number of the black with the number of the white beans withdrawn,
he will find that the ratio of the black beans to the white is always —
more or less — numerically the same. If he were to continue doing
this until the hundreds become tens of thousands repetitively, he
would find that the same general ratio of numbers of black to numbers
of white beans withdrawn, would still hold. This, in brief, exemplifies the meaning of the law of probabilities.

Now, what does this 'law' mean? It means that all things are
related; that they are connected together; and that when certain
things are numerically taken in certain ways, the operation will show
forth numerical results; handled in other ways, the same things
or circumstances will make different appearances, but probably produce similar if not absolutely identical results: the manner of hand-
ling the operation and the things themselves thus handled producing
in all cases certain mathematical consequences. In other words, we
have here the general case of the 'law of averages,' which is so well
known, for instance, to insurance companies. But where is the

'chance' or 'luck' about it? One might consider a lottery, if you will, or a roulette-wheel. A man may keep drawing lots and the chances are nearly all against him, because he has one chance perhaps in a million; yet he may hit the millionth 'lucky number,' as the saying goes, and then he speaks of 'luck.'

Do things, however, 'just happen' so? The Theosophist says no. This is not a helter-skelter Universe, governed by fortuity, by chance, by unreason, by what one may call unrelated or haphazard action of material particles which are called atoms, and so forth. To the contrary, the Theosophical teaching is that of all the great thinkers of all times, and of the greatest thinkers among men of science today: that precedent causes produce effects, which in a sense are the children of what preceded them; and these effects in their turn become causes and produce something else. We call this natural system or operation of Nature, 'Karman' or 'action' — in other words, the so-called law of cause and effect. One may follow this operation of Nature wherever he will, and he will always find that the root precedes the tree, which then produces the seed, which drops to the earth and produces another root followed by another plant and other seeds, and so forth indefinitely. There is neither 'luck' nor 'chance' nor helter-skelter action in this, nor anywhere in the Universe, which is itself the resultant of an endless chain of causation; because if there were crazy, haphazard action then there is no possible reason or rule that the root should produce a tree, nor that the tree should produce a seed which again would produce another root and another tree and other seeds, thus following the consequent regular action demonstrating the law of cause and effect — in other words the law of causation.

Apparent exceptions more or less prove a rule to the mind which is capable of understanding what an exception means; and did we know enough we should see that these exceptions are exceptions only because of our ignorance. For instance, as regards the geniuses in the world: if we followed the law of averages alone, and applied it to the almost universal run of human intelligence, we might argue: It is impossible for such a man as a genius to exist, because the 'law of averages' in the example given takes no note of genius. Nevertheless we know that geniuses exist. Suppose one should gather all the geniuses of the world together and analyse their various characteristics so that we have a full and complete case of all these geniuses before us, lacking not one, and applied the 'law of averages' to them also, we should then find that, granting this number of geniuses, such a one out of the number would be a musician, such a one would be a poet, such a one a philosopher, and so forth. These classes the observing and exacting mind would take note of as varieties or species of the *genus* 'genius': but they would all be geniuses.

Actually there are no exceptional cases in Nature herself. What we humans call 'exceptions' are merely such to our understanding which cannot at the time of examination properly classify them where they belong. There are merely manifestations of causation, link by link, endless and beginningless, and every being, every entity, whether high or low, ordinary or genial, is such a link in Nature's unvarying and at bottom strictly mathematical processes and procedures.

One is brought to believe that the idea of some scientists that 'luck' or 'chance' prevails throughout the Universe, may perhaps be due to their being unconscious mental victims of the old materialistic 'physical determinism,' as it has been called — which is substantially the idea that there is nothing in the Universe except unimpulsed, unensouled, vitally unguided matter, moving in haphazard fashion towards unknowable, or at any rate unknown, ends: in other words a soulless Universe wherein things occur by hap or chance, yet wherein, nevertheless, in some perfectly unexplained manner, cause and effect blindly rule. These scientists have revolted against the illogic of this conception of our recent forebears, and have sought to find in the newer speculative theories of ultra-modern science a refuge in purely mathematical conceptions, where their unvoiced hunger for law and regularity are everywhere manifest, but where there is sufficient vagueness of causative background to admit the intrusion of a cosmic governing intelligence; yet they fail to see that this idea of 'luck' or 'chance' is itself but a falling back into the same old materialistic physical determinism under a different, a new, form and name.

One feels, however, a certain genuine sympathy and unqualified respect for those scientists of this character but of fore-seeing vision like Jeans and Eddington as examples, who in their more recent works do not hesitate to state that to them the Universe and its bewildering operations seem to be like the productions of a cosmic mind.[65]

The mere fact that scientific research in our era of change and development seems to the unthinking to alter its speculative bases

---

65. Consult as instances: *The Universe Around Us* (1929), Sir James Jeans; *The Mysterious Universe* (1930), Sir James Jeans; *The Expanding Universe* (1933), Sir Arthur Eddington; *My Philosophy* (1933), Sir Oliver Lodge.

of thought almost from year to year, so that what is an opinion of scientific men in 1930 is no longer that of the same men in 1935, merely shows that the average man, however interested he may be in scientific work, does not fully realize the progressive nature of scientific research and discovery. Each new step forwards in science should not be looked upon as adding a new brick, or another trowelful of mortar to the building of the Temple of Knowledge, but should rather be considered for what it all is — a manifestation of a relative or complete revolution in the scientific outlook.

For the changing views of scientific men, brought about by the discovery of new natural facts, do not mean that the universe is what these gentlemen think it is, but signify only that these very eminent scientific discoverers are steadily undergoing a radical change of opinion; that there is a flux in scientific thought, of which no man has yet given us the end. Doubtless many ideas which have been broadcast as being scientific during these later years, and subsequently abandoned for other and newer ideas, may be re-called and re-shaped and re-modeled to fit what the future has in store.

Particularly is this possibility the fact in connexion with the extremely vague and unsatisfactory scientific opinions about what it is now popular to call 'indeterminism' which in some ways is as baldly materialistic as was the old physical determinism now going into the discard, and which again to many minds seems to be but the same old physical determinism in a new form. For it should be obvious to any thinking man, that if indeterminism is to be considered as being mere fortuity or chance, or haphazard action, this cannot exist in water-tight compartments in a universe which these same scientific gentlemen so often proclaim to be the work of 'a cosmic mathematician' — i. e., of a cosmic intelligence. Intelligence and chance will as little mix as would cosmic order, implying law and determined action on the one hand, and irresponsible fortuity, implying cosmic disorder, on the other hand.

Consult also *The Architecture of the Universe* by Professor W. F. G. Swann, Director, Bartol Research Foundation of the Franklin Institute. This is an interesting and suggestive work printed in 1934.

One could call attention with equal emphasis to the admirable and amazingly fine scientific work both in research and in philosophical deductions made by other eminent European and American scientific men, such as Einstein, Bohr, Planck, Millikan, and others, all of which tends to run, when all is said, towards the same speculative objective as that to which the English and American scientists hereinbefore mentioned likewise tends. As Galileo said: *Eppur si muove!*

V

The Theosophist is no fatalist. When we speak of the Universe and all in it as being bound in and the result of an inherent chain of causation stretching from the infinity of the past into the infinity of the future, when we say that everything in the Universe is a product, a consequence, a result, a fruit, of previous causes engendering present effects, we bring this forward as proof of the action or operation of countless wills and intelligences in the Universe; or to put the matter with still greater accuracy, the proof of the action or operation of countless wills and intelligences of all-varying power and of all-varying quality rising along the scale of life, which scale virtually has neither beginning nor end, for it, like the Universe itself, which indeed is itself, lies precisely in that chain of beginningless and endless causation; for this chain is not other than the Universal Kosmos acting from and strictly according to its own innate being.

Even as Spinoza, the Netherlandish, Jewish, Pantheist, re-echoed the teaching of the Upanishads of ancient Hindûsthân in stating as the essence of his own philosophical doctrine that the Universe is but a manifestation or a reflexion of the consciousness of the Kosmic Divinity, just so does the Esoteric Tradition derive all that is from this primal, incomprehensible, Divine Source, from which all sprang, into which all is journeying back; and therefore says that the Kosmos and all in It is builded on Consciousness-Substance as its essence. It were sheer stupidity to suppose that between this invisible Divine Source and our gross physical material universe, there are no intermediate grades or stages of inter-acting links, these 'links' being verily the vast ranges of invisible worlds or spheres, which, as hereinbefore stated, are the causal factors in Kosmic Manifestation.

Man, in consequence, precisely because he is one minor hierarchy emanating from the same Divine Source, possesses his proportion, so to speak, of intelligence and will-power, which are inherent parts of his interior constitution. Man, or rather mankind collectively, is one of the numberless hosts of the hierarchical aggregates of intelligences and wills infilling the Universe, each such hierarchy living on and in its own world or sphere, invisible or visible to us. Man is enabled thereby to carve his destiny as he will, because he has in him, in the inmost of his inmost, the same factors which inspirit and govern the Universe; and from this fact flows the ineluctable consequence that he takes his part in fashioning that portion of the

Universe which he can cover within the sphere of his own activities derivative from his will, his intelligence, and spirit. The inescapable laws of the Universe surround him, with which he is inescapably solidary because he is a portion thereof; and out of the Universe nothing may go and into it nothing may come from outside because there is no outside. And because he contains all that the Universe contains, he has possibilities of understanding everything in the Universe: the greatest problems of Kosmic Nature may and must find their solution in him if he penetrate deeply enough into the invisible realms of his own constitution.

What we see around us, our own world, and the stars and the planets, cannot just be there because they are there, or in other words, they cannot be the products of 'chance.' What is 'chance'? Chance is a word which expresses or tells our ignorance of facts. When something happens whose causative relations we cannot trace, we say, popularly, it 'chanced' so; but it should not be forgotten that giving words to things somewhat after the Hebrew legend of Adam in the Garden of Eden naming the beasts as they passed before him, by no means tells us what the things are: naming things is merely a convenience so that we may be able to call them or define them when we wish to speak of them. Man's logical mind demands links of thought; and rejects as unintelligible any conception which is senseless and therefore illogical. Man's mind, being one expression of the energies in the Universe and belonging to it, must function fundamentally after the pattern of that Universe, which is equivalent to saying that because man's mind is conscious and logical, therefore the Universe is essentially conscious and logical; and because man's intellect demands causative links, therefore the Universe *is* linked together and is not a haphazard and insane dream of a kosmic lunatic.

From what has been previously said, therefore, it will be seen that these 'links' in the Universe are the various spheres and planes all interworking and interconnected, and thus forming the kosmic structure. As man is both visible and invisible in his constitution, as he has both body and mind or intellect, and spirit: equally so must the Universe be visible and invisible; for the part cannot contain more than the Whole of which it is an integral portion.

Our globe, the sun, the other planets, the stars, and the nebulae, and the comets, and the atoms and the electrons: whatever body it may be: are all of them ruled and governed after the same general kosmic plan by infilling and inspiring energies which, because they are substantial, have their own inner planes, and express themselves on our physical plane as they work down towards it and through it. These energies originate in, and indeed, in the last analysis are, those invisible worlds.

Everything and every being, no matter how small, no matter how great, is an evolving *Life,* and hence, as every one of these visible bodies in the Universe around us is but an aggregate of such lives, we have here a clue to the real meaning of many of the ancient philosophers who spoke of the suns and stars as being living entities, alive and intelligent, making and unmaking what the Theosophist calls karman. They are what the ancient Greeks called 'ensouled entities,' ζῶα (*zôa*), from which comes the word 'zodiac,' used even in our current astronomical books, and meaning the circle of the 'living ones'; and which the Latin philosophers called *Animals* — a word of course which they used with the original Latin meaning of *animate entities,* and not in the restricted meaning of modern European speech, signifying only the beasts.

Even some of the greatest of the early Christian Fathers taught more or less exactly the same thing: that the suns and stars and planets were 'living beings,' and such indeed is the explicit teaching of the great Greek theologian Origen, as well as of Clement, doubtless.

For the sake of their intrinsic interest, a few passages from Origen are quoted here:

Not only may the stars be subject to sin, but they are actually not free from the contagion of it; . . .[66]

And as we notice that the stars move with such order and regularity that these movements never at any time seem to be subject to derangement, would it not be the highth of stupidity to say that so consistent and orderly an observing of method and plan could be carried out or accomplished by beings without reason. . . . Yet as the stars are living and rational beings, unquestionably there will appear among them both advance and retrogression. . . .[67]

Again Origen observes in his tract *Against Celsus:*

As we are persuaded that the sun himself and the moon and the stars also pray to the supreme deity through his Only-begotten Son, we think it improper to pray to those beings who themselves offer up prayers.[68]

And again in the same tract *Against Celsus,* Origen remarks once more, quite after the Christian manner of his time:

---

66. *De principiis* (First Principles), Bk. I, ch. vii, section 2.
67. *Op. cit.,* Bk. I, ch. vii, section 3.
68. *Contra Celsum,* Bk. V, ch. xi.

For we sing hymns to the Most High only and to his Only-begotten who is the logos and also God; we praise God and his Only-begotten, as also do the sun, the moon, the stars, and all the multitude of the heavenly host.[69]

Furthermore, in order to show the early Christian view about the innate vitality working in and through the celestial bodies as vehicles of that Cosmic Life, the reader will find in the writings of the Latin Father Jerome, the following passage which repeats Origen's teachings:

Respecting the heavenly bodies, we should notice that the soul of the sun, or whatever else it ought to be called, did not begin to exist when the world was created, but before that it entered into that shining and luminous body. We should hold similar views regarding the moon and the stars.[70]

It is also interesting to note that despite the condemnation of the views of Origen and his School by the two Constantinopolitan Councils of the sixth century previously referred to, those views prevailed more or less openly throughout the Christian community, and lasted until a fairly late period of Christian history; indeed echoes of them continued even into the Middle Ages. The ecclesiastical writers of the Dark and Mediaeval periods have many passages with reference to the sun and the stars, which, historically speaking, are understandable only on the supposition that they are more or less distorted reflexions of the views of Origen and his School, which in themselves, as we have already pointed out, were distorted reproductions from original so-called 'pagan' teachings. For all such doctrines as those of Origen just described were already largely degenerate and misunderstood in the time when Origen and his School enunciated them to the Christian community, and were, furthermore, more or less distorted from their original pagan meaning by the theological mental bias of the Christians who later taught them.

It is to the Ancients themselves that we must turn, if we wish to gain a clearer and more definite outline of the original thought; and it may be said in passing, that it is from Plato in especial, and from Pythagoras and his School, that are derived these doctrines which certain ones of the Christian Fathers took over and modified for their own especial Patristic purposes.

The ancient teaching was not that the stars and other shining celestial bodies were in their physical forms 'angels' or 'archangels,' but that each one was the 'dwelling' or vehicle or channel of ex-

---

69. *Op. cit.*, Bk. VIII, ch. lxvii.   70. *Epistles*, 'Letter to Avitus.'

pression of some 'angelic' entity behind it. The truth of the whole matter is this: each and every celestial body, whether it be nebula, comet, sun, or star, or hard and rocky planet like our own earth-sphere, is a focus or psycho-electric lens, if one can so express it, through which pour the energies and powers and substances passing into it from the invisible spheres; and this statement is based on sound philosophical principles and scientific facts of invisible Nature.

Bearing this ancient occult teaching of the Esoteric Schools in mind, it will be at once seen that the Earth as the mother and producer of the animate beings which draw their life from her, is very properly considered an 'animal,' or animate being, and is obviously therefore an entity, an animate and ensouled organism. The Earth even has a mysterious principle of instinct or 'quasi-thinking principle'; and it has also its vital actions and reactions, which manifest as the electro-magnetic phenomena known to science — actually arising out of the earth's *jîva* — electrical storms, magnetic storms, earthquakes, and so forth. Even as the human being in his lower principles is an 'animal,' or animate entity, just so is the Earth in its lower principles an animate being, and is therefore an 'animal'; though it would be misleading and would lead one into too great a mass of confusing details to try to trace too closely the analogies between man's physical body and the earth, in such matters as sense-properties, psycho-magnetic qualities, and so forth. Each has its own evolutionary progress, although the Earth and its physical children are very intricately and closely linked together. As man came into being as a human from a microscopic human seed, so did the Earth, or in fact any world, come into being from a cosmic seed. Just as man is born, so, relatively speaking, and making the necessary changes of circumstance and time, is a world born. Both are born from points or centers of energy; and these points of energy or energy-points, are always imbodied in a more or less large aggregate of atomic substances.

Thus came man forth. Thus came the Earth forth. Thus came the Solar System forth. Thus came the Galaxy forth. Thus came a billion Galaxies forth. And then when the great change of life that men call death comes, man or world or system of worlds is withdrawn into the invisible spheres for rest and peace, and comes out again and begins a new evolutionary course on a somewhat higher scale or plane.

Take a planet as an instance in point: Out of the invisible spheres, in its progress downwards into grosser matter than that prevailing in the invisible world which it left, comes the life-center or seed or energy-point, collecting unto itself, as it grossens and becomes more and more material, what are called in Theosophy life-atoms, which are ready and waiting for the passage downwards of this evolving seed or energy-point. The latter continues its journey into grosser matter, passing through the various inner and invisible spheres earth-wards, or rather matterwards, until it appears in the higher material part of our own World-System, as a nebula, a wisp of faint light that we see in the midnight skies. It then passes through various stages and conditions in the grossening process, one such transitory process being that of a comet; and it finally becomes a planet in a highly ethereal state or condition. The process of thickening or grossening or materialization continues until it reaches such a stage as that of the planet Saturn, for instance, of our solar system; for Saturn, as we know, is less dense than even water is on our Earth. Such a planet is in one of the earliest phases of its existence as a planetary sphere; and as time passes, it will grow still more dense as the planet follows the evolution of its life-course, until it becomes finally a rocky, hard, and solid globe like our own Mother-Earth.

This ancient teaching of both world and man rising into physical existence and growing therein from the small to the larger, and both along the same general energical lines of development, is one which H. P. Blavatsky re-enunciated to the West some fifty years or more ago; but it has not been accepted by modern scientists — except perhaps in the sense of a vague mental suggestion arising in the consciousness of some few semi-intuitive scientific spirits. The birth of worlds has always been and still remains a riddle which scientific research and discovery have not yet fully solved, and consequently there are a number of theories about it, each one in some points bettering its predecessor, and each one in certain points seeming to be less satisfactory than its predecessor.

One such fairly recent planetary hypothesis is the theory of Professor Moulton and Professor Chamberlin, set forth by them with characteristic scientific ability first in 1929 in an interesting pamphlet entitled *The Planetesimal Hypothesis*. The writers here describe their theory of the birth of planets from the sun at some remote period of the past, caused by the disruptive effect of the approach of another sun or star near to our sun, at that time supposed to be without planetary children or companions, thus arousing enormous tides on the surface of the sun leading to vast masses of the solar substance being torn from the solar body; and the collecting of the solar pieces thus wrenched from the sun by means of the commonly known action of gravity, these collections or aggregates of the solar pieces forming the beginning of the respective planets that now are.[71]

It is a lack of knowledge of the existence of invisible and powerfully causal realms, clothing themselves in what thus becomes the garment which we call the physical universe, which is responsible for such theories as the above. All the great religions and philosophies of past times, yea, all the ancient sciences likewise: all possessed and in fact were founded upon this universal and fundamental idea of inner, invisible, intangible, but causal realms, as the foundation and background of their respective formulations in religio-philosophical thinking. Universally they taught that our physical World, including stars, suns, planets, etc., is but the outer shell or garment or veil of an inner, vital, intelligent aggregate of causes, which in their collectivity form or rather are the Kosmic Life. This Kosmic Life is not a person, not an individualized entity. It is far, far beyond any such merely human conception, implying logical limitations as all individualizing necessarily does, because It is infinite, boundless, beginningless, endless: co-extensive with infinity in magnitude, co-extensive with eternity in endless duration. The Kosmic Life is in very truth the Ineffable Reality behind all that is, within all beings and things that are. Spirit and matter both are but two manifestations of this indescriptible because unthinkable Mystery, this Universal Life-Substance, i. e., Universal Consciousness-Substance. Sometimes the Theosophist calls it abstract Space, which is not the same as the mere bald spacial extension of European Science, but is the essential and also instrumental cause, through its agents which are its own offspring, as well as the substantial cause of both spirit and matter, *alias* energy and substance; for spirit and matter, or energy and substance, are really one — two forms, two attributes, two qualities, two manifestations, of the one underlying Invisible Reality.

Space itself, therefore, by which is meant abstract Space, is Reality, the underlying Noumenon or ever-enduring and eternal and boundless, substantial Causation, which in its multi-myriad forms or activities shows itself as the Kosmic Life, expressing itself over the face of the Boundless, and in and through and from the Boundless, as eternal Motion combined with Consciousness and Intelli-

---

71. This is but a brief and imperfect statement of the Planetesimal Hypothesis, but it may suffice to give to those who are unacquainted with it some idea of the theory. It is not the teaching of the Esoteric Philosophy.

gence, and through manifestation as unceasing Kosmic Motion, directed by Kosmic Consciousness and Will.

Shall one then call it God or a God? Why? Such allocation to it of individualized attributes or qualities, limits and bounds its essentially limitless and boundless being. Fundamentally it is Spiritual Entity, Divine Entity indeed, of which we with our imperfect sense-apparatus perceive naught but what we humans call the material and energic aspects. But is Itself 'God,' in the modern or rather old-fashioned Occidental religious sense? Emphatically no, because there are many Universes, not merely one, our own Home-Universe, the Galaxy; therefore are there many 'spaces' with a background of a perfectly incomprehensible greater Space, without limiting magnitude, inclosing all — a Space which is still more ethereal, more tenuous, nay, spiritual, yea, divine, than the space-matter that we humans know or even conceive of in our highest flights of analogical imagining, which, in this lowest aspect called our Universe, manifests the grossness of the physical matter of common human knowledge. Our own Home-Universe is only one among literally innumerable such or similar Universes scattered over the fields of the spaces of Boundless Space, the latter beginningless and endless, each such Universe vitalized and intelligently inspired by the indwelling and inworking boundless Kosmic Life working through such Universe and all its countless hosts of congeners. Therefore, each such other Universe is the physical expression or vehicle of another to us incomprehensibly great and vast Kosmic Entity, even as one man on our own tiny earth differs from another man and from any other animate entity here. The World Universal, Space Universal, is full of gods, 'sparks of eternity,' links in an endless causative chain of cosmic intelligences that live and move and have their being in the vast spaces of Infinitude, precisely as we do in our own Home-Universe on our own smaller scale.

VI

While some of the inner and invisible worlds are of substance and energy, or rather of substances and energies, much more ethereal and subtil than the substances and energies which function in and animate, in fact structurally compose, the visible and tangible worlds, there are likewise worlds much more material and gross than is the world cognised by our physical senses; and these latter are as invisible and intangible to us as are the more ethereal and more subtil worlds, and for precisely the same reason: because our physical senses do not respond to the vibrational rates that these higher and lower worlds possess, but respond only to those particular and restricted vibrational rates that characterize our own particular physical world — indeed only to one small range of the far-flung ranges or scales that even the physical universe contains, which latter is the mother of our senses and also their relatively limited field of action; and it is this restriction of the powers of our sense-apparatus which prevents us from 'tuning in,' to use the modern expression, with the other and widely differing vibrational rates that prevail in the visible and invisible worlds.

The amazingly successful results of scientific research and study in those fascinating fields of discovery which modern scientific thought has grouped under the general name of 'Radiation,' which in the last analysis is but a collective term for energies and matters vibrating in different amplitudes and rates, has demonstrated clearly to us that despite the really wonderful ability of our sense-apparatus in catching and transmitting to our perceiving brain certain portions of the wonderful gamut of radiation, we humans know as yet very little about the amazing mysteries that Nature has even in this one field of its activity.

It has been stated by modern scientific research-workers, that radiation alone covers a gamut of vibrating substances comprising some seventy octaves, ranging from the most penetrating and hardest rays known as yet, first named by Dr. Millikan 'cosmic rays,' through octaves of less amplitude and vibrational degree such as the X-rays, ordinary light, heat, to that form of radiation used in radio-work; and of this entire range or scale or gamut of seventy octaves, our eyes perceive barely one octave at best. Our sense of touch is cognisant but imperfectly of another small patch in this long gamut, which we call heat-rays, for heat is as much a form of radiation as is light itself.

Thus, then, amazing and intriguing as is the ability of our physical optics to translate the radiation which we call light to the brain, it is, after all, but one part in seventy, one octave out of seventy octaves, which they tell us something about — and that something itself is imperfect information. Small wonder it is that the Great Theosophist, H. P. Blavatsky, wrote in her master-work, *The Secret Doctrine*, that our entire physical universe is but concreted or crystallized 'light,' by which term she meant almost exactly what twentieth-century science calls radiation: a statement apparent enough today when it is indeed understood that what we call physical light is but one octave in the gamut of radiation extending in both directions on either side of the light-octave into what are to us in-visible and intangible realms and spheres of force and matter.

If light, then, is the substantial basis of our physical universe, how about the universes, or worlds, or realms, or spheres, of intense activity suggested to us by the right- and left-hand ranges of the radiation which we can neither see, nor feel, nor cognise by any other of our five senses, but of which the industry of modern scientific workers is at present apprising us? As a matter of fact, the Occultist, or student of the Esoteric Tradition, would call this gamut of seventy octaves but a larger portion of that particular field of cosmical activity and substance comprised in the lower ranges of what he calls the Astral Light.

To the Occultist, instead of there being some seventy octaves of radiation, or vibrational activity in matter, there are at least one hundred whose particular range is the physical and astral worlds. Above and beyond these, in point of greater ethereality, lie literally unimaginable fields of cosmic activity, each field or plane or realm possessing its own set of substances and forces, and in consequence infilled with worlds and spheres and beings and things belonging thereto. Here, the careful student may see some beginning of a scientific proof of the statement of the Ancient Wisdom, *alias* the Esoteric Tradition, that there are Worlds within worlds, substances more ethereal existing within substances more gross, the former being the causal *noumena* of the latter; and thus do we see the reason for the ancient saying that the visible, tangible, so-called physical World is but the veil or garment inclosing and covering the invisible and intangible.

Nor is this all: for these invisible or unseen, these intangible, unfelt worlds or universes, are, as frequently hereinbefore stated, the causal *noumena* of what we humans sense and can more or less successfully cognise and therefore know as the World of material substances and forces.

Many are the thinkers in modern scientific work who are approaching, both in inward conviction and in published statement, to the teachings of the prehistoric Esoteric Tradition on a number of most interesting parallels, and indeed in many cases making approximations to what might be called a modern exoteric exposition of archaic philosophy.

Dr. James Arnold Crowther has recently written on radiation in a manner which provides an amazing scientific parallel with one or two of the teachings of the Esoteric Philosophy, and he is by no means alone in his views. He points out in graphic and striking language that the entirety of our globe Earth with all its apparent solidity and its manifest diversity and variety of physical appearances and substances is after all but radiation intimately connected and probably identic with electricity, and yet electrically held enchained so that the radiation is not lost in outer space.[72]

This really thoughtful man furthermore utters a distinctly esoteric tenet in stating that the essential or intrinsic substance of the Universe is radiation which is but another name for force or energy. With such corroboration from eminent scientific sources, the Theosophist might well feel that it is needless further to labor the argument concerning the substantial character of radiation, or to prove that H. P. Blavatsky was perfectly correct in stating, in *The Secret Doctrine* (1888), that the physical world, when all is said, is but concreted or crystallized light, i. e., radiation. As she phrased it: *An lumen sit corpus nec non?*, 'Is light not a body, i. e., substantial, also?'

Perhaps Professor Crowther's most interesting point of agreement with the Esoteric Philosophy, however, is the declaration of his own conviction that the law and order so obvious in the Universe are not the product of irrationality but of reason.

Consciousness in whatever form it may express itself, fundamentally is the noblest and most spiritual form of cosmic energy — indeed, consciousness is the source and origin of all the forms of cosmic force; and as all these inner and invisible worlds exist by and from and through force in its dual form of vital movement and substantial basis, and as these inner, invisible worlds are in fact nothing but forms of force or energy expressing itself in countless fashions and manners, the inescapable deduction therefore is that these inner and invisible worlds or spheres are filled full of consciousnesses and lives — with hosts and countless multitudes of conscious and living and self-expressing entities, operating and functioning in their own respective spheres or worlds even as we are also doing in this part of the kosmic whole, all of which, or of whom, are under the sway of the general kosmic laws of evolutionary development; all, therefore, even as with us humans, advancing steadily and continuously from relative imperfection to ever enlarging perfections.

Just as our physical world, and others like ours that belong to this general material kosmic plane or sphere, have inhabitants of

---

72. *Radiation*, by James Arnold Crowther, M. A., SC. D., F. INST. P., Professor of Physics, University of Reading. This is the second article of the series published under the title *The Great Design*, ed. by Frances Mason (Macmillan, 1934).

many and various kinds and classes, so exactly do these higher (and lower) worlds have inhabitants, which are their own particular denizens, with senses and minds built to know and to respond to the vibrational rates of the worlds in which they are, just as our physical senses here are so built and evolved that they respond to the vibrational rates of that part of the gamut of life belonging to the physical plane on which these senses function and to which they belong organically.

Furthermore, just as Man, for instance, knows dimly of other planes and spheres, because of his more delicate psychical and mental faculties: and will in the future know vastly more about them than he now does, as evolution perfects these interior senses and faculties: just so is it with the inhabitants or denizens of these higher (and lower) worlds: evolution or progressive growth in faculty and sense-organs brings all entities and beings slowly into contact and communication with and knowledge of other planes and spheres, on whatever planes or spheres of action and consciousness these armies or hosts of beings may be at present.

To the inhabitants or populations of any one of these higher or lower worlds, their own matter is as sensible and real to them as is ours to us, and actually, on the other hand and in truth, as *unreal* as is ours to us, when we understand, as we ought to understand, how temporary and therefore unreal our physical matter is. For matter in the higher worlds and composing the higher worlds is force or forces *to us;* and our matter is force — and forces — to the worlds below or rather inferior to our own.

What is called objective existence or being, is that part of the boundless Whole which, on any one Plane or in any one World or Sphere, is cognised by the beings whose consciousness at the time acts and functions there; but this *objective is subjective* to beings whose consciousness contemporaneously acts and functions on other planes or in other worlds or spheres. Obviously, therefore, our entire physical universe is as subjective — therefore as invisible and intangible — to beings whose consciousness at this time is acting and functioning on other planes, as these inner and invisible worlds are subjective to us, and therefore to us are invisible and intangible.

But where are these invisible and to us humans intangible worlds and spheres of the general Kosmos, the Universe, with which we are in kosmic relations only? When we speak of 'superior' or 'inferior,' 'high' or 'low,' in relation to these other planes and spheres, we do not necessarily mean that they are 'above' or 'below' us.

These other worlds and spheres and planes interpenetrate our world and sphere and plane, we moving through them and they moving through us, blending indeed with our physical world, and are as unperceived by us with our gross physical senses, as their inhabitants are unconscious of us and of our own world and sphere.

There is a very striking passage in *The Secret Doctrine* by H. P. Blavatsky bearing on this subject. She says:

> . . . the Occultist does not locate *these spheres* either *outside* or *inside* our Earth, as the theologians and the poets do; for their location is nowhere in the space *known* to, and conceived by, the profane. They are, as it were, blended with our world — interpenetrating it and interpenetrated by it. There are millions and millions of worlds and firmaments visible to us; there [are] still greater numbers beyond those visible to the telescopes, and many of the latter kind do not belong to our *objective* sphere of existence. Although as invisible as if they were millions of miles beyond our solar system, they are yet with us, near us, *within* our own world, as objective and material to their respective inhabitants as ours is to us. . . . each is entirely under its own special laws and conditions, having no direct relation to our sphere. The inhabitants of these, as already said, may be, for all we know, or feel, passing *through* and *around* us as if through empty space, their very habitations and countries being interblended with ours, though not disturbing our vision, because we have not yet the faculties necessary for discerning them. . . .
>
> . . . such invisible worlds do exist. Inhabited as thickly as our own is, they are scattered throughout apparent Space in immense number; some far more material than our own world, others gradually etherealizing until they become formless and are as *"Breaths."* That our physical eye does not see them, is no reason to disbelieve in them; physicists can see neither their ether, atoms, nor "modes of motion," or Forces. Yet they accept and teach them. . . .
>
> But, if we can conceive of a world composed (for *our* senses) of matter still more attenuated than the tail of a comet, hence of inhabitants in it who are as ethereal, in proportion to *their* globe, as we are in comparison with *our* rocky, hard-crusted earth, no wonder if we do not perceive them, nor sense their presence or even existence.[73]

How indeed *could* we sense their presence or even existence, as long as we have no senses evolved to perceive these invisible worlds and their inhabitants and therefore capable of reporting them to us denizens of this our physical plane? Yet we have, nevertheless, our more subtil and interior sense-organs and apparatus of understanding which are the real, inner man: that part of our constitution whose still more interior portions are linked to the inner and higher parts of the cosmos, even as our physical body is similarly, perhaps, indeed identically, connected with this physical world.

---

73. *The Secret Doctrine,* I, 605-7.

The following extract taken from a recent book by the American scientist, M. Luckiesh, echoes H. P. Blavatsky's teaching, though it is probable that this scientific writer was unconscious of the fact. He had been discussing the imperfections of our physical senses as instruments of report even as regards the outer physical world. Then he continues:

This emphasizes the extreme limitations of our human senses in appraising all that may exist in the universe about us. With our mere human senses we may be living in a world within a world. Anything is possible beyond our experiences. Our imagination could conjure up another world coincident with our 'human' world, but unseen, unfelt, and unknown to us. Although we know a great deal of the physical world in which we live, beyond the veil unpenetrated by our senses may be other worlds coincident.[74]

Or again, for what is perhaps an even more remarkable statement running to the same effect, the reader is referred to a book just recently published, written by Professor W. F. G. Swann, which still more clearly shows how amazingly close the best thought of ultra-modern scientists is approaching to the borderland of the Occult. Certain paragraphs in this work set forth in admirably lucid language what amounts to a paraphrase of the last given citation from *The Secret Doctrine* by H. P. Blavatsky.

In this exceedingly interesting work, Dr. Swann writes like a Theosophist born, speaking as he does of the mathematical possibility of different universes, virtually limitless in number, which — if his words are properly understood — could occupy the same space, apparently interpenetrating, but which would be, each one, distinct from all the others, so that beings inhabiting any one such universe would not be cognisant of other universes and the respective inhabitants of these last. This distinction of universe from universe, however, in no wise destroys the possibility, and indeed the probability, that there are relations of a mathematical and perhaps other kind between such mathematically differing universes; therefore, due to these interconnecting or related lines of union, beings in any one universe might find it possible not merely to become conscious of the existence of universes other than their own, but even to pass — in some mathematical manner? — into another universe or other universes and thus to become cognisant of and acquainted with such other universes and the respective denizens thereof.[75]

---

74. *Foundations of the Universe*, p. 71.
75. *The Architecture of the Universe*, pp. 414-5 (Macmillan, 1934).

This might seem an attractive thought to Christians of either the old school or the modern as suggesting the possibility of the existence of the old-fashioned heaven and hell; but one may safely venture the guess that Dr. Swann's intuitive mind was not envisaging so much the establishment of a scientific foundation of the existence of the old theologic heaven and hell, but rather was holding in thought what the modern Occultist or Esotericist means when he speaks of the Invisible Worlds and the inhabitants thereof.

VII

These higher and lower worlds, including our own world, are literally as incomprehensibly numerous as are the atoms which compose physical matter, which latter again but reflects itself in every one of its component atoms. For instance, in a body of physical matter no larger than a bean or a small grape, the number of atoms that form or compose its substance is so incomputably immense that they must be reckoned in sextillions of sextillions; and the higher and lower worlds of the spaces of Space are at least equally numerous, for they are but the 'atoms' of THE UNIVERSE on the scale of kosmic magnitude, and in the other direction, to human vision, that equally unimaginable UNIVERSE on the scale of infinitesimal magnitudes — the one reflecting faithfully the other, and interpenetrating it and interpenetrated by it.

Now such UNIVERSE, on the scale of kosmic magnitudes, is itself composite or compounded or builded of minor universes, varying among themselves, each one, nevertheless, faithfully copying its incomprehensibly great Parent. Each such minor Universe, considered alone, is itself an organic whole or unit, a cosmic molecule formed of incomprehensibly numerous hosts of cosmic 'atomic' entities, 'cosmic atoms.' These last are the various suns and their accompanying planetary systems scattered over the wide fields of space. Each one of such celestial bodies, whether sun or planet, nebula or comet, is likewise an organic entity, composed in its turn of incomputably numerous hosts of entities or beings still smaller than itself. Our earth, for instance, is compounded of atoms ultimately, in their turn built of other still more minute particles or entities called protons and electrons and positrons and neutrons by modern scientists; and these last again are very likely also compounded things, built of infinitesimals still more minute.

The interpenetration and interlocking of the vast hosts of worlds, both great and small, higher and lower, and illimitable in both directions as regards high and low, is the root-idea in the Theosophical teaching of Kosmic Hierarchies. Each one of these Hierarchies has its own summit and its own base; in other words, its own highest plane or world or sphere, and its lowest; and the highest plane of any one such Hierarchy grades off into the lowest of the next succeeding and superior Hierarchy; while its lowest plane, again, grades off into the highest or summit of the next succeeding Hierarchy on the downward arc of descent, and endlessly in all directions; therefore, says the Esoteric Tradition, extending inwardly as well as outwardly. Just as there are worlds within worlds, thus by the same token are there worlds outwards of worlds. Each such Hierarchy is thus inseparably interlocked and interpenetrated by forces and vibrations with every other similarly connected Hierarchy.

Every point of Space, therefore, is the abode of life and of lives, and on many planes to boot; for these Hierarchies are densely populated with all-various kinds and classes of living entities in all grades of evolution, from the Divine, through the most spiritual, down to the lowest or most material, of any such Hierarchy; and every unit of these countless Hosts of lives is a learning and evolving being or entity on its upward way towards ever larger degrees of evolutionary perfection.

We know ourselves more or less as a human host; but how many of us pause to think that other still greater hosts, higher than we are, and lower than we, surround us on every side and form respective parts of the structure of the same Universe in which we, even as they, move and live and have our being! Every point in space represents an evolving entity — essentially a Monad. Intelligent beings — on earth we call them humans — live and exist throughout the boundless realms of the fields of endless Space. Some of them are high in development, some intermediate, some low; but they all work together and their combined actions and substances are the diversified and marvelous gradations of energy and substance of which the Universe is composed.

H. P. Blavatsky wrote:

From *Gods* to *men*, from Worlds to atoms, from a star to a rush-light, from the Sun to the vital heat of the meanest organic being — the world of Form and Existence is an immense chain, whose links are all connected. The law of Analogy is the first key to the world-problem, and these links have to be studied co-ordinately in their occult relations to each other.[76]

Imbodied consciousnesses, and please to note the plural, exist in

---

76. *The Secret Doctrine,* I, 604.

a practically infinite gradation of varying degrees of evolution — a
real Ladder of Life, or Stair of Life, stretching endlessly in either
direction, and thus running through the vast hierarchical system of
the Galaxy, and indeed of virtually limitless Space. There are, therefore, no limits except a hierarchical one, and such hierarchical limitation is but spacial and not actual. But this Ladder of Life is marked
at certain intervals by landing-places, stages, the so-called different
'planes of being,' which are otherwise the different spheres of cosmic
consciousness which expresses itself in the multi-myriad degrees of
consciousnesses.

VIII

It is not our Earth, this speck of cosmic dust, which populates
with its dead the invisible worlds and spheres of the spaces of illimitable Space. We humans are not exceptions nor favorites in Eternity
and in the Boundless Fields of Infinitude. The populations, or inhabitants or denizens, of these other worlds and spheres, invisible and
therefore unknown to us humans, *belong to those other higher (or
lower) worlds or spheres,* as the case may be; just as we belong to
our present physical world because for the time being we live in
bodies arising out of it — out of the substances and matters and
energies of this physical world.

Our essential Self, the Monad, however, does not belong to this
earth. It takes up bodies various and many, and uses these for a
while; then casts them aside and then passes on; but itself tastes
never of death; for its very nature is life, being an integral part of
the Kosmic Life as much as an atom is an integral part of dense
matter; and the dead bodies that the Monad leaves behind are merely
composite entities, not integral entities, or unitary integrals; and
these bodies, being but composite things, of necessity must wear
out, fall to pieces and disintegrate into their respective elements.
The body lives because of and on account of the monadic life which
fills it, and when that life is withdrawn, because the force which
brought about the cohesion of its particles is withdrawn, then the
body of necessity decays. Bodies are dreams, so to say, illusions —
mâyâvi or illusory forms, because temporary, transient, and in themselves, as already stated, are merely fluid composites held together
during any incarnated life of the Monad by that Monad's psycho-
magnetic energy.

But Life *per se* is continuous and flows forth from within: from
these inner and invisible and intangible worlds as a compound stream

of vital force. Life is as continuous inwardly, interiorly, as it is over the fields of the space of our own physical universe. Life is infinitely various in its manifestations. Too bold indeed and too shortsighted is the man who says: 'Life goes so far and no farther. It has limits.' How does he know? Life is limitless, because life is force, or rather, force is life; and life, in one sense, is but another name for the intrinsic movements of Kosmic Intelligence.

Some of the populations of the superior Spheres are far ahead of men of Earth in evolutionary growth; and the substances and matters of their various worlds being so much finer and more ethereal than are ours, their inhabitants would *de facto* seem to us like luminous gods; even the state corresponding to that held by our animals here, on certain such inner Spheres is higher than our own human state is here on Earth. Imagine then, what must be the state of their great 'humans'! On the other hand, the inhabitants of worlds inferior to our own, are of much coarser and more material fiber in all respects than we men of Earth are.

Slowly through the ages, as these populations of the hosts of worlds grow through evolution, as the faculties and senses of these populations thereby unfold and develop; and because these worlds both inner and outer are all of them permeated and infilled by the kosmic vitality; and because all these worlds on the endless Ladder of Life interpenetrate each other: therefore the populations of any one world or plane or sphere will, in the course of time, pass into other realms and spheres and worlds, and thus know these latter, because these populations will become a part of these latter worlds; for these evolving populations shall have bodies and sense-organs and sense-apparatus fit, builded, prepared through evolutionary unfolding, to sense and to report to the perceiving consciousness the nature of, and experiences gained in, these inner worlds.

Indeed, we inhabitants of this our Earth have come here after the manner outlined in the preceding paragraph, ages and ages and aeons and aeons agone; and in the aeons of the far distant future, we shall pass out of this physical world again into these inner realms, doing so collectively as the entire evolving human host: and when that time comes in the distant future, we shall then be as gods, because the divine part of us will have begun to be conscious, and therefore to act and to function, on the planes relatively lower than itself; and in consequence we shall then know and feel and therefore act and function as truly divine beings.

Or, to put the idea in another way: man, and equivalently, beings holding the human stage in all other worlds and on all other planets, visible or invisible, is in his essence a spark of the Central Intelligence-Consciousness-Fire of the Universe. Being a spark of that Central Fire, man is in inseparable alliance with all that the Universe contains, because this Central Fire is all-permeant; and therefore this unity with the Central Fire of the Universe is in all of man's inner constitution — his inner nature; it is written there, so to speak, in bonds of flaming energy; and by following the terms of this his inseparable alliance with Nature, this union of essences, these bonds of being with that Central Fire: by following these bonds of flaming consciousness ever inwards, and ever more withinwards of himself, man can and will in due course of distant time reach highths of wisdom and knowledge utterly beyond present human understanding.

CHAPTER VI

WORLDS VISIBLE AND INVISIBLE — II

IT should be obvious from a careful perusal of the contents of the preceding chapter, of which the present chapter is a continuation dealing with somewhat more technical aspects of the theme under consideration, that the basic conception of the teaching of the Esoteric Tradition in this manner of visible and invisible worlds is, that the Universe in all its parts, which is equivalent to saying in all its hierarchical structure, is fundamentally and throughout alive. It is a living Organism, builded in every part or range of interlocking and interworking forces, playing upon, in, and through, the various grades or degrees of ethereal substances, which last, even from the standpoint of ultra-modern science, are themselves but concreted or crystallized forces.

Each and every one of these forces, considered distributively, is itself a manifestation of an intelligence; and these forces, considered collectively, thus compose the energic aspect of that equivalently vast aggregate of intelligences which in their unity themselves form the collective Third Logos of the Cosmos. These Cosmic Logoi, again, each one the formative or so-called Creative Logos of its own Hierarchy, are actually innumerable in their activities in the fields of Infinitude. Thus, when the Theosophist speaks of a Universe, of a Hierarchy, of a Logos, it is always pertinent to ask oneself: 'Which Universe, which Hierarchy, which Logos is here intended?'

As has so often been stated during the course of the study imbodied in the preceding chapters of this work, the small — whatever its degree of infinitesimal or cosmic magnitude — mirrors the Great, whatever its scale of cosmic magnitude may be; for throughout all Being there runs one universal identic Consciousness, one universal common Life; and in consequence of the foregoing, that fundamentally unitary system of Cosmic Law thus of necessity pervades all manifestation, and reduces all, thus of necessity subordinate to it, to its sway.

It is upon the foregoing grand truth of Universal Nature that is based the sublime principle of analogy throughout the UNIVERSE, inclusive as this last is of all minor universes, hierarchies, systems of worlds visible and invisible, and the countless hosts of living, sensate, conscious and self-conscious beings and entities which are the denizens, inhabitants and populations thereof.

The Esoteric Tradition recognises no so-called 'dead matter' anywhere in Infinitude, for from what precedes it is at once clear that whatever is, and all that is, is *de facto*, in greater or less degree, not only intelligent, i. e., conscious, and often self-conscious, but first and foremost is alive.

The Cosmic Logos has been alluded to as an aggregate, and so verily it is. Yet it is something more than a mere aggregation of entities which in their inseparable union or unity thus form an entity comprising them all and greater than them all. The Logos itself is an Individual, a Cosmic Spirit, and for this reason is called a Cosmic Hierarch — i. e., the 'Supreme Spirit' for its own Hierarchy; for it is the source and origin thereof, as well as the all-inclusive Individual which comprehends within the compass of its own being the hosts of minor beings and entities and things through which it lives and expresses itself.

Just here is one of the most difficult problems of the Esoteric Philosophy: How the One becomes the Many during the course of its manvantaric manifestations, remaining withal apart, and throughout manvantaric time superior to its various component portions. As Kṛishṇa phrases it in substance in the *Bhagavad-Gîtâ:* "I manifest this universe with portions of myself, and yet remain separate and superior thereto."[77]

Just so, as another illustration, is man in his septempartite or decempartite constitution a hierarchical aggregate of hosts of beings over which the spirit of his constitution presides as the Hierarch or Logos, remaining separate and distinct from its children which it emanates during each incarnation; and yet these hosts of beings form in their aggregate man's constitution or the vehicle of his spirit.

It is a fact difficult for most Western minds to grasp that consciousness is both essential or unitary and yet is during manifestation divisible into minor or children consciousness-points. Just as the cosmic consciousness, which one may figurate to oneself as an ocean of conscious life, almost automatically divides itself into droplets, these droplets being the minor component individuals of itself and forming the various hierarchical classes, so is man, the mirror of the Universal Great, an essential or unitary consciousness which, during its manifestations or incarnations, extrudes from its own being or essence hosts of consciousness-atoms, so to speak, droplets

---

77. Ch. x, śl. 42.

of itself, each one of such droplets or atoms nevertheless having its own inherent and innate individuality.

It was this idea which the Buddha-Gautama had in mind when, as his thought has been transmitted to us by later ages, in describing the final resolving of the minor into the greater, the Great Teacher said, "the Dewdrop slips into the shining Sea" — here adopting the beautiful phrasing of Sir Edwin Arnold.[78]

Man, therefore, like every other unitary or monadic being in Universal Nature, is composite, a compound entity, at least during the periods of evolutionary manifestation; and the respective portions of this composite aggregate exist on different planes, or in different worlds, because of differing degrees of ethereality or substantiality or rather of materiality. Thus it is that six-sevenths or seven-tenths — according to another method of enumeration — of man's constitution is invisible, unseen, because resident upon and in, and functioning upon and in, planes of cosmic being far more ethereal than is the physical sphere thereof, upon and in which man's physical body lives.

Following exactly the same line of thought, the teaching tells us of the invisible spheres of the Universe which thus are six-sevenths — or seven-tenths — of the Cosmic Whole, and are therefore invisible and intangible to the sense-organs of physical man.

I

There are two manners of viewing the Universal Aggregate or Cosmic Whole. The first is visioning the All as an immense and individual system of interlocking and interworking worlds or realms or spheres or planes, from the divine of the Universal Hierarchy through all intermediate planes and worlds and spheres, downwards to the physical; and this is the simpler and easier way. The second, and somewhat more difficult of mental visualization or picturing, is retaining the foregoing as the background or framework, and then upon this background or in this framework, mentally viewing the manner in which the Universal Aggregate as an Individual subdivides itself into hierarchical details of structure.

We have then, first, the invisible and to us humans intangible worlds and spheres of the general Kosmos with which we are in kosmic relations only; and second, and as an example of what exists elsewhere, our own Earth-chain of seven distinct and individual

---

78. *The Light of Asia,* Bk. VIII.

globes which are likewise inextricably connected and bound up with the so-called 'Seven Sacred Planets' of the solar system, and the respective sevenfold worlds or globes belonging to each one of these Seven Sacred Planets. These latter, the Sacred Seven, together with the Earth-chain, form a particular Hierarchy within the general solar realm or kingdom, because they are closely united in origin and destiny; and in evolutionary growth and development they form a closely interconnecting body corporate, an especially aggregated part of the solar system.

Every one of the physical globes that we see scattered over the fields of space is accompanied by six invisible and superior globes, forming what are called a Chain. This is likewise the case with every sun or star, and, as said above, with every planet, and indeed with every moon of every planet. It is likewise the case with those wandering radicals both of the Galaxy and of our own solar system, respectively called the nebulae and the comets: all are septiform entities, i. e., all have a sevenfold constitution even as man has, because the Great, as stated above, of necessity mirrors itself in each part of itself. The Esoteric Teaching is, in fact, that there are twelve globes to any chain, though the number seven is commonly used for study and exoteric or open exposition, for the reason that these seven are the lower septenary of the duodenary whole, and because it is obviously easier to study and understand the interconnexion and interworkings of seven things than it is of a larger number.

Each such chain is a cosmic unit or individual, as for instance, the Earth's planetary chain. The other six globes of our Earth-chain are of course utterly invisible and intangible to our physical sense-apparatus or organs, because these organs were evolved to cognise this earth-plane and none other, and the other six globes being existent two by two on three planes of the solar system higher than and superior to, and consequently more ethereal than, our physical plane, where our Earth-globe is. These three higher or inner planes or worlds are each one superior to the world or plane immediately beneath or inferior to it. Thus our Earth-globe is the lowest of all the seven globes of our Earth-chain. Three globes precede it on the downward arc, and three globes follow it in the ascending arc, of evolution.

Now in order more clearly to set forth the schematic delineation of this hierarchical structure of the solar system, or, indeed, of our Home-Universe, the following diagram is given, the names in this case appropriated to the respective planes or spheres being those used for that purpose in Brâhmanism. In the *Vishnu-Purâna,* one of the most interesting of ancient Indian works, the invisible worlds are divided into fourteen *lokas* of which seven belong to the superior class or range, and seven to the inferior. Another name for the seven inferior worlds is *talas;* and in this scheme of enumeration the earth is taken as the midway-point, and is reckoned as the first in the ascending scale, and also the first in the descending scale. There are other methods of placing our own world-system in a hierarchical succession of steps or stages, but the enumeration that is almost always found is either seven of any range or class, or nine, or ten, the differences depending upon the manners of viewing the hierarchical succession of worlds, and therefore of enumerating them as ascending or descending.

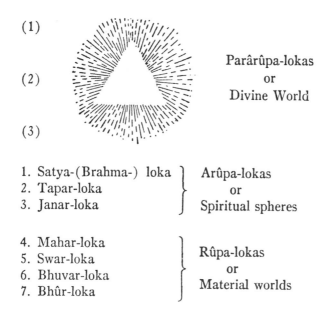

(1)

(2) Parârûpa-lokas
or
Divine World

(3)

1. Satya-(Brahma-) loka	Arûpa-lokas
2. Tapar-loka	or
3. Janar-loka	Spiritual spheres

4. Mahar-loka	
5. Swar-loka	Rûpa-lokas
6. Bhuvar-loka	or
7. Bhûr-loka	Material worlds

The Sanskrit word कोक (*loka*) means 'place' or 'locality,' or, as a Theosophist would say in this connexion, a world or sphere or plane; whilst the word रूप (*rûpa*) means 'form.' Now 'form' is here employed technically — not in the strictly popular sense in which it is used in European tongues; and it signifies an atomic or monadic aggregation about the central indwelling consciousness, thus forming a vehicle or body or transmitter thereof. अरूप (*arûpa*), equivalently, means 'formless,' but this word 'formless' is not to be taken so strictly as to signify that there is no 'form' of any kind whatsoever; it means only that the 'forms' in the spiritual worlds, as outlined in the above scheme, are of a spiritual type or character, and of course are far more ethereal, indeed spiritual, than are the 'forms' of the *rûpa-lokas.*

The technical meaning might better be expressed by saying that *rûpa-lokas* are lokas or worlds where the body-form or vehicle is more or less definitely outlined in, and composed of, matter, ethereal or physical; whereas in the *arûpa-lokas,* or the spiritual worlds or spheres or planes, the vehicle or body or transmitter is to be conceived of rather as an enclosing sheath of energic substance. If one were to speak of the entities in these arûpa-lokas, at least in the higher portions of them, as being clothed in bodies of light, doubtless this expression would more closely convey the real idea, because even in modern physical science, light is substantial — as the Ancient Wisdom likewise teaches it to be, although obviously not the light-substance or light-stuff of our physical world. While the three highest rûpa-lokas are relatively immaterial to us inhabitants of the lowest or Bhûr-loka, and even more so the three higher or arûpa or spiritual spheres, nevertheless they are in all cases as substantial or seeming solid to their respective inhabitants as is our physical sphere to us.

It should be noted further that the seven lokas of this schematic diagram, which include the three of the arûpa and the four of the rûpa, include all the manifested universes — that is to say, the universes subject to manifested imbodiment, counting from the spiritual down to the spheres of most material density, and therefore actually including — though it is not sketched in this diagram — even what is alluded to by the Theosophist as the mystery of the 'Eighth Sphere.' Concerning this last or Eighth Sphere, nothing further can be said in a published work, except the passing statement or incidental comment that it is a sphere even more material than is our Earth, and may perhaps be best and most briefly described as the sphere of 'absolute' matter: in other words, the lowest possible stage or step of our own Home-Hierarchy, in which last stage matter has reached its ultimate in density and physical concretion.

Beneath this last stage begins a new Hierarchy; just as on the highest stage, in other words above our own present Home-Hierarchy, could we consciously ascend along the various stages or degrees or rungs of this Ladder of Life, we should pierce through the laya-center there existing and enter into the lowest existent or prevailing stage of the next Hierarchy superior to our own.

As regards the 'triangle in radiation' or radiating triangle, which the above diagram also presents, and which there is called the

Parârûpa-lokas, this triangle represents in symbolic form the aggregative summit or acme or top of the Ladder of our own Home-Hierarchy, and is to us children of this Hierarchy our Divine World. This Divine World is not only to be considered as the divine Living Seed whence flow forth in the cosmic periods of manifestation the seven grades or steps below it, but it is also the spiritual Goal towards which and into which all shall again be ultimately resolved when such a hierarchical or cosmic period of manifestation shall have concluded its course of evolution in self-expression.

It is seen from the above, that, strictly speaking, any Hierarchy is composite of ten degrees or stages or steps; or, if the highest of all counting downwards, or the first, is considered to be the same as the lowest of the next superior Hierarchy, we have nine degrees or stages or steps descending in successive ranges of worlds or planes. The difference, therefore, between seven and ten, or again seven and nine, is merely a matter of viewpoint and enumeration, and has no significance in itself. Any reader conversant with the theogonical mythological aspect of ancient and present-existing Oriental religions and philosophies, knows how frequently the numbers ten, nine, seven, five, four, and three, occur therein in relation to the various families or groups or hierarchies of the worlds and of the beings and things which respectively inhabit them.

It might be added here in passing that there are certain Oriental Yogins who teach of the Lokas and Talas rather as centers in the human body than as planes or spheres in the universe, which centers, if stimulated under proper training, enable one to attain greater knowledge of all planes of existence. But this teaching is inadequate because imperfect, and is true only because these inner centers are organs, or, as it were, the ends of living wires, to use an electrical metaphor, of which the other ends are fastened in the cosmic fabric, and are of the same substance as that fabric is. It is the teaching of the great Sages and Seers that the cosmical Universe, or the universal Cosmos, exists in a mâyâvi sense exterior to man, although it is likewise the teaching of the great Sages and Seers that the essence of man and the essence of the Universe are one. This last teaching is one which should be emphatically stated.

Theosophy uses the terms given in the preceding table in a larger sense than that employed in the Brâhmanical system. It places not only our physical sphere in the lowest or seventh degree or stage of the above scheme, the Bhûr-loka, but includes therein also our solar system and, indeed, our entire *physical* Home-Universe.

II

In order that the reader of this work, or the student of the Eso-teric Tradition, may have at least an outline in his mind of the manner in which Nature is builded by and through and of and from the lokas and talas, the following observations are written with the desire to contribute something that may be helpful to that end.

The first thought to have clear in the mind is that these various lokas and talas are not separate from or distinct from the universe, and that they do not merely exist in the universe as a complex structure different from it. This idea is all wrong. The universe itself in its vast aggregate *is* these lokas and talas, which are mere names or descriptive appellations picturing the manner in which the universe itself is builded. The idea, therefore, is vastly different from the notions prevailing in the Occident about heavens and hells which exist within the body corporate of an ethereal or spiritual cosmos.

Were it possible, which it is not, to annihilate the lokas and talas, this would annihilate the universe itself; for, as said above, the lokas and talas *are* the universe.

The next thought to retain clearly in the mind is that these lokas and talas are not, distributively considered, water-tight or rather spirit-tight compartments of nature; the truth is the exact contrary of this. The lokas and talas from the highest to the lowest inter-penetrate, interwork, interblend, and all of them together form the cosmic organism. Thus they are an organic unity.

Furthermore, because the Great mirrors into the small, every sub-ordinate hierarchy, or series of subordinate hierarchies, repeats in itself or in themselves with perfect fidelity whatever exists in the Great, and this is because of the all-permeant Cosmic Life and funda-mental or essential Cosmic Law, which, whatever its various rami-fications in these subordinate hierarchies may be, works in identical fashion throughout them all. Thus it is that we have here again the same structural system that has been alluded to in other parts of the present work. Every subordinate hierarchy is an integral part of the Cosmic Whole, and therefore, as said above, repeats in itself and contains in itself all the laws, substances, functions, attributes, whatever it may be, that the Cosmic Whole contains.

As an illustration, our Galaxy, otherwise our Home-Universe, is a Grand Hierarchy mirroring all that is within a Hierarchy still more vast; similarly, in converse order, as our Galaxy is builded of groups of celestial bodies, i. e., the various suns with or without companion-planets, in other words of solar systems, therefore each such solar system is a subordinate Hierarchy faithfully repetitive in laws and substances and functions and of whatever exists in the all-inclusive Galactic Hierarchy.

Now then: Just as the Galaxy is builded of these lokas and talas, all interacting, all interblending, all interconnected, on a galactic scale, thus likewise every solar system in the Galaxy, our own solar system as an example, is likewise builded of lokas and talas, functioning, working, and structurally builded on the pattern set by the Greater Hierarchy, the Galaxy. Again, and following the same rule of repetition, which is but another way of saying the same rule of analogy, every planet in our solar system repeats in the small the same structural system of lokas and talas, such planetary system living within, and functioning within, and builded from, the same substances and forces, and controlled by the same laws that work in the larger Hierarchy, the solar system.

As above stated, every visible planet of the solar system is merely a representative, on this lowest or physical plane of the solar system, of a planetary chain composed of seven manifest globes and five relatively unmanifest globes. The seven manifest globes are to be considered as belonging to the Rûpa-lokas or material worlds, as outlined in the schematic diagram hereinbefore given, whereas the five relatively unmanifest globes are to be considered as belonging to the Arûpa-lokas or spiritual spheres, likewise designated in the diagram just mentioned.[79]

Thus it is seen that of the seven manifest planes or worlds of our

---

79. If the reader will turn to H. P. Blavatsky's master-work, *The Secret Doctrine,* Volume I, page 172, he will find an interesting and useful diagram there of the manner in which both the Lunar chain and the Earth-chain are connected as regards the traveling of the life-forces and monads from the former to the latter. This diagram, of course, is highly conventional but very suggestive.

Or again, if the student is desirous of understanding the manner in which the seven manifest globes and the five relatively unmanifest globes of the complete structural system of our Earth's planetary chain are interconnected and interworking, it is suggested that he turn to the author's *Fundamentals of the Esoteric Philosophy,* on page 487, where he will find a schematic diagram giving the information sought for.

It should be remembered that this latter diagram is likewise conventionalized, and it must not be forgotten that a conventional diagram is not a picture or photograph of the position in space, nor of attributes and qualities of bodies occupying such positions, but is suggestive of the interworking and interconnected units of any one planetary chain of the many such that exist in the solar system.

Solar Systemic Hierarchy, each such solar plane or world comprises two globes of our own Earth's planetary chain, and identically so as regards the respective structures of the other planets of our solar system, except that the lowest globe, the fourth, is alone on its plane.

The following parallel columns of the Rûpa-lokas and the seven manifest globes of our planetary chain will be instructive, and should be carefully studied.

Rûpa-lokas
or
Material Worlds
{
4. Mahar-loka ....Globes A & G
5. Swar-loka.............Globes B & F
6. Bhuvar-loka........Globes C & E
7. Bhûr-loka ....Globe D (our physical
                                            Earth)
}

In the above suggestive comparison of lokas and globes, it is of the first importance to remember that no single solar plane is a single loka acting alone, as for instance in the above comparison where it is stated that Globes A and G belong to the Mahar-loka. It is not to be understood that on this plane wherein function Globes A and G, the quality of Mahar is the only quality active or functioning therein. The truth is that these lokas interpenetrate each other; so that on every Cosmic Plane every single one of the seven lokas and the seven talas is not only manifest, but highly and strongly functional; but on each such solar plane, one of the lokas and one of the talas is predominant in its influence — i. e., one pair of loka and tala is predominant thereon by and through the respective characteristic of each.

Thus our Bhûr-loka of the physical world or of the physical solar system, or of the physical galaxy, nevertheless contains, interconnected with it, and contemporaneously and co-ordinately working through it, all the other lokas and talas, albeit the Bhûr quality is predominant here; and thus it is that because of this predominance of the Bhûr-characteristic, it is commonly called Bhûr-loka with its correspondential tala called Pâtâla. The same rule applies on the other cosmic planes.

Or again, let us take Globes A and G existing on and in the Mahar-loka with its corresponding tala. These two globes, A and G, have the predominating Mahar-loka characteristic; but nevertheless they are shot through and through with the influences and functions and characteristics of all the other six lokas and six corresponding talas, each loka, i. e., every one of the lokas, having its corresponding nether pole, so to speak, which is its corresponding tala.

These lokas and talas, furthermore, grow progressively more material in substance, functions, and characteristics, as they run down the scale from the Satya-loka to the Bhûr-loka; yet, as emphatically stated above, the Satya-loka has its corresponding physical attributes because the Bhûr-loka in its highest or most ethereal portions interpenetrates it; similarly the Bhûr-loka has the functions, attributes, and characteristics, of the Satya-loka, because the Satya-loka in its 'lowest' aspects interpenetrates in and with the Bhûr-loka. Every world, every plane, every sphere, is compounded of all the seven lokas with their corresponding talas, but nevertheless is characterized by the predominance of the functions and substances and forces belonging to the particular loka and tala which are most strongly manifest therein.

And, finally, before leaving this sub-theme of our chapter, the foregoing contains the reason, philosophically expressed, why even the lowest of beings or entities or things contains relatively latent within itself all the attributes and possibilities belonging to the higher realms or spheres — i. e., the higher lokas and talas. Man himself is a luminous example in point. In his present manifested life he is a Bhûr-loka-pâtâla being, yet the ethereal portions of his constitution contain likewise the essences belonging to all the other lokas and talas. The Macrocosm repeats itself in the microcosm — one of the grandest and most sublime generalizations of the Esoteric Philosophy, the Esoteric Tradition, wholly based as the latter is on Universal Nature herself in all its unimaginable beauty of symmetry in substance, force, and structure.

III

Ultra-modern science is coming with every lustrum, or five-year period, closer and closer to certain age-old teachings concerning the nature of matter and force and their origins in and from a common divine-spiritual *prima essentia* or *primum substantiale*. Thus it is the tendency of the minds of our greatest men of science today to derive the Universe and all in it from a pre-cosmic substance-energy, which men like Jeans, Eddington, Einstein, Planck, Younghusband, etc., attempt to describe their conception of in human terms such as 'a Cosmic Mathematician' or 'a Cosmic Artist,' which terms, nevertheless, when analysed, and the somewhat anthropomorphic coloring discarded, verge or tend towards a conception deriving the Universe and all in it from Cosmic Ideation.

Consider this vastly important point faithfully for a few moments. Our best minds thus derive the Universe and all in it from Mind or

Consciousness possessing, obviously, intelligence and artistry in operation of cosmic magnitude. And from Mind, thus varying the strictly metaphysical thought of idealistic philosophers, they derive not only the gross physical universe and all that is in it, but all intermediate stages between. A most significant deduction indeed! It is strictly in line with, and as far as it goes, is faithful to, the teaching of the Esoteric Philosophy, the Esoteric Tradition, that all manifested being and life evolved itself forth, or unfolded itself, from Cosmic Thought. Thus the atom itself and all the *minutiae* of atomic structure from which our gross physical world is builded can with strict logic and propriety be spoken of as imbodied THOUGHT — or, as the Esoteric Tradition would phrase the matter, Cosmic Thought expresses itself in innumerable hosts or armies of imbodying and imbodied entities and beings and things.

Following, therefore, the key-thought lying in the preceding paragraphs, we shall more readily understand how the entire structure of the universe is unfolded, unwrapped, i. e., evolved, stage by stage and degree by degree 'downwards' from the Cosmic Originant: or, what comes to the same thing, from the highest of the lokas and its corresponding and accompanying twin-tala. From Satya-loka with its accompanying twin-tala, therefore, in the beginning of manifested life, whether it be galaxy, or solar system, or planet, came or unrolled or evolved forth all subsequent or succeeding lokas in the downward arc of manifestation, each such loka in inseparable union with its accompanying tala or nether pole. Thus from Satya-loka rolled forth or evolved itself in manifestation the next succeeding loka on the downward arc, which is Tapar-loka; in exactly similar fashion, from Tapar-loka, containing likewise the reflected forces and essence of its parent the Satya-loka, rolled forth or evolved itself the Janar-loka, which thus contains not only its own swâbhâvic characteristics, but likewise includes in minor degree the swâbhâvic characteristics or essences or forces of its parent, the Tapar-loka, and its grand-parent, the Satya-loka.

Thus the unrolling or evolving forth of the universe — or the solar system, or a planet — proceeds in identically similar fashion through the succeeding lokas and talas, i. e., through Mahar-loka, Swar-loka, Bhuvar-loka, finally reaching the lowest of the hierarchical ladder, the Bhûr-loka, our gross, physical World. When the bottom of the Ladder of Life is reached, when evolution in that particular hierarchy, be it galaxy, solar system, planet, etc., has concluded its unrolling matter-wards on the downward arc, then the converse procedure begins to take place: involution succeeds evolution, and all the vast and fascinating pageantry of the manifested hierarchy begins to inroll itself, to ascend what in Theosophy is called the Luminous Arc. This procedure takes place by the lowest portions of the Bhûr-loka beginning to radiate away their energy into finer forms, such radiation gradually ascending through all the scale or degrees of the Bhûr-loka, until finally the Bhûr-loka disappears in radiation, and, what comes to the same thing and is perhaps more carefully expressed, the Bhûr-loka is indrawn into the next higher Bhuvar-loka. The Bhuvar-loka then in its turn begins the process of disintegration, of dissolving, of radiation, and so proceeds until it is withdrawn into the next higher loka, or Swar-loka. Thus the process of indrawing continues steadily until finally, all the lower lokas and talas being indrawn, the Satya-loka is reached, and the same process begins there, until it too finally passes out of manifested existence into what in Sanskrit is called the Amûla-mûla, that is, into Mûlaprakṛiti or Root-Nature, the substantial-spiritual Originant which in the beginning of manifestation was the *fons et origo* of all.

This process of rolling forth and then of inrolling of a universe or solar system or celestial body has been variously described and pictured in ancient literatures, but all have the fundamental conception, derivative originally from the Esoteric Philosophy. The Stoics taught this identic process of the universe being unfolded into its bewildering variety and maze and intricate patterns until the end of possibilities for that cosmic period was reached, when there immediately ensued the beginning of the return journey towards spirit, which took place by the exact reversal of what had produced the unrolling or unfolding. The Universe and all in it thus is inrolled, infolded, involved, finally reaching the period where the Universe that was and all its host of beings, entities, and things, pass back into the essence and life of the Cosmic Spirit, there to rest in unimaginable felicity, consciousness, and peace, until the time comes for a new world-period to begin a new evolution but on a higher plane.

Even in the crude statement of the Hebrew and Christian scriptures may be found very definite allusions to this process, especially to the process of involution, which the Christians called the Last Day or Day of Judgment, when everything shall have vanished and the last accounts shall be settled.

And all the host of heaven shall be dissolved, and the heavens shall be rolled together as a scrowl. . . .[80]

---

80. *Isaiah*, xxxiv, 4.

Or again, in the Christian New Testament is the same teaching:

And the heaven departed as a scrowl when it is rolled together. . . .[81]

Here the somewhat crude yet graphic symbol is used to picturate evolution as the unrolling of a scroll, consisting of one volume of the Cosmic Book of Life or one page thereof; and the reverse process or involution is figurated as a rolling up of the Book of Life or of the page thereof, whereby all things pass away, and what was is no longer to be seen.

IV

The Seven Sacred Planets, alluded to in previous paragraphs, were called such by the ancients because they form with our Earth a Planetary Family. These seven and our Earth are much more closely connected among themselves than they are with the innumerable hosts of other worlds existing both in the solar system and in the general Kosmos. For there are literally scores of planetary chains in the solar system, some much higher than the planetary chain of Earth, some much lower than it. There are entire planetary chains within our solar system, of which we do not even see the lowest globe, for the reason that in these cases these lowest globes are above our Fourth Cosmic Plane, just as there are planetary chains so far beneath our Fourth Cosmic Plane that even the highest globes of these last are below our Fourth Cosmic Plane.

Yet all these planetary chains are as much component parts of the Universal Solar System as our Earth is, or as are Venus, Mars, Jupiter, Saturn, etc. Each such planetary chain, however invisible it may be to us, is an integral part of an organism, or organic union of chains playing their respective rôles on the multi-myriad stages of the cosmic life, and are all of them the habitats of beings — some of them far higher than we, some of them far inferior to us men, in evolutionary development.

All physical bodies in the sky that we see are fourth-plane globes, i. e., globes existing on the Fourth Cosmic Plane, and this statement is without exception, at least so far as our solar system is concerned. Even Father-Sun, which is not really a physical body, i. e., the Sun that our physical eyes can see, is a fourth-plane globe. But it is nevertheless a material body of highly ethereal character, and is matter in the sixth and seventh, or highest, states of matter, manifesting as light, hence as radiation.

---

81. Revelation, vi, 14.

Now the Seven Sacred Planets above referred to are those which we men know as Saturn, Jupiter, Mars, the Sun as a substitute for a secret planet, Venus, Mercury, and the Moon also reckoned as a substitute for a secret planet. They are all most intimately and intricately connected not only with human destiny, but with the destiny of every entity of whatever kind or grade or class that the Earth contains. Including Earth, these eight planets, or in other words eight planetary chains, are the sacred Ogdoad of the ancients, so often referred to in the classical literature of Greece and Rome. As a matter of fact, however, there are not only Seven Sacred Planets, there are twelve of them, although because of the extremely difficult teachings connected with the five highest of this twelvefold system, only seven were commonly mentioned in Greek and Latin literature.

In the same manner exactly the globes of any planetary chain should be reckoned as twelve in number, of which five are rarely if ever mentioned in the exoteric literatures because of the extremely abstract and recondite character of the teachings connected with them. Thus it is that seven globes of a chain are the ones mentioned and partially described by H. P. Blavatsky in *The Secret Doctrine*.

Thus then there are twelve globes of our own planetary chain of Earth, and every one of the globes of this our chain is builded by one in especial, but by all in general, of the Twelve Sacred Planets or Planetary Chains that the ancients in their mystical writings at least hinted at. Our Earth, that is to say the physical globe, Earth, which is the fourth globe of our planetary chain as usually counted, has been especially builded and formed, and is watched over, and in a sense guided by, the planet Saturn assisted in such function and operation by our own physical Moon. Similarly, every other one of the twelve globes of our planetary chain has been built by in especial, is watched over in especial, and is guided in especial, by one of the Twelve Sacred Planets of the ancients. Nevertheless, although each one of the twelve globes of the planetary chain of Earth is the particular ward of one of the twelve Sacred Planets, every one of the other eleven Sacred Planets has combined or co-operated in the past in forming such particular globe of our chain, the predominant influence, however, in such work and guidance flowing forth from that one of the twelve Sacred Planets which is the main Guardian of the globe it guides.

When we speak of the Seven Sacred Planets we must think rather of the ensouling divinities of them than merely of the physical bodies which are seen as spots of light, or with telescopic aid as disks of light. The Planetary Spirit of our own Earth is not the physical body, this rocky earth, although this last has life, the vital force which keeps it together, which makes it what it is — which ensouls it, in other words. This life is the vital manifestation of the Planetary Spirit of Earth, which likewise infills our globe through this permeant life with seeds of mind.

Our Earth is a globe, the Sun is a globe, the stars are globes, because each one of these is the visible or physical body expressing and manifesting the operative vital and mental energy within and behind it, which latter makes it what it is. The interior elements or principles of every such physical globular body are themselves globular, and the outer or physical shell faithfully reflects or mirrors the inner or causal compound structure. Forces are poured into our world or globe constantly from within, and our world or globe in its turn by the same token is constantly pouring forces out of itself. The same may be said regarding the operations and functions of the vital forces in any globe of a planetary chain, and likewise applies and appertains to the precisely similar circulations of substances and matters. These last enumerated circulations of energic substances or matters may be called, if it be so desired, the different forms of radiation, involving radio-activity in all its various phases.

Modern scientists are today beginning to talk of the possibility of 'matter' vanishing or disappearing or dissolving in a burst of energy — or what the Theosophist prefers to call force. In order to realize how subversive this is of the old science of our boyhood-days, it is sufficient to recall to mind one of the main pillars of the physical science of thirty or more years ago: the so-called Law of the Conservation of Energy, which states in substance that the Universe contains a fixed amount of energy, to which nothing can be added and of which not an iota can be subtracted, the energy within such a universe merely changing its forms.

This is a scientific doctrine which the Esoteric Philosophy has never been able to accept in the purely mechanistic or materialistic form in which it was enunciated; and in consequence, students of the Esoteric Tradition recognise with extreme gratification the newer light thrown upon this matter by the more recent discoveries in science, and the revolutionary deductions drawn from these new discoveries made by scientific men. While it may be relatively true, in a universal cosmic sense, that every cosmic body is a closed system, sufficient unto itself, more or less, as regards the forces and substances working within it, yet it has always been the teaching of the Esoteric Tradition that each such cosmic unit or organism, however vast, however small, is but a drop, a particle, a part, of a still vaster Cosmic Life in which such drop or part or minor closed system exists, and from which vaster Cosmic Life the minor unit is constantly receiving streams of forces and substances in continuous and unending flow, and which it, in equal degree, surrenders or returns to the surrounding or inclosing Cosmic Reservoir.

As an illustration, consider the constitution of man himself. Here we have a complex or compounded being, consisting of divers and diverse substances and forces, ranging from the divine through many intermediate degrees or stages to man's physical body. He is thus, in one sense, a closed system, yet he is constantly receiving from the circumambient universe an unceasing inflow of both forces and substances which feeds him and builds him, and which throughout the range of his constitution he thus uses; at the same time, he constantly and in the same unceasing manner returns to the circumambient sphere the forces and substances which he has received and used and which he finally rejects, excretes, or returns whence they came.

Or again, in the same manner, and following the same general rule of analogy operative everywhere, any planetary chain of the solar system, although each one as a unit is a closed system, nevertheless receives from the circumambient solar system, i. e., from the Sun and the different planetary chains other than itself, constant, unceasing, inflows of both force and substance, which are used for purposes of building and experience and are finally ejected or returned to pursue their interplanetary and intersolar circulations.

From these two examples or illustrations, which can be extended indefinitely to each larger inclosing system, such as Solar System and Galaxy, or as between Galaxy and Galaxy, the general reason is easily seen why the Esoteric Philosophy has always looked askance at the old scientific doctrine of the Conservation of Energy, which scientists themselves are at the present time equally suspecting of being at least inadequate.[82]

---

82. The argument in the above paragraphs, involving the rejection by the Esoteric Philosophy of the scientific doctrine of the Conservation of Energy, is of course wholly based upon the fact that this doctrine is entirely mechanistic, is the child of the materialism of the now outlived scientific age, and deals with the universe as a closed system of energies and matter which in their aggregate are unensouled, forming an insensate, unintelligent mechanism. Such a universe is but the physical universe and recognises no spiritual source or background of mind and consciousness.

There is, however, one manner of viewing the mere scientific doctrine which no Theosophist, probably, would refuse to accept. It is the view which would

To put the matter briefly in other words: the Esoteric Philosophy teaches that every such closed system, whether it be universe, or galaxy, or solar system, or individual sun or planet, is an individual, possessing its own unitary mind, character, life, and type.   Being

consider utter Infinitude as the 'Universe,' as the home and limitless field of boundless consciousness, dividing itself into literally an infinite number of hierarchies of minor consciousnesses; and that from this limitless infinitude spring forth into manifested and multi-myriad forms of living existence, the ineffably grand and sublime pageantry of the divisions of Kosmic Life.

Considered after this fashion, the so-called 'Doctrine of the Conservation of Energy' would arouse no particular objection in the mind of the student of the Esoteric Philosophy, although it is probable that he would consider its enunciation in the scientific manner as lamentably short of the reality, and as halting and imperfect in expression.

The 'closed system' called the universe, in this latter view, would be simply Boundless Infinitude, inclusive of all possible energies as well as substances that Infinitude can contain; and it then becomes obvious that with such a conception no forces can be added to Infinitude from outside, because there is no outside: nor can it lose any of its store of forces because there is no 'outside' to which such outgoing forces could flow.

Obviously, to speak of a 'closed system' in connexion with Infinitude is in every way a misnomer as well as a logical absurdity.   The term is here used as illustrative and not descriptive.   Furthermore, what is here said of the so-called Law of the Conservation of Energy applies likewise to the so-called scientific Law of the Conservation of Matter, because in the view even of modern science, force and matter are fundamentally or essentially one.

In similar manner the student of the Esoteric Philosophy can recognise the other so-called scientific Law of the Correlation of Forces or Energies only with immense reserves; and the same remark applies with equal emphasis to the scientific speculation called entropy, or the theory that the available stock of energy in the universe is steadily flowing to lower levels, so that ultimately the available forms of energy will have vanished and there will be no further possibility of inherent movement in the system, for all will have become a dead energic level.

However, these different scientific teachings, briefly sketched above, are workable enough in 'closed systems' such as are found everywhere, because such 'closed systems' are limited both in extent and time.

Methinks, however, that even the idea of a 'closed system' which is inherent in, or the foundation of, the scientific laws above mentioned is fallacious and not true to Nature.   Such a system would be like a clock which once run down or 'entropized' cannot wind itself up again — a picture adequate for the four walls of a study or a laboratory, but totally unlike what is found in Nature herself.   At the best, a natural organic system or so-called 'closed system,' is an energy- or substance-system of the second order, because whatever its own inherent or creative flow of energies may be, it is surrounded by an inclosing

rooted with divine-spiritual roots in the Boundless Universe, it receives in its highest parts a constant inflow of divine-spiritual forces and substances, which permeate throughout its structure or fabric, building and stimulating and inspiring, and which finally in various forms are radiated away from the system in streams of influence or energy — call these streams by what name one please.

We thus have a picture of Individuals, fundamentally spiritual, growing from forces and substances welling up from within-above, and withal communicating their energies or rather forces to all other entities in the circumambient universe. Hence, every sun, every planetary chain, is a Spiritual Individual, fundamentally and essentially a Cosmic Spirit, to use a well-known phrase, appearing through karmic law or necessity at the beginning of every period of world-manifestation, running its evolutionary course therein, and sinking again into ineffable rest and peace when the world-period has reached its culmination and final end — only to reissue forth again from the bosom of the Universe when the time strikes for a new world-period to begin.

v

It was the guiding Souls or Spirits of the Seven Sacred Planets — let us call them Seven, because H. P. Blavatsky wisely enough when she wrote disguised or hid the truth about the Twelve — it is their

---

system of the first order, with whose energies and substances it is permeated throughout.

Of course such inclosing system of the first order becomes itself a system of the second order on account of a still larger system by which it is surrounded and fed. This is Nature: system within system, each necessary to all and each interacting with all.

The doctrine of entropy is derivative from the so-called scientific laws hereinbefore enumerated. But if it is true in the Universe, why is it that entropy has not yet brought about the cosmic death or 'heat-death' talked of, since it has had eternity to do it in? The question is unanswerable from the standpoint of the materialistic science of forty years ago, with its various laboratory-laws created in the study, many of them now sinking into disrepute.

At best, therefore, the scientific hypotheses or theories respectively called the Conservation of Energy, the Conservation of Matter, the Correlation of Energies, and their dependent hypothesis or theory expressed in the term entropy, are all secondary or contingent 'laws,' so-called. It would seem from the observations and deductions made in the present note that they apply as such secondary or contingent laws to closed systems or organic units only, and become mere speculations without foundation in natural facts of cosmic magnitude, when any attempt is made to apply them to the Universe, the Boundless All.

guiding Souls which are the Kosmokratores, or World-Builders, so often mentioned by the old Greek philosophers. It was these Kosmokratores who builded our world, our entire planetary chain. In just the same way and following the same rule of action, our own planetary chain, including our own globe thereof, is a Kosmokrator or World-Builder aiding in the building and guidance of some other septenary (or duodenary) planetary chain: action and interaction everywhere throughout the Universe: everything interlocked and interworking. All the planetary chains, from the beginning to the end of the Solar Manvantara, or Solar World-Period, co-operate in the solidary work of building each others' respective structures, and infilling each other with the respective characteristic energies and radiations particular to and belonging to each such formative unit or Kosmokrator.

Thus it is that all the planetary chains throughout the solar system work together, aid each other, build each other; and all thus work out their common destiny together. As has been seen from the foregoing paragraphs, the Esoteric Tradition teaches that the solar system is alive throughout — as indeed all solar systems are. The solar system is a living organic entity, its heart and brain combined in the Sun; and this system is composed of organs, just as, in the small, man's body is an organism composed of organs and incidentals such as flesh and bones and sinews and nerves and what not.

Likewise, and by the same tokens and following the same rule of reason, each planet of the solar system is an entity, a living entity. Our Moon, however, is an apparent exception, because it is a corpse and therefore cannot be called a living being, albeit its particles as particles are as much alive and as active in their small spheres as are the particles of the human corpse. But although a dead and dissolving entity, it is nevertheless septenary, because it is a chain, although a dead chain, of seven moons which were once a living system or organism. The Moon-chain, therefore, has seven bodies, seven dead bodies, which now represent what was the once living Moon or Moon planetary chain. The planetary chain of which the Moon in its first appearance was the reimbodiment aeons and aeons agone, had itself disintegrated into its component life-atoms, into the atoms of 'blue ether,' which ages and ages later re-collected by psycho-magnetic attraction to re-form, to become, to rebecome, the then new Moon-chain in its entirety. Long before we of Earth shall have attained our Seventh Round, our Moon, and all the globes of the Moon-chain, will have dissolved utterly away. This simply means that their component life-atoms will have then disintegrated and fallen apart, as do the atoms of every decaying physical corpse, and all those then disintegrated Moon-atoms will be drawn to the Earth and into the Earth, because attracted hither by the same psycho-magnetic forces which once builded the Moon-chain and later builded the Earth-chain.

When our Earth shall have reached its Seventh Round and have become ready to project its life-essences, which means its hosts of life-atoms, into 'neutral' or laya-centers in space in order to form the (future) Child of the Earth-chain, this Earth will then be or become the Moon of its (future) Child, the chain-to-be, the offspring of the Earth-chain. But our Earth-globe then will be dead, as the moon now is; and as the ages pass, dropping one by one into the ocean of bygone time, our Earth-chain will in its turn thus slowly and slowly disintegrate, dissolve, losing atoms by uncounted millions of millions every day, every year, to speak in human terms of time: until finally the dead body or corpse of this our Earth, and the dead bodies or corpses of all the globes comprising our present Earth-chain, will have in their turn disappeared into blue ether, and all the life-atoms composing them will have flown to rejoin this new reimbodiment, the chain-to-be. The planetary chains thus succeed one another in a regular series, exactly as the reincarnations of a man succeed one another in an identically similar and regular series.

The teaching about the reincarnation of the human Monad makes this matter of the reimbodiment of worlds very clear, for Nature in her operations repeats herself everywhere, although obviously no two processes in any series are identical in all details. Take a physical body: Every atom that is in a man's physical body — excepting those that are in his body as guests, i. e., in it in transit, just passing through it — every atom, which means practically all atoms composing this physical body, was the same atom, and all were the same atoms, that at one or another time helped to make or form his last physical body in the man's last imbodiment on Earth. Every atom that helps to make this physical body, when the man dies and again returns to Earth will go to form that new human body. The rule is fundamentally the same with the celestial globes, therefore with the planetary chains, and likewise the same with the Solar Chain, the septenary or more accurately the twelvefold Globe-chain of the Sun.

Father-Sun, said the ancient Greek and Roman poets, was encircled with seven radiating forces, with seven rays: twelve rays indeed, being the twelve great powers, the twelve great radiant forces flowing forth from its heart and brain; and each one of these rays,

although aided by each one of the other eleven rays, is the spiritually active agent in building a globe in the planetary chain.

We thus see how intimate and intricate are the connexions combining all beings and things together. Every entity, every force,
every substance, in the solar system, co-operates after its own fashion
and with its own life and substance in building the bodies of every
other being or entity in the solar system. In precisely the same
manner, the solar system itself is interconnected and involved with
the vital processes and structural framework of the surrounding
Cosmos or Universe. Thus, our solar system and all in it is interconnected because interlocked with all the other solar systems of
our Galaxy.

Hence there is the closest line of connexions as among the twelve
Houses of the Zodiac, the twelve Sacred Planets of our solar system,
the twelve globes in any planetary chain in the solar system, and
indeed the Universal Solar System itself. Cosmic Nature being an
organism, an organic entity, it is obvious that nothing within it is
exempt from or can be excluded from whatever is or takes place
within its encompassing range. Therefore each one of the globes
of our own planetary chain, called the Earth-chain, is ruled over by,
and is under the especial guidance of, its own particular or most
closely linked portion of the Zodiac, just as in identically similar
manner, each one of the twelve Sacred Planets also is.

Among the twelve Sacred Planets neither Neptune nor Uranus
are counted, although these two latter planets of course belong to
the Universal Solar System.[83] It should not be supposed that Neptune and Uranus are among the five superior planetary chains which
are connected with the five superior globes of our Earth's planetary
chain.[84]

Just as six of the Houses of the Zodiac are psycho-magnetic and
even spiritual opposites or contraries of the other six Houses of the
Zodiac, being in a sense reflexions of them, so are the lower five
globes of the Earth's planetary chain copies or rather reflexions,
which perhaps is a more accurate term, of the superior five globes

83. The reader should remember to make a clear distinction between what
is called in the Esoteric Tradition the Universal Solar System, meaning every
thing or body or being within the Sun's realm, on the one hand, and that particular group of planets in the solar system most closely connected with the destiny
of Earth and its inhabitants. *Fundamentals of the Esoteric Philosophy* contains
some valuable hints as to this point of study, and the reader is referred to it.

84. See the diagram of the twelve globes composing the Earth's planetary
chain given in *Fundamentals of the Esoteric Philosophy*, p. 487.

of the twelve which make the Earth's planetary chain, working around the two middle globes which thus form as it were the hubs around the central axle.

Furthermore, as already hinted at in the preceding paragraph where an allusion is made to opposite signs of the Zodiac and the opposite globes of a planetary chain, planets are at times in esoteric astrology used as convenient substitutes for others, because in such case of substitution the spiritual and psychical resemblances are very great as between the components of any two such powers.

However, in what is said above, only hints are given because it is all a matter of difficult teachings in esoteric astrology. It may here be said in passing that there is indeed a genuine astrology; there is a great and noble Science based on Nature's recondite and sublime operations, which in ancient times was the genuine 'science of the stars,' but it then included vastly more than what now passes current in the Occident as 'astrology.' This Occidental astrology is but a relic, a fragment thereof, a few tattered remnants of the ancient astrological Wisdom combined with quite recent astrological hypotheses born of the imagination or intuition, as the reader will, of modern students.

The ancient Wisdom-Astrology dealt not only with the influences of the planets and the Sun and Moon and the stars on earth and therefore on human life, but it dealt with those celestial bodies primarily as being wholly animate entities; it showed in a conclusive, and what would be called today a scientific, manner our common origin with them and all other beings in the Universe; it showed not only how they affect us, but it showed also what relations we have with them, karmically and otherwise and both in the past and in the future.

There is, indeed, a genuine Astrology, and it is in very truth one of the main branches of the Archaic Wisdom, the Esoteric Tradition. As to consulting modern astrologers: even the tattered modern astrological remnants contain some elements of truth; but modern astrologers themselves are usually reduced mostly to guess-work, despite all their earnest sincerity and good will. The expert among them, all have a certain mathematical machinery which they manipulate more or less cleverly, and from the different ways in which this machinery works in any one instance they deduce, strive to deduce, the true and proper answer to their questioning, but, when all is said, the results are largely guess-work. If they knew the ancient and sublime Science, they would realize how relatively unimportant the modern descendant of the ancient Astrology is. Yet they believe, as does every student of the Esoteric Tradition, that we are intimately

linked with the stars and the sun and planets, and all other celestial
bodies, including, as the Esotericist believes and avers, nebulae and
comets, not only because they act upon us, but because we act and
react upon them, and likewise because we come from them and go
to them in our peregrinations along the circulations of the Universe
in a manner that is as fascinating as it is marvelously beautiful.

As a modern poet, Francis Thompson, says:

> All things by immortal power
> Near or far
> Hiddenly
> To each other linkéd are,
> That thou canst not stir a flower
> Without troubling of a star.[85]

It is a very truth that even the thought of a human being can touch
with delicate tendril of force the corresponding body of every celestial globe; for in the grand organism which Universal Nature is,
each feeblest vibration or flow of energy produces its corresponding
effect, and the originating agent experiences a reaction therefrom in
magnitude precisely equal to the originating causative act or impulse. This thought contains in itself the substance or essence of
the teaching of Karman.

With reference to the statement that was made in a preceding
paragraph to the effect that neither Neptune nor Uranus belongs to
the twelve Sacred Planets which are most particularly connected with
the building and evolution and therefore with the origin and destiny
of the Earth's planetary chain, it may be well to add here a few
observations, which, although of a more or less fugitive character,
it is hoped will be of some value to the reader or student. Uranus
is a member, as said above, of the Universal Solar System — actually an integral part thereof, otherwise, an organ within the organism
of the solar system. But Neptune is not such by right of origin in
this Solar Manvantara. The planet Neptune is what we may perhaps call a 'capture.' One hears in these days of interesting recent
discoveries along the lines of scientific chemical research and consequent theory, and of equally recent scientific deductions drawn
from these discoveries and theories, to the effect that certain chemical atoms, composed as they are of points or 'wavicles' of electrical
energy, at times become electrically hungry, probably due to the
loss of an electron; and any passing electron is then captured by
such an atom and with the capture the atoms become stable, electri-

---

85. 'The Mistress of Vision.'

cally satisfied. Atoms sometimes lose electrons, which for some strange reason seem to be torn out of the atom and become vagrant in the atomic spaces, and for vast distances outside of the atom. Then the atom becomes 'hungry' again.

Now it is curious that according to modern chemical theory, when an atom captures a wandering or vagrant electron and thus becomes electrically satisfied, its electrical polarity changes. This idea the student of the Esoteric Tradition would call a true idea, true to Nature, and it is really a marvel how some of these physical chemists are approaching with each passing year ever closer to some at least of the doctrines of the Ancient Wisdom. Neptune we may call a capture in somewhat the same manner. It is no proper planet of our solar system. It would be correct, doubtless, to look upon Neptune as a captured comet of a certain age; for 'comets' in the Esoteric Philosophy can be of more than one kind. As a matter of fact, comets are merely the first stage in the evolutionary development of all planets, and of all suns too for that matter, because there are planetary comets and solar or cosmic comets — that is, comets which become planets around a sun, and comets which become suns.

As examples, Encke's comet, if it still exists, de Vico's, and Biela's, are three comets that belong as natives to our solar system. They have through the ages, in elliptic orbits, followed regular paths around the Sun; and as time goes on these ellipses should tend to become more circular, and then these comets, if they are not destroyed before reaching this period in their development, will finally settle in life as respectable infant-planets, young planets. They are what one might call planets in a condition preceding their first Planetary Round. To speak plainly, they are reimbodiments of former planetary chains which are now returning to a new manvantaric course in the solar system.

Since Neptune is a capture, it is not connected with the twelve Houses of our Zodiac after the manner that are so connected the true and proper planets of our solar system. Neptune, furthermore, has no genetic connexion with our solar system, but it does influence our solar system, nevertheless, and that strongly, and will continue to do so as long as it remains one of the bodies thereof. Not only does it change the entire polarity, electrically speaking, of our solar system, but it influences everything within the solar system by that fact. Every cosmic body whatsoever is a living being. As an illustration take a family; introduce a new element into that family by importing into its sacred family-circle an outsider, thus giving a stranger a home in the family-circle. Of course the stranger will affect, and perhaps powerfully affect, every member of the family.

It is just so with the planet Neptune. He exercises an influence, astrologically speaking, upon all men, upon all beings and things on Earth. Yet it is an 'outside' influence, although strictly karmic of course. Indeed, everything that is is karmic; it cannot be otherwise than karman. The cause of all such karmic relations or ties, intimate and close, or more distant and less strong, but karmic in every case, is that all things that are, sprang originally from the same great Heart of Kosmic Being, and thus are not only identic in origin and closely related in all the complicated conditions of existence, but ultimately pursue, although by myriadfold changes of pathway, the same course to ultimate reunion with the Divine Source whence all in their origin sprang.

To repeat: Neptune does not belong to our own Solar System, in the sense that the native and congenital planets do belong, or as the members of a family properly belong to the family; thus it is not one of our Solar family; nevertheless it is a living entity through whose veins, so to say, courses the same cosmic life-blood that courses through ours. We have relations with it, karmic relations, otherwise it could never have been captured by our Sun and its attendant family of planetary chains. It should be remembered also that Neptune likewise is a planetary chain exactly as all other celestial bodies are; but with our physical eyes we see only that globe of the Neptunian Chain which is on the same plane of perception where we ourselves are.

Now, not only is each planetary chain of our solar system a living entity itself, but each is the home of vast, characteristically differing populations. Every globe visible or invisible, of the seven (or twelve) globes forming each such chain, has its own population, inhabitants, or denizens. These seven differing classes or families, which we may equally well call life-waves, are all closely linked together in karmic union and destiny, thus forming a distinct Group of closely allied entities; and therefore, each such Group is most closely connected in evolutionary development and growth with its own particular planetary chain.

Furthermore, the various substances and energies which compose each such globe, are the actual product of the hosts of evolving populations or denizens which work in and use these globes, just as the substances and energies which compose a man's body are the products of his own inner and invisible substances and energies which in their aggregate compose his constitution, sevenfold likewise — plus such peregrinating life-atoms or monadic entities which at any time may be passing through his various vehicles or bodies and thus helping to build these last.

During the course of their common evolutionary journey through time, these seven families or life-waves pass in succession, and following each other, from globe to globe of the chain, thus gaining experience of the forces and matters and consciousnesses on all the various planes and spheres that each such chain lives in and itself comprises.

Our own Earth-chain will illustrate this: All the Monads which came over from the Moon-chain were — and are — divisible into seven great classes, or indeed, more accurately into ten; but the three highest classes of the ten we need not further refer to here. These seven classes of Monads compose the grand Life-Stream divided into seven smaller rivulets, each such rivulet being a monadic family, so to speak; and yet they are all connected together because all belong to the grand Life-Stream or River of Lives just spoken of.

The human family or life-wave, which is one of these seven monadic Families or Classes, passes scores of millions of years on each one of the seven globes of our Earth-chain. Then the life-wave leaves such a globe in order to pass to the next succeeding globe, and continues to do so through all the globes in regular serial order; and on each succeeding globe, after a relatively short interglobal period of rest, the life-wave passes another long term of scores of millions of years; and thus the majestic course of evolutionary development or growth proceeds step by step all around the planetary chain, and through each of the seven (or twelve) globes which compose it.

On each one of these globes the human life-wave functions in a manner appropriate to the conditions and circumstances prevailing on each one of these seven globes, precisely as we now function on, or exist on, or live on, our present globe, the Earth, in a manner strictly correspondential with conditions and circumstances prevailing here. This earth being a material world, the circumstances and conditions correspondingly are material. On the higher globes of our chain, circumstances and conditions are much more ethereal; and on the highest are actually quasi-spiritual.

Furthermore, the time-periods passed by any life-wave on the more ethereal globes on the descending and ascending arcs respectively, are much longer than the time-periods passed by such a life-wave on the more material globes, such as is our Earth.

It must also be remembered that the other six rivulets or Monadic Families, belonging to the grand Life-Stream of Monads which came over from the Moon, are, as just outlined in preceding paragraphs, also evolving on all the seven (or twelve) globes of the Earth-chain; but they do not all evolve on any one globe during the same period of time: in other words, their appearances on any one globe are not contemporaneous. There are life-waves or rivulets which have preceded us, and there are other life-waves or rivulets of entities which are following us, and in both these cases on other globes of our chain. But every rivulet, in other words every one of the seven Classes or Families composing the grand Life-Wave, must pass around all the seven globes of the Earth-chain, and each such passage around all the seven globes of the Earth-chain constitutes for such particular rivulet or life-wave a Planetary or Chain-Round.

These seven Life-Waves, the populations of our Earth-chain, pass around the Earth-chain seven times during the course of their immensely long evolutionary journey; and to complete this planetary evolution requires several billions — that is, thousands of millions — of human years.

Because the populations of the seven globes of our own Earth-chain are so closely connected in origin and in destiny, they form a distinct Group, as above stated, of closely allied entities; and therefore such Group is most closely connected in evolutionary development and growth with our own particular chain, naturally. Man, the individual, is connected with and is evolving with his own essential or particular life-wave; such a life-wave in its course of evolution on a globe, is broken up into smaller bodies which we may call nations; the nation is connected with other groups or other nations, forming one human Family; the Families of the earth all are connected and evolving together and forming the Earth-population; the seven populations of our Earth-chain all are connected and evolving together, forming one Planetary Hierarchy; and with the seven Hierarchies of the Seven Sacred Planets, likewise all connected together, forming one Solar Hierarchy, this is a Kosmic unit on a still larger scale. This is one part of what the Hebrew Prophet, Ezekiel, meant, when he recounted his vision, so called, of 'wheels within wheels' — all revolving, all in motion, as individuals, yet forming a unity of beings in movement on a larger scale.

The Solar Hierarchy, considered as an aggregate, will not combine more closely in evolutionary development with the other or second great division[86] of the Universe and its Kosmic hosts, until

---

86. This 'second great division,' the reader may be reminded, refers to one of the 'two main divisions of invisible worlds and spheres' to which allusion is made in the first part of this chapter.

this aggregate of planetary populations shall have evolved, as it were, out of present vibrational rates of substances and matters and forces. But the time will come in the immensely distant future when this vast aggregate of beings in manifold ranges of consciousness and evolution shall have evolved out of its present planes or systems of vibrational rates, or, more accurately speaking, of states of consciousness; and then they, including of course ourselves as humans, shall have expanded through evolution into wider and more universal cognition and experience of forces and substances, entering into wider as well as profounder phases, of evolutionary growth.

VI

The Universe constitutionally is built, as before said, of various worlds and planes and spheres, invisible and visible, extending endlessly in both these directions of being and existence: endlessly towards what we may call Spirit, and endlessly towards what we may call increasing materiality. Therefore the evolving entity, when it has finished one of these cosmic states, or worlds, or planes, enters a higher state or condition of evolutionary growth; or in other words, enters into and upon a higher world or plane of the Cosmic Hierarchy. But it enters such higher world as a beginner, a 'little one,' as the Christian New Testament puts it, as a spiritual child therein, so to say, as an infant in this to it new and higher world; and this evolving entity's destiny it is to receive such expansion of consciousness there as had occurred in smaller degree before in the preceding and inferior world from which it now has graduated.

One may ask: If we have been growing through eternity, why are we no greater, why are we no farther advanced in evolutionary development, than now we are? The question really answers itself. Kosmic Life, working through the Universe, does so not through the physical Universe alone, but through endless stages or degrees or steps of substances and forces, varying greatly in degrees of ethereality or materiality; and with this working therein of the Cosmic Life which manifests itself in armies or hosts of progressive beings, there naturally follows a constantly growing expansion in the perception-range of psychical and physical sense-apparatus.

The human host, when it shall have attained the highest stage of this present World-System or Hierarchy, will blossom forth as full-blown gods, Dhyâni-Chohans, and, after a long period of release from anything that partakes of even the shadow of the suffering and pain or trouble and trial that belong to the material spheres, they will make ready to enter into another and higher system of worlds, which will be — or indeed already is — to them a Universe far more spiritual, far higher in every sense, than this present Universe is to them.

This is the destiny of all evolving lives, man included: endless growth, endless duration in which to learn to know and to understand all parts of all the world-systems, first of the Solar Universe, then of the Universe of the Galaxy, then throughout future time, and in due serial order, the world-systems of Boundless Space: learning through individual experience, and leaving nothing behind to which they must return; for Nature never tolerates wide leaps ahead in irregular evolutionary development as such evolutionary 'jumps' would be.

It is all a matter of expansion of consciousness. For instance, our human consciousness limited to this Earth and possessing vague concepts and dreams of a solar life, enables us to look outwards through our telescopes into the Galaxy and towards the Island-Universes beyond the Galaxy, and have thoughts about them; but they are *thoughts;* they are not the actual becoming of our consciousness *into* those wider spaces filled with Worlds. But our consciousness expands continuously through evolution: it expands self-consciously, first to comprehend all in the solar system, and then still later in aeonic time to embrace the Galaxy, and finally to embark upon still vaster fields within the limitless ranges of Kosmic Space.

Kosmic Space, however, is in a sense limited, however vast, because the Boundless consists of, and in fact is, limitless aggregations of such Kosmic Spaces or Kosmic Universes; but sheer, pure consciousness *per se* is free of limitations in its *essence,* and thus it can be expanded to cosmic dimensions, or conversely, can be, as we humans say, shrunken to electronic magnitude. A man can constrict, can shrink, his consciousness to the point of being suited for inhabiting an electron, and yet in still deeper profundities of his being be as free as the wild winds or the free bird, because consciousness is not and cannot ever be bounded by material extension, subject to mensuration.

On certain ones of the electrons composing even our physical matter, there actually are entities as conscious as we are, it is quite possible thinking divine thoughts, thinking about the Universe, just as we humans do. The cause or reason of this is that all forms of manifested substance, however small, however great, are offsprings of the Cosmic Intelligence; and hence every particle of the Universe, indeed every mathematical point, is as infilled with Cosmic Consciousness, because rooted in it, as is the Universe itself. Thus it is that consciousness is as functional and as active in the electron and its inhabitants if any, as it is functional and active in any other portion or spacial extension, be it even of galactic magnitude or of reaches still more vast.

We humans are still very imperfect in our evolutionary growth. There are beings on other planets of our solar system — one would not call them 'humans,' and yet they are actually more evolutionally advanced than we human beings are — who think diviner thoughts than we do. There are also beings or entities inhabiting the Sun, and its system of globes in its own chain; and consequently the Sun and its globes have inhabitants thinking god-like thoughts, because having a godlike or solar consciousness.

Turning our eyes from the world of infinitesimals, by the same argument that held in the preceding paragraph, we can aver with equal truth that there are 'electrons' also, of kosmic magnitude. Such might our Earth be called. Consider briefly the scale of entitative beings: first there is the Universe, which we may call a kosmic cell, then aggregates of such Universes consisting of star-clusters and nebulae, which one may term kosmic molecules; then in the other direction in our own Galaxy we have groups of solar systems, each one composed of a sun or suns and companion-planets, which we may represent to ourselves as kosmic atoms — the sun or suns being the kosmic protons, and the planets the kosmic electrons; and, as we know, our Earth, which is such a kosmic electron, is builded up of hosts of entities and things formed of the chemical atoms which in their turn are formed of atomic protons and electrons, thus exemplifying the kosmic pattern or rule of repetitive manifestation; and with the chemical atoms we enter on a minor scale of magnitudes, comprised within the kosmic scale. The little mirrors the Great everywhere and in all things; the atom mirrors and duplicates the Universe. The Universal Life, which is another name for Kosmic Consciousness-Force-Substance, which latter is the inner and all-sufficient cause of our own Home-Universe in and through which this Kosmic Life works, is the vital activity of some vast and incomprehensibly great Kosmic Entity, even as the life or vital activity which runs through and in man's physical body is the lowest form of the vital-conscious cement linking all of man's constitution and powers and faculties together into an individualized unit.

Now such a vast Kosmic Entity of super-Galactic magnitude, might consider us in his thought, and wonder, and think: "Can such infinitesimals have thoughts as I have them? Is their consciousness free like mine? Can it reach into the abysmal bosom of things?" The answer would be, Yes, because Consciousness or Cosmic Mind, is the very heart of beings and things, the essence of beings and things; and when a man allies himself with pure or sheer consciousness, he then enters into the Heart of the Universe, the Heart which is nowhere in particular because it is everywhere, as Pascal said, quoting the thought from previous philosophers. The Hindû Upanishads nobly express this thought: अणीयानणीयसाम् (*anîyân anîyasâm*), "Smaller than the smallest atom"; which in Hindû philosophy is equivalent to saying, vaster than the Universe. It is verily so; for *this* is Consciousness-Mind-Life-Substance.

How is it that the Heart of the Universe is everywhere? It is because our Home-Universe is a Kosmic Hierarchy, to wit: a self-contained entity reaching from its highest, that is to say, its divine Root, through many intermediate grades of consciousnesses and substances and forces extending to its lowest, which is the bottom or end of that Kosmic Hierarchy and which is likewise matter for that Kosmic Hierarchy. The Divine Root is its Divine Hierarch, the Divine Heart of Things; and the worlds visible and invisible combine to form the body of this indwelling Divinity, whose heart-beats make the diastole and systole of the Universe. How does it all work? It works wholly through beings and entities — which thus become the vehicles of its multiform action — on the highest rungs of the Ladder of Life, which beings and entities in their turn and after a similar manner, live in and work through other beings and entities still more material than they themselves are; and so forth and forwards and downwards to the grossest matter of that particular System of worlds, or Hierarchy, or Universe — in our own case, our Home-Universe, the Galaxy.

Moreover, each entity within that Kosmic Hierarchy is itself a minor and therefore subordinate hierarchy, because of being a self-contained entity or 'closed system' having its own highest and its own lowest and all the intermediate grades of matters and forces, thus faithfully copying its pattern, the Kosmic Hierarchy, in which it moves and lives and has its being. The Solar System is one such inferior hierarchy, builded withal as a repetitive copy of its grander and larger Kosmic Parent. Furthermore, in any solar system, every individual planet as well as the central luminary, the sun itself, is an exemplification of a hierarchy still smaller, but patterned and builded as is its containing hierarchical parent. And on any such planet, our Earth for instance — in order to particularize more completely — every self-contained being or entity is a hierarchy still smaller, and this is so *just because* it is a self-contained entity.

A man is such an instance, for he is a being or entity having his highest and his lowest, which last is his physical body, and having all intermediate grades of consciousness and substance which together comprise his spiritual and psychical and passional and emotional and vital activities. But throughout all of it and in all of it there works and lives and dwells the Dominant Self, the Overlord of all, man's highest, his own Spiritual 'Wondrous Being' — this last word being a technical term of the Esoteric Tradition. This Wondrous Being is the supreme Chief, the fountain and origin of the fundamental law or consciousness or conscious life of his hierarchy which is in itself an aggregate of his constitutional structure.

As the Hierarchies in the Universe are virtually infinite in number, the Wondrous Beings therefore are also virtually infinite in number, because every such Wondrous Being is such only for its series of lives beneath it. There is the Wondrous Being, the Silent Watcher, for the Holy Order or Brotherhood of Compassion; there is a Wondrous Being for our Globe, the supreme spiritual Chief, who is identic in this case with the Hierarch or Wondrous Being of the Brotherhood of Compassion. There is a Wondrous Being or Silent Watcher for our planetary chain. There is a Wondrous Being or Silent Watcher for our solar system, whose residence, whose habitat, is the Sun. There is a Wondrous Being or Silent Watcher for the Milky Way, for our own Home-Universe, and so forth forever.

In the other direction of thought and following the same rule of invariable repetitive action in Nature, there is a Silent Watcher or Wondrous Being for every atom; and, as before said, there is a Silent Watcher or Wondrous Being for every man or woman, for every human entity, man's own inner god — the Buddha within him and above him, the Christ immanent, which is the core of his being. This core of his being is a god-spark from and of the divine Solar Entity which vitalizes and overlives the entire solar system, and in whom, as Paul of the Christians said, "we live, and move, and have our being."[87]

Children of the Solar Consciousness-Life are we, even as the innumerable lives composing the cells and the atoms and the infinitesimal corpuscles of man's physical body live and move and have their being in man, their overlord: his vitality, their vitality. So we are linked through this Solar Entity of cosmic magnitude with spaces still more grand, with Forces and Substances, far-flung over and in and through Kosmic Space.

---

87. *Acts*, xvii, 28.

Each link in a hierarchy is essential to that hierarchy. Consider Father-Sun: all within his kingdom are subject to his jurisdiction, and yet all are individually relatively responsible. From his heart are sent forth all the currents of mind and life into the outermost fields of the solar system, and every atom responds instantly and spontaneously and inevitably and continuously to the voiceless mandates flowing forth from the heart of Father-Sun. Yet are not the planets individuals withal, and therefore responsible, each within its own sphere? Are we men not bound to mother-planet as mother-planet is bound to the solar system? And is not Father-Sun but a link in the ascending Chain of Beings comprised within the directing and administrative sway of some Kosmic Intelligence still more grandiose than the Sun?[88]

---

88. The 'Sage of Concord,' the great American philosopher, Emerson, voices the ancient thought of the archaic East, as more or less feebly transmitted to us through great Greeks such as Plato, Empedocles, Iamblichus, Plotinus, and others. In his 'Plato; or the Philosopher,' Emerson writes of the Divine Unity which he calls by different names, as for instance here both Soul and Spirit:

"Soul — one in all bodies, the pervading, uniform, perfect, pre-eminent over nature, exempt from birth, growth and decay, omnipresent. . . . The knowledge that this spirit, which is essentially one, is in one's own, and in all other bodies, is the wisdom of one who knows the unity of things. As one diffusive air, passing through the perforations of a flute, is distinguished as the notes of a scale, so the nature of the Great Spirit is single, though its forms be manifold. . . ."

Or again in his treatise on 'The Over-Soul':

". . . that Over-soul, within which every man's particular being is contained and made one with all other; . . . . We live in succession, in division, in parts, in particles. Meantime within man is the soul of the whole; the wise silence; the universal beauty, to which every part and particle is equally related; the eternal ONE."

And again, from the same treatise:

". . . the heart in thee is the heart of all; not a valve, not a wall, not an intersection is there anywhere in nature, but one blood rolls uninterruptedly an endless circulation through all men, as the water of the globe is all one sea, and, truly seen, its tide is one.

"Let man, then, learn the revelation of all nature and all thought to his heart; this, namely; that the Highest dwells with him; that the sources of nature are in his own mind. . . ."

And finally, the same deep thinker, who in so many passages strikes a note which almost persuades one to believe that his brain had been touched by the thought of the Nirmânakâyas, writes, in his essay on 'Intellect':

As Vergil, the initiate poet and visioner, says in his *Aeneid:*

> Know first, the heaven, the earth, the main,
> The moon's pale orb, the starry train,
> Are nourished by a soul,
> A bright intelligence, whose flame
> Glows in each member of the frame,
> And stirs the mighty whole.[89]

". . . that lofty and sequestered class who have been its prophets and oracles, the high priesthood of the pure reason, the *Trismegisti,* the expounders of the principles of thought from age to age. When, at long intervals, we turn over their abstruse pages, wonderful seems the calm and grand air of these few, these great spiritual lords, who have walked in the world — these of the old religion — dwelling in a worship which makes the sanctities of Christianity look *parvenues* and popular; for 'persuasion is in soul, but necessity is in intellect.' This band of grandees, Hermes, Heraclitus, Empedocles, Plato, Plotinus, Olympiodorus, Proclus, Synesius, and the rest, have somewhat so vast in their logic, so primary in their thinking, that it seems antecedent to all the ordinary distinctions of rhetoric and literature, and to be at once poetry, and music, and dancing, and astronomy, and mathematics. I am present at the sowing of the seed of the world. With a geometry of sunbeams, the soul lays the foundations of nature. The truth and grandeur of their thought is proved by its scope and applicability, for it commands the entire schedule and inventory of things for its illustration."

What Emerson saw in these great men of Greece and Rome, was what he likewise clearly discerned in the majestic and stately thought of ancient India, as in the Upanishads, with which it is certain that Emerson had at least some acquaintance, and this that he saw was precisely those dazzling rays from the body of the Esoteric Tradition which these titan Intellects of the past had been taught and in their turn taught to others.

Finally, Plotinus, in his treatise: 'The Three Primordial Essences,' V, i, 2, 3, 4, makes his thought still clearer:

"It is by the Cosmic Spirit that the system of the world, so myriad-formed and various, is one vast whole. Through this spirit the Universe itself is a divinity; and we ourselves and all other things are whatever we are in our noblest by virtue of this all-permeant Cosmic Spirit. Our individual spirit is identic with this Cosmic Spirit through which also the gods themselves are divine beings. . . . Thus the essence of the spirit is incomparably higher than anything which has form. Honoring the Cosmic Spirit everywhere, it leads us to honor our own individual spirit . . . but over this Spirit Divine there is something loftier and still more divine, the origin and source of the former. . . . In this diviner still all that is eternally alive is contained. Naught is there in it but the Divinest Intelligence; all is Divinity; and here indeed is the home of every individual spirit in peace eternal."

89. Book VI, vv. 742-7. Translation by Conington.

The great Latin poet goes on to tell us that: "Hence also spring the races of men and of beasts, and the lives of the flying things, and the monsters that the ocean bears beneath its crystalline surface."[90]

There, indeed, is the spirit of the ancient Pantheism, differing so greatly from what modern European philosophers mistake true Pantheism to be: comprising no personal supreme divinity responsible for all the evils and the woes which, according to mediaeval theory, 'he' has created his unfortunate children to undergo, and has then abandoned them, mayhap, to eternal torment because they were created by him too feeble to resist the temptations of surrounding nature, also created to be stumbling-blocks, according to the theory. Archaic Pantheism, in its original sense, is the teaching, the belief, the intuition, that back of all, behind all, within all, beyond all beings and things, there is a Divine Essence which lives and moves and operates in billions and trillions and quadrillions and indeed in innumerable multitudes of life-consciousness rays, through all Being: the eternal Consciousness-Life-Substance, super-spiritual, from which the entire Universe flows forth, and back into which it will in due course of the revolving ages return — *that* is archaic Pantheism, the Pantheism of the ancients, of the Ancient Wisdom, of the Esoteric Tradition.[91]

---

90. Book VI, vv. 728-9.

91. The Esoteric Philosophy of necessity is substantially Pantheistic from one point of view, but assuredly never so in the manner in which Pantheism is so consistently, and, it would seem perversely, misunderstood in Western lands, but solely in the sense of the ancient philosophers, which sense has been briefly set forth above. Indeed, every philosophy or religion which contains in its theological structure the fundamental conception of all-permeant Divinity, which is at once everywhere and is outside of time and spacial relations in its essence, but which nevertheless is limitless Infinity — any religion containing the conception in its philosophy of infinite divinity is, *de facto*, basicly pantheistic.

Even Christianity, despite the manner in which its God has been set forth by its theological exegetes, is nevertheless pantheistic in basic idea, as much as any other one of the great religions, although this basic idea has been so cloaked and disguised and emasculated that it is reduced to little but the vague statement that 'God is Infinity.'

Obviously, if Divinity is Infinity, it cannot be a Person, because personality implies limitation; and although the Christian God is stated to be 'without body, parts or passions,' being nevertheless considered to be Infinity, it must be as all-permeant, *ex hypothesi*, as could be desired by the most rigid of abstract Pantheists.

All modern European philosophy seems to be tending in its vision towards

VII

There is no similarity except a wholly superficial one between the Christian God and this ancient conception of an ever Unknowable Principle from which all flows forth, and into which all returns: both, it is true, are said to be beyond the range and reach of any human conception, imagination, or similitude; and it should be obvious that the Christians would have to say this also of their divinity, because if such supposititious divinity is not infinite and eternal, both of which attributes are unthinkable by human beings, he would be a finite deity, a mere small god. But the Christian God is a Creator, demiurge, and this is, after all, a big-small god in the boundless spaces of Infinitude, since creation or demiurgic activity instantly implies limitation because restricted activity within something greater; whereas the THAT of the Theosophist and of the Vedic Sages, indeed of all religions of the Archaic World, is no more a creator than IT is a non-creator.

The usage of the word THAT, the Vedic तद् (*tad*), is simply the usage of a word implying abstraction without qualities or attributes suggesting limitations of any kind, thus expressing the utmost abysms of infinitude and of frontierless duration, and we let it go at that — Boundless Space and Boundless Time; because if we limit IT by attributes or other limiting qualifications, we thereby introduce an illogical conception into our first postulate, that IT is unthinkable and ineffable, and in consequence cannot be described in any fashion. IT IS for ever and for ever.

Lest there be confusion of thought, and the reader suppose that this Ineffable is any one, however great, of the Hierarchs mentioned in the preceding paragraphs, it will be well to say that any such Hierarch is but one unit in the mathematically innumerable Hosts which in their incomprehensible Kosmic aggregate form the various

---

some sort of pantheistic type of expression, and the same may be said of the dreams of the most forwards-looking men of modern science. The Holism of Smuts, which apparently is the Holenmerism — or Divinity everywhere in all parts — of ancient Greek philosophy, and the rather vague but interesting pantheistic speculations of the mystically-minded Younghusband, or again the metaphysical dreams of scientific luminaries like Jeans and Eddington who discern 'a Mathematician,' or 'an Artist' at the 'back of beyond': all these and other examples that might be cited show clearly enough that the human mind is incapable of conceiving Divinity as existing otherwise than as being all-permeant, everywhere pervading, in the spiritual worlds as well as in the physical, and thus as being throughout essentially and typically pantheistic in character.

Divinities or active Demiurges — all comprised within the limitless encompassing SPACE of THAT.[92]

The teaching imbodied in the immediately foregoing paragraphs, does not mean that all the vast ranges of Space and Duration between the Unthinkable and us humans, for instance, is Kosmic emptiness, devoid of Mind and Consciousness and Life and Substance. The truth is emphatically the contrary: these endless realms of Space are infilled with innumerable Hierarchies of beings and entities, Divine Atoms so to say, ranging all the way from the gods through the various Hierarchies of minor beings and entities to men, and extending beneath men to other smaller hierarchies of beings and entities and things. Everything and all throughout is instinct with life and thought and intelligence. Every tiniest atom that sings its own keynote (for every atom is in eternal vibration, and every vibration produces a sound), every entity everywhere, and in all the abysmal deeps of boundless Space, and all the orbs of heaven, as they run along their paths, are, each one and all, but children of the Kosmic Life, offsprings of the Boundless.

What do we see when we look around us? Do we see one man for humanity? There is no such thing as 'man,' but there are men. There is no such thing as vegetation, but there are plants. 'Man' as a term is an abstraction describing a host of human individuals. 'Vegetation' as a term is an abstraction describing a host, an army, of plants. The word 'God' is an abstraction, unfortunately with great limitations, properly to be used only in the same way. The Universe is instinct and filled full with intelligences and lives; and it is this diversity in Cosmic Manifestation which causes the diversity so wondrous, so sublime, in everything around us, so that not even two leaves of a tree are alike, so that not even two

---

92. "*SPACE*, . . . is, in reality, the container and *the body of the Universe* with its seven principles. It is a body of limitless extent, whose *PRINCIPLES*, in Occult phraseology — each being in its turn a septenary — manifest in our phenomenal world only the grossest fabric of *their subdivisions*. 'No one has ever seen the Elements in their fulness,' the Doctrine teaches." — H. P. Blavatsky in her *The Secret Doctrine*, Vol. I, p. 342

The reader's attention is directed to the manner in which *SPACE* is here treated as being not only a 'container' of all things, but vastly more than a mere container, because *SPACE* in the teaching of the Esoteric Tradition is the Eternal and Boundless ALL considered as infinitely alive in itself, and therefore containing a limitless plenitude of consciousness-life-substance expressing itself in the fields of Space in interlocking, interblending, interworking, Hierarchies of the Hosts of consciousnesses. These Hierarchies are virtually infinitely numerous.

atoms are identic. If they were they would be not two but one.

The Christian deity is an evolution for the better from the thundering Jehovah of the Jews, who liked the smells of the sacrifice and whose heart waxed wroth in anger. It is in many ways similar to the exoteric Zeus of the Greeks or the Juppiter of the Romans — yet an evolution, through the mediaeval periods, to the modern theological Christian divinity, who seems to be about as colorless as any timid human conception could make him to be.

The Christian trinitarian idea, or the idea of their God being three persons in one Godhead, is but an echo of the old mystical teachings of the Mystery-Schools. There were many Triads in ancient days, and the Christian Triad or Trinity is but a copy thereof — and an imperfect and distorted copy at that. So little do the Christians know or agree upon the attributes of their own Divinity that the question of the procession of the persons from the Godhead was a rock upon which the earlier Church split in twain, the two parts becoming the present orthodox Greek Church and the Church of Rome. The Greek Church taught that from the Father proceeded the Holy Ghost, and from these two proceeded the Son. The Roman Church followed the belief that from the Father proceeded the Son, and from these twain proceeded the Holy Ghost; and this latter is the historic origin of the famous 'Filioque-clause,' meaning 'and from the Son.'

Returning to the teaching regarding the hierarchical structure of Space, and to the collateral doctrine that the summit or origin or fountain of any such Hierarchy is the monadic essence of a Cosmic Spirit, of high or low degree evolutionally speaking, it may be well to reiterate this teaching in once more emphatically remarking that what men call 'Spirit' is the summit, as just stated, or acme or root, or again the seed or beginning or noumenon, of any particular Hierarchy existing in the innumerable hosts of the Cosmic Hierarchies. Equivalently, what men call Matter or Substance, is in one sense the most developed or the most evolved form of expression of the same Spirit in its radiation *downwards,* in any one such Hierarchy. This is but another way of saying that matter is the inherent forces or inherent powers or inherent faculties of that same Spirit which in their journey downwards into manifestation have been unfolded, rolled out, and self-expressed, and in consequence — and this is the important point of thought — is the nether pole of what the original and originating Spirit is; for Spirit is the primal or original source of departure of the evolutionary activity which brought forth through *its own inherent and spontaneously arising energies* the appearance or manifestation in the cosmic spaces of such a Hierarchy. Between first, the Originant or Spirit, and second, the resultant or Matter, there is all the intermediate range of hierarchical stages or steps, thus forming the Ladder of Life or the Ladder of Being of any individual Hierarchy of the Host of Hierarchies.

Thus it will be seen that these Hierarchies do not exist 'merely in' the Kosmos, nor in any sense do they exist *apart from* the Kosmos; nor are they merely *expressions of* the Kosmos. But they are in very fact the Kosmos itself, because not only do they infill it and inform it, but what the Kosmos or Universe is, it is, because it is they. They are the bone of the bone and the blood of the blood, as well as the form of the form, of the Kosmos. Nevertheless, while the Universe is correctly to be thought of as a vast and incomprehensibly great aggregate or collection of Hierarchies, extending into and through the vast ranges of the invisible worlds, in each such Hierarchy, and *a fortiori* as concerns the Kosmic all-inclusive Hierarchy itself, the inmost of each and every one, the highest of each and every one, never itself departs from its own realm or divine-spiritual condition or state; but unrolls forth from itself the descending stages or degrees of the hierarchical Ladder of Life. Thus as Krishṇa says in the *Bhagavad-Gîtâ,* in substance: "I establish the whole Universe with a portion of myself, and yet remain distinct therefrom."[93]

Just so in the case of a man, his spirit is the primal Originant from which his constitution flows forth in descending degrees of substantial concretion, until the physical body is reached. Nevertheless the spirit in a man is not his physical body, but, as Krishṇa says, the spirit establishes the whole man with portions of itself, after the meaning hereinbefore outlined, and yet remains on its own plane and distinct. This is the heart or genuine substance of the archaic pantheistic idea.

Yet every human being, to mention one hierarchy, is in his essence a spark of the divine fire of consciousness in and of the Universe — divine, spiritual, intellectual, ethereal, astral, as well as physical, in its farthest reaches. A great loss of esoteric and mystical truth in the Occident, a loss due to miseducation in religious thought for nigh upon two thousand years, has been the supposed separate existence of the individual human being from the Divinity which infills the Universe. How is this possible! Nothing is so near as Divinity, nothing is so intimate, nothing is so familiar; for the Kosmic Divinity is that Kosmic Consciousness, that Kosmic

---

93. Ch. x, śl. 42.

Life, frontierless and indivisible, which fills everything and throughout boundless duration infills everything, and of which everything and every being is an offspring — not only human beings, but every other entity and thing in boundless Space.

VIII

There is an infinite and a universal brotherhood among all beings; there are no radical separations, no root-divisions, anywhere; what man thinks, he thinks because the god within him thinks, and his human brain receives the divine thought, and interprets it feebly because humanly, and as we human beings evolve, we shall interpret these divine thoughts of the divine thinker within, more and more perfectly, as evolution, growth, development, bring them forth.

The Universe is our Home. We are brothers, we also are essentially akin to the gods, for their life is our life, their consciousness is fundamentally our consciousness, their being is radically our being, their origin is our primal source, their destiny is ours; and what they are, we in essence are — Children of the Gods!

What a wondrous field of thought this opens to the reflective mind! When man feels himself thus at-one with all that is: when he feels that the consciousness which he calls his own is but a god-spark, so to say, of some vaster Consciousness, in which he lives; and that the very atoms which compose his own body are builded of infinitesimal lives which infill those atoms and make them what they are; when he feels that he can pass along the pathways of his own spirit ever more and more inwards into a closer and straiter union with some self-conscious Entity still more sublime than his own highest: then he feels not only a keen sense of his own high human dignity, but he looks out upon the universe around him, and his heart then broadens, and his mind expands, in sympathy, love, and benevolence towards all other beings and entities and things. Vast sweeps of consciousness open up for him as being his own future; duty takes on a new and gloriously bright aspect; right becomes the law of his living, and ethics no longer are a more or less tiresome code of abstract teaching, but very living and vital maxims of conduct; for he instinctively knows that by living in harmony with Nature's Harmony, he becomes self-consciously ever more at-one with it, and instead of opposing and battling with other entities and things, as the totally wrong ethic of all modern scientific thinking has it, his new vision makes him to become helpful, and he obtains a growing understanding of all others, because in proportion as he understands himself, he understands other beings and entities, also recognising that they are derivatives from the Fountain of Life and Mind and Consciousness which are his own fontal source.

Now, what relation has this expansion of man's consciousness with the invisible spheres and worlds of the Universe? When man, either through evolution in the far-distant future, or by special occult and esoteric training which our Great Teachers can give to those well worthy and qualified to receive it: when man rises above the magnetic and psychical attraction of this our earth-sphere of astral and physical matter, and functions in his higher principles and elements, which are his inner forces and substances making up his composite constitution: then he will be able to function and live and act on and in the inner and invisible worlds and planes and spheres of the entire solar system, as easily as he does on the visible earth to-day; because then he will be an inhabitant of those inner planes or worlds or spheres, with bodies and senses fit and adequate for life there, and with ever strengthening faculties making him progressively fitter there to live and to act. This high state mankind will reach, as a human host, when in the far, far future, evolution shall have brought man to be, self-consciously in thought and in function, the inner god that he even now actually is in his inmost essential Self.

When personality vanishes into individuality, in other words, when the corruptible becomes the incorruptible, when the dissoluble is transformed into the Indissoluble, into the Undecaying, into the Undying: then man shall have attained his final growth in evolution in this present System of Worlds. He then shall have knowledge and vision and consciousness in all fulness, because he shall see and feel that he actually is one in his essential Selfhood with the Divine.

CHAPTER VII

EVOLVING SOULS — I

THE theme of study of the present chapter and of the one which follows turns around what is really one of the most wonderful teachings of the Ancient Wisdom, otherwise the Esoteric Tradition, but the difficulties involved in any even tolerably adequate elaboration of it are simply enormous, mostly because of the novelty of this theme to Western minds.

It is of course true that every portion of the human race in its philosophical or religious literatures has an opportunity of knowing something of what the ancients thought concerning the denizens or inhabitants of the worlds both visible and invisible, but such presentation of the Archaic Philosophy is almost always highly metaphorical, and has become so involved in orthodox religious teaching, that minds have crystallized around these forms, and are therefore unready to receive what appears to be offhand a new and indeed unheard-of explanation of these philosophical and religious fragments.

Nevertheless, an attempt will be made, however imperfect, to draw aside the veil as to the inner meaning of this portion of the archaic Theosophy; and it is hoped that the results of the study contained in this and in the succeeding chapter will provide at least a framework of material upon which the reader or the student may erect a more satisfactory superstructure builded of his own deductions, once his attention has been directed to the source to which he may turn.

Just as one of the fundamental teachings of all the great Sages and Seers was the existence of hierarchies within hierarchies forming the structure of the Universe, and of the worlds both visible and invisible in which these hierarchies of beings lived and worked, so likewise did their teaching contain in more or less elaborated formulation the corollary that all these beings inhabiting these interlocking hierarchies were evolving, growing, progressing — a strictly logical and necessary corollary; for if one postulates a static universe, one must further reason that each and every hierarchical range of beings has existed in its present stage during all past time, and will continue to so exist into an endless future; or, that each class of such beings was at some time 'created' to its present status by the whim of a Deity entirely outside of the universal scheme.

The present writer was once jocularly asked the question why he so often used the expression 'evolving souls' rather than 'revolving souls.' The question, however, was not so unimportant as it might appear to be to the casual thinker. Indeed, the difference between these two verbs, as is shown throughout the entirety of the Jewish Qabbâlâh, in other words the difference between the *evolution* and *revolution* of spirit into matter and of matter again into spirit, is but slight, so far as the two words alone go; so that one may truly say that souls *revolve* along the pathways of life from the eternity of their past into the eternity of the future, yet such revolving obviously involves the idea of *evolving;* and that therefore the doctors of the Qabbâlâh were right when they used the term *Gilgûlîm* to signify this revolution in destiny of an un-self-conscious god-spark — a life-atom of the spirit, so to say — through all the ranges and stages and planes of illimitable duration, and on all the planes and worlds of being, unto perfection, or at least unto relatively perfected unfolding of their innately divine-spiritual capacities.

Yet despite the apparent slight distinction between these two words, a study of the Esoteric Philosophy shows clearly that profound questions of evolutionary growth are involved in this distinction.[94]

---

94. In order not to interrupt the intricate and indeed extremely complicate theme of the line of thought followed in the present chapter, it seems wise to append this footnote as an explanation, however brief, of the difference between 'evolving' and 'revolving' Monads — or what, for purposes of simpler exposition, are called 'souls' in the present chapter. Monads, of course, is the correct term for these beings, but this latter word is uncommon in Western thought except for those who are acquainted with the philosophy of Leibniz for instance.

The reader is requested to remember that the Universe is a vast organism, a living organic Entity composed of myriads of invisible and visible worlds, each populated with inhabitants or races of beings or denizens appropriate in type and character to the respective worlds which they inhabit. All these hosts of beings are in unceasing states of developmental growth. These hosts of beings are divided into great Families which follow paths of experience from the spiritual down through all the intermediate ranges or stages of substance to the physical, and then backwards again to the spiritual. These families may be called life-waves. As these life-waves descend from the spiritual, the process comprises an evolution or rolling forth of matter and a coincident infolding or involution of spirit. This continues until the lowest possible range is reached that any one such life-wave can attain in that Manvantara or World-Period, whereupon the process is reversed and the ascent along the Luminous Arc is begun, comprising a process the converse of what the former was: i. e., an evolution or unfolding of spirit again, and an involution or inwrapping of matter.

When one speaks of the relative perfection that may be and certainly will be in due course of the revolving ages attained by the evolving Monads, this term 'perfection' must not be misunderstood to imply either static immobility after its attainment, or, on the other hand, the reaching of an absoluteness in evolutionary unfoldment beyond which further evolution is impossible. Such attaining of a purely hypothetical 'absolute' ultimate is impossible, because there are no utterly absolute 'absolutes' anywhere in the Boundless. How can there be such? How can an evolving Monad reach an end, whence there is nothing further in the way of growth or farther progress? Could such a one reach an absolute and final end, then he must have started from a beginning; for a sempiternity of an entity or a thing — in other words a thing which is eternal and endless in one direction, the future, but has beginning in the other direction, its commencement — is a logical monstrosity. If we, as examples, being imbodied Monads, had a beginning — speaking of 'we' in the sense of the immortal monadic element in us — then we sprang from something other than ourselves, something other than our highest; but our highest is the highest in the Kosmos, for that highest is indeed that aggregate of divine Powers, logically a Unit, which enlivens and inspirits the Universe, and which is endless in

---

This process continues for the life-wave until it reaches the spiritual realms again plus all the vast treasury of garnered experiences, and after a period of Nirvânic rest, the units composing such life-wave begin a new course similar to the last but on somewhat higher grades all along the line.

Now this process of passing through these different worlds or spheres or planes may be likened to the rolling forwards or revolving of the great Wheel of Life, the individual units of this life-wave thus being properly spoken of as revolving Monads or 'souls.' These revolvings might likewise be called gyrations or cyclings or circlings or wheelings; or again, on account of the travelings through time and space, the process may be called a series of circumrotations or transrotations. The old term for this process was transmigration — a word grossly misunderstood in the West. It could likewise be called metempsychosis, as comprising changes in the 'souls' which follow this long course of developmental unfolding of faculty and power and consequent organ.

Thus then, 'evolving' means unwrapping or unfolding the faculties and powers already in the being or entity but in a latent or sleeping condition; whereas the *path* pursued by these evolving entities being of the nature of a cycling or wheeling or revolving, the entities following such path may be said truly to be 'revolving souls.' The two terms, therefore, are seen to be not only cognate in etymological meaning, but also to express two pictures of the entire manvantaric course of growth and experience that the growing beings pursue.

both past and future, and of which we are monadic sparks, growing monadic essences, evolving Monads, revolving Monads.

I

In order that there may be no misunderstanding as regards the two words evolution and souls, it may be well to explain what is here intended by the use of the terms. Lamentable ignorance is betrayed everywhere in Occidental minds when they attempt to define what they mean by 'soul' and by 'evolution,' for almost invariably those nouns are used in a manner that shows that the ideas connected with them are as indefinite and uncertain as they are inchoate and elementary. The great majority of Western thinkers rarely even stop to analyse what they mean in using these words, yet accept them and employ them in consequence as mere verbal counters, because other people have used them.

But the uncompromising and inflexible logic of the Theosophical philosophy does not permit us to use words with such vague and nebulous meanings, for the student of the Esoteric Wisdom has discovered that it is necessary to speak with care and due consideration of the import of the terms which are employed in all studies appertaining to subjects so profoundly philosophical as well as mystical in character. Furthermore, the student is always obliged to remember that words, in the language of Homer, are 'winged' transmitters of living thought, and consequently are more than mere counters; and although the student naturally has to employ the vernacular of the time in which he lives in order to be understood and to pass ideas into waiting and intelligent minds, nevertheless because of the paucity in European tongues of words of abstract philosophical import, it is frequently necessary not only to invent or to 'coin' adequate words, but also to employ well-known words of accepted currency in their original or etymological significance. The latter usage is exemplified in such words as 'evolution' and 'revolution.' Both these words are of Latin origin. 'Evolution' means the 'rolling out,' the 'unwrapping' of that which previously had been inwrapped or infolded. Its significance, therefore, is self-expression, expression of the Essential Self, the latter being what the Theosophist otherwise calls *swabhâva*, a word derived from the Sanskrit. 'Revolution' is likewise a word of Latin origin, with the same etymological meaning and derivative usages that the word evolution has, but because of the preceding particle represented by the letter 'r,' the meaning is intensified, pointing to repetitive action.

It is obvious that the vast multitudes of beings which compose
the Hierarchies of growing and progressing entities infilling the spaces
of Space, are not in a state of quiescence or inactivity, but contrariwise, are all of them without exception and without regard to degree
of spiritual and intellectual unfoldment, in a state of continuous
motion both in time and in space, as well as in evolutionary growth.
Nothing in the Universe stands still, for this is contrary to the fundamental impulses of Cosmic Life, the most marked of whose attributes
is unceasing activity — at least during the course of a Manvantara
or World-Period.

Now this unceasing motion of these armies of beings, both collectively and distributively as individuals, is *growth:* commonly
growth forwards in evolutionary unfoldment, or in what it is customary to call progressive development, and, much less frequently, activity in a retrogressive line or direction; but it is activity or movement in either case. It is for the foregoing reason that all these
beings which for the purpose of easy understanding and simple
expression we may speak of as 'souls' — imperfect and ambiguous
as this term certainly is — are described as 'evolving,' i. e., as being
engaged in an incessant process arising in inherent impulses of unfolding or unwrapping or unrolling, i. e., 'evolving' innate or hitherto
latent forces and substances within themselves.

Considered from this standpoint, these evolving 'souls,' or more
accurately stated, these evolving Monads, are working out their
destiny through the process of evolution just briefly depicted; but
at the same time they are likewise following courses of repetitive
action in time and space which seem to be best described by the word
'revolving.' They are not merely 'evolving,' i. e., growing in unfoldment, but are likewise engaged in 'revolvings' or 'whirlings' in and
through the different worlds and planes and spheres not only of our
Planetary Chain, but of the Solar System. Just as evolution, or
growth in the unfolding of latent faculty, is both continuous and progressive, so are the 'revolutions' of these evolving monads continuous and likewise progressive in the sense of rising or falling into
higher or lower worlds or spheres respectively.[95]

Biological researchers in European countries from and indeed before the time of Lamarck and Darwin have speculated far and wide
as to the meaning and the cause of the undoubted differences in the
families of so-called animate beings, these differences presenting a
picture of a Ladder of Life or scale of creatures which in some manner

95. See note No. 94, pp. 212-3.

are linked together by close bonds of similarity, and yet present equally marked and often confusing differences as among themselves. Faithful study of these similarities and differences long since brought thoughtful biologists to the conclusion that living beings are closely related, or more distantly related as the case may be, yet related in both instances; and there slowly grew into almost universal acceptance the conviction that all nature was under the sway of a primal impulse, urging on creatures towards progress through growth. This is the so-called evolutionary law or law of evolution; and the word is both apt and descriptive.

It is not the intention in this work to embark upon the otherwise fascinating topic of the differences that exist between the Theosophical teaching of evolutional emanation and the still more or less materialistic biological teaching about evolution which even today holds the field in modern thought — although indeed it is only fair to say that modern scientific ideas about evolution are beginning to wander far from the rather crude, because new and imperfect, ideas that the great Darwin himself taught. It will suffice here to state briefly that the teaching concerning evolution as given in the Esoteric Philosophy is primarily one of unfolding from within and the releasing of infolded or innate forces and faculties which as time passes seek their expression in and through organisms in the form of developing faculty followed by the appearances of consequent organ and organic activity thereafter.

The Theosophist conceives evolution as a process of unfolding beginning within the entity and expressing itself outwards; and it is just here where the Theosophist is obliged to part company with the Darwinian or the quasi-Darwinian or still more modern conception of evolution as being mere accretion following accretion in the bodies of growing beings.

The source of evolution therefore lies within each evolving entity or being itself: within its character or 'soul,' what may here be briefly described as its swabhâva, i. e., its character expressing itself in equivalently characteristic forms. To illustrate: why is it, even on the physical plane and as seen in cases of animals and plants, that a seed, animal or vegetable, which is sown produces always its like? An apple-seed produces an apple-tree always and will not produce a fig-tree nor a banana-plant, nor a strawberry-vine, nor anything else but an apple-tree. The fact is so common and so familiar that it is apt to be passed over without comment. Similarly through all manifested existence. Why? At the heart of that seed, behind it and within it, is its own minor Essential Self, its individual characteristic or swabhâva, which is what the ancient Stoics called a 'spermatic logos' (a seed-logos): in other words a psycho-spiritual essence or Monad, an individuality, which obviously can produce nothing but itself and from itself, because, obviously, if it produced seeds from other than itself, those seeds would not reproduce or grow into similar individuals closely alike to itself. What is there within this seed which governs its direct path in growth? We cannot see this invisible factor; we cannot analyse it in the laboratory. It is the inner latent powers, capacities, forces, energies, i. e., the 'soul' of the being, expressing itself in the new generation or rebirth. Itself expresses itself. The 'evolving soul' reproduces itself in the new life, and does so because it is 'revolving' through the spheres.

This is evolution, 'revolving' as well as 'evolving,' both signifying and implying the coming forth of what is within — and nothing can come forth except that which is within. The rule applies not only to the human kingdom, nor to the beast-kingdom, nor to any other single kingdom of beings, but applies to everything everywhere throughout the entire ranges of the Cosmos, for evolutionary growth is universal. It is in all cases the interior self self-expressing itself.

The innate powers or faculties or capacities, whatever they may be, in the long pilgrimage of human evolution, and indeed of the evolution of every other entity and thing in the Boundless All — all these faculties and powers are not added unto the being evolving in growth, after the fashion of Darwinistic transformism, but are the outward expression of interior causes. Evolution, therefore, is not the accretion unto an evolving individual of parts from without, nor the improvement of organ or faculty by the impact of exterior forces arising in the environment only, which thus form or change the imperfect organ into a better one, but is the throwing outwards of forces and indeed faculties and powers latent in the being or entity itself.

The principle of evolution is well illustrated in the small in the ordinary processes of physical growth, as that of the infant into the child and of the child into the man, with a consequent improvement in expression of faculty met by an increasing usefulness of the organ through which the faculty expresses itself. In living he grows, and in growing he advances by pouring forth that which was in him before, but improved nevertheless at each new going forth into manifestation, at each new age of such rolling out or 'evolution' of latent and sleeping capacities. This is, in brief, what the Theosophist means by evolution.

Theosophists, in addition to being evolutionists in their own technical sense of that word, are also decided emanationists, perhaps even more so than they are evolutionists. This word 'emanation' is also from the Latin, with a meaning very closely akin, at least mystically so, to the meaning of evolution as above described. 'Emanation' is a Latin compound meaning 'the flowing out' of what is within, and one can here see immediately that the difference between the flowing out of what is within, and the unrolling or the unwrapping of what is already inrolled and inwrapped as the substance itself of a being, is very small indeed.

There is a distinction, nevertheless, between these two terms. The Theosophist speaks of *emanation* of the gods from their still more divine parents; yet one might just as correctly speak of the *evolution* of the divine beings governing the cosmos as to say that they 'emanated' from their divine forebears; notwithstanding this, the word evolution is employed more particularly to signify the process of the unwrapping or coming forth into manifested activity or into energic manifestation of the divine into less ethereal parts which are innate and as yet non-expressing within the growing being.[96]

---

96. It would seem advisable to attempt briefly to clarify by a few distinctions the difference which lies between the two words emanation and evolution, both so important in their respective ways. These two words approach each other closely in meaning, yet are not only distinct but different. Emanation, as said in the text above, signifies an outflowing of a Monadic Essence or a Monad from a parent source; evolution signifies the unwrapping or unfolding of what lies latent or rather unmanifest in the constitution of a being. Emanation, therefore, may be illustrated by the case of the Sun which is, during the entire Solar Manvantara, emanating or throwing forth from itself innumerable octaves of radiation. These different forms of radiation are at once force and substance combined, and considered analytically each such form or class of radiation is compounded of radiation-units, force-units, which at one and the same time may be considered to be discrete particles or compounds of energy and equivalently compounds or wavelets of substance. Modern science which is so rapidly approximating to conceptions which are fully as metaphysical and indeed as mystical as anything of its kind that the Theosophical Movement has uttered, speaks of these units of energy as quanta of energy or photons — which is an exceedingly good description for the quasi-astral and quasi-material plane where these energy-quanta or photons are placed by scientific thought.

Consider, therefore, these vast numbers of photons which have been emanated or radiated from the Sun, as individuals, undertaking, if you please, individual peregrinations or pilgrimages throughout the solar system. Each one when radiated begins a cycle of experience precisely as the Monads of the Theosophical Philosophy do when first emanated from their Divine Parent. Each such Monad or spiritual force-unit, if the term can be used, once emanated,

II

Now these growing or evolving beings, thus emanated from their more spiritual forebears, are the causal factors in evolution. They are what we may call 'souls,' adopting a familiar word. They are likewise compounded beings — not pure Monadic Essences. They evolve because they pass through stages: they pass from the imperfect to the relatively more perfect, from the young in evolution to the more mature in evolution, and from the mature to age; and then when the Grand Round of peregrinations or revolvings in the Solar System is accomplished, and the Solar Manvantara comes to its end, these Evolving Souls, thus having reached relative perfection, are withdrawn into the Cosmic Oversoul, and therein remain for the entire term of the Solar Pralaya or period of Cosmic Rest. When the Solar Pralaya in its turn has reached its end, and a new Solar Manvantara is about to open in a new period of Cosmic Manifestation, these perfected Monads then reissue forth to begin a new course of life and activity therein but on higher series of worlds or planes than

---

has begun its cycle of *evolution*, rolling forth or unwrapping from itself by karmic necessity its own latent powers or faculties which in time develop forth appropriate organs through which it expresses itself.

We have, then, first the emanation or flowing forth from the Originant or Source of these hosts of individual Monads which immediately begin their ages-long peregrinations through the different realms visible and invisible of the solar system; and from the instant they are once radiated or emanated from their divine source, they begin to *evolve*, first by automatic unfolding or unwrapping of innate forces or energies, and at a later stage continuing the process through self-devised efforts in bringing out the inner or superior and as yet unevolved parts of their essence.

The reader should note two or three important points in this marvelous process of birth or emanation, and of unfolding growth or evolution. First, each new evolutionary impulse that such an evolving Monad experiences is itself a minor emanation from the heart of the evolving being; second, each such expenditure of evolving energy which in its first form is an emanation, is itself but giving birth to a minor entity which we may call a life-atom, which in its turn begins its evolutionary pilgrimage through the same process of unfolding growth or evolution; and third, it is at once seen from the foregoing that emanation and evolution are really but two forms of the same activity: one the emanative or original, and the other the unfolding or evolutive. So that each emanation can likewise be considered to be a form of evolution, and each new evolutionary impulse can equally well be looked upon as an emanational outflow. Thus it is that the twain are essentially one activity manifesting after two different manners, and it is this difference of manners which is the distinction between the two forms of the fundamental process of developmental growth.

the aggregate in which they had formerly been involved as evolving beings.

In frontierless space there is a perfectly incomputable number, an infinite number, of evolving Monads, which one may here speak of as 'souls' using this word in a very general sense without any technical significance. These 'souls' are expressing themselves in all-various forms, and they exist everywhere and are the causal factors, as above stated, in the complexity and diversity which surrounds us everywhere in universal Nature. Some armies or hosts of them express themselves in matter as material beings and entities; others in the invisible ranges of the Cosmic Ether, or rather in the Cosmic Ethers, as ethereal entities. Other hosts express themselves in the still higher spiritual realms; other hosts again, which through evolution have reached higher ranges of Cosmic Life, express themselves in the fields of super-spirit. One stops here in this enumeration, not because there is any limit at all in the Universe, but simply because human intelligence fails to reach higher than spirit, its parent, or, on the other hand, to anything much lower than physical matter, although in very truth there are endless reaches of inhabited worlds in both these directions of space as well as time.

We see diversity everywhere around us; we never see utter uniformity anywhere, which fact means that the consciousness-centers, the conscious force-centers, which interiorly or inwardly infill and actually *are* Universal Nature, are manifesting in all the various and diverse manners which collectively produce the diversity spoken of: gods, Dhyâni-Chohans or spiritual beings, human beings, beasts, plants, minerals, and the beings of the three Elemental Worlds — call them by these names or by any other names one likes — all of them are hosts, families, multitudes, armies; and those which are the nearest akin collect together because of psycho-magnetic attraction as naturally as drops of water or particles of quicksilver will flow together and to a certain degree coalesce.

It is therefore evident enough that if we speak merely of conscious force-centers in the Universe, or if we speak of 'consciousness-centers' as such, or again, if we speak of 'souls,' and do not limit this word as applicable to human beings alone, then the number of them is infinite; because the whole Universe is full: the Universe is nothing but they, a vast aggregation of them. One may say: Where are they? The answer is: Where are they not? Everywhere. Their number is simply unthinkable in any terms of human numerical mensuration.

The number of souls, however, in any particular Host or Family is limited, because that particular Host or Family itself is finite; but the Hosts or Families themselves are infinite in number, *ex hypothesi*, because they fill all space, and we cannot place a limit to Universal Nature or abstract Space.

Space in the conception and teaching of the Esoteric Tradition is not a mere extension of material dimensions, which is but one of the attributes of matter, which is, so to speak, the body of Space. Space is far more than this; Space is the ALL — whatever is, was, or will be, throughout limitless duration; and in addition to this, Space as conceived of in the Esoteric Philosophy is, in consequence of the foregoing postulate, of endless expanse 'inwards' as well as 'outwards,' therefore comprising everything that human intuition even vaguely envisages as the frontierless Plenum or Pleroma of all Being or rather Be-ness, including the limitless Hierarchies of worlds and planes and spheres from the divine or the super-divine downwards through all intermediate grades to the physical and what is beyond physical matter in further continuation of the spacial concept.

Indeed, SPACE, just because it is whatever is in both Infinitude and Eternity, can otherwise be called the shoreless Life-Consciousness-Substance, at once abstract Being and all Causation, over the fields and in the fields of which pulsates throughout endless time the abstract ideation engendered in and born of ITSELF. It is THAT from which all comes, THAT in which all is and exists, and THAT to which all finally returns.

Such therefore is Space, everything that is; and therefore the number of 'souls' which infill and in a sense compose Space is like Space itself, limitless, frontierless, without beginning and without end. All the wonderful phenomena that we humans sense around us in this our material sphere, in the starry heavens, even in the infinitesimal worlds of the atoms, and all between, are simply the outward expressions of these inner causal individuals, infinite in number, as said, and composing the infinite Hosts or Families of beings manifest and unmanifest.

Even the atom is a 'soul' in a sense, although of course not a human soul, nor an animal soul, nor a plant-soul, nor a mineral soul; but an atomic soul, precisely on the same grounds on which we speak of an animal soul or of a plant-soul. It is an atomic soul because its consciousness-center is manifesting in the atomic or infinitesimal spheres or realms, and the physical atom of chemistry, is merely the physical body of it — a merely temporary vehicle truly, because the incessant repetitive reimbodiment of these atom-souls occurs so frequently when compared with human reimbodiment that they seem to take place with scarcely a perceptible interval of time as human beings understand time.

III

Perhaps it is as well to state once for all that although the term 'soul' is used in this and the succeeding chapter as descriptive of these Hosts or Families of beings and entities, nevertheless this descriptive term is obviously open to many well-founded objections; and this is so because of the strong color of significance which the word 'soul' has acquired in Western minds. The exactly proper descriptive appellation for the individuals composing these Hosts or Families, as hinted in a preceding footnote, is the Pythagorean term *Monas,* which in European languages is usually spelled *Monad.* The value of this word, philosophically, is the implication of individuality which it suggests; for these Monads are distinctly individuals throughout the entire term of their manifested existence, or cycles of revolvings or circumrotations or transrotations in a Cosmic or Solar Manvantara.

They may be looked upon, albeit in somewhat metaphysical fashion, as individualized spiritual droplets or 'atoms' of SPACE as hereinbefore described: component drops of the shoreless Ocean of spacial Being. They are the causal Agents, collectively speaking, of all the diversity in the Universe around us; and in their incessant motion or unceasing action, both collectively as a Host or distributively as monadic individuals they not merely compose but actually *are* both the instrumental as well as the substantial causes of the Hierarchies of the Worlds.

They exist in all-various or multi-myriad stages or grades of evolutionary unfoldment or development; so that with this correct picture, brief as it is, in mind, the student may at once see how it is that the Esoteric Tradition speaks of certain aggregates of these Monads as spiritual beings, others as intellectual or Mânasaputric, others again as life-atoms, and others again as being in that particular grade of their monadic peregrination which makes them appear or manifest or show themselves as the particles of material substance.

Let us try to imagine the immense numbers of these beings or monadic entities existing even in our own small realm of space-extension. A cubic inch of air is a small portion of matter, yet the American scientist Langmuir has calculated that the number of gaseous molecules in one cubic inch of air is so immense that if each molecule were enlarged and changed into a grain of fine sand, these grains of sand would completely fill a trench one mile wide and three feet deep and would reach from New York to San Francisco! How on earth is it possible to pack that number of molecules into one cubic inch of air, one may well ask in bewilderment. And air is only a gas, and the molecules are supposed to be relatively far distant from each other, otherwise they would not have the molecular freedom and mobility that makes a gas what it is.

Again, take the human physical body: it has been estimated that it contains some twenty-six thousand billion cells — each one a fairly large physical entity, for each is composed of entities still more minute which give to that cell all its physical being, all its characteristic shape and even size — which make it all that it physically is. These smaller entities are the atoms, each enshrining a force-center, a consciousness-center, a 'soul.'

We are told that the physical atom is mostly holes, 'vacancies' so called, so-called empty space, and that if we could collect the electronic and protonic centers composing the atoms of which a man's body is builded into one point, that point would be invisible to the physical eye! Why then do we see each other? Because — strange paradox — we are mostly 'empty spaces,' vacancies, which produce upon us similarly composed, the illusion of dimension and bulk. Just exactly as the celestial bodies are seen in the abysmal deeps of Solar Space, so, relatively speaking, are there equivalent distances between electron and electron, of which the atoms are composed, and between atom and atom which again build the molecules, which again make the cells, which again form the physical body of man. Just as these celestial orbs are ensouled, so likewise are the atoms of man's body; for there is one fundamental Law, therefore one fundamental individuality or spiritual characteristic, running through every aggregative body or universe, greater or minor; and thus it is that every part of the greatest universe that our imagination can figurate feels the sway and impulse and compelling sanction of that same fundamental Law: in other words, is instinct with the life and consciousness of that same fundamental all-embracing abstract Individuality of which the said Law is the activity.

We can therefore with strict logical accuracy call an atom a soul, because the atom is a transitory event in the life-history of a force-center, or consciousness-center, or Monad, which is a growing, learning, evolving as well as revolving being. The electrons and protons of the atom are but the bodies or veils of still more infinitesimal force-points, or consciousness-points, which make or form or compose these electrons, or protons, and express themselves through these electrical infinitesimals in the sub-atomic worlds. The number of these protons and electrons in a tiny bit of matter, so small as scarcely to be visible to the naked eye, is so great that we must count them in octillions; that is to say, 10 raised to the 27th power, or, in other words, 1 followed by 27 zeros!

Dr. Robert A. Millikan a number of years ago estimated that the number of electrons which pass every second through the filament of a common 16-candle-power electric lamp is so enormous that it would take the two and a half million people living in Chicago, each person counting at the rate of two per second, and working twenty-four hours a day, twenty thousand years to count them; 3,153,600,000,000,000,000 — 3 quintillions, 153 quadrillions, 600 trillions — of electrons and protons pass in one second through the filament of a 16-candle-power electric lamp! Yet each one of these electrical infinitesimals is the physical expression of an evolving and revolving soul — so incomputably vast, so incomprehensibly numerous are they!

It baffles the imagination and surpasses the utmost reaches of it to attempt to form any mental conception of the quasi-infinite magnitudes, so far as numbers are concerned, of these countless whirling circumrotating entities in a single ordinary human body. Here is literally a case where the infinitesimal merges again into the so-called 'infinite,' much as an inverted cone, after passing the point of its origin again spreads forth into a new 'infinite.' The figure is not so bad, because it may be looked upon as an actual *schematic* or *diagrammatic* representation of natural facts.

Furthermore our scientists now tell us that these electronic infinitesimals are the substantial basis of all physical life; that they are the physical building-bricks of the Universe, being at once either force or matter, according to the way in which one looks at it; and each one of these infinitesimals is an incarnate imbodied force-entity, or, in its last analysis, a 'soul'; otherwise, and yet more accurately, a Monad. To such infinitesimals, the body in which they live and move and have their being — our human physical body — is no doubt a mathematically infinite universe, and the human soul, overlording this vast multitude, is to them a god.

The human soul itself is composed of hosts of minor 'souls,' the life-atoms in and through which it expresses itself: hosts of young and learning entities, just as are the cells, and the atoms of the cells, and the electronic infinitesimals of the atoms, all going to make man's physical body. These hosts of minor souls it is which give to the physical body its form and shape, and endow it with consistency and coherence, and enable it to transmit to the outer world the sublime spiritual and intellectual messages passing down through the intermediate vehicles or inner bodies to the mind of the physical man: love, mercy, compassion, pity, knowledge, the teaching of wisdom: all those noble and beautiful things that spring forth from the very core of man, from the heart of his heart, from the core of his core — from his Monadic Essence, the spiritual Center which is his deathless spiritual individuality.

According to the beautiful Hindû picture or figure or metaphor, man is a living tree of consciousness growing with its roots in the spirit above and its branches bending downwards into the material world. Many souls, one spirit: that is the picture of the nature of the human constitution. For the undying force-point or Monadic Consciousness-Center from which the soul, itself a host of minor souls, issues, and which gives to the soul individuality, thus enabling it as an entity to issue forth as a ray: this inmost point is deathless because it itself is one of the host of consciousness-centers or Monads born from within the bosom of the Mother-Spirit: it is a spirit-center, which has not yet become manifested in this sphere, in this world, on this plane. This spirit-center is breaking through, as it were, on its evolutionary journey, new spheres and planes, and therefore it manifests on these lower planes at first but feebly its latent transcendent powers. We must not misunderstand the meaning of this to be that the Monad is something which is destined in the future to become spirit, and now at this present stage of its evolutionary journey is not yet a spirit; that is not the idea. It must be considered to be a spirit-point, which, during the course of its evolutionary journey in the realms of matter, clothes itself in its own rays of light, and these rays of light are what we call the 'souls' in which it vestures itself. But as each such soul or ray is rooted in this spirit-center, the soul or ray has in the core of its being the very nature of the mother-spirit.

Universal Nature, it will therefore be seen, is the vast aggregate of these infinite Hosts or Families of souls or Monads in infinitely varying grades or degrees of development, a flowing stream of evolving entities, as Herakleitos would have said. They are not all alike, these souls or Monads; if so they would all be one. Each one of them is an individual *expressing itself*; yet they group together naturally into classes or hosts or families, each individual in a class holding certain characteristics in common with all other members of the same class; and for this infinite variety of them obviously all the infinite spaces of Space are needed for their imbodiment.

This fact of natural being, i. e., that certain monads are linked together by similar attributes due to evolutionary unfoldment, is the source of thought whence many modern mystics have drawn their idea of families of souls, which families they call group-souls. The idea is true enough as viewed in the light of the foregoing; yet one must not suppose that these group-souls compose groups or bodies essentially distinct or different from each other, but are aggregates of evolving beings which because of similar karmic unfoldment in evolution are brought together in the same relative times and places.

Moreover, when souls aggregate together in nations, for instance, thus forming a body of human beings, or in animal groups, thus forming a family of beasts, we must not suppose that either such nation or such animal group is distinctly oversouled by a unit mother-soul which thus lasts through eternity. It is the karmic similarities of such individuals of group-souls which bring them together into these groups; although no mystical mind would deny the obvious fact that the collective impulses or qualities which such groups have, together form a sort of psychical atmosphere which these group-individuals breathe and live in. Such an oversoul of a group, however, is not a true entity or Individual.[97]

---

97. While what is said in the text above is strictly accurate and concordant with the facts, it must nevertheless be stated that there is another and more esoteric aspect to this which it is extremely difficult to outline satisfactorily in a published work. However, it is possible that the following observations which are appended here may be helpful. Let it be clearly understood that these groups, last spoken of in the text above, whether national or racial, are not manifestations of an actual entitative evolving and revolving being called the Over-monad, or more popularly the racial 'soul'; such groups, however, whether racial or national, are the representatives on earth of what the ancient Latins called a Genius, which is not an individualized entity pursuing its own individual peregrinations through time and space, but is a vague or diffuse energy or rather force in the ideation of the Planetary Spirit, and which is actually evoked into manifestation because of the combined intellectual, psychical and astral, as well as spiritual, forces engendered by racial or national units incarnating more or less contemporaneously.

Such a Genius, whether racial, as Chinese or Scandinavian as examples, or national, such as French or Russian for example, nevertheless exists as above said in the ideation of the Planetary Spirit, and in far distant ages of the future will find itself again in manifestation when the intricate and complicate combined karman of the same individuals once more brings these individuals together, thus creating more or less the same 'atmosphere' which brings about the manifestation of the same Genius, national or racial, between these two epochs latent in the ideation of the Planetary Spirit.

So far as the individuals or human units of a race or even of a nation are concerned, it must never be forgotten that their simultaneous or contempo-

Understanding clearly the above, the student will not be tempted to confuse such aggregates or groups with another mysterious and yet most common fact of universal nature, to wit, the working of individualized monads, call them spirit-souls if you wish, through groups or aggregates, using these groups or aggregates as vehicles. For instance, a tree is an entity, and among the old Greeks its ensouling Monadic Essence was called a dryad, or hamadryad. A tree, thus, is composed of groups of entities, each aggregate group consisting of individuals closely resembling each other. And yet in and through these aggregated aggregates lives and works the tree-soul. So man's body, for instance, is composed of aggregates or groups of evolving monads or life-atoms, the members of each group closely resembling each other and yet all together forming the physical vehicle through which the human soul works. The human soul, being an individual, could not be said to be a group-soul, obviously, nor could the individualized evolving monadic consciousness or life-atoms or *paramâṇus* of any one such subordinate group be said to be portions of a group-soul, because each individual is an individual, but each works with others more or less in its own line of evolution and more or less of the same evolutionary status.

Here then is the picture: Aggregates of life-atoms closely resembling each other combine with other aggregates of life-atoms closely resembling each other in order to form a vehicle — such as the human body — for an evolving soul of a far higher grade. These aggregated individual entities are groups, but they do not form a group-soul, but are themselves *ensouled* by a soul higher than the aggregates and higher than any individual members of such aggregates.

Now the endless chain of lives, above spoken of as being karmically divided into racial or national families, where humans are concerned, or into other family-groups or hosts: this endless chain of

---

raneous incarnation in a race or nation is a matter only of similar karmic characteristics thus drawing these units together into temporary unity. These human souls themselves very quickly wander from such national or racial atmosphere to find the next or the next succeeding imbodiment in some other nation or race to which their karmic proclivities attract them. This is an exceedingly important point because, among other things, it shows the inherent folly, if not stupidity, of blind and unreasoning prejudices based upon mere nationalisms or racialisms.

As illustration: two Greeks of the time of Pericles or Plato in their next reimbodiment, may, as individuals, find themselves, the one incarnated as a Frenchman, and the other as a Chinese, a Hindû mayhap, or a Russian, or what not.

lives, when all is stated, is but an immense congeries of 'event' succeeding 'event' in the unbreakable chain of cosmic causation, acting as the latter does both in the large and in the small, in the group as well as in the individual. Through the eternities this Chain of Necessity passes, 'event' succeeding 'event.' Man is but such an event also, in his case a consciousness-event, a spiritual event, a psychological event, and a physical event, according to the plane of his being that may be considered at any moment. The gods in the highest heavens are but events of consciousness. The heavens themselves, the celestial spheres pursuing their regular courses above our heads, the worlds visible and invisible, and indeed, all beings and things — all are but events of consciousness; for consciousness is the fundamental thing or basis of all manifested existence; and our phenomenal universe of substance or matter, with all its manifestations of force, or what modern science calls energy, is but the expression, to the minor consciousnesses of the beings passing through it, of the invisible, immensely great workings of the underlying Cosmic consciousness-sphere.

Consciousness, or mind, if the word be better liked, comes first, and out of it flows everything else into manifestation. This, therefore, as is abundantly obvious, is in no wise the old doctrine of scientific materialism, nor in any sense of this word; but is the direct converse of it. The advocates of the old materialism, which is now moribund if not dead, who made consciousness arise in some perfectly inexplicable way out of dead, insensate, unconscious matter, are disappearing — their number is diminishing rapidly; our modern-day scientists are becoming mystics, and our philosophers are becoming scientists. Let our most brilliant and able scientists say what they may or like, the fact is that the whole tendency of modern science, as is clearly shown in the scientific deductions made by the most prominent scientific men, is directly towards metaphysics if not indeed mysticism. Certain of our modern scientists are openly voicing statements based on their researches into Nature, and upon their deductions drawn therefrom, which are as metaphysical, if not as mystical, as many things that may be found in metaphysical philosophy.

Each Hierarchy, each Universe, each god or 'angel,' each man, each animal, each atom, is but a passing phase, fugitive, non-enduring, however long its individual existence; a passing phase of the eternal evolutionary journey of the respective monadic essences which inspirit and inform these different units. A spark of the Cosmic Essence, each such monadic essence works through that particular veil or garment which we call in its passing form a man, or a beast, or a world, or a plane, or a sphere, or a universe; all are 'events' existing, in the words of the modern philosophical scientist, in space-time or time-space, which really is a continuum of consciousness-substance.

What then does all this mean? It means that abstract force, or still more abstractly, conscious Motion, is at the root of every thing, in and behind every being and every thing, at the heart of every thing; and consciousness is the purest form of Cosmic Force — Spirit, in other words. Matter itself is but a vast aggregation of monadic particles: monads, latent, sleeping, passing through that matter-phase; but each and all of them, every individual of them, sooner or later will express itself in individualized action: all will thus self-express themselves, and thus grow; and each phase of this evolutionary growth is an 'event.'

We live our little life and pass. It is an event. We go into a larger life, and live it, and pass by transrotation to the next phase. Both such life and the succeeding phase is each one an event. We go into a phase still more sublime, into invisible worlds, and live there and pass, and these too, collectively are but a larger event. Thus are all things and phases of things events, passing stages through which the evolving entity circumrotates. All these events, therefore, comprise the totality of the adventures of evolving and revolving souls, or more accurately monadic centers, consciousness-centers, throwing forth from within themselves what is locked up within themselves.

There is ever something new. The manifestations-to-be of man's spirit are as great as are the opportunities of boundless infinitude; because his spirit is a child of the Boundless All. It springs forth from it; it is a part of it, it is inseparable from it. It is he and he is It. *Tat twam asi* is the marvelous manner in which the ancient Sanskrit writers of the Hindû Upanishads put it: THAT THOU ART.

IV

The reader is requested ever to keep clear cut and prominent in his mental vision the distinction which the Esoteric Philosophy makes between the Spirit in man and the evolving human child of that spirit which is correctly and accurately called the human soul — itself a projection into active manifestation of the recondite human monad. This distinction has been referred to or pointed out in previous paragraphs of the present chapter where it is more or less definitely stated that the term 'soul' is so ambiguous that its usage is here somewhat protested, but that, nevertheless, and just because it is a useful word because commonly known, it has been adopted as a generalizing term in order to describe the Hosts or Families of learning entities who and which in their immense aggregate form the Evolving and Revolving Souls, the theme of the present study.

By 'souls,' therefore, and speaking with strict accuracy, we do not mean entities or beings immortal, thanks be to the immortal gods! It is the spirit or Monadic Essence in man which alone is immortal; and the human soul, itself a projection of its own Monadic Essence, as just stated, is the partly self-conscious vehicle receiving the spiritual illumination as its guidance from the spirit within. Every human being as a partly self-conscious and more or less adequately thinking creature *is* a human *soul;* but as every human soul, as at present manifesting itself, is very obviously an imperfect entity, as above pointed out, it is not immortal as 'soul.' Who would want to live as he now is in an immortality of soul-imperfection, lasting through endless Duration? Certainly not the present writer. To him such an immortality would be an endless hell. It means that the soul would exist in illimitable eternity, relatively changeless, with all the prospect of possible future growth consisting solely in merely ringing the changes of the small cycle of development experienced by that soul in the physical body in which it had lived in the previous life.

But outside of anything else, what we may wish or not wish has little or nothing to do with Nature's operations. Nature in her majestical procedures is as impersonal as the falling of the rain or the shining of the sun, and it should be perfectly clear that an imperfect being or thing can no more be immortal throughout eternity with continuous and uninterrupted and, as it were, crystallized consciousness, which is an obvious contradiction, than can any other contradiction involving imperfections exist for ever in Nature.

Immortality in imperfection finds no place in eternal Nature; and every human soul is an imperfect entity, because it is a growing entity, i. e., a learning thing, an evolving thing; and therefore it should be quite clear that no imperfection can put on the garments of immortality. Therefore is it again repeated: thanks be to the immortal gods that we grow and learn and advance steadily ever towards a goal which in Nature's illimitable expanses we can never finally reach; for the reaching of such a final goal would mean the sinking into a crystallized immobility of consciousness which is as horrifying in conception, when it is once understood, as it is also revolting to our instincts of truth. The pity of it all is that men want the universe to be as their imperfect brain-minds think it ought to be. If such could be the case, then we should have immortality for arrogant and increasing selfishness, a typical attribute of the lower part of the human soul: immortality for a composite and *de facto* imperfectly evolved entity, which composition signifies ultimate dissolution and precedent suffering and pain.

It is our foolish because undeveloped minds, and hungry because imperfectly satisfied hearts, which dream of 'immortality' for themselves as if it were the greatest boon that could be conferred upon wretched and erring because imperfect entities, such as human beings in their present evolutionary state most certainly are. What ignorance we humans show when we arrogate to ourselves in our presently imperfectly evolved state, an immortality lasting throughout endless duration! Why should we imperfectly developed humans be such only exceptions in an infinite universe, which teaches on all sides, and in every possible manner and way, that human beings are collectively but one group, one family, one stock, among innumerable multitudes, countless hosts of other beings and entities, all of which are growing, all evolving, and some of which hosts are incomparably superior to us humans in developmental or evolutionary unfoldment. Why should we be the only exceptions? Is there anything in Universal Nature that permits us to arrogate to ourselves this supposed immortality — as human *souls,* be it carefully noted — an immortality towards which, blind as most humans are, they aspire?

It is, of course, on the other hand, perfectly true that this yearning for self-conscious continuity in existence is founded on a clear and ever-flowing stream of intuition taking its rise in the bosom of the Spirit within us, and reaching down to our brain-minds and touching them with its holy fire; but continuity in ever-lasting life as the Esoteric Tradition teaches it, is a far different thing from the quasi-static 'immortality' as this word is invariably misunderstood in the West. If there is one thing which the Esoteric Philosophy teaches with an emphasis that is surpassed in no other part of its sublime Message, it is that LIFE is not only all-permeant, i. e., universal, but that every being, entity, and thing, in Boundless Space is at once permeated with this Cosmic Life and is of the very essence of this Cosmic Life.

Yet the reader is earnestly requested to note the vast difference between an unending but ever-changing continuity in life and existence, and the quite impossible, because utterly unnatural, idea of a changeless or eternally more or less static *human* ego or soul supposed to be immortal in its imperfections. The point is that if such ego were to change one iota, it would no longer be the same ego but would have been altered; and the truth is that it is precisely the ego, or self-conscious center, which is undergoing incessant, continuous, and unbroken changes.

The unceasing continuity of consciousness as taught by the Esoteric Tradition signifies the losing of the human ego into its becoming a spiritual ego — no longer the human ego that it was — and proceeding for ever with such 'losing' in an unceasing betterment. The Occidental supposititious immortality is like the possible yearning of the beast, a tiger for instance, to be eternally immortal in its tigerishness, hunting, ravening, slaying, and glutting its appetite with the blood and flesh of its unfortunate prey. Indeed, we humans in the sight of the divinities would be considered unholy denizens of the spiritual spheres were it possible for us to attain them with all our present imperfections, our gross if not animal appetites, yearnings and tendencies, incredibly stupid mental biases and prejudices. Continuous immortality for such beings! Would it not be even unto themselves an everlasting hell?

The average Westerner, the average Occidental, does not even know what true immortality is, or what we have just described as being unending continuity through ceaseless change in progress in the Cosmic Life. It means an unbroken continuation of the self-consciousness of the thing that presently is, that is at present, but unceasingly enlarging through boundless time its ranges of activity and expansion. What men call their 'self-consciousness' is but a feeblest glimmer of the life and mind of the Spirit, i. e., of the Monad, within and above it; so that as these changes in enlargement and expansion continue, we pass from the less to the greater light, from the greater to a light still more splendid, so that what is now but a flickering and imperfect point of brilliance in time expands into the noon-day glory—only to embark into greater glories beyond.

The point of distinction, therefore, that the Westerner desires, although quite unconsciously to himself, is immortality or continuity of his imperfections; whereas the Esoteric Philosophy shows clearly that it is precisely these imperfections, these flickering lights of the imperfect mind, which must be abandoned so to speak, or expanded, speaking more truly, into the greater. The idea is admirably illustrated by considering the differences of understanding as between man and man, two men: each has a feeble ray of self-consciousness; each prefers his own feeble ray to the ray of his brother, were it possible to exchange them; each yearns for immortality in his own limited understanding of the situation, fearing to lose himself, forgetting that only by losing his own imperfections, whose aggregate he calls 'himself,' may he enter into greater things.

This is the lesson that in human concerns is taught to us so clearly by Love. The lover yearns to lose himself in the thing loved, intuitionally feeling and realizing that by so doing he expands himself, widens his sympathies, becomes co-sentient with the thing loved and finally with others; until one day as the process continues he realizes that he has lost himself by becoming the All.

The truth therefore is that there is but one SELF, of which all the hosts of minor selves are but greater or smaller ray-selves. The 'dew-drop' finally slips into the Shining Sea — not to become 'lost' in the Occidental sense of this word, but to expand the dewdrop into the Sea itself. This was the secret teaching of the great Gautama the Buddha; it is the teaching likewise of the noblest spiritual effort in Hindûsthân, the Adwaita-Vedânta of Sankarâchârya; it is likewise the intuition of every great Mystic that the world has ever known.

It is strangely difficult for the Westerner to grasp this sublime thought that by losing himself in the greater, he becomes that greater because the twain are in essence one. The Westerner imagines that when this grand consummation of the Cosmic Manvantara is finally reached, then and there for ever afterwards will ensue an immortality in static crystallization of perfection — which is just what will not take place; and just here again we see how grossly the teaching of continuity of consciousness is misunderstood. For, marvel of marvels, wonder of wonders, when the new Cosmic Manvantara opens its great Drama of Life, after the Cosmic Pralaya, all these individuals composing the uncounted myriads of the Monadic Hosts will reissue forth for a new evolutionary pilgrimage in the new series of Worlds that will then flow forth from the heart of being — worlds which are the reimbodiments of the worlds that were.[98] Is it any wonder that the Theosophist speaks of the ages-long peregrinations of these individual Monads as being, in their operations in manifestation, evolving or revolving Monads or Souls?

98. A new world-system, indeed, but everything is on a higher plane, worlds as well as their respective inhabitants. Each individual entity of the hosts on and in this new World-System thus then begins a new Cosmic Pilgrimage, a new series of evolvings and revolvings, but like the worlds themselves on higher planes than those that last it left.

One of the main objections that may be strongly urged against the Western misconception of continuity in a more or less static but imperfect consciousness is the fierce egoisms that it arouses. Instead of a man's being taught that his humanity is but one stage, and a very imperfect stage at that, on the endless pathway to glories unspeakable in the future, this Western misconception implants in his consciousness the idea that he must 'save' his soul at all costs, bringing about small consideration for others. It offers to him no soul-enlarging views of the future, and fixes in his mind the totally wrong idea that his imperfect self or soul is his first concern. It makes a man egocentric and selfish, and induces into his mind the feeling that it is not necessary to look far within himself simply because there is no 'distance' within himself to look into. This erroneous conception makes him a spiritual pauper, and works to deprive him of that noblest form of self-respect which is born by discovering one's own grandeur, inner grandeur, spiritual grandeur, in recognising soul-kinship with all others around him, seeing in those others limitless wells of beauty, and genius.

A man must learn above everything else to look upon all surrounding Nature, his fellow-human beings first and foremost, with the all-penetrating eye of the spirit. This prevents crystallization of his mind, giving birth to endless prejudices, misconceptions, and egoisms.

When the conviction comes upon a man, no matter what his age, that he has little more to learn either about himself or about the souls of others around him, it is then time that he bestir himself. Not only is it egoism in its most dangerous form, it is the beginning of the crystallization of his inner, ethereal, intermediate nature, which is the wanton parent of all human evil and trouble, and is more productive of even physical disease, and more certainly a leading to an early and perhaps painful death, than any other thing that can affect a man. Every Sage and Seer of the past has told us: "As a man thinks, so is he."

There is an old Sanskrit saying which is often quoted in the Hindû writings. It is this:

यद्यद्रूपं कामयते देवता तत्तद् देवता भवति ।

Yadyad rûpam kâmayate devatâ, tattad devatâ bhavati,[99]

which means: "Whatsoever thing a divine entity yearns to become, that very thing it will become." It is most important to note that

---

99. Yâska: *Nirukta*, x, 17.

this same principle of natural law applies to all conscious beings. A man can deprive himself of his own inner spiritual illumination: he can shut the door against the entrance into his mind of the light from his own inner god, by refusing to believe his own higher instincts and intuitions; on the other hand he can know that he is the manifestation, at present unconscious or more or less conscious, of his own inner god; and that if he can ally himself with that inmost Center of his being, knowledge without bounds then can be his. It is thus that the Great Seers of the past got it.

Katherine Tingley wrote:

> It is that nobler part of our nature that rises to every situation and meets it with patience and courage,— the power that often sweeps into a man's life unawares and carries him out beyond all brain-mind thought into the great broad road of service. . . .
>
> The knowledge of it comes not in any world-startling or magical way, and is not to be purchased save by the surrender of a man's passionate and lustful nature to the God within.[100]

We human beings are composite creatures: we are souls when in the body, and then a dissolving and breaking-up compound after the dissolution of the body, in order that the truly immortal and continuing element in us, our individualized divine and spiritual sparks may then be freed and pass to their own respective spheres of post-mortem rest and experience, each attracted to its own and attracted nowhere else. Thus it is that we build for ourselves after physical death what the exoteric religions, in their imperfect rendering of the original Verities communicated to each religion by its great founder, call the Heavens and Hells.[101]

A 'soul,' then, and correctly speaking, is a growing entity, a *composite* being, which is builded or constructed around what is called a 'Monadic Ray' — an efflux from the Monad its source; that is to say, a soul is a compound of forces and substances; but the divine-spiritual ray, around which the soul-structure is thus builded, *that* indeed is immortal as human beings should properly understand immortality, because it lasts from the beginning of a Solar Manvantara to the end of a Solar Manvantara — in other words, from the beginning of our Solar System to its end: and this Monadic Ray lives as a spiritual being in the bosom of its parent Monad with un-

---

100. *The Wine of Life,* p. 12.

101. This matter of heavens and hells will be dealt with at greater length in a subsequent chapter.

broken continuity of consciousness: it endures throughout without interruption or lapses of continuity.

But 'souls' are not this. Souls, being composite things, must have rest, as all composite beings or entities must; they must have periods of peace and repose for recuperation; and it is in this recuperation that they gain strength for the next expression of themselves in their next incarnation on earth. A familiar example to us humans, which may perhaps make the idea more clear, is the rest and recuperation which our compounded physical body needs at the end of each day. We then sleep and rest and recuperate, and awake in the morning refreshed and ready for the new day's duties.

v

In view of what has been said about the mortality[102] of the human soul, certain unthinking people may ask: What, then, is the difference between a human being and a beast? That is often a knotty question to one who does not understand Theosophy. There is, of course, a great difference, indeed an immense difference, between man and beast; but so far as the *lower or lowest parts* of the human constitution are concerned, there is very little difference in origin and in destiny between a physical human being and a beast.

As the human has a soul, and as the human has a divine or Essential Self, so likewise has a beast a soul — but a beast's soul, not a human soul; in other words, a highly evolved elemental, which has, however, evolved less far than has the human soul, which likewise in its origin was an elemental; but that beast-soul, a highly evolved elemental and in its primal origin a life-atom, is neverthe-

---

102. A more correct phrasing of the thought would be: the conditional mortality of the human soul; otherwise, the conditional immortality of the human soul. It should be clear enough from what has gone before that continuance in consciousness or true immortality consists solely in the human ego's (of which the human soul is a ray) allying itself in self-conscious union with its own divine-spiritual parent, the Monad.

The Monad, *per se,* is unconditionally immortal; the human lower triad, comprising the physical body, the Linga-śarîra or Model-body, and the vitality, unconditionally mortal; that which is intermediate between these twain, to wit, the human ego and its soul, are conditionally immortal, or immortal depending upon whether the soul ally itself with its spiritual immortal source, or so enwrap itself into the mortal triad that its composition is affected thereby and disappears with the disappearance of the mortal triad. In this case a new human soul has to be evolved so that the human ego may express itself therein.

less a soul, the structure of which will reassemble itself around its
own inmost Monadic Ray at each reinfleshment, even as occurs in
the case of man. This Monadic Ray inspires the higher and quite
latent parts of the humble beast exactly after the manner that the
Monadic Ray, which is the innermost of man, inspires him. Yet in
the beast this Monadic Ray is practically unmanifest in the sense
of self-consciousness, whereas in man it has so refined its vehicular
soul-structure, through which it works and acts, that this structure
has been evolved into retaining self-consciousness in incarnation.

The beast thus in a sense is automatically conscious, or directly
conscious; the man is self-conscious or conscious through reflexion
from above; and this difference, as has been said, is simply enormous. The beasts are indeed composed of all the elements of Nature,
of Universal Nature, that compose man: yet between the human
kingdom and the beast-kingdom there is a truly impassable psychical
and intellectual gulf brought about by the inclusion in the human
inner economy of the higher intermediate nature of the human being
— a self-conscious and self-consciously thinking and choosing entity, while self-consciousness in the beasts is as yet quite unexpressed
— at least relatively so. This is a gulf so great that nothing in
Nature can bridge it, *except* the gaining by the beast of self-
consciousness through the conscious imbodiment of the Monadic Ray
in the soul-structure; but this will happen also for all beasts in
the far distant future of another great Planetary Manvantara or
great Planetary Life-Cycle.[103]

It should be quite clear, however, that the Theosophist does not
put himself upon the evolutional level of the beast; and the pious
Christian should be the last to assert this of a Theosophist, if he is
sincere in his own beliefs, because in one of the canonical books of
his own Bible, that is to say, in the book of *Ecclesiastes,* occurs the
following, which the author purposely translated from the Hebrew
original himself rather than use the more or less biased translation
that the accepted European rendering of the Hebraeo-Christian
Bible contains:

> I debated in my heart concerning the condition of the sons of man, as Elôhîm
> [the god or the gods, if you like] made them, and seeing how themselves are
> beasts, they themselves. For the destiny of the sons of man and the destiny
> of the beast are one destiny to them both; even as dieth the former so dieth
> the latter; for there is one spirit in them all; so that the pre-eminence of the

---

103. This future Planetary Manvantara referred to in the text above is
the next and succeeding reimbodiment of our entire planetary chain.

man over the beast is nothing; for all is illusion. All goeth to the one place; all is from the dust; and all returneth to the dust. Who knoweth the spirit of the sons of man which riseth upwards, and the spirit of the beast which descendeth under the earth?[104]

This book of *Ecclesiastes* is supposed to have been written by one whom, in the days of the writer's boyhood, he was taught to consider 'the wisest man who ever lived': the mythical King Solomon. At any rate, the book is entitled *Qôheleth* in the Hebrew, which means 'the Teacher.' This Hebrew book is a mystical work, and in the passages quoted we are told that 'even as the beast dies, so dies the man: they both go to one place; both came from the dust and both return to the dust.' If these words are taken carelessly in their surface-meaning, they teach a crass materialism; but this the Theosophist denies as the intent of this Hebrew work; and a close study of the text, especially in the Hebrew original, shows that another meaning is to be drawn from it than what appears outwardly. But the point is that beasts in modern times are usually, and falsely, considered to be soulless; and all antiquity, while denying that idea, nevertheless made a very great distinction between the intellectual and spiritual powers and faculties of man, and the interior psychological apparatus of the beast. Is it not obvious that Solomon, or the writer of this treatise, whoever he was, taught under cover of superficial words and meanings a hid and secret sense? All the sages of antiquity followed this method of using the metaphorical, the figurative. Their reasons were several, but the main one was that it was universally considered to be an abominable sacrilege to promulgate this sacred and secret lore to those unprepared, who would only abuse it because they could not understand its profound reaches of meaning; and such abuse would work to the positive harm and mischief of one's fellow-men.

In the first part quoted above, the allusion is obviously to the lowest parts of us; and it is true, thank the immortal gods! For who would want or desire or wish for a continuance in endless immortality of these lowest parts of us, imperfect, trifling, foolish, stupid, and ignorant!

Then at the end we are told: "Who knoweth" the difference between "the spirit of the sons of man which riseth upwards, and the spirit of the beast which descendeth under the earth" — showing by this comparison that there is some very real and important

---

104. Chapter iii, verses 18-21.

difference between man and beast; and indeed there is! — a real gulf in moral and intellectual development, which evolution alone can bridge.

The difference is briefly this: that man is a self-conscious being, which, as before stated, signifies consciousness reflected upon itself, thus producing self-consciousness, and this is a distinctly spiritual quality, for thus does consciousness know itself. This is an unfolding or unwrapping of latent faculty and power brought about by and through evolution — it means not the mere adding of experience to experience, or of emotion to emotion, or of thought to thought, or of idea to idea, as evolution is commonly mis-supposed to be, for this would amount to an accumulation of scraps into a mere heap or pile without inhering co-ordinating and unifying power. This is materialistic Darwinism applied to intellectual and psychical evolution; and the Esoteric Philosophy positively rejects this scheme as being both utterly inadequate to explain the facts that are, and, on the other hand, as being but an attempt *a posteriori* to apply the unproved evolutionary scheme or hypothesis to the facts of Nature. To accept such an hypothesis it would first have to be proved that it is true in Nature and to Nature, both as causal agent and effectual product. Neither has been proved.[105]

---

105. The fascinating teaching of the Esoteric Tradition dealing with evolution as it is taught in the Ancient Wisdom will be more fully unfolded and elaborated in later chapters of this work. Nevertheless, for the purpose of avoiding possible misunderstanding on the part of the reader, as to the basic urge or impulse or force causing and bringing about the evolutionary development of beings and things, as Evolution is thus explained in the Esoteric Tradition, it may be as well briefly to state the fundamental principle here. This fundamental Principle or Cosmic Urge, is conscious Mind — or still more accurately expressed, an unfolding of individual Minds from life-atoms to gods, through inner propulsion — from the urge to self-expression rising within evolving entities themselves. Evolution is, therefore, no chance, or fortuitous, or hap and hazard process; it is distinctly an unfolding of faculty, developing the appropriate organ, and both brought about by the working of conscious minds — the as yet unexpressed conscious mind in every living being or thing. It is therefore a process of development originating within an organism, all organisms; instead of being, as Darwin and other later materialistic theorists taught, blind chance operating to bring about the dominance of superior over inferior creatures.

This materialistic conception of one of the grandest and indeed most sublime processes in Nature, is, as elsewhere stated in this work, already moribund if not dead; and modern biology, keenly alive to the mistakes of its former propagandists, is now searching with relatively unveiled vision for an evolutionary theory accordant with all the facts thus far known of manifested life — and

In man the process of unfolding has proceeded so far, that the psychical life-atoms which make the structure of the human soul are of a much higher grade than they which compose the structure of the soul of the beast, and therefore in man they express much more fully the faculties and powers of the Monad, of the Monadic Ray, which flow through them — yet not fully expressed. If the structure of the soul of man were capable of expressing all the faculties and powers of his spiritual Monad, then man indeed would be a true human god walking on earth; and that in very fact will be his destiny in time to come; but he is not it yet.

If the student examine himself, and if he examine his fellow humans without prejudice or *parti pris,* he will find many interesting things, which if he has at all a philosophical mind, will demand a

---

lives. The change that has come over biologists in this respect during the last twenty or thirty years has been revolutionary; and it would be a simple matter to cite the opinions on the point openly proclaimed in recent years of the foremost and cleverest of biologists. Let it suffice here to cite the opinions of three well-known men, biologists and other, as illustrations of the amazing and most welcome change in the manner of viewing the evolutionary process that modern research and deduction have brought forth.

Professor C. Lloyd Morgan, University of Bristol, England, has recently stated very plainly that in his view, Evolution throughout and in all directions, and from the beginning of time to the present, is a "great scheme," which statement is of course obviously true if we take the word *scheme,* as Professor Lloyd Morgan intends it to be taken, as meaning a process of purpose and objective — for a scheme to be a scheme must be purposive, otherwise it is mere chance action.

Dr. Hans Driesch of the University of Leipzig is equally emphatic in his statements, just recently made, to the effect that the theories of both Lamarck and Darwin are insufficient, because chance and contingency in these theories are taken as the 'causes' of both phylogenetic and evolutionary procedures in Nature; and although he states that he does not consider either the Darwinian or Lamarckian theories to be completely wrong, and admitting natural selection as a fact, he qualifies the latter as being wholly negative and a mere factor in the evolutionary process. He affirms with emphasis his conviction that evolution is certainly not due to chance but to purposive design and planning in Nature which are due to intrinsic mind.

Finally, it was the late Professor Sir J. Arthur Thomson, University of Aberdeen, who exclaimed when writing of the marvelous mechanisms so universally found in the bodies of both living and so-called inanimate entities, that if these marvelous mechanisms were to be ascribed to an automatic machine, our ideas as to causes would have to be shifted to the designer of such supposedly automatic machine.

more satisfactory explanation than merely the fact that the discover-
er has found them. He will find understanding, judgment, discrimination, will, love, compassion, pity, and many other such noble
and very beautiful attributes. He will likewise find that his consciousness is colored with other energies — passions, hates, envies,
jealousies, malices, and many more such evil attributes.

Pursuing his examination still farther into his own inner make-up
(and what study can possibly be more interesting than this to any
thoughtful man or woman?) he will find yet other things: instincts,
intuitions, illuminations; also blindnesses, wilful ignorances, perver-
sities of various kinds. He will sometimes find his nature so contrasted with itself, so torn among its own qualities, as it were so at
war with its own elements, that, if these states or conditions exist
in large degree, he has what modern psychology rather absurdly
calls 'double' or 'multiple personality' — actually seeming to be one
person at one time and another person or persons at other times;
and indeed the facts are thus, though the ascription of this title —
'double' or 'multiple personality' — to these facts is hardly one that
a Theosophist would accept. Man indeed is 'legion,' to use the
figure of the Christian New Testament, only he is not alone the
legion of imps or of elemental forces therein supposed, but likewise
a legionary host of elements of light and inspiration; for in his inmost he is essentially a 'creator' in the sense of being a producer,
continuously sending forth from within himself all-various powers
and streams of ethereal substances which eventuate in ordinary
human consciousness expressing itself in these legions of manifestations which have just been sketched. These are all from him and
of him, for he is their parent; but none of them is he, for he is
above and superior to them in his essence.

We immediately see here one great psychological reason why
the entertaining of these vagrant impulses and wandering thoughts
and more or less incoherent ideas which tramp through our consciousness, can be productive of no good, for they distract the attention away from the Central Fire of the man, which is his Essential
Self, the Monadic Ray.

All the above is but another proof of the old, old saying touching man, that he is a microcosm, copying in the *small* all and whatever the Universe or the Macrocosm itself contains, for he obviously
is an inseparable part or portion of the Universal Whole, and with
equally obvious reason again, he, the part, cannot contain something that the Whole lacks. Man is manifold precisely because the
circumambient Universe is manifold. Conversely, man the micro-

cosm is to the philosophical and clear-seeing eye of the Sage a living proof of what the Universe is in the great.

What is lacking in such cases of 'double' or 'multiple personality,' is that the individual sufferer's own egoic stream of consciousness seems at times to be submerged or overwhelmed with these other and phantasmal apparitions of 'personality.' It would be wrong to say that anything is 'lacking'; it would be more correct to say that the man or woman has not yet found himself or herself; and one sees an exemplification of this imperfect psychological state of mind and consciousness in the growth of little children into youth, and how easily they follow the distracting influences of what is called 'the world.' No, nothing is lacking in such cases of dissipated or dislocated consciousness, for the central egoic Self is always there; but the man has not yet learned to ally himself — his lower ordinary human self — with his own spiritual Self, and hence follows psycho-mental will-o'-the-wisps of impulse and thought and emotion instead of the central Light. It is the benign and calming and unifying influences of the spiritual Self, which any man may ally himself with *if he will,* which produce the great and strong and virtuous men and women. All these lower psychological affections that have been mentioned belong to man's lower nature.

Now there exist in the beasts — but nevertheless exhibiting only in the rarest cases the psychical dislocations observable in man, because they have not man's mental and emotional apparatus governing them — there exist in the beasts passions, memories, instincts, strange operations of the beast-consciousness, which almost seem to approach to intuition at times, also limited knowledge of things, likewise hates, loves, and contrarieties of various kinds, just as man sees them and feels them in himself. If they were not in him he could not understand them in others; he could not understand them in the beast. But one does not find in the beast, judgment for instance, as man knows it so well, nor discrimination, nor creative intellectual power, nor recognition of abstract truth, nor impersonal love. The love of a beast is very beautiful sometimes; but it is a purely personal love, and therefore limited.

Pondering upon these similar or differing attributes and qualities, one descries the cause of the difference between man and beast — a difference of degree in evolutionary growth, but nevertheless not of kind, nor again of spiritual origin. The beast has everything in it that the man has, but mostly latent, unmanifest. In the man it is more or less manifest; and the destiny of man in the future, of course, is more and more so to ally himself with the higher parts and faculties of his nature that he in time becomes self-conscious of so doing, and therefore becomes conscious of entering 'into his own kingdom.' He becomes his own master instead of the slave of his whims and fugitive passions, and no longer eats of the 'husks' that the swine eat of. Becoming thus self-conscious, he begins to recognise himself for what he truly is; and coming to know himself for what he is, he acts in accordance with this knowledge, and verily becomes more and more a Man.

VI

Everything is interlocked and interlinked and interblended with everything else. We are bound together by bonds which can never be broken. We of the human host, leaving aside the other incomputable numbers of hosts which infill and indeed make the Universe — we of the human host alone, limiting our attention to ourselves for the moment — have duties to perform to each other, which the Theosophist in particular never dares to be blind to — however inadequately he may fulfill these obligations. We are bound together by unbreakable ties; and no man can live unto himself alone, nor think unto himself alone, nor feel for himself alone. He may cheat himself into imagining that he does this; but he inevitably suffers from it. Nature, which is infinitely merciful in its widest operations, because it is inwardly controlled by Divine Beings, nevertheless and for that very reason, is inflexibly and ineluctably just.

We Westerners are extremely egoistic, for we imagine that we as human beings are favored creatures in a Universe where no favor exists — because infinite mercy involving ineffable justice cannot contain either suggestion or actuality of favoritism of any kind! How much greater and grander is the other view, the view of the entire world of ancient times! This view we can understand so clearly and have our understanding greatly enlightened by it, if we use one simple key. What is this simple key? The realization of our *oneness with the All.* It is a wonderful and sublime thought, and is the root, the foundation, of all the greatest philosophies and religions that human Genius, inspired by the inner god of the first promulgator of each one such philosophy or religion, has given to the world.

One is reminded in this connexion of a well-known passage in the Christian New Testament, the deeper significance of which passage is rarely grasped. Here in the Christian New Testament a story is told about a certain lawyer who was questioning Jesus, the Syrian Sage and Avatâra, in an attempt to catch him tripping, if possible, in his interpretations of the Jewish Scriptures. This lawyer asked Jesus:

Teacher, what is the great injunction in the Law? Jesus said to him: Thou shalt love the Lord thy God in all thy heart, and in all thy soul, and in all thy consciousness.
This is the prime and great injunction.
The second is exactly like it: Thou shalt love thy neighbor as thyself.
In these two injunctions hang all the Law and all the prophets.[106]

A man who loves the Divine — called in this New Testament passage the 'Lord thy God' after the manner of speaking in those days — is a lover of All. In loving all, he loses all self-love, and self-love, as is obvious, is a limited and restricting emotion and consequently is the root of all selfishness and evil in the human world. Self-love narrows the vision, and cripples the wings of the Soul, which in this case is the true Self; but the All-lover loses the small in the infinitely great; he loves all and sees even the glimmering good behind the seeming or actual evil that exists in the world. This is the real meaning that Jesus had in mind when he uttered this noble doctrine. The man who loves the All, obviously loves all beings and everything; and it is therefore not wonderful at all that the great Syrian pursued the path of his thought in saying that the second injunction was exactly like the first: 'Love thy neighbor as thyself' — for this is precisely what a lover of the All would necessarily do, because his neighbor in his inmost essence is the same as he in his inmost essence. The man who loves his neighbor, necessarily loves himself — but his best, highest, and finest and loftiest Self.

VII

Our study has not carried us far from the theme of the present chapter 'Evolving Souls' because the reflexions which have occupied the last few pages have been illustrative of how Nature is knitted together in all her parts — infinite variety living in a fundamental unity; and that this infinite variety is but a manifestation on this plane of the ever-active workings and movements of the Hosts of beings and things marching steadily forwards and upwards on their evolutionary path, a path whose beginning is lost in the immeasurable past of Time and Space, and whose continuance is discerned as losing itself in the immeasurable vistas of the Future.
Consciousnesses everywhere, of multi-myriad grades or stages in

---

106. *Matt.*, xxii, 36-40.

evolution, very high, high, intermediate, low, and very low, from gods to life-atoms, yet all progressing, all evolving, all revolving through the worlds and planes and spheres visible and invisible: all engaged in following one general path of evolutionary progress, yet as individuals pursuing roads which most intricately cross and re-cross each other, thus bringing about the interlocking and inter-blending karmic destiny of all things.

Intuitions in the minds of great men, whether we accept or reject their particular and individual contributions to human thought, occasionally break forth in noteworthy statement, and the devoted student of the Esoteric Tradition finds it a fascinating study indeed to compare, to analyse, and to examine, the published convictions of great men of today with the teachings of the great Sages and Seers of the past. The similarity as between the two, often very striking, is of the nature of proof that man's essential selfhood will not be crippled by current philosophies or sciences, but expresses itself in kindred subjects in all ages and everywhere. Modern scientific men in particular seem to be casting off the fetters of intellectual confusion and to be striking out new pathways for themselves into the unseen worlds, often boldly declaring their inmost feelings as to the Divine Consciousness which is all-permeant in the Universe. As Einstein, the well-known author of the modern Relativity-Theory, is reported to have said:

It is enough for me to contemplate the mystery of conscious life perpetuating itself through all eternity — to reflect upon the marvelous structure of the universe which we can dimly perceive, and to try humbly to comprehend even an infinitesimal part of the intelligence manifest in nature.

Einstein's voice is but one of many in our days, all proclaiming, some more boldly than others, some with more timid conviction, the same or similar ideas. What a welcome change is all this in scientific outlook from what existed in the days when the Messenger of the Masters, H. P. Blavatsky, wrote her great work, *The Secret Doctrine!*

CHAPTER VIII

EVOLVING SOULS — II

THE all-inclusive philosophy-religion of the Esoteric Tradition, and therefore likewise its modern representative, Theosophy, divides the Universe, and consequently Man who is an inseparable part of that Universe and who therefore also has in him everything that the Universe has, into four general, basic Planes, so to say, or perhaps more accurately Worlds of Manifestation; and these Planes or Worlds of Manifestation should not be considered or conceived as being in the shape of or constructed after the manner of a rising (or descending) stair; but rather as being interior to or inwards of one another: that is to say that these four Worlds or Planes are — counting from the grossest and most material 'inwards' or 'upwards' — each one finer and more ethereal than the grosser and more material one which incloses it and thus imbodies it, and through which it therefore works and manifests.

These four great Planes or Bases or Worlds are the spheres or domains of operation of the four lower basic or elemental principles of the septempartite Kosmos or Universe; and the same rule of partition in consequence holds true for the human being.

These four are as follows:

The first and highest is the Divine, the domain or world or sphere of activity of the gods — the highest spiritual entities belonging to the Universe, in this case our own Home-Universe, which includes all within the encircling zone of the Galaxy or Milky Way; but there are vast numbers of other Universes, some far higher than our Universe, and some far lower than our Universe. In all these Universes the countless hosts of beings which infill them and populate them are ranged, more or less as they are in our own Universe, in four general divisions having their respective habitats according to their respective grades.

There is no beginning and there is no ending in this hierarchical Chain of Lives; and if the student will pause a moment for reflexion, he will readily see the reason for this. How can there be an ending, how can there be a beginning, of Infinity, of the Boundless All? — for these hierarchies are countless in number and fill the Boundless All. Probably no sane man in these days would say that the human species, the human race, with its habitat on this speck of cosmic dust which we call our planet, is the only race or species of beings in the Boundless All which has unique capacity for thought or of consciousness, and of self-consciousness in particular — a divine quality in its origin. We do not know, we cannot therefore say, where such powers and faculties begin in their development on the endless hierarchical Ladder of Life, because obviously such beginning is without existence, except at best illusory, and then only by comparison; and we do not know, and therefore we cannot say, where such hosts of evolving and revolving beings end, simply because we know of no ending — an idea equally illusory and for the same reason. All we know is that we ourselves are here, as conscious, self-conscious, thinking entities, thus proving the existence of such beings in the limitless fields of Space — inner Space and outer Space. For it were but a vain speculation and a dream of empty fantasy to suppose that we humans are exceptions, unique, without peers, in all the rest of Boundless Space! The idea is grotesque, and admitted as an argument would immediately call for an explanation as to why we humans should be the sole exception in infinity. If a man sees a sunrise and thereafter goes blind and never sees a sunrise again, he has a perfect right, as a logical being, to say, "What I have seen must come again and must have been before; for it *is*."

As said, the highest of the four Worlds or Planes or Bases above spoken of is the Divine, the domain or habitat of the most evolved beings existing contemporaneously in any one period of our own Home-Universe. The next lower of the four Worlds or Planes or Bases is the Spiritual, or the domain or habitat of the Monads. This word *Monad,* as before stated, is a Pythagorean term, and it should not frighten one by its supposed strangeness. It is a descriptive term of the nature or character of those entities who have attained self-consciousness in relative or hierarchical fulness — especially so far as all the beings below them in the same hierarchy are concerned. The word *Monad* is Greek, and means a 'unit,' an 'individual' — therefore what the Esoteric Tradition calls a self-conscious individual life-center or Jîva. The Monads are embryo-gods, in fact, or perhaps more accurately speaking young gods at school, the school-house in this instance being the Universal Solar System in all its ranges of visible and invisible worlds — or indeed we may speak of the school-house and now term it the Cosmic University, and identify it with the Galaxy or Milky Way.

The third World or Plane or Base, and next below the Monadic or Spiritual, is the realm or field of operations of Souls of various kinds. They are rays from the Monads and can thus be re-called,

withdrawn, into the parent-source. There are, as already said, countless multitudes of these Souls in our Home-Universe. They may
properly be called embryo-Monads: entities growing towards rebecoming their own inner and as yet unevolved monadic essence, just
as the Monads or embryo-gods are growing towards divinity, towards
becoming divine beings or gods by evolving in the manner in which
evolution has been explained in preceding chapters, i. e., by unfolding or unrolling the inner essence.

Fourth and last of these Worlds or Bases or Planes, and below
the preceding, is the habitat or domain of other countless hosts of
entities, which, for lack of a better term in European tongues we may
call 'life-atoms' or even 'atoms,' provided that we adopt this last
term also from the ancient Greeks of the Atomistic School, such as
Leucippus and Democritus, and give to this their term the significance which with them it originally had. These atomic entities
are not the physical atoms of chemistry, necessarily, which last are
but the material reflexions or mirrorings, so to say, of the real
life-atoms just mentioned. These atoms, or more correctly 'life-
atoms,' are the energic centers within and behind the physical atoms
which thus ensoul these physical atoms, and which therefore make
the physical atoms what they actually are, and hold them in coherency as the individual units of physical matter. The physical atoms
are the concretions of substance around the energic outflow from these
life-atoms. Furthermore, these life-atoms are called in Sanskrit also
by the term we have given to the Monads, i. e., Jîvas; though it
should be stated in passing that this Sanskrit word जीव (*jîva*), thus
used in two senses because of its appositeness, is properly used in
strict accuracy to mean only the fundamental monadic life-center
itself — which term is therefore applicable to entities on the other
and superior Worlds or Planes or Bases equally as well as it may
apply as above stated. Thus the intrinsic meaning or significance
of *jîva* is life-center, provided that we include in this conception the
containing of mind and consciousness.

For the present moment one could perhaps, without wandering
too far from strict accuracy, say that the life-atom is virtually the
same as the ensouling vital force of the electron of modern chemical
physics,[107] with this most important condition or proviso, however,
that this life-atom, as just stated, is in itself ensouled by an elemental

---

107. This statement, however, being subject to a future modification when
our scientists shall have acquired greater knowledge of precisely what the
chemical electrons are.

soul — a proviso which of course the modern chemist would probably boggle at before admitting because he knows nothing whatsoever of 'elemental souls' or elementals; or at any rate, if his thought occasionally wanders away from his laboratory into the realms of philosophy, and he has adumbrations of this idea, he very rarely incorporates his philosophic reflexions in language or textbook!

I

It may be just as well for the sake of clarity, and in order to round out even this brief presentation of this aspect of the teaching of the Esoteric Tradition, to define with somewhat greater particularity just what it is that is called an Elemental in our Cosmic Philosophy. First and foremost, then, and as a statement of first importance, an Elemental should be considered to be an evolving and revolving 'soul' in its earliest or elemental stages — a life-center *in its appearance in this material sphere;* and attention should be drawn away from any ideas about form or 'shape' that the elemental may or may not have. The form or shape is a matter of no importance whatsoever, at least in this definition, because, as a matter of fact, the elementals or elemental lives, as being the nature-sprites of the elements, change their presentations of form or shape with a rapidity which can only be likened, and truly likened, to the rapidity with which the 'forms' or 'shapes' of forces manifest themselves.

Indeed, the elemental is just that: an elemental force or energy which is ensouled by a jîva.

Every ray of sunlight, every little 'whirling devil,' as the Arabs call them, on a dusty road, every water-spout, and even every raindrop, imbodies an elemental or group of elementals; every electric spark is one elemental or a collection of elementals; every twitch of a nerve in the body is the effect of the action of one or more; but this does not mean that the elementals are miniature entities of human form pulling a nerve, or whirling water, or throwing raindrops down, or with a tool making the miniature cyclones of whirling dust that are seen on the road.

Every atom in a physical body, such as man's body, is the physical encasement of a psychic elemental or nature-spirit, itself more highly ensouled with a jîva. We talk by the aid of elementals; we digest by their aid; breathe by their aid; love by their aid; write by their aid; live by their aid; sin by their aid. In fact we are surrounded with them; they actually form every part of us, and take part in every thought or emotion we have and in every action we do — and this is because they are nature-forces, nature-sprites, therefore even individuals in a certain true sense. They exist as individuals and are of immensely different kinds and of immensely many classes. There are some of them that are titans in size, loftier than the loftiest mountain, miles high; and there are others that are atomic in size; and between these two extremes there are all-various sizes and varieties of them.

Think of the varieties or kinds of radiation that modern scientific discovery is so cleverly unveiling to our knowledge and for our use, these ranging from the extremely small, infinitesimal, vibratory forces called cosmic rays, then X-rays, towards others passing through the radiative ranges that we call heat and light, and increasing in amplitude or size until we have the long waves used in 'radio' — a mile or so in length.

There are other ranges which scientific men suspect but have not yet subjected to experimentation and proof. These different rays may illustrate the point of the differences in quality and kind of these elementals, because each such ray is the activity or function, or is brought about by the activity or function, of an elemental, which thus expresses its own characteristics in the type of radiative wave which it produces.

Elementals are simply nature-spirits or nature-sprites, in all-various degrees of evolutionary unfolding. A stroke of lightning is a cosmic elemental at work, in action. What Occidentals, translating the word *Maruts* of the East-Indian Vedas, quaintly call 'wind-gods' or 'storm-gods,' are cosmic elementals but of exceedingly high class; indeed these Maruts, it may be said in passing, are really elementals evolved or unfolded to so high a degree that they may verily with truth be called self-conscious spirits of Nature.

Man was himself an elemental which through evolution or unfolding inner capacities has grown from un-individuality to monadic individualization — at least so grown in part, because there is no end to the same growth before him. Man is at the same time a mass of elementals subordinate to him, just as he himself is subordinate to the gods, who also formerly in far past Cosmic Periods were then elementals, but who now have evolved and revolved through the stages of 'evolving souls' into being gods. This bare and brief statement is true indeed, but it is only a microscopic fraction of the truth about the subject.

The elementals, therefore, are the great and semi-automatic communistic workers or quasi-conscious agents in Nature, imbodying not only their relative proportions of mind and consciousness, but

likewise the hierarchical ranges of the higher minds and consciousnesses who use them in this manner, and thus bring about the multi-
myriad forms of work in the Universe. Consequently, these ever
active and, from the human standpoint, incessantly 'industrious'
nature-sprites, are everywhere, and are the instrumental means or
causes for bringing about the doing of whatever is done anywhere,
and this is the case equally with works of high intelligence or in
works of low. A man writing a book does so by and with the aid
of elementals that he temporarily enslaves to the mandates of his
mind and will; the same man lounging in a chair or swimming in
the sea, or riding a horse, or a bicycle, or driving an automobile, or
sitting in church or in a meeting, or in the séance-room studying the
so-called 'phenomena' that are present there — all these actions are
performed by and with and through the aid of elementals.

When certain mediumistic humans are present in these séance-
rooms, it happens that at times the elementals go out of control, as
it were, and then they show their presence by twitching things or
jerking things, or making strange and unusual noises. A house
where such things happen is a house containing what the Germans
call a *Poltergeist,* or what is sometimes called a spook, or what other
peoples call a *bhûta,* or a *jinnî,* or what not; and most people then
would say that the house is 'haunted.' In the presence of certain
mediums whose human principles are so poorly co-ordinated and
controlled that these principles are, as it were, loose and do not
function properly — in other words, when the human principles do
not automatically obey the higher mind and will of these individuals
— the elementals sometimes go 'out of hand,' and occasionally so
much so, that the most astonishing things may happen, such as raising or tipping of tables, or throwing down crockery in a closet if
the 'medium' be near, or tripping him up and making him fall, or
making his bed shake or rise on a leg — indeed it is possible for
them to work all kinds of pranks in such cases. It is all a matter
of nature-forces flowing from the 'medium' in unregulated and quasi-
anarchic fashion. Once that the rationale and nature and cause of
these phenomena are understood, it is at once seen that there is
nothing at all 'weird' or 'uncanny' about them, no more so than is
an attack of hysterics, or an attack of rheumatism, or a bad stumble
when walking — all of which events are instances of the facts just
outlined.

The word 'elementals' is simply a generalizing term meaning
'nature-forces,' whether cosmic or infinitesimal in magnitude; and
it is most important to remember that all elementals are undevel-

oped, i. e., unevolved, entities because arising in the Cosmic Elements. As said above, the gods are self-conscious beings who in past Cosmic Periods were elementals, but who now have passed out of that stage into the divine stage, and at present are the powers of Light and the typical relatively fully evolved exemplars of self-conscious beings in the universe. A human, also relatively evolved as he is but in a lower degree than the gods are, in far past time was also a nature-sprite or Cosmic Elemental.[108] What else could he have been? He is a part of Nature; he is a spiritually and intellectually individualized nature-force; he has gained a certain degree of self-consciousness; in other words, he has brought forth from within his Monad, out of his Monadic Essence, into manifestation, some of the divine and quasi-divine powers for ever living there.

Yet every time when a man is overcome with either a human or a beastly passion, for that series of moments he is more or less in the grip of, under the sway of the dominating power of, an elemental or group of elementals which normally belong and function in the lower parts of his constitution and which he uses when in full control of himself as forces automatically following the mandates of his mind and will for higher purposes.

So, taking into account the ensouling elemental, the life-atom may properly be called an embryo-soul, because it is an individualized vital force, each one a center of consciousness of its own specific type and quality, having a cohering individual form, yet withal linked with the mightiest as well as with the feeblest by innumerable tendrils of vital cohesion in the Boundless All. For universal Nature in all her divisions or hierarchical ranges is by them interlocked and interlinked in every way and in every 'direction' and in every 'dimension,' by unbreakable bonds of Cosmic Vital Essence.

II

All these four main Classes of beings, here reckoned as four, are not only evolving but likewise are revolving, and not only as aggre-

---

108. "In sober truth, as just shown, every 'Spirit' so-called is either a *disembodied or a future man.* As from the highest Archangel (Dhyan Chohan) down to the last conscious 'Builder' (the inferior class of Spiritual Entities), all such are *men,* having lived aeons ago, in other Manvantaras, on this or other Spheres; so the inferior, semi-intelligent and non-intelligent Elementals — are all *future* men. That fact alone — that a Spirit is endowed with intelligence — is a proof to the Occultist that that Being must have been a *man,* and acquired his knowledge and intelligence throughout the human cycle."

—H. P. BLAVATSKY: *The Secret Doctrine,* I, 277

gated classes but equally so as individuals. The Atoms, or life-atoms, the invisible partly conscious lives which infill the Universe and which in very fact compose the so-called 'matter'-side of the Universe, grow slowly by evolving through the aeons, and steadily thus become greater and ever more perfect expressions of the locked-up potencies or powers or faculties which from eternity are in the essence of their core. As this revolving evolution proceeds, self-consciousness begins to appear, thus unfolding, growing steadily in ever greater degree. Self-consciousness, it must be remembered, is reflective or reflected consciousness — consciousness reflected upon itself as it were, and therefore consciousness knowing itself as consciousness. When self-consciousness is finally reached, these life-atoms are then become Souls; and these Souls, likewise in exactly similar manner, are evolving and revolving and thus growing in unfolding, becoming ever more and more fully what is lying within themselves, in their own core. Each entity anywhere can manifest forth only what is inherently and intrinsically *itself;* but of course as this 'self' is rooted in its turn in the Boundless All, it is obvious that evolution or self-expression is at once endless and beginning-less, and also gradually unfolds in both growth and change, the pathway of development reaching into and progressively expanding with the limitless fields of Boundless Infinitude. What a sublime thought! In this idea lie the keys of the whole of the Esoteric Philosophy, in so far as this portion of its teachings is concerned.

That particular Monadic Ray which manifests through the composite which in life we call the human soul is our Essential Self; and the human soul through which it so manifests was in far past time, aeons upon aeons agone, a life-atom, a life-center; in other words it was then an elemental soul, evolving and revolving through the spheres towards its goal, humanity.

Thus, then, these 'souls' as they evolve, as they grow or *become* more and ever more their Essential Self, become in course of the flowing of endless time what we call Monads: not because a soul changes into a Monad by growth through accretion, as before explained, but because of unfolding, unrolling, bringing out what is already within itself, in the Monadic Essence. These Monads, again, evolving and revolving through the spheres, as the aeons pass on into the frontierless ocean of the Past, finally become Divinities, or gods, or super-spiritual beings, by precisely identical unfolding of the inner essence.

Does then evolution end here? How is such an ending possible? It has already been said that logical absolute beginnings and absolute endings are unthinkable, except as of conditions and states of entities; for such conditions or states are always but the results of compositions and of component and temporary passages through space and time, no matter how long a time any such composition may endure.

In our own Home-Universe or Galaxy, which of course is here taken as the type of all other Universes or Kosmical Hierarchies, we see that when the evolving and revolving entities reach, through unfolding of the inner essence, the stage of divinity which is the highest state in our Universe, then their course of long evolutionary development, their Cosmic Pilgrimage, is run. What then happens? Progress they no farther? How can they stop or stay for ever there? Such an idea is logically both meaningless and intellectually absurd, in view of the nature of things as already set forth in the present and preceding chapters.

We humans are now where we are, and are what we are, having *become* such, in the beginning more or less unconsciously to ourselves, by exercising our inner faculties and powers of intelligence, of will, of judgment, of choice, of discrimination, and of such parts of wisdom as we have. In other words, as Katherine Tingley has phrased it, we have *become* what we are by more or less conscious 'self-directed evolution'; and as we progress more and more, and become greater and greater in the Cosmic Scheme of things; as our faculties expand from within and come forth into manifestation in ever increasing and larger degree: thus the more shall we use our divine faculty of will, this divine faculty of choice and judgment, and thus carve our own destiny more grandly towards becoming divine beings, as and how we will to do so.[109]

We are moving towards that divine destiny now as self-conscious

---

109. "The Secret Doctrine is the accumulated Wisdom of the Ages, and its cosmogony alone is the most stupendous and elaborate system: . . . Everything in the Universe, throughout all its kingdoms, is CONSCIOUS: *i. e.*, endowed with a consciousness of its own kind and on its own plane of perception. . . . The Universe is worked and *guided* from *within outwards*. As above so it is below, as in heaven so on earth; and man — the microcosm and miniature copy of the macrocosm — is the living witness to this Universal Law and to the mode of its action. . . . The whole Kosmos is guided, controlled, and animated by almost endless series of Hierarchies of sentient Beings, each having a mission to perform, and who — whether we give to them one name or another, and call them Dhyan-Chohans or Angels — are 'messengers' in the sense only that they are the agents of Karmic and Cosmic Laws. They vary infinitely in their respective degrees of consciousness and intelligence; and to call them all pure

human beings, for even now we are as embryo-gods, evolving and revolving Monads essentially; but it will be long, long ages yet before men even know with relative fulness what and who they essentially are.[110] We are passing now through merely the present temporary stage of our long, long, aeonic Cosmic pilgrimage, always advancing to greater stages and larger degrees of perfection: coming out of the visionless past, a past so far distant and mysterious with its hid secrets of bygone time, that no system of human thought throws any light upon it save the Esoteric Philosophy, which in very truth gives as satisfying an explanation of the road over which we have thus traveled as it does of the distant future towards which we in common with all others are steadily marching.

There is neither caprice nor favoritism in Nature and its controlling and governing Spiritual Powers. Man is the architect of his own soul, the builder of his own bodies, the shaper of his own mind, the maker of his own destiny. Obviously the realization of this fact confers true dignity and self-respect upon the individuals of the human species; for it implies that man has the power of free

---

Spirits without any of the earthly alloy 'which time is wont to prey upon' is only to indulge in poetical fancy. For each of these Beings either *was,* or prepares to become, a man, if not in the present, then in a past or a coming cycle (Manvantara). They are *perfected,* when not *incipient,* men; and differ morally from the terrestrial human beings on their higher (less material) spheres, only in that they are devoid of the feeling of personality and of the *human* emotional nature — two purely earthly characteristics."
— H. P. BLAVATSKY in her *The Secret Doctrine,* I, 272-4

110. J. E. Boodin, Professor of Philosophy at the University of California, at Los Angeles, has no hesitation in using plain words without mincing them when referring to certain varieties of human egoism, one of the chief of which is the tendency of certain human beings to look upon themselves as virtually perfect imbodiments of the Absolute, if not the Absolute itself. Such a human egoist Professor Boodin plainly calls a "stupid ass."

Very true words, indeed, and one may apply them with distinct effect to those shallow philosophasters who preach that the 'Absolute' — whatever this highly debatable term may mean — is but a few removes, at most, from the comparative insignificance of even man's human monad.

Yet how vastly more comprehensive is the sublime and subtil doctrine of the Adwaita-Vedânta of the Avatâra Śankarâchârya — an echo in this matter, faithfully stated, of the Esoteric Philosophy — that the eternally Ineffable Kosmic SELF-hood is the Root of All and of all beings and entities and their Goal, for ever receding into increasingly sublimer vistas as the progressing and evolving Monadic Hosts, throughout endless Duration, unfold towards it ever more and more for ever!

will and choice, however limited it may be in the present because of his past karman. This faculty or power of discriminative will is godlike, because only the gods, those divine beings who have passed through the human stage in aeons long gone by and have now gone beyond us: only they have this wonderful power of acting in full and untrammelled will and consciousness in carving out the destiny of themselves, that a man in his present stage of evolution does more or less imperfectly and more or less without discrimination.

Obviously, the exercise of free will and its employment to carry these operations into effect, imply instant and immediate responsibility in the human agent, and this all along the line between causal thought and effectual act. The life-atoms in which we live and work on all planes of our being — not merely the life-atoms of this physical body, but the life-centers, the life-atoms, of the intermediate and more ethereal vehicles which 'step down' the tremendous energies of our spiritual nature — all these life-atoms are beings on their upward way for which we are more or less responsible, in so far as our thoughts and acts more or less mold their future. By our thoughts and acts we bind ourselves to these life-centers by bonds of ineluctable destiny, bonds which are unbreakable, and which become part of the fiber of our being and affect us powerfully until we have straightened out the tangles and smoothed out the knots.

These life-atoms, whence came they? Came they to us by chance? Nay, they came to us because we are their parents, and in consequence are responsible for them. The meaning of this may be illustrated by a very simple fact. Put an acorn into the soil and let it grow. In time it will produce a noble tree, an oak, and this oak will give birth to many other acorns proceeding from its heart, from itself. In a somewhat similar manner these life-atoms are our own children, the offspring in their essence of our spirit. For what are they, really? Not only elemental souls, but, if one may adopt the terms of the physical body, they are blood of our spiritual blood and bone of our spiritual bone. We are to them as gods. They come into manifestation from the highest parts of our nature originally, as our spiritual thoughts; for a thought is a force or energy, and being a force it is a substance; therefore it is a thing; and being ensouled by a spiritual energy it too is what we call a soul.

Yes, these life-atoms sprang from us, even as we sprang from the gods in a somewhat similar way. Here is the reason explaining why man has a divine nature, because each one of us, as individuals, is rooted in one of these gods, each one of us springing forth from that evolving god in the beginning of our own present Cosmic evolution: coming forth from that divinity as an un-self-conscious god-spark, in the highest part of that divine being when formerly it was evolving in a past Universe, in other words when that divinity was a man or some other being equivalent to a man, or mayhap inferior or superior to a man.

Even as the life-atoms of our own bodies and of our own intermediate nature have sprung from us, from our own essence, so we sprang forth from the higher nature of such at present divine beings in far past aeons, as thoughts colored with the attributes of the mind and emotion, doing so as the emanation of a force or as a ray; and we then ourselves began to grow and evolve along the Cosmic Pathway upwards which now has culminated in our present humanity and will continue to be our way of evolutionary growth into the dim vistas of the incognisable future.

Universal Nature works after the same manner everywhere — for there is but one universal rule and law of natural existence involving many changes. The birth of a little child from the physical mother on earth is an exemplification of precisely the same rule of action that prevails everywhere in the Great and in the small. Details of the rule differ very widely indeed; but the details are nothing as compared with the rule itself. It is the principle or the law that is important for consideration in the present theme.

Progress through evolving and revolving is the great course of Cosmic Life — growth, evolution, evolving out that which is within, pouring forth that which is locked up within: and in exact proportion as any entity is enabled to self-express itself, to express its own inner faculties and powers, just in the same proportion can it be classified as inferior, intermediate, or high. Even the life-atoms which compose the human body, being themselves the embryo-souls or elemental souls mentioned above, are centers of consciousness, and therefore also are they conscious forces; for force and matter are fundamentally one thing: in other words, Spirit and Substance are fundamentally and essentially one. Were they not, then we would have in the Infinite, two Infinites — an absurdity: an infinite extension of forces on the one hand, and a correspondingly infinite extension of matter on the other hand, but, *ex hypothesi,* eternally different and not springing forth from the same incomprehensible Reality back of both and within both.

The Boundless All would then contain two Infinites — one which we may call the light-side or day-side of Nature, consisting of the incomputable hosts and multitudes of beings which have grown to divinity, to godhood, through all the intermediate stages; and on the other hand, another infinite of material beings and things. This is a logical and also a natural impossibility. The two sides of Nature, the light-side and the matter-side, are essentially and for ever one.

So, then, any such life-atom is, on its lower or vehicular side, the body-side, substantial; and on its superior side or energic side, it is really a center through which pour out into manifestation, through which are unfolded, are unwrapped, are sent forth, all the powers and substances inherent in the being or entity, innate in it, and belonging to an inner stream which is the Monadic Ray, otherwise the characteristic individuality of the spiritual being. It is a thought to pause over and to try to comprehend: the marvelous manner in which Universal Nature is builded, and consequently the manner in which man's constitution is builded; for man is an inseparable part of the Universal All, a microcosmic copy of the all-inclusive Macrocosm.

Everything works for everything else; everything helps everything else. There is in Theosophy, in the Esoteric Tradition, but one 'heresy,' to use a popular Western term, which we call 'the heresy of separateness' — the idea that anything can stand alone and be essentially different from the Universe of which it is an inseparable part. No, everything is interlocked, and interlinked, and bound together with everything else. Nothing is absolutely alone in the Boundless.

The Universe, then, actually is imbodied consciousnesses. This is a wonderful idea, a real key to knowledge and wisdom. The Universe is full of consciousnesses; and indeed, there is naught but consciousnesses in the Universe, for the macrocosmic aggregate of these consciousnesses is the Universe itself. There is no matter *per se;* there is no spirit *per se;* they are two phases of the underlying REALITY. Yet these two phases manifest spirits on the one hand, and matters on the other hand. Nor by the former word is meant excarnate human beings only — nothing so childish as that. Divine entities are here implied, also entities less than divine, entities still more inferior to these last, also human beings, and the hosts of evolving and revolving souls beneath the human stage, and also those other hosts again higher than the highest we can conceive of, when we speak of 'the gods,' and those above the gods.

Matter is, according to the dicta even of our greatest ultramodern scientists, naught but concreted forces so to speak, and this is an old idea among students of the Esoteric Tradition everywhere on earth, an idea which is older than the enduring hills.

Now these imbodied consciousnesses just spoken of are the vast armies or hierarchies containing their respective subordinate hierarchies which infill and in very truth compose the Universe, and in exactly analogical fashion infill and compose the substance of subordinate parts of the Macrocosmic Whole, such as the solar system.

III

As was stated in the beginning of the present chapter, the Esoteric Tradition, in addition to other manners of dividing the Universe into its component parts, likewise divides it into four great Planes or Bases or Worlds, respectively called the Divine, the Spiritual, the World of Souls, and the physical-material Spheres. These four generalized Planes or Bases are the four lower Cosmic Planes of the septempartite solar system; the three higher Planes or Bases being technically called the Arûpa-worlds, even as the four lower planes of the Cosmic Septenary are called Rûpa-worlds.[111] H. P. Blavatsky, in her literary master-work, *The Secret Doctrine*,[112] gives an exceedingly interesting and suggestive schematic diagram of the manner in which the Ancient Wisdom has divided these seven basic Planes or Worlds of the Solar Universe. She speaks of the 'highest' three of these seven Cosmic Planes as being *arûpa* or what to us humans is 'formless' — not that they are formless to their own inhabitants, which would be absurd, but formless in the human manner of looking at things.

The four lower Planes of the Cosmic Seven she names as follows, beginning from the fourth and running downwards to the lowest or Plane of the physical material World:

> ARCHETYPAL WORLD;
>
> INTELLECTUAL IDEATIVE OR 'CREATIVE' WORLD;
>
> SUBSTANTIAL OR FORMATIVE WORLD;
>
> PHYSICAL-MATERIAL WORLD, i. e., the world of concreted bodies or 'shells,' using the word 'shells' here in the sense of integument, carapace, like the shell of an egg.

As said above, these four or Rûpa-worlds, being thus the worlds of 'form,' are in consequence the four Cosmic Planes on which the seven manifest globes of the planetary chain exist, and consequently

---

111. See ch. vi, 'Worlds Visible and Invisible — II.'   112. Vol. I, p. 200.

it is in these four lower Cosmic Planes that are found the larger part of the visible and invisible worlds which, in man's present evolutionary stage, most closely are involved in his destiny because of the peregrinations he makes in and through them as an evolving and revolving Monad.

This same teaching of these four generalized Cosmic Planes or Worlds is mentioned with more or less clearness in many if not all of the ancient religious and philosophical literatures of the world. They are particularly spoken of in the Hebrew Qabbâlâh — the Theosophy of the Jews, a Theosophy, which, however much it may have been modified by later Christian hands and minds, is a derivative from the archaic Qabbâlâh of Chaldaea, the form that the Esoteric Tradition took in Mesopotamia.

The Qabbâlâh, as above stated, is perhaps unusually clear and outspoken among ancient Traditionary Schools in its descriptions of the nature and characteristics of these four basic Cosmic Planes. The Qabbâlâh calls these four Cosmic Planes, counting from the highest downwards to our physical-material plane, by the following names:

1. 'Ôlâm Atzîlôth — World of Emanations
2. 'Ôlâm-hab-Berîâh — World of 'Creation'
3. 'Ôlâm hay-Yetzîrâh — World of Formations
4. 'Ôlâm ha-'Asîâh — World of Labor or Works

These four Qabbalistic worlds are a faithful copy in systemic form of the teaching of the Ancient Wisdom, and as will be seen from the foregoing are identical in all essentials with the four lower Cosmic Planes that H. P. Blavatsky has in *The Secret Doctrine* as stated.

Be it carefully noted that the Qabbâlâh likewise contains in its teaching of these four worlds, the hierarchical structure of the Universe as taught in the Ancient Tradition, since it gives to each one of these four basic Worlds a hierarchy of ten Sephîrôth.[113] Thus there are ten Sephîrôth in the first World or World of Emanations, al-

---

113. The Hebrew word *Sephîrâh* (plural *Sephîrôth*) means a spiritual or angelic being, and likewise the spiritual or angelic quality or attribute which such being imbodies. The Sephîrôth, ten in number, of any such scale or cosmic plane, are, collectively, the divine beings active on such plane both 'creatively' or rather formatively, and also substantively or substantially. They correspond to the Hierarchies or Classes of spiritual-divine beings in other world-religions or world-philosophies, in which various names are given to them. In the Esoteric Tradition they are most commonly called Dhyâni-Chohans.

though these highest ten are rarely alluded to. The next succeeding world in the descent likewise contains ten Sephîrôth, thus forming a hierarchy belonging to this second World, but inferior to the ten Sephîrôth of the preceding World of Emanations: yet the ten Sephîrôth of the World of Emanations work in and through their offspring, the ten Sephîrôth of the second World. The Third or World of Formations likewise contains its hierarchy of ten Sephîrôth, with their own individual characteristics, but yet imbodying and 'stepping down' the characteristics of the ten plus ten Sephîrôth of the second World superior to it. Finally, the lowest of these Qabbalistic worlds contains also its hierarchy of ten Sephîrôth which not only has its own characteristics belonging to its own world, but likewise imbodies and 'steps down' the ten plus ten Sephîrôth of the three superior worlds above itself.

It might be added that the last or lowest or fourth world of this Qabbalistic series is also called 'Ôlâm haq-Qelîphôth — the World of Shells: this last being but another way of describing the fourth or lowest world of the Qabbalistic world-system of four. The student should note very carefully that in this Qabbalistic hierarchical World-System, each superior world reproduces itself in the world inferior to it, which is its emanation, so that there is a Chain of forces and substances and hosts of evolving and revolving 'souls' working by Circulations throughout this Qabbalistic world-system of four divisions — thus reproducing here again with fidelity one of the most sublime teachings of the Esoteric Philosophy.

Says the *Zôhar:*

> The Divine animated all parts of the Universe with characteristic and appropriate spiritual beings, and thus all the hosts exist.[114]

It is further to be carefully noted by the reader that this ancient Qabbâlâh thus makes the essence of the Universe Divine as the source from which all proceeds, with which all and everything is permeated with mind and consciousness and forces, and into which everything and all beings in the distant fulness of time will return — a faithful reproduction of the teaching of the Esoteric Tradition as regards the periods of Cosmic manifestations called Manvantaras and the periods of Cosmic rest called Pralayas.[115]

---

114. *Zôhar,* iii, 68a.

115. Goethe had the same conception of the origin of the Universe in and its ultimate return to the Divine:

"Die ganze Schöpfung nichts ist und nichts war als ein Abfallen und Zurückkehren zum Ursprünglichen." — *Wahrheit und Dichtung,* 8

IV

Fundamental unity underlies all things and all beings and all worlds throughout eternity; and this fundamental unity is not what the West calls 'God,' for this word because of its conventional Western coloring is deplorably inadequate to express the Illimitable Vast and the Incomprehensible and utterly Unthinkable Life-Consciousness-Substance which this Fundamental is. But the numberless multitudes and armies of evolving and revolving beings are, as said before, divided into Individuals in all-various stages or degrees of evolutionary unfoldment, and all advancing on the upward Way. So that each such individual being or Monad by unfolding from its own essence more and more what therein lies, grows steadily into larger reaches of Mind, into ever-expanding ranges of Consciousness; for each such individual Monad is but a life-center, a droplet, in the shoreless Ocean of Infinite Life.

Every being or entity that is, therefore, is a part, as it were a life-atom, of a Being or Entity still more great than it, yet all evolving and revolving upwards; and these hosts of evolving and revolving beings are not only limitless in their numbers, but even as aggregated hosts are incomputable, so numerous are they. Where indeed can one stop, i. e., find an ending? Where can one say: "Here a being begins, and there it must end?" Has anyone ever seen an absolute beginning of any being or thing with 'nothing' preceding it: or an absolute ending thereof, with 'nothing' following it? The mere statement would show us clearly that such are logical monstrosities — fleeting pictures of the mind brought about by the working of that imperfectly developed faculty within us which Plato called the 'phantasy.'

There are of course beginnings and endings of conditions and states of beings and things, but only to these beings or things as traversing certain and particular conditions and states. Thus is the human soul to be viewed: it has a beginning as a condition or a state of the vital soul-structure, inclosing its portion of the divine Monadic Ray; and it has an ending as a *human* soul, because it had a beginning as a soul. This is obviously true because it is an evolving entity, therefore subject to continuous change, implying a passing from change to change, until, from being a merely *human* soul it has unfolded or unwrapped or evolved a larger portion of the Divine Essence within itself. Then it is no longer a 'human' soul but either becoming or already become a spiritual soul, later to unfold itself into becoming the full self-expression of the Monad which is its own core of being or heart of hearts, thus attaining divinity.

Thus as a *human* soul it is an imperfect entity, a composite thing, builded of force and matter, more accurately of spirit and substance — the twain in either case fundamentally one. It, the human soul, functions as a vital soul-structure around the Monadic Ray, during the period when man is in his physical existence on Earth, Globe D of our Planetary Chain. This soul-structure is built of hosts of life-atoms which, in fact, in their aggregate *are* this soul-structure, as a structure or composite. It is this composite soul-structure that the Monadic Ray uses to work through, to self-express itself through, just as the human soul in its turn uses and works through the life-atoms which compose man's physical body, which of course is just such another composite, vitalized organism or structure, but on a much lower plane, the physical.

Similarly, everything everywhere in our own Home-Universe, when considered as a vehicular entity is a composite builded of smaller entities inferior to the being or entity which uses them by working through them, after having first emanated such composite vehicular structure.

One of the most fascinating teachings of the Esoteric Tradition is that which deals with the interlocking and interworking and inter-blending hosts of lives which, as above said, not only infill any one Universe, but in point of fact *are* that Universe. Yet — and this is a point of the first importance — any such Cosmic Hierarchy or Universe, considered as a unit in the Boundless All, has its own characteristic swabhâva or individuality, the all-permeant, intelligent, Life-essence which pervades and inspirits every part and division of such a Hierarchical Unit, and which, therefore, for such Hierarchical Unit is the Oversoul thereof, to adopt Emerson's term. Such Oversoul again is but a unit in a hierarchical aggregate of still vaster magnitude, both in time and space, and this interlocking and interlinking and interblending of hierarchies within hierarchies, or conversely, of hierarchies inclosing hierarchies, is the rule throughout Infinitude.

Thus, and by strict analogical reasoning, any subordinate being or entity which is an Individual in such a parent- or inclosing hierarchy, is itself compounded or composed of hosts of beings or entities inferior to itself, which we may inadequately but descriptively generalize under the appellative term 'life-atoms,' themselves in manifold degrees or stages of evolutionary growth. For each such minor being or entity, here called life-atom, is itself an evolving and revolving and therefore changing because growing unit. For in such

Individual, the hosts which it incloses form and compose its various vehicles or bodies, or sheaths of its consciousness; and the far larger number of them are the offsprings or 'children' of the inclosing Individuality itself.

As an instance in point, or illustration, consider the case of an individual man. *Man is the parent of all the minor beings or lives or life-atoms which compose his various vehicles or sheaths of consciousness* — with the exception of those migrating or transmigrating, i. e., revolving minor lives or life-atoms which, following their own evolutionary courses, are at any instant passing through his various vehicles or sheaths, and this throughout all time. His very body is born of and composed of the entities, the 'invisible lives' — with the exception of the migrating lives or monads just mentioned — which have flowed forth from his own heart of hearts, from the core of his own being, from the inmost of the inmost of his own nature in past lives on earth as well as in the present life; and each one of these subordinate and inferior lives or monads is in itself a more or less progressed life-atom, or psychic atom or evolving and revolving soul — the name does not matter much, provided that the idea is clear that they are life-centers, partly evolved consciousness-centers or monads, and therefore are distinctly evolving entities themselves.

This may be illustrated, perhaps, by the nutrition of the physical body. The food that we take into our bodies: the water, which is also food, that we drink: the air, which is also food, that we breathe: — what do we take out of these things? A certain portion is rejected; as, for instance, as regards the air, a part reissues from the lungs, a part has been absorbed; and the same rule holds good with regard to solid food and drink. In other words, we absorb and assimilate, we take into ourselves, only that which is or has been parts of us — and have been parts of us because belonging to us as once having issued forth from our essence; and the parts which are not native to us, which we, electro-magnetically, to use popular scientific language, cannot assimilate: which are not drawn into us by the alchemy of astral electro-magnetism, so to speak: we reject and cast thus forth again.

One may suppose that there is not a particle of physical matter on our earth which has not been through our bodies in this and in other incarnations, and many times so. Through air, through water, through food, and on each taking of a meal, the body is nourished only by those portions which are native to it; in other words, its own atomic children, so to say, its own offspring, which are the 'souls,' the atomic souls, which originally came forth from the vital center which man is, and which are now drawn back to him and which he takes again temporarily into his being. It is they which build him up, nourish him; and in doing so, they re-enter into their parent, abide for a while within the sphere of his ethereal or electro-magnetic nature, reissue forth again on peregrinations particular to themselves, and again return to him, only to repeat the same cycle endlessly, although as individuals they are steadily growing because evolving, which means unfolding. The same rule applies with equal accuracy to the invisible sheaths or bodies of man's composite constitution.

Again, the same rule of peregrination, or of migrating and transmigrating or circumrotating and transrotating beings and entities, applies throughout the Universe, so that every being or entity which is, is in a continuous and unending series of revolvings through the various worlds or ranges or spheres which form our solar system, whether these worlds and spheres be visible or invisible. Yet these revolvings through the spheres invisible or visible are not in any sense working at hap or hazard, nor by chance or fortuity, but strictly according to natural laws, among which some of the most important are the spiritual, intellectual, psychic, astral, and physical, magnetic attractions or repulsions which direct the 'revolving souls' hither or thither at all times and everywhere. Yet each such peregrinating and evolving and revolving Monad, is a 'child' or offspring of some one of the countless Hierarchies which infill the Universe in the manner hereinbefore sketched.

In precisely the same manner is man a child of the hierarchical Home-Universe or Galaxy in which he lives: in his highest nature, a spiritual offspring or child or *emanation* of the Divine Hierarch that is the Self-conscious Divine Heart of our Universe.

All this may seem very mystical and abstruse to those who are unaccustomed to the philosophy of the Esoteric Tradition, but even a modicum of serious investigation will show the earnest student how fascinatingly coherent and logical and therefore satisfactory these teachings are.

Modern scientists in their researches and discoveries are approaching the frontiers of some of these strangely beautiful teachings of the Esoteric Philosophy, and in so far as they do this one can render due homage of admiration and respect to their labors, which in many cases are the fruit of self-forgetful and self-sacrificing devotion to what to them is the search for Truth.

A modern scientific writer, Geoffrey Martin, recently voiced thoughts in the daily press that are extremely familiar to every student of the Esoteric Tradition, as the following brief citation illustrates. He says:

Every scrap of nitrogen in our bodies once floated in the primeval atmosphere ages before man or beast or plant arose. Every particle of nitrogen in every living thing that creeps upon the earth, in every flower that nestles on the ground, in every tree that grows aloft to heaven, once streamed in the primeval winds of our planet. There is no atom of nitrogen in the air that has not at some time or other in the course of its existence throbbed through the tissues of a living plant or animal, not once but many times.

The writer here speaks of nitrogen as an instance in point, but the Theosophist applies the same principle or rule to every kind of substance of physical matter, and indeed likewise to all the various kinds of mental substances, and to the spiritual ethers as well. Yes, our wondrous philosophy goes much farther, goes to the roots of things, and tells us that though we take things into our bodies as nourishment, they cannot throb with the pulses of the heart and in the tissues of our body unless they are essentially a part of and belong to it; otherwise they are cast out or rejected after a temporary sojourn therein. Nothing can enter the soul and abide there unless it is native to that soul. And what is more, each such entrant or life-atom, or peregrinating monad, enters and leaves the body or the soul at its own stated times. This is one of the minor aspects of the wonderful teaching of the Esoteric Philosophy called the Circulations of the Universe, about which it is hoped to say something more anon.

All these infinitesimal entities, call them monads, or life-atoms, or 'evolving souls' of minor degree, that come back to their respective parents and issue forth again, can be called 'souls' therein in exactly the same way that this Universe of ours is filled with the souls of the Monads which infill it and make it what it is, and of which limitless multitude our own human host is but one family.

The reach and import of this teaching is simply immense. It shows that a man, or indeed any other being or entity whatsoever, is a well-spring of 'creative' activity, pouring forth, as in the case of man, from the unfathomable deeps of his own nature — which is the same thing as saying from the unfathomably deep womb of the Universe — a continuous and ceaselessly flowing stream of invisible lives: let us call them life-atoms, as before. Physical Nature, which is but the copy or the mirror of invisible Nature, pictures the same marvelous fact to all men who are not inwardly blind; pictures this same wonder to every truly seeing eye: and does so in the well-known fact that all beings and things produce from themselves their likenesses. Even the plants, for instance, as long as lasts their state of existence on this physical plane, produce seeds, which grow into other plants of the same exact type, which in their turns produce other multitudes of seeds anew. Every being or entity is continuously doing the same on every plane of its existence, for every being or entity is a well-spring of 'creative' activity.

V

Turning our thoughts now to a previous portion of the study of the present chapter, containing, as this chapter does, one of the most difficult to explain of all Theosophical doctrines, and concentrating our attention for a few moments on the matter of the soul-structure previously mentioned, and its evolutionary progress, we may ask a question that must have occurred to many students: If, as has been stated, the nature of an evolving human soul is a compounded structure, a composite entity, and therefore mortal in character, going to pieces when its life-term is ended: what part of it persists and enables it as a continuing entity to evolve?

The answer to this question has been dealt with, albeit briefly, in a previous chapter wherein is discussed the Secret Doctrine of Gautama the Buddha, to which the reader is now again referred. Here, it may be said that while the facts are as above stated in this question, nevertheless it is not the composite soul-structure itself which was ever said to persist beyond the portals of death, but the individual life-energy, or power, or spiritual ray or influence, which works through each compound entity or structure and holds it together in coherency — it is this individual Monadic Ray which endures; for it is this inworking power or life-energy, individualized as a force, which gathers together the life-atoms of that compound structure of the human soul at each new incarnation on Earth, and, having thus gathered them together again, self-expresses itself anew through such new-old compound; and does so as the Ego of the new incarnation.

Thus also is it in the case of the physical body of that new incarnation on Earth, for this physical body is obviously a compounded entity or structure, and yet precisely the same rule prevails with regard to the physical body as prevails with regard to that structure of far more ethereal matter, of psychical substance, which we call the human soul. The rule of Nature is the same in both cases. The physical body is composed of its own component elements, the physical life-atoms and their vehicles the chemical atoms which form the physical vehicle through which the human soul works and manifests itself on this physical plane: and this human soul is itself the expression, the individualized Force, of the spiritual ray which is the Reincarnating Ego.

In other chapters of this work the manner in which the life-atoms of both the soul-structure and of the physical body are gathered together again in order to compose the new complete vehicle in each case for the new incarnation of the Ego will be more clearly elaborated. Here let it suffice to say that this new gathering together is a new vehicle, it is true, yet composed of the same identical life-atoms that composed both the soul-structure and the physical body of the last preceding incarnation or life on Earth. If it were possible to dissolve our physical body at will, to disintegrate the life-atoms of which it is composed so that it vanishes, and if it were possible to collect by an effort of the will the same identical life-atoms anew into the same human bodily shape, we would have the entire picture of the process of incarnation before us, for that is precisely what happens when a new incarnation on Earth takes place — although such 'effort of the will' is virtually automatic rather than self-conscious in this case.

Yet both these vehicles, soul-structure and body, are in the new incarnation improved somewhat over their state or condition of development of the last preceding incarnation, for evolutionary growth by stages and changes is Nature's first law.

Thus therefore is it that the human soul, although a composite or compounded entity or structure, formed of the life-atoms belonging to the psycho-mental plane or world, or what is often called the psychological sphere, through which the spiritual or Monadic Influence or Power before spoken of works, albeit mortal in structure, yet provides the field of activity or of operation for the Reincarnating Ego; and, furthermore, the soul-structure itself improves and rises in the evolutionary scale by means of the refining influences and work upon its structure of the Reincarnating Ego, so that the time will come in far distant future aeons when the human soul itself will have evolved forth into an individualized and durable center of consciousness — in other words will have become through evolution a Monad — surrounded with a host of subordinate entities which were its former life-atoms and which are now, at this stage, human souls in their turn: the Master-Center being the thus evolved Monad, still overshadowed or enlightened by the Divine Monad which formerly worked through it when it was the human soul.

Now this compound entity which we call the 'soul' is composed, as has so often been said before, of the psycho-mental life-atoms which are native to the plane or to the world or to the sphere — call it what you will — which is the habitat or the domain of such evolving soul, even as the physical body is similarly composed of the life-atoms belonging to the physical habitat or domain wherein such physical body takes its rise. The soul then is not formed of the physical atoms of chemistry, as is the physical body; yet the body is a copy or a mirroring of the soul: the body mirrors the soul of man — an old saying of the poets and philosophers;[116] and this saying is essentially true, though, doubtless, if we desired to be punctilious we might find fault with the various ideas which the poets and philosophers have used in order to express this great truth. The body mirrors forth that more subtil and ethereal entity which we have called the soul.

Yet even the physical atoms of chemistry which build the physical body are, as it were, but the secretions and consequent excretions, or manifested parts, of that same Monadic Ray from which the soul itself takes its life and structure, thus building around itself its own garment of ethereal matter thrown out or emanated from within itself. Just as the sun clothes itself in its own light emanating from itself, flowing forth from its own heart, so does the Monadic Ray secrete and excrete from itself these different groups of life-atoms, each group native to one of the planes through which the Monadic Ray passes, thus building around itself its own different garments of light, as we may call them, for light is force, and force is substance, and substance is matter, of course.

As the body builds its own flesh and bones, surrounded with the outward shell of skin, so in much the same manner does the Monadic Ray when it descends into incarnation anew upon the Earth, throw forth from itself, emanate out from itself, and likewise gather and collect around itself, a concretion of its own most material substances on any one of the various planes through which it descends, and this structure of life-atoms on the psycho-mental plane we call the human soul — the vehicle of the qualities and attributes and powers of the essence of the Monad, working through the Monadic

---

116. As evidenced by Spenser, the English poet who, citing a common opinion of antiquity, writes in *An Hymne in Honour of Beautie,* lines 132-3:

"For of the soule the bodie forme doth take;
For soule is forme, and doth the bodie make."

Ray, that Monad's child, which Ray in other words is the Reincarnating Ego.

The above, however, gives but one-half, more or less, of the substances or aggregated life-atoms composing the structure of the human soul; the other half, more or less, being the vast number of life-atoms thrown forth or secreted and excreted from the Monadic Ray in other lives, and which return by psycho-magnetic attraction to the Monadic Ray when it descends to reincarnation anew on Earth.

This thought also gives the key to a most important matter, which is the generation of new-born elementals by the evolving and revolving soul-entity, these new-born elementals becoming at their generation parts or portions or native individuals of what is called the material planes or spheres;[117] and thus building up from the light-side of Nature, in other words the spiritual part of Nature, that flowing river of energic substances which manifest as the material or substantial or dark or night-side part of Nature.

Many students doubtless have asked themselves where and how the material side of Nature, considered as an aggregate of evolving individuals, is recruited, if throughout the endless eternity of the past every individualized being or entity has been progressing and evolving towards divinity or the light-side of Nature. Obviously the thought involved in the question is a pertinent one, because the endless eternity of the past seems to give time enough to have refined all the substantial side of Nature into divinity. The foregoing then is the explanation of this most fascinating and profound subject, although it should be obvious to every thoughtful and reflective mind that the brief and rather sketchy explanation just hereinbefore given is at the very best the mere outline of what is in itself a fundamental doctrine of the Esoteric Tradition.

The root-thought of this question, pertinent as it is, is the illusory belief in the mind that at the beginning of the cosmic manifestation

---

117. Quite so; and expressed with sufficient accuracy. But this statement of the generation of those especial Elementals whose native realm is karmically placed in the material planes or spheres, in no wise precludes or takes the place of the other equally true and equally important fact that the evolving and revolving soul-entity generates other classes of Elementals on the other planes and spheres through which it passes in its evolutionary revolvings or pilgrimage.

In other words, the Monad through its various sheaths or vehicles, including the soul-structure, is a continuously emanating or so-called 'creative' center or focus, producing or generating or emanating on each plane through which it passes Elementals karmically appropriate to and fit for each such plane or sphere.

all possible emanation for that Cosmic Period once and for all took place, and that thereafter the entities thus manifested and thus beginning their aeons-long pilgrimage through the visible and invisible worlds, have but to continue evolving and revolving until the vast aggregate thus originally emanated, both individually and as a collectivity, reaches the divine perfection from which it all originally sprang. As said, this idea is entirely illusory and therefore wrong. The truth of the matter is that emanation or origination is a continuous process even during the Cosmic Time-period, and it is precisely this unending stream of newly-born monadic units which provides the amazing and fascinating and endless variety in Universal Nature that the most unobservant intelligence discerns everywhere: beings in the lowliest stage of their evolutionary journey, beings farther advanced in their pilgrimage, higher states or stages still of other evolving and revolving beings and entities — these grades rising along the Cosmic Ladder of Life until the mind staggers in an attempt to follow its reaches into the dim vistas of both space and time.

All this, however, must not be supposed to exclude the equally important fact of Nature that these countless hosts of evolving and revolving 'souls' are divided, as indeed they obviously are, into Families or Groups or aggregates; and it must be remembered also that Nature's processes of growth or evolutionary unfolding take place by means of secular or periodic or cyclic impulses or surges, like the waves of the incoming tides, following each other, both waves and tides, in regular and unending succession.

Every entity is a self-contained being, an energic 'engine,' to use a term borrowed from mechanics, whether that engine be on the divine plane, or the spiritual plane, or the intellectual plane, or the psycho-mental or emotional plane, or the vital-astral plane, or the physical plane; and being such a vital 'engine,' it produces what is within itself, constantly throwing forth streams of vital force — these streams themselves composed or builded of units which we may call life-atoms, each such life-atom imbodying an elemental. Everything thus works for everything else. No man nor indeed any other being can be in Nature a complete and isolate law unto himself or itself. Man, for instance, must obey overruling natural powers which intrinsically and in their essence are likewise his own spiritual constitution. Obedience in this sense is the noblest rule in life, because the highest; and upon this fact is founded the teaching as well as the human intuition of what men call substantial ethics or morals. Man's obedience is a duty to these controlling powers of the Universe, divine-spiritual in their originating operations, which gave him primal birth in the Universe, and towards reunion with which he is now evolving and revolving on his long, long, long cosmic pilgrimage. He began as a life-atom, ensouled by an elemental in the beginning-time of the manifestation of our Universe; during its changes he grew; he evolved; he poured forth those qualities and faculties from within himself at this or at that or at the next and at each succeeding stage; and by so pouring forth and exercising his innate powers, he grew from the inferior to the better; and the process continued until he became what he now is — a human soul, a composite entity formed of other life-atoms: a soul to which the Monadic Ray of his inner constitution has given birth and in which soul he is now self-expressing himself, as that Monadic Ray: doing so in this soul formed of these hosts of life-atoms, teaching them, his own children, and leading them also on and upwards: which is a godlike thing to do.

And he, this human, this man, where may he stop on the pathways of destiny? Where can he stop? There are no beginnings and ends, considered as absolutes; there are only relative beginnings and ends of equally relative conditions or states. A man is continuously in growth, even as the life-atoms are growing: the life-atoms composing all his vehicles — invisible and ethereal, and exterior and visible — which are likewise entities on the upward path. In time to come, the human, by continuously more and in larger and fuller measure pouring forth from within himself the spiritual attributes of his own divine-spiritual source, over-enlightened by his own god in proportion as he so pours forth from his heart of being, from his heart of hearts, his own inner capacities and powers, causes the life-atoms of his body likewise to respond ever more quickly, more magnetically, more electrically, to the impulses which impel him forwards; and in this manner elevates also, and aids in their evolution, the minor monads or ensouled life-atoms. Thus it is that man grows by evolution or unfolding on all planes, becoming more and more, as endless time flows on, a fuller and more perfect exponent and manifestation of the inexpressibly wonderful faculties locked within his own heart of hearts, the divine core of his being.

CHAPTER IX

THE EVOLUTIONARY PATHWAY TO THE GODS

ETERNITY stretches in one direction behind and in another direction in front of us, and along and within this eternity the numberless multitudes of beings and entities which have been studied in the preceding chapters have been evolving — and will evolve — for ever. This progressive growth or development is continuously in action throughout Universal Nature — nebula or comet, star or planet, atom or electron, all exemplify it on one side of the picture; and, on the other side, gods, cosmic spirits or Dhyâni-Chohans, men, the beasts, and all so-called 'animate' entities of whatsoever kind and wheresoever situated.

Universal Nature itself may be thought of as being in two divisions: first, countless hosts of beings and entities of widely varying degrees of development in evolution and possessing proportionately *self-consciousness* in accordance therewith — that is to say in widely varying degrees; and, second, countless hosts of beings and entities in inferior evolutionary development, and composing in their endless aggregates what is popularly called the material side of Universal Nature — these being the habitat or home of the self-conscious beings and entities of the former division.

Technically speaking, this essential carpentry of the Universe with its inspiriting Hosts may be called Monadism and Atomism,[118]

---

118. These two terms, 'Monadism' and 'Atomism,' are placed in opposition merely for purposes of illustrative description. Actually, Monadism and Atomism are but two words descriptive of the same essential fact — the inherent and unceasing urge in Universal Nature to manifest or self-express itself in and through Individuals. When these Individuals are viewed as belonging to the higher or so-called divine and spiritual worlds, they are called Monads; and when these Individuals self-express themselves in the worlds or realms of substantial being or matter, and because they therein express themselves as discrete or individual points, they are properly referred to as Atoms in the original Greek sense of the word as used by Democritus and Epicurus as signifying Indivisibles. The point is important, and should not be overlooked.

It might be added in passing that some of the great religious philosophies

signifying the consciousness-side of Nature and the so-called 'unconscious' side of Nature. These two form the evident dualism of and in Nature, but it must be remembered that this dualism exists in the periods of Cosmic Manifestation only.

However, these two divisions just mentioned grade off into each other imperceptibly, so far as our own Home-Universe is concerned; and the intermediate parts or portions of the Cosmic Whole between the two relative extremes or divisions comprise the hosts of beings and entities in whom spirit and matter are more or less evenly balanced, and who and which are called by different names in the Esoteric Philosophy — verily offsprings of heaven and of earth, our Human Family being one of such hosts. Elsewhere than on Earth in our own Home-Universe or Galaxy the same intermediate parts or portions of the Cosmic Whole consist of beings and entities occupying the same relative positions that the various stocks or groups of beings and entities do on our Earth itself. Like the human race on this Earth, beings corresponding to men on other planets aspire towards divinity and are evolving out of the darkness of imperfection of the material side of nature into becoming gods, capable of taking a relatively fully self-conscious part in the Great Work of the light-side of the Universe.

I

Inspiring principles of religion, philosophy, and science, have been taught in all ages and among all races of men: they have governed the lives of men and have made these men better therefor because they satisfy the intellect as well as the heart and soul; they give hope, and are therefore inspiring.

For example, let us take from a Celtic people, the Welsh, two Druidic Triads. The first runs:

Animated Beings have three states of Existence, that of Inchoation in the Great Deep or Lowest Point of Existence [the atoms]; that of Liberty in the State of Humanity [the self-expressing monad in man]; and that of Love, which

of the ancient world, such as the archaic religion-philosophy of Zoroaster the Persian, were positively dualistic in type and character for purposes of formulated teaching and definition to the masses. Yet even these so-called dualistic religion-philosophies were, without exception, founded upon an esoteric doctrine or basis — a faithful echo of the archaic Esoteric Tradition — which taught the primordial Unity of Cosmic Being with a voice as insistent as was that which taught the public formulation of cosmic dualism in manifestation.

is happiness in Heaven [the gods, rays from whom exist in humankind as the divine part of us men].

The second Triad runs thus:

There are three necessary occasions of Inchoation [beginning]: to collect the materials and properties of every nature [the aggregation of atoms in order, for the formation of corporeal vehicles or bodies, small or great as the case may be, and on different planes]; to collect the knowledge of everything [the intrinsic and natural function of the learning monad, the learning soul, the growing human conscious entity]; and to collect power towards subduing the Adverse and Devastative, and for the divestation of Evil [which is the work of the gods].[118a]

Let us turn now to the Latin poet Lucretius. Lucretius has been greatly misunderstood in modern times. He was a disciple of the Greek philosopher, Democritus, or rather, perhaps, of that other Greek atomistic philosopher, Epicurus, who was a follower of the Democritan atomistic system. In connexion with the latter name, the very adjective, 'epicurean,' in our modern ears, rings unpleasantly. To Europeans it seems to signify a man or a woman who follows naught but pleasure, making that an end in life. But this misunderstanding is downright unfair. These men were two really great thinkers, who, one may say in passing, actually laid the foundation of the modern scientific doctrine of the atomic structure of the material world.

From their theories, only a few hundred years ago European chemists and physicists obtained the fundamental ideas of modern physical chemistry; and the latter even adopted the early Greek exoteric meaning of the word 'atom'— which, of course, is from the Greek — as signifying an indivisible, something that can no longer be divided: although since the most recent discoveries of physical chemistry, it is known that the atom is indeed a true divisible. These early European chemists did not understand what those two

---

118a. In *Barddas* (a collection of manuscripts in Cymric) the Rev. J. Williams ab Ithel, M. A., translates these triads as follows:

"13. The three states of existence of living beings: the state of Abred in Annwn; the state of liberty in humanity; and the state of love, that is, Gwynvyd in heaven.

"17. The three necessary occasions of Abred: to collect the materials of every nature; to collect the knowledge of everything; and to collect strength to overcome every adverse and Cythraul, and to be divested of evil; without this traversing of every state of life, no animation or species can attain to plenitude." — p. 173

men, Democritus and Epicurus, who were really great in their way, actually meant. They meant indivisibles, as the Greek word 'atom' itself shows, as signifying that which cannot be cut or divided. In other words, Democritus and Epicurus and their early School meant precisely, although in physical-astral relations, what the Theosophist calls Monads. It is quite likely, indeed probable, that Democritus taught a Monadism identic with that taught by the Esoteric Tradition. They indeed taught Monadism — the existence of spiritual consciousness-centers, spiritual Individuals; and they have been misinterpreted as teaching the existence — as earlier European chemists did — of little hard round bodies, incompressible and virtually eternal, which until very recently were supposed to be indivisible, and moreover the ultimates or originals of matter.

Lucretius, then, in his noble poem, *De rerum natura* ('On the Nature of Things'), most eloquently describes the Democritan and Epicurean system of philosophy. A few citations are hereinunder given:

I shall proceed to tell thee of the entire system of celestial things, and of the gods, and to unfold to thee the first principles of all things, from which Nature produces, develops, and sustains everything that is, and into which Nature again resolves all things at their dissolution: these first principles in explaining our theme we are accustomed to call matter, and the generating elements of things, and to call them the seeds of all things and to give to them the name of 'primary bodies,' because from them as primaries all later things are derivatives — [119]

In other words, in all important points, this is a fair approach to the Theosophical doctrine of Monads ensouling Atoms.

And again:

Reason and the study of Nature must be the dispellers of the terrors and darknesses of the mind . . . of the human soul — and our first philosophical principle is this, that NOTHING IS EVER DIVINELY PRODUCED FROM NOTHING.[120]

Somewhat later in the same first Book, he declared:

Furthermore, Nature resolves every single thing into its own fundamental elements, and DOES NOT REDUCE ANYTHING TO NOTHING.[121] [122]

---

119. Book I, lines 48-56.   120. *Op. cit.*, Book I, lines 149-51.
121. *Op. cit.*, lines 249-50.
122. Note the echoes of this thought in more modern times:
     "Kein Wesen kann zu nichts zerfallen." — GOETHE
          "All that is at all
          Lasts forever, past recall." — BROWNING

If the reader be under the sway of European orthodox religious teaching, he might say readily enough that this ancient Roman Epicurean was teaching personal immortality; on the other hand, the Epicurean philosophy has been mistakenly supposed to teach that man is a bundle of physical atoms only, which bundle or aggregate falls to pieces when he dies; and that hedonism, or the doctrine of seeking mere pleasure in life, is a natural and logical outflowing consequent therefrom. But Lucretius did not teach either idea. He taught in this respect somewhat as the Theosophist holds: to wit, that the central spiritual core of man is an indivisible entity, an Atom, or indivisible Individuality, an indivisible consciousness-center, which expresses itself necessarily through lower atomic aggregates, inferior to it, because in no other wise can it have contact or contactual relations with this physical sphere.

This continuous process of ever greater self-expression on the part of each and every spiritual Monad is true evolution as taught in the Esoteric Tradition, Nature furnishing but the surrounding stimulus, thus calling out the latent powers and faculties of the indivisible spiritual Monad in its aeons-long peregrinations through the visible and invisible spheres, and therefore during the course of its equally long evolvings and revolvings. These lower atomic aggregates, just spoken of, in their turn of necessity also self-express themselves as aggregates, because in some degree they are alike to the inner Monad, governed each one or guided each one by its own monadic core, enlightened and illuminated by that divine-spiritual Monadic Center within each. But this is not all the doctrine alluded to here, this enlightenment or illumination actually being a flow of primordial force expressing itself through the intermediate nature of the being or entity and therefore ultimately through the physical body in which all these beings or entities respectively live and are imbodied, and thus experience the relativities of the physical world.

Deduction: Having this indivisible Essence and Center or Monad in ourselves — which in its own nature is immortal — therefore, as before stated, being the droplets of the Cosmic Essence, we are in this respect deathless; which means that the essence of us is deathless, and being deathless that essence is logically birthless, because there is no such thing as an infinity which begins—an infinity having only one end, so to say. That spiritual-divine part of us never had a beginning and it never shall have an end. It is the living spiritual-divine Monad, of which Cosmic Life is the essence; and Cosmic Life is eternal. For Intelligent Life, after all, is but an expression of the finest and noblest form of Cosmic Consciousness-Substance.

Our whole inner nature is, as has been said, a sheaf or bundle of force-substances, which in their aggregate form the entire constitution of man; and through this composite sheaf or bundle the divinity at the heart of us expresses itself — expresses itself therefore through our human selfhood, which is the intermediate part of our constitution, i. e., of this sheaf.

II

The entire constitution of man, as should be sufficiently obvious from what precedes, is an integral and inseparable part or portion, not only of the surrounding Kosmic Whole, but likewise an integral and inseparable albeit compounded part or portion of that minor division of the Kosmic Whole which is the solar system. Not only this, but the human constitution, which means obviously the constitution of every individual human being, is an equally integral and inseparable part or portion of a still smaller division of the Kosmic Whole which we may call the Earth-system or the planetary chain of Earth. These statements should be clear enough because if a being is a portion of a grand whole, a portion integral and inseparable thereof, such being is obviously likewise an integral and inseparable part or portion of any minor but inclusive subdivision of the Kosmic Whole, in which such minor division the being lives.

We thus come to an exceedingly beautiful, profound, and suggestive deduction, to wit: every such being, or integral and inseparable part, is not only builded of the essences and substances and forces and attributes and qualities of its inclusive hierarchy — whether subdivisionally or larger — but is likewise coeval with the beginning of the Universe itself: nay, not merely coeval with the beginnings thereof, but because it is of the very substances of the Universe itself, it is coeval and identic with the Universe.

This entire Earth-system includes those Monads (or spiritual centers) which individually, i. e., distributively for the hierarchy of the Earth-system, are each one a human being now, and on whatever globe of the planetary chain, and also all other beings which such Earth-system incloses. All have existed since the very beginnings of our planetary chain in time and space; nay, more, as already stated, we are coeval not only with our solar system, but likewise with the Galaxy; and in a still grander sweep of being we are coeval with and identic with however vast a range of the Boundless Kosmos we choose at any moment to look upon, for purposes of convenient thought, as the fields of our destiny in the future.

We were with the Sun, with the Earth, in the very morning of Time, though not then in bodies of flesh; and we helped to build this planetary chain as well as this Earth of ours, because, not only are we its children but we are collectively and individually integral parts thereof. This last fact is obvious. Even our bodies, our physical bodies, are of the substance of which our Mother-Earth itself is composed; and every atom that now sings its musical hymn or note in our bodies has likewise sung its paean in the Sun and in other planets and in the inter-planetary spaces during its unceasing peregrinations — in this case as a life-atom — in ages past during the course of its evolving and revolvings.

In thus emerging from spirit, as stated above, Nature proceeded steadily and systematically to enshroud itself in veils or garments of increasing materiality, as has already been stated when sketching an outline of the teaching concerning the Cosmic Worlds or Planes or Spheres; and continued so doing until it reached the limit possible, in that direction of increasing materiality, for this present great evolutionary Period or Cosmic Adventure. Turning this lowest point, the evolutionary stage of grossest materiality possible for the planetary chain in this Cosmic Manvantara, the entire Earth-system or planetary chain began to reascend towards spirit once more, but now with incalculable fruits of experience gained by every being and entity and thing composing the Earth-system: experiences gained, furthermore, by sojourning in the matters and qualities and attributes of this presently existing Cosmic System of planes of substances and forces.

So that in the present stage of evolution on earth, developmental or evolutionary growth takes place from without inwards, because, having begun the ascent towards spirit, the procedure henceforth will be the involution of matter into spirit and the evolution of spirit, just as on the Downward Arc or descent into matter the procedure of developmental growth was the involution of spirit and the evolution of matter. That is to say that at present we are advancing towards and into the inner and invisible planes and worlds and spheres which we passed through on our Downward Arc. This means that not only every more progressed being, such as man, is so evolving, but also that the entire manifested Nature on our Earth (elsewhere likewise, but here for the moment the discussion concerns our planetary chain alone) is doing so likewise.

In other words, the idea is that henceforward there is a gradual, secular, and steady dematerialization of matter towards ethereal tenuity, and finally the mergence into Cosmic Spirit of all beings and entities and things, comprising a veritable River of Lives carrying with it all results of this Cosmic process in the shape of experience, bringing about evolved faculty or developed power.

Having thus merged into Cosmic Spirit, for a vastly long period of time in these highest or spiritual realms or worlds or spheres, the Evolutionary Wave or River of Lives ceases its pulsing progress for aeons, reaching as it has the merging of the 'River' into the Kosmic Ocean of being — and in this case the reference is to the Cosmic Spirit of the Solar System. The entities and beings of all-various classes composing such Wave or River re-enter into the ineffable Mystery of the Divine-spiritual, where they take their rest and repose through the ages of the ensuing Chain-Pralaya, or resting-time, and there assimilate and build into the fabric of their respective monadic essences the fruitage of the vast evolutionary experience gained in the period of cosmic manifestation which as a Wave or River of Lives they have left behind for their interval of spiritual rest and recuperation.

When the cosmic clock again points its hands to the time for a new evolutionary period of manifestation of the planetary chain, then this same Wave or River of Lives, composed of these almost incomputable hosts of entities or beings, begins a new evolutionary course, but on planes higher than or superior to those of the preceding Life-Period through which the Evolutionary Wave had passed — planes of more refined substance than those of the preceding life-cycle.

It is quite possible for an imbodied human being to get some adumbration of the state of things or rather of the state of consciousness, if we can so phrase it, during the Pralaya of a Planetary Chain or even during the Solar Pralaya — the resting-time of the entire solar system. This is done by remembering that Pralaya is dissolution or death; and the Pralaya of a solar system or of a planetary chain, the Earth-chain for instance, signifies that its higher principles have gone into still loftier and more sublime spiritual realms and spheres for their periodic rest; and that the lower quaternary of the solar system or any other system such as a planetary chain, is then dissipated into its component life-atoms, which likewise then rest during their long dreamless sleep. Thus stay all things and beings until the reawakening comes for the new Manvantara, whether of a solar system or of a planetary chain, though it should be remembered that the rest-periods of the life-atoms are vastly shorter than is the rest-period of highly evolved spiritual beings, because the life-atoms within a relatively short time again become active and pursue anew their ceaseless peregrinations of evolvings and revolvings hither and yon through larger spaces still, until the reawakening of the resting System, whether of solar system or of planetary chain, magnetically attracts them back to such new reawakened System.

Thus it is that during such Pralaya of a system, the higher principles thereof, i. e., the spiritual and intellectual parts, are in their Nirvâna — equivalent to the Devachan of the Reincarnating Ego of the human being after physical death; while the life-atoms of such system follow their peregrinating wanderings in precisely the same manner in which the life-atoms of man's physical body follow their peregrinations while the Reincarnating Ego of the man is in its Devachan. These hints thus do indeed give us some adumbration of the state of things or of consciousness when such a Planetary Chain is in its rest-period.

Again, some idea of still greater clarity may be had of what takes place in the Pralaya of a system, by a human being who is trained through initiation to 'see,' and this vision may be had by such trained ego self-consciously entering into what the egoic human consciousness experiences during what the average man calls dreamless sleep. This state is technically called तुरीय (turîya) — a Sanskrit word meaning 'fourth,' and is the highest state of Samâdhi, which is indeed a Nirvânic condition of human consciousness. Putting the matter in other words, the Turîya-condition of human consciousness is a virtual attaining of spiritual self-conscious unity with the Âtman or essential Self of the Man, and implies a virtual identification of the Ego thereby with the Cosmic Spirit. Otherwise phrased, this condition is a becoming at one with the essence of the Monad.

Thus the initiated Adept can at will reach this state of spiritual consciousness with fair ease. But the average good man, whose higher principles are to a certain extent at least active, may also get some, however faint, understanding of the consciousness existing in the Pralaya of a system; but it is obvious that his power and ability to do so are incomparably feebler than are those of the trained and initiated Adept.

The fact of the mergence into Cosmic Spirit of all beings at the time of the Solar Pralaya, or dissolution of the solar system, is what H. P. Blavatsky referred to, at least in part, when she says: "Theosophy considers humanity as an emanation from Divinity on its return path thereto." When Divinity is thus reached it is obvious that the individual Monads merge their respective monadic consciousnesses into their Divine Source, and thus, at least for the period of the Pralaya in question, partake of the character and vast

reach of the Consciousness of the Divine Originant — only to re-
emerge therefrom, again as Monads, when a new Manvantara opens.

III

These ideas were taught even in early Christianity — in the
very origins of that particular religion. Those who have not examined the evidences for this statement — evidences both historic
and theologic — probably have no idea what immense changes came
into the understanding of Christian fundamentals, and therefore into
the method of the presentation of the Christian religion, since the
time of its first and greatest propagandists.

Take the case of Divinity as an instance in point. Clement of
Alexandria, a very early Greek Father and indeed one of the greatest, and all his school for a long time after his period, talked and
wrote of the gods as actual beings, and only sometimes called them
'angels.' Origen of Alexandria, who was almost contemporaneous
with Clement and who was an even greater man, did precisely the
same thing after the same manner more or less.

Origen, in his polemical writings against Celsus,[123] says that
there are passages in the books of the Hebrew scriptures where the
'angels' therein referred to are spoken of as being 'gods'; and any
Hebrew scholar knows that this statement is verbally true.

The very Christian Arnobius, who lived in the fourth century,
refers to the matter as follows:

Gods, angels, daimones, or whatever other name they possess — [124]

— thus identifying, and confusing, these divinities under the different names which different schools of pagan thought had called
them by.

Augustine, also of the fourth century, and one of the most important and influential of the Christian Fathers in later centuries, speaks
of the spiritual beings whom the ancients called 'gods,' as being
identical with the beings whom the Christians then called 'angels.'[125]
This was undoubtedly the consensus of opinion of the fourth century — a hundred years, more or less, after Clement and Origen.
Already the decay of original or primitive Christianity had begun,
and as time went on, the word 'gods' was dropped from theological

---

123. *Contra Celsum*, Bk. V, ch. iv. Celsus was an erudite 'pagan' philosopher
who criticized — and criticized very successfully — the new-fangled religion
then being popularized in the countries around the Mediterranean Sea.

124. *Adv. Gentes.*   125. *De civitate Dei* (City of God), xix, 3.

usage. It first became unpleasant to the orthodox ear and then was considered to be positively heretical.

Lactantius, also of the fourth century, another greatly considered Christian Father, who refers to the famous Roman philosopher and statesman Seneca's account of the spiritual beings directing the world and holding their spiritual posts or positions by, through, and from, Divinity, contends only that it were better to call these spiritual beings 'angels,' as being a term to be preferred to that of 'gods'; and he protests against worship of these Christian 'angels' as gods. He further quotes an oracle delivered by the Pythoness at Delphi — the famous ancient Greek oracle, as everyone probably knows — in which oracle the gods are called the 'Messengers,' that is to say, the 'angels' of Zeus.

'Angel' is a Christian term adopted from the Greek word ἄγγελος (*angelos*). The Greek meaning of this word is 'messenger,' and this word originally signified the 'messengers' between states, or between man and man; and in one department of Greek philosophy also signified the intermediaries or messengers between the gods above and the beings existent in the lower spheres, i. e., the messengers passing to and fro, carrying messages from men to the gods, and equivalently, carrying the gods' messages to intelligent beings below, thus forming, in fact, one of the 'Circulations of the Cosmos':[126] one of the methods of union and intercommunication between the invisible worlds in all their ranges and the outer or material worlds in all their ranges. This of course has nothing whatever to do with modern 'spiritism.'

The word 'angel' was early taken over or adopted by the primitive Christians and employed to signify those spiritual intermediaries between Divinity and the human species whose function was that of messengers or envoys between man and 'God' or 'God' and man.

In connexion with this term 'angel,' it may be as well to state that it has been used more or less constantly in the Occident from the beginning of the Christian 'dispensation' to signify certain spiritual beings who not only were 'angels' in the original Greek sense of the word, as Messengers, but also as including hierarchies or families of spirits intermediate between man and Divinity. All this is but a feeble echo of the archaic teaching, common to all the ancient

---

126. For a clearer understanding of the high signification of the expression, 'Circulations of the Cosmos,' the reader is referred to later portions of this book wherein an attempt is made to set forth the vastly important teaching which goes under that title, and its wide and profound meaning.

world, that between the spiritual realms and the material world in which man lives, there are indeed different hierarchical families or hosts of spiritual beings, of which hosts or families the human race itself is really one — but a 'fallen' host, fallen because sunken or descended from an original spiritual state into fleshly incarnation on earth. Thus it is that European mystics from very early times, re-echoing the archaic doctrine which is one portion of the teaching of the Esoteric Tradition, have spoken of men as being 'fallen angels' — a statement perfectly true in itself, but entirely inadequate in descriptive power because lacking the background of the profound philosophical teachings which the Esoteric Tradition alone gives.

The subject of 'fallen angels' is a very interesting one indeed, and provided that we change the noun 'angels' and substitute in its place the noun 'gods,' we shall have a meaning which in its philosophical and religious implications and reach of significance is simply immense, one which lies in the background of all the great world-religions of the past, and which indeed, in its philosophical meaning, lies also in the background of the great world-philosophies of the past.

But what then are 'fallen' gods or angels? We find in all the religions and philosophies, legends given in a mythological form of the existence of beings of spiritual nature who 'fell,' that is to say who 'lost' their spiritual status and condition and became beings of nonetheless continuing individuality in the lower or material worlds. Thus they are actually Wanderers or Searchers for knowledge and wisdom in those lower worlds, and are likewise beings and entities possessing individual wills: beings in fact who form the different hierarchies of the lower spheres, which is but another way of saying the different world-systems: these are the 'fallen gods,' the 'fallen angels' so called.

One may see here a direct reference to the 'Garden of Eden' mythos in the Hebrew Testament of the Jews. Adam and Eve living in their paradise represent one aspect of this more or less universal mythos, for it was only when they ate of the 'Tree of Knowledge' that they lost their original spiritual status of innocence and quasi-un-self-consciousness, and left their paradise in order to become the seed, according to this curious Hebrew legend, of the humanity of the future. But there are of course other aspects of the general theme, that is to say, other secondary mythoi or legends having this general theme as their common background.

The Christians have called these beings 'fallen angels'; and Milton, in his great poem, *Paradise Lost,* uses the typical Christian, in fact the Puritan, ideas of his time in Britain, in order to write anew the age-old mystical teachings regarding beings who were originally sparks of cosmic divinity, lights of the Central Fire of Life, who had become *individualized,* and therefore who had become learners, growers, evolving beings.

Therefore are the 'fallen gods,' the 'fallen angels,' those who have left the pure spiritual condition or state in which no *personalized* individuality exists — and which state is the bare, sheer, pure, un-self-conscious life in cosmic consciousness — in order to become individualized entities, evolving individuals, growing and thinking beings, with a developing will and with developing individualized intelligence.

See the contrast: from being sparks of divinity, sparks of the Central Fire of Life so to say, they become bright, fiery intelligences, each one destined in the future to carve out its own individual career. How? Through growth, through evolution, through unfolding or unwrapping innate and latent capacities: through *becoming.*

Thus then are the legends or mythoi concerning the 'fallen gods,' the 'fallen angels,' the kernels of many of the ancient mystery-doctrines. The Christians had the legend. One may read about it under one form in the *Book of Revelation* so called. The ancient Greeks had it in their mythological legends concerning their Titans, who were cast into the lowest deeps of Tartarus by the decree of the almighty ruler of Olympus, Zeus, the meaning being that they had begun to exercise independently their own innate powers of intelligence and will, by contrast with the ocean of Cosmic Intelligence and Life, which from our human individualized standpoint, is un-individualized, pure, sheer consciousness.

The verity of this fact, this growth towards an individualizing consciousness, starts into instant prominence before our vision, as we trace the armies of manifested beings and entities and things backwards to realms beneath the human stage. The families of beasts are less individualized than are men. The vegetation has a more general and still less individualized consciousness than have the beasts. The rocks exist in what may be called a unitary form of consciousness with but slight individualization; and beneath the rocks we have the various atomic elements; and back of these, the hierarchies, usually graded into three classes, of the Elemental Kingdoms, existing in a quasi-individualized way, and manifesting the generalized cosmic forces.

The ancient Persians, copying the Babylonians who had preceded them, likewise had their myths of a War in Heaven, of a Rebellion against the Mighty Powers of Heaven; and these 'rebels' were they who in the Perso-Babylonian mythic cycle 'fell' or were 'cast out.' They were the 'fallen gods,' the 'fallen angels' of the religions and philosophies of the Mesopotamian and high-land countries surrounding the great plains of the Euphrates and the Tigris.

So likewise, in ancient India, in archaic Hindûsthân — the Motherland of religions and philosophies, as it has been called — do we read of the Asuras, who had rebelled against the Suras or 'gods.' Indeed, the Asuras or 'not-gods' — for thus we may translate the word *asuras* — were originally Suras or gods; but they 'rebelled' and fell, and thus found themselves in a never-ending struggle with the Suras, who, so to say, were crystallized in impassive 'purity.'

So this 'fall,' this 'rebellion,' is really nothing but the entering upon the pathway of evolutionary progress, the beginning of all these numberless hosts who 'fell,' or were 'cast out,' to use mythological terms — the beginning, indeed, of the exercise of individual will-power, individual intelligence; the beginning of the exercise of 'self-directed evolution.'

Such then are the 'fallen gods,' the 'fallen angels.' We humans are they, at least one host of them; but we do not compose more than one host of them, for the human army is but one multitude, one family, of the almost boundless aggregate of hosts which form the entire Universe that is perceptible by sense or conceivable by mind.

When the stirrings in the heart of each Monad, of each divine spark, in their aggregate forming these hierarchies, first began in an impulse for self-manifestation, for self-growth: when the first impulses towards the exercise of individual will-power and intelligence began to stir in the core of the core of these monadic intelligences, of these bright shining lives: then they 'fell' or were 'cast out,' which words really mean, as the ancient tradition explains them, that they 'descended' into the material worlds in order to learn the lessons that the worlds of manifestation could give to them. Leaving in the beginning of time their high spiritual status and condition as un-self-conscious god-sparks, so to say crystallized in impassive purity, cycling down through the worlds visible and invisible, they entered upon the sublime Adventure of self-evolution, of self-growth, of *self-becoming,* and of bringing to each one of their enshrouding quasi-conscious veils or sheaths of consciousness, an ever expanding consciousness of each one's own inner being; for the most wonderful thought in the archaic evolutionary scheme is this: that not only is the spiritual Monad itself evolving, revolving in unceasing peregrinations, but it thus aids in the evolution of every one of these enshrouding garments or veils in which and through which it expresses its own transcendent powers.

In using the word 'fall' or 'cast out,' the reader should not misunderstand these phrases to mean so much the idea that superior intelligences spurned beings below them and thus drove them into lower spheres, for this is entirely wrong; the truth is that the phrase 'cast out' or the word 'fell' merely signifies that when the karmic evolutionary stage had arrived in which these beings seeking further experience had to begin a new evolutionary course, they embarked upon it from their own inner impulses, karmically brought about by the seeds of action and attraction gathered up in previous world-cycles before these beings entered into their last pralayic rest-period.

Taken in conjunction with the other Theosophical teaching of the course of Nature's working, involving the passings or peregrinations of the hierarchies of beings from higher to lower spheres, so that these beings may learn in each new Manvantara or World-Period new lessons appropriate to the new conditions, we see at once that the so-called 'rebellion' is but a somewhat poetic and graphic way of expressing the fact that their urgings impel them downwards in their evolutionary course, which brings them into immediate opposition, so to speak, with the already more fully developed spiritual agencies in the higher spheres.

IV

Evolution takes place on every one of the planes which form the inner constitution of every composite being or entity; and we have, therefore, (a) divine evolution; (b) spiritual evolution; (c) intellectual evolution; (d) the evolution of the psycho-mental human soul; (e) astral evolution; and (f) evolution of the physical body. This is but another way of saying that man is a Microcosm or Little World containing in himself hosts of inferior entities through which he manifests himself, each one of which inferior entities is a learning and evolving being; even as the Macrocosm or Great World of the Universe contains in itself its own hosts of learning and evolving beings and entities in their almost endless series of hierarchies.

Moreover, evolution is teleologic, that is to say, it is purposive, working towards a destined end. But this purposiveness in evolution, this inherent urge or drive to betterment, is in the entity itself, and is not imposed upon it from without, either by a god or gods existing outside of and separate and different from the evolving entity, or, on the other hand, by physical nature alone. Nevertheless, all these hierarchies exist each within the vital compass or sphere of a still larger and grander hierarchy, so that the encompassing influences of these larger hierarchies flow constantly through the minor hierarchies which each such larger unit contains. Thus is Nature in all her divisions and compartments mysteriously and most wonderfully and inextricably interlinked and interlocked and interworking and interblending.

Physical nature furnishes one phase of the environment or fields of possible experience within which the various hosts of monadic essences work; and it is in these physical fields of experience that the various races of physical bodies which biological science calls by various names such as Classes, Orders, Families, Genera, and Species, of physical living beings, exist, and are the means for the continuous self-expression of the evolving hosts of Monads or con-sciousness-centers.

It is the realization of this inner focus of energy, inherent as an individual in every evolving unit, which is lacking in the scientific conception of evolution — an ignorance likewise of the existence of inner and invisible spheres in which the physical world is rooted, and from which the forces which infill this physical universe flow.

It was because he lacked this fundamental conception in his theory, that Darwin could see no farther than his vision of the evolutionary process as a series of mere additions to, or in some cases subtractions from, the physical equipment of, or bodies of, evolving entities brought about by what he called 'natural selection' or the 'preservation of favored races in the struggle for life.'

That teaching, while it prevailed as the last word of science, and because it was more than half imperfect, destroyed a proper viewing of the universally working forces in Nature as all striving but in different manners towards a common end — for greater perfection in the self-expressing activities of the inner inspiriting lives; and because Darwinism was thus essentially materialistic both in conception and in outlook, its moral effect on the human soul was disastrous on the one hand and crippling to the ever inquisitive researches of the human intellect on the other hand.

It taught that man was but a developed beast, more accurately a developed ape; that there was naught but gross physical matter in the world, uninspired, insensate, and indeed dead; that fortuity or chance was the basic law or rather procedure — if such it can be called — bringing about improvements in bodies by means of haphazard adaptations; that spirit and spiritual ideals were but dreams;

that these did not exist in themselves, but were the results, in some mysterious and unexplained mode, of chemical action in the cells of the brain; that when a man died that was the utter end of him, as a well-known English biologic evolutionist said in substance in a letter printed some years ago in the *Westminster Gazette:*

The only immortality that modern biologists believe in, is the immortality of man's descendants

— which of course is no immortality at all to the individual, and is equivalent to teaching utter individual extinction or annihilation, and therefore is a preaching of most gross materialism. It is absurd in any case to speak of 'immortality' in connexion with physical bodies which are obviously but transitory and very impermanent vital-chemical compounds; and in a sense still more ridiculous to misuse the word immortality merely to signify that living bodies have offspring which in their turn have offspring which again produce offspring; and thus as long as the stock endures. This is not immortality in any sense.[127]

The effect of the teachings of Darwin on the human mind has

---

127. It is really too absurd, when the facts are carefully scrutinized, to talk of 'immortality' in connexion with the physical body. One can only express one's amazement that scientific men of supposedly sober mind and acquainted with the impermanent and utterly mortal nature of flesh should use the term immortality in connexion with man's physical integument even in the sense of its application to generations succeeding each other. Outside of the fact that immortality means something which is not mortal, as flesh most certainly is mortal, it is misuse of graver import to employ a term applicable in religious philosophy alone, to describe not only a biological fact but one merely signifying a series of physical beings.

But setting the foregoing reflexion aside as obvious enough, had the West even the remotest understanding of what true immortality is, such misuse would have been impossible even in the distorted sense in which it is commonly employed either in religion or in philosophy as these two are understood in the Occident.

True immortality signifies unbroken continuance or continuation of an individual consciousness of whatever grade or degree of evolutionary development; and the only instances where such immortality becomes possible are the cases of Jîvanmuktas, or 'freed Jîvas,' or equivalently, 'freed Monads.' Now the Monad can be 'freed' in the technical sense of liberation from the whirling changes of the wheel of life in material existences with its concomitant series of imbodiments only when such Monad or Jîva in its evolution reaches a state where it becomes self-consciously able to pass at will from body to body with retention of full consciousness, and employing such series of selected bodies for the pur-

been disastrous, as above stated, not only because it tends to destroy the vigor of man's innate moral responsibility, but also because it is less than half true; and the result has been a progressive increase in the dying of ideals in the modern world; that is to say, and otherwise expressed, the gradual loss of spirituality. The baneful influence of materialism as such has laid its pall of hopelessness and human despair over the entire civilized world; and it is only within comparatively recent times that biologists, through honest study and much deeper investigation of Nature than ever before was made, have, almost in despite of their own scientific prejudices, rescued because of their present greater knowledge some still glowing embers of Truth from what at one time threatened to be the ashes of human hope.

In reference to Darwin's so-called scientific principle of 'Natural Selection,' it is interesting to examine, however briefly, some of the pronouncements which upholders and propagandists of this biological teaching have uttered, as being significant of what is to the Theosophist a soulless and morally dangerous teaching, for many years past abroad in the world, and permeating the thought-life and consequent outlook and activity of those who fell under its sway.

First then, a paragraph from a book written by Professor George McCready Price, *The Phantom of Organic Evolution*. Professor Price very possibly is a Christian (?), and of course his outlook is

---

pose of fulfilling its chosen mission in the world of 'shells'— our material spheres.

This is real immortality, as signifying that the Jîva is expressing its own transcendent powers which, whatever else they may be, in their grandeur are certainly not mortal. Yet even here, in these cases of 'freed Monads,' such immortality can endure only for the period of Cosmic Manifestation in which the Jîva or Monad finds itself in its evolutionary course. Once 'freed' in the sense above described, it has immortality for the remainder of the Solar Manvantara, but when this enormously long time-period itself comes to an end, then even the Jîvanmuktas or freed Monads must follow the River of Rising Lives sweeping all with it into spheres of spirit loftier still than those which are the spiritual spheres during the course of the Manvantara of the solar system last passed. In accordance with Cosmic Law, when the next Cosmic Manvantara begins its course, after the long Solar Pralaya or rest-period, then these Jîvanmuktas, in common with all other individuals of the River of Lives, reissue forth anew for a still vaster and grander cyclical Pilgrimage in the then opening great Drama of Life.

It is this seizing of the Kingdom of Heaven by strength on the part of an imbodied Jîva or Monad — i. e., the entering the Path of Immortality, which is the true road or Pathway to the Gods.

colored by his private convictions, but nevertheless what he says is true enough.

The merest tyro in the study of organic evolution can see that the doctrine of survival of the fittest, or natural selection, makes some of the most morally objectionable characteristics manifested by animals and men the ladder by which all true progress has been attained. In other words, those qualities among the lower races of men, or among the animals, which we rightly regard as objectionable and blameworthy, such as selfishness, vindictiveness, and a heartless disregard of the feelings and desires of others, have been made by Darwin and his followers the chief factor in their scheme of organic evolution.[127a]

Professor Price here uses language which some people may think rather severe, but those who thus think have certainly not studied the case which he thus so clearly and truly arraigns. Another writer could have used language even more graphic and far stronger, and yet have fallen short of stating the whole truth.

Turn now to John Fiske, the great American Darwinian Evolutionist, who says:

Those most successful primitive men from whom civilized peoples are descended must have excelled in treachery and cruelty, as in quickness of wit and strength of will.

Professor J. Arthur Thomson writing on heredity, says the following:

Tone it down as you will, the fact remains that Darwinism regards animals as going upstairs, in a struggle for individual ends, often on the corpses of their fellows, often by a blood-and-iron competition, often by a strange mixture of blood and cunning, in which each looks out for himself and extinction besets the hindmost.

Huxley joins the chorus in the following words:

For his successful progress as far as the savage state man has been largely indebted to those qualities which he shares with the ape and the tiger.

It is small wonder indeed that the world is in the perilous state in which it now finds itself, if its shaky ethical sense is founded on no more stable and stronger foundation than that derived from a materialism which bases the loftiest and noblest intuitions of the human spirit upon appetites, impulses, and the beastly qualities which man shares with the most savage representatives of the animal kingdom! The causes of such materialistic nightmares, for they are nothing but scientific nightmares, have arisen in a complete, and in certain cases it would almost seem in a wilful, ignoring or turning

---

127a. Page 180.

aside from every noble quality and impersonal attribute which the human constitution contains. One might well ask the scientific gentlemen who write in the above strain, whether they have never known of other qualities, attributes, impulses, powers, and faculties in the human constitution, besides those beastly instincts which we share with the beast, and which, when unleashed, sink man to depths of depravity that even the beasts are incapable of reaching.

The argument becomes immediately preposterous, because it wilfully turns its face away from everything that the human constitution contains which makes man man, that has built the great civilizations of the past, that has brought about the efflorescence of all the activities of human genius, that has established the great works of moral splendor and intellectual light which have given hope and inspiration and inestimable comfort to the human race for ages past. On the basis itself that these materialistic evolutionists lay down, they fail to show any origins for such sublime qualities in the human soul as self-forgetful devotion, impersonal love, the strong ethical instinct of altruism, and the spiritual and intellectual fruits of its activity which the human spirit has produced in the world.

The snarlings and growlings and yelpings and shriekings of jungle beasts have nothing in common with these, and, on their own showing, their origin cannot be traced to something so radically different.

It should never be supposed — and one cannot see how it ever could be supposed — that the Theosophist is a disbeliever in evolution, for he most certainly is one of its strongest propagandists and upholders; but it is evolution in the sense that has so frequently been outlined in Theosophical literature, and which has on several occasions been briefly set forth in this present work. Darwinism at best — and the phrase is here repeated, *at best* — teaches an imperfect and secondary or even tertiary aspect or portion of the great Evolutionary Drama of life; nor is the Theosophist ever forgetful of the years of self-sacrificing study and labor that Charles Darwin, Russel Wallace, and others of their school have devoted to the study of the physical bodies of beings. Yet no scheme of evolution, no evolutionary hypothesis or theory, which throughout ignores ninety-nine percent of the factors in the problem, as Darwinism does, can be accepted by any thoughtful Theosophist as a comprehensively inclusive explanation of the otherwise undoubted fact that development in growth and consequent unfolding of both faculty and organ are among Nature's fundamental laws and operations as regards the so-called animate kingdoms, including the plant-world; and the Theosophist, furthermore, looks upon the entire Universe in all its parts and portions or kingdoms as undergoing the same process of developmental unfolding.

The reason is that the Cosmic Spirit, the abode of mind and consciousness, is all-permeant and therefore the ultimate impelling urge behind the evolutionary process which operates everywhere. Of course it is obvious to any thoughtful mind that Nature which is fundamentally conscious does make selections, not through fortuity nor by chance as the Darwinistic hypothesis alleges, but more or less consciously; but all such 'natural selection' is, at every turn and instant of time in the evolutionary course of the evolving entity, governed and controlled by the spiritual impulse or urge within the evolving entity itself.

Nor again does the Theosophist deny in totality the truth of Darwin's idea of the survival of the fittest, because ordinary observation shows us that the fittest in a set of circumstances is by far the most probable to be successful in it; but we must remember that this reasonable understanding of these two secondary or tertiary 'laws' are not what is meant in Darwinism, which preaches, when all is said, a sheer materialism and that entities evolve haphazard, by chance, without an inner spiritual urging power, leading to unfoldment of faculty and consequent organ. Darwinism recognises no indwelling impelling spirit urging its vehicles towards progressive unfoldment; and just here is where the Theosophist and the Darwinist part company.[128]

No Theosophist would deny that ape and tiger and shark and fox and wolf and ox and parrot and all the rest of the animate hosts

---

128. But why belabor the matter which already is dead and well-nigh a detail of biologic history? Materialistic Darwinism is moribund, i. e., dying if not dead; and the newer views held by most modern biologic researchers, even of the more materialistic type, differ greatly from the Darwinism so loudly voiced by men like Haeckel and Huxley.

In another great branch of modern science, that of Physics, voices are being raised in the teaching of a most welcome departure from the old materialistic ideas of a bygone time; and a host of men, headed by such great figures as Einstein, Jeans, Eddington, Planck, Bohr and others, make little hesitation in stating that in their best considered judgment, back of and within all material existences there is a cosmic Cause or Causes, which they variously describe as Mind, Mind-stuff, or by some equivalent term. This is a far cry, and a welcome one to hear, from the dogmatic preachments of the last quarter of the nineteenth century, which century was the heyday of materialism, and in which period H. P. Blavatsky wrote her master-work *The Secret Doctrine*.

of life have qualities which men possess also; but the former have them because ultimately these creatures were derived in their primordial origin from primal man himself. The Darwinian scheme is in many respects an actual inversion of what took place in the past. So it is small wonder that man should have characteristics of the beast in him, such as those of the ape and the tiger, but it would be truer to say that the beasts have these characteristics in them, because derived in far past aeons from imperfectly evolved humanity itself. But man's moral sense, his dominating intellect, his aspirations soaring on the wings of the spirit, are qualities which no beast ever yet has shown — only because no beast is as yet a Man, which means that no beast has yet unfolded from within itself the spiritual and intellectual and psychological powers and qualities and attributes which are there latent indeed, but not yet unwrapped, unfolded, as they occur in man, albeit even in man more or less still imperfect.

As an example of the effect of biologic and other materialism upon the minds of even the relatively great men who lived when the materialistic theories were completely dominant over men's souls, more or less from the middle of the nineteenth century onwards to its end, one might cite from the works of a number of such noted characters, and in all cases in their writings trace the soul-destroying influence of these materialistic vagaries. As an instance in point, one might refer to Friedrich Wilhelm Nietzsche, the German philosopher who died in 1900 in an insane asylum. He was an evolutionist according to the materialistic biologic teachings of his time, and his otherwise really brilliant mind would certainly seem to have been distorted and warped by the Darwinian and Haeckelian teaching of humanity as arising out of beasthood. Undoubtedly in the course of his philosophical studies and writings he said many beautiful things and therein lay the danger to his readers, because all beauty is magnetic and sways human souls by its power.

In this first quotation that is hereunder made from Nietzsche, he adopts the style and manner of a self-appointed prophet — but fortunately egoism of this character always in the end destroys its own effects. He wrote:

Here is the new law, O my brethren, which I promulgate unto you. Become hard; for creative spirits are hard. You must find a supreme blessedness in imposing the mark of your hand, in inscribing your will, upon thousands and thousands, as on soft wax.[129]

---

129. *Also sprach Zarathustra,* 'Von alten und neuen Tafeln,' p. 287.

This teaching seems to be little short of monstrous, and in flagrant violation of all the spiritual instincts of compassion of the human heart, which instincts raise man among others above the level of the savage. In this second quotation, made from him, which follows hereinunder, Nietzsche attains the ultimate reach of his egoistic vision:

Such ideas as mercy, and pity, and charity are pernicious, for they mean a transference of power from the strong to the weak, whose proper business it is to serve the strong. Remember that self-sacrifice and brotherliness and love are not real moral instincts at all, but merely manufactured compunctions to keep you from being your true self. Remember that man is essentially selfish.[129a]

Such are, first, the result of false religious teachings, and second, of false scientific teachings, upon the minds receptive to them, and especially subject to the voice of authority. Contrast this brutal egoistic animalism with the Theosophical conception of all existence as a continuous stream of imbodied lives and consciousnesses, of living beings following a pathway which ultimately through future ages of evolution will lead to wisdom and knowledge unspeakable, also to impersonal love without bounds, without encompassing frontiers, which takes in not merely all humankind and all below humankind and all the Earth and all on it and in it, but the entire Universe!

This teaching, as has already been set forth, is based upon the fact that the Universe is intrinsically and essentially conscious and what man would call moral in its operations, because the Universe is founded in and is the evolution from the Cosmic Mind and Cosmic Life.

v

Has this evolutionary pathway to the gods an ending? Nay. As said before, there are no absolute ends in very truth, because such absolute ends and beginnings are dreams of illusion, and at best are but the beginnings and ends of the transitory conditions or states of consciousness through which the evolving hosts of beings progress throughout endless time. Evolution nevertheless is cyclical, and in this cyclical sense only it may be said to have a beginning, a culmination, and an end — which temporary end is but a new beginning along higher lines.

This fact is so perfectly obvious that even the most recalcitrant Darwinist, or the most positive and determined materialist, is not blind to the fact. Even from Darwin's day, it was noted and commented upon that as the geological record is progressively uncovered and becomes better known, there is one very interesting fact

---

129a. *Also sprach Zarathustra,* 'Vom höheren Menschen,' p. 417.

which is observed with greater clearness and more fully, and it is this: there seem to have been in past ages on Earth evolutionary waves or cyclical periods during which one or another stock *apparently* 'suddenly' appears in the geological record, advances steadily to its culmination or maturity of development of form and power and size, and then fades away and apparently, in some cases, as 'suddenly' disappears, while in other cases remnants are carried on over into the succeeding age.

Such cases of succeeding evolutionary waves are very noticeable in three instances — possibly because these three are the best known — first in the Age of the Fishes, which took place during what it was once usual to call the Primary or Palaeozoic Era.[130] This was the geological era when the sea swarmed with fishes of all-various kinds and sizes, which fishes then represented, *as far as the geological record shows,* at least the supposedly highest known forms. This last supposition, the Theosophist does not admit as a fact.

The second of these waves, which occurred during the so-called Secondary Era or period of time, is what is called the Age of Reptiles, when reptilian monsters of many kinds and often of huge body, were, so far as the geological record shows, the masters of the Earth.

---

130. The names of these different geological ages used in the present work, and as shown probably with greater clarity in the succeeding chapter, were the popular names in scientific vogue when H. P. Blavatsky wrote her great work, *The Secret Doctrine,* but due to the greatly changed opinions concerning the time-periods of the geologic record which have taken place since 1888, it is quite possible that the names of the three periods alluded to in the text do not correspond with strict exactitude to the more recent pronouncements of geologic science.

This is a matter, however, of indifference, for it is solely a matter of nomenclature and of placing these three evolutionary waves, mentioned in the text, in accordance with whatever geological age the most recent deductions of geological science would claim for their appearance. The days of Lyell and Geikie and others — great names in their time — have passed, and the geologic time-periods which the most eminent geologists of the last quarter of the nineteenth century considered to be sufficient for these respective geological eras, the geologists of our later times find to be entirely inadequate.

The Theosophist is concerned solely with the facts in the case, and pays but little attention to time-periods or geological nomenclature, to both of which he is perfectly willing to adapt himself once that the more modern views in geology have proved their worth.

It should be stated, however, that from the standpoint of the Esoteric Tradition, the lengths of the time-periods called for by the latest geological researchers are in most if not all cases greatly excessive.

The third instance occurred during the Tertiary — or perhaps it began in the last period of the Secondary, and continued into the Tertiary — and this third evolutionary wave or cyclical period we may call the Age of the Great Mammals, which then in their turn, succeeding the Reptiles, were the masters of the Earth — and still are in their presently existing forms.

In each of these three cases, as the geological record is studied, we can see the respective beginnings of a kind: we can discern the growth in size and physical power, the culmination or the maturity or full efflorescence of the particular stocks. Then we see decay and a final passing of the bulk of the animate beings belonging to each particular evolutionary life-wave, thus making place for the new and succeeding stock, which in turn has its relatively complete dawn, appearing with a certain suddenness in the geologic record. The new stock reaches its fulness in the expansion of its physical powers and size, and then again in its turn passes away, and so forth. Wave succeeds wave, each wave reaching a higher level of evolutionary unfolding activity than did the preceding wave; and each wave in its turn is followed by another succeeding wave, bringing on the scene beings or entities and things of a 'new' and different evolutionary type.

This itself has always been one of the mysteries of geology, and, as far as the present writer knows, no adequate explanation has ever yet been given of the relative suddenness with which some of these stocks appeared on the scene, and apparently, after having passed ages on Earth, seemed to disappear with equal suddenness. Whence came they and what brought about their sudden appearance and relatively evolved forms? We do not know, say the geologists.

It has been customary to say that the fishes gave birth to the reptiles, and that the reptiles gave birth to the mammals, to the great mammalian beasts, and these great beasts — or at least a certain line of them — brought forth man through the highest of their own type, which, as supposed, was the anthropoid ape. But the difficulties in the way of the acceptance of this theory are far greater than any arguments which have been advanced in favor of it.

The Theosophical teaching runs directly to the contrary. It sets forth that while it is perfectly true that these evolutionary waves succeed each other, each such wave represents or manifests the coming on the scene of physical existence on our Earth of a 'new' Family or a 'new' Host of evolving entities. It says, furthermore, that each one of these hosts has its dawn, its noonday, and its

evening, and that the physical bodies in which these monadic hosts
of evolving entities dwell, die or pass away in due time, and that
the hosts of monads, having used these bodies, thereupon pass on
to inhabit vehicles or bodies of a higher evolutionary character
which these monadic hosts themselves bring forth from within their
own respective monadic essences by emanation.

Thus if we consider, by way of illustration, an evolving entity
in that phase of its evolutionary journey, on and through our Earth,
called the Mineral Kingdom — which means a spiritual Monad
passing through its temporary mineral phase — we find the teaching
to be that in the course of long ages, through the process of unrolling
or unfolding the innate qualities and attributes and powers flowing
forth from the Monad itself, the intermediate or psychological nature between the Monad and the Mineral Kingdom becomes a fitter
and more perfect vehicle of self-expression for the evolving Monad,
so that ultimately the peregrinating monadic unit creeps out of that
temporary phase of its journey called the Mineral Kingdom, perhaps as a lichen, then perhaps later, as the ages pass, appears as
the lowest of the higher plants. Constant perfecting of the intermediate or psychological vehicle between the Monad on the one
hand, and the plant-body on the other, brings this intermediate
vehicle into a still more sensitive and quasi-conscious condition, so
that this intermediate vehicle becomes fit for inshrining the Monad in that temporary phase of its evolutionary journey called
the Beast-Kingdom.

Thus the Monad working through its intermediate vehicle passes
on into the Beast-Kingdom, where there is a larger measure of progressive unwrapping in higher or more spiritual qualities and attributes and powers flowing forth from the inner and 'overshadowing'
Monad itself, till the thus sensitized beast-nature becomes more fit
to express in still larger degree, still higher and nobler qualities and
attributes and forces flowing forth from the Monad; and at this
point, we find the journeying, evolving and revolving, Monad manifesting in the Human Kingdom.[131]

---

131. It is imperatively necessary at this point for the reader to avoid misunderstanding this teaching to mean or to imply, that it is the spiritual Monad
— in itself a divine and self-conscious being — which itself becomes, let us say, a
stone, and after its peregrinations in the Mineral Kingdom passes out of it and
becomes a plant, and after peregrinating in the Vegetable Kingdom later *becomes*
a beast, and after peregrinating in the Animal Kingdom finally *becomes* a Man
— i. e., enters the Human Kingdom. This is not the idea, although some coun-

The foregoing, therefore, does not mean as in the Darwinian theory that the mineral turns into a plant, the plant turns into a beast, and the beast turns into a human being. It would be entirely wrong to imagine the Monad of a Newton or of an Einstein, for instance, having been at some remote period in the past but a speck

---

tenance could be lent to this mistaken conception by the well-known Qabbalistic axiom so familiar to students of the Esoteric Tradition, that "the stone becomes a plant, the plant becomes a beast, the beast becomes a man, and the man becomes a god." This axiom is literally true, but it must be understood in the light of the teachings of the Esoteric Tradition.

The Monad, which is the Originant and continuously impelling spiritual urge back of all evolutionary unfoldment of an evolving entity, is, as said above, a self-conscious divine being, but due to the karman of its past lives in the former Cosmic Manvantara, it is inextricably involved as a unit in helping to make and to guide the entire body of evolving beings and things in the present Cosmic Manvantara. This it does by what may be called an emanation of a ray from itself, shot down from itself into the lower and even into the lowest of the interlocking hierarchies forming the body corporate of the Universe, which now is itself these rays, thus individualized as a stream of quasi-conscious force-substance which manifests itself first in the Mineral Kingdom; then each ray working out of it, after doing its work therein, enters the Vegetable Kingdom, and working through this it enters into the Animal Kingdom, and after its revolvings therein have been completed, it enters the Human Kingdom. When its evolutionary peregrinations in the Human Kingdom have been completed it finds itself entering still higher Kingdoms as a divinity — which is rejoining its Parent Monad, plus its vast wealth of experiences. The aggregates of individual rays make the different Kingdoms.

These experiences are not gained in the Darwinian sense by accretions from the various Kingdoms through which it has passed or is passing or will pass, but by a constantly progressive unfolding, or unrolling, or unwrapping, of its own inherent and innate monadic essence — the various Kingdoms thus giving the ray not only opportunity for its own unfolding, but likewise the ray aids in developing or evolving the various Kingdoms through which it passes.

The difference, therefore, between the esoteric teaching of evolution and that taught by Darwinism and the newer forms of evolutionism is thus seen to be simply enormous; and it is precisely to this difference of such immense import, that the student's attention is called with emphasis. The difference or distinction, therefore, is the contrast between evolving spirits building themselves bodies in the material worlds through which they express themselves, on the one hand, and, on the other hand, the materialistic teaching that matter unaided and mistakenly supposed to be insensate or dead produces from its own inherent incapacities spirituality, the noble powers of the intellect, the delicacy of the psychological nature, and the wonder and to science deeply mysterious adaptations which physical bodies exemplify and display in such profusion.

of mineral substance with no previous spiritual history behind it, which slowly through the evolving aeons grew to humanhood, un-impulsed by a spirit, and as the growth in some utterly mysterious manner of lifeless, insensate matter, according to the ideas of the old and now dying fatalistic determinism. The esoteric teaching of evolution means that the soul of the life-atom manifests in different bodies *on different planes,* both contemporaneously and in suc-ceeding time-periods. The soul of a life-atom, for instance, which really is an elemental, is at one phase of its evolutionary journey a mineral life-atom — or expresses itself thus. The soul of the same life-atom at a later date expresses itself in physical life as a plant life-atom. The soul of this plant life-atom after a long while imbodies itself in a phase of its evolutionary unfolding from *within* in a beast-body. The soul of the same life-atom later self-expresses itself by means of imbodying its radiating qualities in a human body. The soul of the same life-atom later self-expresses itself as a god; and so forth. This must not be misunderstood to mean because of the repetitive use of the phrase 'life-atom' that the evolving ray from the monad mentioned in the previous footnote is always a 'life-atom.' The idea is that the tip of this ray, so to speak, enters the physical sphere as a life-atom in the Mineral Kingdom, and that the same monadic ray in a later age expresses its still further unfolded powers as a life-atom in the Plant-Kingdom, and thus onwards up the scale.[132]

A god is a being which, as an original life-atom, has attained divine self-consciousness. Every god has, as a journeying psycho-spiritual Entity, passed through the man-stage; every man, as a journeying psycho-spiritual Monad, has passed through the beast-stage; and here is the especial point to remember: every man as a psycho-spiritual Monad has manifested as a beast in some manvan-tara, *but not in this.* In exactly similar way, every beast, manifest-ing as a psycho-spiritual Monad, has passed through the plant-stage in some manvantara, and finally in like manner, every plant, mani-festing as a psycho-spiritual Monad, has passed through the mineral life-atom stage, just as every mineral life-atom had previously been an elemental life-atom, and so forth.

Words, those 'winged messengers' as Homer calls them, can mis-lead thoughts so easily; and here we must not misunderstand these

132. In a later chapter of this book the reader will find a closer study made of the septenary constitution of an evolving entity, and the matter therein contained should clarify this teaching still further, for those interested.

words or these phrasings of the thought to signify that the higher stage *has been* the lower stage. This is wrong. As explained before, evolution as taught in the Esoteric Philosophy shows a countless host of Spiritual Individuals, called Monads, pouring forth from themselves qualities and attributes and powers which build up bodies in the lower realms of progressively increasing sensibility and power of response to the inner monadic urge, and thus it is that the monadic ray, thus shot down into the lower realms, builds around itself vehicles at each stage more or less fit for the Monad's efforts at self-expression in these different spheres. From this it should be abundantly clear that the man actually *has not been* the beast, but the ray passed through the beast-stage first, and when it had finished that series of circumrotations or revolvings, it had brought forth from its own being the already latent human qualities, and thus built up human bodies for their expression. In an exactly identical way will the god already within the core of the human being finally be brought forth into manifestation as a self-conscious divinity. Thus similarly with all the other classes of beings which fill the Universe full.

VI

Evolution, according to the Ancient Wisdom, is fundamentally the activity of spiritual powers manifesting throughout the spheres of Universal Being. It is entirely a spiritual process, being the manner of working of the indwelling hosts of consciousnesses which are the fabric or framework or web of the Universe itself.

Everything that is, is an aggregate, a composite, of these hosts of Monads, of Divine Sparks, offsprings from the Cosmic Central Fire of consciousness which exist in all degrees of evolutionary unfolding, from what we humans call gross matter, and even beneath the gross matter that we know, up through the beings beneath man, through man, through the beings higher than we humans, which higher beings in the Christian religion are called 'angels' and 'archangels,' etc.: and in other religions these superhuman entities are called gods, or devas, or by other names: the names changing in the various religions or philosophies. And where shall we, where can we, stop in following this hierarchical ladder of life? There are no endings, just as there are no beginnings; for the hierarchical series ranges, cyclical-fashion, through and over the fields of boundless infinitude.

Man is man because of his divine faculties of lofty intelligence, of spiritual intuition, of understanding, of capacity for knowledge, of love, of his sense of duty, of his moral sense — a godlike thing this last also; he is such indeed because he represents better and in larger and fuller degree than does any one of the inferior Kingdoms, the innate spiritual powers which are self-expressing themselves through his psycho-mental and physical apparatus, built up through ages past from the incessant evolutionary urge working from within.

We humans are 'fallen gods,' 'fallen angels' with capacities divine, active or latent, enshrined within our minds and souls. We shall return to the high spiritual status or condition which we left in the beginning of the present period of cosmic evolution, in other words, to our former status of divinity which we had left, but in doing so reaching higher levels than those from which we departed. We shall in time re-enter — and one may here use the mythological phraseology of the ancients — the Bosom of the Divine in far distant future aeons, but then we shall no longer be un-self-conscious god-sparks, as we were when we began our aeons-long pilgrimage, but shall re-enter that Divine as fully self-conscious gods, having gained fulness of character, vast experience, and the full blooming of individual will-power and wide self-consciousness.

Fallen gods! But not 'fallen' in the ordinary human sense of evil doing. Nay, but only in the archaic mythological sense is this word here used; not in the sense of any modern religion crystallized in formalisms, nor in that of any of the priesthoods, ancient or modern; but in the sense of the true spiritual Visioner, of the Seer. This 'fall' is really an entrance upon the evolutionary path of constantly unfolding progress which originates in the Heart of Things, and results ultimately in bringing out, from within the individuals of the countless monadic hosts, that which is within, and manifesting it and developing it, in order to become, first, beings beneath man, then through various stages to become man and, passing through the human stage, ultimately to become something superhuman, until divinity is finally attained once again, but as self-conscious freed Monads — Jîvanmuktas!

We fall to Earth; but we rise again! Indomitable is the spirit within us. Nothing can daunt it nor conquer it, if only we do use it. It is indomitable, for it is the energy pouring forth through our own individual wills from the very heart of the Universe; and all evolution, all growth, all achievement, depend upon the degree with which we ally ourselves with this spiritual river of consciousness and force flooding our inmost being. All evil will pass away when men understand this and act accordingly, for evil is the running contrary to the operations of Spiritual Nature — the setting of the individual will against the mighty and impassive consciousness of the Universe. Thus do we fall, thus are we 'cast out'; but blessed be the immortal gods, it is thus also that we poor humans learn through pain and suffering and distress. Evil is the man who chooses evil for his god, and evil will be his ways; great will be his suffering and tribulation; but sooner or later the divine spark of impersonal divinity in universality will stir in his soul, and then will he hear the voice of his inner god. Far distant it may be for most, but growing more compelling and more insistent as time flows on. Indeed we are fallen gods, fallen angels, learning, growing, evolving god-sparks.

The urge behind evolution, and the objective which this urge is impelling us towards, is simply the divine hunger in the Universe to grow greater, to advance, to unfold: *Excelsior!* It is innate in the Universe. Why this is so, no one can say. Perhaps the gods do not know. All we men can aver is that it is so. Everything grows and yearns to grow greater, to become grander, to rise, to advance, to evolve, and the objective is to become at-one self-consciously with the Boundless — something which never can be reached! Therein is infinite beauty, for there is no final ending for growth in beauty and splendor and wisdom and love and power. The Boundless Universe is our home.

What we may call a blind striving or struggle for betterment in the atoms, becomes in man a self-conscious yearning to grow, to unfold, to become ever more the divinity within himself, arising in a recognition, now quasi-conscious, that man is a son of the gods. This same urge becomes in the gods a divine knowledge that they are inseparable parts of the Universe, and are growing to take a vaster self-conscious part in the Universal Labor.

All possible things are latent in the core of the core of the being of each one of us; they are like sleeping powers of the Universe; and this core of the core of the being of each one of us is man's own inner god, the Cosmic Dhyâni-Buddha within him, the Divine Christ immanent within him: the living Osiris of the ways of Infinity.

CHAPTER X

ESOTERIC TEACHINGS ON THE EVOLUTION OF
HUMAN AND ANIMAL BEINGS

IN several preceding chapters of this volume an attempt has been
made to draw aside, to some extent at least, the veil which for
long ages has more or less closely curtained the teachings of
the Esoteric Tradition as regards the fascinating subject of evolutionary unfolding; and however inadequately this has been done,
it is probable that the attentive reader will have gained some notion
at least of the basic idea upon which the esoteric teaching concerning evolution reposes: to wit, the gradual and secular unwrapping
or rolling forth in manifestation of attributes, qualities, and powers,
lying latent in the invisible essence of every entity or being progressing on its upward way along and through the ranges of Cosmic
Life, and consequently along and through the Hierarchies of the
Worlds Visible and Invisible.

A master-hand had already pointed to the secret teaching concerning evolution behind this Veil, and had raised it sufficiently to
allow the perspicacious and intuitive reader to obtain glimpses into
the scenes that this Veil hid. Yet it is doubtless no exaggeration
to assert with some emphasis that, despite the presentation made
by this master-hand, there are even today, nearly fifty years after
this pioneer-effort, very few students, Theosophists or others, who
have any clear ideas even of the fundamental principles of the
esoteric teaching concerning the nature, character, and complex
processes that are involved in the evolutionary theory as unfolded
by the greatest exponents of the Esoteric Philosophy.

The master-hand, just alluded to, was of course that of H. P.
Blavatsky, aided by two of the Masters of Wisdom, and the literary
work which was then given to the world was *The Secret Doctrine*.

This lack of an adequate understanding of the extremely difficult
subject of evolution is certainly not to be ascribed to any imperfection, or faults, or inadequacies, of treatment, in H. P. Blavatsky's
greatest literary effort; but is properly explained by two facts: first,
the novelty of the teaching itself, and the unfamiliarity of esoteric
thought to the minds to whom this novel teaching was given; and,

second, because even in *The Secret Doctrine* what was delivered to the public was all that was deemed by the great Authors thereof proper and wise to give out of the Esoteric Arcanum at that time and to a generation, which, in religion, philosophy, and science too, was a generation largely of self-satisfied pharisees and sadducees — in other words, to a generation of minds satisfied either with empty ritual or swollen with pride in the achievements of a science wholly materialistic.

H. P. Blavatsky herself pointed to the twentieth century as the time when at least the basic or fundamental thoughts contained in *The Secret Doctrine* would begin to be understood as having been neither invented by her nor as being merely speculative hypotheses, but as reposing on the everlasting foundations of Nature itself so far as the teachings went, and as comprising the principles of an Ancient Wisdom which far antedates the Vedas, and, indeed, runs back into the mists of prehistory.

It is perhaps the magnificent simplicity of the esoteric teaching concerning the character, nature, and processes, of evolutionary or developmental unfolding, which is at once extremely attractive to intuitive minds and in many cases repellent to other minds which, refusing to believe in their own innate powers of intuitive discernment, hesitate at each forward step, boggle over imaginary difficulties, and largely trust to the dictates issuing from the mouth of established scientific authority.

Magnificently simple as the esoteric teaching about evolution certainly is, it is none the less in its profounder ranges extremely difficult adequately to grasp because of the immense reach of the teaching into every range of Cosmic Life, and, more than anything else perhaps, because of the fact that it involves or comprises the fundamental, essential, and inseparable oneness of the root of each and every evolving entity with the life-web of the Universe itself. This last teaching alone, of the essential oneness of every evolving unit with the fabric and structure of the Universe, is so unfamiliar and novel to Western minds, that it takes no short time-period of assimilation and digestion, after comprehension, before its import can properly be seized.

An attempt, therefore, will be made in the present chapter to throw at least a little more light on the nature of the evolution of sentient and so-called non-sentient beings and things, and especially to clarify the very recondite and difficult branch of the main thought involving the evolutionary appearance of primordial man, and the origination of the animal phyla or stocks from Man. A Theosophical writer, in any attempt to unveil or to explicate a teaching of the Esoteric Tradition, is faced with really great difficulties and of several kinds, when he tries to make at least fairly clear to minds more or less untrained in philosophical and especially theosophical thought some of the far-past history not only of the human race but of the great stocks or classes of animate beings which have in the past peopled the earth and/or which people it today.

It would be a hopeless and indeed a thankless task to attempt to make any reconciliation of somewhat extensive character of modern-day scientific evolutionary hypotheses with the teachings of the Esoteric Tradition. It is probable that even an imperfect attempt at reconciliation cannot yet be satisfactorily achieved, because modern scientific evolutionary theory utterly ignores, is indeed unconscious of, vast stretches in time of the past evolutionary history of the once widely distributed stocks of living beings of many kinds which at different and successive periods of time formerly inhabited this globe. Any attempt to make even a partial reconciliation of modern-day biological thinking, whether in botany or zoology, with the esoteric records, is almost hopeless, because, although biological science has advanced far since the days when H. P. Blavatsky wrote *The Secret Doctrine,* it is still too early to find common bases of thought between modern biology and the Ancient Wisdom, and to erect upon it the structure of fact and theory which would be satisfactory both to the biologist and the esotericist.

The only thing that can be done is to tell the facts of past evolutionary history by drawing attention to the esoteric records and teaching, and then point in a general way to the constantly increasing new discoveries of biological and palaeontological science as being material corroborative of the secret records.

Further, when one realizes how rapidly science itself is changing, biological science especially, it will be more clearly understood that any such attempt at reconciliation of the biological theories of our own present time with the ancient science, i. e., with the ancient esoteric teaching, would also be almost a waste of time, because the biological science of ten or twenty or thirty years from now, will doubtless be very different from what it is today, and the work, if not having to be done all over again, would call for repetitive efforts in justification of the ancient records, and explication of the meaning of new facts thus discovered and explanations of new theories drawn from these new facts, which by the same token would, within a short time, be themselves replaced by something newer still.

What the present chapter has to say is therefore difficult, not from any one standpoint alone, but from several, as already stated. Moreover, it is inconvenient in plain words to explain the processes of the physical reproduction of creatures as such processes occurred in far past geologic times, because these processes are now in large part utterly unknown on earth, at least in the human kingdom — indeed, probably also in any of the other animate phyla; and although there still remain today remnants or hang-overs, as it were, of these now far past processes, just as there still remain in the human body the vestiges, the survivals, of organs or forms of organs that were active and vitally functional in former stages of evolutionary development that the human race has passed through, nevertheless, these survivals of organs or organic functions are not yet accepted in scientific theory as proclaiming what they themselves otherwise clearly and silently prove — that even the beings of our day are biological records of what the human race at one time passed through. Some of these organic but now non-functional remnants of a biological character would seem to show clearly that the human race at one time was androgynous or hermaphroditic in form and function, that is, in biological reproductive type; nor, even were this fact of a former androgynous condition of the human race admitted, would it carry the prehistory of the human race fully back to its primal origins. In other words, human hermaphroditism was but an intermediate or so to speak middle-way stage between the first originating protoplasts and humanity of the present-day human beings.

I

To begin our study: How did the animals or beasts originate from Man? In the first place, it is not the Theosophical teaching that in the present Fourth Round, *this* great Life-Cycle on our globe, Earth, *all* the animal-stocks originated from man, or mankind. Only the mammalia did so *in this Fourth Round*, i. e., the beasts with breasts (*mammae*) and with a vertebrate skeleton and reproductive functions which from the beginning up to the present day have continued to be more or less like our own — and which underwent the same cyclical changes in structure and function that occurred in the evolutionary unfolding of the human race. All the other animal-stocks, especially the lower Orders thereof, are evolutionary hold-overs in this present Fourth Round or Life-Cycle from the great evolving animal-stocks that were in their heyday of evolution in the Third Round or Life-Cycle on this globe, Earth. To put the matter in other words, all the beasts or animals or animate entities in the many and widely differing evolutional stages beneath the human and the other non-human mammalia, are with us today as hang-overs from the Third Round, but it should not be forgotten that they are largely *specialized* in this present Fourth Round.

There were large numbers of stocks of beings which in long past times had their evolutional heyday on this globe Earth, and even during this Fourth Round, but which now have completely vanished from the scene, leaving only their fossil records or remnants behind. The great Reptiles are an instance in point of illustration of this statement, despite the fact that many of the reptiles which have lasted through the ages even unto our own day are evolutionary hang-overs or hold-overs which, for one reason or another, managed to survive through the different geologic Eras till the present. These *śishṭas,* or remnants, or seeds of life of these hold-overs from the Third Round above spoken of, were, in the majority of cases, already on our globe Earth at the beginning of the Fourth Round, before what the Esoteric Tradition calls the 'First Root-Race' of 'men'[133] put in its appearance on this Globe in this Fourth Round.

The First Root-Race and the early part of the Second Root-Race of protoplastic 'mankind' were, as stated in the adjoined note, astral men. Though called men by courtesy, they were not truly human as we now understand the term, because they were mindless — i. e., the Sons of Mind, the Mânasaputras, had not yet incarnated in them and thus had not yet infilled them, even in small degree, with the divine flame of self-conscious intelligence and thought. Thus, too, were they likewise unmoral beings — not 'immoral' in the usual sense of the word, because the moral instinct had not yet awakened within them. They were as unconscious in this respect as are the beasts today. Yet this statement must not be misunderstood to

---

133. They were 'men' only by courtesy, as it were, or, speaking still more accurately, they were the original protoplastic sketches of the true Man or mankind that was to follow in far later ages. They are called 'men' simply to identify them as having been in their own evolutionary time-period the true roots or originants of what their descendants in strict line later became — mankind; nor is this 'First Root-Race' to be considered in any wise as being animals or beasts, or the primordial supposititious beast-stock from which mankind of today derived in evolutional series, to which present mankind should trace back its direct evolutionary ancestry. We repeat: They were not beasts, whether mammalian or non-mammalian, but were the astral prototypes, the protoplastic originants, and existing in different great Families or Orders, from which present mankind has descended in lineal and uninterrupted life-stream.

signify that they were 'evil' in their lives and deliberately and wilfully chose the pathways of 'sin.' It should be obvious that if these beings were unmoral they could no more do 'immoral' acts than they could do deliberately and self-consciously noble moral acts. They were, so to speak, under the virtually infallible although unrecognised guidance and directing power of spiritual instinct, which kept them both from moral and physical injury, much as the plants today are neither moral nor immoral, but are guided with almost infallible prescience by the generalized spiritual and intuitional instinct working in and through them.

These beings of the First and Second Root-Races of 'mankind' were mentally very much like little children: just as today our little children are mindless — not meaning, however, that our children lack mental capacity in latency, or rather the potentiality of mind. This is obvious, because mind *per se* does not manifest its sublime powers in the unborn child nor in the newly born child, nor even in the child in its earliest years. Mind, as such, begins to manifest itself, and progressively so, only as the years pass by, and while the child in its growth shows the opening of the functions and qualities and operations of mentality. The little child today is mindless in this sense, but nevertheless has the latent capacity and inherent but unevolved powers of mind.

The First Root-Race was astral. It was also more astral or ethereal than the Earth upon which it lived. As the ages passed, this First Root-Race slowly grew more material in structure, i. e., the astral slowly thickened or condensed, became more concreted; but still even the Second Root-Race which followed the First and which in point of fact was merely the First Root-Race become more concrete and material, was likewise distinctly semi-astral, was indeed a gelatinous, filamentoid race, physically speaking. Both the First Root-Race and the Second had neither bones, nor organs, nor hair, nor a true skin. As regards lack of bones, as offering a possible objection to the existence of a tenuous physical body having a more or less coherent form, it might be pointed out that even the grossly material shark today has no true bones, strictly speaking. Its firmer parts are cartilaginous, and so was largely the internal structure of the last part of the Second Root-Race.

In physical substance one might even go so far as to say that the Second Root-Race, so far as their bodies were concerned, were somewhat like the jelly-fish, possibly. It is not here meant that they were jelly-fishes, because they certainly were not, and any such deliberate misunderstanding of the statement would be absurd. They too were human by courtesy because they had not yet evolved or developed into functional activity the main and striking characteristics, attributes, and elements of the human stock, which are in truth, psychical faculty, mental faculty, and spiritual faculty, working in combination through tenuous and invisible sheaths, which again combine to express themselves through a physical body.

They were 'shells' in the sense that they were not yet self-consciously infilled with the spiritual-intellectual Dhyâni-Chohanic essences and powers, just as a little child from its birth is a human 'shell' in the above sense, until the slowly incarnating Dhyâni-Chohanic essence, or the psycho-mental fluid of the incarnating ego of it, begins to manifest itself through and in the physical body.

II

The First Root-Race propagated itself by fission, that is to say, by a portion of the parent breaking off, such portion growing to be like its parent: i. e., a part dissolved off, or separated itself off, from its parent, very much after the fashion that living cells today follow, i. e., by division. A living cell today is a gelatinous,[134] semi-astral, entity without organs as we understand them, without bones, without hair, and without a true skin.

Without going too deeply into the more recondite teaching which concerns the history of the First Root-Race, which would be both impermissible and probably useless because of the great difficulty in conveying the intricate ideas, it may nevertheless be said with some approach to accuracy that the First Root-Race in the earliest portions of its evolutional unfolding might almost be called huge astral

---

134. The word 'gelatinous' is here used because fairly descriptive of that intermediate stage between solid flesh and the ethereal yet quasi-visible tenuity of the lower astral. Flesh is, in fact, thickened or condensed astral. There is no need to boggle over a difficulty here, for the reason that the thickest or densest astral and the most tenuous physical matter are virtually the same. The two realms, the lower astral and the ethereal-physical, here melt or merge into each other; and there is absolutely no division-line between them. The heavier astral is so close to the tenuous physical, that, as said above, the distinction is impossible to make except theoretically. These two merge into one. Consequently, it is correct to speak of a thinly gelatinous substance as a thickened or condensed astral substance; and this statement is made deliberately and without reserve. There is no true dividing-line between astral and physical.

cells or 'Pudding-Bags.'[135] These huge and highly ethereal or astral Cells were living creatures of course in the sense that they lived, reproduced their kind, and were infilled with the astral essence of the lowest of the Dhyâni-Chohanic fluids. As time passed on, during the evolutionary career of the First Root-Race, these Cells, albeit constantly undergoing minor changes of shape and size vaguely reminiscent perhaps of the *amoeba,* little by little but steadily and surely, gradually became more and more alike unto the astral type around which they were slowly crystallizing through the ages; so that when the Second Root-Race appeared on the scene, this new racial stock — really an evolutionary continuation in time of the First Root-Race — already had begun to show a distinct although as yet highly imperfect outline in form of what was in ages later during the ending of the Third Root-Race to become bodies of human shape, possessing human characteristics, although even then, during the later Third Root-Race, still imperfect human bodies when compared with the human physical frame as it is known today.

Nature repeats herself everywhere. Just as in the case of a single human being: its first physical appearance is a microscopic cell or egg slowly passing through the repetitive stages of the evolutionary course which the race has traversed in the past, until having finished its various modifications and changes of intra-uterine development, the embryo now become human is born as a child, and from birth onwards begins to manifest progressively the inner psychical, mental, intellectual, and spiritual faculties which make man truly man. Here we have in a thumbnail sketch, so to say, a close repetitive evolutionary picture, of the stages of evolutionary development passed through in successive and serial order by the First, the Second, the Third, and the Fourth Root-Races — our own present human stock, in all its various species or varieties, being what the Esoteric Tradition calls the Fifth Root-Race.

Furthermore, here likewise may be seen the evolutionary process as hereinbefore explained, as signifying an unrolling, unwrapping, unfolding, of qualities, attributes, characteristics, powers, functions, etc., which are already innate or latent or unexpressed in the essence of the evolving being.

The Second Root-Race propagated itself by gemmation, i. e.,

---

135. This is a semi-humorous but graphically descriptive term originally given, it would seem, by H. P. Blavatsky to the individuals of this Root-Race. The term could likewise to a certain extent be applied to the individuals even of the early part of the Second Root-Race, but not much later than this.

by 'budding.' Instead of a portion of the parent separating or dividing off, as was the case in the First Root-Race, the process followed in the Second Root-Race was repetitive of the former but in the small. A small part of the body, i. e., a bud, separated from the parent, dropped off from the main trunk, and thereafter began to grow and to develop into a being which was in all important respects alike unto the parent. About the middle period of the life-cycle or duration of this Second Root-Race, these buds grew more numerous, and became what zoologists would probably call human 'spores' or 'seeds,' or what H. P. Blavatsky with even more accurate metaphor, called 'vital sweat.' Thus many of these buds at certain seasons, after the parent-entity had become mature, would leave the parent-body as do the spores or seeds of plants today. These seeds were then taken care of by Nature and were developed in what was in all respects the proper environment, quite closely similar to the manner in which the seeds of plants are cared for today. Millions might indeed perish, but other millions would successfully grow into beings alike unto the bodies of the parents which gave them birth.[136]

Then, after several millions of years, began the Third Root-Race, which was a development or evolution of the Second Root-Race; and this Third Root-Race was still more material or concreted than was the Second. The jelly-like substance of the Second Root-Race had now become what one might call tender flesh composed of cells, beginning to surround and cover bones, and to acquire skin and hair, and likewise containing either rudimentary or fairly well developed physical organs. The method of reproduc-

---

136. The reader is requested carefully to note and carefully to retain the fact that in the above description of the different methods of what were in those far-distant and earliest periods of the human race perfectly natural methods of reproduction, however strange they may appear to the modern man, the argument in the text for the time being, as is sufficiently obvious, is concentrated upon this fact of physical reproduction more or less exclusively. But not for an instant should the far more important fact be lost sight of, or forgotten, that these methods of reproduction were connected with the then 'physical' bodies of earliest mankind, the argument or picture drawn in the text ignoring for the time being all matters pertaining to the inner or invisible constitution of early mankind, touching upon matters connected with this last only lightly and inferentially.

The truth is — just as it is also the truth today — that the physical body copies servilely, slavishly, and as best it can in its poor way, the inner and far more important evolution of the *real* man which is continuously in action in the invisible and intangible parts of the very complex human constitution.

tion of this more advanced race, the Third Root-Race, was hermaphroditic or androgynous; that is to say, the two sexes existed in
every individual of this early and middle Third Root-Race.[137] The
psycho-magnetic activities within those 'human' individuals, of this
far-distant geologic past, produced a fertile germ which was cast off
from the body as an egg, somewhat resembling the process that
takes place in birds and certain reptiles today. These creatures produce eggs from which their young grow and develop to maturity.
Just so was it with the early androgynous, egg-bearing, Third Root-
Race of some twenty million years agone or more. The egg was
matured, and in those days it took a long, long time — at least it
would so seem to us of today — for one of the 'human' eggs to become matured, and for the infant finally to issue forth from it,
alone and unaided. At one time a year or more was required before the egg was broken and the young issued forth from it very
much as the chick does today from the hen's egg.

As the ages slowly dropped one after the other into the ocean of
the past, the later Third Root-Race, as stated in the adjoined footnote, gave birth to the beginnings of the Fourth or unisexual Root-
Race. By this time the androgynous Race had long aeons before
passed away, the sexes had 'separated,' and children were born from
the womb in the manner which at present occurs. It is interesting

---

137. This matter is not so easy to explain, and the reader is requested to
overlook inadequacies or insufficiencies in exposition which cannot be avoided
in view of the lack of space. In strict accuracy, it is really wrong to say that
'the two sexes existed in every individual,' because this confuses the idea: if
the phrase be understood literally, it says that every individual of the Third
Root-Race was a man and a woman in one body, which was not true — at any
rate not true for the greater portion of the history of the Third Root-Race, and
possibly not exactly true even in the period immediately preceding the so-
called 'separation of the sexes' and the appearance of true sexual mankind in
the last portion of the Third Root-Race.

The idea rather is that for the greater part of the time through which the
Third Root-Race lasted, the hermaphroditic or androgynous condition was
rather that of a double functioning of organs appropriate for hermaphroditic
reproduction, somewhat as it may still be seen in certain lower representatives
of the animal kingdom and among certain plants.

During the last portion of the Third Root-Race, however, this double function or hermaphroditic condition slowly modified itself or changed over into
a state of things in which in each individual the particular characteristics of
one or of the other sex became predominant, this in turn finally resulting in
the birth from the womb of individuals of distinct unisexual or one-sex type.

to note that in the beginning, when the sexes first began to 'separate,' such a being might have been considered to be very unusual, a *lusus naturae*, a 'sport' of Nature, but finally these 'sports' found themselves to be in the majority, and the present method of reproduction became the invariable rule, or nearly so, so that an androgyne (the rule was now reversed) came to be considered a teratological monster.

III

Long before the appearance of the Second Root-Race, evolution was in full swing — evolution *as evolution* (speaking now from the matter-side) contrasted with involution — and it continued its work of unfolding the matter-side of beings, i. e., developing and specializing their bodies, both in organs and in organic functions, until the turning-point was reached of this present Fourth Round or great Life-Cycle, which turning-point occurred at the middle of the Fourth Root-Race, which by common agreement or convention modern Theosophists call the Atlantean Race because the center or focus of the great and brilliant civilizations which then flowered over a continental system covering the Earth more or less, was centered where now stretches the Atlantic Ocean.

Then as evolution *as evolution* stopped its work, and involution began — the reverse process;[138] and thereupon what is called the 'door into the human kingdom' closed. This great natural fact of

---

138. As is explained several times elsewhere in the present work, the idea is that on the downward arc of descent into matter, the evolving and revolving monads or 'souls' evolve or unfold or unroll forth matter and involve and inroll spirit; but when the turning-point alluded to in the text above is reached, the reverse process automatically ensues, spirit evolving, albeit slowly, its transcendent powers, while matter *pari passu* involves its own characteristics. The result of this wonderful process of Nature thus gives us a picture of spiritual beings gradually clothing themselves or investing themselves in the garments or veils of material substance, otherwise 'bodies'; and on the upward arc, gradually through the evolution of spirit, etherealizing these bodies slowly to become as the ages pass, and on the ascending arc towards spirit, vestments of what we may truly call 'light' — at least towards the end of the Chain-Manvantara.

The planetary chain with its seven (or twelve) globes, itself follows the same downward and upward course; so that the globes of such planetary chain are at one period in the beginning of their evolutionary course spiritual, then ethereal, then astral, then physical, and on the upward course, etherealize themselves again as matter slowly resolves itself towards the spiritual substances from which it was originally born, and which it again thus slowly rebecomes.

biological history meant not only that no longer could entities inferior to the human kingdom enter the human kingdom by an evolving forth or unrolling forth of what was within them, but it also meant that no longer could new phyla, as the modern biologists call them — that is to say, new racial stocks — be produced from the then existing seeds of life, for the reason that the processes of unfolding, of starting new stocks, of originating new families, orders, and classes had come to an end. Evolution, or the differentiation of the one into the many, had ceased, i. e., its impulses had faded out, that is, for this Fourth Round; and therefore while more specializations of what already existed could and did continue, in some cases even to extreme degrees, no new orders or great stocks of distinct animal or vegetable entities could henceforth appear for the remainder of the great Life-Cycle or Round of this Planetary Chain.

Involution was from this turning-point the manner of Nature's universal working on this Globe, Earth; and involution means the infolding of matter and the coincident evolution or unfolding or unwrapping or coming into manifestation through the vehicles already materially evolved of hitherto latent spiritual, intellectual, psychical, and therefore consequent and effectual physical functions, processes, and senses. Evolution as here used means the unfolding of the potencies latent in *matter*, and the *in*folding or *in*volution of spiritual qualities; this involution thus providing a treasury or repertory of faculties and functions which became progressively more recessive as the evolution, or the unfolding, of *bodies* proceeded. At the turning-point above mentioned there occurred the last fading out of the evolutionary process of differentiation in matter, and thereupon the involutionary process thereof began: that is to say the infolding or gradual etherealizing and final disappearance of bodies, bringing about a coincident and accompanying and gradual release or manifestation of the faculties and functions and organs infolded by the preceding process of evolution on the Downward Arc, or Shadowy Arc, into matter.

We have, then, first the evolution of matter and the accompanying involution of the spiritual; but from the turning-point the process is reversed, and we have the moving towards spirit, therefore the involution of matter and the evolution of spirit. On the Downward Arc or Shadowy Arc, matter unfolds or evolves itself in myriad forms, and spirit infolds or involves itself. From the turning-point onwards, when the Ascending Arc or Luminous Arc is begun, involution begins, which means the involving of matter and the unfolding or evolution of spirit and its faculties and powers. The two processes interwork.

The generation and birth and growth of the human child may probably be cited as an example by way of illustration. From conception until the mid-point or turning-point of adult life, it is the body which grows and develops faculty and power and organ, while the spiritual and intellectual and psychical faculties are more or less recessive or involved — latent, if the word be preferred. From the mid-point of life, say early middle-age, the reverse procedure is seen to take place in the normal individual. The body and its functions become less active, less important for the purposes of human life; and coincidentally and *pari passu,* the evolution of the noble spiritual and intellectual and psychical faculties and organs occurs, as man develops mind in its strength and power, and what is commonly called 'soul' and its fine qualities and attributes.

As before said, the animate stocks which had not reached the human stage at the great turning-point above mentioned could thereafter no longer evolve upwards on the rising arc, and must in consequence wait their turn for their natural and perfectly proper evolutionary development in the manner above described, until the next great Planetary Manvantara or Life-Cycle or Round.[139] But

---

139. Here again one encounters a difficulty, not in the teaching itself, but in any adequate explanation of it in the compass of a single chapter of a work like the present. What is stated in the text is perfectly correct; but the reader should remember the following really important point if he is interested in matters of which the present chapter treats. While it is true that during the next or Fifth Chain-Round, the animate stocks below man, which means the beasts in this connexion, will again appear on this Earth and continue their evolutionary course, repeating what happens during this Fourth Round, but in conditions and circumstances which the Fifth Round will bring forth, nevertheless because the entire Planetary Chain itself is now in the process of *involution,* the barrier into the human kingdom will become ever more difficult to pass, so that, as a matter of fact, the lower animate stocks beneath the human, dating even from the turning-point above spoken of in this present Fourth Round, will all show a tendency to die out and disappear from the evolutionary life-stream.

This does not imply in any sense, however, that Nature here shows any favoritism to the human stock and to the anthropoid apes, for such favoritism is merely a human quality, and Nature knows it not. This will happen to the Kingdoms beneath the Human because they are belated in their respective evolutionary courses, whereas the Human Kingdom and the anthropoid apes, being 'on time' so to speak, when the turning-point arrived, were enabled to press steadily forwards because having within themselves already awakened those spiritual and intellectual and psychical faculties and powers which fitted them to swim in the upwards-rising evolutionary stream, comprising and bringing about the unfolding of the faculties and functions of spirit as hereinbefore described.

the human stock and the higher anthropoid apes which were already in existence before this turning-point, which took place at the middle of the Fourth Root-Race, could and did continue their upward or spiritual course, *involving* the functions and organs of matter, and beginning, although slowly, to *evolve* the organs and functions of the spiritual and intellectual and psychic powers and forces latent and lying waiting within them. The single exception, therefore, to the animate stocks below man, as stated above, is the simiidae in their highest representatives, that is to say the anthropoid apes — and possibly the cynocephalus; the reason for this being that they had a strain of genuine human blood in them before the turning-point above spoken of was reached.[140] The anthropoid apes, therefore, are an exception to this fact of a barrier to further developmental unfolding of the lower animate stocks. These apes are destined to become human beings of a low grade in the next or Fifth Chain-Round, the next great Planetary Life-Cycle, millions and millions of years hence.

IV

Now then, after this picture we come to the direct question: How did the mammalia originate from the human stock? The mammalia originated from the human stock somewhat after the following manner, and the reader is requested to bear in mind that the outline here given is a mere sketch. Before the Lords of Mind, the Mânasaputras, evolved spiritual beings of an intellectual type, had begun even their first approaches to imbodiment in the then mindless humanity (which imbodiments happened in the last part of the Second and took place fully in the middle part of the Third Root-Race during this present Fourth Round) — before the Lords of Mind had done more than project from themselves a feeble ray of self-conscious intelligence and of ethical instinct into the then evolving Second Root-

---

The turn of the Kingdoms below the Human will come in the next imbodiment of the entire planetary chain; and then the Kingdoms inferior to the human, etc., will find the fields of life ready for them for their own respective evolutionary expansion in power and faculty, with the added compensation, if the term be permissible, of becoming unfolded human beings on a chain imbodied on planes superior to what exists at present.

To the reader who knows little or nothing of the teaching of the Esoteric Tradition concerning planetary chains and their individual reimbodiments, it is suggested that he read pertinent passages in H. P. Blavatsky's *The Secret Doctrine*, Volume I.

140. See *The Secret Doctrine*, Volume II.

Race, this Second Root-Race was mindless, as was indeed the First. It did not possess the psychical and physical instincts and barriers that now infill and control the human consciousness and therefore act and react upon the physical bodies. This fact of psychical instincts, and the barriers raised by them, is very important. Unless one understands this idea of the natural psychical barrier or inhibition forbidding, and therefore preventing, the miscegenation of a higher with a much lower stock, he will understand with difficulty the explanation of this very important and involved and intricate theme of study.

As before said, the bodies of this mindless Second Root-Race were, as bodies, the vehicles of the life-atoms of all kinds of evolving entities seeking manifestation: seeking to unfold, to unwrap, i. e., to evolve; because in that early geologic period of time, all the stocks from the 'human' down to the protozoa were under the natural urge and instinct to evolve ever newer corporeal forms. All the entities on the planet were still running down the Arc of Descent or Shadowy Arc, and unfolding and therefore differentiating through evolution. All the stocks had an inner urge, powerful, masterful, to express themselves, i. e., to unfold what lay latent within them, exactly as the acorn is urged from inherent life-impulses to grow after germination, and thus to unwrap or evolve the oak already lying invisibly latent within it, and exactly as the human embryo must unwrap or evolve itself and produce itself as a human child.

The consequence of this evolutionary urge of all beings was that the spores, the drops of 'vital sweat' above alluded to, of the later Second Root-Race and of the early Third, were in large part guests in the 'human' bodies of these two Races, drawn to those bodies by karmic psycho-magnetic attraction, and thus helping to build the physical frames of those bodies — exactly as the cells of man's body today are animal-cells, guests in man's body and aiding in its building and coherence, for Man is their host and uses them in his own physical vehicle. Even the human body today, one may repeat, is builded of animal-cells, each one greatly inferior to a human being, yet in their aggregate inferiority forming the human body — or at least a large part of it — through which the psychical and mental and spiritual apparatuses of the inner man work.

Now these cells or life-germs, using the bodies of the Second Root-Race as their hosts, were cast off in a then perfectly normal way from these human bodies, and grew, each cell, according to its own swabhâva, which means according to the essential urging characteristic or individuality which is the life-center within each such cell. Even today, if the psychical bar or barrier just mentioned did not now exist with such intensity and vigor of operation, a vast number of the supposedly human spores or seeds cast off in one way or another, would grow, i. e., would evolve, and would become the starting-points in certain cases, of new phyla, although in all cases of status inferior to the human. These cells thus cast off from the protoplastic human bodies of these early races, in many cases grew and became the starting-points of new stocks of creatures which in their originating cells had passed through the human body in germ, and were cast off therefrom, exactly as germs or life-atoms pass through our bodies today and leave them in one way or another.

Every seed, every spore, is the dwelling or house or body of an evolving entity, of a psychical life-atom — call it in its such stage an Elemental, a term which is strictly correct for this period of its existence. Of course, every life-atom has everything in it *essentially* that a man or a god has; but no life-atom can express on any one plane, which means on any one globe of a planetary chain, more than its then existent evolved or unfolded capacities permit it to express or unfold or evolve. Exactly as a man today cannot be a god, because he has not yet evolved forth the god within him, although the god is there, latent, or dormant, asleep — more accurately it is we who are asleep and cannot express the god within us — just so every vital cell, every reproductive germ, contains within itself the potentiality not only of the divinity latent within it, but it also contains within itself numerous lower quasi-psychical life-impulses, which, could they only find expression or come out, would produce an inferior creature, whether it be an elephant, a giraffe, a horse, a cat, a dog, or some biological 'sport' which past history shows has not yet appeared on earth.

The reasons therefore why such cells or reproductive germs in man today do not evolve forth into new phyla or animate stocks beneath man, are the two set forth: First, evolution, *as a process of unfolding new bodies and starting new stocks* has permanently ceased for the remainder of this Round. The evolutionary urge has faded out, and involution has taken its place. It should be borne in mind that whereas there can be no evolution without an accompanying involution, in one sense — as for instance, the involution of matter and the corresponding and *pari passu* evolution of spirit, or *vice versa* — nevertheless, using the terms as above described, during the geologic periods when one of the two is predominant, the other then and there is recessive.

The other and second reason, above alluded to, is the psychical barriers and inhibitions already described, working powerfully against such originations of new animate stocks. The influence of the human psychical fluid in man's constitution at the present time is so powerful and over-masterful in its effect on the germinal cells or life-atoms which help to build man's bodies, that these germs or cells have become passive thereto, and actually inactive so far as the ability to evolve forth from themselves the beginnings of new animate stocks — considering likewise the effect of the 'door into the human kingdom' having closed, which door really is naught but this tremendous psychical barrier just spoken of. To adopt an expression taken from modern biological experimental science, the human life-fluid or psychic essence is dominant, whereas the hosts of germinal cells or psychical life-atoms through which the human psychic fluid works have become recessive both as individuals and as naturally divided into hosts.

If we human beings could project ourselves back into the time and into the physical laws which governed the procedures of evolution or unfolding at the time when the Second Root-Race lived, we should find things happening which would appear exceedingly strange to us with our crystallized notions of how 'things should be.' A human individual would find that the vital or reproductive germs from his body — 'sweating,' to use H. P. Blavatsky's term — if falling from that portion of his organism where the reproductive plasm has become seated and perfected, would reproduce a second human like unto its parent, even as at present; but if this 'vital sweat,' these spores of vital psychic-astral fluid, fell from some other portion of his body, say from what modern histology calls the somatic plasm of a cell, these falling cells or germs would not grow into human beings like unto the parent, but would, in millions of instances, if the environment were favorable, grow into beings of curiously differing characteristics who would be the beginnings of new phyla, new animate stocks.

The main point is the following: every vital cell or reproductive germ is in itself a storehouse or repertory of unexpressed types; and if there be no natural inhibition, no psychical barrier or bar to its expression, the type having the strongest urge for manifestation would be the one to emerge as dominant, and grow into a representative entity which would be the beginning of a new stock of creatures.[141] This no longer occurs because of the strong psychical-vital

141. The reader will kindly note the word 'type' used in the sentence in the text. The text briefly describes or outlines the case of a single life-germ

human force which over-masters and thus controls every such re-productive germ, barring or inhibiting the self-expression or mani-festation of all types inferior to the parent, which inferior types thus become utterly recessive and in consequence non-self-expressing, and whose function at present is merely to aid in forming and hold-ing in vital coherence the physical body as a whole.

Now all these animals or beasts that came forth from the then human bodies in the manner described, many of them the far-distant 'parents' of the beast-stocks which now are on Earth, and beginning with the last part of the Second Root-Race and continuing up to the central part of the Third Root-Race — all these animals or beasts were mammals. Why? Because they were the highest kinds of evolving beast-monads, although inferior to the evolving human monads, and which naturally drifted — drawn thereto by psycho-magnetic attraction — to the Kingdom next above themselves — the Human Kingdom, which already at that time was beginning to take unto itself the foreshadowings of the mammalian type or character.

---

or psycho-vital reproductive spore falling from its parent and growing into a creature or being different, perhaps in large degree, from its parent, the reason being the inherent swâbhâvic impulsion of a psycho-vital character, latent in the invisible fluid of such falling reproductive spore. This does not mean that the Esoteric Tradition teaches the unity of genesis of the human race from a single individual or from two individuals somewhat after the type of the He-braeo-Christian mythos of the romantic event which took place in the 'Garden of Eden'; but, to the contrary, teaches a distinct polygeny, meaning by this term that an indefinitely large number of such reproductive spores might, could, or did, fall from the bodies of the early humanity contemporaneously, and as these psycho-vital reproductive spores themselves belong to classes or families, it be-comes obvious that thus would appear the beginning of new stocks of creatures, individual, of course, born from another parent or possibly from the same parent; and, furthermore, that as these psycho-vital reproductive spores or germs were, as just stated, themselves members of widely various classes, a single 'human' individual body could thus have shed from itself, or cast off from it-self, or 'sweated' out, offsprings of lower evolutionary kinds at different times.

Nor should this last statement be misunderstood to mean that these proto-plastic 'humans' did not give birth to 'children' like unto themselves — 'humans,' for they most certainly did, as stated above in the text. If the life-germ which fell or was 'sweated' out came from a portion of the parent-body which already had become adapted to or set apart for 'human' reproduction, the 'human' spores falling from this part grew into 'human' beings like unto their parents.

And, finally, the Esoteric Tradition does not teach a monogenesis of any of the stocks which were thus originally 'born' and 'filled the earth.' Polygeny was the rule throughout, in all cases in those very early ages.

But did not the animals, like the human stock, have an inner urge behind them, causing them to evolve along their own lines, once that their originating individuals had appeared? The answer is obvious: Yes, certainly. The important thing to remember in this complicated natural fact, is the following: all the Kingdoms of Nature below the Human Kingdom aspire towards the Human Kingdom, psychically yearn upwards to become human; and during their aeons-long evolutionary pilgrimage, the Monads evolving in the beast-bodies cast off beast-body after beast-body, gradually rising along the scale or Ladder of Life until the Human Kingdom is reached, at which point they enter into the lowest class of human vehicles, but not as beast-monads, but as human monads, albeit of the lowest type.[142] It is the human type to which all the lower kingdoms tend in evolutionary course; and this wonderful truth of Nature, so suggestive and instructive when properly understood, is now becoming so obvious that certain intuitive biologists and biological palaeontologists are beginning to recognise it, or at least to have some adumbration of it. They are, however, as yet but few. Men like Dr. Robert Broom, President of the South African Association for the Advancement of Science, are noteworthy instances in point; although, indeed, Dr. Broom's theory differs from the Theosophical teaching inasmuch as he makes Man to be a descendant of some formerly living anthro-

---

142. It will be fatal to a proper understanding of this complicate teaching if the reader supposes that the beast-monads are essentially different from monads of any other kind. This is entirely wrong. The difference between 'monad' and 'monad' is solely a difference in the evolutionary stage reached by any monad because of its having brought forth from itself some of its inner spiritual-psychic essence or fluid. We speak of the 'Mineral Monad,' 'Vegetable Monad,' 'Animal Monad,' 'Human Monad,' 'God-Monad,' etc., only by way of description or for descriptive purposes. All these different Classes of Monads are sprung from the same primordial Cosmic Spirit and therefore each one has within itself, or locked up within itself, infolded within itself, all the capacities, powers, faculties, attributes, etc., that all others have. These different classes of Monads are therefore classified in the above manner solely to describe their different standings or stages in the evolutionary ladder of life.

Thus the beast today is not a Man because it has not as yet unfolded or unwrapped from within its own essence those characteristics or qualities or attributes which we call human; but some day it will unwrap them all and then it will be a Human Monad and will take unto itself a human body.

Distinguish carefully therefore between this teaching and the utterly erroneous idea that these different classes are from eternity Monads of essentially distinct and different type or kind. They are one in Spirit, many in manifestation.

poid ape. This idea Theosophy or the Esoteric Tradition does not accept. Theosophy shows the apes as derivative from man, in their case more particularly from certain degenerate groups of the great Fourth Root-Race — an occurrence which took place probably in the Miocene geologic period; although here it should be pointed out with some emphasis that the Theosophist does not give to the duration of the Tertiary Age the over-long time-extension which modern palaeontologists give.[143]

The matter of time-periods is here touched upon with great reserve, and this for several reasons. When H. P. Blavatsky first wrote *The Secret Doctrine* geologists then very grudgingly gave to the different geologic periods what Theosophists looked upon as sufficient time for the evolution of the First, Second, Third, Fourth, and Fifth Root-Races respectively. But today modern geologists give us a great deal more time than is required even by our occult records. Our records show that it is some 320,000,000 years since sedimentation began on this globe *in this Fourth Round,* nor does this long lapse of time fully include the evolution of the three Kingdoms of the Elementals which preceded the mineral activities beginning such sedimentation mentioned above. Of course the four Root-Races which preceded ours, the Fifth, did not require all these 320,000,000 years for their evolution, because the First Root-Race appeared on this globe in the Fourth Round long after the mineral-activity had begun; long after the Vegetable Kingdom had awaked; and even after the Animal Kingdom had awaked from its obscuration — except of course, the higher division of the Animal Kingdom, the Mammalia, which in this Fourth Round *followed* man, as has already been stated, and whose appearance was brought about in the manner hereinbefore sketched.[144]

---

143. Consult footnote No. 145, *infra.*

144. It should be remembered in connexion with the serial appearance of the different Kingdoms, that, so far as Man and the Animal Kingdom are concerned, the animals — but not the mammalia — preceded man in their appearance on this Globe D on the Downward Arc, that is to say they fell into matter more rapidly than did the Human Kingdom, because being of a more material type, the attraction of the material Globe D was stronger upon them than upon the Human Monads.

Furthermore, it may just as well be stated here that the separation of the sexes occurred among the animals or beasts before the same event took place in the Human Family. Thus it was that not only did the huge beasts of various kinds of that early geologic period clothe themselves with gross physical vestures before the Astral Man did the same, but they likewise separated into male and

324THE ESOTERIC TRADITION

For when the First (or distinctly astral) Root-Race appeared on this Globe, there were then present on it many groups of the Vegetable Kingdom which were the śishṭas or remnants of the Vegetable Kingdom as it was in the preceding or Third Round; and also there were a number of groups of different animals, although these were animals below that stage which is now called the 'mammalian.' There was, in fact, an amazing welter of protozoa and crustacea, and fishes, and reptiles, and birds — although very few reptiles and birds — but no mammals. The first mammals appeared as unimportant 'sports' in the very last part of the Second Root-Race — or it is possible that these first and unimportant mammalian representatives appeared during the first third of the Third Root-Race.

v

A little may be said, by way of two or three more hints, with respect to geologic time-periods. Mankind 'separated' into opposite sexes about eighteen million years ago, during the Third Root-Race, according to the occult records, or in what geologists in H. P. Blavatsky's time called, in defining geologic time-periods, the late Triassic or early Jurassic of the Secondary Age.[145] Humanity was then

female from the preceding androgynous state before the human stock followed the example set by what were then its forerunners — the beasts.

At the beginning of the Ascending Arc, the position of forerunners became reversed; for, the climb towards spirit having begun, the spiritual attractions consequently acted most strongly on the most spiritually developed stock of that time; so that man, from the beginning of this ascent, slowly took the place which he now holds as the leader and forerunner of all the Kingdoms behind him, all of which unconsciously aspire to the human stage.

145. In regard to the use of geological terms by H. P. Blavatsky in *The Secret Doctrine*, it is a matter of importance in order to be prepared for any possible scientific criticism, for interested readers to remember that the Great Theosophist spoke in terms of the time-measurements adopted by geologists and astronomers of fifty years ago, more or less, which were, however, really nearer the truth than most of the guesses tentatively accepted by geologists today. When H. P. Blavatsky spoke of 'Jurassic,' etc., and stated that man existed at such-and-such periods, using the geologic terms then popular and in vogue, she was using the *short* calculation then current, which could fit in, in a general way, with the age of '*separated*' humanity ('Vaivasvata's humanity') as given in the esoteric records — let us say, 18,600,000 years and odd centuries. But retaining the same names for the time-periods that H. P. Blavatsky then used is too apt to create confusion, because of the lengthened time-periods that modern geologists give to those same geologic Eras, and thus the esoteric statements

a fully physicalized Race, although not so grossly physical as was the Fourth Root-Race of the Atlantean Era which followed the Third Root-Race of some eighteen million years ago. The early Third, as well as all the Second, stretched back even to a longer period in bygone geological time than the eighteen million years spoken of, possibly as far back as twenty-five or thirty million years from the present era of the Fifth Root-Race. Some twenty-five or thirty million years ago mankind was in the Second Root-Race, whereas the First Root-Race stretched still farther back into the remote mists of geologic time.

It is extremely difficult also from another point of view for a Theosophist to locate these different Root-Races in the modern geologic Ages, for the reason that geologists themselves disagree as to the length of these different geological time-periods. Then, also, it must be remembered that preceding even the beginnings of the purely astral, or ethereal, First Root-Race, there were between two and three hundred million years of evolutional development belonging to the Animal Kingdom (but not including the mammals), the Vegetable Kingdom, the Mineral Kingdom, and the three Elemental Kingdoms.

Geologists today are basing what are to the Theosophist their exaggerated time-periods on the fairly recent discovery of radioactivity in the rocks, which they believe provides a reasonably trustworthy method of calculating the time elapsed since the rocks were formed. This radio-activity, which is the disintegration of certain heavy elements, is supposed to have taken place with no change of speed during all the ages during which these radio-active minerals

---

and those of the most modern geology, in regard to the number of years in the respective geologic periods, no longer harmonize.

H. P. Blavatsky, however, was well aware of the possibility of such enlargement in time of the geologic Eras by modern geologists, and she specially referred to it on page 693 of the second volume of *The Secret Doctrine,* where she writes:

"It may make our position plainer if we state at once that we use Sir C. Lyell's nomenclature for the ages and periods, and that when we talk of the Secondary and Tertiary age, of the Eocene, Miocene, and Pliocene periods — this is simply to make our facts more comprehensible. Since these ages and periods have not yet been allowed fixed and determined durations, . . . Esoteric teachings may remain quite indifferent to whether man is shown to appear in the Secondary or the Tertiary age."

As the Tertiary has now been extended far beyond the few million years accepted in 1888, the 'Vaivasvata-humanity' would be included in its more recent epochs, provided of course that the modern geologic time-estimate be accepted.

have lain in the rocks where we now find them. As a reason for rejecting the modern time-periods estimated by this method (and on which there is such disagreement that the best modern textbooks of geology point out carefully that they depend upon yet unproved assumptions), it is necessary to point out the following: the radio-active changes referred to were brought about and are now continuing, as elsewhere explained, because of the fact that the Earth and all on it are now on the Ascending Arc or Luminous Arc, and consequently undergoing the processes of dematerializing, thus bringing about the breaking up or disintegration, which modern physics and chemistry call 'radiation,' of the coarsest, grossest, heaviest, of the chemical elements. On the Descending Arc, the Shadowy Arc, up to the middle of the Atlantean Race, all the chemical elements (which means the body of the Earth) were condensing and therefore concreting; and radio-activity as now understood was unknown as a fact in Nature. From the turning-point at the middle of the Fourth Root-Race, the Earth and all on it has been steadily albeit slowly etherealizing; and consequently radio-activity will become more and more pronounced, and chemical elements and chemical compounds will become, and are indeed becoming, albeit very slowly, less heavy and less concreted. The heaviest now known which are not at present radio-active, will soon — speaking in terms of geological time-thought — also become radio-active. In other words, the process of radio-activity will in future ages take place in all the chemical elements and compounds, beginning with the heaviest and grossest, and running up the scale towards the lightest and simplest. Consequently, when the geologists base their presently exaggerated time-periods on what they understand of radio-activity, they should properly so do, i. e., make their beginning only from the mid-point of the Atlantean Race, when this radio-activity first began.[146] But because they do not know of a Descending Arc and an Ascending

---

146. When was this mid-point of the Atlantean Race? In view of the close secrecy that has always veiled in obscurity all accurate chronological computations by the Guardians of the secret records of the Ancient Wisdom, it is very difficult in a work intended for the public to venture upon accurate statements of this character. However, a hint may be given, and it may be said that as we are at the present time almost at the mid-point of our present or Fifth Root-Race, and taking into account certain other time-factors which need not be mentioned here — it may be said that the mid-point of the Fourth or Atlantean Race took place between 8,000,000 and 9,000,000 years ago. When radio-activity first began in this already remote period, it was but slight, but very slowly increased in extent. It will continue to increase for the range of chemical ele-

Arc, they think that radio-activity began with the first incrustation of our globe. For this reason, to the student of the Esoteric Philosophy, the geological time-periods, reckoned as based upon radio-activity, are highly speculative and inaccurate at the best, and at the worst thoroughly wrong.

VI

To return to the main argument or theme of this chapter, it is to be remembered that the lower Kingdoms tend towards man as their evolutionary goal on this Earth, and this not only because man has preceded them: man is far older than they, man has blazed the trail, which they instinctively and unconsciously follow. He has made and left the astral molds behind him out of which he has grown to greater things; and the inferior beings of the Animal Kingdom, trailing along behind, follow the path that he has made and thus copy him, as we humans indeed copy those beings now far in advance who have preceded us, i. e., the Dhyâni-Chohanic Races — and these Dhyâni-Chohanic Races, because manifesting or self-expressing a portion of the septenary constitution which in man is still but slightly active, might with truth be said to form a Kingdom above the Human, just as man can truthfully be said to form a Kingdom above the Animal, and for precisely the same reason.

Man preceded the mammalia and also gave birth to their original phyla or stocks in the manner hereinbefore outlined or sketched. Once these mammalian stocks were begun, thereafter each pursued its own rapid evolutionary unfolding from within, breeding true to type, and yet developing, i. e., evolving, each one such stock, along its own particular swâbhâvic or characteristic line of developmental evolution. But when the turning-point, the middle point of the Fourth Root-Race, was reached, thereafter all that the evolutionary impulse or urge working in and through and behind these various

---

ments and compounds running up the scale towards the simpler, as before said, as the millennia of the future slowly drop one by one into the past.

Thus it comes about that in the etherealizing process which our Earth-globe is now undergoing, the heaviest and grossest of the chemical elements and compounds will first become radio-active, radiating their substance away with increasing speed, and will be followed by the next or less heavy and gross, the process continuing until the end of the present Fourth Round in particular, and, with intervals of the reverse process during the downward arcs of the succeeding Rounds, proceeding until the Seventh Round will have reached its climax or end. By that time, the Globe and all on it will have returned to the highly ethereal state or condition of matter that prevailed through the First Round.

animal stocks could produce, was — what? *Specialization*—specialization, indeed, in all its manifold and mysterious and intriguing complexities, aiding in producing the fascinating varieties and species and classes of beings which formerly existed and those which at present exist and are discoverable around us. It was evolution on large and 'creative' lines until the 'door into the Human Kingdom' closed, and thereafter the evolutionary impulses produced bewildering specializations, this being evolution in the particular as contrasted with evolution in the general. The animate stocks beneath the anthropoids, as already has been stated, cannot go higher for the rest of this Round-Manvantara or Planetary Life-Cycle. They will die out before the last, or Seventh, Round is reached, because they will not be able to rise along the Ascending or Luminous Arc; to speak in the vernacular of today, they will not be able to 'make the grade.' As long as they live and propagate their kind, if there be any evolution or unfolding towards a higher phylum on the scale of life, it will be extremely limited only, nevertheless there will continue to be a large amount of specialization in many directions. All that these animate stocks *can* do is henceforth to specialize. The elephant, for instance, with its long so-called 'trunk' or proboscis, and its huge ears, is highly specialized in proboscis and ears, but it will nevertheless always be an elephant as long as the elephant-stock lives during the remainder of this Planetary Life-Cycle.

Two more examples of minor evolution, called specialization, as contrasted with grander evolution proper, i. e., unwrapping and unfolding of impulses on general lines towards higher kinds of beings, are the bat and the whale. Both are mammals, both are of the mammalian type, as much as man is. Yet one, the bat, left the earth, took to the air, and became a flying creature with a flight which, in its ease and swiftness and silence, is more perfect than the flight of most of the true birds. The other, the whale, left the land and took to the water. Although as much a mammal in type as man is, it took to the water and therein it acts like a fish, looks like a fish, swims like a fish. These are strange and vastly interesting specializations, and they are 'evolution' in the etymological sense of the unfolding of innate faculty; but they are not, strictly speaking, evolution in the larger and more technical sense of the unfolding of future type-characters including larger capacities. For all the rest of this Manvantara or Planetary Life-Cycle, that is to say, for the remainder of this Fourth Round and for the Fifth and the Sixth Rounds, the animals, if they continue in existence as a Kingdom until the Sixth Round, will be specializing in multimyriad ways, but truly *evolving* no more. The human race, however, will 'evolve' by 'involving,' paradoxical as it may sound: evolve forth spirit, and involve matter.

It should be evident to the perspicacious reader and student that the tenor or argument of the present chapter is one dealing largely if not wholly with the developmental evolution of physical bodies, whether of man or beast or plant. The reason is that it is necessary for any extending of the teachings of the Esoteric Tradition to include physical evolution in this work of exegesis in order to explain its cause, its character, and something at least of the time-periods in which it takes place. Yet it is of the first importance to remember that the evolution of the physical body, whether of man or of beast or of plant, or indeed of the mineral, is but the result, an effectual consequence, of the causal evolutionary processes which arise in the invisible constitution of evolving beings, and merely expresses such results thereof through the physical body as the physical body is capable of following.

In other words, and selecting man as an example in point, it is the inner man which really is evolving, and who passes from life to life through the ages selecting in each new imbodiment such body as in each instance happily may be somewhat improved over its last physical vehicle. It must never be supposed that it is the physical man which evolves primarily, and that it is the inner, spiritual, intellectual, and psycho-mental, Man which trails after or follows the evolution of the physical vehicle, as one whose mind has been colored by modern scientific evolutionary teaching might at first superficially suppose. It is the exact opposite of this which happens. It is the inner man, the Monad, which through the ages and by slow but progressive stages unrolls or unwraps or unfolds from within its own essence ever larger measures of spirituality, of intellectual power, of psycho-mental sensitivity, and of astral ethereality. All these combine in expressing, however feebly, their powers through the physical vehicle, and slowly through the ages refine and improve such physical vehicle both in functions and in organs, for the physical vehicle is plastic, and follows and copies the molding of the invisible inner Worker.

How can one explain these things easily to a modern scientist who knows nothing of the astral worlds and still less of the spiritual and intellectual worlds, although indeed he may be beginning to point to what even now remains in botany and zoology — in biology, in other words — of the vestiges or records of what took place in these now distant ages of the past? How can one explain that what now remains as remnants or vestiges of disused organs, were the regular and common appendages and procedures of fully functional organs in that distant past; or again that the stock which has been longest on the earth obviously is the oldest and therefore the most advanced stock, and this stock is the Human. It obviously takes time to grow, i. e., to evolve; and it is only the rolling ages which in their revolving courses have conducted man from the Elemental he was in the opening or beginning of the Drama of Evolution in this Solar System, to his present status of being the most important because most evolved or unfolded animate stock on the earth today.

It is indeed no easy task, nor work of a day, to convince a generation of hard-headed scientific men of the esoteric teachings concerning evolution, except first, along the lines of general reason and logic, and by insisting that all known facts in the case be given their due meed of consideration courageously; and that all such facts must be taken into account and not shelved because of already ingrained scientific prejudice or preconception; and second, by pointing to what is after all a vast number of hitherto unexplained biologic facts, which if they are not forced into an unnatural setting of modern scientific dogma, nor forgotten, are eloquent in mute testimony of modern scientific evolutionary hypothesis and theory as being imperfect because inadequate to cover all the facts; and what is much worse, because unphilosophical, that such modern hypothesis or theory more or less completely ignores what is by far the larger part of man's constitution — spirituality, the moral sense, the powers and characteristics of intellect, the faculties of judgment, discrimination, and the power of analysis; and most important of all, those moral faculties which are always found where true spirituality exists, which to any thoughtful mind no evolutionary theory yet propounded has ever endeavored to explain: and with the moral sense, those other qualities or human attributes which men call love, devotion, self-abnegation, self-sacrifice, and others like unto these.

VII

Now what is the process of consolidation by which the early astral and semi-astral Races of mankind evolved or unfolded into the physical condition — and of course the reference is here made to the physical bodies or vehicles? Any difficulty in understanding the principles involved lies in the fact that students of H. P. Blavatsky's teachings are too prone to take literally the words in which her teachings are given, rather than generally and constructively and synthetically as teachings: i. e., their thoughts are led away by the *words* that she uses in attempting to describe difficult things. Thus they omit to synthesize or bring together in proper co-ordination the many statements she makes — most of them from the esoteric records. Yet nothing is really more simple or more easy.

What is now and here said has reference to this Fourth Globe in this Fourth or present Round only, omitting other than fugitive references to preceding Rounds in order to avoid confusion of thought. The First Root-Race, then, was a highly ethereal race of beings vaguely yet more or less distinctly having the present human shape, *reminding* one strongly of the present human shape in fact: but could one see individuals of this First Root-Race today, our attention would be immediately caught by what would be to us strange differences and remarkable yet fugitive shiftings or changings in outward lineament or form — a quasi-fluid Race, in fact; an astral race, therefore, just beginning to be physicalized in matter. They were likewise translucent or transparent — or would be so to our present Fifth-Race vision. The nearest present-day thing to which one may liken them, perhaps, would be a cloudiness in the air, or a highly heated air-current with its dancing effect on the eye, or again, perhaps, a cloudy gas. This does not mean, however, that they were formless in outline as is air or a cloudy gas. They indeed had a form, but far less *fixed* than is the gross heavy body of man today, and they were transparent because ethereal in texture, and consequently made no fossil-impression on the earth at that time, the reason for which appears in the following paragraph.

The Earth at the opening of this Fourth Round, i. e., this Fourth Globe itself at that time, was also more ethereal than now it is, nevertheless as compared with this First Race of 'human' protoplasts, it was relatively hard and condensed; in other words, the First Root-Race in its beginning, and indeed throughout its entire course, was more ethereal than the Earth then was. Both the Earth and the Races which inhabited it, consolidated steadily until the middle period of the Fourth Root-Race, when the maximum of condensation or consolidation was reached, i. e., the extreme degree of consolidation or physicalization of matter possible during the present Chain-Manvantara of seven Rounds. Since the time of the middle of the Fourth Root-Race, which also happened to be the middle of the Fourth Round and therefore likewise the middle of the entire Chain-Manvantara — for the time-periods in this case converged to a point — both the Earth and its inhabitants, such as man, have become somewhat etherealized again. The flesh of the men of the

Atlantean Race, for instance, was grosser and coarser and more solid than is the flesh of our Fifth-Race folk, and both the Earth and its inhabitants will become more and more ethereal as the aeons of time in the future slowly drop one after the other into the past; until, at the end of the Seventh Round, aeons upon aeons hence, the Earth and its then future humanity will have reached the highly ethereal stage, more or less, that prevailed during the First Round.

Another reflexion which it may be useful here to state: when the astral First Root-Race of humanity began to concrete or consolidate and thus to become more physical, it of necessity and naturally used material already existent on this globe, and this was material which had been cast off and left behind by the forwards-evolving human stock during the preceding or Third Round. The use of this material by evolving humanity in this Fourth Round naturally aided the evolution of the life-atoms composing such formerly used substance, and the life-atoms of such material or substance naturally were impregnated with the influence of the higher astral material of the growing and evolving human stock during its evolutionary course in this Fourth Round.

From the foregoing, the beauty of the archaic teaching that man is a microcosm, a copy in the small of the Macrocosm, should be apparent. Man, both as an individual and as a stock, or humanity, is the repertory, the depositary, the treasure-house, of only the gods know how many as yet unmanifested future great phyla of animate beings, who will in the future far, far distant ages yet to come, in a new Chain-Manvantara or Great Planetary Life-Cycle, then flow forth from him as his off-throwings, in a manner more or less identic with that which brought about the origination of the great animate stocks hereinbefore briefly explained. Just as we are children of the gods, so are the beasts, the higher beasts, the mammalians especially, our off-throwings or offsprings; all belonging to a lower Kingdom than the Human, yet both collectively and individually on their upward way to become in future ages members of a new Human Kingdom — not the bodies alone, but definitely and positively the as yet imperfectly evolved Monads, now inhabiting their imperfectly evolved animal bodies. As a matter of fact, all the creatures of the Third Round which at that time filled the Earth, were the offsprings or off-throwings of the then imperfectly evolved human stock; and in those now far distant times of the past, all the then beings of the lower Kingdoms were unconsciously produced, unconsciously thrown off, from the then 'mankind,' thus owing their origin to the then imperfect, because imperfectly evolved, 'human' physical stock. In other words, it was *man* who threw off at various periods during his long past aeonic evolution the root-types which later *specialized* into the Vegetable and Animal Kingdoms. Indeed, the same thing is true of the Mineral Kingdom, but in the First Round, which preceded the Third and Second counting backwards. All of which is equivalent to saying that MAN is the oldest of all the stocks on Earth.[147]

To continue: the Second Root-Race was more condensed, more material, more physicalized, than was the First — considerably more so. The Second Root-Race, especially at its middle part and towards its end, was no longer transparent, nor would it seem so even to our Fifth-Race vision today. One might look upon the bodies of the individuals of the middle Second Root-Race, for instance, as being albuminous, somewhat like the white of an egg, having a definite form, having even the rudimentary beginning of bones and organs, hair and skin; but all as yet imperfectly developed, imperfectly condensed — mere sketches or foreshadowings. But although it was consolidating or physicalizing, it was still too ethereal to leave any fossil impression or fossil records on the then Earth, which, although itself physicalizing or consolidating, was not doing so as rapidly as was the Second Root-Race itself.

In all this description, it should be remembered that this whole process of condensation is not that of an astral 'meeting' a physical, and joining with it, but of astral beings physicalizing themselves, or materializing themselves, from astral into physical or material beings.

At about the beginning of the Third Root-Race, and continuing on to the middle of this Race, this process of consolidation or physicalization meant that the bodies of the latest Second and early Third were changing over from astral into physical substance; and as those early Third Root-Race beings were becoming distinctly

---

147. The MAN here referred to must not be misunderstood to mean the highly evolved human being that he is now, for the man of the present time is the last word in evolution that the developmental processes of unfolding have as yet brought forth — the highest type attained up to the present. The MAN referred to in the text signifies the great Family or Hierarchy of evolving Monads which through those long past periods were individually and collectively passing through all the intermediate stages between their first appearance in the Solar System and Man as he is today. The Man of that far past time is called 'Man' only by courtesy, for the innate, latent, locked up powers, capacities, potencies, functions, and organs which make man man as he is today, were as yet not unfolded, as yet not unwrapped, and therefore man was merely the 'presentment' of what he was to become, and now actually has become.

physical — indeed now heavily gelatinous — the bones were making their distinct appearance, although as yet soft. Organs and their respective functional activity were now beginning to appear. The filamentoid structure of the Second Root-Race had thus given place to tendon and muscle and organ and flesh, although still quite gelatinous or cartilaginous. From the middle to the end of the Third Root-Race, this process of condensation of the astral into the physical, or the changing over of astral into the physical substance, proceeded apace, so that at the end of the Third Root-Race, when the androgynes of the middle Third had already become the sexed beings of the latest Third, this latest part of the Third Root-Race was a fully developed and physicalized humanity as we now understand it, with bodies of fairly solid flesh, with organs relatively fully developed, with skin and hair and bones and all the other zoological characters that we now possess; and this process of physicalization or condensation thereafter continued without interruption to the middle of the Fourth Root-Race, when the reverse process, or etherealization, entered into activity; and although very slight in its beginning, this etherealization of the Earth and all on it has continued ever since and uninterruptedly, although slowly, up to the present time, and will proceed henceforth to the end of the Chain-Manvantara — to the end of the Seventh Round.

Another point of noteworthy importance is the fact that the First Root-Race were titanic in size when compared with the stature of our present humanity. They had form, indeed, but no *physical* appearance, as we now understand the term, as already stated. The Second Race were still titanic in size, but smaller than the First. The Third Root-Race comprised beings who were still huge in size as compared with our own pygmy-humanity of today; and finally, the grossest and coarsest Race of all, the Fourth Root-Race, even more physicalized and dense than we are, were, at least up to the middle-point of their growth, relatively huge creatures, thirty to twenty to ten or twelve feet in stature, thus showing the progressive decrease in physical size down to our own Fifth Root-Race humanity with its five or six feet average in size.

Thus we see that, following this thumb-nail sketch of these earlier Races of evolving 'mankind,' we notice not only a progressive increase in materiality or condensation or thickening or consolidating of bodies, but a coincident and regular and progressive decrease in size from the First to the present Fifth Root-Race. Thus as the Races consolidated and grew more material, their physical stature coincidently steadily decreased. It should be noted, however,

that although from the beginning of the point of etherealization at
the middle of the Fourth Root-Race the remainder of the Fourth,
and the Fifth up to the present, have been slowly becoming less
grossly material or dense in physical substance or structure, nevertheless the decrease in size has continued during the Fifth Root-
Race up to the present day — an interesting detail which is worth
noting. This does not necessarily imply that the succeeding Sixth
and Seventh Root-Races will continue to grow smaller until the end
of the Globe-Manvantara closes with a pygmy or Seventh Root-
Race. At any rate, the important thing to note in this connexion is
that spiritual and intellectual and psychic faculty and capacity do
not of necessity depend upon bulk or magnitude, for bulk in point
of fact has little bearing on the matter.

The difficulty of the foregoing picture lies perhaps in the visioning to oneself of the gradual solidifying of an originally ethereal
series of Races through the ages into a physical series; but this
difficulty, once the general idea is grasped, should vanish. Of course
it is difficult, on the other hand, adequately to picture to ourselves
all the details of the physical structure and functions and organs
of these early Races, because there is little if anything on Earth
today to give us exact ideas of what their details of structure and
function were. But reasoning by analogy and keeping in mind the
gradual physicalization of the astral — i. e., the consolidation or
solidifying of the astral into the physical — some fairly clear notion ought to be grasped by any thoughtful student.

As a matter of fact, the same process, but in the small and
greatly foreshortened, so to speak, does take place even today in the
growth of the human embryo. The embryo begins its existence as a
microscopic speck of human protoplasm, a life-germ thinly gelatinous, which gradually hardens as it grows until it becomes a fleshy
embryo, which in turn hardens still more, and finally is born as a
human babe. The hints that embryology gives to the thoughtful
student are illuminating. For instance, back of and behind and
within this consolidation of the astral into the physical, there is the
constant evolutionary urge towards growth and developmental unfolding of the growing human embryo, continuing later in the growing child, urging and guiding it in its evolution to full manhood.
Here, then, is the picture in the small of the general process that
takes place.

The student should see here, therefore, and taking into consideration the various points of teaching that have been briefly elaborated
in this chapter, how it is that the earliest Root-Races could have

left no geological record in the rocks. They could not do so, because they were too ethereal to make an impression on the then comparatively more condensed Earth when their bodies died and were cast off. It should also be remembered that the First Root-Race strictly speaking did not 'die' at all, but each 'generation' melted into its own progeny in the very beginning; and even in the later parts of the First Root-Race when fission took place, the parent became as it were a sister to its daughter, thus, as said above, 'melting into' the next generation.

Towards the end of the First Root-Race and during the beginning of the Second Root-Race, when fission gave place to budding, the process was pretty much the same because 'death' had not yet come upon the scene, the older generation in almost all cases simply disappearing into its daughter buds, leaving no physical trace or remnant or what is now called 'fossil' behind. Towards the end of the Second Root-Race, however, the bodies had become sufficiently condensed or solidified or concreted or 'individualized' actually to die, so to speak, when their store of vital activity had been exhausted; and in this case, had circumstances been favorable, the relatively solidified bodies of the last Second and early Third could indeed have left impressions or 'fossils.'

The bodies of the late Third Root-Race easily could have made a physical impression or left fossilized remnants behind, and there is a possibility that some such fossil remains may ultimately be discovered or uncovered; but this is a bare possibility, and one might almost say that it is extremely unlikely, having in view the tremendous volcanic and seismic and cataclysmic geologic events that have occurred secularly and at periodic intervals geologically speaking since the days of the middle and later Third Root-Race. Continents since then have sunken beneath the oceans, and new lands have arisen from beneath the waves in many parts of the globe, and the constant grinding of rocks through volcanic and seismic activities would have tended almost infallibly to break up and ruin any such geologic records of the fossil-remnants that ages ago doubtless existed.

All the astral processes that took place in these early ethereal astral Races, were perfectly harmonious with life on the physical plane as it then was, just as much so as is the life of the gelatinous jelly-fish today; and the reader should note with attention that there is nothing at all that is miraculous or marvelous or contrary to Nature about it. Simply figurate first, the incorporeal Races becoming ethereal, i. e., astral, and then, second, slowly becoming condensed and physicalized into relative solidity through the geologic Ages that have elapsed since this globe became the scene for activities of the Life-Waves of this Fourth Round.

VIII

The student should bear in mind also the esoteric teaching concerning the life-waves following each other around the planetary chain from globe to globe and through them all in serial order omitting no single globe; and the manner in which each Kingdom or life-wave follows the one preceding it. It is in this manner that he can get some idea of the way in which a globe awakens from its obscuration or dormancy, to become anew the scene of the evolutionary cyclical courses of incoming life-waves, each such life-wave comprising its own several or characteristic types or stocks of Races, minor races, and family-groups.

The different life-waves which thus succeeded each other in the past history of our globe and which will in precisely identic manner succeed each other in the future history of our globe, and indeed of all the globes of the planetary chain, are composed of or formed of groups or classes of spiritual, intellectual, psycho-mental, and astral Monads, each such group or class of Monads comprising individuals more or less holding the same degree or stage of developmental evolutionary unfolding. These Monads, speaking generally and collectively, are called by various names in the Esoteric Tradition — in the Esoteric Philosophy. The highest classes of them we may group under the generalizing term of Dhyâni-Chohans, spiritual beings of the most advanced or progressed evolutionary type that belong to our planetary chain; the second general class we may group together under the name of Mânasaputras, whose predominant characteristic or attribute is intellectual; the third group or class, inferior to the latter just mentioned, and comprising beings of what we may truly term a psycho-mental type or character are commonly called, for descriptive purposes, Pitris, a Sanskrit term meaning Fathers — just as the superior preceding class, the Mânasaputras, likewise a Sanskrit term, are grouped under this name which means Sons of Mind; the lowest general class or group we may briefly describe as psycho-vital-astral Monads, likewise technically called Pitris, and forming the lowest or last evolved of all the four general classes just mentioned.

The above paragraph outlines the four main Groups into which the Monads naturally fall. Nevertheless, and speaking in a more accurately distributive manner, there are ten or seven Groups or Classes or Types into which the evolving Monads find themselves as evolving or unfolding beings, pursuing each one its evolutionary journey, and distinct from the others, yet all intimately and very closely interlocked and interlinked and in a sense interblended.

It is these seven (or ten) Classes thus grouped, according to the innate capacities of the individuals composing each group, which form the entirety of the hosts of Monads thus evolving in seven (or ten) hierarchies through the visible and invisible worlds or spheres to which allusion has been made in a former part of this work, these invisible and visible worlds or spheres in the case of our planetary chain being the seven manifest and the five unmanifest globes of this planetary chain.

Speaking in a more technical theosophical manner, there were, as already stated, seven (or really ten) classes of Monads or Pitris — using the word *pitris* here as a generally descriptive term — four of these seven classes being relatively gross or inferior to the higher three.[148] These four lower classes are the ones which builded the physical and the vital-astral bodies or sheaths which became in far later ages the evolving physical mankind; the three higher classes of these manifest seven supplied man's highest and intermediate principles. These higher and these lower classes worked together through the ages, and in due course of cycling time, and strictly following lines of karman, builded or produced the First, Second, Third, and Fourth Root-Races, as each played out its drama on the stage of time; and these likewise are the same monadic individuals which compose our own Fifth Root-Race, and will compose the Sixth and the Seventh Root-Races to follow us.

The Chhâyâs or 'Shadows' — that is to say the astral bodies of the lower Pitris (who are the four lower classes just above referred to) — were projected into the physical: which simply means that they consolidated or solidified or condensed into the physical. Thus the astral-ethereal bodies of these, the lower Pitris, finally *grew into* the physical bodies, or, more accurately, finally *became* the physical bodies, by condensation, of the late Second and early Third Root-Races.

---

148. These four Classes mentioned in the present paragraph should not be confused with the four general groups or classes of Monads spoken of in the preceding paragraph. In that preceding paragraph the thought concerned the four great types of the Monads; in the present paragraph the reference is restricted to the four lowest classes of the seven manifest groups.

For the reader interested in the processes of evolution as taught in the esoteric records of the archaic ages, no study could be more profitable than that of H. P. Blavatsky's great work, *The Secret Doctrine* — the first volume if his interest is captivated by more cosmogonic matters, and the second volume thereof if his interest runs rather to matters of the evolution of the human and animal races or stocks.

While it is perfectly true that the Great Theosophist left unsaid vast portions of the teaching of the Esoteric Philosophy in this matter, nevertheless she gave innumerable hints of, and made as many illuminating allusions to, those portions of the teaching of the Esoteric Tradition which she and her Teachers thought improper to give out more fully at that time to a highly materialistic and skeptical generation. There are few studies more illuminating that the student, Theosophical or other, can undertake, and few more instructive, than a rigorously logical and continued investigation of the roots of the evolutionary teaching as given in H. P. Blavatsky's master-work, wherein are unworked mines of esoteric doctrine.

CHAPTER XI

THE TURNING OF THE WHEEL — THE PAST

OUR civilization is at present a civilization in transition. Things are changing, and changing so rapidly that what one evening considers to be settled, the following morning finds undone. People today are beginning to ask themselves questions which it never occurred to them to ask a generation agone; and these questions are of many kinds, but especially those pertaining to religious, philosophical, and scientific matters. The more philosophical minds among men are beginning seriously to question: What is civilization, after all? Is it a steady advance in merely mechanical knowledge? Is the civilized polity of the world the result merely of a period of discovery of natural physical facts, made utilizable for man's benefit or for his destruction, and indeed, mostly for his destruction? Or is civilization the manifestation of the powers of the spirit and of the soul of men? By all past standards and by the defects that observing minds are but too conscious of today, the answer would seem to be: the latter, surely; for a civilization without spiritual and morally intellectual bases becomes but a fabric of barely legal conventions, based upon self-interest and mutual fear.

Civilization is not a mere knowledge of, nor a cultus of, mechanical laws, and their useful derivatives; civilization is fundamentally the work of men's hearts; it is also the work of men's intellects; it comprises the work of men's aspirations. No civilization can rest permanently upon soulless machines, although these latter have their proper place. Indeed, machines themselves would never be produced unless there were a more or less stabilized civilization based on ethical law, in which machines as such could be made useful appurtenances of man's profit and comfort. No sane man condemns machines as such; but when the prince is in the palace, and employs the machines around him for the uses to which they are proper, which of the twain is the more important, the man or the machine?

Disraeli, the English statesman and Jewish philosopher, himself a 'Victorian,' as the English say, of the Victorian age of which he writes in clever and graphic phraseology, said many years ago:

The Victorians talk of progress because by the aid of a few mechanical inventions they have succeeded in establishing a society which mistakes comfort for civilization.

"A civilization," says Oswald Spengler, "is the transitory flowering of spiritual forces." So say we. Transitory, because by the laws of cycles, or repetitive action inherent in Nature, things come, have their day, decay and die, in order to come again in the course of cycling ages. The seasons come and go; the stars and planets follow their cyclical ways; night follows day; decay follows growth; and so forth. For millions of years civilizations have existed in the past; they were the result of the continuously repetitive action of natural forces, a fact upon which Nietzsche based most of his philosophical work, and which one may truly believe to be the best part of all his otherwise more or less erratic writings, to wit: that Nature moves in cycles and thus repeats herself, and that things, civilizations included of course, go and come again and again: have their life and pass, and return. All Nature follows the same general course of cyclical or repetitive action; and similarly so do men, for they are born and die and come again.

It is the teaching of the Esoteric Tradition that on other planets, even of our own solar system, there are great and sometimes grand civilizations — as they would appear to us men — wrought and builded up by the inhabitants of these planets, some of which are far higher than our own, and which are such as our planet will be more or less like aeons upon aeons hence, when we shall have evolved to the greater spiritual and intellectual stature that we shall attain in ages to come; and there are other planets far inferior in quality and evolutionary unfoldment to that which our own globe Earth has thus far attained.

Spengler further remarks:

Cinema, Expressionism, Theosophy, boxing-contests, nigger dances, poker, and racing — one can find it all in Rome. Indeed, the connoisseur might extend his researches to the Indian, Chinese, and Arabian world-cities as well.[149]

True; one can find most of these things, perhaps all of them, issuing forth, flowing forth, from human hearts and minds in any period of brilliant civilization, largely because the same egos — or aggregated groups of them, reimbody themselves more or less contemporaneously, and thus make a civilization anew which is very largely akin to the civilization which they made in past ages.

149. *The Decline of the West*, Vol. II, p. 103.

That Spengler thus quaintly classifies Theosophy among such things as the cinema, expressionism, nigger-dances, and what not, only shows that this brilliant German writer knows nothing whatever of genuine Theosophy, and doubtless imagines that it is some new-fangled modern religious cult, although no objection can be taken to its mere insertion in a list or category, except on the ground of incompleteness, because to be complete one would have to include in such an hypothetical list Christianity and all its works, modern civilization and all of its strivings, and everything else — Spengler included.

Well might we say that the past also knew of such men as Oswald Spengler. He also has lived in the past, and others like him, such as the historians and satirists and skeptics and materialists of the different ages, like Juvenal in Rome, and Pyrrho in Greece, and Chârvâka in ancient India, and many others.

I

It is the course of everything, human nature included, after birth, or first appearance, to grow and to attain maturity and to wax strong: then decline sets in, old age follows, then the degeneration of senescence and decay, and finally death ensues. This cycle of change and repetitive phase occurs with and in civilizations as noticeably as it does with man's physical body. Yet while the sun is setting on one part of the earth, it is rising elsewhere. In times of decay, of spiritual loss to the organism, men hunt for truth perhaps more fervidly than in the hot morning of aggressive youth; but they know not, as a rule, whither to turn in order to find it; nor do they know how to take and use the gems of wisdom from the treasuries that their forefathers have bequeathed to them. They have, in such periods, lost the path, as it were; and the consequence is that they search everywhere, in good ways and in evil. Such was the situation during the decline and fall of the Roman Empire, to point to a well-known historical episode by way of illustration; and such to a certain extent is likewise the case with our own civilization today.

The Roman historians of the centuries following the accepted date of the opening of the Christian Era tell us, as for instance Ammianus Marcellinus in the fifth century, that religion and philosophy were so degenerate then, and scientific inquiry and discovery had so nearly ceased — and Ammianus was a thoughtful and learned inquirer — that the ordinary run of men of that degenerate period sought for truth and guidance in life by running to consult fortune-

tellers often of dubious reputation, and real or pretended astrologers
— astrologers in this period of Roman civilization being the so-called
'Chaldaeans' and 'Babylonians.' These inquirers were hunting for
truth and for guidance in life, and for other things much less com-
mendable than this noble objective; and knowing not whither to
turn for certain help, they did as experience and history show people
will always do when they are at an utter loss and have come to an
unknown turning in the road: they ran to speculation and games
of chance — to the many forms of divination, for instance. The
old and in many ways highly ethical and majestic state-religion of
their forefathers was nearly extinct, while the new religion of twin-
birth in Alexandria and Judaea was steadily spreading its power
and influence over the Roman Empire. It was to be many long
centuries yet before the then future rays of the rising-sun of knowledge were to shine anew over those highly civilized lands bordering
the European Inland Sea; in fact, European history shows us that
those rays began to illuminate European intellects only about the
fourteenth century, some little time before Christopher Columbus,
according to the accepted tale, rediscovered the New World lying
to the setting sun, far across the Atlantic Ocean in the West.

But what does Ammianus Marcellinus, for instance, tell us of
the methods pursued by the people of his own time in their search
for spiritual and mental anchorage and guidance? They hunted
for truths and direction in goblets filled with water: they divined by
means of a ring attached to a string, and held over the top of a goblet,
and if, due to a quivering or shaking of the holding hand, the ring
touched the rim of the vessel, thus making a sound, they drew
weighty conclusions from certain rules of alleged interpretation. The
choice of a husband or of a wife was often thus determined; or in-
vestments were made or not made thereby; or this or that or some
other course in life was followed or abandoned. Palmistry was
another eminently popular method of divining truth and the future;
or astrologers were consulted.

It will be remembered that the Roman State, and in later times
the Roman Emperors, frequently passed laws or issued imperial
rescripts directed against the practice of the then prevailing method
of astrological divination, the practitioners of it being at repeated
intervals expelled from Roman territory, and the degenerate art
itself forbidden under the sanctions of law, and the law-breakers
made subject to serious penalties. All this official supervision and
interference took place, not because the great majority of even highly educated men thus doubted the reality of a genuine Science of

Astrology, a fact which the Esoteric Tradition also avers; but because great Seers or Sages no longer moved publicly among the people and taught it publicly, and the true Science had degenerated into a merely pseudo-art practised as a means of gaining influence and position, or as an easy method of obtaining a livelihood. It is indeed small wonder that the Roman State took stringent measures of precaution and often of repression, because frequently unhappy and sometimes fatal consequences ensued, and the running after the will-o'-the-wisps of fortune was seen to be to the detriment of public morals and individual welfare and happiness. People lost their fortunes from following astrological advices; some committed suicide, or even murder, or other crimes; others went mad; some joined political secret societies banded together against the general policy of the Empire or against powerful political influences — and the Romans, while exceedingly tolerant in all matters of religion as such, or social affairs as such, were always very jealous of secret political organizations, against which they invariably proceeded with relentless energy and with all the instruments of repression that the Roman laws put into their hands.[150]

Much as it was in Ammianus' day, so is it with us today—though

---

150. There were many forms of running after what would today be called psychic adventures during the time of the dissolution of the Roman Empire, and one of the most commonly practised and severely punished by the State, when it was discovered, because of its highly detrimental effect on the ethical and spiritual fiber of men, was what was called necromancy or traffic or communion with the shades of the dead. This took a number of forms, some too disgusting and revolting even to mention here, and others not revolting indeed but singularly familiar to modern ears.

The poets and historians of Greece and Rome in many instances refer to these various practices, and did so from remote ages, even including the great Homer, who in his *Odyssey,* Bk. XI, vv. 30-224, describes the evocation by Odysseus of various persons from the infernal regions and his communing with these ghosts, these astral simulacra and reliquiae of dead men, remaining in the lowest regions of the Astral Light.

Ovid, Vergil, Lucan, and many more touch upon these unpleasant themes. Lucan, in his *Pharsalia,* Bk. VI, gives a graphic description of the then common beliefs of the Graeco-Roman world in the power of the Thessalian witches of 'bringing down the moon from heaven to earth' by means of unholy incantations, and their necromantic intercourse and practices with the shades of the dead, and describes how Sextus, the son of Pompey, driven by fear, goes to the Witch Erictha in order to learn the outcome of the war then waging.

There are a number of passages which would well repay careful study, and

very probably in no such advanced degree. The old religion, popular and all powerful in European countries for some fifteen hundred years past, and similarly in countries settled by European colonists, is now going by the board, at least so far as its dominant and in some cases powerful steadying influence is concerned; and multitudes of good and earnest men and women in the Christian churches are attempting to rescue what remains that is of permanent good and of intrinsic value. People are hunting today, even as they did in the time of the decline and fall of the Roman Empire, for spiritual guidance, for intellectual truth, and for mental and spiritual peace; and also today one notices everywhere, just as in the days of the degenerate Roman Imperium, advertisements of fortune-tellers and of diviners and of astrologers so called, and what not.

Methods of divination have always had an appeal for the mass of people in times of trouble and when nobler resources failed them. Such huntings for a resolving of doubts or difficulties have always existed in all times and in all places; and exist today among us, too. Perhaps the Hebraeo-Christian Bible is consulted at such times, or it may be divination by means of opening a book of poems, or possibly of prose, or even a newspaper, or by what is modernly called the methods of 'numerology.' The book or paper is taken, the eyes are shut for a moment, the finger placed at seeming random on some part of the consulted print or writing; and the word or words

---

the following two extracts from Lucan, *Pharsalia,* Bk. VI, are examples in point:

"Coetus audire silentum,
Nosse domos Stygias, arcanaque Ditis operti,
Non superi, non vita vetat. . . ." — vv. 513-5
"Haec ubi fata, caput spumantiaque ora levavit:
Adspicit adstantem projecti corporis umbram,
Exanimes artus invisaque claustra timentem
Carceris antiqui. Pavet ire in pectus apertum
    .   .   .   .   .   . " — vv. 719-722, etc.

The common idea among the Mediterranean peoples, mentioned above, that the Thessalian witches could 'bring down the moon,' has always seemed utter nonsense to European classical scholars, simply because they have never understood what the phrase meant. However, anyone who has passed through the Third Degree of the initiatory rites will grasp the idea instantly, as indeed can anyone, but in less degree, who has received some intuitive knowledge of esoteric symbolologic method of speech, and who knows something at least of the rôle that the moon plays in the economy of Nature, and of how her emanations and influences and her functions can be to some extent modified by the masterful will of even a human magician — of the 'left-hand,' of course.

or general sense of the sentence touched are supposed to be a guide — if only it could be interpreted correctly! All these ways are truly specific types of divination, so called, which had and still has almost innumerable forms.

In ancient times, however, when the Spiritual Wisdom of the ages, the Esoteric Tradition, still exerted enormous influence over the minds and hearts of men, because it was more or less commonly known in its more easily understood truths, there were true methods of arriving at some knowledge of the future at least, but always such methods took a legitimate and proper form, and were recognised and approved of by the State, and were placed under the control of the wisest and noblest men of the Commonwealth. We may instance the Greek Oracles in their prime. It has been the fashion in Europe since the final downfall of Greek civilization — and in our own days also it is still the fashion of our literati — to ridicule these Oracles of the ancients and their pronouncements, such as those of Apollo at Delphi, or those of Trophonius, also in Greece, mentioning here only two of the several that existed and were for ages so highly revered by all.

The cause of this ridicule is a non-understanding of the nature and meaning of the ancient Oracles, and an entire misapprehension of their reaches and functions, or in many cases it arises in religious antagonism due to ignorance and prejudice. But let us ask ourselves a simple question: Is it conceivable that one of the most intellectual and naturally skeptical and mocking peoples who have ever lived on earth in historic times should send solemn embassies of State to consult these Oracles, notably the Oracle of golden Apollo at Delphi, unless through the centuries the minds and hearts of those keenly alert and intellectual Greeks — who have given us so much that is still basic in our own civilization today — had been trained by experience and swayed by conviction to believe that what the Oracles had told them at intervals through the ages, in times of stress and solemn supplication to the gods, was based on truth, and that they did wisely in doing their best to understand and follow the oracular responses when received?

These Oracles invariably gave their answers in symbolic language and in indirect form. This very indirection, this symbolologic method, has been the butt for the repeated satire and ridicule of modern or near-modern European scholars and students, simply because these men have not understood the principles involved nor the reasons why the responses took such form. It is human nature to make fun of what it does not understand! The famous answer given by the Oracle of Apollo to an embassy sent by Croesus, King of Lydia, will illustrate the point. Everyone knows the story: King Croesus of Lydia was at the time greatly disturbed by the movements, political and military, of the Persians, whose empire was widely contiguous with his own realm. Persia was then a mighty realm to the east of Lydia, and the Persians themselves were an aggressive people, highly intelligent, highly civilized, and ambitious, as such people always are in their prime. The question put to the Oracle in substance was this: "Shall King Croesus, in order to protect his own empire and people against the possible danger of a Persian invasion, make war upon the king and kingdom of the Persians?" In substance the answer came: "If King Croesus wars on the Persians, King Croesus will destroy a mighty empire."

It should be noticed here that if the answer had been a simple affirmative or negative, there would have been involved into the situation a direct and positive interference by divine power — according to Greek ideas — in human affairs; for the fundamental religious and philosophical principle of all ancient conduct was that man must work out his own destiny for his own weal or woe, and by the gifts of spirit and mind and heart and body which he has. The gods never interfere in the exercise of man's free will except as adjuvants or helpers to better things for the common good, when man himself has first acted in that direction. Hercules would not help the wagoner to pull his cart out of the ditch into which the wagoner's carelessness had let it roll, until the man himself first put his own shoulder to the wheel and shoved with all his own strength. Thus was it left to the mind and heart of King Croesus himself to decide what course he ought to follow, a course of self-seeking in imperial aggrandizement, or one for the common good of all concerned; depending in the first instance solely upon his own sense and intuition of what was right to do and wrong to follow. This is simply the foundation of all morals. But the Oracle nevertheless gave an answer and in answering spoke the truth, thus including a solemn warning combined with a reaffirming of the moral law in its response to the Lydian embassy. King Croesus decided to make war on the Persians and their King Cyrus; and King Croesus lost his own kingdom: he destroyed in very truth a mighty empire!

No one among the ancient Greek philosophers or wise men, and no Theosophist today, learning wisdom and the truths of Nature under Theosophy the Interpreter, supposed or supposes that Apollo, God of the Sun, sat or stood somewhere invisible in personal form and dictated his answer in unclear words to the Priestess, the Pythoness, who sat waiting the inspiration on a tripod, and who, receiving them, conveyed the words thus received to the stately embassy of Croesus, King of Lydia. No, the idea was this: Even as there always have been great Seers, so also can any normal human being, by purity of life, by aspiration, and by study, so clarify and purify the inner man, that the Solar Ray — to follow the Greek idea, that part of us which they said is a part of the spiritual Sun — may convey truth to the receptive mind of the Seer. In olden days, the Priestess of Apollo was always a young virgin, but in later times, during a certain war, a terrible thing happened at Delphi in the Temple of the Oracle there, and ever afterwards the Oracle was represented by an elderly woman of spotless life.

As long as the Oracles in Greece functioned, they never failed the inquirers who questioned them, whether these were States or individuals; and the Greeks thus had a sure source of spiritual help, and a steady and never-failing intellectual support, as long as they themselves sought the proper way and thus were, in the main, expectant of obtaining an answer that was not a response to aggressive human selfishness. The interpretations of the answers received, through the ages, were frequently entrusted to the noblest and wisest in the State, if the matter were of public import.

The habit of referring to the Hebraeo-Christian Bible as a means of divination is not today as popular nor as widespread as once it was; but there are still people who look upon this collection of scriptural writings in somewhat the same light as their forefathers did, and consult it in somewhat the same manner that the ancient Romans followed when using for the same purpose the Sibylline Books. In an article called 'The Bible Today: A Modern View of Inspiration' by Frederick Keller Stamm, he says:

> There has been a radical departure from the idea that the Bible contains mysteries beyond our reason, revealed and guaranteed to us as true, either by marvelous signs such as miracles, or by the infallible pronouncement of the official church. The authority of the Bible is based on the revelation of self-evidencing truth. We have been released from the view which expresses itself in the dictum, "If anything is in the Bible, it must not be questioned, it must simply be accepted and obeyed," and a truer approach to authority has been opened to us by saying, "If it is in the Bible, it has been tried and found valuable by a great many people. Question it as searchingly as you can, try it for yourself, and see whether it proves itself true."

The reason for calling attention to this ultra-modern view of the Hebraeo-Christian Bible, and Bible-consultation for purposes of divination, is that here in this extract we see clearly a very modern

re-echoing — although in the form of disapproval — of the old idea
that truth is found in a book, which, though it be no longer considered to be infallible, is yet one of the best books, perhaps the very
best, to consult when in trouble or sorrow, or, mayhap, when searching for the best path to follow in the midst of life's problems. This
itself is a form of minor divination, speaking generally. One is no
longer expected, however, to look within the Bible for the truths of
Nature; one is to search within it for help and consolation; and if
one can get anything good out of it, it is excellent! Well, nobody
probably will object to this sort of mild divining-process, for it is
quite harmless, and if such vague search is all that the truth-seeker
is after, it may lead him on to consult others of the magnificent
literatures of the world — those of the other great world-religions
and world-philosophies; and there, in very fact, the searcher will
find noblest treasure-houses of spiritual and intellectual thinking,
valuable beyond anything else in the world. But, after all, is there
nothing but problematical help of a meager and tenuous kind to be
gotten out of the Hebraeo-Christian holy book?

II

It was with the closing of the Mystery-Schools that spiritual
night descended over the Occident.[151] Their degeneracy had been
steadily increasing for several centuries before this event, and their
formal abandonment was really contemporaneous with what one
may describe as the definite downfall of the old Roman Empire.
Men in the countries surrounding the Mediterranean had become involved more and more in selfishness and the affairs of the material
world, and this had brought about the loss of the inner union or
contact with the spiritual consciousness, which the Mysteries themselves had been originally established to support and bulwark.

The epochs and episodes of European history, especially in the
lands surrounding the Inland Sea, that ensued after the downfall

---

151. This closing of the Mystery-Schools and the consequent abandonment
of their rites and the formal initiations that in a very late and degenerate age
still took place in them, occurred in the sixth century by reason of a Decree or
Rescript of the Emperor Justinian, and there would seem to be little doubt,
at least to the mind of the impartial student of esoteric history, that Justinian's
action was consequent upon a petition presented by the then thin and feeble
band of Pagan philosophers who felt that the Mysteries had become so degenerate, or were about so to become, that it was better to bring about their
cessation by their own act than to allow them to continue to become worse.

of the Roman Empire of the 'Pagans,' and the religious ideas which then began to appear and spread apace with the coming on of the Dark Ages — in fact, leading to those Dark Ages and very largely responsible for them — is a subject of general knowledge. Nevertheless, even in an era of crumbling spiritual and intellectual ideals, and the consequent bewilderment which men of all classes then feel, as was the case after the actual breaking up of the Roman government and general polity, it would be both historically inaccurate and trifling to suppose that the eternally inquisitive and searching mind of man brings forth no new ideas and finds no 'new' bases of thought thus providing at least some kind of intellectual anchorage. As a matter of fact, and as has been hinted at in the previous pages of this chapter, such periods of transition are always marked by unusual and often vigorous forms of mental activity, precisely as we see it today all over the world in our own era of transition, involving as it does the dissolution of former principles of thought and conduct and the novelties both spiritual and intellectual which are perceptible today at every turn.

In addition to the new religious ideas which were then daily gaining wider vogue in both the Eastern and Western parts of the Graeco-Roman world, there was what must have been to thinking men of the time an almost embarrassing or bewildering influx of 'new' thoughts and 'new Movements,' these novelties being not solely of a religious character but also philosophical, mystical, and what today would be called scientific — although the 'scientific' portion of these innovations was the least noteworthy and least popular.

As said, a certain part of this influx of what were then considered to be novel ideas pertained to what now would be called matters appertinent to scientific investigation and study, such as the astronomical notions derived mostly from Claudius Ptolemy, the Alexandrian astronomer-astrologer and mathematician, who flourished in the second century of the Christian Era, and who wrote what was at the time considered to be a remarkable book, which, by its original Greek title, was called *He Megale Syntaxis,* which may be translated as 'The Great Composition' — meaning, in other words, a Complete Outline of Astronomy, which work the Arabs later took over distorting its title as *Almagest.*

Part of Ptolemy's work — and a far larger part than has been commonly recognised by modern scholars — was based on astronomical and astrological ideas taken over from the Mesopotamian regions, Babylonia and Assyria, in addition to scientific improvements and elaborations that Ptolemy himself introduced on the basis of astronomical and astrological science as it was commonly known and taught in Greece and Rome.

There were really great astronomers in Mesopotamia in earlier days; and it is a point to remember, that back of and within the wording or phrasing and figurative expressions of these old astronomical ideas there lies an esoteric significancy or explanation which is truly wonderful when properly understood.

It may be said that the parts or portions of his book which the great Alexandrian astronomer took over from his predecessors, the Babylonian astronomers, were somewhat as follows hereinunder, although it should be stated that Ptolemy of necessity having in mind the psychological and intellectual characteristics and peculiarities of the Greek and Roman worlds, more nimble and critical and intellectual in temperament than mystical in tendency and mental bias, 'wrote down' and reshaped, and veiled much that it is quite likely that he himself as a truly profound mind clearly understood, but was reluctant to have pass current under his name among peoples untrained in the method of mystical thinking, for ages so popular in the lands of the Euphrates and the Tigris.

These ancient Babylonian astronomer-astrologers taught that the Universe — meaning our own Home-Universe, which is all that is inclosed within the encircling zone or boundaries of the Milky Way or Galaxy — is composed or builded up of interlocking or interacting worlds or spheres of different degrees of ethereality from the spiritual to the material, and that these hierarchies could be envisaged under the figure of a scale or ladder of existence, the true Cosmic Ladder of Lives, this Ladder consisting of ten degrees or steps or 'rungs' ranging from earth, or the grossest matter known, upwards and inwards to the tenth or most ethereal degree or step, which tenth degree, or, more accurately speaking, the all-inclosing Ocean of Space, was called the *Primum Mobile*—'the first movable.'

These ten degrees or steps on the Ladder of Life, of Kosmic Life, and forming by means of the aggregated hierarchies the substance itself of our own Home-Universe surrounding us, these ancient astrological-astronomers set forth or taught somewhat after the following manner: first and lowest, Earth; next, the Sphere of Water; then that of Air; then that of Fire; these being the four common Elements universally recognised in the ancient World as the basis of a complete Hierarchy of ten degrees, the six higher degrees usually being left unnamed, except that the fifth from the bottom was frequently called Aether — otherwise the Quintessence, i. e., the Fifth Essence.

Then, leaving the Sphere of Earth, came the Sphere of the Moon;

then that of Mercury; then that of Venus; then that of the Sun; then the Sphere of Mars; then that of Jupiter; then that of Saturn; then the eighth, or the Sphere of the 'Fixed' Stars; then the ninth they called the Empyrean — the Cosmic Sphere in which move the Wandering Stars or comets, and in which the nebulae are seen; then the tenth and last, the *Primum Mobile,* surrounding as with a crystalline shell the entire universe as just enumerated. The usage of this word 'crystalline' did not mean actually real crystal or glass, as it sometimes has been really stupidly misunderstood; but the reference is to the transparency or translucency of interstellar space: we in our modern days would probably call it the surrounding ether. This Kosmic Hierarchy thus considered to include everything that the spacial reaches imbody: this consistent and coherent and self-contained Universal Whole: the ancient Mesopotamian sages said was itself contained in or included in the limitless and unbounded and surrounding 'Waters of Space' — in other words, Infinitude.

Ptolemy took these ideas over from the Babylonians more or less modified by himself in the manner above stated; and far later the mediaevalists during the European Dark Ages, who drew their astronomy from Ptolemy's great work, taught, as did he, that there were ten interlocking and interpenetrating spheres which in their aggregate compose our Kosmic Universe. It is obvious that they did not fully understand Ptolemy, however; and moreover, that their ideas regarding cosmogony and the cosmogonical structure and its operations, were very largely influenced by the misunderstood meaning of the first chapter of the Hebrew *Genesis* and the notions of the early Church-Fathers. Nevertheless, in this tenfold Universe of their conception, the mediaevalists retained a fundamental and vastly important principle of the archaic astronomical teaching of the formerly universal Wisdom-Religion, whether we call it the Esoteric Philosophy or the Esoteric Tradition or the Wisdom of the Gods or Archaic Theosophy.

It is clear enough that Theosophy or the Esoteric Tradition cannot be held responsible for the distortion of such fragments of its truths as have percolated through the minds of the mediaevalists to modern times in Europe; yet among its most important doctrines, as has been set forth elsewhere in this work, that of interlocking and interblending and interwoven Hierarchies, ranging from the divine to the physical, occupies a highly important position in its teachings concerning cosmogony, and its elaboration of this theme is one which is satisfactory in eminent degree to both intellect and one's sense of analogical reasoning, and is curiously in line, when properly understood, with many ultra-modern scientific ideas.

The adduction of this instance of how a fundamental and far-reaching teaching of the Ancient Wisdom passed through and from its Mesopotamian presentation into the Greek mind of Ptolemy and others, thus profoundly affecting the psychological atmosphere of the Graeco-Roman world, is an illustration of the manner in which truths are transmitted not only from generation to generation but from people to people, often, alas, in such distorted form or formulation that it is oftentimes difficult for students of such latest distortion of the original teaching to find out just what that primal Doctrine was in its purity.

A number of other examples or illustrations might be adduced here were it at all necessary to the main argument of this chapter, or needful in order to trace the turning of the vast wheel of time and destiny; but as every competent scholar, and every well-read student of the religious and philosophical history of the nations which dwelt in the lands surrounding the European Inland Sea, is fairly well acquainted with the manner in which mystical and religious ideas and philosophically mystical thoughts passed from land to land, it would be a waste both of time and of space to enter more largely upon this theme here.

The steady march of not only religious and philosophical ideas but historical events from Orient to Occident is so well recognised that even the Christian has sung: "Westward the course of empire takes its way."[152] There are a large number of works which have been written imbodying the studies and the conclusions of their authors on this steady progress in both time and place of ideas, and these works exist in virtually every cultured and literate European tongue. Christianity itself has been traced by some rather over-enthusiastic scholars and literati of a more or less dilettante character to ideas which were widespread in the Greek world at about the time of the accepted beginning of the Christian Era, some of these literary dilettanti, with more enthusiasm than critical judgment, even tracing the main body of Christian theological doctrine to Egypt, or to Assyria and Babylonia, or again to one or more of the schools of Greek philosophical and mythological thought, forgetting that the material imbodied in Christianity as a whole is a direct offspring, not from any one source of thought percolating from a single point, but from the common and more or less commonly accepted ideas which had

---

152. Bishop George Berkeley: *On the Prospect of Planting Arts and Learning in America.*

wide currency in the Graeco-Roman world for a century or two preceding the opening of the Era called 'Christian.'

It is probably true that only those who have investigated the matter with real literary thoroughness and with the thoughtful care required, can appreciate how greatly the Graeco-Roman world was a true intellectual melting-pot or alembic of many different religions and philosophies at the time when Christianity arose, and that ideas, systems of thought, doctrinal biases or tendencies, and novelties in the way of religion and philosophy, had percolated to and permeated all strata of human society, so much so that the great cities around the Mediterranean like Alexandria, Antioch, Athens, Carthage, Rome, and others, were like great intellectual emporia or markets, wherein ideas jostled each other — ideas often of the most disparate character, so that Indian thought brushed elbow with Druidic, and teachings even of the North Germanic peoples strove for place and power with other equally interesting and profound notions coming out of Syria, Persia, and elsewhere.

The illustration, therefore, which is given above, is merely adduced by way of example; and it has been selected because of its basic and wide-reaching importance in a religious and philosophic sense, for it imbodies not only cosmogonic and theogonic and therefore theologic principles, but bears powerfully upon mystical matters and the loftiest ethical principles.

It is probable that in all history as known to modern scholars and students, no more fascinating picture could be presented than that which the Graeco-Roman world offered at the time in question of the manner in which the turning of the Wheel of Thought and Human Destiny acts in its unceasing revolutions. For ages nations remain relatively separated from each other and to a certain extent apart in thought, receiving but small and apparently unimportant infiltrations from outside; then as the Wheel continues its turning, new life comes in flood, in spate, sweeping down barriers between peoples and nations, mixing and reforming, modeling and remodeling, so that once separate peoples, jealous of national characteristics and power, become melted into larger racial units. There is a really amazing similitude or similarity between our own world in transition today, and the world as it was in transition in the centuries just mentioned.

Yet everything passes. It would seem to the impartial and thoughtful student of human history that things were in the making, when the Roman Empire began, which promised to bring about an expansion of human thought and an enlargement of political frontiers which might have involved all of what is now the nations of Europe, had the onflowing course of time and events and the bright promise which seemed to have dawned at about the time of the foundation of the Roman Empire under Julius Caesar and Octavian not been checked in some as yet but obscurely understood manner; and instead of a continued ascent towards greater things, the course of destiny took a distinctly downward path, culminating in the deep and intellectually obscure valley of the Dark Ages. In these Dark Ages thenceforth there remained but vague memories, forgotten and half-forgotten recollections of the glory that was Greece, and the political splendor that was Rome.

III

The profound religious and philosophical ideas current and almost popular in the Graeco-Roman world when Octavian lived were now nearly passed away; but feeble rivulets of the once mighty river of human thought still flowed on, giving, nevertheless, to the Dark Ages such spiritual and intellectual inspiration and stimulating thought as human minds then could receive and use. Still, all through the Dark Ages, here and there, could still be perceived feeble glimmerings or flickerings of what was once a Great Light; and it was these feeble flickerings or glimmerings which actually became the seeds of the later intellectual awakening in Europe which men call the Renaissance. This awakening was later enormously aided by the rediscovery of some of the grandest works of Greek literature after the conquest of Constantinople by the Ottomans and the consequent dispersal of the contents of libraries over the intellectually darkened West. Thenceforward human thought began to strive anew to burst the bonds of dead-letter and cramping dogma; and bitter indeed the struggle later became.

It is comforting to the earnest student of life and of the intricate pathways of human destiny to know that although the human race, or rather branches of it or portions of it, may at times, in its evolutionary journey, pass downward into the valleys of obscuration both spiritual and intellectual, nevertheless humanity is watched over and guided, yet strictly according to karmic law and justice, by Titan Intellects, Men of advanced evolutionary unfoldment whose Great Work it is to instil into human consciousness from time to time, as the ages flow on, ideas not only of natural verities but of spiritual and ethical worth. Humanity is at no time abandoned of these Elder Brothers of the human race; but even in the darkest epochs of human history individuals are selected or chosen because of innate spiritual and intellectual capacity, and often unknown to themselves are occultly inspired with new and brilliant and stimulating ideas of which such chosen individuals thus become the voices unto their fellow-men.

Likewise, from time to time when the ages become ripe for it, special envoys or Messengers are sent forth from the great Brotherhood of these Seers and Sages who strike anew the old, old strings of human inspiration and thought, and who thus become the visible and publicly active Teachers and Saviors of the human race, appearing as they do among this people or among that.

Often, again, epoch-making ideas or brilliant suggestions are deliberately, and with noble humanitarian purpose, set floating in human minds, these ideas passing oft-times like wild-fire from brain to brain; and thus unusual men, although far inferior in spiritual penetration and in intellectual power to the Teachers above mentioned, are set intellectually aflame by these permeant ideas or thoughts, and become themselves subordinate though often imperfect helpers or inspirers of others.

Newer ideas forming the basis of later and more important discoveries in Europe thus appeared at different times in the Middle Ages. Examples were the theories and studies of Nikolaus Krebs of the fifteenth century, and of Pico Count di Mirandola of the sixteenth century, and especially the cosmogonical and astronomical notions of Kopernik (Koppernigk latinized as Copernicus), the German-Pole. As every school-boy knows, these new ideas and the literary works which they gave birth to aroused a vast deal of antagonism on the part of the authorities, ecclesiastical and civil alike, in European countries. Indeed, the men who thereafter adopted these new ideas, followed later by the unfortunate Galileo and a rapidly increasing host of thinkers, suffered the all too common fate of pioneers in human thought; but as is always the case when truth is with them, their ideas and their work finally prevailed.

Nikolaus or Nikolas Krebs was born at Kues, near Trier, Germany, in 1401 and died in 1464. The son of a poor boatman was this remarkable man, who later was made a Cardinal of the Church of Rome, and called, from the town of his birth, Cardinal de Cusa. His extraordinary genius in investigation, and in what was then broad-minded and courageous exploration of the mysteries of the Nature surrounding him and of the inspirations of his own inner nature, brought upon him charges of heresy including that of pantheism; and it is likely that only the personal friendship of three

Popes, who seemed to stand in reverential awe of the genius of this great man, saved him from the fate which later befell Giordano Bruno, and still later, but in less degree, Galileo.

Cardinal de Cusa has often been called a 'Reformer before the Reformation' — this statement being both graphic and true. He anticipated, in many if not all of its essentials, the later discovery of Copernicus in astronomy, as regards the sphericity of the Earth as a planetary body and its orbital path around the Sun; and he also did no small pioneer work in popularizing such ancient Greek learning and thought as then existed in more or less imperfect Latin translations of older dates. In his book, *De docta ignorantia,* is found the following passage:

The world may not be, possibly, absolutely boundless, yet no one is able to figurate it as finite, because human reason refuses to give it limits. . . . Just as our earth cannot be in the center of the Universe, as is supposed, no more can the sphere of the fixed stars be that center. . . . Therefore the World is like an immense machine, having its center everywhere, and its circumference nowhere. . . .[153] Hence, because the earth is not at the center, it cannot be motionless . . . and although it is much smaller than the sun, it should not be concluded from this that it is more vile. . . . We cannot see whether its inhabitants are superior to those who dwell nearer to the sun, or in the other stars, for sidereal space cannot be destitute of inhabitants. . . . The earth is, most probably, one of the smallest globes, yet it is the cradle of intelligent beings, noble and perfect in a sense.[154]

---

153. The ascription of this graphic figure of speech to the Frenchman Blaise Pascal as its inventor is inaccurate and indeed wrong. It is here seen that two centuries before Pascal, the famous German philosopher and theologian Nikolaus de Cusa wrote, as above quoted, in his most notable work *De docta ignorantia:* "This world resembles a vast mechanism, having its center everywhere and its circumference nowhere" — *machina mundi quasi habens ubique centrum et nullibi circumferentiam.*

In the same work, this great man anticipated the ideas and teaching of Copernicus and Galileo, stating in the clearest words that the Earth is not the center of the universe, and that just because the Earth is not at the center of the World, therefore it is in motion. He also went beyond both Copernicus and Galileo in his declaration that not even the mighty sphere of the 'fixed stars' is in the center of the Universe, for that "center" is "everywhere," as above quoted.

Cusanus was a soul born into earth-life centuries before his 'proper' intellectual period, and he was made to suffer for his attempts to enlighten the then prevailing spiritual and intellectual gloom. Such seems to be the lamentable fate of all who come before their natural time — whether by choice, or otherwise!

154. *De docta ignorantia* ('On Learned Ignorance').

This is a remarkable statement for a Roman Cardinal to have made; and more than one student of this great man's work has wondered if there were not in the inner life of this noteworthy mediaeval thinker an inner guiding Genius or Daimon who led him intellectually on and guided his thoughts in such directions that the inner doors of his own being were thereby opened, so that he could see through them more deeply into Nature's arcana. In a period of European history when the Earth was thought to be flat and immovable and the center and only center of the Universe, and when the Sun and the Moon and stars and other celestial bodies were supposed to revolve around it, he taught the sphericity and rotation of our Earth! He taught that this Earth was not the only globe in sidereal space to give birth to intelligent beings; and other things now accepted as common knowledge found in every elementary school. His knowledge of natural truths most probably first came to him from reading what remained in literature of the works of the ancient Pythagorean and possibly Neo-Platonic thinkers and scientists. One may truly ask oneself, whether this man ever held — albeit privately — the ancient Pythagorean doctrine of the metempsychosis of the soul, and its repetitive reimbodiments both in human flesh and possibly elsewhere.

Two hundred years and more after Nikolaus Krebs, there lived the Frenchman, Blaise Pascal,[155] who wrote:

Let man not stop in contemplation of simply the objects which surround him. Let him contemplate Universal Nature in its high and full majesty. Let him consider that dazzling luminary, situated like an eternal lamp, in order to illuminate the universe. Let the earth seem to him to be a mere point by comparison with the vast circle that this star describes; and let him stand amazed in reflecting that this vast circle itself is but a point, very small with regard to that which the stars that sweep around the firmament embrace. But should our vision stop there, then let our imagination pass beyond it. Imagination, again, sooner grows weary than Nature does in furnishing still larger bounds. All that we see of the world is but an imperceptible spot [point] within the ample bosom of Nature. No idea can approach the sweep of its spaces. We may expand our conceptions to our utmost: and we give birth to atoms in size only. Nature is an infinite sphere, of which the Center is everywhere, the circumference nowhere. . . .[156]

It is thus that another great man in his way attempts to describe — Infinity! Even here, apparently, in this otherwise remarkable picture of a thoughtful mind struggling for freedom, one discerns

---

155. 1623 — 1662.   156. *Pensées,* ch. xxii.

the crippling effect of the then prevalent geocentric theory of Nature; and yet the fine figure of speech with which Pascal closes this passage, probably drawn from Krebs as above stated, is virile with the suggestion that though Pascal may have openly conformed to the geocentric idea, his intuition rejected it as an astronomical truth.[157]

This sublime idea that the Divine — and necessarily therefore what we call Infinite Nature — has its center everywhere and a limiting boundary or circumference nowhere, while likewise a purely Theosophical idea, is also a very ancient one. It was, for instance, taught by the Pythagorean philosophers in ancient Greece. It was and still is taught by all the schools, by all the thinkers — and magnificent thinkers some of them were — of all the schools of the ancient Hindû philosophies and religions. It was in the background of the teaching of all the Sages of all the ages; and, in more modern times, it has reached us also as the splendid speculation of certain great men.

What, indeed, is this Universe in which we live: this Universe of which we for ever are inseparable parts, component portions thereof, and therefore either self-consciously or unconsciously co-operating agents in the Great Kosmic Labor? We cannot ever separate ourselves from the ALL, for we are parts of IT. What are we then in our inmost being? An answer to this question obviously answers the former query. We are essentially Monads: eternal, unitary, individual, life-centers, consciousness-centers: and, because of the very stuff of the Cosmic Stuff, deathless, ageless, unborn, universal in essence. Therefore each one such Monad — and their number is infinite, since the Universe is infinite, since the Kosmos both invisible and visible is without any limits or boundaries whatsoever except as aggregated hierarchies, extending in all directions limitlessly, everywhere, inwards and outwards — therefore, each one such Monad-center or fundamental-spiritual Life-Atom is mystically and factually a center of the Universe, whether such central point be one of us humans or an inhabitant of some far-distant sidereal body, a living entity or 'life' on one of the immensely distant so-called 'island-universes' that our modern scientists describe to us as existing outside the encircling zone of our Milky Way — each one

157. Yet, strange mystery indeed, some of the most enlightened of the ancient Sages taught a doctrine which when properly understood in its secret or esoteric implications, shows that aside from the mâyâ (illusion) of the geocentric, and as taught in the Middle Ages utterly false, idea, there is imbodied in it a verity delivered unto those who were found worthy to receive it.

such Monadic center is the center of the ALL, for the simple reason that, as an old teaching of ours has it, the Divine or the ALL — the invisible or divine-spiritual side of Invisible Nature — is THAT, which has its center everywhere, and its circumference or limiting boundary nowhere.[158]

This sublime conception alone furnishes food for reflexion for a lifetime; because it shows why each one such spiritual center or each one such Monad is in its inmost the central point of the Boundless All, having its center or centers everywhere. Furthermore, such reflexion shows us that there is a Path leading into the inmost of the Boundless All, which — paradox of paradoxes — can never through eternity be reached; and this Path is each one of us: every human being is himself this Path leading inwards for ever to the ever-unattainable 'Heart' of the Boundless Universe. Every center everywhere, every Monad, every living entity in the inmost of its inmost, is that Path himself or itself; and this is precisely what Jesus the Syrian Sage, the Avatâra, speaking of his own inner divine Monad, had in mind when he uttered his 'dark saying,' "I am the Way [Path], the Truth, and the Life!"[159]

No longer did the advancing knowledge concerning astronomical truths permit the teaching that our physical Earth, this small Earth on which we live, is the sole and only center of the Boundless Universe, and that all the planets, the Sun, and the Moon, and the stars also, circle around our Earth in concentric spheres. These newer teachers in the fifteenth and sixteenth centuries of European history harked back to the old doctrine of Pythagoras of Greece and of his school, and often to the Neo-Platonists and their philosophical verities, whence these mediaeval Europeans drew as from a perennial fountain of wisdom and knowledge. The newer science now taught that the Sun is the center of our solar system, and that the planets revolve around this central Sun, and that the Earth is one of these planets so revolving.

These innovators were treated rather badly. When Columbus

---

158. "The Highest of all is ubiquitous yet nowhere in particular. Furthermore, the highest Divine is at once everywhere in its fulness for it is the 'everywhere' itself, and, furthermore, all manner of being. The highest Divine must never be thought as being *in* the everywhere, but itself is the everywhere as well as the origin and source of all other beings and things in their unending residence in the everywhere." — Plotinus: *Enneads*, 'Free Will and Individual Will,' VI, viii, 16

159. *John*, xiv, 6.

appeared before the doctors of the University of Salamanca and argued his case that the world was spherical and that there must exist continents beyond the Western Sea, he was told in substance: "You are wrong. It is impossible; the Bible does not teach it, and the Bible contains the truth of God." The Fathers of the Church knew of this fantastic doctrine of a rotund and spherical Earth, and they deliberately and pointedly rejected it. "Turn to Lactantius, for instance," they said, "and you will see what he has to say of Pythagoras and his teaching of the spherical nature of the Earth."

Lactantius' squabbling irony reads funnily today to us men of a wiser age, a kindlier age, indeed a more thoughtful age. Speaking of Pythagoras, the great Greek philosopher, he calls him "an old fool who taught old wives' fables" such as metempsychosis, and the sphericity of the Earth, and the heliocentric character of our solar system. He delivers himself of the following spiteful invective:

That old fool invented fables for credulous babies, as some old women do who have nothing else to do!

The folly of this foolish old fellow ought to be laughed to scorn!

How can people believe that there are antipodes under our feet? Do they say anything deserving of attention at all? Is there anybody so senseless as to believe that there are men living on the under side of the earth, whose feet thus are higher than their heads? Or that the things which with us grow upright, with them hang head downwards? That the crops and trees grow downwards? That rains, and snows, and hail, fall upwards to the surface of the earth? . . . These people thought that the earth is round like a ball . . . and that it has mountains, extends plains, and contains level seas, under our feet on the opposite side of the earth: and, if so, it follows that all parts of such an earth would be inhabited by men and beasts. Thus the rotundity of the earth leads to the idiotic idea of those antipodes hanging downwards! . . . I am absolutely at a loss to know what to say about such people, who, after having erred in one thing, consistently persevere in their preposterous folly, and defend one vain and false notion by another; but perhaps they do it as a joke, or purposely and knowingly defend lies for the purpose of showing their ingenuity in defending falsehoods. But I should be able to prove by many arguments that it is utterly impossible for the sky to be underneath the earth, were it not that this my book must now come to an end.[160]

Alas! Why did not the self-satisfied and egoistic Lactantius give us of his own arguments? Surely they would be interesting reading today!

The theological doctors of Salamanca further said in substance to Columbus: "You take your life in your hands, and the lives of

---

160. Lactantius: *The Divine Institutes,* Bk. III, ch. xxiv.

your officers and men, if you sail so far out into the unknown sea!"[161]

Had Columbus listened to his opposers and objectors, and had he renounced his project: had he not had the royal favor and aid: how long would it have been before some other hardy spirit would have embarked from a European port, sailing westwards to imperishable fame? It surely would have come to pass; but this in no wise detracts from the merit of the enterprising Genoese. During his transit of two and a half months' duration, he had a near-mutiny among his men; for after sailing so many weeks, and seeing no land, the men, believing in a flat earth, thought that the time was not far distant when they would come to the rim or edge of the earth and there would fall over and off it in a titanic Niagara into empty space, or into the bottomless abyss. Nevertheless Columbus persisted, and sailed his three little vessels westwards over the stormy Atlantic. Today the tomb of Columbus bears the engraven inscription: *Á Castilla y á León nuevo mundo dió Colón:* To Castile and to León, Columbus gave a new world!

The doctors of Salamanca were not alone in their mistaken and fantastic ideas. The entire Christian world held the same notions, with the exceptions of the noble-minded few who were courageous enough openly to state their faith, and perhaps many others who lacked the courage openly to confess their beliefs. What did Martin Luther have to say of his contemporary, Copernicus? He said:

> People listen to an unknown astrologer who tries to show that the earth rotates, and not the heavens nor the firmament nor the sun and the moon. Everyone who hankers after being thought clever forthwith devises some new-fangled system, which of course is considered to be the very best of all systems. This fool desires to overthrow the entire system of astronomy; but Holy Writ tells us that Joshua commanded the sun to stand still, and not the earth.

But Martin Luther was not the only one of his day to turn against the heliocentricism of Copernican astronomy, his co-worker in Germany, Melanchthon, wrote in his turn of Copernicus as follows:

> Our eyes themselves prove to us that the heavens revolve around the earth in the space of twenty-four hours. But certain men, whether from love of novelty, or in order to display their ingenuity, are teaching that it is the earth that moves; and they assert that neither the eighth sphere nor the sun revolves

---

161. It is a well-known fact of history that Columbus nevertheless sailed westwards in his three small vessels, with a body or crew of officers and men numbering a hundred, more or less. He left Palos on August 3, 1492, and in somewhat less than two and a half months of sailing, touched at an American island, on October 12th, Old Style, 1492; or New Style, October 22nd.

around the earth. . . . It is simply a lack of honesty and decency to declare such fantasies in public, and the example is pernicious. It is the part of a sound mind to take the truth as revealed by God and to accept it.

What did Calvin say about Copernicus?

Who is it who dares to place the authority of Copernicus above that of the Holy Ghost?

Even when Galileo, in the first third of the seventeenth century, appeared before his ecclesiastical examiners and set forth his theories of the nature of the Universe which surrounds us, and of how, as he put it, the Earth is not the center of the Universe, and that the Sun and the stars and the moon do not arise in the east in the morning, pass over our heads during the day, and set in the west in the evening, thus partaking of the supposed revolving sphere of the heavens moving around the immovable Earth, his theories — which were those of Copernicus, and others which Galileo had accepted — were condemned as heretical, contrary to 'faith,' and therefore untrue. These judges of Galileo were no doubt earnest men and thoughtful men, after their poor lights, doing what they believed to be the best for the welfare of their fellows; but belief and good intentions are no guarantees that men possess truth: good intentions are not enough, for men must have knowledge, men must know truth.

These cardinals and bishops in solemn conclave assembled declared:

That the earth is not the center of the Universe, and that it moves even with a daily rotation, is indeed an absurd proposition, and is false in philosophy; and theologically considered, at the least is erroneous in Faith.[162]

Karman makes short work of human ignorance, and of human pride, the offspring of ignorance. Galileo was right from the astronomical standpoint, which is the standpoint of visible nature, and he thought with his teachers, the ancient Pythagorean sages, and taught what they taught, as he understood it; for Galileo, despite his in-

---

162. "Terram non esse centrum mundi, nec immobilem, sed moveri motu etiam diurno, est item propositio absurda, et falsa in philosophia, et theologice considerata ad minus erronea in fide." — Congregation of Bishops and Cardinals, June 22, 1633.

The original Italian, in its Roman dialectal form, of the Latin sentence above, is thus given in the Sentence, or 'Sentenza,' as follows:

"Che la terra non sia centro del mondo, nè immobile, ma che si move etiandio di moto diurno, è parimenti proposizione assurda, e falsa in filosofia, e considerata in teologia, ad minus erronea in fide."

quisitive mental apparatus, was no initiate as many of the Pythagorean sages were.[163]

IV

It would, of course, be an exceedingly interesting study, having both its pathos and its diversions, to trace the gradual opening and expansion of European intellect from the downfall of the Graeco-Roman civilization to the Renaissance in Europe, and thus onwards or forwards to the times when European activity took a definitely scientific and in many respects a materialistic turn — let us say the age of Newton and his immediate predecessors. But this work has been admirably well done by many writers holding different views; nor is the present work such as to require the inclusion of this study in its pages. It suffices merely to point to the manner in which the great turning Wheel of human Thought, and therefore of human Destiny, has taken place through the revolving centuries.

It is quite probable that no open or public Theosophical effort, such as was begun by the founding of the Theosophical Society in New York in 1875 by H. P. Blavatsky and others, could have taken place at any period between the time of the closing of the Mystery-Schools under the Emperor Justinian and the beginning of the nineteenth century — an observation which applies to Europe and later to America of course; and it is unquestionably true that the appearance of H. P. Blavatsky with the Message that she brought to the West in the time when she came was well fitted into its proper cycle, and its consequences foreseen.

This does not mean that the Great Brotherhood made no effort to aid and help during the long centuries intervening between the two periods just mentioned, for the exact contrary is the case, as already has been stated. A number of minor movements of a more or less

---

163. As a matter of historical interest, it may be stated that it was only in 1757, on the eleventh of May, that Pope Benedict XIV signified his consent to expunge the clause of the decree of March 5, 1616, which prohibited all books teaching that the sun is stationary and that the earth revolved around it. Again, it was only on September 11, 1822, that the College of Cardinals of the Inquisition agreed to permit the printing and publication of works at Rome teaching the Copernican or modern system of astronomy, and this decree was ratified by Pope Pius VII on September 25 of that year. Yet it was not until 1835 that Galileo's prohibited works were removed formally from the Index.

"Dichiarono permessa in Roma la stampa e la publicazione operum tractantium de mobilitate terrae et immobilitate solis, juxta communem modernorum astronomorum opinionem," — *Olivieri*, p. 97, or *Hist.-polit. Blätter*, p. 588.

veiled mystical and philosophical character usually working under the guise or garment of conventional religion took place and did what work they could do. Individuals also were aided and in many cases inspired in the degree to which such inspiration could be received by their imperfectly developed spiritual and intellectual and psychical faculties, to promulgate a few at least of the ideas of the Archaic Wisdom, in such manner and after such forms, however feeble they may have been, as to meet with some possibility of success in impressing the minds of different ages.

The modern Theosophical Society and its members have been in the past fifty years or more somewhat in the same relation to established authority, religious and scientific, that Copernicus and others and their respective followers held to the generations in which as individuals they lived. Even as those often noble-minded and self-denying men were not infrequently called by discourteous and impolite epithets, such as imbeciles, idiots, dreamers, heretics, and what not, so were modern Theosophists in the beginning of their work called by the same or closely similar names; but that period of sometimes angry and always ignorant denouncement is today virtually ended. Yet even at present, so strongly are the passing ideas, whether of a religious or scientific character, held to, that when our Theosophical doctrines are voiced before audiences unacquainted with their tenor and their import, it is not unknown still to find otherwise perfectly intelligent, kindly, and well-meaning people indulging in critical remarks which are often as diverting as they are shallow. As for instance: "Why, that statement is not right. That is not what the scientists teach. I do not believe that. There is no foundation in Nature for it."

These unthinking ones forget that there is nothing so changeable as science itself — few departments of human thought which are so mutable — and thank the immortal gods that it is so mutable! True Science, as represented by its most noble exponents and students, is always advancing and always learning; and that fact is to its greatest and highest credit, and is the one thing more than any other, perhaps, at least from one standpoint, for which we all should be grateful to these high-minded and often self-sacrificing men who are devoting their lives to searching as far as they can and may into Nature's secret and recondite places for ever more light. Yes, Science is changeable, very changeable; it changes with every lustrum or two, so that what is supposed to be truth — accepted scientific truth — today, in five or ten years from now will be discredited and considered to be — as exactly it is — just one more step forwards on the path of discovery: although while it was considered a truth, it had mathematical demonstration, it had, perchance, a modicum of philosophical demonstration, and all the other methods and ways of scientific thinking and research were collected and brought together in proof of and support of it.

This is just as it should be, but to the reflective mind the situation is one which demonstrates clearly that the changing and therefore passing views of any one scientific generation, to be succeeded by another and others, are no permanent or durable intellectual foundation upon which to base and erect a superstructure of thought to take the place which Religion and Philosophy, derivative from Nature's structure and operations alone, can occupy. This observation is directed specifically to the totally erroneous idea so widely current in modern times that scientific views are the religion and philosophy of the present. Mankind were, indeed, in a perilous situation were the only *true* Religion and *true* Philosophy, which it can know, the scientific ideas and notions and teachings and deductions which inside of a generation may be utterly overthrown for something new, for something novel. Here is the reason why the Theosophist, while holding in his heart and mind immense respect for the work of scientific men, as aiding in the emancipation of the human intellect, nevertheless is obliged to look upon scientific hypotheses and theories as being just what they are — ideas of a generation, to be followed by newer ones. The student of the Esoteric Philosophy, the Esoteric Tradition, is as convinced as he can be of anything human in this world of changing scenes and shifting thought, that sooner or later mankind as a whole will once again become keenly conscious of the fact that there exists in the world a WISDOM which once was the common property of the human race over the earth, and which, as several times before stated in this work, is what the Theosophist calls by various names, such as the Esoteric Tradition or the Esoteric Philosophy or the Wisdom of the Gods, and in modern times by the term Theosophy. It is only this WISDOM, which is KNOWLEDGE of THINGS-IN-THEMSELVES, which can adequately feed the hunger of the human intellect and supply the spiritual and ethical needs of the human heart. How great is the need for this KNOWLEDGE — the knowing of things-in-themselves: i. e., the essence of things, what the German philosopher, Kant, had in mind with reference to the essence of an individual existence as *Das Ding an sich!*

The pathway to Wisdom for any individual human being is *within*. Those human beings who became the great sages, became such because they followed that inner pathway leading ever more inwards, until each individual of them became at-one with his own inner god and therefore *knew* truth, because the inner god of each one of us is an inseparable part of the infinite Universe. They thus learned what the Universe is, how it works, how it functions, yes, even what the real form of the Kosmic Figure is. Guardians of the mystic, archaic Wisdom-Religion as they are and have been through the ages, it was from them that the ancient peoples learned of the truths of Nature: through and from them, and also because of the exercise of the same inner faculties of vision by individuals, and from the keen powers of observation that we know that they possessed, as we ourselves do — once we learn to trust our inner powers and to confide in them as being what they are, the *only* source of knowledge. A robot is an amazingly clever mechanical construction, but it is obvious that a robot is unable to grasp the truths of the Universe and to understand them, because it is not a MAN.

Mighty men indeed were some of these ancients, men whose names today even are revered. Nevertheless in many cases it has been customary in Occidental countries during the small period of time of fifteen hundred years or more last past, to speak of them as being individuals whose scientifically untutored faculties and aspiring but more or less untrained understanding nevertheless brought forth those marvels of religious and philosophical 'ingenuity' which were the great systems of human thought which even today our greatest men study and revere. How normally sensible thinkers of our times have ever been able to voice the imbecile theory of past human ignorance, such as it has until recent times been all too popular to suppose, with the known intuitional power and strength of intellect that the great and greater among the ancients had, is a fact which is a perennial cause of amazement to every thoughtful spirit.

But the explanation is simple enough, and it is this: that during the last fifteen hundred years or so, there was practically no organized scientific research into Nature, and no knowledge of Nature whatsoever, except the small and half-forgotten remnants of knowledge that came over into the Dark Ages from those ancient nations surrounding the Mediterranean Sea. Indeed, intellectual progress and the accumulation of scientific data were virtually unknown, with certain rare exceptions that are the more notable because of their rarity. Slowly growing knowledge of Nature, in other words the advancing science of European civilization, in time broke down the self-sufficient religious and quasi-mystical egoism of our forefathers of the Dark and later Mediaeval periods, and there then succeeded to the self-sufficient egoisms of mediaeval times, the equivalently self-sufficient egoism of the new-born spirit of discovery and research.

It is true that various scientific men made great advances in knowledge of Nature after Galileo's day. From that fateful day for Galileo, June 22, 1633, when the solemn conclave of cardinals and bishops officially condemned his teachings as false, up to the time of Laplace, the great French astronomer, wonderful strides ahead were made in knowledge of the physical universe in which we live. But concurrently there ensued very definitely a progressive losing of the intuitive sense of the existence of inner and ethereal and spiritual worlds, and hence to a certain extent also, a loss of spiritual values, so that there began to grow in the minds of men a narrow materialism which reached its culmination in our own age in the closing years of the nineteenth century, say about 1900.

But this materialism which then waxed so strong and widespread in its influence over men's souls, met and underwent a totally unexpected series of intellectual shocks brought about by newly discovered truths of Nature, which new truths were almost wholly the discoveries of scientific men themselves who had, as it were, almost suddenly begun to obtain new and dazzling insights into hitherto unsuspected verities lying behind and within Nature's physical veil.

However, even as late as thirty years ago, many scientific thinkers and speculators were so desperately afraid of dropping back into the old ruts of mediaeval scholastic thinking, that they deliberately blinded themselves to the necessary deductions and inferences which the succeeding generation of scientific workers, pointing to the facts of Nature, have now made known to all.

In the first days of modern physical discovery practically all the researchers into Nature were more or less under the influence of mediaeval thought, of mediaeval ideas; ideas, that is to say, of so-called 'witchcraft,' and heaven knows what else of that kind of stuff; and of the ideas then held with regard to the atomistic theories of Democritus and Epicurus and of Lucretius: in short of the atomistic school of ancient Greece. This modern atomistic philosophy began definitely to be widely influential in the beginning of the nineteenth century, and it was an intellectually wholesome and salutary thing as far as it went; but unfortunately it went too far in a literal interpretation of the work of the ancient Greek atomists, and thus became in time the crass materialism so popular in the nineteenth century. The student of physics forty or more years ago was then taught that the physical universe is all that there is: that it had no inner spiritual roots, that it hung, as it were, in and from nothingness, or in the so-called hypothetical ether — in other words was rooted in nothing of a spiritual character; and that it was nevertheless a self-contained system; that the amount of energy in that hypothetical universe so set forth was fixed, determined; that nothing could enter it from without, and nothing could leave it. These two foundation-stones, these two pillars of the older science of our fathers, were the 'physical correlation of forces' and the 'conservation of mass' — likewise the 'conservation of energy.'

The idea of the 'correlation of forces' was actually, if analysed sufficiently, that spiritual thinking, that the play of man's emotions, that the exercise of intellectual thought, and that the psychic movements of his soul, could be transmuted, transformed, into physical motion; and this we do not deny, for these various operations of man's inner constitution are in fact the result of the action of forces; and the physical proof of it is that they can move physical things. I lift my arm; I walk; I think; I talk; I can in moderate degree change the aspect and course of Nature; I do all these things that a man does. Now, what is it that is the driving power behind these operations of mine? It is energy, or force, which in these cases is the working of the soul or spirit; and what does the name matter which we for the moment give to this force? In one aspect we can call it force or energy; in another aspect we call it the functions of consciousness and life.

Equivalently, therefore, according to the old idea of the 'correlation of forces,' friction of molecules, or some electrical machine, or heat, can produce the works of genius of the ages, because these forces can be transformed, according to that old theory, into spiritual and intellectual and psychic work! The great freethinker of his day, Colonel Robert Ingersoll, once made the statement in substance: "Is it not wonderful that a piece of bread in the chemistry of the human body can be transmuted into the immortal works of Shakespeare?" This, to the Theosophist, is simply a foolish statement; it is impossible to imagine how such alchemy could be done. But human *thought* can do it. Whereas bread nourishes the physical body in which that living thought lives and works, it is the living thought and not the bread which produces the work of genius![164]

---

164. The famous German chemist, von Liebig, has well expressed his disgust at the grossly materialistic ideas of his time in writing as he did: "I would more readily believe that a book of chemistry or of botany could grow out of dead matter, than believe that a leaf or a flower could be formed or could grow by merely chemical forces." He but echoed the archaic wisdom and thinking.

Scientific knowledge and discovery forty or more years agone were exceedingly egoistic, and dogmatic in a thoroughgoing way. One might summarize the view of the scientific student of the last quarter of the nineteenth century somewhat in the following words: "The marvelous discoveries made by scientific research within the last three or four generations have completely unveiled the mysteries of Nature to modern vision. There remains little more to be discovered in Nature or to be wrested from her bosom; but what the scientists of the future can do, will be to develop in detail the complete knowledge of Nature already gained."

There, not exaggerating a single thought, lay the substance of accepted views of science itself, and of its achievements, at that time. It is, however, one of the pleasantest reflexions that the modern man can make that the most prominently outstanding figures in science today, the true leaders of their scientific collaborators, are coming to unite in holding an incomparably wiser and loftier conviction concerning Science and its proper work for mankind. Ultra-modern Science is steadily and indeed rapidly becoming distinctly metaphysical and mystical, however much these terms may displease many scientific men who are still more or less within the psychological and mental confines of the last generation. The greatest men of science today, in different ways, and by means of different methods of approach, seem, to judge from their writings and published statements, to have come to the definite conclusion that back of, behind, and within all physical Nature, there is constructive Mind, Consciousness, and mathematically working and guiding Intelligence of cosmic magnitude, permeating and guiding all things.

CHAPTER XII

THE TURNING OF THE WHEEL — THE PRESENT

I T was to a strangely self-complacent world that H. P. Blavatsky came when about to launch the public part of her mission in the last quarter of the nineteenth century — strangely self-complacent and thoroughly self-satisfied, and yet, as is always the case in such eras, a world-psychology which was shot through and through with intellectual discontent and spiritual hunger. Ease and grace both of mind and soul were conspicuous because of their absence, to employ what sounds like an Hibernian mode of speaking; and because of this intellectual *malaise* and the feeling of insecurity in so many lines of human consciousness, it was the time of the beginning or inauguration of those many and various new movements of human thinking and feeling which since then have reached such widespread proportions.

Officially, however, the Western World was divided into two camps, each armed to the teeth and each regarding the other with both suspicion and deep distrust because of the 'conflict' between religion and science which had been waged for the previous two hundred and fifty years, more or less. The religious camp, with its many factions, each distrustful of all others yet united against the common foe, was haughtily nursing the deep wounds received in the long struggle, yet refusing to recognise the case as it stood; and on the other hand were ranged the scientific forces, equally haughty, and arrogant, and swollen with steadily mounting pride over their supposed victory. Although neither camp officially made advances towards the other, at least a species of neutrality or truce had been tacitly made between them; yet here again both these camps, antagonistic to each other, instinctively united to frown down with haughty and contemptuous pride aught that seemed to either to attack what had come to be considered either's special prerogatives or field of activity.

The tale has been well told by many quick and ready pens, and there is no need to elaborate or even to sketch the story here, for it is one which is known to everyone having more than an elementary instruction in history. The way had been, to a certain extent, prepared for the coming of the Great Theosophist, aided by her collaborators, because of the then relatively recent introduction into the thought-life of the West of somewhat at least of the great philosophical and religious and mystical thought of the archaic Orient. Such men as the Frenchman Anquetil-Duperron and the English Orientalist, Sir William Jones, and their many later followers, especially in Germany, had, through the introduction of several varieties of Oriental Studies in the Universities and the publication and diffusion of at least some driblets of this ancient Oriental learning, brought into the consciousness of the Western World a realization, albeit feeble as yet, of the fact that the great religious systems and philosophical schools of other parts of the world, outside of Greece and Rome, contained a message of genuine and deep spiritual and intellectual worth and import, which could no longer be ignored or set aside on the formerly frivolous grounds that it was 'polytheistic nonsense' or 'irreligious heathenism.'

Everywhere even then, rapidly growing groups of thoughtful men and women who had become deeply interested in religious and philosophical matters, zealously labored in these new fields, uncovering what was to the West novel proofs and examples of the fertility of human philosophical and religious genius wherever found on the globe. Moreover, other far less socially 'respectable' movements were taking birth, such as what later came to be called 'New Thought,' or the peculiarities of the then different sects of the 'Deniers,' and last, but certainly even then the most numerous, the thousands and perhaps hundreds of thousands of men and women who had become, at any rate temporarily, fascinated and intrigued by the claims of the Spiritists and the phenomenal occurrences which took place in their circles.

Yet all these latter movements lacked the worthiest and noblest of foundations on which to build a proper temple wherein the always soaring genius of the Human Spirit might take up its abode, and these foundations are Philosophy and Religion, derivative or flowing forth from Nature's own self — from her structure and her operations and laws. 'Nature' here does not mean solely Nature's physical shell, as its parts or particles are studied in the laboratories of the schools or in the secluded privacy of one's library, but means what the Esoteric Tradition states it to mean: the Heart of things, and therefore and in especial, the shoreless and invisible inner realms of the Universe.

I

It was indeed to a frigidly unsympathetic world that H. P. Blavatsky brought her message and into which she launched her work:

a world contemptuous of all that to it was 'new' or unknown, because so perfectly self-assured in its convictions, both in science and in the established religions, that the last word had been uttered in either camp. It is a curious picture when one considers it and reflects for a moment upon it. Here comes a woman of middle age, knowing little or nothing of the jargon of the Schools, and though a gentlewoman to her finger-tips both by birth and breeding and education, yet markedly unconventional to Western eyes, joining, at least to a certain degree, the Spiritists, partly in order to show them the real facts behind the phenomena that these latter were so zealously studying; and when rejected by them because of her lack of spiritistic 'orthodoxy' and because of her stated truths which were too unwelcome to be received and too profound to be easily understood, then inaugurating or founding a society of her own through which she immediately proceeded to pour into the Western mind with all the native genius that she so abundantly possessed and with the wealth of talent that she lavished thereupon, a stream of what seemed to the average Occidental an almost incomprehensible medley or farrago of 'heathenish' ideas combined with the then last word in modern science; offending the social susceptibilities of people with her incessant smoking of cigarettes after the manner of Russian ladies; but most unwelcome of all, perhaps, in her insistent and reiterated affirmations, delivered with real, genial power which was so peculiarly her own, that there exists in the world a majestic Brotherhood of Great Men, true Sages and Seers, whose life and entire work are devoted to watching over the spiritual and intellectual destiny of men: — it is small wonder, when one reflects over this truly amazing picture, that the Great Theosophist was not only misunderstood but even in some cases heartlessly and perseveringly pursued with invective and libel.

A curious picture, indeed; but what is wonderful about it is not the novelty of the picture so much as the fact that she succeeded in accomplishing her mission, single-handed, at first; and sole and alone and unaided[165] by any other in the beginning, wrought what really was a marvel: she not only broke through the hardest substance

---

165. Assuredly no one will suppose for a moment that this mentioning of H. P. Blavatsky in the text as having almost alone and single-handed begun her great work, is in any wise an ignoring or slurring over of the really great pioneer work that was done at H. P. B.'s side by her first two most important, because most prominent, collaborators: Colonel Henry Steel Olcott and William Quan Judge; the former the first president of the Theosophical Society and the

known to man — the human mind — but the breach once made and the Theosophical Society once founded, she really achieved what history will some day recognise to be the fact, the diversion of the heavy and powerfully-flowing stream of Western thought then running downwards, into a new orientation or direction.

It was not to a world such as the world of the twentieth century slowly became, wherein the cry of everyone seems to be like that of the ancient Athenians, 'for something new,' for novelties, that H. P. Blavatsky came. One may well ask oneself just what it was she did in order to give her Message initial currency in the world then divided between religious dogmatism on the one hand and scientific materialism on the other. As a matter of fact, she did everything that a greatly intuitive mind and the impulses of a heart equally great could do. She drove her wedges of thought into any logical opening that offered itself and that promised to widen into paths fit for her Message to be launched upon. She neglected no opportunities, she missed no chances. As above alluded to, it was thus that she worked for a while with the Spiritists because they were at that time far more open-minded in the reception of new ideas than were either the self-satisfied church-people on the one hand, or the equally dogmatic and self-satisfied scientific thinkers on the other hand.

By every means possible to her she made her Message to become more or less known: the newspapers began to print columns of chit-

---

latter probably H. P. B.'s most understanding and faithful student and defender.

It is not the intention of the present work in any wise to embark upon the very painful and disastrous events which, shortly after the Great Theosophist's passing, brought about the breaking of the Theosophical Society in twain.

The work of Mr. Judge is so well known and was of such wide-reaching nature that it needs little more than to mention it to show how faithfully the Great Theosophist was supported during her life by him both in written and spoken work and by his unceasing Theosophical activities.

Colonel Olcott, likewise, undoubtedly an honest man at heart, did most admirable work for the Theosophical cause, especially as long as H. P. B. herself was alive and was enabled by her profound genius and knowledge of him to guide his activities by her example. There were others, after the founding of the Theosophical Society, whose work it is not easy adequately to commend.

The observations in the text are intended solely to point out that it was almost alone and single-handed, indeed quite alone and single-handed in the beginning, that H. P. Blavatsky, after a number of years passed in travel and preparing herself for her great Task, turned to the Occident and began her work, reaching New York in 1873, where later with Colonel H. S. Olcott, Mr. W. Q. Judge, and several others, she founded the Theosophical Society in 1875.

chat and gossipy talk about her personality; she and her Message were written about and talked about and gossiped about everywhere; although there is no doubt at all, as is proved by the written records of those who then knew her best, that her sensitive mind and heart suffered greatly at times from the grotesque and often parodied misunderstanding of herself and of the Message that she brought to the Western World, on the part of the newspapers and the general public.

But the main thing was adoing, which was that her Message was going out to all and sundry, and was entering into receptive minds everywhere, and was being welcomed by them, and was thus beginning to be recognised at least in some small degree for what it was. She laid all her talents, all her intellectual and psychological powers, indeed all her life, on the altar of her work; she gave up everything that a woman cherishes as most dear: name, personal happiness, fortune, social status, even reputation — for as regards this last, as said above, she was scandalously slandered at times by those who misunderstood or who feared the Message of which she was the aggressive and incessantly active Voice.

This Message was a religious one; this Message was a philosophical one; this Message was a scientific one: it was *her* Message indeed, yet not hers. She was the Messenger, but she neither invented it nor composed it nor syncretized it haphazard and piecemeal from the reading of articles in encyclopaedias and reference-books dealing with the world's great religions and philosophies.

Such an idea is ludicrous to the competent scholar who knows her history and the work she did, and indeed would be absurd to any one of competent judgment who has honestly studied the already accumulated evidence. One has but to look at the articles in such encyclopaedias as then existed to recognise that she would have found very little indeed in those works in any wise akin to the majestic System of universal and incomparably profound truths that she so widely disseminated. It is only in fairly recent years that Western scholarship has come to know somewhat of the deeper reaches of the profound religions and philosophies of the archaic world and of the Orient, and to do something more than a simple chronicling of data found in the more or less misapprehended Oriental literatures.[166]

---

166. The reader should not suppose from the foregoing observations that the Esoteric Philosophy, or the Esoteric Tradition, is solely of East Indian or Hindû origin, as a hasty perusal of the text might perhaps induce the inattentive reader to presume. The majestic Wisdom-Religion of Antiquity was at one

Moreover, she herself never had studied philosophy as such; she never had studied religion as a science; she was an excellent modern linguist in her native Russian and in French, and to a certain small extent in German. English she then spoke but haltingly. To say that this great soul, wonderful woman as she truly was, but with a mind untutored and untrained in technical philosophical, religious, scientific, and linguistic studies, could have invented the majestic System based on the recondite truths of Nature as found

---

time the universally diffused and accepted belief or religion-philosophy-science of the human race, and its vestiges or remnants may still be found by careful research imbodied in every great religion and philosophy which the literatures of the world contain.

It is no more Oriental than it is Occidental, no more Northern than it is Southern, no more Chinese than Druidic, no more Greek or Roman than it is Hindû; and it was as devotedly studied among the Mayas and the Aztecs and Peruvians of ancient times as it had been in China or the forests of Northern Europe. Even the so-called savage and barbarian tribes as they are found today, degenerate descendants of once mighty and civilized sires, have their carefully treasured Traditions of a far-distant past, although the inner significance or meaning of these branches of folk-lore is now utterly forgotten by their fallen and degenerate custodians.

Special emphasis is laid in the text above on the fact of H. P. Blavatsky's constant reference to and illustration of the branches of the Esoteric Philosophy as she found it in the Oriental religious and philosophical literatures, only because it is in these literatures of still highly civilized peoples that the existence of the ancient Wisdom of the Gods is most easily demonstrated and proof of its once universal diffusion found.

In *Isis Unveiled*, H. P. Blavatsky's first work of monumental size, she took pains to show the once universal diffusion of the Ancient Wisdom in every land and in every clime and among every people, using material that was then at hand for her work in illustration and elaboration; whereas in her still greater work, *The Secret Doctrine*, her literary labors in illustration and proof and the elaboration thereof were largely based upon the majestic religions and philosophies of Hindûsthân, for the reason just set forth.

It is important that both reader and student understand this matter, because in recent years there is a tendency among a few to suppose that India alone, or perhaps India and China together, with minor allusions to the literatures of Greece and Rome, were over-emphasized by the Great Theosophist in her literary labor. This opinion is entirely erroneous and without any foundation in actual fact, as the competent scholar may discover for himself by adequate study. Let it therefore be said once again that the Wisdom-Religion of Antiquity was and is the property of no particular race or time in world-history, but once was universal over the globe and was the common property, the common spiritual and intellectual heritage, of every nation, and that it has existed in every clime.

evidenced in the world's religions and philosophies, in the short space of time which we know she could have had to compose such a System, is, in all its reaches as an idea, a perfectly incredible supposition.

She herself in substance once said, in answer to the remark of some fanatic religionist who understood neither her nor the philosophy which she brought: "You say, my friend, that you think I myself composed all this. Nay, I cannot accept that. Had I done so, I were indeed a miracle myself! It would be a more marvelous thing, were that the case, than is this System itself which I give to you from my Teachers. I am but their mouthpiece in that respect."

Her Teachers and the Inspirers of her great work, according to her own self-effacing statement, were two of the members of the Great Brotherhood of Sages mentioned before, two Great Men, men of Buddha-like souls, who took the karmic responsibilities upon their shoulders of making themselves thus karmically answerable[167] for the sending out of a new spiritual and intellectual Message to mankind, which Message, by virtue of its innate vigor and the persua-

---

167. To a mind still tainted with the thorough-going materialism of thirty or forty years ago, as, alas, the larger part of the European and American psychology still is, because of the sheer mental inertia and weight of former intellectual standards, the immense import of the idea contained in the text above will seem either nebulous or, possibly, even a downright exaggeration. The Occident has well-nigh lost all sense of the great natural law of Retribution active throughout every sphere of the Universe; and because of the loss of this sense of rigidly retributive action in Nature, there has grown up in Western psychology a feeling that a man can do pretty much what he desires to do, can act pretty much as he will, without of necessity thereby falling under the sway of an ineluctable and all-seeing Justice.

In the West chance or fortuity seems to be looked upon as being everywhere: that if a man act so as to escape the consequences of the sanctions of human law he has little else to fear from the movements or operations of Universal Nature herself. This is a deplorable mistake, and it is high time that the truth about the matter be emphasized at every turn of thought.

No Occultist worthy of the name could ever hold such an idea, for he realizes that the very foundation of the Universe is rigid and inflexible operations brought into action by consciousnesses of whatever grade, each individual consciousness according to its standing on the Ladder of Life; and that, consequently, no man can act, nor even think, nor feel, without placing himself instantly under the sway of compensatory or retributive action, which will pursue him or follow him until the movement thus set in motion by him has run its course to the very end.

It is a matter of the gravest character, and of far-reaching import, in any wise to touch or to affect the thoughts and feelings and thereby the lives of

sive power of the teachings which it contains, would induce men to think, and to think towards sublime and lofty ends, and to do so despite themselves. Yet it should not be forgotten that H. P. Blavatsky herself, while messenger and mouthpiece in one sense, had of necessity a most unusual spiritual, intellectual, and psycho-mental constitution superior to and evolutionally ahead of the average of men, to have been capable of transmitting to us so successfully the wonderful Message that in fact she did transmit, and that has so widely, and yet with such invisible and subtil power, molded the thought of Europe and of America and indeed of Asiatic countries, since 1875. It can probably be said with perfect truth and without exaggeration that no other religio-philosophical movement has ever

---

others, for in so doing we set in motion causes, *verae causae*, which, thus awakened, are sleepless and Argus-eyed, and dog the footsteps for weal or for woe of him who has thus acted.

Here is the root of the Theosophical teaching of Karmic Retribution, and in it is involved the principle of that mysterious and in some senses dread Law of Universal Nature, which the Occultist-student of the Esoteric Philosophy briefly describes in the Sanskrit term, Karman.

Any man who involves himself in any wise in affecting the life and therefore the destiny of others, by that fact becomes bound to those others, and cannot free himself from these bonds until he himself has undergone all the effects, the consequences, flowing forth from the original cause or causes. It is indeed a most serious thing, a heavy responsibility, to touch the lives of other men; and this responsibility is the greater, the greater is the original actor who thus brings about the weaving of the karmic web of destiny in which he involves himself when thus upon him has fallen the influences of his thought and consequent actions. Nature will exact retribution to the uttermost farthing, or, contrariwise, will bring about compensatory reward in exactly similar manner.

It is of course inevitable, and indeed our duty, to aid, to help, to support, to succor, each other to our utmost; but this is all in accordance with Nature's primordial law of Cosmic Harmony, and the consequences flowing from such action are always beneficial to all concerned; but it is another matter entirely when the thought or action is inaugurated for purposes of the self-interest of the actor, or for ignoble or egoistic reasons of any kind. In this latter case, the actor is working against that primal Cosmic Harmony just spoken of, because he sets himself up as a unit and for selfish reasons as against the common good. Retribution will follow him to the bitter end.

Thus it is that the sublime work of the Great Brotherhood is a constant laboring in the cause of all that lives, helping, aiding, stimulating, spiritual and intellectual attributes and qualities wherever they are found in human individuals, and consequently striving to increase the sum of human wisdom, happiness, and peace.

The extremely subtil and difficult doctrine of Karman imbodying as a teach-in past times done anything at all equal to what the Theosophical Movement has accomplished in the world in the short space of its sixty years of work.

Who then can seriously doubt, having in view the true psychological marvel that she wrought, that H. P. Blavatsky appeared as a true spiritual and intellectual Teacher, and as one in the regular succession or series composed of other Teachers, both those who have preceded her through the ages, and, as the Theosophist teaches likewise, those who will follow her in times to come. The ages pass, and each age brings in a new generation of men, and each generation of men receives light, it is true, from the generation which preceded it, from its fathers. But generations rise and they fall, physically

---

ing the descriptive working of the Law of retributive justice in the Universe, should not be confused on the one hand with the soulless insensate and mechanistic determinism of the now moribund materialistic ideas of a generation or two agone, nor, on the other hand, with the nebulous and vague but nevertheless interesting ultra-modern scientific ideas clustering about what is at present called Indeterminism —a very natural revolt and reaction of the scientific intellect against obviously incomplete and inadequate physical determinism, formerly so popular.

This is not, however, saying that either of these two ideas is entirely devoid of some modicum of natural truth. Karman, or the operation of infallible and inexorable retributive and compensatory justice in the Universe, is derivative, in the last analysis, from the actions of Colossal Minds in the Cosmos, interworking and interlocking and interblended, and existing in various evolutionary grades or degrees, and yet all working or operating through equivalently interlocked and interblending and interoperating hierarchies extending from the divine to the grossest matter.

Thus Karman is not Fatalism, nor again is it arbitrary moral irresponsibility, which Free Will is so often misunderstood to be. Every being or entity in Boundless Space has its own modicum of free will which it uses or abuses or misuses in accordance with its evolutionary degree of interior unfoldment; and each such being or entity has free will in progressively greater degree, in rising proportion, as such being or entity penetrates to higher and deeper states of consciousness, or rather *Mind*, within its own essence or constitution. In other words, the more a being or entity becomes the imbodiment of higher states of mind or intelligence or consciousness within its own constitution, the more does it exemplify and imbody and express a larger measure of free will.

Finally, therefore, Karman is actually seen to be in no wise fatalistic, but both radically and operatively an expression of free will interacting and interblending in function with other free wills with which it is inextricably interlinked and involved.

For a further elaboration of this subject see *infra*.

in civilization as well as spiritually in light, and also in the intellectual, the ethical, and the mental courses which men follow in producing the civilizing influences of human life. Yet in these generations which thus follow each other in time, there is always a crying need for guiding minds, for a Light given anew from age to age; for a new lighting, phoenix-like, of the old spiritual and intellectual fires. There is always need for another Passer-on of the same Light which lighteth all men.

Yet, although in the foregoing paragraphs we have endeavored to render due meed of homage to the Great Theosophist because of her own grandeur and spiritual worth, doing so with hearts filled with gratitude for what she brought to us, nevertheless it is of the utmost importance for the reader to remember that the matter of highest value and of greatest worth is not, after all, H. P. Blavatsky's own noble self, but the Message which she brought, and of which she was the ever self-abnegating mouthpiece and interpreter.

Our gratitude runs to the woman, indeed, yet it is not upon her personality that we must fix our vision and our reflexions, but upon her Message and upon her Work, determining to carry it into the future whole and complete, unadulterate and unchanged, elaborated and enlarged by new additions drawn from the same Sublime Source, as time goes on. It is thus principle and principles rather than personalities which should receive the greater part of our devotion: neither the Messenger apart from the Message, nor the Message as divorced from the Messenger, but each receiving its due meed and portion of our reverence and devotion. As the Great Theosophist herself would have said in substance: "I am as nothing; pass on to others what I have brought unto you. This is nearly everything."

II

H. P. Blavatsky came at a critical period in world-history. Religion in the Occident, as has been already stated, was mostly dogmatism in opinion, and forms of service, because the Christ-spirit worked not as a living inspiration and ideal to follow in the different ecclesiastical organizations. Science had already introduced a scientific materialism — or quasi-philosophical negationism — into men's minds and consequently into their inner outlook on life, so that they had lost all abiding faith in their own spiritual intuitions, and indeed the vast majority had forgotten that they had such, and had lost the instinctive recognition that there is an interior and invisible Universe, the roots and foundation of the outer material spheres, which latter are but the lowest and least expressive garment of the indwelling Divinity.

Men, furthermore, had lost all their sense of a lively faith that there is an inherent moral law in the world, administered on a colossal scale and with inflexible and infinitely impartial justice, to which men, as inseparable parts or portions of the Universe itself, were by the fact subordinate, and from which moral and spiritual administration of affairs, taking place both on the cosmic scale and in the small, there was no possible hope of escape, either through favoritism or through any sort or manner of propitiation.

The loss of the indwelling sense of this utterly and impartially just course of events, with its consequent loss of human dignity as partakers of and co-laborers with such moral sanction, had therefore deprived men of all faith, both instinctive and intellectual, that both collectively and individually they would reap in the course of cycling time what they themselves at any time sowed.

The result of all this was that in those days the human race as a whole, especially in the Occident, having lost the directing light of the spiritual Star which guides mankind through the ages, and thinking themselves to be but beasts of a somewhat better kind than the apes, and that they were destined to annihilation when the body died, were rushing with accelerating speed for the maelström of gross material sensualisms — the sensualities of an utterly material existence. This, as every occultist knows full well, had it proceeded farther than it did, would have involved the loss of hundreds of thousands and indeed, in time, of millions of human souls, in addition to heaven knows what untold spiritual and intellectual misery and moral injury to hosts of men and women, whose intuitions were still alive indeed, but blighted and blinded, and who in their intellectual suffering knew not whither to look for light. The churches gave it not for they had it not; albeit a great many noble men and women illuminated the ecclesiastical organizations by their presence within them. The scientists never had it. They were searching only and researching, hunting desperately; but they had not yet found.

Then came H. P. Blavatsky with her Theosophical Message. Laughed at and derided at first, scorned and persecuted for years, she worked alone until she found a few true helpers; and by means of her indomitable, her inflexible will, and her magnificent intellect, and her amazing spiritual intuition, she taught and she wrote and she built up a society devoted to stemming the tide towards the Abyss, and to diverting its stream into nobler ways — and it succeeded. A new impulse was forced at high pressure into the thought-atmosphere of the world. Attention was attracted by the work of the Theosophical Society to other sources of wonderfully inspiring thought: to amazing and lofty philosophies, to profound and inspiring religions. New words imbodying grand ideas entered into the language of the West. The truth of the teaching of Reincarnation, which was then only partially known by scholars and called by them 'transmigration' or 'metempsychosis,' and which was scorned because considered to be merely a literary relic of 'ancient heathenish superstition' — people of the Occident forgetting that even in their day, as today, three-fourths or more of the human race still hold that belief — the truth of the teaching of Reincarnation began to insinuate itself into human understanding and to percolate into all departments of human society, so that today it has become common knowledge — as far as it is understood — and is frequently met with in literature and in the drama, in picture and in sermon, and, however much misunderstood, has now become more or less tacitly accepted by untold millions.

With the coming and work of the Theosophical Movement many new thoughts besides that of Reimbodiment began to sink into and to permeate the consciousness of men. The protagonists of the old theology became less dogmatic in their pronouncements, apparently more charitable in statement, more kindly. Scientific researchers in all lands coincidently began to have what were to the time strange stirrings of new ideas in their minds, due to their marvelously efficient and far-reaching work in discovery. The existence and action of new forces burst upon their astounded vision which had been almost trained to look for nothing radically new but only for novel permutations of what already had been uncovered by research. Scientific men as a body became less cocksure in assertion, more careful and more sincere in statement, and therefore more truly scientific, as every true devotee of science should be.

The veil was lifting; truly magical things were about to happen in all lines of research where the inquisitive intellect of men commenced to discern and to intuit what up to that time had not been considered to be possible — new and unguessed fields and realms of the physical sphere. The world was suddenly startled by hearing of the work of Crookes, Becquerel, Roentgen, and others in 'radiant matter,' leading on to the discovery of the so-called X-rays — a marvelous and most unsettling revelation to the cocksure materialism of the time, proving the existence of an interior world or realm which was utterly invisible and intangible by the sense-apparatus which we have, and to which all were then more or less enslaved.

Following this, came the work of the Curies, of Rutherford, of Soddy and of others. Radium was discovered. Men's thoughts took a new turn. They began to think along new lines, or rather along the old lines which the church had forgotten and modern science had not yet rediscovered.

Great things grow in the silence. In the silence lies the seed, and in the silence it brings forth what is in its heart. Thus all growth takes place. The Great Theosophist cast into the world the seeds of thought of the Message that she was sent to bring; and thereafter quietly, in the inner silences of men's minds and hearts, those seeds took root and grew, and like the plant that will burst the rock into which it sends deep its roots, so did these seeds of thought sown by her strike deep roots into human souls, breaking the adamantine hardness of custom and prejudice and predilection — and anyone who knows anything whatsoever of human nature and of the lessons of history will realize how hard and unyielding are the prejudiced minds of men.

III

H. P. Blavatsky herself had described a part of her mission as that of being a breaker of 'the molds of mind.' It is no exaggeration to say that since her time all departments of human thought have moved with startling rapidity along the lines of thought that she laid down, and in the direction towards which she pointed with emphatic gesture. The scientific speculations and teachings and theories and hypotheses which exist today were in large part if not entirely unknown when in 1891 she passed on to what she called 'Home.' Yet she taught the essentials of all these things, now recently discovered, in her great work *The Secret Doctrine*. In it *all the latest discoveries of modern science* are outlined at least, and in some cases even sketched in detailed outline. In fact, in this profound and most suggestive book the ground-work may be seen for the superstructure of scientific theory that then was to come and now is with us.

It is difficult for us men of today, who live in and under the psychology of our own time, adequately to realize the woful restrictions of religious and philosophical thought that existed when H. P. Blavatsky came to America in 1873. The word 'soul' was then actually *tabu* in circles valuing social polish and good form. A man was considered superstitious who thought that there was anything in him of a permanent nature besides the vibrating atoms and molecules of his brain, which were supposed to give to him the 'sensation' of consciousness; and among countless millions the accepted idea was that when a man died everything of him died, and that this was the end of all of him. *Non omnis moriar* — 'I shall not all of me die' — was an intuition of very real fact which had died an inglorious death, choked and smothered by the evil and relentless embrace of the abominable psychology of a shallow but egoistic materialism.

On the other hand, other millions of people thought, or thought that they thought, that the soul might be an intangible something, indeed — nobody knew quite what: perhaps the same as the spirit, perhaps not — which, if a man were good, when he died went to heaven; and if he were bad while he lived on earth, when he died — well, nobody knew just what did happen! The old idea was that the bad soul fell into an eternal hell of material fire, in which throughout eternity it would suffer the pains of the damned in an asbestos-like body. But this idea for generations had already been renounced as pure superstition by virtually everyone except a vocal few in positions of authority, or by unvocal multitudes whose chief characteristic was that they were a mere sequacious herd, believing unthinkingly whatever they were told.

In either case the idea, if accepted at all, was an eternity of unearned bliss or an eternity of unearned horrible physical suffering, as the destiny of that nebulous ghost-like wraith of uncertain lineament, and still more uncertain characteristics, which those who still accepted the idea spoke of as the human 'soul.'

Let us briefly consider some of the scientific ideas then popular. The materialists, a wholly dominant school, said that the world was made of dead, insensate, unensouled matter, and that this matter is composed of various chemical elements — which last fact of course nobody ever denied. These various chemical elements in turn were shown to be composed of atoms. Those atoms were considered to be indivisible, hard little bodies, which therefore were practically eternal. It was said: if the atoms are not everlasting or eternal we do not know it, and we fancy that they are. No one ever heard of a beginning of them, and no one has ever heard of an ending for them. Eternity stretches backwards into the infinite past as well as forwards into the infinite future. Whence then came they unless out of the eternity of the past, for here they are? They must indefinitely exist or be eternal, otherwise how came they here?

Sir Isaac Newton, in following but misunderstanding his Greek teachers, nearly all of them of the famous Atomistic School, spoke thus of the atoms, for he understood them to be merely ultimate particles of physical matter and nothing more. They are, he said:

Solid, massy, hard, impenetrable, moveable Particles . . . so very hard, as never to wear or break in pieces; no ordinary Power being able to divide what God himself made one in the first Creation.[168]

Newton was a scholar: he was a religious man after his own manner and after the religion of his time, yet he was an industrious student of Greek philosophy. He particularly favored, as is evident from his writings, the teachings of the Greek Atomists such as Democritus and Epicurus, who taught — and their teaching has been grossly misunderstood by modern times, even by Newton — that the ultimate particles of life and of cosmic being are 'indivisibles.' Therefore they gave to these indivisibles the appellation of *atomoi,* a Greek word meaning things that cannot be divided or cut into two or more pieces — in other words, 'indivisibles.' The real meaning of the term as thus used by Democritus and Epicurus, and by their followers, when their rather vague expressions are correctly understood, is that these 'atoms' are spiritual atoms, the consciousness-centers of things, cosmic spiritual sparks.[169]

Neither Newton nor the often really great scientists who followed him in later generations knew the real meaning of the ancient Atomistic School in its adoption and usage of this term, and in consequence they took over the word itself from the old Greek literature and used it as the name by which they designated the "solid, massy, hard, impenetrable, moveable particles" of Newton.

Although the prevailing scientific opinion or view of Nature in the middle and later years of the nineteenth century was predominantly, if not wholly, abjectly materialistic, nevertheless a number of great men at different times voiced their objections to it, and occasionally did so in no uncertain language.

Thomas Henry Huxley, the eminent English biologist, chemist, writer, and what not else, was so disgusted, although he was a fervent Darwinist himself, with the materialistic chemical theories of his day, that he imbodied in one of his essays the following significant and telling paragraph:

I must make a confession, even if it be humiliating. I have never been able to form the slightest conception of those 'forces' which the Materialists talk

---

168. Newton's *Opticks.*

169. These Greek *atomoi* are really what in the Esoteric Philosophy, and in its terminology adopted for the West, are called by the Pythagorean term Monads — signifying spiritual unitary Individuals or Individualities, which *de facto* are indivisible, everlasting, at least for the time-period of a Solar Manvantara, a length of time so vast that it is expressible only by fifteen figures.

about, as if they had samples of them many years in bottle. . . . by the hypothesis, the forces are not matter; and thus all that is of any particular consequence in the world turns out to be not matter on the Materialists's own showing. Let it not be supposed that I am casting a doubt upon the propriety of the
employment of the terms 'atom' and 'force,' as they stand among the working
hypotheses of physical science. As formulae which can be applied, with perfect
precision and great convenience, in the interpretation of nature, their value is
incalculable; but, as real entities, having an objective existence, an indivisible
particle which nevertheless occupies space is surely inconceivable; and with
respect to the operation of that atom, where it is not, by the aid of a 'force'
resident in nothingness, I am as little able to imagine it as I fancy anyone
else is.[170]

In those days, everything that was, was supposed to be dead
matter and nothing else; but yet in some very mysterious way, which
nobody could understand, which nobody really knew anything about,
there were certain 'forces' in the Universe which were continuously
operative likewise, and which worked upon and moved this 'matter.'
To the question: "Whence came these forces?" the answer was,
"We do not know; but as matter is the only substantial thing in the
universe, they must arise out of matter in some way unknown to us.
Let us then call them 'modes of motion.'" Are the forces then
matter? Answer: "No, because they move matter." Are the forces
then different from matter? Answer: "No, because they arise out
of matter."[171]

---

170. *Science and Morals.*

171. As Plato expressed it, some twenty-five centuries ago, in words which
were as descriptive of materialistic fortuity in his time as they are true today:

"They mean to say that fire and water, and earth and air, all exist by
nature and chance, and not by art [plan], and that as to the bodies which
come next in order — earth and sun, and moon, and stars — they are created
[formed] by the help of these inanimate existences, and that they are sever-
ally moved by chance and some inherent influence according to certain affini-
ties of hot with cold, or of dry with moist, or of soft with hard, and other
chance admixtures of opposites which have united of necessity, and that on
this manner the whole heaven has been created [formed], and all that is in
the heaven, including animals and all plants, and that all the seasons come
from these elements, not by the action of mind, as they say, or of any god,
or from art [plan], but as I was saying, by nature and chance only. . . .
And that the principles of justice have no existence at all in nature. . . ."

— *Laws*, X, 889; translation by Jowett

Plotinus also rejects this materialistic naturalism, and very properly and
cogently, on the same grounds that are familiar to modern thinkers:

"The most irrational theory of all is that an aggregation of molecules

No wonder that men of penetrating intellect revolted from this paradox, nay, were repelled by the obvious contradictions. Yet the materialists doubtless did their best to give some adequate explanation of the nature of force and of matter. They had nothing better to offer than a lame hypothesis, and this lame hypothesis they actually rode to its own death. But so great was their influence, so all-pervasive at the time was the materialistic conception of things, that only a few brave and intuitive souls ventured to question these scientific dogmas, for that in truth is just what they were.

We have learned much about Nature since that time. We now know that the atom itself is 'mostly holes,' so-called and mis-called 'empty space'; and for all that we know, the protons and electrons and neutrons and positrons, etc., etc., which compose the atom are themselves composed of particles — shall we say wavicles? — still more minute. And, if so, are these still minuter particles — or 'wavicles' — in their turn again simply divisibles? Who in the ranks of ultra-modern science can tell us? Where shall one stop, where can one stop, in following with the mind such a conception of the nature of substance?

Our modern scientists are wiser by far than were their predecessors; and they certainly know more than the latter did. Our moderns have learned many new things, and they are today enthusiastically discussing philosophical and scientific problems that fifty years ago would have been considered cause for ostracism of their proponents, had they been offered in any scientific gathering. One of the last of these remarkable adumbrations of truth is the scientific dictum — which also is a theosophical teaching — to the effect that force and matter are essentially one; that what we call matter is equilibrated or crystallized or concreted force, or forces; and, vice versa, that what we call force may with equal propriety be called liberated or free or etherealized matter — one or other of the many forms of what it is now customary to call 'radiation.'

Thus two of the old absolutes of science have been discarded as such. Gone is the old idea, which European thinkers have held for heaven knows how many hundreds of years, that there are certain absolutes, as popular language terms them, existing cheek by jowl with each other in the Universe, and yet in some perfectly unaccountable way blending together and making the Universe as we see it. These logical contradictions in conception have been some

---

should produce life, that elements without intelligence should produce intelligence." — *Enneads*, IV, Bk. VII, 2; Guthrie's translation, p. 58

of the greatest stumbling-blocks that scientific thinkers for three hundred years or more have had to meet and have had to explain away as best they could.

Two more such 'absolutes'[172] were considered to be time and space. For ages it was thought in the West that there actually is an entity, so to say, called 'time,' quite distinct if not utterly apart from matter and from force. Sir Isaac Newton himself wrote:

> Absolute, true, and mathematical time, of itself flows in virtue of its own nature uniformly and without reference to any external object.[173]

He thus makes of time an absolute something or entity, independent in its own essential existence of everything else, *per se* independent of space, *per se* independent of force, *per se* independent of substance. Now what does he say about space?

---

172. The literary Theosophist, who is careful in the choice and use of his words, employs the word 'absolute' in current speech and in technical Theosophical writing, because it is a convenient term with which to express the radical or original or perfected state or condition of whatever entity or thing one may be discussing at the time; but in so using the word 'absolute,' it is done in a strictly relative sense; for there are a virtually infinite number of absolutes, in this relative sense.

Accuracy in the use of such words of highly technical philosophical or scientific character is something which should be strived for, because with good literary tools accurately employed, the descriptive and expository work of a philosophical writer is thereby rendered easier, albeit he has to face the very natural, and in one sense proper, objections of those who care less for verbal accuracy and who care more for the principle of using 'common words in their ordinary acceptations.' The argument is of course a good one; but equally good and indeed better is the argument that one should use words employed in a technical manner in as strictly clear and descriptive a sense as possible.

Not a few writers on philosophical and similar matters who are careful in their choice of words, use this term 'absolute' in its proper sense as meaning 'freed,' 'perfected,' 'completed.' Sir William Hamilton in his *Discussions*, 3rd ed., page 13, footnote, remarks upon this word: "The *Absolute* is diametrically opposed to, is contradictory of, the Infinite." This is 'absolutely' correct, because 'absolute' is the English word derived from the Latin, *absolutum*, meaning 'freed,' 'unloosed,' and hence is an exact English equivalent word of the Sanskrit philosophical term, *moksha* or *mukti*, signifying spiritual freedom or release for the period of a cosmic manvantara from the cycle of imbodiments or peregrinations in the material worlds, and is therefore closely similar to, if not exactly identic in meaning with, the other Sanskrit word of such wide usage, Nirvâna.

173. Newton's *Principia*, Definitions, Scholium I.

Absolute space, by virtue of its own nature and without reference to any external object, always remains the same and is immovable.[174]

Today, however, such an ascription of independent existence, or entification, to space on the one hand, and to time on the other hand, has come to be considered extremely doubtful, and is, indeed, rejected by a rapidly growing body of scientific and philosophical thinkers. The new idea about space and time as forming not absolute entities *per se,* independent of and in consequence different from each other, but as being rather two aspects of a continuum containing both, is largely due to the labors of Dr. Albert Einstein, although the idea is not a radically new one, and was known to and accepted by one or more of the philosophers of ancient Greece. It is quite possible that the intuition of such a space-time continuum, as it is now called, has formed the subject of the private cogitations of many thousands of thinking men, at least those of a somewhat metaphysical bias; and, indeed, everybody knows that it is actually impossible to divorce space and its substances from time and its movement, because it is impossible to conceive of duration apart from things which endure, or on the other hand, it is impossible to conceive of space without duration in which it exists; so that the two ideas are radically interwoven in human consciousness.

Thus the idea may be said to have been lying latent in the consciousness of everybody, but nobody seemed to have taken the pains to understand it, or had ever dared to propose it as a logical philosophical and metaphysical as well as natural reality, to wit: that all things whatsoever and wherever they are, are fundamentally relative or related to each other, or together both in 'time' and in 'space,' and that consequently the old conception of absolutes in these matters is untenable.[175]

This idea has revolutionized modern scientific thinking; it has overturned the commonest and what was at one time apparently the most solidly founded conceptions of quondam orthodox science — for that in very truth is what it was, *orthodox* — and the world, which is never particularly noted for its independence in thinking, is in consequence vastly amazed. Yet every thinking man and woman

---

174. *Op. cit.,* Definitions, Scholium II.

175. The point here is that it is both logically impossible and therefore unnatural to divorce time from space or space from time — which is the same thing; because, as just said in the text, the one is unthinkable, except as a phantasy, apart from the other. Strictly speaking, CONSCIOUS SPACE, or Space-Duration, is the only Reality. This should be carefully borne in mind.

knows perfectly well that any force in operation proceeds inseparably both in and from time, and in and from space, and does this concurrently; and 'time-space' or 'space-time' is just this conception, is just this thought: that time, and space or matter, and force, are all three one thing, or one event manifesting itself in tri-form or triadic manner: one phase or facet or aspect of it being duration or time, another phase or aspect or facet of it being the force of it or the energy of it, and the other phase or facet or aspect of it being the matter of it or the space of it, but all three are one fundamentally — much like the various Triads, or triune Entities, or Trinities, of ancient mystical religious thought.

The physical body exists; it is matter; it is force; it lives in time; and yet you cannot separate from the physical body, either in thought or in actuality, the matter of it, or the force of it, or the time-element of it, because the combination of these three as a single unit: time-force-space: in any particular phase of manifestation of it, is that body.

The Universe is in exactly the same case; it is time-space-force or space-force-time; and therefore anything whatsoever is an *event* of time-space-force: a passing phase, in which time is involved as an aspect, in which matter or space is involved as an aspect, and in which force is involved as an aspect, of the triune whole. But behind time, behind force, behind space: behind or within or above and around these three aspects: there is THAT — the Reality, of which everything that exists in time-space-force is an 'event.'

Precisely because of these transitory or ever-flowing series of events, which are in constant flux and change from predecessor to successor, did the archaic Wisdom speak of the entire manifested universe and therefore of all individuals or entities or component parts of it as well, as being *mâyâ* or *mahâmâyâ* — or Illusion. The profound import of this teaching of mâyâ, or of the illusory and transitory nature of all manifested beings and things, has not yet dawned on the Western mind, but is beginning to do so, as is seen by the wide and rather sudden vogue which the modern doctrine of Relativity — at least in its principles, and apart from mere mathematical expositions of it — shows clearly enough.

The Universe is a coherent and consistent Whole, one vast Organism, or more accurately still, one mighty Organic Entity, every part of it related to every other part, everything in it in relation to everything else in it, and any one part of it subordinate to the whole. Some scientists state that some at least of the factors governing atomic physics do not appear to follow in all respects the same laws that govern macrocosmic phenomena, and give to these singularities in atomic structure and operation the name of 'indeterminism,' though why it should be supposed on any grounds of logic that the minute, which in its infinite particles compose the Whole, should not follow even in a single detail the macrocosmic operations of the Whole, in no wise appears.

The truth probably is that ultra-modern physicists and chemists see only what we may call the very large or general workings of the atomic physical operations, and have not yet penetrated more deeply into the smaller minutiae thereof, and are not as yet more than very partially acquainted with any of these operations. Inversely, astronomers see only the minutiae of macrocosmic physics, and are but just now beginning to have some intuition that there are very general and super-macrocosmic laws or operations of universal Nature of which the cosmic minutiae are but details. The still wider view of things which the future is infallibly destined to bring, unquestionably will reconcile under one common generalization what now seems to be the differently explicable singularities or partialities which puzzle modern research. It stands to reason that atomic physics sees but one phase or aspect, and that macrocosmic physics sees inversely another aspect, of Universal Nature.

IV

It is the modern Relativity Theory that has brought about so large a part of the revolution in modern scientific thought, and has done so more largely than any other factor. It cannot be said that the Theosophist approves of all the mathematical proofs that Dr. Albert Einstein, the formulator, or at any rate the main popularizer,[176] of modern Relativity has elaborated and published in demonstration of his hypothesis. Not at all; nor necessarily, again, the

---

176. As a matter of fact, Einstein was not the originator of this speculative but in some respects truthful theory of things. The credit for the first, if rather vague, formulation of that theory in modern times seems to lie with a Hollander, H. A. Lorentz. At any rate, Lorentz's Transformations — which are mathematical formulae expressing certain endeavors to reach the relations of things as based upon their co-ordinated interplay with each other — formed the mathematical basis of Einstein's first calculations. Einstein used these mathematical Transformations as they were, and with their help and by means of his own studies, illuminated by real flashes of intuition, he was enabled to combine various fundamental, mathematical, and therefore natural, principles into a systematic form, which finally took the shape of the 'Doctrine of Relativity' which bears his name.

rather restricted mathematical manner or mode under which he presents his proofs; nor again, his understanding of the operations of Nature as he cites them in substantiation of his demonstrations — not necessarily at all. But certain fundamental ideas are the same in Theosophy and in this wonderful new hypothesis, which has revolutionized all modern scientific conceptions, and has brought about a virtual overthrow of the fundamentals of scientific thought of a generation agone.

The beautiful thing about this hypothesis is that it introduces Metaphysics into Physics, although this perfectly true observation will arouse the ire, probably, of the larger body of still 'orthodox' scientists, who seem to be as afraid of Metaphysics as they are of Mysticism. Metaphysics literally means 'beyond physics,' and physics means anything that pertains to the ordinary physical world of perception that falls under the notice of our senses; and in consequence what can be more 'metaphysical' than the truly invisible, intangible, infinitesimals of the world of atoms and electrons which are as completely out of the scope or range of observation of any one of our senses as thought itself is!

This hypothesis also strongly tends to do away with purely speculative ideas, of what Plato would call 'phantasy,' that certain things are 'absolute' in a Universe wholly relative throughout, and thus brings us back to an examination of Nature as Nature is, and not as mathematical theorists have tacitly taken it to be — and as all too many of them still do, even of the ultra-modern school.

When first enunciated, this theory was not widely accepted, and this was to be expected. Every new discovery has a hard time at first in finding acceptance; then it becomes popular, and everybody takes it for granted; then comes a later time when it becomes crystallized as a more or less dogmatic teaching, and is then inevitably subject to misinterpretation and misconstruction; it becomes scientifically sectarian or orthodox, or becomes a scientific tenet with almost the inertia of a religious dogma; finally there springs forth some new idea, the child of some new man, some new luminary, in the scientific world, who gives to us a novel view or version of natural truth, and the old tenet, the old idea, the old dogma which is now crystallized and more or less misinterpreted, finds its way into the limbo of rejected ideas — where it is given the quietest burial possible with the least amount of publicity!

Relativity is not what it is often popularly misunderstood to be — the doctrine that nothing whatsoever in the Universe is other than relative, which would mean that there is nothing continuously fundamental or universally basic or enduringly real anywhere, whence or from which all other things within its encompassing sphere flow forth; or, in other words, that there is no positively and eternally real or infinitely fundamental background of unchanging Reality. The point is that Relativity, when properly understood, refers to all manifestations whatsoever, because manifestations are beings and entities and things evolving forth or rolling forth from an inner and superior enduring and unchanging Reality.

Of course, all manifested things are related also to this primordial and universal Source; but the beings and entities and things in their interlocking and interwoven relations with each other are obviously all relatives. In other words, just as the Esoteric Tradition and all its religious and philosophical offsprings through the ages teach: there is a relativity in manifestation or manifested outpourings from the heart of Eternal Reality, because these outflowings or manifestations are essentially and inherently all related together, yet all, for the term of their cosmic appearance, are transitory and therefore 'unreal' in the sense of being mâyâvi productions of the ONE. It is evident that there can be no relativity in One, for relativity implies differentiation into multitudes or units which then have interactions and relations.

Mathematical and physical Relativity is, or rather should be, the search for the Ineffable Reality which is suspected even now in many scientific quarters to lie within and beyond and behind relative things — in other words, behind the phenomena of the Universe. Its fundamental postulate is that this Universe in which we live is composed of relatives, as already stated, everything being relative to every other thing, yet all working together; that there is *no thing* 'absolute,' that is to say, purely and wholly independent of other things, among these relative things, as was formerly taught — neither what is commonly called space, nor time, nor matter, nor forces. All these are the macrocosmic 'events,' to use the Relativists' own technical word: the forms which a relative universe takes or assumes at certain times and places as it passes through, or perhaps more accurately as it itself forms, the 'space-time continuum' — again to use the jargon of the Relativists.

However, the Relativists, unfortunately, are still bound by the conception that physical matter, the physical world in short, is the only world there is, or at least the only world whose existence they will admit, and some even go so far as to say that there are no other spheres of being and no possible states of matter or time or space or consciousness than those which they think they know — i. e., no inner and spiritual worlds on the one hand, and no worlds more material than ours on the other hand. One does not presume to question this attitude of mind in so far as strictly physical science is concerned in its necessary limitations; but it would seem needful to point out that this mental attitude of self-satisfied vision in restrictions — which is just what it is — literally slams the door of discovery in the face of any easy entrance into larger spheres of thought. No man can advance far if he does not believe that a farther advance is possible. The theory of Relativity is founded on unquestionable essentials or points of truth, but the deductions drawn in many cases by many Relativist speculators appear to be mere 'brain-mind' constructions or phantasies.

There are some seven points of thought on which we may say that this ultra-modern scientific relativist theory of the nature of the Universe and of its operations is practically the same as the teachings of Ancient Theosophy, the Esoteric Tradition: nor does this statement imply that every point hereinunder listed has been set forth in formal fashion by scientific writers, but simply that these seven points seem to be necessary deductions, or actually teachings, of the modern scientific relativist theory. The seven points are suggested as follows:

1. That all things and beings are relative to all other things and beings, and that nothing is absolute, i. e., apart from — and existing as an absolute entification separate from — all other things and beings in the entirety of the Universe.

2. That force and matter are fundamentally one thing; while Theosophy says that force and matter are two macrocosmic forms of phenomena of the underlying and eternally causal and vivifying REALITY: KOSMIC LIFE.

3. That force and matter are both granular or corpuscular or atomic, so to say, and necessarily so, both being manifested and differentiated forms of the same underlying essential Reality.

4. That Nature in its forms of manifestation is illusory to us; that is to say, that things and beings are really not in themselves as our senses interpret them to us humans. In other words, we do not see the Universe as it is, because our senses are imperfect receiving instruments and therefore inadequate reporters. There is a great lesson to be drawn from this idea — if nothing else, at least the lesson of modesty!

5. That our Universe is not infinite; that is to say, boundless;

but only one of innumerable other Universes; and that it is rounded, more or less, in conformation, which, therefore, because of its self-contained nature and the global activities of its forces, is the so-called 'curved-space' of Dr. Einstein; this signifying that all movement in it, reduced to the last analysis, must necessarily pursue lines or pathways within that rounded Universe which follow the general conformation of the Universe.

6. That Time, Space, Matter, and Force, are not singular and individual absolutes in themselves, any one separate from the others and different from them, as formerly so confidently supposed; but that all are relatives, and interdependent and interlocked, any one in the other three in existence and in function; and all of them manifestations or phenomena of the underlying fathomless Reality before spoken of — the limitless Kosmic Life.

7. Because our Universe is rounded in conformation; and because it is filled full of countless forms of forces all at work; and because force is substantial, force and matter being fundamentally one; and because force and matter are inseparable by nature: therefore all the many forms of force or energy follow pathways or lines of least resistance; in other words, force cannot leave matter nor matter divorce itself from force, both being essentially one. Hence, all pathways of force or energy, or lines of least resistance, follow curved paths, because the Universe itself is of rounded or global type — force thus returning into itself after following its courses. Nevertheless, force of higher forms, of kinds not imbodied or englobed, or encrusted, so to say, in physical matter, could and must have intercosmic circulations, which are the bonds of the Universe with the Boundless Space surrounding our own Home-Universe, and are the links between our own Home-Universe and other Universes. It should be added here that although the forces in the Universe of necessity follow in operations the conformation of such Universe, nevertheless it is the Universe itself which is the product of or builded of and from these Forces, and not *vice versa*.

v

In connexion with our consideration of the foregoing seven points, it must here be pointed out, however, that modern Science is a very changing and very changeable thing, exactly as it ought to be because it is advancing steadily in knowledge, and that a thing which by its very nature changes from year to year cannot be taken as an ultimate or final teacher of truth. Thank Heaven that it is so, because if it were an ultimate or final statement of truth, it would then have reached its utmost limits, and in a short time it would be as dead as a door-mat, and its representatives would have become a true corporation of amiable 'moss-backs' mutually patting themselves on the shoulder, in a common and foolishly exultant pride over their conquest of the universe. Science is always approximating, ever coming nearer and nearer, to the truth, which it will, nevertheless, never attain in fulness; for that would be equivalent to saying that the human mind is capable of encompassing infinity, which is absurd. The progressive and therefore changeable views of science in every way provide the right atmosphere and frame-work of scientific study, and all this is just what it ought to be.

Therefore let us be on our guard lest we take any one scientific theory or hypothesis or deduction and say: "This is Science's latest declaration; being the last, it must be the most perfect, and therefore probably it is the Truth." No, it is not necessarily true; but it is the latest honest endeavor to approximate to truth: it is the latest theory about scientific discoveries, but it certainly will be displaced in time by the next-forthcoming theory, which will be a still closer approximation to truth — perhaps! Scientific thinkers not infrequently go back to theories which were once held as true and then abandoned when new light was received from wider and deeper research: the annals of Science contain many cases where a truth has been learned by temporarily abandoning a theory which in still later days has been proved to be truer than the newer one which superseded it.

All honor, therefore, to the great men of scientific research who are great enough and broad enough mentally to change when change is necessary — great enough to change even their bases of thinking, when new lights come into the purview of their vision. But for all that, and abating not a tittle of our reverence for honest study and discovery, where are there any unchanging disclosures of natural truth in modern science — disclosures of new facts in Nature which later research and newer discoveries will not overthrow or prove to have been misunderstood facts? Complete reliance upon an ever-changing thing which in some scientific quarters all too often becomes a dogmatic scientific religion, is blinding oneself to what is Science's greatest glory — its continuously enlarging field of vision brought about by changing ideas. Hence, to accept any step in scientific progress as the ultimate, as was so often done even by thoughtful scientific writers at the end of the nineteenth century, is simply attempting to build a temple upon ever-changing quicksand.

There are today in the scientific ranks men as scientifically dogmatic as ever the religionist in Occidental countries has been dogmatic in his religious beliefs. Any new discovery, any new fact, any new theory, particularly, is welcomed by these men with a very cold reception indeed, if it do not conform, at least on most points of contact, with orthodoxy in scientific thought!

As an illustration: some time ago, at Harrisburg in Illinois, there was found in a lump of coal of the Carboniferous Period a stem of an angiospermous plant. An angiosperm, as those who have studied botany know, is a plant which contains its seed in a capsule or pod or encasement of some kind; and this type of plant has always been supposed, according to the popular Darwinian evolutionist theory, to have been the very latest development of structure in time, and to have been preceded by the gymnosperms, or plants with more or less naked seed. The angiosperms are the prevailing form in the world today, while the gymnosperms were the prevailing form in the earlier and earliest geological periods. Examples of gymnosperms are pines, firs, larches, etc. The point of this discovery is that an angiosperm-relic was found among the fossils in an Era in which the gymnosperms alone have been popularly supposed by Darwinians to have had existence. In other words, a plant of a fully developed type supposedly belonging to a far later geologic Era was found, according to reports, in coal-deposits belonging to periods far preceding the alleged earliest evolution of this type. This discovery has received a mere and scanty mention and no more than that in a scientific paper which fell under the present writer's notice, and seems otherwise to have been ignored.

Is this a case where scientific theories were more true than the facts of Nature herself, i. e., if the discovery is an authentic one as seems to be unquestioned? Was this remarkable discovery set aside and ignored, although a fact of Nature, because it did not conform to scientific hypotheses? If so, is this Science, or the consequences of scientific dogmatism?

Another illustration: some time ago, at Scofield, Utah, in a deposit of the Cretaceous Period, which period belongs to the Mesozoic Age, there was found, according to report, what has been described as the entire fossilized foot of a one-toed horse. The one-toed horse is the very latest type in development of the Equidae, according to the Darwinian theory and other modern evolutionist theories; and this type is that of the horse today, the five-toed type having hitherto been found solely, it would seem, in geologic deposits of the Eocene

Period of the Tertiary Age — an Age which, as everybody knows, came millions of years later in time than the Cretaceous Period.

The Cretaceous Period, as remarked above, belongs to the Mesozoic or Secondary Age — an entire geologic epoch or stage before the appearance of the Tertiary deposits. Thus, according to the evolutionary theories based on all discoveries of horse-fossils hitherto made, the foot of a modern-type one-toed horse is found in a geological Era when even the primitive five-toed horse of the Eocene had never yet been heard of — or in other words, before Nature produced it!

It is of course within the bounds of possibility that these two illustrations, which have been intentionally taken from unacceptable discoveries, are no genuine discoveries at all but downright frauds, and one can imagine in his mind's eye wicked and perversely minded deceptionists deliberately planting or 'salting' the spots where these discoveries were made; but as no one, as far as the present writer knows, breathed a word contesting these discoveries, nor has offered any proof, however intangible, that these 'finds' are fraudulent, and as they have been passed over in utter silence by the entire scientific world, as far as the present writer is aware, the suggestion that they are frauds seems to be as arbitrary and unfounded in fact as one could well wish for. Time will show. One is reminded of the fate of the Calaveras skull and of other similar instances of discovery which have been rejected as unfounded but which a later day has proved to be as well authenticated as many things that are commonly accepted because falling within the frontiers of scientific hypothesis and unconscious prejudice.

Darwinians and other evolutionists are usually so certain of the history, as they have traced it, of the development of the horse through the periods of geologic time, that they even describe the five-toed beast of the Eocene Period as a small five-toed mammal not much larger than a modern fox; yet, if the second of the two discoveries above mentioned is authentic, there has been found the fully carbonized foot of a one-toed horse in deposits of the Cretaceous Period. This discovery, which if it can be proved to be authentic — and, as above stated, no one apparently has as yet disproved it — is ludicrously subversive of the evolutionary scheme of the accepted geologic history of the Equidae, and has been entirely ignored by responsible biologists and geologists, as far as one has been able to ascertain. If the discovery is an authentic one, it is a case of another scientific 'conspiracy of silence.'

The great men of science, however — the really great men — are always open-minded and indefatigable researchers for new light. It is rather the scientific popularizers — and they are very numerous — who are oft as dogmatic and as set in their ways of thinking as ever any dogmatic religionist has been, and sometimes they are fully as unreasonable. Some of these men have in very truth wrought more mischief in the world from a misunderstanding, and therefore because of a misteaching, of the truths of Nature, than the great-hearted men of science have ever been able to neutralize. The voice of these latter, the truly great, is always modest and their declarations are invariably restricted to ascertained fact. The consequence is that when they give to the world the results of researches and studies in the form of scientific deductions their voices are listened to with high respect and with an understanding recognition that their speculations are always as least well founded in theory even if a later day prove them to be erroneous.

Ultra-modern science is far more open-minded, as a whole, than was the science of a generation agone, when too many men actually insisted upon reading into Nature what they wanted to find there. Preconceptions, prejudices, prejudgments, too frequently represented the state of mind with which a large number of the scientists of thirty or forty years ago greeted any new fact of Nature or any new discovery that was brought to their attention; and the supporters of every such new fact or discovery had to fight a desperate battle for recognition before it was acknowledged as even a possibility. This was human nature then, as it is human nature now. If the facts did not conform to accepted theories, heaven help the facts!

VI

Today Science is everything to men, a goddess by whom they swear, and whose oracles are becoming the code of conduct by which men live. In former years Western thought turned to modern science in a pathetic reaction from the intellectual revulsion and rebellion brought about by dogmatisms of unreasonable, outworn religious creeds. Today men do not refer everything back to accepted religious statements as our more pious forebears did. Yet a new and in some respects a more truly religious spirit is nevertheless finding its silent way into men's minds and hearts. Having overthrown the old standards both of thought and conduct, humanity is desperately searching for new ones. Men, both individually and collectively, are becoming more inwardly critical and not so outwardly dogmatic. They are searching as they never have searched before, for some foundation in religious thinking which will give to them peace and hope; and in modern science they think they find it — at any rate, until very recently, they thought that they had found it. It was a sound instinct in a way, because it was an instinct which expressed itself in the thought: "We men are collectively a part of Nature. Nature is governed by inescapable law. It is throughout coherent and consistent with itself. Therefore, if we can really only understand it, and get the truth of Being in this manner, we shall know Reality — or as much of Reality as our minds can encompass. That Reality is in us as fully as it is in Nature." This instinct is thoroughly sound, for indeed it is no mere instinct at all, but a spiritual intuition; and truly, there can be no greater or nobler religion than this: the instinctive recognition of one's spiritual as well as material utter oneness with the Universe and the new and lively sense of moral responsibility that is thus born within us.

Science is becoming philosophical; indeed, 'philosophical' is an inadequate word, in a sense, because to Western ears it implies merely dry reasonings and dusty volumes of almost empty verbiage; science actually is becoming metaphysical and mystical, as observed elsewhere in this work. The cogitations and literary studies of the great modern scientific mathematicians, say what they may to the contrary, are as truly metaphysical — i. e., pertaining to ideas and substances 'beyond physics,' or beyond visible and tangible worlds — as are a vast number of the philosophical and religious ideas and fundamentals of thought which are found in the great Systems which have survived through many ages the most exacting intellectual probing and the loftiest spiritual investigation.

How can it be otherwise than that science, like every other human activity, should slowly or rapidly change as the case may be, with the incoming of new light and with the steadily enlarging treasure-house of garnered facts. We must never forget that the affairs and pursuits of men are, in the last analysis, the manifestations of the thoughts and ideals of men; and the thoughts of men always follow three distinct and separately characteristic types, as history abundantly demonstrates. They are: a religious era, always followed by a scientific era, invariably followed by a philosophical era, which ushers in again a new religious era, which gives way in its turn to a new scientific era, followed anew by a philosophical era; and thus the Wheel of Life turns continuously around. H. P. Blavatsky came to do her great work in a scientific era, and therefore her books were largely composed towards and shaped to breaking the scientific molds in the thoughts of men, although obviously her magnificent genius dealt beautifully, splendidly, as every reader of her works knows well enough, with equally great philosophical and religious questions likewise. This philosophical era that was due to come is now with us, or beginning to come to us. Science is becoming decidedly philosophical; day by day, year by year, the scientists are drawing more and more deftly and cleverly aside another and still another corner of the Veil of Isis, the spiritual Guardian and Inspirer of Nature, the fostering Spirit behind things; and with each such partial withdrawal of the Veil hiding the immaculate sublimity of Truth, do we see that the greatest of the men of science — not all of them but indeed many of them — are approaching closer and closer in their ideas to some of the fundamental Theosophical doctrines. These great men no longer dogmatize, even scientifically, but they pass their lifetime in research into and discovery of the facts in Nature; and now, as yet very dimly indeed, darkly as yet, they are receiving intimations of how Nature's worlds are builded and of how the forces invigorating and inspiriting these worlds work and urge upwards the countless hierarchies of entities and beings inhabiting them. There is thus a growing understanding of Nature, not of the physical sphere alone, but intimations of the existence of vast reaches of worlds existing in the Universal Cosmos, and indeed, likewise true intuitions of inner and spiritual realms which are the true causal and productive factors of the marvelous spread of things in the bosom of the Boundless All.

Science, if it proceeds steadily forwards and is not halted in its stride by the outbreak of some karmically cataclysmic disaster, is on the brink of wonderful discoveries. The bandages which man's egoism has placed over the eyes of the Goddess of Research, Science, have, to a certain extent, fallen away. The Goddess looks into the future and therein glimpses the faint outlines of what the generations of men in the future will be busy with. The attitude of her devotees today is no longer one of a wholly absorbing self-satisfaction with what has been achieved; they no longer consider past conquests in science as a completed and closed book of natural revelation, for in them today appears a divine hunger for a larger and more inclusive truth — a yearning which will not be stayed or put aside — for a greater light, for more light for ever.

CHAPTER XIII

BEHIND THE VEILS WITH SCIENCE — I

W E live in a wonderful web of worlds in Nature — worlds that are becoming, at least in their physical parts, more understandable to Occidental minds through the very remarkable discoveries that are in making in our times by the great men of science: discoveries in many respects remarkably corroborative of the Ancient Wisdom, the Esoteric Tradition, and thereby showing us in ever larger degree how amazingly the Sages and Seers of olden times interpreted Nature well and aright when such interpretations are examined in the light of modern scientific research and discovery. These discoveries, especially the very latest 'inventions' of our ultra-modern scientists, go far in elucidating the real facts, the causes behind the phenomena of the material Nature that surrounds us. Indeed, modern research and discovery, and the interpretation of the discoveries thus made, are elucidating, that is to say bringing into the light, and in many astonishing ways, the real meanings of some of the great teachings of the Sages and Seers of past times, who, up to our own epoch, have been all too often mocked at by the wiseacres of recent generations as being visionaries living in the dreams of the childhood of the human race. Were this true, most wonderful children were they! Marvelous children indeed, possessors of genius surpassing all that we have in our own era!

It is an interesting fact of human history, whose import is all too often forgotten even by the cleverest of European scholars, that the profoundest of philosophies which human genius has given birth to and elaborated are all of very hoary age, born in long past millennia; and it is asking too much of human credulity to suppose that the 'untutored mind' and the supposititious 'simple confiding and child-like trust' of primitive man, or of barbarian man, or of their relatively recent descendants, could have thought out such consistent and indeed highly scientific systems. Precisely the same observation may be made of the great and wide-spread religious systems of the archaic ages. The more these ancient philosophical and religious systems are examined, are studied, are analysed, the more is the modern imagination captured by them, because of their

subtil psychology, because of their often immense intellectual intri-
cacy, and because of the depth of spiritual penetration which they
manifest; and, last but not least, the reflexion grows upon one that
such highly elaborate and symmetrical systems of human thought,
swaying the minds of so many millions for so many ages, are obviously not the product of the minds of men inferior to the best that
the twentieth century itself has produced.

Or, in the case of human languages: philologers and linguists
have often expressed their astonishment that some of the languages
even yet spoken, albeit imperfectly, by what are now many of the
barbarian and savage peoples of the earth, should be so elaborate
both in vocabulary and in syntax. Of what possible use can such
languages be to barbarian or savage peoples of the present day,
whose simple lives and physical wants show no causal reasons for
such extended vocabularies and such intricacies of grammar! If
languages are the product of human genius and experience, as unquestionably they are, how is it that barbarian and savage man, who
had no need of so many words nor for such intricate grammatical
and syntactical relations, produced them? If a man had never seen
nor heard of an automobile, nor of an aeroplane, nor of an electric
light, it would be astounding to find these words in the vocabulary
of the language he uses imperfectly, and one would naturally question: Whence came these terms into his speech?[177]

Thus it is that not only language, but the surviving in existence
of these highly elaborated and metaphysically accurate religious and
philosophical systems, prove what to the reasoning mind is the
only explanation possible of the facts — that so-called modern barbarian or savage peoples, instead of being 'primitive,' as commonly

---

177. The point in illustration here is not that the savage or barbarian having
these terms in his language understands them, but that he does *not* understand
them, since they are words or names retained from pre-history in his language,
and which in his sight are either entirely inexplicable or are words used in tribal
mystical ceremonies, or in tribal initiations, or in their mythology as signifying
their divinities, or the powers or tools or instruments of the gods. The words
remain, but their real significance has been utterly forgotten.

It is, however, to be remembered that such linguistic fossils are of extremely
uncommon occurrence when dealing with things or events of a purely physical
or material character; but such fossils are very numerous when dealing with
more abstract things, such as pertain to philosophy, religion, mysticism, and the
like. The reason is that words dealing with physical things are more likely to
die and pass out of currency almost with the passing of the things themselves
when no longer in use; whereas words of religion or mysticism remain.

thought, are the degenerate descendants, the modern human relics, of civilizations of far past times, whose very existence has been lost track of in the night of pre-history, and who retain today but surviving remnants of what was once a highly developed culture.

The only exception to this, perhaps, at least the most noteworthy exception, is the Negro, who, instead of being a degenerate of once mighty sires, is 'primitive' as meaning a human stock still in its infancy or childhood, and destined at some time in the future to play a truly civilized part in world-history. But then the Negro will no longer be a Negro, for he will have mixed with many and different racial strains — a process of miscegenation which even now is taking place, despite the laws which the White Man in many countries has passed in the hopeful endeavor to stop it.

These civilizations of pre-history were indeed a fact, although virtually an easily attainable proof of their existence has long, long since vanished, save for relics or forgotten or half-forgotten and degenerate representations, such as has been briefly hinted at above. Every one of these great civilizations or races of archaic pre-history was at different times and in different manners guided and led by Great Men, whom it is convenient to class under the inclusive phrase Great Seers and Sages. No race of men and no part of the globe has existed without such high spiritual and intellectual guidance and over-seeing; although the continents on which some of these highly progressed, noble, and cultured civilizations were born and lived out their destiny, have ages since sunken under the waters of what are now the seas which roll their waves where once archaic man lived and builded.

These great Sages and Seers were as much the product of evolution, i. e., of unfolding and unwrapping of innate and latent genius, as are the outstanding spiritual and intellectual figures of today and of the annals of known history. Human beings of surpassing ability, spiritually and intellectually speaking, in part through initiation and in part by means of natural evolutionary unfolding, can pass behind or into or through the enshrouding veils of matter which so closely hem us in, and thus reach directly into the causal worlds and study these at first hand, returning from this most wonderful of human Adventures, enriched with garnered experience.

Yes, those Great Sages and Seers cast their percipient consciousness behind the veils of the outward seeming, doing so self-consciously, and saw things as they are at the Heart of Nature, following the threads, the marvelous reticulum, the intricate web-work, of invisible Nature into the inmost recesses reachable by them, and wherever that web-work exists, which is equivalent to saying every-where; and on their return to ordinary human life they cast their knowledge thus gained into the systematic philosophical, religious, and scientific formulation, which, in all the ages of the past, was the Mother-System of the great World-Religions and World-Philoso-phies, and which today in its modern presentation is called Theo-sophy — God-Wisdom, the Wisdom of the Gods, in other words the Esoteric Philosophy, or the Esoteric Tradition.

It is to be remembered that those ancients looked out upon the Nature surrounding them more or less just as we ourselves do. They had among them the Great Men, hereinbefore mentioned, 'Superior Men,' to use the old Chinese term; likewise all the human host of the past, and during all the hundreds of millennia of the past, also obviously included as the majority what we may call 'middling men,' that is to say, average men, just as most men and women today are average; and they likewise numbered among themselves 'inferior men,' just as we have them today. But it was these Great Men, these highly intuitive men, these men of expanded consciousness and titanic intellect and flashing spiritual vision, who saw, and seeing, who understood, and who, understanding, were able to formulate the System, the Mother-System just spoken of.

They believed, therefore, in a Universe builded on invisible causes — brought forth from invisible causes, and in consequence function-ing and operating through the qualities and attributes and powers flowing forth into exterior physical manifestation from those in-visible causes. The material universe which they saw, they said, is but the garment or veil which shadows forth, manifests, transmits, which lets us see, the working characteristics of those forces thus flowing forth from and out of the originant causes contained in the hierarchies of invisible worlds and their inhabitants. They said that these invisible causes are very frequently highly self-conscious invisible Beings, therefore living spiritual and intellectual entities, very much as we ourselves are self-conscious beings and living in-tellectual entities and therefore are originators of causative opera-tions which flow forth from our own thoughts and energic impulses into concrete manifestation around us. Man thinks and feels; he in-tuits and is conscious; because the Universe itself is a manifestation of consciousness and feeling, therefore of conscious forces and self-conscious powers. The Universe is, in fact, they said, but imbodied consciousnesses; and the human host is but one of the hierarchies of conscious beings thus infilling the Universe; and in very truth, making that Universe and spiritually and intellectually informing it.

Now what is Science — the supposed intellectual hope of modern humanity? It is the result of four things combined: human experience, human experiment or research, human reflexion or thinking, and correlation of the knowledge thus gained into systematic form.

This is precisely what the System which we call Theosophy is, and as it is presented to the world today. It is the result of innumerable ages of human experience, of human research and experiment by the Great Sages, the Masters of Life and of Wisdom, and of their deep thinking and reflexion, casting this Wisdom-Knowledge into systematic formulation. It is the result of their correlation of the knowledge that they have wrested from the womb of Nature and have formulated into systematic exposition. Such Great Men still live as a Brotherhood. They are humans of relatively immense spiritual and intellectual grandeur, whose flashing vision has penetrated into the deepest arcana of matter or substance, and of force or energy; and they have been able to do this, because the faculties and powers within them which allow them to do it are directly derivative from the same faculties and qualities and powers which operate in the Universe itself; and in this sense they are but discovering what they themselves essentially are, which is equivalent to saying, finding what the Cosmos essentially itself is. Human ability to do this arises in the fact that man's constitution is wholly derivative, both in general and in particular, from the Universe in which he moves and lives and has his being. Man but repeats in himself and in the small, as the microcosm, whatever Great Nature herself is and contains as the Macrocosm.

As the mystic Jakob Böhme wrote:

> For the Book in which all mysteries lie, is man himself: he himself is the book of Being of all beings, seeing he is the likeness of Divinity. The Great Arcanum lies in him; the revealing of it belongs only to the Divine Spirit.[178]

Man as a ray of this Divine Spirit can ascend along that ray until he is enabled to read all the pages that his thus developing consciousness allows him to read in this Book of Life and Being of the surrounding Universe and of himself.

These Great Men know truth instantly when they see it, for their consciousness is becoming universal in proportion and relative to their inner development or evolution. Having raised themselves into self-conscious union, in greater or less degree, with the All-Self, they thereby become proportionately conversant with and operate upon

---

178. *Epistle* IX, par. 3.

the fields where the All-Self is and operates, and this is everywhere. Nor do they laboriously have to work among millions of details and carefully to sift therefrom the facts which constitute recorded scientific experience and knowledge.

This Wisdom which they have discovered and gathered is as certain and sure in fundamentals as are the principles of mathematics — a branch of this Wisdom. Like mathematics it is wholly self-consistent and its proofs are found in itself, which is equivalent to saying *found in Nature*. It is ordered Knowledge therefore; in other words, Science *per se*.

I

Let us see then, by brief study in this and in the following chapter, how near Modern Science has approached and is approaching to this Sacred and Secret Science of the archaic ages. Certainly we are living in a marvelous age. Our modern scientists are becoming more than scientists — they are becoming scientific mystics. Our chemistry is becoming alchemy, a super-chemistry. Our astronomy is becoming more and more like ancient astrology, for our astronomers no longer try solely to find out the exact modes of the movements of the celestial bodies and where they ought to be at certain specified times, and more or less what the physical composition of these celestial bodies is, but they are casting their minds, as did the ancient Sages and Seers, forwards and backwards in an endeavor to try to pierce the veils of the phenomenal seeming; and this very effort in itself is one of the noblest exercises of the human intellect; for it is in fact a yearning to pass beyond mere brain-mind thinking into the realm of invisible causes, into what is in sheer truth the realm of metaphysics,[179] and scientists in certain other branches of human research are, perhaps only half-consciously, attempting to do the same thing.

Professor A. S. Eddington, when writing recently of Space, Time, and Gravitation, openly says that theories of materialistic physics reach no ultimate realities whatsoever — which of course is a statement of obvious fact. Nevertheless it is significant to have this

---

179. "It is plain that the physicist is becoming deeply involved in metaphysics. . . . The physicist might have gone for advice to the philosophers, but in that case he should have become more confused than ever, since philosophy has followed no definite method and is for the most part in the grip of the old physics which has now broken down. We may hope that out of the new physics may evolve a more intelligent metaphysics." — *Three Interpretations of the Universe*, pp. 168-9 (Macmillan, 1934). Quoted by the kind permission of the author, J. E. Boodin, Professor of Philosophy, University of California, at Los Angeles.

acknowledgement by one of the most eminent men in ultra-modern scientific research, for it shows that scientific thinkers today are rapidly advancing out of the realms of an imagination captured and held shackled in the bonds of a now outworn materialistic conception of Nature into fields of actualities, and to a great extent are freeing themselves from the formerly universally prevalent attitude of scientific egoistic self-sufficiency that one's own conceptions of Nature are cosmic realities.

Unfortunately, the candid observer of the trend of scientific thought, especially along the new mathematical lines presently so favored, must acknowledge that even yet there remains no small bias to look upon the conclusions of mathematical investigation, often based upon very shaky premises, as actualities in themselves. We must never forget that the mathematical mill produces finally only what is put into it: in other words, and to change the figure of speech, mathematical deductions or conclusions are logically based upon certain premises upon which are wrought certain mathematical operations; and if these premises be supposititious or speculative, or not actually founded throughout on natural fact, the conclusions derivative therefrom are bound of necessity to carry the imprint or taint — if the word be pardoned — of the defects that the premises themselves contain. In other words, again, mathematics *per se* are no absolutely certain instrument for uncovering or discovering or unveiling verities in Nature, but are a fairly perfect instrument for tooling whatever premises may be subjected to them. Mathematics are a means or rather a method of abstract thinking concerning relations among things; but cannot be used apart from the original premises upon which mathematical work is done.[180]

---

180. "Mathematical physicists have enjoyed the atmosphere of mystification which their complicated formulae have made possible. They have informed us that we must not try to make any sensible models of the primary level of nature. We must think of it merely as mathematical waves or curves of probability. We must not ask what the waves are waves of. They are just waves in the equations. Recently there has been a reaction from this mystification. Physicists are beginning to recognise . . . that our mathematical models, however complicated, are merely symbolic statements of the data we derive from sense-experience. . . . The chemists have held aloof from the mathematical orgy and have tried to make workable the more imaginative models of Rutherford and Bohr. . . . A recent experiment by Jesse W. M. Dumond at the California Institute of Technology shows that the earlier imaginative model of the atom by Rutherford and Bohr contains important truth." — *Three Interpretations of the Universe*, p. 159. Quoted by the kind permission of the author, J. E. Boodin.

Professor Eddington poetically and very truthfully says that we form theories about life and the Universe which are shaped in our own image and patterned after the forms of our own minds. These are true and wise words, and everybody who thinks about the matter knows it perfectly well. It stands to reason that the human mind can think only thoughts that the human mind contains. This indeed is very true. We begin to realize that we see the shadows of the thinking of our own minds, the images of our own thoughts, instead of cosmic realities *in themselves* that science all too frequently has hitherto fondly imagined those shadows to be.

Professor Eddington is in many respects an intuitive man; he is one of those rare minds who can, by the force of pure native genius, at times by intuition — if one like the term better — cast his understanding, when the mood to do so is upon him, through and beyond appearances into noumena, i. e., into the causal realms behind the phenomena; although naturally, because he is no initiate, his intuitions are often halting, and his vision by the same token is often, despite his best will, imperfect. All human steps of progress in thinking and in discovery are slow and faltering at first, as must be the case with human researchers.

Some little time ago, in speaking before a meeting of the English Royal Society, he probably amazed that gathering of eminent men by his declaration in regard to the need of a radical modification of our ideas concerning the nature and dynamical characteristics of the electron, which, as we all know, is now supposed to be the ultimate — or nearly the ultimate — element of physical substance; and he went on to say, as we understand, that such a modification was a necessity and was timely: in other words, that it was high time that such a change in conceptual outlook should occur with regard to our views of the range of consciousness in Nature.

This new attitude is a distinctly encouraging one; and the Theosophist can do no otherwise than voice his sincere commendation of the new visioning of Nature that is coming to scientifiç men.

A. Wolf, Professor of Scientific Theory, London University, in an English paper, quotes Eddington as follows:

It is Professor Eddington's theory that they [physical occurrences] all partake — everything partakes — of the nature of mental activity, of consciousness, or sub-consciousness, sometimes of a low and sometimes of a higher order, and these mental activities can be described by other and higher minds, but all things have a consciousness of self, which is different from their appearance in the consciousness of other minds and from the description.

Professor Eddington here is quoted as saying — and saying truly, thus echoing the ancient Esoteric Wisdom of Immemorial Time — that the Universe is infilled with consciousness expressing itself through innumerable consciousnesses, and that to a certain extent we can interpret them; first of all, however, understanding that we interpret them strictly according to the framework of our own specific and peculiar consciousness. Hence any such descriptive interpretation, as we humans must necessarily figurate it, is *de facto* imperfect because of our own imperfectly developed consciousness; nevertheless, every entity everywhere, whose consciousness we might attempt to interpret and to describe, has its own understanding of its own consciousness, which it understands better than any other one can understand it or interpret it or describe it to be. This seems to be his meaning, and it is obviously true.

In a review several years ago of Professor Eddington's book, *The Nature of the Physical World,* appeared the following:

> Perhaps the most important aspect of these new ideas is to be found in the insight they give us into the limitations of exact science. Instead of knowledge of substance, science gives us knowledge purely of structure, and instead of revealing a strict determinism in Nature, science has to be content with probabilities. But is the whole of our knowledge confined to what can be reached by scientific methods? Professor Eddington suggests that our own consciousness gives us a clue to the actual nature of the material of which science tells us nothing but its structure. We have peculiarly intimate knowledge of certain collections of atoms — namely, our brains. It is our own succession of feelings that constitutes the stuff of what is described by an outside observer as 'brain-matter.' Accordingly, Professor Eddington suggests that the stuff of the world may be what he calls 'mind-stuff.'

People of olden times, and even of recent times, frequently used to call essential matter by the name of Mind, but now, following Eddington, for a time at least, they will call it 'mind-stuff.' The name is thus changed a bit, but the idea or thing is the same — although the ancients, in speaking of mind-stuff, it must be carefully noted, meant something purely spiritual, indeed at times super-spiritual, the Cosmic Soul, in fact; whereas ultra-modern scientists have risen apparently no higher in conceptual allusion than to ethereal substance — one remove or at best two removes beyond and within the physical sphere.

More than forty years ago, H. P. Blavatsky wrote in her magazine, *Lucifer,* upon the subject of consciousness as existing in the atom. Her article was called forth by another article written by the well-known journalist and contributor to various magazines, George

Parsons Lathrop, and dealt with the religious views of Mr. Edison. Edison was at one time a member of the Theosophical Society. She said:

Edison's conception of matter was quoted in our March editorial article. The great American electrician is reported by Mr. G. Parsons Lathrop in *Harper's Magazine* as giving out his personal belief about the atoms being "possessed by a certain amount of intelligence," and shown indulging in other reveries of this kind. For this flight of fancy the February *Review of Reviews* takes the inventor of the phonograph to task and critically remarks that "Edison is much given to dreaming," his "scientific imagination" being constantly at work.

Would to goodness the men of science exercised their "scientific imagination" a little more and their dogmatic and cold negations a little less. Dreams differ. In that strange state of being which, as Byron has it, puts us in a position "with seal'd eyes to see," one often perceives more real facts than when awake. Imagination is, again, one of the strongest elements in human nature, or in the words of Dugald Stewart it "is the great spring of human activity, and the principal source of human improvement. . . . Destroy the faculty, and the condition of men will become as stationary as that of brutes." It is the best guide of our blind senses, without which the latter could never lead us beyond matter and its illusions. The greatest discoveries of modern science are due to the imaginative faculty of the discoverers.[181]

How true that is! Probably there has not been one single great scientific discovery, arising out of the process of brain-mind reasoning from *a* to *b* to *c*, and eventuating in success: but always there was the yearning for truth, the intuitive visioning; then suddenly came the light, and the thing was seen — however dimly, however imperfectly sketched. To continue:

But when has anything new been postulated, when a theory clashing with and contradicting a comfortably settled predecessor put forth, without orthodox science first sitting on it, and trying to crush it out of existence? . . .[182]

Scientists today are becoming the best friends of Theosophists, i. e., students of the Esoteric Tradition; but in those days there was a deal of scientific dogmatism: a wretched, miserable, haughty dogmatism, just as much of it as there was in the churches — of a different type to be sure, yet equally dogmatic in its way. If a man in those days even spoke of the 'soul,' though he spoke of it *sotto voce*, he was considered to be just a trifle soft-headed, or mayhap soft-hearted; in any case it was thought that something was wrong with him somewhere.

---

181. *Lucifer*, April, 1890, article 'Kosmic Mind,' Vol. VI, p. 89.
182. *Op. cit.*, pp. 89-90.

Man in those days was considered by the scientists to be an 'animate machine.' The Universe was also a mechanism that ran itself. There was no spirit, no soul, no life anywhere; mechanisms everywhere, machines which ran themselves—and nobody knew how! To continue the citation:

Is it then, because consciousness in every universal atom and the possibility of a complete control over the cells and atoms of his body by man, have not been honored so far with the *imprimatur* of the Popes of exact science, that the idea is to be dismissed as a dream? Occultism gives the same teaching. Occultism tells us that every atom, like the monad of Leibnitz, is a little universe in itself; and that every organ and cell in the human body is endowed with a brain of its own, with memory, therefore, experience and discriminative powers. The idea of Universal Life composed of individual atomic lives is one of the oldest teachings of esoteric philosophy, and the very modern hypothesis of modern science, that of *crystalline life,* is the first ray from the ancient luminary of knowledge that has reached our scholars. If plants can be shown to have nerves and sensations and instinct (but another word for consciousness), why not allow the same in the cells of the human body? Science divides matter into organic and inorganic bodies, only because it rejects the idea of *absolute* [i. e., Universal] *life* and a life-principle as an entity: otherwise it would be the first to see that *absolute* [i. e., Universal] *life* cannot produce even a geometrical point, or an atom inorganic in its essence. . . .

Now to lay at rest once for all in the minds of Theosophists this vexed question, we intend to prove that modern science . . . is itself on the eve of discovering that consciousness is universal [Eddington's mind-stuff] — thus justifying Edison's "dreams." But before we do this, we mean also to show that though many a man of science is soaked through and through with such belief, very few are brave enough to openly admit it. . . .[183]

The sporadic utterances of some of our modern scientists show how true were the above words of H. P. Blavatsky. Sir James Jeans, in an interview published in *The Observer* (London), when asked the question: "Do you believe that life on this planet is the result of some sort of accident, or do you believe that it is a part of some great scheme?" replied thus:

I incline to the idealistic theory that consciousness is fundamental, and that the material universe is derived from consciousness, not consciousness from the material universe. If this is so, then it would appear to follow that there is a general scheme. . . . In general the universe seems to me to be nearer to a great thought than to a great machine. It may well be, it seems to me, that each individual consciousness ought to be compared to a brain cell in a universal mind. . . .

---

183. *Op. cit.,* pp. 90-1.

And he significantly concluded the interview with the statement: "I do not think I have the right to give a definite opinion on any of the questions that we have discussed this afternoon." Why not? Once that a scientific man states that what he says is his own opinion, definite or otherwise, he certainly has as much right to give it as have other scientists who seem to manifest no such reluctance or hesitation in making statements of a far more aggressively assertive character. One certainly is driven to commend such modesty, with the regret, however, that scientific modesty is not always as strongly vocal as it might be.

The great German scientist, Max Planck, in a similar interview, published in *The Observer*, when asked, "Do you think that consciousness can be explained in terms of matter?" replied:

No, I regard consciousness as fundamental. I regard matter as derivative from consciousness. We cannot get behind consciousness. Everything that we talk about, everything that we regard as existing, postulates consciousness.

Citations might be made from a number of other equally great scientific luminaries all running to the same definite conclusion, but it is unnecessary to do so here. The main point is that some of the greatest, perhaps the greatest, men of science today are beginning to re-echo one of the fundamental philosophical postulates of the Esoteric Tradition, that 'Mind' or 'Consciousness' is of the essence of the Universe, and that such 'Mind' or 'Consciousness' is perforce operative and self-manifesting in every part or point of the incomprehensibly vast Cosmic Whole.[184]

---

184. In passing, it seems appropriate here to allude to a beautiful and thoughtful book, *Plant Autographs and Their Revelations,* written by one of the most remarkable scientific men and thinkers that have appeared in the last century or so, the Hindû scientist, Sir Jagadis Chunder Bose. Before his time, it was commonly thought that plants were not animate entities; that they had movement and substance, indeed, but that they had no individualized life or 'soul'; that they had no actual circulatory system; that they had no nerves; that they had no feelings. Indeed, as regards a circulatory system, it was thought that such could not exist in a plant-body, even in the face of the seasonal mounting and descent of plant-sap, which truly marvelous phenomenon no scientist has ever explained because no one has ever understood it — and such explanation as might have been made from such knowledge as was then to be had, was oversaddled by the dogmatic conviction that the human beings and the beasts were the only ones possessing life and more or less voluntary action.

Now this remarkable Hindû proves through his exceedingly clever apparatus, electrical and otherwise, for the study of plant-life and for recording the pulse-

So that beyond, behind, within everything, the atom for instance, and within the electronic infinitesimals composing the atom, is a consciousness-center — or what the Esoteric Philosophy calls a Jîva, and which, adopting the Pythagorean word, made familiar to European philosophers through Leibniz, we may call a Monad, or unit of Individuality. Indeed, according to the Ancient Wisdom, every atom is an organism, an organic living entity, an atom thus being the vehicle or manifestation of a transcendent but imperfectly expressed 'soul' and ultimately of a god enshrined therein. In other words, the soul-life of the atom is an intermediate portion of the invisible and ethereal atomic structure which flows forth from the monadic center or root at the 'back of beyond,' so to say, of each physical atomic unit.

The modern scientist is already preparing the way for this larger conception when through his researches he can declare that the atom is no longer considered to be a blindly driven, senseless, lifeless, inert particle of dead matter: driven by blind fate, urged by fortuity, attracted hither and yon by haphazard chance, but is a composite entity made up of electrical points or charges.

II

The Danish physicist, Bohr, in 1913, evolved a conception of the physical atom which was exceedingly interesting, approximating in certain degree to the Theosophical view, and which — despite the modifications of the Bohr theory which have been made since 1913 — explains electro-magnetic and other phenomena of Nature with almost uncanny precision: to wit, that the physical atom is a sort of solar system in miniature, or, conversely, that our solar system or any other solar system is a cosmic atom. Each such atom has its atomic 'sun,' which the scientists today call a *proton,* or aggregate of protons combined with electrons, and also has its planet or planets which are called *electrons,* whirling with incredible speed about their central atomic sun. In the case of the hydrogen atom,

---

beat and functions of life in plants, that plants have indeed nerves and are plant-conscious — not animal-conscious nor human-conscious, but plant-conscious; that they can be poisoned, and cured through the administration of the proper antidote; that they become tired; that they must have rest; that they have a circulatory system, and a nervous system also; that they are very much alive, in other words. The apparatus for this most fascinating study was invented by Sir Jagadis C. Bose himself, and great credit is due to him, not merely for that, but for his method in applying his apparatus to the study and consequent explanation of the circulatory and nervous channels in the plant's body.

which is modernly supposed to be the primordial building-brick of physical matter, there is but one planet or electron, with its one proton or atomic sun.

The great value of Bohr's conception was that it is analogical; that is to say, it follows the pattern laid down by other and larger structures and processes of Nature. What Nature does in one place, very logically and indeed of necessity she repeats in other places, because she follows one ultimate fundamental law or course of action operative throughout her entire extent. Bohr's entire conception is an unconscious tribute to the very ancient and esoteric doctrine of Analogy. For analogy is a method of reasoning based on Nature herself and on her alone; and, despite many disclaimers to the contrary, some of them rather irritable, it is becoming more and more in modern times apparent as a mode of reasoning, perhaps only half-consciously followed by our ultra-modern scientific theorists or theories. It must be noted, however, that there are such things as false analogies only too easy to fall into, which are in consequence misrepresentations of Nature's functionings and events, and against these false analogies the student has to be constantly on guard.[185]

Bohr's theory that the atom is a kind of miniature solar system, whatever defects this theory may in future be proved to have, at least is correspondential to all Nature as we know it. It is based on analogical reasoning; it is not a mere hypothesis arbitrarily evolved to meet a supposed need, or a supposed want, of a passing phase of ultra-modern physics which confessedly is still but an ambitious infant. It is precisely this combination of analogical reasoning, however half-consciously done by Bohr, with the other scientific idea of the substance of matter being essentially force, which renders the Bohr atom so attractive, at least in its general outline, to the Theosophical student. Time will show how much of truth Bohr's

---

185. There is another still more recent conception of the structural character of the physical atom, still more ultra-modern than was Bohr's. It is due to the work of physicists such as Schroedinger, de Broglie, and others, whose opinions may be found in any work of modern physics.

To the Theosophist, the newer conception of the internal structure and functions of the atom is as interesting and temporarily as acceptable as was the Bohr-atom. Either structure is in essence an electrical entity, whether it be diffuse as Schroedinger said, or more strictly patterned after the manner of our solar system as Bohr said. The point of importance is that the composition of the atom, whatever its structure and internal organization may be, is electrical, i. e., an entity builded of forces, expressing themselves as matter; this is strictly in line, as far as it goes, with the teaching of the Esoteric Philosophy.

picture of the atom contained,[186] and how much of truth is involved in later theories of atomic structure — time and experiment as conducted by our really remarkable leaders in physical chemistry. Whether future research will show that Bohr or any later worker was the more exact in evolving a conception of atomic structure, matters not in the least for our present purpose; the essential conceptions seem to be more or less the same in pretty nearly all modern theories of atomic structure, to the effect that the atom is built mostly of etheric spaces, and that the particles of the substance that it contains consist of electricity variously compounded of its 'positive' and 'negative' qualities or parts.

Thus therefore the physical world so seemingly solid to our senses, reduced to its ultimates, is mostly 'emptinesses' or etheric spaces, with almost innumerable particles of negative or positive electricity, electrons, protons, positrons, etc., mutually acting and interacting, and by their common labor producing all the physical world and likewise all its component parts.

Incredible is the rapidity of movement which is assigned by modern scientific theory to these electric particles. Dr. E. E. Fournier d'Albe wrote in *The Observer* of London several years ago about the orbits of these electrons and their rate in speed and time as they pursue their supposed orbital course around their atomic protonic sun:

> In this miniature solar system [of the atom] the year would be represented by the time of one revolution [of an electron] round the central 'sun,' and as these revolutions take place at the rate of about a thousand million millions [or one quadrillion in American numeration] per second, it is clear that while we watch, even for a moment, untold ages and geological eras of atomic time are passing by.

Professor W. F. G. Swann gives a still more modern view of atomic time as founded in an electronic revolution or electronic year when compared with human time.[187]

There are beings in this Universe whose time-movement is so slow that were our solar system, which today has been called a 'cosmic atom' by certain intuitive scientists — one of the teachings of the Esoteric Tradition — to be conceived by them as an atomic system, then the revolution of our planet Terra around our central luminary, which revolution we call a year, would be an incalculably small period of time to them — in fact smaller to them than is the

---

186. See footnote No. 180, page 408.

187. Vide *The Architecture of the Universe*, pp. 56-7 (1934).

revolution of an electron around its atomic sun, which constitutes an atomic year, small in time to us. On the other hand, to infinitesimal beings whom we may imagine, if you please, with perfect justice, as living and having their life-period on an atomic electron — one of the atomic planets — one of our years would be a quasi-eternity.

The life of our Universe, while contrasted with infinity is but the wink of an eye, so to speak, yet to us it seems as quasi-eternity, for it lasts for many trillions of human years; and after the same manner of thinking, man's life is but a fleeting instant in endless duration, although it is of immense time-length as contrasted with the bewilderingly rapid appearances and disappearances of infinitesimals in the atomic world.

We are told also by scientific thinkers that the atomic distances separating electron from electron and these from their protonic center or sun are relatively as great in the atom as are the distances in our cosmic solar system separating planet from planet and these from our sun, and there is no reason in the world why this most suggestive teaching or declaration or statement of ultra-modern science is not perfectly true. One must remember that to ourselves all things in this Universe are relative, as stated before, and in consequence that such supposedly fundamental things as space and time are as relative as all other things contained by them. Indeed, in one sense of the word, both space and time, as is taught by the Esoteric Philosophy, are *mâyâvi* or illusory in the sense that neither the latter nor the former, when we give to the term 'space' the meaning of extension, is external in the European sense; and because in European usage the terms 'space' and 'time' are both directly related to physical things or 'events' and therefore distinctly temporary, neither can be called 'absolute,' and this, according to Einstein, is perfectly correct in this aspect or portion of his Relativity Theory.[188]

---

188. The frequent reference to Einstein and his Relativity Theory as found in Theosophical writings does not imply a wholesale acceptance of this theory, and especially not of the mathematical deductions drawn therefrom. It is the fundamental idea of relation, or of relativities, that the Theosophist finds to be true in Nature, and therefore equally true to the teachings of the Esoteric Tradition. Yet the Theosophical student has always envisaged the high probability that after the Einsteinian theory has run its course, or has had a certain vogue, some new mathematician will come to the fore with another theory, perhaps more novel even than that which Einstein evolved, and this new theory would either greatly modify the relativity theory of Einstein, or perhaps even supplant

The atoms which compose our bodies are builded thus, according to modern scientific ideas, and therefore are infinitesimal copies or repetitive reflexions of that larger Cosmic Atom which human knowledge calls the solar system. Just as the interplanetary spaces are empty, or nearly so, of visible physical things, and are therefore called emptinesses, so are our bodies mostly such 'spacial vacancies.' But it must not be imagined for a moment that these 'vacancies' are actually 'nothingness'; that idea is enormously absurd. These spacial vacancies, so called, are filled full with ethereal substances even as the cosmic spaces of our solar system and the greater kosmic Spaces of our Galactic Universe are filled full with kosmic ether.

III

The most interesting deduction that we could and indeed should draw from the foregoing reflexions is — just as the Esoteric Philosophy has taught from immemorial time — that what we humans call physical appearances of things are but transitory 'events' or illusory and fugitive episodes, on and in that particular Cosmic Space of the solar system which we call our physical world; and that in point of fact, this physical world itself is mostly composed or woven of 'holes' or so-called and mis-called 'empty spaces.' We say 'empty' only because our gross physical senses, such as the organs of sight and touch which have been evolved to cognise and to report only things of physical matter, tell us nothing of the inner and invisible, because highly ethereal, worlds and spheres and realms, which we

---

it because of the newer theory's superior scientific worth and accuracy in prediction and explanation.

Some such newer theory already seems to have come to birth, according to report, and is the mind-child of an Indian scientist and mathematician, Sir Shah Sulaiman, M. A., LL. D., who is Chief Justice of the High Court of Allahâbâd, India. This new mathematical prodigy — the present writer here refers to the theory and not to the eminent Hindû whose child it is — is stated to be more powerful in prediction and more accurate in explanation than is the theory of Einstein; and among other things it is claimed for it that the mathematical equations of this theory reduce to the equations of Newton as a first approximation and to those of Einstein as a second approximation.

As instances of its greater accuracy in prediction, it is stated that this new theory of Sir Shah Sulaiman foretells almost perfectly, if not perfectly, the amount of the shift of the Fraunhofer lines in the Sun's spectrum; and, as concerns the deflection of star-light as it passes close to the sun, this new theory is stated to be far greater in accuracy than is that of Einstein.

thus collect under the single term 'etheric spaces' or 'empty spaces.'

Probably the actual so-called solid physical units — let us call them electrons, etc. — which compose the substantial part of my physical body, when closely assembled, thus leaving to one side the 'empty spaces,' could be compressed into a volume little larger than a pin-head. So that we see immediately that so far as mere volume or spacial extension is concerned, our physical bodies are indeed true illusions as regards bulk, yet very real to us because our sense-organs live in this world of 'bulky' illusion.

As an example: I enter a railway train. I take a seat. My body touches the seat, presses it, apparently, and physically deforms it; the seat is screwed to the framework of the car, into the wood-work, which in turn rests upon the metal carriage, which in turn rests upon the wheels, which roll over the steel rails, and the rails rest upon the earth, and the earth is builded of various particles of soil — stone and what not. Yet at each one of these steps in our picture there is no absolute physical contact whatsoever between any two of them — no physical contact between any two of the series.

I am but apparently touching the chair on which I sit. Not a particle of my body actually touches it: the electrons of which my body is composed are repelled by the electronic vibrations of which the chair-seat is composed. The chair is screwed into the wood of the car of the railway coach; but those screws do not actually touch the wood, although they have broken it. This wood is again clamped to the metal body of the car. To us these clamped links seem tight and solid and absolutely in contact; yet not a particle of that wood actually touches the steel. The steel-carriage rests on the axles of the wheels, yet not a particle of that resting steel actually touches, is in absolute physical contact with, the metallic substance of the wheels. The wheels as they roll along the tracks actually do not touch the railroad-tracks at all; they roll along on ether. Every particle of the wheel which seems to touch the track and *vice versa,* consists of electronic and other particles of negative and positive charges, and they repel each other. The rails supposedly rest solid-ly on the earth, yet the same statement of fact is true there likewise; the rails are not in absolute contact with the earth. The earth itself is composed of these various electronic and other materials, and yet not a single mathematical point of any one of these materials has absolute physical contact with any other; they are held apart by electric repulsive forces, residing in the electrons, protons, etc., of which the atoms are builded. What an illusory world it is we live in!

Hence we see something of what 'matter' is: it is, first, the atomic forces or vibrations as well as the balancing among themselves of these forces; working, second, in open spaces relatively as vast as those which form the solar system and the Universe around our physical earth. 'Matter' therefore, as we humans find it, is really an illusion; for first we do not see it as it is, and, second, not seeing it as it is, we imagine it to be something that it is not.

Take as an instance the constitution of an atom of hydrogen, the simplest atom as yet known to science. The hydrogen atom is composed of two electric particles, one positive, called the proton, which according to theory is the central sun of the atom, and one negative particle, called the electron, which is the atomic 'planet' whirling around its central nucleus or proton with vertiginous speed. A quadrillion times mayhap — some scientists say more than one quadrillion times — does it circle in its orbit around its atomic sun in the short space of one human second. What is the result of this vertiginous movement, as we humans sense that result? Tiny, infinitesimal, as this whirling electron is, its speed is so great that, if we had the power to put our finger upon it, or even tried to touch it, we should feel resistance arising from the incredible speed of the whirling of this electron around its central sun, forming as it were a streak of something solid, or a belt or shell which to our gross physical flesh would then be sensed as highly tangible. We would sense it as what we call 'matter,' and yet this 'matter' is but a charge of negative electricity, in other words of force.

We may indeed ask ourselves: What is matter? What is the material side of being? We now know that 'matter is mostly holes'; matter is mostly spaces; matter is mostly 'emptinesses.' It is obvious that if we consider our solar system, we see that the larger part of it is what is called vacuity or space, the sun and the planets forming but a small part of the space within the confines of it; and so is it exactly the case, according to the theory, with the atom. The protonic sun and the electronic planets are but a very small part of the space which the atom contains; and yet out of these 'empty' atoms is built up all the physical matter which we know of, of any kind whatsoever, from the most ethereal gas to the most dense of metals. Truly is our physical world essentially an unreal world, an illusory world.

Eddington gives us in his book, *The Nature of the Physical World,* an admirably phrased view of the modern scientific conception of physical matter, pointing out that 'matter' has been dissolved by ultra-modern scientific specialists into points of energy existing in a void. Professor Eddington in thus speaking of a 'void' filled with atoms scattered sporadically, recalls to mind very curiously what was taught by the old Greek theorists of the Atomistic School of philosophers, a School supposed to have been founded by Leucippus and Democritus, who taught that the 'ultimates' of all things are atoms and a void. But their teachings have never been properly understood by moderns. They did not mean by τὸ κενόν (to kenon) — which are the Greek words usually translated by 'vacuum' — 'void,' what this word is understood to signify in modern times, utter or absolute emptiness. They meant an absence of the matter which is subject to perception by the senses of man; but the very basis of their thought was the existence of an ethereal field or ocean in Space — when properly understood, SPACE itself — which by comparison with the grossness of illusory physical matter was called the 'Void.'

In modern times this ethereal cosmic substance has commonly been called ether; and, indeed, the Greeks themselves often spoke of *aether* from which our moderns have taken their word 'ether.'[189]

---

189. In view of the confusion of ideas almost universally prevalent in scientific circles as well as in philosophical, a confusion with equal universality shared by the average 'man in the street,' concerning the nature of ether, or aether as the Theosophist prefers to write it, it may be as well to subjoin the following suggestions as aids to the thought of the reader or student.

The ether, or ethers, of scientific speculation of the nineteenth century, is by many thoughtful scientists today discarded as an outworn or outmoded idea; and not a few of the most progressive men of science today seriously question whether there is such a thing as the cosmic ether. Certain ones of these ultra-modern scientists, such as Eddington, for example, are inclined to look upon the terms 'ether' and 'space' as interchangeable — and Eddington is even now beginning to write 'aether' after the manner of the ancient Greeks.

In strict accuracy it is quite wrong and without other foundation of fact than mere theory to suppose that space and aether are one and the same thing or identic, at least this is the fact in the view of the Esoteric Philosophy, in which Aether, cosmically speaking, is the material substratum of manifestation or differentiation or rather substantial substratum thereof, and therefore is virtually identic with what in the Ancient Wisdom is technically called Âkâśa or even what is almost the same thing, Mûlaprakṛiti or Root-Nature, or Root-Space. Now it is obvious that in any particular cosmic hierarchy, the Mûlaprakṛiti or Âkâśa thereof, otherwise its Aether, fills all the space of the said hierarchy and therefore is to be considered as virtually identical with the space of that hierarchy, being the Mother-substance of the said cosmic hierarchy.

Yet as these Cosmic Hierarchies are literally innumerable in the bosom of the Boundless and are therefore to be considered as infinite in number, the respective aethers of these incomputably great numbers of Cosmic Hierarchies

The Esoteric Philosophy does not postulate the existence of any such thing as an utterly *absolute void,* which would be, apparently, identic with the old theologic idea of nothingness. The conception when carefully analysed is seen to be but phantasy, as

---

are to be considered as all contained within the still more incomprehensibly vast Space of Boundless Infinitude. But this does not mean that Space is therefore an 'infinite emptiness' or mere spacial containment, in other words that Space is but a frontierless container; for this would be philosophically inaccurate and therefore faulty both in conception and in the reasoning flowing from the conception.

Space is in fact the term used by the Esoteric Philosophy to signify the Boundless cosmic deeps themselves, without frontier, without beginning, without ending, *being* from eternity unto eternity; whereas the Cosmic Hierarchies as they appear in their cyclical manifestations bring forth by evolutional emanation from within themselves the fields of aether, which from inner up-surging impulses directed by cosmic intelligence develop forth the diversity of differentiation.

From the foregoing it should be clear that while aether for any comprised 'portion' of Space is co-extensive with the space of such comprised portion, the aether therefore is a production in and of the all-inclusive spacial deep of that hierarchy. Again, from the foregoing we are obliged to draw the philosophical deduction that space is virtually interchangeable as a term with what we may call Divinity — not any 'one' divinity which would mean limitation, but the abstract frontierless and timeless Divinity of boundless duration and frontierless being.

The student of the Esoteric Philosophy smiles, yet smiles with sympathetic understanding, when he hears the 'ether' of science, whether accepted or rejected, described as a 'jelly' or when he hears attributes given unto it such as fluidity or rigidity, etc. What the scientists really mean when they speak of ether is truly the root-nature or Mûlaprakṛiti or Mother-substance of any one cosmic plane, and of course our scientists mean the physical plane or physical world, for it is the only world they know anything about. As a matter of fact, there is a Mûlaprakṛiti for every Cosmic Hierarchy, otherwise an aether for every such hierarchy; and the 'ether' or 'ethers' of the science of the nineteenth century was or were merely the grossest and most material lees or dregs or sediment, so to speak, of the original Mûlaprakṛiti of the Physical Cosmic Plane.

Still, there are signs that our forwards-looking and thoughtful scientists are beginning to have intuitions more closely approximating the teachings of the Esoteric Philosophy, as witnessed by some interesting statements on the matter of the ether made by Eddington in his most recent book, *New Pathways in Science* (1935).

The main thought for the reader therefore to bear in mind is that, as said above, every Cosmic Hierarchy has not only its primordial or general or cosmic aether, which is its Mûlaprakṛiti or Âkâśa or Mother-substance, but that every one of the seven (or ten) Planes of such Hierarchy has as its root-substance or root-nature a subordinate aether of its own. All these subordinate aethers interblend.

Plato would have phrased it, an illusion of the mind reacting on its own thought when dealing with etherealities. Obviously, *something*, whatever its nature or being may be, and however ultra-ethereal this *something* may be, must exist to provide the space within and upon which the various electric particles composing the atoms have position and function. Were modern science once to grant the existence of invisible, because extremely ethereal, worlds or realms of space, many of the phantoms which now trouble its dreams and harass the imagination of the mighty men who are the devotees thereof would instantly disappear, for these ethereal worlds existing within the physical universe would be seen to be the background and container of the latter, and of which our physical universe is but the outer shell or garment or veil. The very lowest part of this range of invisible substance may as well be called 'ether' as by any other name, provided that the idea be once grasped.

This word 'ether' is a convenient term, although it does not mean very much to modern scientific speculation because nobody understands precisely what is meant by its use; but it is employed in a vague and generalizing way to signify the field of action of electromagnetic forces; and this to a Theosophist is a limitation so unreasonable that while he accepts it as a provisional scientific theory, he does not accept it as a natural fact.

The Ancient Wisdom teaches that the ether is not merely matter of one grade or of uniform density or existing only on one plane, but that it is septiform or sevenfold counting from its most ethereal parts to its densest — just beyond the range of the physical. Its most ethereal parts we call, in our own technical Theosophical terms, Âkâśa,[190] or the highly spiritual-ethereal substance-energy infilling

---

190. It is perhaps proper to call attention here to the fact, not so commonly recognised, even among Theosophists, that the manner of presenting the relation of Âkâśa and matter adopted in the text above, is, strictly speaking, inaccurate, and is followed only for purposes of easier illustration. In fact it is the Âkâśa which is the infinite *sub-stance* or spiritual substratum of all manifested being. What we humans call 'matter,' in all its manifold forms, is simply the lowest dregs or heaviest lees, so to speak, of Âkâśa. Thus, Âkâśa is but another name or term for what with equal technicality is called in the Esoteric Tradition, Mûlaprakṛiti — Root-Nature. Out of Âkâśa come forth all beings into manifestation, from within the boundless fields of Âkâśa itself in its multi-myriad degrees of spirituality, ethereality, or materiality; and back into the Âkâśa return all beings and things for their variously long periods of rest or recuperation, only to reissue forth therefrom anew when again the cycle of manifestation opens a new drama of life, whether Kosmic, Solar, or Planetary.

and in a true sense composing what is popularly called Space — or less accurately, spacial extension. There are therefore many grades of ether.

For instance, consider the ether, so called, which surrounds the Earth, which ether is kosmic in extent, and in which every molecule and indeed every atom of our bodies, every molecule of everything that exists, and every atom and every electron and proton of every atom, are bathed as in a boundless ocean. This 'ether' seems to us tenuous, thin, ethereal, and yet, according to ultra-modern scientific theories, it is incomparably more dense than is the densest known 'physical' substance. Obviously, for does it not permeate and interpenetrate all? It permeates and interpenetrates our grossest physical matter, as water will a sponge; and, as shown above, our physical matter is mostly spaces, 'holes,' 'emptinesses.'

A British scientist, Sir J. J. Thomson, recently has stated his conclusion that the density of the ether is 'two thousand million times that of lead'— or, as Americans would say, two billion times denser than lead. Such is the character of this intangible, super-gaseous-like thing or entity called ether, which is everywhere and pervades everything. Lead is one of the most dense of our physical metals; and yet the ether, which permeates everything, according to this hypothesis, is two billion times more dense!

Yes, says the Ancient Wisdom, the lowest parts of the ether actually are far more dense than are our densest metals.[191] So that

---

191. The reader or student is earnestly advised and indeed warned to be on his guard during the perusal of the present work, against accepting too easily or too 'literally' — as the popular phrase runs — the words 'dense' or 'density,' and 'tenuous' or 'ethereal' as found in this and the following chapter and possibly in other places, where the varying stages of concretion of matter or substance are alluded to. This warning is given because of the extreme difficulty in finding in any modern European language terms adequate or sufficiently subtil to express exactly what is found in Nature's grades or stages of essential substance or of matter.

To illustrate: there is perhaps no word which is so vague, with such slight precision in significant definition, as is the word ether, because it has been used in science until recently to signify one thing, while Theosophists have used the same word to signify a similar but not identic thing; and in making an effort exactly to place the different stages or grades of substance or matter, adjectives have been used which, though giving an adumbration of the idea it is desired to express, are nevertheless feeble in conveying the thought. These adjectives are 'dense,' 'tenuous,' 'ethereal,' 'essential.'

Even modern science has never had any precisely exact understanding of the

our physical world is not the most 'material' thing in the universe. There are planes or grades of substance-matter far more dense than are our own, even as there are planes and grades of substance-matter incomparably more ethereal and tenuous than is the physical. That

term 'ether' which it formerly used so commonly, and there was always a more or less diffuse or vague frontier of meaning surrounding this otherwise useful term.

In esotericism the difficulty is one thousandfold greater, for the simple reason that there are 'ethers' or substances in tenuous and ethereal conditions or states 'above' physical matter, and other 'ethers' in variously 'dense' or compacted states or conditions 'lower' or far grosser than physical matter is; yet the one term 'ethers,' just because it is conveniently vague yet suggestive is applicable both 'above' and 'below' that cross-section of Nature which we call the plane of the physical sphere.

But this again is not a sufficient explanation of the difficulty. The 'ethers' below or grosser than the physical sphere, although in certain instances enormously denser and more complicated than is physical matter, nevertheless permeate physical matter and fill all its holes so to speak, precisely because physical matter has these 'holes' or intermolecular, interatomic, and interelectronic spaces or 'emptinesses.' It is just these 'holes' or 'emptinesses' which not merely are filled with these sub-physical 'ethers' but actually *are* these sub-physical ethers; and yet the most dense and compact and gross of our physical matters, such as lead or gold, etc., are permeated and all their interatomic spaces filled with these ethers, which by analogy we may call either 'dense' or 'tenuous' according to the manner of considering the situation.

The sub-physical 'ethers' to our ordinary sense-apparatus are so far outside of the sense of touch, for instance, that being unable to touch them directly, they seem to us to be extremely thin or tenuous, just exactly as the fingers are unable to 'touch' or grasp air, and yet atmospheric air is a relatively 'dense' gas.

The matter therefore, as may be intuited by the thoughtful student from the preceding paragraphs, is one which is extremely difficult adequately to describe; and it is for this reason that in order to convey this, that, or some other viewpoint which may at the moment be in mind, the same particular 'ether' or 'ethers' are indifferently described as being 'tenuous' or 'dense,' according to each case. Take a particularly difficult thought as a striking illustration: consciousness or mind-stuff, or thought, is so fine and subtil, so tenuous and ethereal, that philosophy and religion from time immemorial have looked upon it or them, as being, cosmically speaking, the essence of everything, permeating everything, washing through everything, or underlying and inhering in everything; and this usage is fully justified because it is, abstractly, perfectly true; but let us likewise note just here that if Cosmic Mind or Consciousness is thus all-permeant, and the essence of everything, it must be more minute, more infinitesimal, than the most compact, dense, concreted entity that it is possible to figurate in the imagination; and therefore although it is so essentially and cosmically tenuous, mere logic

incomparably more ethereal and tenuous part is what we human beings call 'spirit'; and the other far denser and grosser part is what we call absolute 'matter'; but this entire range of substance from spirit to grossest matter is, in the Theosophical teaching, the septiform range of the Âkâśic background of the Universe — *of our Universe*. The entire Kosmos or Kosmical Universe is composite of vast ranges of ethereal substances and beings and entities and things and of other vast ranges of material grades of substances and beings and entities and things; and in that portion of it which we call our solar system, man and all other beings and entities and things therein move and live and have their being, each of such units withal imbodying with its own essence a spark of something infinitely more sublime, which 'something' we may call, if we wish, the Divine Central Fire of Consciousness-Life-Substance. It not merely imbodies this spark within itself, and at the core of its being, but that spark is in very truth the unit's own ultimate essence. Therefore and because of this the unit man in his essence is universal, because that essence is in inseparable identic unity with the universal Divine Fire just mentioned.

The words employed in any such explanation are more or less of necessity metaphors, it is true, but while being metaphors or verbal symbols, they nevertheless represent positive actualities or

---

compels us to add that it is infinitely more dense, because underlying it, than even the ether of modern science, which is '2000 million times that of lead,' i. e., two billion times denser than lead.

Or, to phrase the same striking paradox in other words, Cosmic Consciousness is Cosmic Force, and force and matter are fundamentally identic; and this force is 'denser' and more 'compact' than the densest matter is and yet it is incomparably more 'tenuous' and more ethereal — and this precisely because it is both.

The author hopes therefore that with this note of warning, the reader will not take amiss nor stumble over in perplexity any statement made in this work about the 'ether' or its 'density' or the 'tenuousness' of substance and matter, which he may meet, and which may seem to him to be statements involving contradictions.

Finally, it should be pointed out that this difficulty illustrates very clearly somewhat at least of the enormous philosophical import of the archaic teaching of the Esoteric Philosophy about the mâyâ or mahâmâyâ — Illusion, cosmic or otherwise — which comprises so important a part of its teachings, and which bears directly on this difficulty itself. The entire Universe surrounding us in all its phases of manifestation, high or low, essentially mâyâvi, or illusory, to us humans; which does not mean that the Universe is non-existent *per se,* which would be an absurd supposition, but that we percipient and intelligent beings do not understand it *as it is in itself, an sich* as the Germans say.

realities, and it is in the growing understanding of these realities or actualities that we come to comprehend ever more greatly the real meaning of the Esoteric Wisdom lying in the background of all the great ancient religions and philosophies, because all these last were based in their reaches of thought on the fundamental teaching of the identity in essence of the Infinite Universe with all its offsprings.

IV

The well-known and widely read English physicist, Sir Oliver Lodge, who also in many respects is entitled to the name of philosopher, has recently given his opinion on what he considers to be the nature and origin of 'matter,' so called;[192] and what he says in this passage is so closely akin in divers ways to the teaching of the Esoteric Tradition on the same point, that it is well worth quoting here. Sir Oliver writes:

. . . matter should, as it were, crystallise out of an unmodified spatial ether, the original seat of all the energy in the universe. According to this idea matter becomes the palpable part of the ether — the only portion of it which affects our organs of sense, and therefore the only portion which is incontrovertibly *known* to us. . . . We can trace the physical operations back and back as far as we can, but not without limit. Sooner or later we arrive at something which is not physical, which has more analogy with our minds than with our bodies, and which we sometimes call idealistic and sometimes spiritual.[193]

Unfortunately, one cannot always follow the eminent English physicist in all his scientific deductions and philosophico-scientific ideas. The citation that follows is one which contains, to the Theosophist, a great deal of truth, yet it cannot be accepted by the esotericist in the manner in which it is stated.

Sir Oliver Lodge writes:

---

192. *My Philosophy*, p. 24 (1933).

193. The esotericist feels compelled to register an emphatic objection to the idea contained in this word 'unmodified,' although the balance of the citation would seem to be such as one can gladly welcome as a new and far-sighted contribution to the general theme here under discussion. The point is, that the 'ether of science' of which Sir Oliver Lodge here writes, far from being 'unmodified,' is in every possible sense of the word already enormously modified or changed as compared with primordial spiritual world-stuff, otherwise Mûla-prakriti or Âkâśa. The ether of science is so highly modified that it is but one degree only less material, i. e., more tenuous, than is physical matter; for the ether of science really is the dregs or lees of Âkâśa, and physical matter can properly be considered to be these lees or dregs aggregated or solidified.

I venture to make the, possibly absurd, prediction that life will be found to be something that interacts with matter through the agency of the ether of space, that it is displayed and not originated by matter, and that it can exist in unsensed fashion quite apart from its material manifestation.[194]

One must make the following comment on Sir Oliver Lodge's idea that "life will be found to be something that interacts with matter through the agency of the ether of space." This is not only unscientific in view of the latest declarations of a number of men as great, if not greater, than Sir Oliver, but it cannot be strictly accurate because of the apparent distinction made between life and 'matter' as supposedly entities of radically different type or character; and also for the simple reason that, as said before, force and matter, or spirit and substance, are fundamentally *one* — not fundamentally two. It is this unfortunate divorce of life from matter, or of force from matter, in past years, that has worked such intellectual havoc not only in the scientific circles but, in past centuries as well as today, in religious circles as well. There would seem to be no possible or genuinely solid reason for this radical distinction or divorce except the unfortunate presupposition that life must be something different in essence from matter or from force, whereas they are but different manifestations of the one universal underlying reality.

Probably one cannot weigh too heavily upon the vast and far-reaching importance of clearing our minds once and forever of the old Western religious, and since Descartes' time[195] scientific, idea or notion that life and consciousness, and supposedly force likewise, are all distinct and of essentially different character from what we call 'matter,' or, more accurately, substance. This radical dualism in European thought has been the fecund and extremely fertile mother of more spiritual and scientific perplexities, phantoms, and consequent wanderings from the truth, than any other single cause operative in the same direction for ages past. It has been, apparently, a fundamental postulate of Western theology since the time of the fall of the Roman Empire; but it is particularly on the writings and ideas of the French philosopher, Descartes, that we place full responsibility for the influence of this totally erroneous conception over the minds of all scientific men since Descartes lived.

The radical distinction that he drew between these two sides of Nature, and which is the basic idea of Cartesianism, has swayed scientific thought almost without objection since his time until the

---

194. *Ibid.*   195. 1596 — 1650.

beginning of the twentieth century. It was about the year 1900, more or less, that there set in the new and far truer idea of the fundamental or substantial or essential identity of 'matter' and all forms of 'energy,' or, as the Theosophist would say, substance and force — the physical reflexions on our plane of cosmic Pradhâna and Brahman, i. e., Cosmic Root-Nature and its inspiriting and perpetually co-existent Cosmic Mind.

The Esoteric Philosophy has always rejected this divorce of the inseparable twain as wholly unnatural and therefore utterly untrue. They are in essence ONE: but appear in our illusory universe as twain because of their unceasing interactions and intermodal activities as the two aspects or veils of the one fundamental Reality.

So far as life interacting with matter *'through the agency of the ether of space'*[196] is concerned, there seems to be no possible objection to this, only a Theosophist would prefer to say that life works through that part of the ethers — note the plural — of space which are intra-atomic and hyper-intra-atomic, that is to say, the ethers within, and within the within, the substance and the structure of the atom. These ethers, thus aggregated, are the same as the 'ethers of space'; the term here showing, of course, that there are in actuality many ethers, and not merely one. There are as many ethers, as a matter of fact, as we can say that there are 'matters.' One may also add that while it is just said in a general way that the ethers of space are the same as the aggregated intra-atomic ethers, one does so only in order to be more clearly understood; because the hyper-intra-atomic ether that is here in the mind's eye, is actually much more tenuous and ethereal than is the lower part of the interstellar ether, or, perhaps more accurately, than is the lowest interplanetary ether of our own solar system.

There are indeed and in very truth ethers within ethers as our percipient mind plunges more and more into and within the abysmal recesses of atomic structure: as we go farther and farther into and within the ranges of atomic substance and energy. The physical matter that we know is soaked through by these ethers, especially by the lowest of them, very much as water permeates and soaks through a sponge. Hence we may, perhaps, use this figure of speech and say that our matter is sponge-like, 'full of holes' relatively, and compared with which the ether — even the lowest of the ethers — is exceedingly tenuous. Thus to declare, as Sir Oliver apparently does, that life is distinct essentially from matter and 'works through ether'

---

196. Italicized here for emphasis.

and thus links up with matter, is to say something that one feels bound rather strongly to object to, not merely on the ground of philosophic logic but in view of the latest discoveries and deductions of other eminent men of science.

The truth therefore is that life is inseparable from both force or energy and matter, because it is the causal substance of both these, both these being fundamentally one, as before said — life in fact being the actual and universal source of both force or energy and matter, and in its incomprehensibly manifold activities may, for the purpose of easy illustration, perhaps be called the Causal Energy of the Cosmos, which is thus infinitely more 'energetic' than 'energy' itself.

That life is "displayed and not originated by matter" is of course, an admirably true statement; matter merely displays it, manifests it, and thus proves it, but most emphatically does not 'create' it. No one today, presumably, will deny this. It is a very archaic Theosophical teaching; and the words "not originated by matter" show how greatly Sir Oliver Lodge has freed himself from the older scientific ideas that there is no such thing as a perennially vital fluid *per se* or vital essence *per se,* and that the phenomena of life are merely manifestations rising in some mysterious and inexplicable way out of the bosom of matter.

Further, when Sir Oliver says that "it can exist in unsensed fashion quite apart from its material manifestation," one must applaud this statement as being unquestionably true. It is a brave thing to say, because even today few scientists have had the courage to put it in that way. Yet by this approval, there is emphatically no intention to imply any consent to the view that life is essentially different from matter and has itself no material manifestation, for this is not the fact. Between pure force or energy as such, and the gross physical world as such, there must be connecting grades or steps of force-substance; because it is obvious that pure force or energy can no more act upon pure matter than can heat or electricity produce effective work without intermediary links which are the machinery or engines combining the factors. Steam cannot be applied to work unless you have the proper mechanism for placing the energy of superheated water at the point of operation. An internal combustion-engine can do no work unless connected up with the proper mechanism at the points where results are desired. All this is known to everybody. Yet we do see physical things move, and to move the matter of which they are composed they must be energized. These things act, they do things, and when they are humans or beasts we say that they have 'life,' that they are 'animated' entities. But what fills the gulf between the gross physical matter and the intangible force or energy which moves it? There is in fact a vast scale of substances-forces decreasing in materiality between gross matter and pure energy; and each rung of this scale, each stage or step thereof, is called in our terminology a 'plane.' These planes provide the ladder of communication between pure force or energy on the one side and gross physical substance or matter on the other.

Matters exist, therefore, in all-various degrees of tenuity or ethereality, or concretion or density; but there is life *per se,* in individuals manifesting as a vital fluid belonging to each one such grade or stage or plane of material manifestation — and these vital fluids in their aggregate form what we may call the Universal Life, manifesting in appropriate form on any one plane and functioning therefore through the various matters of that plane.

This is but another way of saying, therefore, that the Universe is full of gods; and not merely of gods or highly spiritual beings alone — call them by what name you will — but of multi-myriad beings beneath them in all-various stages of evolutionary growth; and, furthermore, also of beings superior to gods in evolutionary growth. It is impossible in the Boundless to set limits or frontiers in either direction, for this would be a violation of the fundamental postulate of the Esoteric Philosophy.

v

When we raise our eyes at night, when they are no longer dimmed by the splendor of our own day-star, and see the sparkling worlds bestrewn over the violet dome, we also see what is popularly called 'empty space' in which these sparkling worlds are; but the Theosophist prefers to speak of this interstellar 'ether' as 'open space,' because in point of fact there is no real emptiness anywhere. What we call 'open space,' or, if you like, 'the cosmic ether,' is simply that aggregate, that vast and incomprehensibly great composite, of invisible worlds and substances and forces and energies which our imperfect physical, optical sense can take no cognisance of.

If we turn in the other direction to the infinitesimal spaces of the atom and the intra-atomic ether, we see the same natural principles of elements and figure operative there also. In these infinitesimal spaces the physical atom is builded more or less precisely on the model of our own physical universe — for each atom is mostly open spaces, and only occasionally could we see scintillating electronic stars flashing upon our vision — points of electric energy which our modern scientists call electrons, and by other names.

But what do we mean when we speak of our Universe — our own Home-Universe, which is only one of many such Universes; for in point of strict fact, there is a quasi-infinite number of such Universes? We mean the Galaxy, the Milky Way: all that is contained within the encircling zone of that wide-flung belt of thousands of millions of stars, among which our own sun is a relatively insignificant member. Astronomers tell us that the Milky Way is more or less like a lentil in shape or a thin watch;[197] and they say that this Galactic aggregate of stellar bodies is so enormous in physical extent that light, which travels 186,000 miles or more in a human second, would take 300,000 years to pass from one extremity of the diameter of the Galaxy to its other extremity — in other words, through a plane traversing the middle portion of it; they also say that it is about 10,000 light-years in thickness.[198]

---

197. Such is the shape commonly ascribed to the Galaxy by astronomers of the last generation. More modern research and investigation has changed the Galactic spacial figure somewhat, so that our ultra-modern astronomers are of the opinion that the Galaxy is more or less the shape of a cart-wheel, a more or less flat body with protuberant globular center which in a cart-wheel is the hub.

A number of admirable photographs taken by the magnificent telescopes of the present day prove that a large number of extra-galactic systems approximate to the cart-wheel shape very closely, as is instanced by the nebula NGC 4565 found in *Berenice's Hair*.

It is of course obvious enough that such a galactic or constellational figure or form represents a fairly late stage in the history of a Galaxy, such as our own Galaxy is, and consequently it must have been preceded by other shapes differing somewhat from the cart-wheel shape; thus in this manner the astronomers trace back the different forms of galactic or constellational evolution to what they now suppose to be a primordial form in Kosmic Space — i. e., a vast and slowly rotating mass of highly tenuous cosmic gas. The Esoteric Philosophy runs parallel with this idea to a certain extent, but would insist upon the fact that the mere tracing of the changing structure or form of a galaxy, while interesting enough, tells us little or nothing of the causal factors in the galactic evolution which are of a spiritual, intellectual, and psychical character. The Galaxy, like every other entity in the Universe, is an individual builded up of minor individuals; so that the component minor individuals enclosed within the surrounding life-sphere of the Grand Individual thus form a hierarchical system, with its own spiritual-intellectual-psychical *swabhâva* or individuality.

198. The above estimates of 300,000 light-years and 10,000 light-years, are, of course, tentative, but, within only a year or two of the writing of this chapter,

Now these Galactic spaces, themselves small when compared with still vaster kosmical relations, are nevertheless almost unimaginable expanses for easy human understanding; and they strongly suggest that the entire Galactic System is but one of many similar kosmical units scattered over the illimitable fields of Space, thus making of even our Galaxy but a body of minor molecular extent by comparison. Yet the same system of vast open spaces, relatively speaking, bestrewn with atoms: and in the atoms themselves and with the same relative significance, vast spaces in which live electric points called electrons and so forth: prevails in the infinitesimal world, as above pointed out.

It would therefore most certainly seem that in this really sublime and most suggestive conception we find the principles of the teaching of the Esoteric Tradition that Nature — using the word here in the grandest sense — repeats herself everywhere throughout her own structure, and is builded and operates strictly throughout on analogical principles. "As above, so below; as below, so above."

As Emerson so beautifully says:

> Atom from atom yawns as far
> As moon from earth, or star from star.[199]

How did Emerson get this idea when ultra-modern scientific teachings and conceptions regarding the constitution of matter and its atomic structure, were in his time perfectly unknown, if not from the whisperings or inspiration of his own inner god?

Consider some of the suns whose tiny scintillating points our eyes may descry on any clear night — cosmic atoms indeed, whose glorious splendors our imperfect sense of sight reports to us as merely scintillating points of light. Yet what in fact are these suns? Some of them are 'dwarfs,' but some of them are 'giants,' or indeed 'titans,' in volume; yet these titan suns, to beings constructed on a vastly larger pattern than we are, would be very small, possibly microscopic; and again, vastly larger than those enormous suns appear to us, would they appear to beings whom we humans would consider and properly consider to be of infinitesimal dimensions.

Our own Sun in its physical dimensions and by comparison with others greater than it, may be called a dwarf-sun. Its diameter is stated to be but 866,500 miles. It, too, is a kosmic atom of its kind, and just as every atom of infinitesimal size, our sun is ensouled

---

seem to meet with scientific approval as being fairly accurate estimates. Time may, or may not, change them, as knowledge of the matter becomes greater.

199. *Fragments on Nature and Life.*

by its own spiritual-psychic 'life-atom' or Monad of stellar character. Now let us turn to view an example of a giant sun, to the star Arcturus. This sun is indeed a giant, 21,000,000 miles in diameter: a giant when compared with the diameter of our own Sun of 866,500 miles. Yet this stellar giant, Arcturus, is an infant in comparison with Betelgeuze, the diameter of which is more than ten times larger, reckoned at 215,000,000 human miles; and Betelgeuze would practically fill the orbit of Mars of our own Solar System if we could place it there. Our own Sun, in comparison with it, if we could place them drawn to scale on a sheet of paper, would appear as little more than a pin-prick or pin-point, and Betelgeuze would have to be represented by a circle 250 times as large. But what is Betelgeuze in size, in comparison with the titan-star, Antares, of 400,000,000 human miles in diameter — more and by much more than would be required to fill the entire orbit of Mars. Antares, in fact, has a diameter which is reckoned at 450 times that of our Sun.

What then are these suns? Each one is a cosmic atom, a part of a vast cosmic body corporate in which it moves and lives and has its being, more or less exactly as the atoms of the physical body live within that body and help to build the matter of which it is made. Yet each, whether sun or atom, is a living being itself, the maker and giver of all life to the minor lives dependent on its existence.

This is one aspect or phase of the Theosophical conception of Relativity, as taught in the Esoteric Philosophy, which Theosophical relativity-teaching covers vast ranges of philosophical thought, involving indeed the whole range of Universal or Cosmic Nature. The modern scientific relativity-theory, as elaborated by Einstein and his admirers, is but a mathematical and quasi-philosophical adumbration, a reaching out for, an attempt after, a more or less blind groping for, the Archaic Doctrine, ages upon ages agone pushed to its ultimate logical limits in religious, philosophical, and scientific research by the great Sages of the past, and which aspect of the Archaic Doctrine we call, adopting an old Sanskrit philosophical term, a phase of the 'Doctrine of Mâyâ.' This word *Mâyâ*, popularly translated 'illusion,' when briefly and simply explained, means that we humans do not see the Universe as it actually is, but that we cognise it only as our senses report it back to us; and that there is a fundamental and eternal Reality behind things — or Realities, if the word be preferred — of which all the phenomenal Universe or Universes are but transitory expressions, however long-enduring in time, and therefore are properly to be studied under the guise of relations, or as being relatives — relative to each other, yet each and all expressing differentiated aspects or 'productions' of the Reality behind and within.

In the Orient, as for instance in the Vedânta-philosophy of Hindûsthân, this conception of cosmic as well as individual illusion is likewise called Mâyâ, the meaning there also being that the Universe as we see it is an illusory presentation, or, in other words, that we do not see it as it actually is. This idea is fundamental in all archaic Oriental thinking. It was equally known in the Hither East and to all philosophers of the Mediterranean nations, at least as a reasonable theory, and is a fundamental postulate in the Theosophical Philosophy. Our ultra-modern scientists today are beginning to tell us more or less precisely the same thing — at least inferentially, indirectly, and by skilfully elaborated scientific deduction.

The main stumbling-block in the way of the acceptance of this grand idea by European philosophers and thinkers in the past, has been the psychological conviction under which they labored that the physical universe contains certain absolutes such as time and space, and therefore that space and time and substance are 'real things' in themselves, all working together according to some unknown 'absolute Cause,' as they expressed it, behind all, and thus producing forth the Universe as our imperfect senses cognise it to be.[200]

---

200. The reader or student may perhaps wonder that little or nothing has been said in the course of the present work about a theory of ultra-modern science which seems to have attained some large vogue of scientific popularity, to wit, the notion or theory of "an expanding universe," or, even more extraordinarily quaint, the notion of "expanding space."

The reason is that the present writer has not considered it of sufficient importance to give it any *locus standi* in a work dealing with the teachings of the archaic Wisdom-Religion, although the theory certainly is most quaintly interesting as a specimen of the manner in which ultra-modern scientific mathematicians are growing unconsciously both subtil and abstrusely metaphysical. It is an exceedingly good sign of the times in one way, provided that these speculative theories or theoretic speculations are consistently remembered to be just that, and not facts of nature; although the energetic claim is always proffered that modern metaphysical scientific speculation is based on observational facts alone. Yet this claim is obviously untrue. Mathematics, *per se*, cannot prove anything, although it is one of man's finest and most subtil methods of reasoning, and will return to the mathematician exactly what he puts into it. Mathematics, therefore, brings answers through correct reasoning, concerning what has previously been laid down as premises or postulates.

It is really interesting to observe how some of these mathematical theorists lean so greatly upon their theory or theories. Supposedly, science is co-ordinated knowledge based on facts of observation; and from such facts of observation,

VI

In closing the reflexions, philosophical, scientific, and otherwise, which comprise the bulk of the matter in the present chapter, one may add to them the concluding thought by way of a summary, that the tendency of ultra-modern scientific thinking seems to be a steady and continuous approach or approximation to certain fundamental or essential postulates or axioms of the Esoteric Philosophy or Esoteric Tradition. The idea now seeming to gain headway in scientific

theory or hypothesis is supposedly deduced or born. But a great many scientists today seem to think that if they openly state a theory, that theory should guide the understanding, or deductions, to be drawn from observational facts. Thus the always genial and frequently humorous Eddington, one of the most eminent and kindly of modern scientific thinkers, so believes, apparently, as is shown in his last book, *New Pathways in Science*, (1935), p. 211.

This is really curious logic. There can be no scientific theory without observational facts; theory is born from the observed facts. Yet according to the above notion, the theory born from the facts must be turned about to decide whether the observational facts themselves accord with truth — seemingly a curious fallacy in reasoning and imbodying a vicious circle. The theorist in such cases gets all the profit from both beginning and end of his thinking, and poor Mother Nature has to do the best she can in the outer cold.

Pretty much the same confusion in highly metaphysical 'stunts' of reasoning seems to have given birth to the idea of the so-called "expanding universe," or, worse still, to the notion of "expanding space." The present writer speaks subject to correction by the great men of modern science, but if he understands the situation, the main observational fact which brought about the birth of the theory of an "expanding universe" is the shift to the red of certain lines in the spectrum of far distant stellar or galactic astronomical objects. This the present writer believes is called the Doppler effect, meaning that if a distant astronomical object is approaching us there will be a shift towards the violet-end of the spectrum; and contrariwise, if the distant celestial object is receding from us, the shift of the spectral lines will be towards the red. Admitting the truth of this, it is risky to say the least, to suppose that because the observed shifting of these spectral lines to the red is the greater the farther the celestial body is, *therefore* the farther the celestial body is the more rapidly is it receding from us; because it is quite possible to suppose, equally by theory or hypothesis, that there may be other causes producing this shift.

For instance, the so-called 'constant' of the invariant velocity of light: this today is one of the clauses in the modern scientific creed; yet one may suggest with some confidence that the future may show that light itself is greatly affected by passing through the vast distances of interstellar space and meeting on its way even the thin and tenuous interstellar ether. Query: Can light itself suffer retardation when passing through the incomprehensibly immense distances of

circles that the entire physical universe, is, when all is said, distinctly illusory in character, so far as merely human conceptions go, is typically of the substance of the Esoteric Doctrine; and only the gods know how far this idea will lead intuitive scientists of our day behind the Veil if they pursue it faithfully into its farther reaches, undismayed by what must be to them the startling novelty of the new regions of thought into which they are thus led.

When we consider also the very just and inspiring idea that many modern scientific thinkers now have of the nature of ultimate

---

intergalactic space? Why not? To consider the velocity of light as invariant, i. e., as a universal constant, may be sufficient for all ordinary astronomical purposes, but the present writer is one who believes that the velocity of light is no such universal invariant constant as is supposed. Hence the shifting towards the red end of the spectrum may be due to change in the light itself, as regards either diminution of velocity, or, possibly, an as yet unknown fact of absorption; and consequently the suggestion is made that some future day will bring about a change in the present theory of light. Either one or both of these suggested causes, or something like them, the future may show to be true.

The recession of the galaxies of 'outer space' is stated to be proceeding at a rate of speed strictly proportionate to the distances of the galaxies from us. Thus a galaxy 120 million light-years from us, by this quaint modern theory, is supposed to have a speed of recession of 12,000 miles a second. Now, suppose we continue with the idea: at 2000 million light-years distance, we should, by this quaint theory, expect to see a galaxy receding at 200,000 miles a second. This is a speed a good deal greater than the speed of light itself, which is supposed to be a constant, and the maximum possible speed in our universe of relativities — according to the modern relativity-theory. How about it?

The scientific 'reserves' are here rushed to the front in the shape of the renowned Einsteinian theory of finite space which cannot have distance beyond a certain amount, and by thus — always in theory — making the universe finite or closing it up, it is obvious, by theory, that light itself cannot wander too far. Convenient to say the least!

But even these 'reserves,' due to the fertility of the Einsteinian scientific imagination, seem to be dissolving into intangible mist — or mystification — because, if recent reports which have appeared in the press are to be given credence, Einstein himself, a truly great scientific mind, is stated to be no longer certain that 'space' is 'finite,' but that it may be infinite, after all. The theory of light considered as an invariant cosmic constant, also, has just recently received some severe jolts. (See the report of the French scientist Dr. P. Salet, to the French Academy of Sciences, and the latest measurements of light-velocity made in 1933 at Pasadena, California.) Evidently, since the supposed expanding universe theory is based upon one important observational fact only, the shifting towards the red-end of the spectrum of light received from distant galactic universes, and as light as an invariant constant is now

or primordial causation, and of the essence of things, both of which these men ascribe to the substance and functions and operations of Cosmic Mind, one has real cause for pausing in contemplative thought and wondering just how far this latter conviction will lead the scientific world. With the Universe appearing as illusory, and the substance of the Universe arising in Cosmic Mind and therefore governed by the attributes and qualities thereof, the esotericist sees in these two scientific conceptual postulates alone a relatively complete breaking down of the barriers brought about by the labors and deductions of the men of science themselves, which have hitherto separated Esotericism from Science and made the latter so reluctant even to consider the former's existence as other than the imaginative phantasy of peculiar people.

---

being questioned, it is clear that the theory of an 'expanding universe' or, worse still, of 'expanding space' reposes on the shakiest of foundations.

Thus it is that one theory is made to bolster another: observational facts are forced into the Procrustean bed of theories born from their own bosom, and we thus return to the beginning of our reasoning just like Einstein's "curvature of space" — we are just where we began. The present writer prefers to believe that the theory of light as a constant or invariant, is merely an interesting theory; but that light like everything else in the universe, is relative, in pretty much the sense of the relativity-theory of Einstein himself, and therefore that light is not an absolute or a universal and invariant constant, but that it is subject to change or changes in its relations with other things.

Nor must it be forgotten that the so-called "observational facts," on which the theory of the "expanding universe" is founded, are indeed facts, but facts from which deductions have been drawn in order to form metaphysical mathematical theories which, undoubtedly, time itself will show to be fallacious in more than one direction. Perhaps it is just because the whole idea is so speculative and theoretic, that our modern scientific mathematicians are so ultrasensitive about their ideas being called 'metaphysical,' for in philosophy shaky metaphysics of this type would be run out of camp in short order.

The present writer submits the foregoing observations with the hope that the argument will be understood and that it will not be considered presumptuous for a layman to criticize the 'mind-born' children of scientific professionals. At any rate, of one thing we are sure: that, deny it if they will, repudiate it as they please, the numbers of men in the scientific camps who are becoming with every passing year more and more 'mystical,' are growing constantly larger. The truth is that modern scientific mathematical speculation is shot through and through with a curious modern mysticism originating in the minds of the mathematicians themselves, although the present writer is well aware how greatly words like 'mysticism' and 'mystical' are disliked by the very minds which are most inclined to trust to it. Strange paradox in human psychology!

CHAPTER XIV

BEHIND THE VEILS WITH SCIENCE — II

O NE of the most important axioms, postulates, or fundamental conceptions, of the Esoteric Philosophy or Tradition is that the Universe and all in it, great and small and all things intermediate, is builded in and upon and guided from within outwards as well as from without inwards by CONSCIOUSNESS, which includes in its qualities or attributes or characteristics those other phases of Cosmic Being which men call Life, Mind, Substance. Yet it must be remembered that this term Consciousness, when applied to the Universe, is a generalizing term only, an abstraction, and that it is equally proper, and to many minds incomparably more accurate because more descriptive, to speak of the Kosmic Universe as being infilled with Consciousnesses, existing in structural hierarchies, and as being, distributively speaking, infinite in number.

These consciousnesses exist, or rather are, in virtually innumerable grades or degrees or stages of evolutionary development, and are structurally arranged according to Hierarchical Families. Thus it is that everything in the Universe, considered as an individual expression of an indwelling and self-expressing Monad, is not only a point or individualized atom of the Boundless, but in its inmost essence is philosophically to be considered as identic with the Universe itself.

All space, infinitesimal and cosmic, is filled full of forces and substances in all-various grades and degrees of substantiality, of ethereality, and of spirituality. Such relatively physical force-substances as electricity and light may be cited as entitative examples or instances in point. For what are electricity and light, and indeed any other force-substance? They are, without exception, emanations from entities of cosmic magnitude: emanations — and the word is repeated for emphasis: in other words, the Boundless as above stated, is full of Cosmic Entities, each one of which has its own Universe acting as its own individual 'bearer' or 'carrier'; and the vital forces or energies in any such Cosmic Entity are the identical forces, the energies, the substances, which infill that Universe, and therefore, because substantially of the nature of consciousness, direct it, guide it, control it, and are in fact that inner and eternal urge behind all the outer seeming, the outer phenomenal appearances.

As it is thus in the case of such Cosmic Entity, precisely so is it also in the case of the physical atom. In the atom as in the cosmos: the same rule, the same principles, the same energies, the same substances, and the same structural operations prevail, because both atom and cosmos are forever inseparable parts of the Boundless All, and therefore mirror or reflect, each according to its power and capacity, the Spiritual Primordials which the Boundless contains. Hence all these: cosmos and atoms, inner and invisible, and outer and visible, worlds and planes and spheres, considered as a cosmic composite: all are what we call not only the veils and garments of the Cosmic Life, but the expressions of that Cosmic Life itself.

Is Consciousness then different from Force or Energy? No, Consciousness or Mind is both the root and focus of Force or Energy, the very soul of Force or Energy, and being such, it is substantial, although not 'matter' as we understand 'matter.' Our grossest physical matter is but the concretion of sleeping or dormant consciousness-centers or Monads; in other words, it is but a vast aggregate of psycho-magnetic consciousness-centers, dormant, sleeping, so to say. When they awake to kinetic movement, in other words, when they awake to individual activity, these 'sleeping' Monads, existing and forming the matter around us, begin their respective individual evolutionary journeys upwards again towards that freedom of Spirit, of pure Consciousness-Force, from which in the beginnings of things they originally 'fell' — to use the old saying of the ancients — into matter, which is thus their own collective concretion.

This last thought or suggestion, gives the key to a clear understanding of what the Forces of Nature really are in themselves. They are essentially cosmic entities manifesting themselves in an energic fluidic form; and this fluidic form or activity is what we humans sense as Nature's Forces. They are, in other words, and more accurately, the emanations or outpourings of the collective or aggregative Cosmic Consciousness.

We may take gravitation, electricity, magnetism, heat, chemical affinity, light, as instances, because these are the cosmic forces that most usually come under the observation of human beings. They are all forces, i. e., emanations or outpourings from an individual Source, this Source itself being one of the cosmic entities with which Space is filled; and these entities themselves in their turn are ultimately to be traced back to their origins as outpourings or emanations from the general or universal Cosmic Consciousness. Being forces they are likewise substantial, because matter and force are fundamentally or essentially one. Likewise, and in exactly similar fashion, Spirit or Consciousness and Essential Substance are intrinsically and fundamentally one. So that whenever there is force or energy, or its manifestations, such as gravitation, such as electricity, such as magnetism, such as heat, such as chemical affinity, such as light, it — whatever it may be — is likewise as substantial as it is energic; therefore from what previously has been said, it is likewise essentially consciousness expressing itself as consciousnesses.

In the teaching of the Esoteric Philosophy (and one may venture the prediction that the science of the future will discover it to be the fact some day, even as Einstein and others are already showing the truth of it concerning gravitation as being the same fundamentally as cosmic electro-magnetism) heat and light, as said, are substantial, and just because they *are* forces. Being forces manifesting as energies, they have in them the same essential factors and qualities that the human entity has, although not expressing themselves as these essential qualities and factors do in the human entity. These aggregative factors and qualities are to be grouped as consciousness. Nevertheless these various Forces of Nature — and one may take gravitation as a single illustration in point — are not in themselves (and please mark carefully this important distinction) each one a consciousness, but each one such force is rather the manifestation or self-expression of a cosmic consciousness or cosmic entity: the emanation, the vital fluid, expressing itself as the phenomena of gravitation, of some living, conscious, cosmic entity behind.

The Forces of Nature, then, are the vital fluids, to use very easily understandable terms, or the nervous energy, so to say, working in the Cosmos, of spiritual beings from whom this vital electricity or nervous energy flows, in whom this vital electricity inheres, and working and operating in their circuits around the vehicular being of the spiritual entity which thus emanationally gives them birth; or to put it in another way: each such cosmic force is the outflowing from some cosmic entity of its characteristic vital fluid of the particular grade belonging to this entity's lowest cosmic body-parts.

It goes without saying, and as a matter of logical course, that this vital force or cosmic electric energy is inherently and throughout guided, automatically to us humans, by the mind and will of the cosmic entity or entities from which it flows in emanational series — each unit in such series being what we humans call this, that, or some other one of the Forces of Nature. In this picture it must likewise be kept in mind that these cosmic entities in themselves form an interlocking and interwoven hierarchy of lofty Spiritual Intelligences; and because their individual or respective swabhâvas or characters are nearly akin, they co-operate in producing the entirety of the cosmical phenomena or operations which commonly are grouped under the one term — Nature.

Human nerve-aura, human magnetism, will perhaps illustrate this point in the small, as working in even such derivative phenomena as the circulation of the blood or the digestive functions in the human body. None of these, among other functions of the human body, considered alone, is physical man. In their aggregate, combined with the framework of the body, they form physical man, but in themselves they are functions brought about by the interplay of the emanations of man's vital essence, and thus form the operative economy of his body, and are ultimately derived from the real Man of consciousness and thought. These operations and functions, which eventuate in producing and 'running' the physical body, emanate from the man himself by and through the medium of his permeant consciousness and through the instrumentality of his will, acting more or less automatically in the physical body, fortunately for us, perhaps, in our present state of imperfect moral development; but acting nevertheless in him partly consciously and partly unconsciously, in the latter case automatically, precisely as the Forces of Nature act — but on the macrocosmic scale — in the Universe surrounding us.

I

Verily, spirit and substance are essentially one, and hence force and matter — their physical expressions — are essentially one, being also merely differing grades or degrees of the ethereality or substantiality of the underlying and fundamental Essence, cosmically the Source of Things — the Source or origin of the planets swimming in the celestial ether as well as of gross physical matter under our feet and belonging to our mother-planet Terra: of everything, in short, including Man himself of course, who in his inmost is a being of spirit, an inhering and inseparable part or portion of the Cosmic Essence above mentioned. The Forces of Nature are therefore the substances of Nature in ethereally fluidic form; and at the root or origin of both is pure spiritual Force-Substance, which is the same as Consciousness — Mind. Since these *equi-valent* factors exist or rather *are* in Man, therefore do they all exist in the Universe; for the part, Man, contains only what the whole, the universe, contains, otherwise we shall be faced with the incongruous absurdity that a relatively infinitesimal part of the cosmic whole contains something that the whole lacks — which is impossible.

When the Esoteric Tradition states that there is no such thing as gravitation *per se,* which means that the scientific explanation of gravitation once so popular is no real truth, does this statement mean that we deny one of the obvious facts of Nature? It most certainly implies no such denial. The entire Esoteric Philosophy, considered as a grand system of Philosophy-Religion-Science, is wholly based on Universal Nature, and almost wholly on spiritual Nature, because the physical nature known to us is but the outward shell of vast hierarchies of invisible and causal character, expressing themselves as best they can and may through this physical or enshrouding veil or body. It is merely denied that gravitation as a technical word involving ideas belonging to the older science and which therefore imbodies a certain hitherto orthodox scientific explanation — it is denied only, that this explanation of the natural facts falling under the term gravitation is a true explanation. It is averred (and in this point the Theosophist agrees with Sir Isaac Newton, who first gave a formulated law of gravitational attraction to the Occidental world) that the fundamental cause of gravity has not yet been discovered, and that it is essentially a spiritual force or power.[201]

---

201. The reference here to Newton is to statements made by him in certain letters of his to Bentley, and these statements have always been entirely ignored by former scientific writers, although they are true. These were certain letters written by Sir Isaac Newton to Richard Bentley in the years 1692–3; and in these letters, among other things, Newton expressed his strong opposition to the idea that gravity was a property inherent or innate in matter and also of the idea of *actio in distans,* or action at a distance, without an intervening medium or without intervening media, active or passive.

In Newton's letter to Bentley, dated Jan. 17, 1692-3, Newton expresses himself as follows with respect to the nature of gravity: "You some times speak of gravity as essential and inherent to matter. Pray, do not ascribe that notion to me; for the cause of gravity is what I do not pretend to know, and therefore would take more time to consider of it."

In another letter to Bentley, written in the same interval, 1692–3, Newton expressed himself as follows: "It is inconceivable, that inanimate brute matter, should, without the mediation of something else, which is not material, operate upon and affect other matter without mutual contact, as it must be, if gravitation, in the sense of Epicurus, be essential and inherent in it. And this is one reason why I desired you would not ascribe innate gravity to me. That gravity should be innate, inherent, and essential to matter, so that one body may act upon

Gravitation, or Gravity, according to the scientific theory of only a few years ago, was supposed to be a sort of thing in itself, whose origin was unknown, it is true, and whose operation was expressed in the well-known scientific formula of the relations of two bodies as regards mass and the inverse square of the distance. It actually is a secondary phenomenon, i. e., an effect of invisible forces

---

another at a distance through a vacuum, without the mediation of any thing else, by and through which their action and force may be conveyed from one to another, is to me so great an absurdity, that I believe no man, who has in philosophical matters a competent faculty of thinking, can ever fall into it. Gravity must be caused by an agent acting constantly according to certain laws; but whether this agent be material or immaterial, I have left to the consideration of my readers."

It is abundantly evident from the first sentence of this second citation that Newton himself without doubt held to something "which is not material" as the agent or medium causing and controlling gravitational action; although the last sentence would seem to imply desire to obscure his real opinion, possibly because of a disinclination to attribute immaterial or spiritual agency to gravitational action.

Although in many ways a disciple of the ancient Greek philosophers, Newton unquestionably repudiated the mistaken opinion — based upon mistaken exoteric statements of the ancients themselves — that Democritus and Epicurus taught the fortuitous and chance action and re-action of dead, insensate atoms in an utterly empty void. It has been before pointed out that the real meaning which Democritus and Epicurus and their followers gave to the term 'atom,' i. e., 'individual,' was what the Esoteric Philosophy calls a *Jîva* or Monad. It remained for the materialistic school of modern scientific thinkers from Newton's day to choose the course with regard to the nature of gravity which Newton himself rejected, as is shown by the second letter to Bentley above quoted from.

Methinks that after all is said, Empedocles was not so far wrong in his teaching of cosmic 'Love' and 'Hate,' two principles in nature working both in the universe itself and in and among the atomic individuals which compose that universe. Whether this 'Love' and 'Hate' be called by other names more familiar to modern ears such as Attraction and Repulsion, is a matter of indifference; the point here being that both are the manifestations of the vital force or energy of invisible cosmic entities of differing grades or degrees in evolutionary development, such vital magnetic outflow being strictly dependent upon the amount of the respective emanations and the distance separating two or more individuals thus involved in mutual action or re-action — a statement which reminds one strongly of Newton's law of gravity acting according to the respective masses of two or more bodies and likewise depending upon the inverse square of the distance separating them.

On the whole, and although there is much that is attractive in Einstein's mathematical theories, many minds will find this idea preferable to the purely

working in and through the visible world and hence flowing into this visible world from inner and invisible realms or planes. In other words, as Sir Isaac Newton put it in substance: gravitation is the effect of a spiritual agency; but whereas Sir Isaac Newton evidently supposed this spiritual agency to be 'God,' the Theosophist says instead that it is but one of the manifestations of the inherent activity of conscious cosmic electro-magnetism operating through and by the instrumentality of spiritual *agents,* spiritual beings — in other words, gods, if the good old term may be used without offense to the sensitive ears of the wiseacres of the West.

After Newton's time his gravitational hypothesis considered as a law of Nature held undisputed sway — the entire body of scientists, almost without exception, quietly ignoring the great Englishman's private conviction that gravitation was due to spiritual agency. Then came the usual Nemesis of all materialistic lop-sided theories — the appearance of another and startling theory evolved out of the consciousness of a representative of a later scientific generation. Einstein has been the cause of much upsetting in scientific circles of classical and supposedly unshakable scientific postulates or axioms, and it is probable that not only all the scientific world, but all thinking men, were at first amazed and indeed bewildered by some

---

theoretic notion that gravitation is in some way dependent upon, or brought about by, or caused by, 'curved' or 'crumpled' space.

The simpler Platonic idea that the circle or the sphere is the most perfect form in Nature to which she automatically tends, seems both more reasonable and accordant with fact than the highly metaphysical albeit mathematical conception of a supposititious 'curvature of space' — as if space which is an abstraction *per se,* could be spoken of as if it were a limited material body only.

The Esotericist would have far less objection to the Einsteinian hypothesis of space-curvature if it were supplemented by two fundamental principles of Nature which Einstein seems to have ignored in his mathematical work, to wit: (a) that any 'space,' in the Einsteinian sense, is but a portion of spacial extension and is included in a still larger spacial extension or body, and this latter itself is again included in 'space' or spacial extension larger still, and so on indefinitely, *ad infinitum*; and, (b) that the different 'spaces,' or body-extensions, of the physical Universe are but an outward shell or veil or garment of inner and ethereal as well as spiritual Worlds or Spaces, which are the causes of whatever appears in the physical worlds.

With these considerations in view, it is at once seen that the Einsteinian hypothesis, while exceedingly clever and in some ways intuitive, deals with but small parts or portions, so to speak, of abstract SPACE ITSELF, and being thus limited, is, *de facto,* but a partial explanation at best, and therefore is imperfect.

of his views when they were first published. And yet it is most interesting how some at least of these views have captured the scientific imagination, thus proving, it would seem, that even the most dogmatically inclined minds were privately dissatisfied with what they had learned in the lecture-halls and orthodox schools of scientific thought.

II

Dr. Robert A. Millikan some time ago developed a certain hypothesis which had originated in the consciousness of a German scientist, Dr. Werner Kolhoerster, to the effect that there are certain forms of radiation in the universe — up to that time unknown and unsuspected — appearing no one then knew whence, but whose existence could no longer be denied, and the nature and action of which could be tested by proper study and experimentation. Dr. Millikan elaborated this hypothesis or theory and by a good deal of difficult and conscientious work has proved the existence of what has since been called the 'Cosmic Rays'— a form or forms of radiation apparently streaming into the earth on all sides from outer space. These Cosmic Rays, as they are now called, are in Dr. Millikan's opinion radiation streaming forth from matter in the making, forces or energies which arise as the elements of physical matter are born anew from the disintegration of precedently existing atomic corpuscles. They represent the most material form of energic vibrations hitherto known, because on the scale of radiation mentioned in a former chapter, they are found far beyond the ultra-violet portion of this scale, and are therefore radiation or rays incomparably 'harder' and more penetrating than are either the X-rays or the γ-rays. It has been supposed by Dr. Millikan himself, it would seem, that these cosmic rays may reach us from the nebulae of space — or from some of the nebulae at least.[202]

If this great American scientist's ideas are shown by future research and discovery to be correct, we see here a striking illustration of how force is turning into concrete matter, physical matter; and the theory is most suggestive because it not merely suggests, but actually sketches, the cyclical vanishing of matter into radiation

---

202. While it is quite true that the precise or exact origin or origins of the so-called 'cosmic rays' has or have not yet been absolutely discovered, there seems to be no doubt about the fact that these cosmic rays are born in the fields of space outside the Earth, because they reach the Earth as radiation apparently coming from all quarters of outer space with virtually equal intensity.

and the concreting or concretion of such radiation into physical matter again. As Dr. Millikan himself expresses it, in substance — 'creation' is still going on, and we see no reason to suppose that there ever was a beginning, cosmically speaking, or that there ever shall be an end, of the cyclical process.[203]

---

203. Here again, if the present writer has correctly understood Dr. Millikan's ideas of this process of cyclical destruction and regeneration by means of radiation, it would appear that his idea is that the stars radiate substance from themselves which in some as yet unexplained manner (apparently) rebecomes electronic and protonic particles in the abysses of space separating star from star. The cyclical process therefore seems to be, briefly, that atoms or atomic bodies are dissipated into radiation in the bosoms of the suns or stars of interstellar space, and that this radiation in the trackless fields between the stars is again aggregated into electrons and protons which combine to form atoms, which in their turn again are concreted to compose the bodies of stars, which thus furnish the theater anew for the same cyclical processes of destruction and regeneration already described.

There is a good deal in Millikan's theory which is extremely attractive to the Esotericist because of approximations to the Esoteric Philosophy that Millikan makes on several points which his theory covers; but one is nevertheless obliged to enter a caveat as regards the idea that the universe through eternity involves the process by which radiation becomes matter which in its turn vanishes again into radiation only to re-enter upon a new cycle of concretion into matter, and that this process — so true in some of its aspects — continues throughout endless duration without longer solutions of continuity or interruption of time-periods than those suggested by Millikan's theory, however long may be the intervening time-spaces between the vanishing of matter into radiation and the latter's rebecoming matter.

The truth is, as the Esoteric Philosophy teaches it, that any such process as Millikan in his theory approximates to, or adumbrates as a natural fact, at certain vastly long intervals of time recurring in regular serial and cyclical order throughout eternity, is interrupted or marked by what the Esoteric Philosophy calls the Cosmic Pralayas — or enormously long periods in which a Universe, large or small, vanishes from visibility into invisibility, such dissolution or 'death' of a Universe meaning the beginning or opening of the Cosmic Pralaya or Cosmic Rest-Period. When each such Cosmic Pralaya in its turn comes to an end, as it infallibly does in the serial cyclical order above alluded to, then the individual Universe which had thus dissolved or vanished from the scene, begins a new period of Cosmic Manifestation or Cosmic Manvantara, which, from the instant of its beginning, involves a vast series of evolutionary changes bringing said individual cosmic unit into appearance on the cosmic scene again.

This period of active evolutionary manifestation is followed when completed by a new cosmic Rest-Period; and thus throughout endless duration.

It should be carefully noted, however, that each such new World-Appearance

The usage of this word 'creation' above is adopted here because it conveys some comprehensive idea, yet care should be taken to note that the word 'creation' is not used here in the old Christian theological sense as meaning something made out of 'nothing,' but in its original Latin etymological significance, which is that of 'formation' of something which is thus caused to 'spring forth,' as, for instance, the Latin poets and philosophers sometimes called a man's son by the term *creatus* — the past passive participle of the Latin verb *creo,* to 'form,' to 'make,' to cause to 'spring forth.' The secondary idea involved in this word, therefore, is the formation or the springing forth into manifested being on our plane of physical matter — or indeed on other planes — of new appearances of individualized entities, and that this process of formation is *continuous,* and that the world, or universe for that matter, is a changing and constantly evolving one; with the reservation, however, that universes, solar systems, and indeed every other manifested being and thing, after a period of manifestation, disappears from the scene for a term of rest. Thus it is that worlds appear and disappear, just as man himself dies and after his devachanic term of rest and recuperation is reborn anew on Earth for a new lifetime, only to die again, which death is followed by the next rebirth and so forth through the ages.

Only a short time ago, relatively speaking — as is exemplified in Herbert Spencer's *Synthetic Philosophy,* as he called it — the Universe was supposed to be all matter which was supposed to give birth to energy or force in a manner which no one understood; and furthermore, it was taught that the Universe was slowly 'running down.' An illustration then frequently given was the coiled spring of a watch, which was slowly unwinding — such was the idea; and when the universe was totally 'unwound' or 'run down,' it was supposed that there would be nothing left but infinite fields of atoms, sleeping or dead, and spread through something vaguely called 'space.' Everything would then be completely ended — and people of those days were not even quite sure if the dead atoms themselves would be there — as atoms. Spencer, it is true, himself had some vague notion that the Universe in some inexplicable way would wind itself up again in order to start a new evolutionary course of 'life' — a true intuition, imperfectly understood as it was by him. But he seemed to be somewhat notably singular in this optimistic outlook. Yes,

---

or Cosmic Manvantara, takes place on a somewhat higher — or it may be lower — Cosmic Plane, than the one on which it had previously lived its former manvantaric existence. The "Sparks of Eternity" appear and disappear endlessly.

in those days, there was supposed to be nothing but dead, insensate 'matter' out of which arose its marvelous offspring 'energy' or 'force.'

But in our own days, scientists are beginning to deny that there is any matter *per se* at all; they say now — at least many of them so say — that there is nothing but 'force' or 'energy.' May we not ask, Why run to this other extreme? Why not take the things of Nature as they are, instead of running off into imaginary vagaries of the speculative mind? After all, what does it matter what we call this underlying reality of things — whatever it is? It may be called 'force' or 'substance'; the Theosophist calls it Spirit-Matter.

There is a very real difficulty that our modern scientists have to face, and it is a difficulty that students of and writers on the Esoteric Philosophy likewise confront, and this difficulty is the lack of a comprehensible terminology sufficiently expressive to enable them to state with accuracy and succinctness exactly what their new discoveries and the deductions drawn therefrom imply. They are perforce obliged to use, more or less just as Theosophists are, the phraseology — scientific or otherwise — of recent generations, when so much less was known of Nature than is known today; although it is of course true that new and often graphically expressive terms are almost yearly coined to fit in with the advancing knowledge and the new insights that are gained into the arcana and secret processes of Mother-Nature. Discovery runs more swiftly ahead than does language. In consequence, when one reads at times of some new discovery, or ponders over some new deduction of a truth from what already is known, as given by various researchers into natural laws and operations, the wording and even at times the conclusions drawn are apt occasionally to strike one as being rather quaintly humorous — all allowance being made for new ideas and thoughts expressed in old terms: new wine in old bottles!

One writer, commenting on the discoveries of Millikan, recently said in the daily press:

In view of the newly-discovered facts brought to light by recent and more precise measurements of cosmic rays, it seems probable that ordinary matter is being created in the stars, the nebulae, or in the depths of space. Or, as Dr. Millikan himself puts it, "The heretofore mysterious cosmic rays, which unceasingly shoot through space in all directions, are announcements sent through the ether of the birth of the elements. . . ."

Why should it be supposed that matter is in 'creation' in the stars, in the nebulae, and in the depths of space, and nowhere else? Why limit 'creation,' formation, the new springing forth again, the new manifestation, to those three and in one case rather vague, localities? The reason doubtless lies in modern chemical — or may we not be venturesome and call them alchemical? — theories regarding the breaking up of atoms and their component electronic and protonic particles in the deep hearts of the suns where these minute corpuscular entities are subjected to such almost incredible conditions of heat and pressure. One is tempted to suggest or to predict that the time is coming, and may not be so far distant, when it will be discovered that the interiors or hearts of the various suns are not at all existing in conditions of such incomprehensibly intense heat, although it is true enough that the outmost ethereal layers of the suns have certain heat of their own, brought about by chemical action.

On the other hand, it is perfectly true that the interior of any sun is a most marvelous alchemical laboratory in which occur changes: molecular, atomic, and electronic: which it would be utterly impossible to reproduce in any chemical workshop. It is the teaching of the Ancient Wisdom, the Esoteric Tradition, that every sun, as indeed every other individual celestial body, is the outward veil or the body, or vehicle, of an indwelling Spiritual and Intellectual Agent or Presence or Solar Spirit — let the reader use what descriptive name he may choose. It would be perfectly and indeed easily possible for such a Spiritual and Intellectual Agent to exist and to do its work in a sun, even were the interiors of the different suns the vast and incomprehensibly hot furnaces that ultra-modern science supposes them to be.

Yet it is our firm conviction (a) that the interiors of the suns are not such super-heated furnaces, chemical or alchemical or otherwise; and (b) that the time is not so very far distant when intuitions of this great truth will dawn upon the minds of our greatest scientists themselves, and thus they will introduce a still newer and even more fascinating field of research than what has been opened to the astonished gaze of scientific men during the last twenty-five years or so.

The point that one would like to make here is that even on this Earth there is constantly taking place a marvelous series of chemical and of what one may truly call alchemical processes, which are not different in kind from what takes place either in space, or in the nebulae, or in the interiors of the suns, but which are different perhaps solely in degree. The interior of the Earth is another of Nature's marvelous laboratories wherein wonderful and to us men almost unknown things are constantly happening; and, indeed, the same may be said of the unceasing laboratorial work of Nature in the higher and highest ranges or strata of the Earth's atmosphere, and its unceasing interplay of forces and substances with the fields of outer space — whether this be done through the medium of radiation of various kinds, or partly by radiation and partly by as yet undiscovered natural means.

It seems to be notably unreasonable to the student of the Esoteric Philosophy to suppose that the Earth is 'dead' in the sense of having ceased its play and interplay of forces and substances with the spacial realms of the solar system around it, for this supposition we believe to be entirely unwarranted. It has been for numberless ages past the teaching of the Wise Men, the great Seers and Sages, of the entire globe, that 'matter' in many of its multi-myriad forms or conditions is unceasingly evolving forth, springing forth, on our Earth as well as in the most distant sun or remotest nebula shining with its faint and intriguing light in the abyss of interstellar space. Every part and portion of Mother Nature, and this applies universally, so to say is an alchemical laboratory; and the workings in that laboratory are those of interacting forces and substances which are always and unceasingly throughout time evolving forth or *producing* what is in themselves — i. e., their own characteristics, or the respective swabhâva of each individual case.

But more specifically, What is it that they evolve forth or produce? *It is what is commonly called substance or matter* in one or in many of its ranges or types or characteristics of existence.

In connexion with the so-called 'creation' of matter, a clever writer, Alden P. Armagnac, some years ago gave a neat summary in the daily press of Dr. Millikan's views, at least as held some time ago, regarding the so-called 'cosmic rays.' The writer says, quoting in substance from Dr. Millikan:

These rays are the invisible messengers of creation.

Creation, he said, is still going on — not merely the creation of new worlds or of living things that people them, but the birth of the very particles of substance from which rocks and animals are made. His study of the cosmic rays, he added, revealed the first direct, indisputable evidence that beyond the stars, perhaps even on Earth[204] too, four of the universal substances are daily

204. This is excellent, indeed; and is corroborative of the teaching of the Esoteric Philosophy that the Earth itself should likewise be regarded as an ever-active and never-tiring chemical or alchemical laboratory as has been already stated. It is a hopeful sign or portent that our great men of science are coming to the realization that Mother-Earth itself is no dead and inactive agent, but is as fully 'creative' in its relatively small way, as are the far more active stars in their usually immensely greater bulk. Nature's operations are universally identic.

being born from hydrogen and helium gas. These substances are oxygen, the life-giving gas; magnesium, whose blinding light makes night-photographs possible; silicon, of which the earth, glass, and sand are largely made; and iron. And the mysterious rays from afar, possibly from the great spiral nebulae that astronomers know as half-formed universes in the making, are simply energy hurled forth from the atoms in the mighty travail of new creation.

In other words, the rays are messengers telling us that the universe isn't running down. Rather it is being built up and replenished by continual creation of its common substances from the two simplest substances of all; two gases that are extraordinarily abundant throughout the stellar world.

These two gases are hydrogen and helium; and the example of the birth of elemental substances from which the others of the chemical elements are derivative is most apposite and instructive. Our ultra-modern chemistry no longer believes in the dozens of natural elements, whose names and symbols once occupied several columns in our text-books of chemistry, as being the invariant and indestructible building-bricks of the physical world. Yet this idea of the indestructibility and invariant nature of the chemical atoms was universally held by chemists only a few years ago, relatively speaking, excepting possibly by a few intuitive minds. Times have changed and ideas and consequently things dependent upon ideas have changed with them. In our day the idea of absolute and indestructible elements of matter has gone by. No more 'absolute' matter, no more 'absolute' force, or absolute this, or absolute that: things have become relative throughout, each to each, and all to all. This is a great advance in conceptual knowledge, because it is obviously a better visioning of Nature herself, which is equivalent to saying that the idea is true — or relatively so! But while things and beings are all relative to each other and none is absolute, this fact obviously does not change their essences, nor their essential characteristics as individuals.

The lightest of physical atoms known today is the hydrogen atom, which consists of but one electron and one proton. Perhaps the next lightest atom known is helium, which consists of four hydrogen atoms in combination, with their protonic-electronic nucleus. But mark this: something drew those four hydrogen atoms into combination in order to form what is called an atom of helium. What was it? And mark this also: the helium atom is said not to weigh, although made of and composed of four hydrogen atoms, as much as four hydrogen atoms are supposed to weigh when taken separately. Something equivalent to weight was lost in the combination-process; and that something was matter or mass, which during the process of combination was alchemically transmuted or evolved into energy, which left the new systemic helium atom and became a ray — shall we say one of these cosmic rays? Here then is a case of the transmutation of matter or of the changing over of a portion of matter into an equivalent amount of energy.

The idea of the sempiternal nature of the physical atom is only the continuance of the ideas of the older but still fairly recent chemistry as imbodied in coherent theory by Dalton[205] during the early years of the nineteenth century. This idea of the physical atom as being an indivisible, everlasting, elementary body is now no longer held by the more modern school of physical chemists, who, since the discoveries in radio-activity first dazzled their eyes, are coming to know well enough that the disintegration — in other words the death — of the atom into other conditions or states of matter is the very probable cause of the birth of the various elements of physical matter. For manifestation of activity is always accompanied with an expenditure of force or energy, whether we can trace it or not. This is a fundamental postulate of modern science, and it is a very true one. Each such expenditure of force or energy means one of two things, we may suppose: a building-up process, an integration, or a process of disintegration. This is likewise an axiom in esoteric cosmology, and hence one may say that some at least of Millikan's ideas are welcome because in them one hears a certain portion of our own teachings expressed in modern scientific and mathematical form. It suggests closer approaches to the Esoteric Philosophy, to come later.

Millikan is quoted in the daily press as saying:

We have known for thirty years that in radio-active processes the heavier atoms are disintegrating into lighter ones. It is therefore to be expected that somewhere in the universe the building-up process is going on to replace the tearing-down process represented by radio-activity.

Thus is science showing clearly that atoms like everything else have their period of life, come into being, grow, reach their maturity, undergo decrepitude and decay, followed by death — disintegration; and that then they come again into being, because, as Millikan clearly indicates: 'creation' is continuous — within the Manvantara, say we. This is a dynamic, changing, and constantly evolving world, instead of a merely disintegrating one; and as some atoms disintegrate, thereby giving birth to other atoms of somewhat different kind,

---

205. 1766 — 1844.

why should not this rule apply to all kinds — otherwise, how came they into being?

The Ancient Wisdom teaches and has always taught what science has in part discovered and is on the threshold of understanding more clearly, namely, that all forms of matter are radio-active, had we but the means to perceive it; and that if we do not see any instances, or at least only a few instances if any, of lighter atoms being formed into heavier ones, it is because our planet, Earth, is in the second or ascending arc of its evolution, i. e., its involution, so that disintegration of the heavier into the lighter elements is the first to take place, and it will be ages before easily observable radio-active processes affect the lighter groups of atoms. In the preceding or descending arc along which our planet ran, aeons of ages agone, the converse was Nature's procedure, but only towards the end of the descending arc did the atoms become truly physical and no longer quasi-ethereal or ethereal. On this descending arc the lighter atoms all had the impulse, or showed the tendency, to integrate into the heavier, because the vital essences of the Earth were steadily descending into matter and were expressing themselves in increasingly more material forms and conditions. Now, since we have passed the mid-way point, physical matter is very slowly passing away or disintegrating into more ethereal forms and conditions of substances and force; and necessarily the heaviest elements, such as uranium and thorium, etc., are the ones that tend, first and most, to feel this inner urge or impulse of the universal vital activities of the planet.[206]

'Creation' — adopting here the word so often used in modern scientific works such as those already cited from — has always been going on in different parts of space, while at the same time in other parts of space the process of disintegration or dissolution has the temporary upper hand; for the fact is that worlds, and aggregations of worlds, are born, live, grow to maturity, have their period of mature efflorescence, then decay, and finally die, just as everything else in the Universe does; for the Universe as a whole and in all its parts is an evolving Universe, therefore growing, which means changing; and because it is composed of virtually an infinite number of discrete, that is individual, entities — we may illustrate this by pointing to the atoms — of many kinds and of differing grades of ethereality, of which each has its own life-term or period: it is obvious that each

---

206. For a brief sketch of the manner in which this takes place, consult chapter x, 'Esoteric Teachings on the Evolution of Human and Animal Beings.'

one and every one of these individual entities copies in its own term or career what happens in the Universe of which it is an integral and inseparable part, because perforce, the part must obey the general laws, functions, operations, and structure of the Universal Whole.

III

Returning to the idea or teaching of the Esoteric Tradition regarding the integration and disintegration of worlds and universes, it is most interesting to note that adumbrations at least of the fundamental conception involved in this process are beginning to break into open and ready scientific minds. Sir James Jeans, for instance, speaks as one who had received an inspiration or thought-wave from some one of the great Sages and Seers when he writes:

> The type of conjecture which presents itself, somewhat insistently, is that the centers of the nebulae are of the nature of "singular points," at which matter is poured into our universe from some other, and entirely extraneous, spatial dimension, so that, to a denizen of our universe, they appear as points at which matter is being continually created.[207]

His 'singular points' — a remarkable phrase for it suggests that these 'singular points' are what the Esoteric Philosophy calls 'laya-centers,' which idea imbodies a profound philosophical conception as ancient as thinking man — are, apparently, those 'points' where intercommunication between cosmic plane and cosmic plane or sphere and sphere takes place. There is such a laya-center, or to use Dr. Jeans's phrase, 'singular point,' at the heart of every entity that is — such as a sun, to take a graphic illustration. Every atom contains one such general atomic laya-center; every corpuscle, every granule, every globe in space, every human being, every individualized aggregate anywhere, contains such a laya-center. Every human ovum contains one such; and it is through the laya-center in that human generative particle that the incarnating entity comes into incarnation: as it were sends its life and its energic ray through it, thus furnishing the urge behind the growing entity and causing the development of the unborn infant to birth, and then through infancy and childhood to adult manhood. In fact, the vital germ of every seed that is contains at its heart a laya-center from which and through which the entity growing to maturity from that seed draws its

---

207. This is a noteworthy passage, and is found in *Astronomy and Cosmogony*, p. 352; by permission of the Macmillan Company, publishers.

streams of vitality and the spiritual potencies which build it into the being it is to become.

Jeans speaks of 'dimensions'; and one may ask in passing, why not use plain words in order to imbody his really noteworthy conception? Why should he not say 'other worlds' instead of using the vague and when all is said rather questionable term 'dimensions'? Does this fact show the influence over even a great modern scientific intellect of the familiar fear that it is unsafe to use words conveying old and familiar but yet true thoughts? If so, the great English scientist is not alone in scientific circles in this aversion from employing many old but graphic and truthful terms and expressions, because most scientists apparently are averse from using words which in their minds are too closely linked with bygone religious and philosophical notions. For this very understandable aversion one has no little sympathy and still less blame, yet in a way it is rather unfortunate.

At any rate, he calls these other and inner worlds 'dimensions,' probably according to the new-fangled idea of there being more than three dimensions in and of matter, e. g., four dimensions and five dimensions, and perhaps still others. It seems to be becoming a mathematical bias for mathematicians to think that they think that such dimensions are possible; one can only point out, however much one may object to the use of the term, that there is, nevertheless, a true intuition behind this very striving towards newer and more comprehensive conceptual ideas.

However, there is no need to quibble over words; the essential idea here is that this great modern scientist points with a true intuition to the Reality behind the physical seeming, behind and within the visible and tangible.

Laya is an age-old Sanskrit term which means 'dissolving center' or 'resolving center.' Matter, transforming itself upwards into a higher and more ethereal plane, in other words in leaving our physical realms, passes into such superior plane through *laya-centers* or points or channels, which are open doors as it were, or canals of both egress and ingress. Equivalently, therefore, these laya-centers are the points or channels or canals where the substances or matters of the superior planes pass downwards and enter our physical universe under what is to us the guise of forces or energies, which is really matter in its sixth or in its seventh and highest state. These forces and energies transform themselves first alchemically and then later chemically into the various 'matters' of the physical world, and thus in time become the chemical elements that are known.

In *The Secret Doctrine*, we find the following profound, significant, and indeed *prophetic*, passage, written by H. P. Blavatsky:

We have said that Laya is what Science may call the Zero-point or line; the realm of absolute negativeness, or the one real absolute Force, the NOUMENON [or Causal Beginning] of the Seventh State of that which we ignorantly call and recognise as "Force"; or again the Noumenon [or Causal Beginning] of Undifferentiated Cosmic Substance which is itself an unreachable and unknowable object to finite perception; the root and basis of all states of objectivity and subjectivity too; the neutral axis, not one of the many aspects, but its centre. It may serve to elucidate the meaning if we attempt to imagine a neutral centre — . . . . A "neutral centre" is, in one aspect, the limiting point of any given set of senses. Thus, imagine two consecutive planes of matter as already formed; each of these corresponding to an appropriate set of perceptive organs. We are forced to admit that between these two planes of matter an incessant circulation takes place; and if we follow the atoms and molecules of (say) the lower in their transformation upwards, these will come to a point where they pass altogether beyond the range of the faculties we are using on the lower plane. In fact, to us the matter of the lower plane there vanishes from our perception into nothing — or rather it passes on to the higher plane, and the state of matter corresponding to such a point of transition must certainly possess special and not readily discoverable properties. Such "Seven Neutral Centres," then, are produced by Fohat [Cosmic Consciousness-Energy] who . . . quickens matter into activity and evolution.[208]

The above words were written in 1888. Forty years later, in 1928-9, Sir James H. Jeans writes of his 'singular points,' and thereby displays a genuine intuition of the esoteric truth and the teaching concerning it. But as yet Sir James sees only the appearance of matter *coming into* our own physical world from what he mistakenly calls a 'dimension,' which is really the invisible or next succeeding World above ours, a superior Cosmic Plane. But he does not point out — which should be pointed out — that these open doors or channels, these laya-centers, or his 'singular points,' equivalently serve for the passage of the matter of our world which has become through evolution highly etherealized, back again into the force or forces from which it originally came, thus vanishing or passing upwards in a burst of energy to its first and primordial stage, and thus establishing a dual circulation from within outwards and from without inwards: from our world inwards into the spheres superior to ours, and, indeed, into spheres inferior to ours also, if the passage happens to be degenerative and thus follows the downwards tendency.

---

208. *The Secret Doctrine*, Vol. I, p. 148.

Nor is there any reason why this passage of matter from the higher to the lower, or conversely, from the lower to the higher, should cease anywhere during the vastly long life-term of a Universe in manifestation or in Manvantara. There is not the slightest reason for thinking so; carrying the thought of laya-centers as exist-ing in inner worlds, as they most certainly do, we are perforce obliged to conclude that other and later stages follow in the pro-gress upwards and inwards of such wave or stream of advancing substance until, at the great last stage for any Universe, it re-becomes the brilliance and substance of the Cosmic Consciousness governing such Universe, which consciousness always was its own root, and from which it originally emanated or flowed forth. Where then can we, may we, put limits or endings to consciousness, to mind, to force, to substance and its illusory child, matter? The matter of our plane becomes and is the energy of the planes below it. The matter of the planes above ours is the source of the forces or energies which stream downwards into our plane on their way to become one or other of the forms or manifestations of 'matter' on this plane. The inflowing streams of force or energy simply *traverse* the phy-sical universe, and thereafter in due course of long ages pursue their pathway into other and inner planes of being.[209]

---

209. The course of the reflexions contained in the above text brings us almost irresistibly to the ultra-modern conception of all forms of physical matter as being derivatives of radiation in its manifold manifestations. It is no far cry, but an almost inevitable deduction, to suppose that physical matter as our senses report it to us, is, when all is said, easily describable as concreted or crystallized radiation or light, to adopt a familiar term — not so much the one octave called 'visible' light, but light in its more general significance imbodied in the word radiation. We must remember that 'radiation' now means the many 'octaves' of radiative activity from the 'cosmic rays' to those used in 'radio'-work.

The idea is not at all new, although for hundreds of years it has been either forgotten or quietly overlooked. Newton in his *Opticks* had a sufficiently clear conception of the idea when he wrote:

"Are not gross Bodies and Light convertible into one another, and may not Bodies receive much of their Activity from the Particles of Light which enter their Composition? . . ."

And again:

"The changing of Bodies into Light, and Light into Bodies, is very conformable to the Course of Nature, which seems delighted with Transmu-tations."

The great English scientist never wrote a more admirable thing than this; and one can only marvel that for so long a time it has been so utterly ignored.

All matter therefore is ultimately force or energy, and all matter likewise may be ultimately considered to be pure light, which is both substance and force crystallized, so to say, into material form and shape; hence the world we live in, in its ultimate analysis, is light or radiation, crystallized or concreted light.[210]   Thus all things therefore: nebulae and comets, suns and planets; and, on our Earth, stones, vegetation, animals' bodies and our bodies too — all are crystallized or concreted light or radiation, or, what is the same thing, forces balancing other forces or energies and holding them in more or less stable equilibrium.

IV

The Berlin scientist, Planck, likewise a scientist of international renown, has helped most effectively to break down the barriers once supposed to exist between matter and 'energy,' by the enunciation of his Quantum Theory.   In attempting to account for the operation of certain natural forces in the light of more recent discoveries, more particularly certain electro-magnetic phenomena which have always been obscure, an intuition came to him one day to the effect that what is called 'energy' is, like matter, composed of discrete quantities, that is, unit-quantities; and that 'energy' is not a continuous flow.   At any rate, if energy or force is conventionally conceivable as a continuous flow, much as a stream of water is, we are

---

210. Instances where intuitive modern scientists are approaching the confines of some of the teachings of the Esoteric Philosophy are so numerous that it would require too much space to do more than make an occasional selection which for its appositeness and modern scientific substantiation of the Theosophical teaching becomes particularly interesting.   Thus, Sir James Jeans in his *The Mysterious Universe*, p. 83 (quotation by permission of the Macmillan Company, publishers), states:

". . . the tendency of modern physics is to resolve the whole material universe into waves, and nothing but waves. These waves are of two kinds: bottled-up waves, which we call matter, and unbottled waves, which we call radiation or light. If annihilation of matter occurs, the process is merely that of unbottling imprisoned wave-energy and setting it free to travel through space. These concepts reduce the whole universe to a world of light, potential or existent. . . ."

One is strongly reminded of the declaration of H. P. Blavatsky, the Great Theosophist, that it will one day be discovered by scientific research that what we call our physical universe is but condensed or concreted or crystallized light. This statement was made by her in 1888, and was then considered to be merely the play of her mind, indulging in phantasy. Her justification has arrived!

nevertheless now driven to the thought that energy or force, which is thus like water, is divisible into particles, or in other words is discrete in type; as water is composed of the atoms of hydrogen and oxygen, so energy or force is now conceived of as being composed of corpuscles or particles or charges — called 'quanta.' As matter is composed of atoms, generally speaking, so force or energy is now considered to be composed of 'atoms' or corpuscles, likewise. Planck, developing his intuition into the form of a theory, evolved forth a conception of these energic corpuscles or discrete particles — or whatever is the best manner in which to describe them — to which he gave the name of *quanta* — a Latin plural, meaning 'so-much-es.' These *quanta* are units not of 'energy' alone, but of energy multiplied by time — most simply understood by the time during which any one of such units acts as a definite quantity, as for instance, an electrical discharge; and each such *quantum* or unit, as it is conceived, combined with the time-element, is called an 'action.' Here the terminology of ultra-modern chemical physics is followed as far as these extremely metaphysical and mathematical concepts may be grasped by others than the inventors of them.

From what has been already studied and discussed, it should be abundantly evident to every thoughtful mind, that our Universe in all its phenomena and appearances is illusory; that physical matter in itself is actually the most unsubstantial and unreal thing we know, because we know it only by imperfect reporters — our physical senses — which report but a small part of the cosmos — one or two tones of the gamut of the Song of Life, as it were: only of these few notes do our physical senses tell us of the vast range of vibrational activity that the Universe contains.

Next, it should be evident that force or energy, while substantial, is more ethereal and of a finer and more subtil character than is matter; and that our Universe, our World, or indeed man, or any entity, is infilled with force or energy, which, while substantial, is yet more ethereal than the vehicle or body upon which it works and in which it works.

Further, it is likewise evident that the forces or energies which play through matter and govern it and control it and guide it, are of many different kinds: the physical, the ethereal, the still more ethereal, and so on upwards and inwards until spirit itself — the Cosmic Originant — is reached. From here, from this Originant, begins the ascent of a still more spiritual Hierarchy in every sense of the word; and so onwards, *ad infinitum,* at least as far as human understanding can follow the rising scale which Universal Nature is.

Thus again, viewing the picture from the matter-side and what is beneath it, we can find in this direction no ultimates either. The electron is not an ultimate, for the teaching is that there is something still beyond, still within, in a sense still more infinitesimal, which builds up or constructs the electrons and protons, etc., of which our physical-material universe consists, these infinitesimals being parts of inferior magnitude, although by no means necessarily of inferior energy or potency.

We literally do not know how far we may go in the direction of this kind of divisibility, nor would one even venture to suggest a limiting boundary, unless indeed it be the illuminating Theosophical teaching of the substance-matter or mother-substance of any Cosmic Hierarchy reaching frontiers of 'inwardness' or 'outwardness' which we may call the frontiers of homogeneity. Such homogeneous substance would be but one of the landing-places, or hierarchical ultimates in either direction of the endless Stair of Life or Ladder of Being; so that penetrating in thought still farther, we perceive that what we call homogeneity, as translated to us by our sense-observation and mental concepts, is but the beginning of another and higher — or conversely lower — range or scale of hierarchical life-entities.

In connexion with what was said *supra* concerning the existence and nature and functions of laya-centers, it may be as well to point out here that these laya-centers can, from one viewpoint, be graphically described as originating points between Cosmic Plane and Cosmic Plane, or neutral centers so to speak; and as the junction-line or uniting substance between Cosmic Plane and Cosmic Plane is always the highest of the lower sub-hierarchy fusing into and becoming the lowest substance of the succeeding or higher hierarchy, it is evident that this fusion-substance or line is of homogeneous character. It must be remembered that Nature repeats herself throughout her entire structure, as has been explained before. Thus these laya-centers are not only channels or canals of communication between Cosmic Plane and Cosmic Plane, but, otherwise viewed, could truly be called individualized points or monadic hearts or centers. Their number is literally beyond our powers of human computation and in consequence may be stated as virtually quasi-infinite.

Be it remembered also that these laya-centers are at one time of their existence dormant or passive or latent until awakened into functional activity, after which they become foci of intense motion, and so remain during the life-period or life-term of the being or entity or thing which they through their functional operation bring into manifested being, and, in a very true sense of the word, *ensoul.*

V

Our modern scientists say that the ultimate or rather simplest physical atom today is the hydrogen-atom. But let us ask ourselves a question of fundamental import: How comes it that it is here, i. e., how comes it into being, and whence comes it into our physical universe? The mere fact that one may say that it is there or here answers the question in no wise whatsoever; it is merely inverting the question or the query into an affirmation. It will one day have become common knowledge that there are things still more ethereal, still simpler, so far as physical matter is concerned, than is the hydrogen-atom.

There are signs that what was at one time called 'Prout's Hypothesis' is rapidly gaining favor today in the minds of at least a large number of thoughtful scientific men, although even Prout's Hypothesis may seem revolutionary to no small number, even in our own age which is becoming familiar with the pranks of electrons and the elfin movements of their careers. The English physician and chemist, William Prout, who died in April, 1850, evolved the idea from his studies of Nature, and taught it with sincere enthusiasm for a long time during the latter part of his life, that what the ancients called the *prima materia*, or πρώτη ὕλη (*prote hyle*) — i.e., primary or primordial physical substance — is what European chemists know under the name of hydrogen, from which gas he thought that the other elements as listed in the chemical tables were formed by some as yet unknown process of solidification or condensation and final grouping. The hypothesis gained some small currency for a while, but was finally abandoned when it was discovered upon closer research that the other chemical atoms were not exact multiples of the hydrogen-atom.

But the case is now different because wider research since Prout's day and new discoveries have explained what seemed to be the main difficulty in Prout's hypothesis as just stated above. This later and more accurate research-work in chemical physics, largely due to the labors of Thomson, which were taken up and carried to a successful conclusion by F. W. Aston, showed that some at least of the so-called chemical elements actually consisted of a mixture of two elements which have identical chemical properties but actually possess differing atomic weights. These were called by Soddy *isotopes* — from the Greek compound ἰσο-τόπος (*iso-topos*), signifying having the same place in the chemical table. Chlorine for instance with atomic weight of 35.46 was thus demonstrated to be not a single unitary element but a mixture of atoms possessing chlorine-properties, but with the respective weights 35 and 37. Similar results were obtained with several of the other elements; so that the atomic weights of the other elements in the chemical tables thus far examined are at present known to be very nearly whole numbers, which actually are, as Prout pointed out, multiples of hydrogen. As Dampier-Whetham states:

Prout's hypothesis, that they are all multiples of that of hydrogen, has now been proved to be true, the slight discrepancy being both explicable by and of surpassing interest in the modern theory of the atom.[211]

If our ultra-modern physical chemists are right, and the hydrogen-atom is composed of but two corpuscles — a single electron with a companionate proton, which together form the hydrogen-atom (and we may for the moment let it go at that) the electron and the proton must *de facto* be each one a self-contained and self-enduring yet composite entity; otherwise neither could exist as an individual unit. But while this is so, or may be so, it would seem to be vain and allowing ourselves to fall under the sway of a fond delusion to suppose that because as yet we cannot trace things farther back, the electrical corpuscle is the ultimate entity of physical being. All that can be said is that such electronic unit is the last stage in analytic investigation that has thus far been reached. As a matter of fact, it may as well be stated here once for all, for what use it may be to those who are interested, that the Esoteric Philosophy regards every physical unitary entity, however ethereal or gross, however large or small, whether macrocosmic or ultra-microscopic, as a composite; and hence the deduction is to be drawn that even these so-called 'ultimate' particles of physical substance are themselves divisible into still other component units — were our resources of investigation sufficiently large and our technique sufficiently skilful to enable us to carry our work into the ultra-infinitesimal.

One might aver: Show me anything that has physical, i. e., material existence, however sublimated or ethereal it may be, which is at the same time truly homogeneous and therefore entirely non-composite. If it were such, it could not be physical material, the very meaning of which words signifies composition, construction — in other words, heterogeneity.

The idea of all this is, therefore, that the roots of things, their foundations as it were, are in the inner and invisible worlds; in

---

211. This extract is taken from Dampier-Whetham's *A History of Science*, p. 391 (1931). (By permission of the Macmillan Company, publishers.)

consequence, the true explanations of things are to be found likewise in the inner and invisible worlds; furthermore, the seeds of things, or their monadic essences, are in the inner and *spiritual* worlds; and there we also live in our own inner and spiritual consciousness.

VI

Few indeed realize how immense are the forces and powers of the invisible realms or worlds. Leaving aside for the moment our own invisible sheaths of being — i. e., our invisible clothing or garments between us and the spirit, and still higher inwards to our Divine Spark, the Monad — few indeed realize, that the atoms of even our physical frames imbody and therefore enclose truly terrific forces, which, because they are so amazingly balanced in more or less stable equilibrium, hold these bodies of ours in coherent and enduring form and shape. Yet we as monadic beings in our inmost manage in some wonderfully instinctive manner, outside of our ordinary human understanding, to hold together in fairly stable equilibrium those fearfully powerful and almost incomprehensible forces that constantly play through us, so that we exist on this physical plane as corporeal entities and do so almost unconsciously; and we are not torn to pieces by these natural genii that we unconsciously imprison within our physical frames!

It has long been a dream, more hopeful than as yet practicable, that man could harness the immense sources of power in the atomic world. It has been estimated by a recent well-known scientific thinker that a single cubic centimeter of the earth is so packed with electrical power, that if the latter's positive and negative poles could be divorced and concentrated at points a centimeter apart, the attraction between them would be a force equivalent to a hundred million million million tons!

One hundred quintillion tons! Think now, how many cubic centimeters of matter are contained in our physical bodies; and reflect over the incomprehensibly stupendous play of forces, and balancing of them, that occurs at every instant and all the time, incessantly; consider also how this physical body of ours retains its form in adulthood relatively unchanged as the years go by; how, from a microscopic human seed it grows through infancy and youth on to manhood, changing and evolving during those transitory periods most marvelously and, from the first, working steadily and without intermission, teleologically towards one end: human adulthood, doing so under the gripping and infallibly directing control of the inner and invisible monadic entity, as we call our spiritual Self. What a wonder it all is!   It is this amazingly powerful inner and invisible monadic being, controlling these immense forces of the etheric realms of Nature, which molds us both astrally and physically—to say nothing for the moment of the still more subtil forces working in the psychologic and spiritual fields of our being — and which thus makes us what we are physically; and as just hinted, behind these psychologic and astral parts of us there is the vastly more wonderful spiritual entity, controlling forces still more marvelous and more amazingly subtil — for the spiritual monadic entity is the root of our being.   Unthinkably vast as the source of energy is which is locked up in the atom, it differs both in potency and in quality from those far higher and more potent spiritual wave-lengths of energy of the spirit which pass from star to star.

In far distant future aeons, when evolutionary development shall then have carried us far along our future path of destiny, we shall come into self-conscious control of the still more mysterious and wonderful powers and forces and faculties of the spiritual parts of our constitution, which at present work in us and through us in a manner that seems automatic to our present lower and limited psychologic consciousness, now expressing itself, this latter consciousness, as thought and will: the composite faculty and power which enables us to raise an arm or some other part of the body, or to think consciously to definite ends, and doing so more or less as we will.

Sir Oliver Lodge, in his *Ether of Space,* says that the available energy, could man only harness it, lying in one cubic millimeter of etheric matter, which is a particle no larger than the head of an ordinary pin, is enough to supply a million horsepower working continuously for forty million years!

Such things does science tell us of this seemingly empty space, this 'emptiness,' which is in reality the etheric world of the plane next superior to our physical plane, in other words what in Theosophy is called the cosmic astral plane.   Our senses therefore do not report to us faithfully, or, perhaps better, they cannot report more than what they themselves can gather from within the range of etheric vibrations that they have been evolved, or have learned, to utilize. They are very imperfect instruments.   When we recollect that our own gross physical sphere, which seems so material and so dense to us, is, after all, nothing but a vast agglomerate of electric charges, which are resident in the bodies of the different atoms of which physical matter is composed, and which electronic 'sub-atoms' are as widely separated from each other, more or less, as are the celestial bodies in our own physical sphere; when we recollect all this, there is small difficulty in recognising the fact that beings with a sense-apparatus different from our own could easily enough look through the physical bodies of us humans and through the physical body of our Earth as if these were — 'empty space.'[212]

---

212. So closely are all the parts of Nature and its functions linked together as an interworking web of not only 'space-time' but of what we may call 'force-matter,' that it is now coming to be suspected that nothing at all in the Universe can be excepted from this general rule — and this is one of the fundamental postulates of Esotericism.

The five human senses, for instance, as expressed through their respective organs, are themselves the products not only of evolution in the common understanding of this term, as signifying unfolding or development, but likewise the products of interworking and interwoven forces active in the various matters which compose the Universe.

Furthermore, it is the teaching of the Esoteric Tradition that even the senses of man, with their respective sense-organs, numbering five at the present time, but to number seven, if not ten, in the distant future, were not all evolved or unfolded simultaneously, but appeared one after the other in serial order, albeit there were always in every sense the sensory adumbrations of the other senses or of the other sense-organs before they appeared in the relative perfection that they later attained.

Thus the present five human senses, with their respective organs, appeared in the following order as regards time and sequence: *hearing* was the first sense developed; *touch* followed it; then in regular series came *sight, taste,* and *smell.* It is interesting to compare this series of five organs with the 'octaves' of radiation which modern science has now discovered and is studying with such care and interest. The senses are expressions, one and all, of various forms of 'radiation,' i. e., of forces working in material substance; although in these cases the radiation or radiations are as much of a psycho-mental character as they are physical, as demonstrated in the organs through which they work.

No one can as yet say just how many octaves of radiation exist. Theoretically, and in fact it is thus taught in the Esoteric Philosophy, these octaves of radiation extend indefinitely in both directions of what we may call the 'scale of radiation.' If we take the ordinary scale, and consider the visible radiation of light in its sevenfold varieties as the central part of this scale, and consider the right hand to be the ultra-violet range, followed by octaves of still shorter wave-length, and if we take the left-hand as being a series of octaves of radiations of longer wave-length, we have here a scale which corresponds singularly with the five human senses as thus far developed in connexion with their respective organs.

Thus, beginning at the extreme left-hand in the range of long wave-lengths, we have, as thus far discovered, the wireless waves covering some eleven or twelve octaves as thus far known, and which express themselves as sound, thus corresponding to our sense of hearing. Passing along the scale towards the

Indeed, had we the 'etheric eye,' we should perceive the intra-atomic ether in which we physically live, and we should be invisible to each other as physical bodies; only an occasional electron would flash like a streak of light across our vision — an electron symbolical

---

right, and thus through octaves of wave-lengths which grow progressively shorter, we pass through those waves which produce in us the sense of heat, i. e., touch, which thus follows hearing. Continuing our journey to the right and thus traversing octaves of waves of steadily decreasing length, we reach the range of visible radiation with its sevenfold spectrum, and thus find our organ of sight responding here to the impacts upon it of wave-lengths which it can receive and translate to the mind. Continuing our journey through the scale to the right, and thus entering into wave-lengths of constantly decreasing length, i. e., entering into shorter wave-lengths, we enter the ultra-violet range of the scale, which, could we see the facts, we would recognise to correspond to our sense of taste, represented by its functional organ in the human body; and continuing our journey to the right and into wave-lengths growing still shorter, we enter into the range of the X-rays, which correspond to our sense of smell.

Two other senses, with their corresponding organs, will be developed in the human body before our time-period on this globe in this Fourth Round is ended, and these two senses hitherto undeveloped or of which we have only intimations, will, by comparison with the radiation-scale above spoken of, be discovered to correspond with the wave-lengths which are found towards the extreme right end of the radiation-scale, thus far known — i. e., reaching into the end of the X-rays and into the beginning of the γ-rays.

Then, when evolution in the far distant future brings forth the three senses which will be evolved or unfolded before humanity leaves this planetary chain, scientists of that distant time will realize that these three senses, as yet utterly inactive in man, will correspond in their regular serial order as they unfold with what in that time will be the farthest reaches of the radiation-scale towards the right — i. e., wave-lengths still shorter than the γ-rays, and which we may briefly describe under the generalizing or collective term 'cosmic rays.'

Of course this does not mean that the radiation-scale in Nature ends there. It merely signifies that the perfected humanity of that far future will have become responsive to radiation, and self-consciously so, which now is but slightly understood or only suspected.

As concerns the many ranges of different radiations on the scale of Nature, it is interesting to remember that these octaves are virtually endless; science is beginning to have some adumbration of this fact. As pointed out by Sir James Jeans in his book *Through Space and Time,* p. 53 (1934; quotation by permission of the Macmillan Company, publishers): "Our ears can hear eleven octaves of sound, but our eyes can only see one octave of light." Logically this could seem to mean that our ears as a sense-organ are far older and therefore more capacious in function than are our eyes. The difference between ability to sense and interpret eleven octaves as in hearing, and one octave as in sight, while not

of electric energy. But there is something more in man, by which he may learn and look out upon universal and invisible Nature, than his mere sense-apparatus: it is the faculties and powers of his own

---

immense is certainly significant, and should be remembered in our conclusions.

Be it noted also that in Occultism every one of the human senses, considered now as psycho-mental, vital-astral organic functions, contains within itself the potentialities and capacities, albeit latent, of every one of the other senses. Thus, the sense, and to a less extent the organ, of sight, contains not only its own capacity and particularized function — vision — but likewise, more or less latent, the other four senses of hearing, touch, taste, and smell. Similarly so with the other senses, which, each one, contains the potentiality and latent functional capacities of the other four.

Every one of the seven great Root-Races of mankind succeeding each other serially in time, brings out into full functional activity, and likewise in regular serial order, one of the seven senses, although including each of the as yet undeveloped senses, in imperfect manifestation or unfoldment. Thus:

First Root-Race towards its end has evolved the sense of Hearing with its appropriate organ, but likewise manifests, though very imperfectly, the other six senses.

Second Root-Race towards its end has evolved the sense of Touch with its appropriate organ, but likewise manifests, though very imperfectly, the other five senses.

Third Root-Race towards its end has evolved the sense of Sight with its appropriate organ, but likewise manifests, though very imperfectly, the other four senses.

Fourth Root-Race towards its end has evolved the sense of Taste with its appropriate organ, but likewise manifests, though very imperfectly the other three senses.

Fifth Root-Race towards its end will fully evolve the sense of Smell with its appropriate organ, but likewise manifests, though very imperfectly, the other two senses.

Sixth and Seventh Root-Races towards their end will evolve each its own appropriate sense, with its appropriate organ; and thus the series of seven completely developed senses, each with its appropriate organ and organic function, will all be in activity at the end of the Seventh Root-Race on this Globe in this Fourth Round.

First Root-Race: Hearing
Second Root-Race: Hearing and Touch
Third Root-Race: Hearing, Touch, and Sight
Fourth Root-Race: Hearing, Touch, Sight, and Taste
Fifth Root-Race: Hearing, Touch, Sight, Taste, and Smell
    etc.

It is thus seen that each sense contains in potentiality the radicles or rudi-

inner god, of practically infinite capacity, of practically infinite possibilities, because it is linked inseparably with the God-Nature of the Universe, and therefore is it able to go to and to reach the roots of things, in other words, to Cosmic Reality itself, for this inner god is an individualized but identic part of that Cosmic Reality.

When the science of the future shall have realized that physical beings cannot exist without an inner focus of energy — call this inner focus 'soul' or by any other name one may please to adopt — then the truly philosophical science of the future will with every year tend to become more definitely and more fully in line with the Esoteric Philosophy, the Esoteric Tradition. When the science of the future shall have come to understand, and in understanding to realize, that the physical world is but the expression of the forces or energies and ethereal substances flowing into it, and thereby composing it, from spheres and worlds which to our present sense-apparatus are invisible — and which we may call the 'soul' of the physical world — then too shall we in all probability, indeed of necessity, see the science of that future day becoming with the passage of each year more and more Theosophical.

Science is even now very rapidly moving in the direction just outlined; and the signs are growing daily more numerous that the brilliant minds of ultra-modern scientific thinkers are becoming restive under the rapidly accumulating facts of discovery for which there has as yet been evolved or found out no unifying and satisfying philosophical system, bringing them all together into a definitely coherent and satisfyingly logical synthesis.

Unfortunately, this marriage of Science with the Father of all human Wisdom, the Esoteric Philosophy, has not yet been reached, and altogether too large a part of ultra-modern science is still soulless, and this descriptive word is not here used with any desire to be disrespectful to nor forgetful of the really magnificent work of our scientists in all countries in doing whatever they can and may

---

ments of all the other senses which will follow at any time; and, as a matter of fact, as is well known to students of Occultism, all these senses are but specializations of what might be called the interior and unifying Source of them all. The reader is referred to the author's *Fundamentals of the Esoteric Philosophy* for an explanation of how the Originants, whether a planetary chain or any other evolving entity, unfold and roll forth from themselves, in regular serial order, the chain of manifested 'events' which in their aggregate produce the entirety of a manifested being or entity. The matter is too complicate fully to explain in a footnote, nor would it be wise even to attempt to do so.

to unveil Nature's secrets — and this they are most certainly trying to do and to a certain extent are doing. They are using all their efforts, mental and other, to penetrate behind the veils of the outward physical seeming. Truth is perhaps the holiest thing that man can aspire to have, and unquestionably today the best minds in science are seekers after Truth.

When that future, hereinbefore alluded to, shall have arrived, science then will have become distinctly religious, but in a cosmical sense, and not in the restricted sense which this word 'religious' is ordinarily understood to have in Occidental countries. Then, in those future times, a new and very beautiful Religion of Nature of a truly spiritual type will take the place of the present period of agnostic uncertainty, for it will be not *a* religion, but Religion, founded entirely and wholly throughout on the facts of the Spiritual Universe.

CHAPTER XV

WEBS OF DESTINY — I

THE title of the present chapter, 'Webs of Destiny,' has been chosen with deliberation because graphically descriptive and therefore highly suggestive of the manner in which conscious and self-conscious beings enwrap themselves in the consequences or results or effects which flow forth from thoughts had, emotions felt, and actions done by reason of inner impulses.

The Esoteric Philosophy rejects as both puerile and philosophically untenable in every sense the notion prevailing today in the Western world to the effect that hap or hazard, chance or fortuity, whether in the great or in the small, and in any wise and in any manner, is the cause of either circumstances or environment or of the directing impulses which beings have and follow while living in the environment which at any time may be theirs. When considered with some degree of attentive thought, it clearly becomes evident that a Universe which contains chance or blind fortuity in any smallest degree must be a Universe which is lawless, anarchic, and based on neither reason nor mind; and when the matter is presented in this rather striking fashion, probably not one man in a hundred million would consent to accept the prevailing notion as true.

Conversely, therefore, what men popularly call chance or hazard or even fortuity, is merely what knowledge or research or investigation has not yet brought sufficiently to light as being a link or links in the chain of universal causation; and such words therefore are merely vocables descriptive of human ignorance — or, if the words be preferred, of knowledge not yet attained.

Nature, using the word in the largest sense possible, or what we may call the Universal Kosmos, is organic, an Organism, builded up of and from literally innumerable minor beings and entities and things which distributively and individually are each one likewise an organism; for Nature, as has been before frequently stated, is repetitive throughout her boundless structure, so that what prevails in the small is but a reproduction or mirroring or reflexion of the Cosmic Reality, whether considered as cosmic intelligence or mind or substance, which throughout prevails in the mighty whole.

Thus, in consequence of the foregoing reasoning, All Nature may be viewed as a vast and incomprehensibly great Cosmic Web, into which everything that is is woven, because forming a component part of the Cosmic Whole; and it is from this fundamental conception or conceptual philosophical idea that the Esoteric Philosophy, in its own forms of graphic or descriptive expression, speaks of the relations of all beings to each other and to the environing Cosmic Whole as of the nature of a Web — an inextricably interwoven, interlocked, interlinked, and interpermeant fabric of lives.

Thus it is that Man, as such an individual minor organism, is throughout eternity interwoven and interlocked with the environing cosmic strands of the great Web of Life; and he therefore repeats, perforce, in all his ideations or feelings and their consequent results, the Cosmic Pattern or Law and Substance which form the Universe in which he lives and moves and has his being. Every thought he has, every emotion he experiences, and every action consequent upon the impulses arising from these thoughts and emotions, is thus to be seen as forming a most intricate and fascinating Web of Destiny which man is constantly weaving around himself, and which, in very truth, is from one point of view *himself*.

Nor should the foregoing philosophical reflexions in any wise be supposed to imbody the idea of Fatalism, or that man is the mere puppet or blind and will-less victim of an inscrutable destiny which tosses him hither and yon, whether he will or whether he nill. Such a conception as this last is totally erroneous. It is not the teaching of the Esoteric Philosophy, and is not intended to be understood in anything that may be said in the present chapter or elsewhere. On the contrary, the teaching of the Esoteric Philosophy, the Esoteric Tradition, is that man is a *willing* agent throughout his beginningless and endless course of destiny — in other words, he constantly exercises his modicum of Free Will. His will is free precisely in proportion with the degree which he has attained in rising towards self-conscious reunion with the spiritual divinity which is his own individual inmost essence, i. e., his Monad, the Self of his many human selves manifesting as reincarnations or reimbodiments in the spheres through which he passes.

The general doctrine of the weaving of such Webs of Destiny as man is continuously involving himself in by means of the exercise of his own free will, is what is called in the Esoteric Philosophy by the Sanskrit term *Karman* — the doctrine that everything, thought or emotion or inner impulse, is followed by ineluctable consequences or results or effects, which thus man involves himself in, and by so doing weaves the strands of the web of destiny in which at any moment he finds himself. Probably the general teaching has never been more graphically expressed than by the Great Theosophist, H. P. Blavatsky, who wrote as follows:

Those who believe in *Karma* have to believe in *destiny*, which, from birth to death, every man is weaving thread by thread around himself, as a spider does his cobweb; and this destiny is guided either by the heavenly voice of the invisible *prototype* outside of us, or by our more intimate *astral*, or inner man, who is but too often the evil genius of the embodied entity called man. Both these lead on the outward man, but one of them must prevail; and from the very beginning of the invisible affray the stern and implacable *law of compensation* steps in and takes its course, faithfully following the fluctuations. When the last strand is woven, and man is seemingly enwrapped in the net-work of his own doing, then he finds himself completely under the empire of this *self-made* destiny. It then either fixes him like the inert shell against the immovable rock, or carries him away like a feather in a whirlwind raised by his own actions, and this is — KARMA.[213]

And again she says:

. . . the closer the union between the mortal reflection MAN and his celestial PROTOTYPE, the less dangerous the external conditions and subsequent reincarnations — which neither Buddhas nor Christs can escape. This is not superstition, least of all is it *Fatalism*. The latter implies a blind course of some still blinder power, and man is a free agent during his stay on earth. He cannot escape his *ruling* Destiny, but he has the choice of two paths that lead him in that direction, . . . for, there are *external and internal conditions* which affect the determination of our will upon our actions, and it is in our power to follow either of the two.[214]

It is evident enough from the graphic descriptions thus extracted from *The Secret Doctrine* that man's free will is free precisely in proportion as he the more unites himself with the divine Prototype within him which is his own inmost Monadic Self, the latter being, so to say, a spiritual droplet in the Divine Ocean of the universal Mind-Consciousness-Life-Substance. But as every human being is a composite entity, formed into a unitary being by the congruency of several monadic entities which thus compose his constitution, and which by their continuous and incessant interaction and interworking make him the complex being he obviously is, it is evident, as said clearly above in the extracts from H. P. Blavatsky, that the ordinary human being, or the physical-astral man, is often, as such a vehicle,

213. *The Secret Doctrine*, Vol. I, p. 639.
214. *Op. cit.*, Vol. I, p. 639.

the unconscious or quasi-conscious victim or slave of karmic causes set in motion previously in other lives, of which the present physical man is in no wise conscious, has in no wise willed, and of which therefore he is the 'victim.'

Thus it is that there is what superficially it is proper to call 'unmerited suffering' in man's destiny, because the thoughts and acts of others are continuously at work helping to build the same web of destiny in which the man himself is enwrapped. We are continuously giving and taking to and from each other; and thus it is that our individual Webs of Destiny are so intricately and inseparably interwoven. Nevertheless, granting all the above, which is obvious enough to any perceiving and reflective mind, were we able to trace back to their ultimate causal sources the reasons why this or that or some other mishap or mischance or suffering falls upon us, we would see very clearly that even the entirety of all this so-called 'unmerited suffering' is in its origins due to our own thoughts, emotions, or actions — long since forgotten and passed from our consciousness, but active just as effectually as if we remembered. As H. P. Blavatsky again writes so well:

Nor would the ways of Karma be inscrutable were men to work in union and harmony, instead of disunion and strife. For our ignorance of those ways — which one portion of mankind calls the ways of Providence, dark and intricate; while another sees in them the action of blind Fatalism; and a third, simple chance, with neither gods nor devils to guide them — would surely disappear, if we would but attribute all these to their correct cause. With right knowledge, or at any rate with a confident conviction that our neighbours will no more work to hurt us than we would think of harming them, the two-thirds of the World's evil would vanish into thin air. Were no man to hurt his brother, Karma-Nemesis would have neither cause to work for, nor weapons to act through. It is the constant presence in our midst of every element of strife and opposition, and the division of races, nations, tribes, societies and individuals into Cains and Abels, wolves and lambs, that is the chief cause of the "ways of Providence." We cut these numerous windings in our destinies daily with our own hands, while we imagine that we are pursuing a track on the royal high road of respectability and duty, and then complain of those ways being so intricate and so dark. We stand bewildered before the mystery of our own making, and the riddles of life that *we will not* solve, and then accuse the great Sphinx of devouring us. But verily there is not an accident in our lives, not a misshapen day, or a misfortune, that could not be traced back to our own doings in this or in another life. . . .

. . . Karma-Nemesis is no more than the (spiritual) dynamical effect of causes produced and forces awakened into activity by our own actions.[215]

---

215. *Op. cit.*, Vol. I, pp. 643-4.

Or again, with equal penetration and inflexible logic the same writer states:

An Occultist or a philosopher will not speak of the goodness or cruelty of Providence; but, identifying it with Karma-Nemesis, he will teach that nevertheless it guards the good and watches over them in this, as in future lives; and that it punishes the evil-doer — aye, even to his seventh rebirth. So long, in short, as the effect of his having thrown into perturbation even the smallest atom in the Infinite World of harmony, has not been finally readjusted. For the only decree of Karma — an eternal and immutable decree — is absolute Harmony in the world of matter as it is in the world of Spirit. It is not, therefore, Karma that rewards or punishes, but it is we, who reward or punish ourselves according to whether we work with, through and along with nature, abiding by the laws on which that Harmony depends, or — break them.[216] [217]

---

216. *Op. cit.*, Vol. I, p. 643.

217. The strictest and most impartial justice rules the Worlds, for it is the result of the Kosmic Harmony permeant everywhere, and broken only by the exercise of the free wills of beings who foolishly, and in vain, attempt to sway this cosmic equilibrium. The very Heart of Universal Nature is compassion or what many call Infinite Love, which means Infinite Harmony.

It is truly a non-understanding of the fundamental principle of this Kosmic Harmony as outlined in the text above which has been the rock on which have split into two currents the two main bodies of human philosophical thought concerning the character and nature of Free Will in man. One School, the Fatalists, have denied it *in toto*, or nearly so, whether the members of this School belong to the class which invokes an Almighty Autocrat assigning unto man his lot in life, from which he has no escape; or whether it be the other class: that of the absolute Materialists, who see no free will in man, but see him only as a plaything or bit of jetsam wholly subject to the rigid determinism of their school — the result of blind chance or fortuity.

The other School is that of the Autonomists, or absolute Free-Willists, to coin a word, who seem to think that man is wholly or very largely an entirely independent willing agent, different from the Universe in which he lives so far as his will goes, and therefore possessing unrestricted voluntary action.

The Esoteric Philosophy rejects both these notions as being neither of them founded on fact, and takes the middle line: that the will of man is partially free and partially bound or restricted by the karmic consequences of his past actions for weal or for woe; but that he can attain an ever-increasing measure of freedom in his will proportionately as he unfolds or evolves an ever-increasing and larger measure of the divine force which is at the spiritual root of his being, and by which he is linked to the Cosmic Consciousness, the Cosmic Will.

Indeed, this is shown clearly enough when one considers the wide ranges, or distances rather, which separate the different Kingdoms of Nature. Thus, those Monadic Rays which are aggregated or grouped in such enormous numbers in the simple unism of the rocks, and which are in consequence bound and limited

And, finally, in connexion with the nature or character of this universal and eternally active operation or *habit* of Universal Na-

---

in mind and action, nevertheless aspire to higher things and essay to climb out of the Mineral Kingdom into the larger measure of intelligence and will in the Vegetable Kingdom; out of which in turn they slowly climb — out of these restricted fields of mind and will into the still larger measure of liberty and action that is offered in the Animal Kingdom; the members of which in their turn in precisely similar fashion, and possessing the dawn of mind and the beginnings of free choice, are striving to leave their relatively limited fields in this respect and to climb upwards into the Human Kingdom, where self-conscious voluntary action is accompanied with the exercise of a relatively free intelligence.

It is only a superficial study of this most difficult of all Theosophical doctrines, Karman, which could induce anyone to believe that its explanation, as given hereinbefore in the text, could ever bring about a selfish or cruel ignoring of the claims upon us humans which our fellow human beings perpetually have. Woven as we all are together in intricate and complicate webs of destiny, man with man and these with all other things in the Universe, it becomes an obvious philosophical and religious postulate of the first order that co-operative aid and mutual help and the carrying of each other's burdens, and the refraining from evil-doing in any manner or guise whatsoever, is the first law of our own destiny.

It is precisely upon this incomprehensibly intricate web of interwoven destinies that reposes our conception of ethics or morals as being no mere human convention, but as founded in the primordial laws of the Universe itself. As H. P. Blavatsky so nobly puts it in her phrasing of a passage from the Sacred Books of the East from which she quotes: "Inaction in a deed of mercy becomes an action in a deadly sin." (*The Voice of the Silence,* Fragment II, 'The Two Paths,' p. 31, orig. ed.)

Whether we will or nill, we cannot avoid affecting others for weal or for woe, and if we by means of the exercise of our self-choice, otherwise our free will, affect others to their undoing or to their injury, the majestic and inscrutable and unerring law of Cosmic Justice and Compassion instantly moves into action, and we shall feel the inevitable punitive consequences upon ourselves in this or in some later life. This is Karman.

Thus, in the life of every individual human being, there is "not an accident in our lives, not a misshapen day, or a misfortune," as H. P. Blavatsky says in the text above, except what comes to one from one's own thoughts and feelings and actions in this or in some former life. There is no chance or fortuity in the Universe, and if anything could happen to us that we ourselves were not in some manner, near or distant, concerned with, or that we did not originate, then there would be gross injustice, fortuitous cruelty, and ground for genuine despair. We make our lives great and sublime, or mean and ignoble, and all stages between, because of what we ourselves think, feel, will, and therefore do. It is only the human physical man with his human soul which often suffers

ture, which the Theosophist calls Karman, the Great Theosophist, in answering a question "But what is Karma?" says:

As I have said, we consider it as the *Ultimate Law* of the Universe, the source, origin and fount of all other laws which exist throughout Nature. Karma is the unerring law which adjusts effect to cause, on the physical, mental and spiritual planes of being. As no cause remains without its due effect from greatest to least, from a cosmic disturbance down to the movement of your hand, and as like produces like, *Karma* is that unseen and unknown law *which adjusts wisely, intelligently and equitably* each effect to its cause, tracing the latter back to its producer. Though itself *unknowable*, its action is perceivable.

. . . For, though we do not know what Karma is *per se*, and in its essence, we *do* know *how* it works, and we can define and describe its mode of action with accuracy. We only do *not* know its ultimate *Cause*, just as modern philosophy universally admits that the *ultimate* Cause of anything is "unknowable."[218]

I

Webs of Destiny! We have seen somewhat of the character and significance of this grandly descriptive phrase. Such a web of destiny in the life of man indeed is not only the man himself, but the intricate tangle of circumstances in which he has involved himself; woven, as above stated, of unseen but tremendously strong strands of thought and feeling and will resulting in action. Life itself is the Great Web, a Web woven by living beings, 'creators,' each one in its own sphere, of those particular strands which each brings to the weaving of this Web of Life as its contribution to the general whole. It is precisely these multitudes of living beings and creatures and things of all-various types and kinds, which make life so complex and which play so large a part in the web of destiny which every man weaves around himself.

These multitudes of beings and creatures are not only those which exist on our small earth, but in very truth comprise in their number

---

'unmerited' karmic retribution for what the Reincarnating Ego did in other lives; but for this 'unmerited' suffering, Nature has provided ample recompense and reward in the special devachanic interludes between lives, as H. P. Blavatsky so truly says in her *The Key to Theosophy* (p. 161).

When a man refuses to extend a hand of help, or to assuage the tears of suffering, or refuses to aid those whose piteous call reaches him, he is but a semifiend in human shape, and Nature's retribution, guided by infinite Mind and Wisdom, will search him out through the ages and reach him some day, and then he will say: "Why has this fallen upon me? It is unmerited. I have done nothing to merit this suffering."

218. *The Key to Theosophy*, p. 201.

likewise the almost innumerable series of hierarchies, great and small, visible and invisible, which in the large weave the Cosmic Web. For indeed the Universe is filled full with spiritual beings and entities — call them 'gods' or 'spiritual beings' as Theosophists and others do; or 'angels and archangels' as the Jews and the Christians do; or 'ṛishis' and 'devas' as the Hindûs do; or 'Dhyâni-Chohans' and 'devas' as the Buddhists do; or 'Theoi' and 'Dii' as the ancient Greeks and Romans respectively did: it matters not at all what term is given to these various hierarchies of beings thus called by different names in different nations and peoples, as long as there abides the fundamental conception that these energizing beings and entities — these causal intelligent and quasi-intelligent Forces — form the very roots and the hierarchical structure both of the noumenal and of the phenomenal Universe in which we live, and thus provide for that Universe the entirety of the causal forces and energies which infill and move and agitate it. "Mens agitat molem," as Vergil, the Latin poet, so truly said in his *Aeneid*.

These causal forces express themselves in and through the phenomenal Universe in many and divers and diverse manners, for they are the noumenal or productive agents of the so-called Forces of Nature that are so often spoken of, and concerning which so little is really known. Electricity and gravitation, for example, which even in our ultra-modern science have become, because of recent truly occult discoveries, veritably mystic as well as mysterious, are such expressions on our plane of the noumenal Powers, the latter manifesting as such phenomenal appearances on the very lowest plane of their respective hierarchical lines. We may actually speak of either of them as being either the force or the energy, on the one hand, or the substance, on the other hand, of Invisible Beings, for they are both.

We humans verily are the children, the offspring, as the ancients put it, of these inner energizing forces, of these noumenal gods, of these spiritual beings, who exist in all-various degrees of evolutionary development; and who exist, as just stated, in hierarchical or scalar degrees or states; and therefore are we in our own highest parts also such gods — but, as we may say, 'fallen gods,' fallen into the material worlds, out of which and through which we are slowly working our way back to our Divine Cosmic Source, as the Universal Wisdom of the ancient times taught.

All these multitudinous hierarchies, composed of the divine, spiritual, and ethereal, as well as physical beings just mentioned, for ever do their work under the unerring sway of that incomprehensibly mysterious and occult Habit of Nature, or POWER, which we call Karman. This word itself is a Sanskrit term, and as a word it means only 'action' or 'working.' Such is the meaning of the mere word, of the vocable alone. But it is in Theosophy a highly technical word, and as such it has a recondite and wonderful significance. What is this technical meaning? It can briefly be expressed in four English words, when considered as imbodied in a teaching: 'the doctrine of consequences' — otherwise, and more popularly phrased, the universal 'law of cause and effect.'

The Esoteric Tradition repudiates, and on grounds swept by its inflexible logic, any idea of there being 'chance,' 'fortuity' — whatever these words may really mean — in the boundless Universe. Certainly nobody can give a satisfactory definition of 'chance' or 'fortuity' as a fundamental attribute or quality existing in Nature herself. When carefully examined, the idea is seen to be a mere phantasy; and, as great men even in the West have said: "We use the word 'chance' in order to describe our ignorance of things that we do not yet understand causally." Things happen, the origins of which are unknown or not understood. Not understanding them, people ascribe them to 'chance,' 'fortuity,' or say that 'it happened so.' Nevertheless our minds are logical in their operations, and when the forces and energies flowing into this physical universe appear here, we see in them consistency and coherency throughout; we see that they appear in logical and connected sequences, apparently always the same if the circumstances and conditions be the same, and we therefore say 'a law of Nature.'

But where, pray, is the law-giver? A law presupposes a law-giver. One sees in this term the influence of the old Occidental theology, just as one sees in the terms 'chance' and 'fortuity' the still-living influence of the now moribund if not dead scientific materialism of former generations. The Theosophist prefers to use the phrase 'the operations of Nature.' Modern scientific thinkers, unconsciously approaching the Theosophical doctrine, speak of 'the law of cause and effect,' and in doing so unconsciously to themselves state a fundamental postulate of the Esoteric Philosophy.

Truly, Nature exists in all her operations; and all the beings in Nature exist; but when we talk of 'laws of Nature' do we mean certain operations of natural forces that pursue always the same courses, and that these forces have been set in motion by some great supreme Individual whom men call 'God'? Obviously were that the fact, then this great supreme Individual, a Titan, Cosmic Man, if you like, fashioned by man's imagination after man's own structure, inner and outer, would *de facto* be responsible for everything that takes place in the Universe supposedly created by such a Being and working according to the laws imposed and set in motion by such a Being as the supposititious supreme law-giver. This would reduce man and all other entities, conscious and quasi-conscious, and all things, merely to natural automata; and to ascribe to such natural automata the possession of a free will which neither by origin nor nature they would have, and, not having, could not use, is a mere *petitio principii* — a begging of the question.

Such an idea is an 'easy way' to shoulder off on to somebody else or something else the responsibility, spiritual, intellectual, and ethical, for what we ourselves do or have done for good or for bad, for weal or for woe, for ourselves and for others. But the inflexible universal logic of the Esoteric Philosophy does not permit us to do this. Man is but one of an innumerable host of beings, imbodied Consciousnesses, who infill the Universe. Nowhere do we find anything other than these hierarchies of beings, these consciousnesses active during the Cosmic Manvantara, and each individual of these hosts weaving its own Web of Destiny, its energies pouring out of its own inner being and directed by the intelligence streaming from its own spiritual and mental foci. It is the combination and incessant interaction and interweaving of all these intelligences and wills and their consequent activities unceasingly operative in the Universe that account for the inequalities that we see around us: as much for the imperfections that we see and of which we are more or less sensible, as for the beauty and splendor and the order and law of which we are likewise conscious.

II

It is this interaction and in minor cases ensuing conflict of wills which is the origin of all the evil in the world — not only among men but among the beings strung all along the rungs of the ascending Ladder of Cosmic Life, from the supergods downwards through all intermediate stages to men; and the evil or disharmony which is apparent among the beasts and in less degree in the plants and minerals is due to exactly the same cause. There would be no evil or disharmony on Earth, so far as human beings are concerned, if it were not for this conflict of human wills, which is another way of saying the wrong exercise or use of that divine faculty — a god-like power working within us — our relatively free will.[219]

---

219. Plotinus, in answer to a general question as to what it is that has brought peregrinating souls to forget their divine origin and thus to become oblivious

It has been said by Occidental writers, miseducated to believe certain things that have no real existence outside the educational, religious, philosophical, and scientific fads of the Occidental world, that the origin of evil in the world, and its continuance, form an unsolvable mystery. Verily it does not. What indeed is evil? What indeed is good? Are they things in themselves, or are they, as is perfectly obvious, solely conditions, states, through which beings and entities pass? Evil is disharmony, because it is imperfection; and good is harmony because it is relative perfection. Again, these two, human good and human evil, apply almost solely to the particular hierarchy in which we humans move and live and have our being. Evil is not an entity; it is not a power or an energy or a force which flows forth from the heart of some thing or some being, unless we restrict it to human evil-doing, and then assuredly it is just that. Abstractly speaking, it is the state or condition of an evolving being or entity which has not yet fully placed itself in accord and concord with Nature's fundamental laws: the condition or state of a being or an entity or a group of beings or entities in greater or less degree opposing the forwards-moving evolutionary Stream of Life. Evil may also be called that course of action brought about by the individual or individuals which has not or have not yet evolved forth the latent divinity within, and therefore is always traceable to its origin in the misuse and abuse of will and intelligence by a being or entity which finds itself in temporary inharmonious condition with its environment because of its own imperfections.[220]

---

of their innate spirituality, thus bringing about confusion and evil, remarks:

> "The evil in souls [which likewise means largely the evil in the world] has its source in the self-will of the souls themselves, and in their longing for self-expression thus bringing about imbodiment. Pleasure came to them in this false freedom, which in turn brought them to long for their own motions and ways of doing, so that thus, drifting idly farther and farther, they were swept along the paths of evil and wrong, even finally losing all recollection of their primordial home as rays of the divine. . . . just so the wandering souls forget both the divine and their own intrinsically spiritual character." — Enneads, 'The Three Primordial Essences,' V, i, 1.

220. The fact that human evil, and by analogy evil of other kinds in the world, arises out of the depravation of the will of individuals towards evil-doing, which means doing contrary to or more or less opposed to the fundamental spiritual currents of the Universe, as a theory is found even in Christianity, and in the works of one of its most respected and eminent writers, to wit: the ex-Manichaean and ex-Neo-Platonist, Augustine. This old writer whose influence in the Christian Church has always been a powerful one, has the follow-

Good, as said above, is relative harmony, and therefore relative perfection; and evil therefore is relative disharmony, born of relative imperfection. Neither good nor evil as conditions exist apart from each other. There could be no 'good' things in the Universe unless there were 'evil' things which by contrast set off the former. Contrariwise, there could be no 'evil' things in the Universe, our Home-Universe, unless there were 'good' things by which alone the former appear in contrast. Evil is not created out of nothing. Good is not created out of nothing. The former is disharmony, the latter is harmony. Consequently they are two poles of the same causal origin. There cannot exist such a thing as evil apart from imperfect or inharmonious things or entities, and there is no such entity *per se* as 'evil' which exists apart from entities or things who or which are relatively 'evil.' Precisely the same observation may be made, *mutatis mutandis*, with regard to good.

Paradoxically speaking, evil is a condition through which we humans pass as we grow to become better. This better, however, is 'evil' to a larger and loftier better, and this larger and loftier better is imperfect and inharmonious and therefore relatively 'evil' to something still grander, and so on *ad infinitum*. Good is not spirit. Evil is not the nether pole of spirit, which men call matter; because that would be saying that matter is essentially evil, which is not true. Evil is imperfection, whether spiritual or material, and is whatever is imperfect and passing through the stage or phase of growing to something better. If such stage or phase of growing be a very low one, we humans can properly and justifiably speak of 'malignant evil.' If that stage or phase of imperfection be only slightly inferior to the stage of humanity in which we as human beings at present should be, we properly speak of small or slight evil.[221]

---

ing to say in his *De civitate Dei* ('The City of God'), Book XII, chapter vi:

"The will is not depraved by inferior influences [or things], but it is the will which depraves itself by its inordinate appetite for following inferior things."

221. A caveat should be entered here lest the words in the text alarm those sensitive souls who prefer to think that there is positive and individual evil in the world existing as an entity. It should be understood that evil, however abominable and ignoble and wicked it may humanly be, is nevertheless the result of the misuse of man's relatively free will — a divine thing. Why some people should prefer to believe in a devil who is continually lying in wait to trap the unwary steps of men, rather than to believe that man himself by aspiring to the divinity within him can cease from evil-doing, is just one of those

There is no 'devil' in the Universe, wrongly supposed to be the ever-active suggester of evil and the arbiter of its crooked ways. Equally so, there is no anti-polar god in the Universe, who is similarly and wrongly supposed to be the creator and suggester of good, and the arbiter of its working. Either and both involve the matter of evolutionary growth, of unfolding progress, of passing from imperfection to a less imperfect stage or condition or phase, and continuously. Matter is not evil *per se*, as some schools have wrongly held in the past; and for precisely the same reason, Spirit is not good *per se*. That is to say, neither the one nor the other possesses this or the other condition or state *absolutely*, and for eternity. A spiritual entity is growing, is evolving or unfolding, just as much as any material being or entity is in growth or in unfolding of inner and latent capacity and power. Nevertheless, precisely because spirit, and the hierarchies of spiritual beings which manifest more largely spirit, are nearer to Nature's divine heart — i. e., to its fundamental essence and laws — therefore spirit and spiritual entities are, collectively speaking, more perfect, obviously therefore better, and equally obviously therefore less 'evil,' than matter and material entities are, because these latter are much farther removed from Nature's heart of divinity — i. e., Nature's fundamental essence and her therein inhering laws of harmony.

Nor does evil *per se* become good *per se*, which is an absurdity. That is like saying that one state becomes through growth another state, which is absurd. If this were so, we should have one individu-

---

strange psychological problems that are traceable back to the erratic and wandering mind of lower man.

Moreover, let it here be stated once for all that the Esoteric Philosophy does *not* teach that human beings become good only by deliberately choosing evil as a course of action and learning by it, as some may deliberately misunderstand the words in the text to mean. This would be teaching a species of diabolism running directly counter to all the precepts of the Philosophy. Giving oneself up to evil by choice is the infallible and sure way to spiritual and intellectual and ethical degeneration, and is what is called in the Esoteric Tradition, 'following the lunar path.' It can result only in spiritual wickedness of the worst kind, bringing about a 'loss of the soul.'

These words therefore are not merely conclusive, they are extremely graphic, and are a most emphatic warning to those whose erratic genius may lead them to misinterpret and therefore to distort the simple but luminous and philosophical teaching, which, when once properly understood, fills human life with hope and brilliant promise, because it shows how man may rise out of the mire of worse things into better and then best, thus making of himself a man-god on Earth.

ality retaining its individuality in order that it might continue to be the same being — and yet becoming another contrary individuality, which is absurd. Evil *per se* is not an entity which can grow or become good *per se* — i. e., evolve into some other supposititious entity. Thus, length is not an entity which exists, although there are things which are long; similarly, there is no such thing *per se* as depth, although there are things which are deep. Length and depth do not exist as entities. They are abstract conditions or states of entities.

How can 'evil' become divine? How can imperfection *be* perfection? How can disharmony *be* harmony? How can hate *be* love? Evil never becomes divine, because evil is not a thing which grows. Childhood is not a thing. It is a condition or state or phase through which a growing entity passes. Stupidity is not a thing, nor does it ever become intelligence. It is a phase, a condition, an imperfect state of evolution, or growth, of beings. It is quite wrong, therefore, to say that evil becomes good. Only beings or entities 'become.'

This fallacy, that evil will in time become good, is born of the idea that the origin of all is good, and therefore that evil will re-become what it once was. But is it not a trifle bold to suppose that the origin of all is good? Good and evil are wholly human terms; being human terms they have human connotations. It is like ethics. The ethics of a South Sea Islander are not the ethics of a European, nor of an American — that is, let us hope, in all details! In certain senses or fundamentally in certain relations perhaps we may say yes. The ethics of a devil-worshipper are very different indeed from my ethics; but yet in each case they are 'ethics' to the being who follows them and practises them. Good and evil are human terms, and we call good what men understand to be harmonious: harmonious relations with other beings and things. In fact, as is notorious enough, what some men might or would call evil, other men might actually call relative good. Deduction: when we speak of divinity, dare we endow that incomprehensible — what shall we call it? Being? No; Essence perhaps is a better word: shall we endow that which to us in its fulness, and in its amazingly beautiful and often perplexing operations and characteristics, is incomprehensible Life, with the attributes of the good and the evil that we men understand? Who would dare so to limit, to circumscribe, the Boundless Life? In this connexion, all that can be said is that the heart of incomprehensible Kosmic BEING is law and order and impersonal love and impersonal harmony; that out of this incomprehensible heart of BEING flow the origins or seeds of all that is, including the innumerable hosts of Monadic Individuals; that these Monadic Individuals, in the beginning of their evolutionary journey through Kosmic Time-Space, are learning Monads; and that as these embryo-entities continue their journey through Time-Space, because of wrong choosings of will and intelligence, they pass oft through 'evil shadows.'

It is so easy to say that 'God is love'; but when we say that 'God is love,' do we not immediately perceive that infinite love must include also what we men call evil? Can infinite love, which is boundless, both in space and time, exclude from its encompassing infinitude even the greatest erring creature which in its origin had flowed forth from its own heart? Infinite love is infinite compassion, and includes even the erring and the ne'er-do-wells everywhere. The 'heart' of the Universe is ineffable Harmony, but not all beings anywhere and everywhere are harmonious. The Universe is filled full with all kinds of creatures, with all sorts and grades and stages of evolving beings and entities; but the 'Heart' of Divinity includes them all, for it is their Parent and their Source, and is the ultimate Goal towards which all and everything is evolving through innumerable ages on their return pilgrimage to Itself.

Shall we hold the heart of divinity responsible for what an erring child does? Shall we and dare we say that there is such a thing as an infinite and eternal crime? The idea is monstrous, for it is incredible and inadmissible on any ground of argument or of thought. What we do know is that it is the weak and erring hosts of imperfectly evolved beings and entities, who pass on their pilgrimage through many valleys of shadow, which some men call sin: imperfectly evolved beings and entities, who nevertheless, all of them, are children of the Cosmic Life. But to hold the Cosmic Life, to hold the Cosmic Heart, responsible for what these innumerable armies and hosts and multitudes of evolving beings and entities do, is incredibly absurd.

What is Divinity? Is it 'a Big Man up there,' as the untutored savage thinks? A Big Man 'up there' who makes good and tolerates evil; who makes good creatures and makes evil creatures? If one say that 'God' is responsible for any evil and erring part of infinity, however small the part may be: if one say that 'God' 'created' such an entity, this is to make that supposititious 'God' individually and eternally responsible for whatever the hapless and irresponsible creature may do in the future forever, for, *ex hypothesi,* Eternal and Infinite Wisdom foresaw the infinity of the future, and 'created' the creature for whatever pathway it is destined to follow. In such case in both logic and even human justice — to say naught of infinite love and wisdom — is not the true evil doer the supposititious 'God' himself?[222]

The Theosophist summarily rejects this evil thought, for to him it is blasphemously evil. To him the Heart of Being is compassion absolute, harmony absolute, infinite wisdom. But what is this 'Heart of Being'? In the last analysis, and when due allowance is made for the frailties of human understanding and the imperfections of human speech which interpret the relatively feeble efforts of that understanding, we are bound to admit that this Heart of Being is not the frontierless, beginningless, and endless infinitude and eternity, but the Hierarch, the chief hierarchical Guardian, of our own Kosmic Galaxy, our own Home-Universe — the divine-spiritual Being or Entity beyond all possibility of human investigation or description, but who by comparison with Kosmic Entities still vaster and still more incomprehensibly sublime, is but a relatively minute godling.

The Theosophist therefore rejects the idea that 'God' creates certain multitudes of men unto evil, which is exactly the idea ac-

---

222. The Church-Father Lactantius, writing 'On the Anger of God,' chapter xiii, quotes Epicurus, who puts the problem of evil in the following curiously significant way:

"Either God wishes to remove evil from this world, and cannot, or he can and will not, or he neither can nor will, or, to conclude, he both can and will. If he will and cannot, it is impotence, which is contrary to the nature of God; if he can and will not, it is wickedness, and that is no less contrary to his nature; if he neither will nor can, it is wickedness and impotence at once; if he both can and will (which alone of these conditions is suitable to God), whence comes the evil which exists in the world?"

The pious Church-Father naturally disagrees with the above. The argument, however, which he makes against Epicurus is not only weak but sidesteps the main question: i. e., what is the origin of evil?

The great St. Augustine, in one of his Letters to St. Jerome, states emphatically that not even new-born infants can escape eternal damnation except by being baptized. The Jewish Rabbis boldly stated that God alone was the author of evil, and pointed to exactly the same doctrine as taught in the Bible in passages such as are found in *Isaiah,* xlv, 7, where the Hebrew prophet writes: "I form the light, and create darkness: I make peace, and create evil."

On the other hand, the entire civilized world, outside of Jewish and Christian sources, stated that evil proceeds from imperfect beings themselves who refuse to accommodate their will and their doings to the divine laws which rule the Universe. Hermes, for instance, in the treatise called the *Crater,* says: "Evil does not proceed from God, but from ourselves, who prefer it to good."

cording to the logic of at least one old theory; or, contrariwise, that 'God' creates other certain multitudes of men unto eternal good, which is likewise exactly the teaching of another and contrasted old theory of the West — if we may dignify this belief by the name 'theory.' To the Theosophist, either idea or teaching is indeed blasphemous, because it makes the supposititious creating 'God' wholly and for ever responsible, and thus makes him likewise the original doer because 'creator.' According to this theory, being infinitely wise, infinitely powerful, such a 'God' knew at the instant of creation all that his creature would become, would do through eternity, and therefore according to this old teaching 'God' deliberately created certain men unto eternal damnation — or contrariwise.

Lest these words be thought to be unfair, one ventures to quote here, with due respect to the many fine men and women who may still accept it, Article XVII of the Thirty-nine Articles of the Church of England, as these Articles were laid down in Convention assembled in 1562–3, to wit:

Predestination to Life is the everlasting purpose of God, whereby (before the foundations of the world were laid) he hath constantly decreed by his counsel, secret to us, to deliver from curse and damnation those whom He hath chosen in Christ out of mankind, and to bring them by Christ to everlasting salvation, as vessels made to honor.

This seventeenth Article is mild in its tone and doctrine as compared with the Doctrine of Reprobation of the Westminster Confession of Faith, which was formulated at Westminster also, by a Convocation of English Divines during the period 1643—1649. It should be remembered that Reprobation is a technical term in Christian theology, and means the doctrine that "God has predestined some to everlasting death." This Westminster Confession of Faith was largely drawn up by clergymen having strong Calvinistic leanings, and in its Article III, 3, 4, we find the following:

By the decree of God, for the manifestation of his glory, some men and angels are predestinated unto everlasting life, and other foreordained to everlasting death. These angels and men, thus predestined and foreordained, are particularly and unchangeably designed; and their number is so certain and definite that it cannot be either increased or diminished.[223]

---

223. This Article III of the Westminster Confession of Faith is logical enough provided that one can do such violence to his intuitions as to admit the obvious premises upon which it reposes, to wit: an Infinite and Eternal Creator of the World and of Man, who is both Infinite Wisdom and Infinite Power; for

Abomination of this sort was never taught in ancient times when the great Mysteries of antiquity prevailed in their mighty influence over human souls; which Mysteries taught men not merely how to live but also taught them the secrets of Universal Nature, and therefore likewise of man's interior constitution and his being, and his origin and his destiny. Nor, may one add, was it the teaching of the Avatâra Jesus, called the Christ, nor is it the teaching of the Brotherhood of the Masters of Wisdom and Compassion and Peace. It is a dark and ignoble idea, evolved from the obscured minds of mediaeval theologians and in the early ages of the Christian Era.

The Theosophist accepts no such God, for such a god is very truly man's own creation, created by man's weak and erring and imperfect mind, when projecting its own imperfect imaginations on the background of infinity. Instead, to the Theosophist the heart of the Universe is the source of all life; the source of all intelligence, the source of all order, the source of all regular procedures, the source of everything that in man's inmost heart and highest mind he aspires towards, in order by such aspiration to ennoble his own life and dignify his existence. Indeed, it is the supremest and highest part of man's own constitution, for his inmost essence is

---

it is obvious that could such a being exist every act of his would be directed by eternal wisdom and foreknowledge, and hence every created being would be created to do exactly and precisely what Eternal Wisdom foresaw it would do and created it to do.

The ascription of free will to such a created automaton is but a *petitio principii*, a begging of the question, and would be but the hollowest and most wicked of cosmic mockeries by a creator, for such creator, according to the hypothesis, in his Infinite Wisdom created beings, and knew beforehand all that such created beings would be or do.

Indeed, the above Article of this Westminster Confession not only recognises this but positively affirms it, stating that certain men and angels are "predestinated unto everlasting life," and others "foreordained to everlasting death." Such a 'God' to the Theosophist is simply a phantom of the imagination of perverse and obscured minds, however sincere they might have been.

When one adds to the above premises, the other premiss equally universally accepted, that this creator is Infinitely and Eternally Good, the strict logic mentioned above instantly vanishes — unless, indeed, one choose to consider such a Cosmic 'God' as a Cosmic 'Demon' — and then why speak of him as 'Infinite Good'? One can only wonder when the teachings and immortal precepts of the Christ-man, whom Christians follow as their Master, and whose life is a perpetual exemplar of beauty and love and wisdom, will be understood and followed; and the somber and often terrible — because so inhuman — phantoms of the imaginations of Mediaevalists once and for ever abandoned.

identic with the divine-spiritual Essence of the Kosmic Universe.

The foregoing observations and reflexions do not signify, however, that the teachings of the Esoteric Philosophy, the Esoteric Tradition, in any wise ignore the existence in the Universe of all imperfectly evolved spacial and durational phases of the Cosmic Life, nor, on the other hand, the great multitudes of evolving or unfolding or growing beings who still are plunged in the lower deeps or densities of the many phases of existence in the so-called material world. Indeed, the Titan Intellects of the human race have long ages since as carefully explored these left-hand realms or mansions of life as they have carefully explored and understood the great mansions and realms of the Cosmic Life which belong to what is technically called the rising or Ascending Arc of manifested being. Minds of even greater penetrating power, and wisdom still more impersonal and permeant, than those even of the Titan Intellects of the human race, have transmitted unto the latter, who in turn transmit their knowledge to those who are found worthy and well prepared to receive it, wide and profound ranges of Cosmic Verities, of which the average human being has no conception, nor does he even dream of the existence thereof.

There are hierarchies of spiritual, quasi-spiritual, and ethereal beings and entities which exist in and inhabit the material hierarchies, and they are of as many kinds in their respective ways as are the other hierarchies at the other or spiritual end of the scale. There are, in fact, beings whom we may qualify as entities of 'spiritual wickedness' even as Paul of the Christians taught.[224] What then is meant by this expression 'entities existing in a state of spiritual wickedness'? Obviously, and speaking generally, this phrase refers to those entities who, because of their imperfection, combined with their modicum of free will, although belonging to the spiritual realms, produce a certain disharmony there, and consequently they are evil in that state.

Furthermore, this difficult phrase refers also, and much more specifically, on the one hand to beings possessing certain intellectual and psychical development, but who have deliberately chosen to follow the 'path of matter'; and, on the other hand, it refers to the so-called Mâmo-Chohans, as they are termed in Tibet, which are those somber and mysterious entities who in their aggregate are the karmic agents or controllers or guardians of the matter-side of the Universe. Lords of the dark, the dark Lords, the Mâmo-Chohans

---

224. *Ephesians,* vi, 12.

individually are, as it were, Monads who were of some material development even *before* the time when they began their pilgrimage in *this* Cosmic Manvantara, through the lower spheres in order — in the far distant future — to become men, and later to become self-conscious gods of Light. They are at work or in operation all around us, and continuously so. It is really they who hold the material worlds in hierarchic coherence. Nevertheless it is through these material worlds that the Lords of Light work; it is in the material worlds that the Light Lords clothe themselves with and in bodies. 'Material' as just hereinbefore used, is not restricted in its meaning to our physical spheres only: the term as here used comprises the vehicular side of the Universe, the substantial side as contrasted with the energy-side, the spirit-side — the vast and interworking Hierarchies of Light.

Now these various classes of beings 'of spiritual evil' above mentioned, are not by any means all of them Mâmo-Chohans; they also contain among their number entities much farther advanced along the evolutionary pathway than even human beings are, although most of them have arisen to their present status out of the human stock; and in most cases, perhaps in all, these deliberately ally themselves, in the wickedness of their spirituality, with the Mâmo-Chohans and thus become what Mankind has always vaguely intuited as the 'forces of evil.' They are in fact spiritual sorcerers who are, or who make themselves to be, the active agents on Earth and in other material spheres for the unevolved matter-portion of Life, and therefore are what humans call 'evil' influences coming from the 'dark side' of Nature. As a matter of fact, every human being who deliberately does an evil deed *from choice*, i. e., because he loves the evil thing for its own sake, is an agent of and for spiritual wickedness. This is so because he is then using spiritual and intellectual forces for unholy and wicked purposes and ends. This again is possible because man is a god in his essence, and in his higher nature his will is supreme — if only he knew how to apply it here in the world of men; and thus it is that he can use spiritual energies by his will and apply them to evil uses, wicked uses.

Every individual everywhere, human or other, is pursuing its own pathway of destiny, weaving its own web, but not merely around itself, for *it itself* is that Web of Destiny, because it is a web of character, therefore composite of a mingling of forces and substances which belong to its sevenfold (or tenfold) constitution. Here then is the simple explanation of how evil or wickedness arises in the world: because of the intricate and wayward action of multitudes of individuals using their relatively free will and relatively unfolded intelligence; and because these imperfect entities often choose wrongly and to the detriment and injury of other similar individuals around them, because of ignorance and passion, this conflict of wills brings about the complicated interweaving of the strands of the many Webs of Destiny. This is the great cause, at least among men, of the suffering and misery of which we are all as human beings so painfully conscious.

The explanation itself is exactly correspondent with all Nature that we know; it answers completely the intuitive sense of justice that whatever touches our own life originates in ourselves and that we are our own parents and our own children, so to say; for what we now sow we shall reap; and we reap what we have sown in this or in another life and naught else. No outside God creates misery and unhappiness and destruction to come upon us, any more than does an outside God surround us with unearned joy and fortunate conclusions of the acts that we undertake; for in either of such cases neither of these states would we ourselves then be responsible for. We ourselves build ourselves; and in doing so we co-operate with other hierarchies to build the Universe — i. e., that particular portion of the Universe in which we are.

III

All the beings and things, therefore, that everywhere we cognise, are really individual Webs of Destiny. The Universe itself is such a Web of Destiny, builded by the wills and consciousnesses of the beings and entities and things which infill it, and which actually compose it — all operative or rather co-operative in producing both its invisible and immeasurably wonderful Worlds, and the outward manifestations comprising the gorgeous natural sights that we see; yea, and the imperfections that we see also.

For every point in Space may be considered to be the domicile of a Monadic entity, this point being ensouled and inspirited by its own deathless and stainless Monadic essence, i. e., its own Consciousness-Center, which expresses itself through such infinitesimal 'point' as best it can, thus progressing in the weaving of its Web of Destiny on its journey upward and back to the spheres of ineffable Light. The worlds above us, the stars and planets, are all living beings, growing beings, evolving beings; and these worlds themselves, all of them and without exception, are filled full with other subordinate beings and entities, each one itself similarly engaged in weaving its own individual Web of Destiny, which is itself, and which by such weaving is pouring forth from itself as it learns better how to do so ever larger portions or streams or floods of its guiding conscious spiritual essence. Moreover the natural phenomena that we see around us are but the effects or results in our physical universe of the action of multitudes of intelligent entities in the invisible realms, of whom we vaguely intuit or feel or sense the powers and qualities and attributes and forces, as they flow into our sphere of life.

In this continuous action which perdures throughout the course of the immensely long Cosmic Manvantara, every such being or entity acts and interacts with multitudes of other beings more or less like unto itself, and because of this interwoven hierarchical structure of the Universe, every entity everywhere, no matter what its size, is but one of the entities in the 'life-stream' of some still greater being. As it has been explained at more length in previous chapters, Nature's structure is hierarchical throughout, so that her multitudes of Cosmic Planes which compose her own Being are repetitive each of the Plane higher than itself, and thus it is that any Individual Unit is comprised within the life-stream and constitution and substance of another Cosmic Individual Unit of far greater magnitude.

This thought at first sight may seem very mysterious and difficult to understand, but the composition of a man's body will furnish a simple illustration of Nature's repetitive structure. A man's mind controls the conscious motions of his body; and his so-called and mis-called 'sub-conscious mind' likewise controls the so-called involuntary actions and involuntary and reflex-movements of whatever kind they may be. Remove this mind or this consciousness and death ensues, leaving what we call 'dead' bodies. What takes place in 'dead' bodies? Decay, dissolution, a breaking up of the organic union into its constituent molecular and atomic parts. The controlling and guiding and energizing power has left the body which thus remains 'dead'; the inner forces no longer inflow into or stream into that physical body and move it, either to agitate it or to give it peace, as the case may be, according to whether these inflowing forces proceed from the lower or the higher part of man's interior constitution. Yet our body, considered as a physical vehicle, is composed of nothing but vast hosts of infinitesimal entities, each one of which has the same right and title to be called a 'learning entity,' a 'consciousness-center' on its upward way, as the man himself has, with his dominant and enclosing consciousness and will. During life, over all these vast hosts of entities in the human body—and they are practically numberless, so great is the multitude of them — the human spirit, the human consciousness, the human mind, is their combined overlord and has them all in its enclosing and guiding grasp.

So, on the macrocosmic scale, is it with the Universe; and there are innumerable hosts of such Universes, as our modern scientists are beginning to recognise when they talk about 'island universes' outside our own Home-Universe comprised within the encircling zone of the Milky Way.

We thus see that we are interlinked and interlocked by the inseparable and ineluctable bonds of a Cosmic Consciousness, these bonds expressing themselves as an all-permeant will and intelligence. Yea, every force in the Universe thrills through our being, and every substance in the Universe has done its proportionate part in building us up and therefore has given to us somewhat of itself. Thus it is that all the ancient mystical Schools have spoken of man as being the Microcosm or 'little world' containing in itself portions of everything that the Universal Parent contains and is. Therefore, because we are all parts of one all-inclusive Cosmic Consciousness and its vehicular expression, the surrounding Universe, we are all now and here together, and therefore do we feel others' doings upon us, even as they feel what we do to them. This is why also the expenditure of a certain amount of its own native energy by any entity will instantaneously act upon surrounding Nature, which in its turn automatically reacts thereto. This reaction, however, may be instant or it may not take place for a long time; in some cases the reaction may be delayed even for aeons, but in all events and in all cases surely the reaction will somewhen occur, for it is inescapably determined by the factors involved in the equation itself.

This doctrine, expressive of the fact that we are all but parts of a greater Being is not to be misunderstood to signify the teaching of Fatalism, as already briefly discussed elsewhere. Fatalism is the idea — it can hardly be called a teaching, it is rather the notion or speculation — that man and all other entities, conscious and unconscious, un-self-conscious and self-conscious, and no matter where, are the blindly driven motes of a soulless cosmic mechanism controlled by some overpowering, overdominating force, which some think acts altogether as chance, hazard, altogether and everywhere as fortuity: blind, soulless, insensate, involving aimless wandering anywhere, purposeless, coming from nowhere, and all without any defined objective whatsoever.

This is the view of one form of Fatalism — that of the old materialistic School — which happily is now become an outworn and virtually abandoned belief. The other fatalistic view, rather more difficult to describe, because there are or have been several varieties or shades of opinion about it, is that men and all other things in the Universe are the puppets of an inscrutable cosmic Force, which probably possesses intelligence and will, and, as it were, exercises these attributes in producing the cosmic phantasy of Creation, and in which naught but itself has any true power of self-choice.

There is but little to choose between these two Schools, for they are as alike as two peas in a pod, except for the ascription of names to the one which are not used in the other; and the giving to one of certain supposititious qualities which are only names after all, because they are vacuous and empty of substance.

European scientists long since discerned the existence throughout the Universe of a Chain of Causation, and it has been and still is called the law of cause and effect; for its existence is so obvious in Nature's structure and in her operations, that although one cannot understand the origin and meaning of this dark and mysterious law, as it seems to be, nevertheless its presence and its operations are perceptible everywhere, not only in ourselves, but in all things and beings that surround us.

The most modern or ultra-modern notions regarding this law of cause and effect are, however, undergoing some very curious and interesting changes. The old physical determinism of the effete and now moribund materialism of our fathers, has practically vanished, due to the new light that more recent scientific discovery and philosophico-scientific deduction therefrom have thrown upon the nature of the universe surrounding us.

Our scientists seem to be bewildered, and in some cases proceed to what one can qualify as being nothing other than illogical explanations of the causes and meaning of the physical phenomena which they are laying bare by their very conscientious work. Reacting from the old and fatalistic determinism above mentioned, many eminent scientific men today are speaking of a 'principle of indeterminacy,' but just precisely what the significance or inner meaning of this term or phrase implies, it is extremely difficult for an outsider to say — and after a careful study of many scientific works in which this principle of 'indeterminacy' is mentioned, one feels almost driven to conclude that the eminent gentlemen who have coined this phrase are themselves in doubt as to just what they mean by it.

Are we to look upon this so-called 'indeterminacy' as signifying that the atoms or the electric particles composing the atoms have a modicum, however small, of free will which causes them to act in

an apparently erratic and wilful manner, often contrary to expecta-
tions? Or, mayhap, shall we suppose that 'indeterminacy' as the
term is used, signifies a state of things where hap or hazard or
chance or fortuity or cosmic lawlessness rules everywhere, every
atom refusing to be bound or restricted within those frontiers of
causal concatenation which even the old materialism defined as determinism? Who can say what these bigwigs of our scientific laboratories themselves think—and, perchance, even they themselves know
not! Yet some great scientists (e. g., Einstein, Planck, etc.) *do* admit causality in 'indeterminacy.' Such an atmosphere of nescience,
or possibly better phrased, such an attitude of agnostic 'indeterminacy,' prevails in scientific minds, that one retires from a sincere
and searching study of much of modern scientific work with the feeling that nothing really definite or certain is known anywhere, and
that the cocksureness and dogmatic orthodoxy of the science that
was, has been replaced by amazingly conscientious work in new discovery which thus far has been productive only of bewilderment
and guesswork in scientific circles.

The Theosophist can accept neither the 'deter-
minism' of the old Materialism nor the 'indeterminacy' of the modern scientific schools, nor again the various varieties of Fatalism
which have at different times prevailed among philosophers and re-
ligionists, for they find none of these to meet the needs of man's
intellect, nor the intuitions of his spirit, nor the aspirations of his
soul; nor does any one of them respond in any wise adequately to
the instincts of his moral sense. Neither 'chance' nor 'Kismet' is
satisfactory; although he sees in both these views certain adumbrations of the cosmic reality — that infinitely universal, never-erring,
and wholly impersonal Operation of Nature which he studies under
the term long since given to it — KARMAN. This is the doctrine of
ineluctable consequences, otherwise called in ordinary human speech,
the Law of Cause and Effect, which we may likewise speak of as
the all-permeant Law of Causation and Effectual Results.

The Theosophist, as much as the veriest fatalist, if indeed there
be such a being, believes in this chain or concatenation or stream of
interlocked or interwoven circumstances existent everywhere in the
Cosmic Life, and he believes in the consequent fact that every being
or entity everywhere, and every act done by any being or entity anywhere, and every thought or emotion felt by any being or entity
anywhere, is the enchained effect of some precedaneous cause — in
every case arising in the chain of causation in the being of some
living entity. Moreover, universes, worlds, solar systems, nebulae,

comets, planets, cosmic spirits, men, elementals, life-atoms, matter, and all the various planes and spheres of being: in fact all things: are not merely the resultants or consequences of each one's preceding and individual aggregate of karmic causes. Each one for itself is originating new karmic causes constantly and from itself in combination or in interconnexion with all others.

IV

The question yet remains: What originates these causes operative in and building the Webs of Destiny which we are studying? We here put our finger, so to speak, on the true solution of this problem which has so vexed and perplexed the minds of men for ages: What originates causes? The teaching of the Esoteric Philosophy, the Esoteric Tradition, is: There never was a 'beginning' of such origination. A hard saying, perhaps. But the explanation is simple enough when the key-thought is grasped. Every cause in the Chain of Causation which stretches from eternity to eternity is but the effect of a precedaneous cause which in its turn is but the effect of a cause preceding it, and so forth *ad infinitum;* just as, looking forwards into what men call the future, every cause produces its effect, which instantly becomes a 'new' cause in turn followed by an effect, which instantly becomes a 'new' cause and so forth, *ad infinitum.*[225]

---

225. The phrasing of the very subtil and profound thought of the text above should never be misunderstood to mean that Karman and its action in time is merely mechanical and soulless. It is a fundamental doctrine of the Esoteric Philosophy that all Karman of whatever kind, of whatever class, and of whatever degree, is guided and controlled and therefore directed fundamentally by Cosmic Consciousness, and secondly by the multitudes of interlocking hierarchies each conscious in its own degree and manner, which infill and indeed compose Space. Karman is thus essentially not only a 'function' of consciousness but is, in the manner above described, consciousness itself in action. The human mind with its imperfect development and therefore necessarily restricted range of vision cannot follow the movements of Cosmic Consciousness because of the immense amplitude of its vital motion, so that the human mind at best can conceive of Cosmic Consciousness existent in Cosmic Space as a shoreless Sea apparently immutable and incomprehensibly still.

It is like the inhabitant of an infinitesimal particle forming a part of the human body imagining to itself the time-interval between two human heart-beats which would be to it a quasi-eternity; the sevenfold denary number of human heart-beats in a single human minute (say 72) would be to it of a rate utterly and inconceivably slow, and covering to it a time-period which would seem endless. Thus the motions of even an organ of the human body are of

Here then is the Key: and in illustration of it as a general teaching let us turn again to man as an instance in point. Man is a composite being. His highest parts are pure divinity, therefore are pure consciousness, therefore pure mind, pure will, pure force. Having these qualities aggregated into a unity, and thus being an individual composite of both force and substance, not only interacting but acting exteriorly and receiving effects from the outside world, he is, therefore, an 'actor' in the original sense of that word — one who originates acts: who moves, who does: because the heart of him, the core of him, is this central divine consciousness, this pure divine mind-will-energy; and this unity is by its very nature perpetually active and at work, cosmically speaking, even in the lowest of things; therefore in man, as in every other being or entity or thing. This divine mind-will-force, this inner divine consciousness, always is attempting to self-express its transcendent powers through the veils

---

magnitude so great, of amplitude so immense, that the infinitesimal percipient consciousness can intuit its existence or being, but cannot take it in.

The truth is, however, that the Cosmic Consciousness during the Cosmic Manvantara is in unceasing motion and indeed throughout the Cosmic Pralaya likewise, but just because Cosmic Space is divided up in particular hierarchies forming worlds and planes, and these in turn are again on the hierarchical analogical principle divisible into entities still smaller, we can perceive that as these amplitudes of movement or magnitudes in space become smaller, as we humans understand the matter, the stage finally is reached where human intelligence can begin to see and to grasp these cosmically smaller groups and their movements. The various Galaxies forming Families in Space, then a single Galaxy, then the Star-Clusters, then a Solar System, then a planet — thus we can descend the scale in our thought and perceive the small encompassed within continuously increasing ranges of greatness, and the small enclosing continuously decreasing ranges of other magnitudes reaching the infinitesimal.

Throughout it all KARMAN is incessantly active; and it should be carefully noted for a correct understanding of the idea, that each minutest point in Cosmic Space or in the Cosmic Consciousness may be considered to be a Monadic Center, itself participating in the Karmic Cosmic Labor. Everything and every being and every entity, great or small, collaborates on its own scale in the ranges of karmic action, and therefore is an agent of this mysterious, and to us humans, incomprehensible, operation of Nature's own essence which for purposes of easy description we may call the 'Law' of Karman — through Infinity guided by Ineffable Mind.

It is no wonder that really great scientific minds occasionally have an intuition of the truth and that such men as Einstein, Jeans, Eddington, etc., now openly declare that in their judgment the essence or fundamental stuff of the Universe is — Mind! The cycle of human thought has thus made a complete round!

of matter which in man, just as in all other beings and entities, enshroud it. The essential nature of this divine unity is wholly free,
because being pure, unfettered consciousness — a droplet, so to say,
of the Cosmic 'Shining Sea.'

Moreover, this fundamental and supreme cosmic self at the
heart of beings and things, is altogether 'above Karman,' to speak
popular language — although indeed it is the very origin and source
of all possible Karman, and therefore naturally has its own Karman
which we may specify as being divine — and consequently is never
affected by such lower Karman for the very simple reason that this
divine entity may be called itself the fundamental operative Con-
sciousness-Mind-Substance of the Universe. It is the causal Harmony of that Universe, therefore likewise the causal Harmony of all
beings and all things included in that Universe; and therefore it is
the very root and fount and source of all the operations of Nature
whatsoever: the root of Karman itself. To say in other words just
what Karman is would be extremely difficult, because it is and it
involves the profoundest cosmic Mystery — the nature and operative activity of the essential being of Cosmic Consciousness-Mind-
Substance-Force itself.

Acting incessantly throughout all manifested differentiations, it
encloses within itself all imperfect expressions thereof. But it is
only these differentiations or imperfections which work imperfectly.
Obviously, it is only the previously involved which later evolves: in
other words, evolution or unfolding follows involution or infolding;
and that which by its very nature is the Absolute Perfection or divine
unity of the Universe is the causal root or source of all and every one
of the so-called operations of Nature — of the so-called 'laws of
Nature.' Thus we see why this divine part of man's composite constitution is causally unaffected by the lower natural operations which
are nevertheless its own outflowings, except in so far as these outflowings are destined in future aeons to return unto itself.

When this supreme consciousness of a being or of an entity like
man can so self-express its own transcendent powers, as somewhat
and sometimes it can and does in individuals of the human race, then
we have what is called really free will; and in proportion as man
unwraps and unfolds, i. e., evolves forth, these inner and transcendent faculties and powers, which are the core of him, and which are of
the very nature of this transcendent consciousness within and above
him, by so much does he possess in ever larger degree this wondrous
attribute or faculty of free choice, free action, free will. For free
will is one aspect or energy of that ever-unbroken thread of con-

sciousness-mind-substance-force which unites us with Boundless Infinity. No man has free will ungeared from the Universe, as so many superficial thinkers are apt to imagine; for this would mean that he is outside the Universe. Man has free will in greater or less degree depending upon his individual development, because his inmost core, the heart of the heart of him, is literally Infinity, or what the Vedic Sages called, refusing to employ any attributive adjective — THAT. His free will, therefore, in ever-inextricable unity with his other divine-spiritual attributes and qualities, is the element or principle that links him with the Cosmic Ultimate, because his utmost or inmost SELF is identical with the Heart of Parabrahman.[226] Evolution, therefore, in addition to the incessant and progressive unfolding of faculty and power and organ, means likewise growth or unfolding of free will — all because of the fundamental fact that evolution signifies the slowly progressive but incessant unfolding into ever fuller expressions of the Parabrahmic Essence within and above the man.

Free will, therefore, increases both in power and freedom in proportion as the evolving man advances upwards on the Luminous Arc of Nature, i. e., on the consciousness-side of the Universe; and it likewise decreases as the evolving man recedes from the consciousness-side towards an ever greater descent or 'fall' into absolute matter, which in the last analysis may be described as crystallized or passive Monads, which move, as it were, in perfect automatism with Nature's own operations there.

V

The student of ancient literatures, particularly those of the Orient and their more or less modern commentaries, has doubtless met with observations, particularly in the latter, to the effect that when a man has reached the status or condition of Mastership of and in life — in other words, when he has become one of the great Sages and Seers, or indeed, perhaps has reached a still more lofty stature in spirituality — he is then 'above Karman,' above karmic reaction, and thus has passed beyond its sway. Such statements need to be taken with

---

226. Parabrahman is a Sanskrit compound which means 'beyond Brahman'— पर (*para*), 'beyond,' and ब्रह्मन् (*Brahman*), 'the Cosmic Ultimate' or 'the Cosmic Spirit.' The term thus signifying 'beyond Brahman' has not only reference to all the incomputably numerous multitudes of Hierarchies beyond the Brahman of our own Galaxy, but is more particularly a descriptive term pointing to the utterly unthinkable and therefore indescribable divine Deeps of Infinitude.

great reserve and should be examined with equal care. Now it is perfectly true, according to the teaching of the Esoteric Philosophy, the Esoteric Tradition, that an evolving Individual, such as man, may and indeed can achieve so high a status in spiritual evolution by unfolding from within himself his inner transcendent powers which act always in accordance with Cosmic Law, that he thereby becomes a direct and self-conscious collaborator and agent, in his own sphere of course, with these Cosmic Laws; and thus he may be truly said to be 'above Karman,' in so far as the term Karman here applies to his own evolution and character and activity as a Man — however high may be the stage thus attained by him.

Yet it is also and equally true that the *universal* Karman of Cosmic Being is the ultimate background of activity of the karman of the individual, because any individual whatsoever is inseparable from Cosmic Being — from the Universe. Moreover, it must be said that the highest god in highest heaven, so to speak, is as much subject to *universal* Karman as is the humblest ant climbing up a sand-hill only to go tumbling down again.

Is there then a contradiction either in ordinary logic or in metaphysics between these two statements? There is not, although indeed there may be one of the numerous paradoxes that the student of the Esoteric Philosophy finds constantly confronting him. The following is offered as an explanation of the paradox. A man or any entity, whatever the high state of evolutionary development attained may be, passes beyond, as above said, the sway or sweep of the karmic action of the hierarchy to which he belongs when he has become at-one or in complete unity with the loftiest part or portion of such a hierarchy. For the time being, the glorified man has reached quasi-divinity, because he has allied himself with the divine-spiritual portions of his own hierarchy; and as all the movements of his nature are then entirely harmonious and in accord with the hierarchy with which he is divinely and spiritually in strait union, it is obvious that thus being at one with the spiritual nature of that hierarchy, and thus 'working with Nature,' he is beyond the stage where as a subject of the hierarchy he comes under the sway or 'rule' or 'control' of the general field of karmic action in that hierarchy. Hence that hierarchical karman has no further sway over him, for in that hierarchy he has become a Master of its Life, because he is an Agent of its inmost impulses and mandates. His mind and consciousness have slipped into the Shining Sea.

Nevertheless, so far as the Universe is concerned, and because hierarchies in the Boundless All are numberless, the particular hierarchy to which he belongs and in which he now finds himself a Master of Life, is but one of hosts of hierarchies, some of them far lower, and others far higher. As compared with the Boundless All — the frontierless spaces of Infinitude — his own hierarchy, however great, shrinks to the dimensions of a mere mathematical point, so to say, and becomes simply an aggregated hierarchical atom in the fields of Universal Life.

All this means that as the evolution of such a man or entity progresses, and the time comes when he leaves his own hierarchy for larger spheres in the Cosmic Life, he enters into still vaster and sublimer spheres of experience and of consequent action, wherein, at his entrance, he finds himself on the lowest rung of this new cosmic Magnitude on the Ladder of Life, and thereupon immediately falls under the sway or 'rule' or 'governance' of the still greater karman of this sublimer hierarchical sphere.

Thus it is seen that a man may indeed rise above the karmic sphere of the relatively limited hierarchy in which he may find himself, by becoming spiritually at-one with that hierarchy's own inmost essence, and thus an Agent, an obedient Servant thereof. Yet existence in, or his karmic peregrinations or pilgrimage through, any such particular or limited hierarchy, is seen to be but the taking of a single cosmic step higher or upwards on the limitless 'Ladder' of Cosmic Life through the interwoven and interlocked and interacting Worlds of which the Kosmos itself is builded.

Now the main faculties or attributes in any evolving being, such as man, which bring about this evolutionary ascent through the Spheres, as just briefly sketched, are first the unfolding Will, becoming progressively freer as man evolves more largely, guided and over-seen and directed by the progressively unfolding faculty or attribute of consciousness or rather mind; the twain evolving strictly together and relatively in equal measure — *pari passu,* with equal step. As said elsewhere, man's will at any moment, whether of his past or of his present or of his future, may justly be said to be partly fettered or bound and partly free — the 'freedom' steadily increasing as the evolving Individual becomes ever more at-one with the divinity at his core, which is his own Higher Self and which is likewise the source of the consciousness or mind which guides his will into action.

Thus it is in the Spirit of a being, in his inner spiritual sun, in his inner consciousness, that resides the source or fount of free will, expressing itself always outwards through the encircling and enshrouding ethereal veils of the being's sevenfold constitution. The more evolved the entity, the greater the freedom of its will and consequently of its chosen actions. Free will is one of the constitutional and therefore innate or rather inherent attributes or powers that man has — and it is a godlike quality, in its origin a truly divine attribute. Yes, even though the entire forces of the cosmos impinge upon him on all sides continuously and without an instant's cessation, as completely during earth-life as in the ante-natal and post-mortem periods, he nevertheless has his portion of unfolded or developed free will with which he may carve his destiny as he wills it to be, for good or for evil for himself and his fellows.

It is of course not denied that there are mechanisms in the Universe, for there certainly are, nor is it denied that the Universe in its outer form as we understand it — that cross-section of the Cosmos which we call our physical sphere or the wide dimensions of our physical universe — is mechanical in its physical operations. To be sure it is; so indeed is our own physical body. Everything moves according to so-called 'mechanical' laws in the worlds that we at present cognise. These 'mechanical laws' are the outermost and physical expression of inner and ever active spiritual and ethereal forces; and just herein lies the solution of the riddle of life. The physical universe is in incessant movement; and it moves by reason of, and solely by reason of, the indwelling intelligences and wills which are on all the almost innumerable steps of the inner hierarchical Ladder of Life, from the highest Dhyâni-Chohan or archangel down to the least unfolded or evolved elemental. Behind the mechanisms there are the inner and invisible and ever active mechanicians; behind and within the machines there are the invisible motive powers, the movers.

Thus, in a sense, we human beings, too, may be looked upon as living mechanisms of a spiritual and intellectual type, animated and inspirited each one of us by the indwelling and over-enlightening divinity; and we weave our Webs of Destiny in which, alas, we entangle ourselves all too frequently, as we travel through time and space, winding and unwinding the strands of the web that our own goodness, or mayhap our own folly, has led us into making. Just as does the spider weave its own gossamer web out of the substance of its own physical self, so in somewhat similar manner do we human beings weave each one our Web of Destiny from the forces and substances drawn from within ourselves — our will, our intelligence, our emotions and feelings, and our substance — knotting and unknotting these delicate strands of thought and feeling. Wonderful it is that the Web of Destiny which each one of us thus weaves, is himself!

CHAPTER XVI

WEBS OF DESTINY — II

THE fundamental basis of the teaching which imbodies the setting forth of the building of Webs of Destiny is the sublime fact, openly taught or at least hinted at in most of the greater systems of religion and philosophy of the ancients, that every individual, wherever situated or living, and of whatever character, and of whatever status on the evolutionary Ladder of Life, is in essence identic throughout with the Universe in which all beings and entities and things move and live and have their being.

Whether the student turn to the profound philosophies of ancient Hindûsthân, or consult what remains to us of the religio-philosophical systems of the Greeks and the nations surrounding the Mediterranean Sea, he will find that this most profound and basic of all doctrines is discoverable everywhere. Man, as an example in point, is not only an integral portion or factor of the Universe, and inseparable therefrom, but he draws all his life and being and their manifold and multi-myriad expressions from the Cosmic Source primarily as Spirit, but secondarily likewise from the interlocked and interwoven Cosmic Hierarchies of which his own Human Hierarchy is but one.

This sublime conception was in the back of the mind of the Buddha-Gautama in his teaching regarding what later was called the Great Heresy, i. e., the wholly illusory and false idea that any entity or being whatsoever is different from or in any wise irresponsible to the Whole. It has always been the characteristic philosophic failing of all Western thought — with a few notable exceptions — to consider man as different from or distinct from the encompassing Universe; and this characteristic Western philosophic error has, with the few notable exceptions hinted at above, permeated not only all Western religion in all its forms, but likewise all Western philosophy and equally all Western science.

Fortunately however, the pendulum of thought in this respect seems to be swinging slowly back to the archaic idea, which once, ages ago, was universally accepted over the inhabited globe. It is so important to get this fundamental conception clear, that one need offer no apology for reiterating it whenever possible. It should be the basic idea or teaching of every system of thought worthy to be called religious, philosophical, or scientific. Due to the work of the Theosophical Movement in the modern world, the spirit of this fundamental concept as one of the grand facts of being is slowly permeating and in consequence influencing modern European and American thought; and this influence is especially noticeable in the writings of men of foreseeing and intuitive minds.

Modern Theosophists are doing their best to promulgate this teaching which works so powerfully to human good, and which is so strong an influence in forwarding all movements founded on a basis of philosophic and scientific as well as religious altruism. As an instance of the manner in which this sublime teaching is being broadcast into all receptive minds, the author of the present work quotes hereunder a number of passages, striking in their accurate philosophical and ethical presentation of it, from *Y Fforwm Theosophaidd*.[227]

In the apple are seeds which contain everything that is in the appletree; new appletrees can grow from them. We are apples on the tree of the universe; in us must be everything that is in the universe. By search within we could find out what secrets the stars hide from us; why the Boundless is strewn with an infinity of universes; what suns are for, and what planets; and why there are human beings and for what reasons they prosper or are miserable. It must be so; self-knowledge must be the key to all knowledge, just because the universe produces us and all the forces, powers, capacities, faculties and essences that are in it go to our making and are latent in us also. As we are conscious beings, so is the universe. As we have many grades of consciousness in us, so there is an infinity of grades of consciousness in the universe. As we can evolve: can master the lower elements in our being and develop higher and higher consciousness and character in ourselves, so is the universe evolving, and all the infinite myriads of beings that make it up. And as you cannot find or imagine, and there cannot be, a higher or truer purpose for our existence than that we should so evolve, so it becomes certain that evolution is the great business of all existence. The stars are evolving, and the atoms; the gods of the Milky Way and the infusoria in a drop of water. There is no particle of matter but is the embodiment and final outward expression of an evolving entity; and there is no human being who, if he knew his business and the purpose of his existence, would not set his mind to freeing himself from the things in himself that keep him down, and growing in himself the things that would make him valuable to humanity.

---

227. 'The Welsh Theosophical Forum,' published by the Welsh Section of the Theosophical Society: Dec., 1934, issue. These paragraphs quoted are selected from two or three extremely interesting and indeed profound passages which are undoubtedly from the pen of the talented editor, Kenneth Morris, D. LITT., who is likewise President of the Welsh Section of the Theosophical Society.

And again, on another page of the same excellent periodical:

. . . if we go within ourselves, rising above the animal self that desires and is the seat of the passions, and the personal self which identifies us with our external and separate being; beyond the impersonal self in us which thinks and reasons, into the spiritual self, which does exist in us and can be discovered, and which when we discover it we find to pour out love and compassion, impersonal, desiring no return for its beneficence, upon all beings, we have come into the very presence, and are manifesting the nature and powers, of that inmost Self in us which is universal, and which is "the love that moves the Sun and the other stars."

And Dr. Morris continues his noble theme of thought in the following passages extracted from the same issue of 'The Welsh Theosophical Forum':

Study your Seven Principles of Man. Here we are, personal selves, lower manases. But there is latent within us a Higher Manas, the power to think as the greatest of humanity have thought, waiting for us to develop it. And there is a Buddhi: the power of a Buddha to love and warm the universe with radiant compassion. And there is Âtman, the Universal Self, in which is infinity. There is Will, an impersonal universal thing that comes at the call of desire. People fail in getting what they desire because their desires are multitudinous and contradictory, and because desire has the less command of will the less it is impersonal. If you want things for yourself you are much less likely to get them than if you want them for humanity.

That means that if one's heart is set on the purposes of the Theosophical Society he is attracting into himself all the time currents of universal will power, and all the time becoming stronger. His will and purpose are waking within the personal self of him the Higher Self: vibrating the notes in the personal self octave which set vibrating, because they correspond to, the octaves Manas, Buddhi, Âtman. The powers and faculties of the Divine Universe come pouring into his personality as he needs them, and he becomes equal to any task, however impossible, that comes his way. So your value to this Work depends on the amount of your desire for its success. If your mind is running on and uniting itself with that desire in all your spare moments, and if that longing underlies your occupied moments: because it is impersonal and unselfish you are drawing into yourself the will of the universe, against which no impossibility can stand. It acts in two ways: It awakens the powers of Manas, the Thinking Self, and you become more and more able to express great thoughts for the service of your fellows; and the powers of Buddhi, the Spiritual Self, which are, to be of effective assistance to men, to draw them from evil courses and to protect those about you and awaken in them divine aspirations.

The foregoing paragraphs are most admirably conceived, and expressed with equally admirable lucidity and force. It is precisely as the author of them has pointed out: the weaving of the Web of

Destiny, which every individual, will he, nill he, is constantly and forever engaged in, is, as stated in the preceding chapter, not only the weaving of his own future destiny, which in very truth is his future self, but is likewise the contribution of the Individual to the common weaving by all beings of the larger Web of Destiny which composes what we men call the Universe.

But consider for a moment the converse way of stating this great thought: If indeed it is a very truth that each Individual does his part in aiding in the building or weaving of the Web of Destiny of the Universe of which he is an inseparable and integral portion, likewise the converse of this is equally true: that our own Universe with its sublime divine-spiritual Hierarch of whom we are all the children and offspring, as Cleanthes the Stoic so nobly said, is incessantly and throughout the Cosmic Manvantara perpetually engaged in its Sublime Labor of infilling all the beings and entities and creatures within its far-flung realms with its own Essence, its own Intelligence, its own Mind, its own Force, and in consequence likewise its own Will.

What a marvelous conception this is, when we reflect that although we are as Individuals inseparable parts and component factors in the mighty Whole, yet no such component Individual is a mere automaton or will-less or unintelligent puppet of an inscrutable and soulless Fate; but that every such Individual, because of its participation in the being of the Cosmic Essence throughout unending time, has its own portion forever of that Cosmic Essence, and thus in very truth is a being with free will but only in so far as by self-directed and self-devised efforts it has freed that will; and thus it carves its own future Destiny, weaves its own Web of Destiny about itself, which indeed is verily itself.

Karman thus is seen to be of the timelessness and essence of the Universe Itself, and indeed of the frontierless Boundless; and every such evolving individual, revolving through the many Spheres of the Universe, is not only itself making its own individual Karman by weaving its individual web of destiny, but is likewise aiding as an Agent thereof in weaving the Karmic Web which the Universe itself is engaged upon.

I

Our human minds in studying such matters as these are all too prone to fall under the mighty psychological sway of the Cosmic Mahâmâyâ, or World-Illusion, which we ourselves help to form, and it is because of this psychological bias which our minds have that we are too apt to take a limited view of things instead of rising into the free spaces of our inner spiritual being and there cognising Truth at first hand — Cosmic Reality.

As an illustration of this wholly illusory and yet mighty power in which as human beings we are so greatly entangled, one can instance our complete subservience to the ideas of Time, which we humans, reasonably enough, yet from the absolute standpoint wholly wrongly, divide into what we call the Past, the Present, and the Future; whereas could we, would we, only recognise the real facts in the case, we would instantly see that these time-divisions are but illusory presentments of the Cosmic Mahâmâyâ, and that in very truth there is neither past, nor present, nor future, as existing realities, but solely and only an eternal NOW.

In view of the foregoing, one is driven to ask oneself the very pertinent question: Is Karman itself an aspect of this World-Illusion — so real to us who are in it because partaking of its character, yet so unreal from the standpoint of Reality? Or, again, shall we not more truly say that Karman is of the very nature and substance and essence of Reality itself, and that it is, therefore, the real Cosmic Cause or Productive Power of the Cosmic Illusion itself? Methinks that somewhat of either question contains the truth; nay, rather that both questions state the truth in interrogative form; for it would seem obvious enough to the thoughtful mind that if Karman is the Cosmic Cause of the World-Illusion and therefore of all the minor Mâyâs which enwrap and enfold us as evolving Individuals, it is both precedaneous to and productive of and nevertheless involved in this World-Illusion or Cosmic Mahâmâyâ, and this last seems to be unquestionably the fact.

Our imperfect minds it is, which, unconsciously all too often to ourselves, act under the sway of the time-compulsion, and thus mislead us into taking unnecessary by-paths of destiny; and just here is probably the cause of the confusion which some few conscientious and earnest students of Theosophy have been led into when studying the working of Karman itself — the most difficult of all the teachings of the Esoteric Philosophy. It is utterly erroneous to suppose that the 'Past' can ever be separable or separate from either the Present or the Future; it is our illusion of time which brings this confusion about. To us it is very real, and it is indeed true enough to us, who likewise are creatures of Mâyâ in a sense; and it is therefore quite proper to take cognisance of the Past as well as of the Future in their bearing upon the Present, but it is wrong to consider any one of these three as being independent of or ungeared from or dis-

connected from the other twain, for the three in reality are fundamentally one.

One has instinctive and whole-hearted sympathy with the noble
words of one of the Masters written to a one-time prominent Theosophical worker, Mr. A. P. Sinnett, for the great writer deals briefly
with this question of the time-illusion. He says:

> It is my utter inability to make you understand my meaning in my explana-
> tion of even physical phenomena, let alone the spiritual rationale. This is not
> the first time I mention it. It is, as though a child should ask me to teach
> him the highest problems of Euclid before he had even begun studying the ele-
> mentary rules of arithmetic. Only the progress one makes in the study of Arcane
> knowledge from its rudimental elements, brings him gradually to understand
> our meaning. Only thus, and not otherwise, does it, strengthening and refining
> those mysterious links of sympathy between intelligent men — the temporarily
> isolated fragments of the universal Soul and the cosmic Soul itself — bring them
> into full rapport. Once this established, then only will these awakened sym-
> pathies serve, indeed, to connect MAN with — what for the want of a European
> scientific word more competent to express the idea, I am again compelled to
> describe as that energetic chain which binds together the material and Immaterial
> Kosmos,— Past, Present, and Future — and quicken his perceptions so as to
> clearly grasp, not merely all things of matter, but of Spirit also. I feel even
> irritated at having to use these three clumsy words — past, present and future!
> Miserable concepts of the objective phases of the Subjective Whole, they are
> about as ill adapted for the purpose as an axe for fine carving.[228]

Being ourselves, therefore, of the great Mâyâ of the Universe,
although linked to its inmost Heart of Reality by our own inmost
heart of being, it is natural that the processes and operations of our
mind — itself in very truth, and in more ways than one, a product of
illusion — should follow those operations and functions of Nature
so really wonderful in themselves which surround us on all sides,
and which, however illusory or mâyâvi they may be, nevertheless
contain within themselves the essence of a Reality which is the
Divine. Chiefest and most mysterious of all these operations and
functions and workings of Universal Nature, undoubtedly is that
inscrutable and in its ultimate functions incomprehensible Factor in
Nature which we call, or phrase for purposes of easy understanding,
the Karmic Law, or, more simply, Karman.

It is neither Fate nor fortuitous action, but, being rooted in the
Unthinkable, itself is of the very essence of Cosmic Mind and therefore is itself a function of the Cosmic Mind. We may call it cosmic
destiny; we may call it Necessity if we wish, provided that we ascribe

---

228. *The Mahatma Letters to A. P. Sinnett*, p. 29.

to this word Necessity no erroneous attribute of blind fatality. The ancient Greeks — at least the noblest minds amongst them — understood clearly enough this Theosophical conception of Necessity, or inflexible and ineluctable destiny; and whether we consider it under its name of *Adrasteia,* or Nemesis, we shall be considering it under one or other of its most easily comprehended phases.

The essential meaning of Destiny or Necessity, as the ancient Greeks taught it, was somewhat as follows: If a man sow wheat or barley or rye, he certainly will not reap oats or maize or some other corn, some other grain: he will reap only what he has sown. If he put a grain of wheat into the ground it will produce wheat and nothing else — first the blade of the wheat and then the growing plant and then the yellowing seed which when garnered and sown again will produce in its turn and in due time other wheaten grains.

Hesiod, the great Greek poet and philosopher, sang that the so-called 'Fates' were three; or rather perhaps his meaning was that Destiny or Necessity must be considered from three aspects: Past, Present, and Future; and Hesiod, in common with other Greeks, gave to these three aspects of Karmic Destiny the following names which he figurated as divinities: *Lachesis,* which presided over the Past, which meant for any human individual all that he had thought or felt or been and all that he had done. This word *Lachesis* comes from a Greek root meaning 'to come about.'

The second divinity represented the destiny or necessity of the present time, which the ancient Greeks called *Klotho,* derived from a Greek word meaning 'to spin'— that destiny which a human being at any present time is spinning for himself: in other words, he is presently weaving the Web of his future Destiny.

The third of the divinities was *Atropos,* a Greek compound, which means 'that which cannot be avoided or turned aside'— the future destiny, derived from the present weaving, as above said, which web, again, is woven according to the lines of thought and action of the past.

The past is what has made the man wnat he now is; and according to that past he now spins in the present the web of himself, and this web presently in spinning will eventuate in that which may not, cannot, be turned aside or stayed in the future, and which therefore becomes Necessity, Destiny, that which the man will reap as the fruitage of his own thoughts and feelings and actions — his own soul- and body-harvest of the future. This Chain of Causation and Consequence is the pathway that we human beings have trod in the past; and the pathway that we shall tread in the future will depend entirely upon what we now are making for ourselves for that future. What is the future indeed in itself? Is it something ahead of us? No, verily. It is what we with mental ineptitude call the 'past'; for, strictly speaking, there is nothing but an eternal NOW, as said before, which is but another way of saying a functioning of the the essence of Cosmic Consciousness.

This thought is beautifully expressed by a modern thinker who puts it as follows:

> The future does not come from before to meet us, but comes streaming up from behind over our heads.

II

Karman is the 'doctrine of consequences': that what ye sow ye shall reap now or at a later time, and this also is Destiny or Necessity, that which results from the actions done and the actions left undone, the thoughts thought and followed, and thoughts thought and not followed; for everything whatsoever is dogged and shadowed by its effect, whether it be positive and direct or negative and indirect; and this compound is the karman, i. e., the weaving of the Web of Destiny by the transcendent consciousness, of any being or entity whatsoever. And as the Universe is infilled with these beings and entities, as the Universe is nothing but these imbodied beings and entities, it is therefore imbodied consciousnesses, weaving garments of their own, weaving their own characters, their own Webs of Destiny, and everlastingly interacting and re-acting each upon each and each upon all and all upon each.

Paradoxical as it may seem, we are continually altering and changing the karman of every friend we have, of everyone we love, or indeed, we know; because we are changing ours, and all human beings are inextricably interconnected and amazingly interlocked; really so; and no human being can at any time live unto himself alone. We are responsible to each other. We are affecting each other's karman all the time, and in some cases tremendously, whether we will it or not. Every time one person meets and passes another person in the street, in an infinitesimal degree each is affecting the mind of the other. Each may have changed the direction that the other first took in walking. That very change may have brought to one of them an automobile-accident. Contrariwise, their passing in the street may have made one of them change the direction of his going home and possibly saved him from an automobile-accident.

It would seem of the utmost moment and of the first importance again to state with as much emphasis as it is possible to put into words, and to do so just here in this study of the nature of Karman and its action, that such illustrations as the above should never be misconstrued or misunderstood to mean that the action of Karman is at any time or in any sense or in any wise of a fatalistic character; nor is it on the other hand in any wise to be considered the same as, i. e., identic with, or even similar to, what the Western mind, due to scientific mis-education in the past, almost automatically leaps to as an explanation when such illustrations are used — i. e., that the nature and action of Karman is in any wise of a chancy or fortuitous or haphazard character.

The former error would give the impression of Karman as being the operation of an overmastering Power whether conscious or not, to whose action man is but a helpless puppet; and the latter error comprises the idea that Nature is soulless and insensate — Nature herself and all in her, man therefore included, again being but blindly moved or driven or agitated puppets, possessing neither the willing and guiding consciousness which can rise above fell circumstance, nor any capacity or power to carve out with a will the future that lies ahead. The fundamental fact or idea which it is the purpose of the preceding and of the present chapters to endeavor to elucidate is that Universal Nature herself, as well as every Individual within her encompassing realms, is instinct with consciousness, mind, choice within karmic limits, and therefore each and all possessing according to the degree of evolutionary unfoldment its portion or modicum of free will.

Yet the above in no wise diminishes the force of the statement that every thing is a link in a Chain of Causation, for in the making or production of this Chain, every Individual, high or low, great or small, has its own part to play — and plays it. Every Unit or Individual in Universal Nature, therefore, affects powerfully or weakly as the case may be every other Individual or Unit in the Mighty Whole. Some do it almost automatically, and others do it more or less with a self-consciously directed will; but however it may be done at any time and in any place, it is always done with consciousness and will behind it all.

Thus it is that we humans affect each other, weakly or powerfully, according to each individual case, and it is just this action and interaction of Individuals upon each other, incessant and ever-unceasing during the great Manvantaric Cycle, which produces the immense and complicate situations and conditions in which every evolving Individual finds itself at any moment in time and space.

In consequence of the foregoing, it should be abundantly clear that a human being, for instance, can affect any other human being or group of human beings in accordance with his own power or strength to do so. If such actions, producing effects upon others, originate in or be motivated by wholly impersonal thought and will, for the good of the others or for the common good, ethically speaking such actions and their consequent effects produce what one may describe in the Theosophical vernacular as 'good karman,' and the reactive effects or consequences upon the originator of such actions is often extremely beneficial, and at the worst productive of a mild sort of what in the Theosophical vernacular one may describe as 'relatively bad karman' — the 'badness' or unpleasantness in this last case arising in the fact that no human being is all-wise or all-good, and obviously therefore his judgment preceding any such action may very easily be both faulty because limited, and faltering because of weakness of will.

Yet no normal human being should ever hesitate to act and to act strongly for the benefit of others and to do his utmost to help others at any time and in any place, where and when such help is needed and especially in those cases where appeal for help is made. It is his bounden duty to do so, and to the best of his ability, and in accordance with his wisest judgment and best understanding. It is only a moral and intellectual coward who will refrain from rendering help when it is seen to be needed or when call for aid comes, or who will turn aside in stony-hearted indifference in similar circumstances. Such direct action or indirect action is immediately productive, in the individual thus refusing his aid, of a chain of karmic consequences which some day will find him out and which will fall lightly or heavily upon him in direct ratio to the causative situations which gave them birth.

On exactly the same lines, and following precisely the same law of reaction, does Karman act or react upon such human beings who, from one motive or another, themselves act upon others for personal gain or who from selfish motives attempt to impose their will upon others, who consequently suffer therefrom — either immediately or at a later date. The motive in either case is what distinguishes the making of 'good' karman or 'bad' karman.

Just as it is the bounden moral and natural duty of a human being always and in every set of circumstances impersonally and unselfishly to aid others for their good, equally so is it his moral and natural duty to refrain at all times and in all circumstances from acting selfishly and for personal gain upon the lives of others. The former case arises in motives which in their essence are divine; the latter case arises in motives which in their essence we may qualify as being devilish or diabolic. It is when human beings affect others to the detriment of these latter, that there arise those very frequent cases or states which bring about what is called 'unmerited suffering' — the unmerited suffering of those who are thus the karmic 'victims' of the selfish or selfishly thoughtless deeds of others.[229]

To act with a deliberate intent to sway the will of another is always wrong. To set out consciously to interfere with the karman of anyone else would be simply practising what it has become popular to call 'black magic,' and this is so even if the motive be originally good. Every man should indeed do all in his power, by means of reason and persuasion, precept and example, to prevent another man from consciously doing evil, and likewise to try to make him do better: not by imposing one's will upon this other, but by precept, by example, by kindliness, by suggestive thoughts, by pointing out the new and the better way. But if such wholly proper action is deliberately taken, and the mind of the other does not react to it from its own inner impulses and knowledge because of recognising its moral worth: in other words, if the other does not react from choice, but is made to react because of another's will being imposed upon him, which is what a hypnotist does, this indeed is diabolic, and we can qualify it as diabolism, as black magic unadulterate.

If a man loves another greatly, can he not save his friend from future sorrow by taking upon himself his friend's karman? The question is purely academic in a way, because when the last word is said, the karman of the friend is the friend himself, and therefore the answer in general is comprised in an emphatic negative; nevertheless, there is a possibility, not indeed of taking upon oneself the friend's karman, but of shouldering by means of a powerful will and a high intelligence directed to that end, a certain portion, be it large or small, of the consequences which in the normal course of Nature, with heavy and perhaps crushing effect, would fall upon the friend. The secret in such a situation lies in allying one's own life intimately with the life of the one whose heavy karman it is thus hoped to aid

---

229. With regard to cases of 'unmerited suffering,' which involve an interesting but relatively unimportant side-issue in any set of karmic consequences, more will be said in later paragraphs of the present chapter. At present the really important thing is to obtain some fairly clear idea of just what Karman is and its manner of action, both in Nature herself and in the complicate relations in which individuals are entangled — always traceable back to some originating cause in themselves. Karman is caused, and suffered, by the original actor; not otherwise.

in carrying or exhausting; but it must be remembered that for the one who attempts such noble action there is a consequent and inescapable 'making of new karman' — i. e., originating new karman by such thought and consequent action, which the one thus assuming the burden makes for himself as a chain of future effects or consequences which he himself will have to work out or exhaust.

Thus it is possible to involve oneself in the karman of another, and the doing of this is in every case fraught with either suffering or danger to the one who attempts it. As a matter of fact, it is constantly done by human beings blindly and usually, or at least often, from either selfish or ignoble motives; but there are cases, and they are relatively numerous, in which one does this with one's eyes more or less open to the perilous consequences that may ensue, and if such action is taken solely for the benefit of the one it is hoped and desired thus to aid, the motive is both impersonal and indeed sublime, and therefore the resultant karmic effects will be in no case stained or soiled by any tinge of a selfish originating cause.

In those cases where such noble and altruistic action be taken for the benefit of all that lives or for the results which it is hoped will benefit a large portion of mankind, it is a Buddha-like thing to do, it is a Christ-like thing. It is, as said above, a perilous procedure for those who have neither the wisdom nor the lofty discrimination of a Buddha or a Christ; but the motive in all such cases without exception is always holy, and therefore of necessity in time always redounds to ennoble and strengthen the character, and to enlarge and purify the intellect and moral nature, of those who so act.

Karman acts equally powerfully where the originating will is strong and the directing intelligence is great; for obviously, such action is as much karmic as is ignoble action; the former bringing great benefit to the actor, just as the latter brings suffering and pain in its train. To illustrate: Take the instance of the Buddhas of Compassion. One of the noblest doctrines of our esoteric philosophy deals with the existence and nature of the work of these Buddhas of Compassion. It tells us of their utter self-sacrifice for the benefit of the world, and how they deliberately renounce, for ages perhaps, their own evolutionary unfolding or advancement in order to return into the world of men for the purpose of compassionate help, and that they not only by precept and example show us the Path to the Gods, but they actually live and work amongst the multitudes of intellectually blind and only partially morally conscious mankind. Like the Dhyâni-Chohans of Compassion in their own sphere, out of their infinite pity they reach downwards into our own sphere, and pass lifetimes, it may be, in this sphere of relative spiritual darkness.

Such action on the part of these great and noble Beings is in all cases wholly voluntary and therefore self-chosen; yet in one very true sense of the word their great self-sacrifice and renunciation of individual progress may be called karmic. Yet, though karmic, it does not involve the degradation of their lofty spiritual stature nor the losing of the karmic reward or compensation which at some time in the future will infallibly be their guerdon. Indeed, the strict contrary of this is true, for although their action is voluntary, it is a voluntary action taken for the benefit of all that lives, and this being in character of the nature of the divine, the consequences flowing therefrom will be of corresponding type. Although greatly misinterpreted and misunderstood, the Christian Church drew its doctrine of vicarious atonement from this source. The Esoteric Philosophy, however, does not admit that there is any substantial truth in this Christian dogma, for as it has been understood for centuries in the Christian Church it is directly counter to and violative of the fundamental principle involved in karmic law — to wit, that no human being can escape either in whole or in part the karmic fruits or consequences of his actions, in their turn born of his thoughts and feelings.

Like many and perhaps all of the fundamental tenets or dogmas of Christianity, it was born in and from a greatly misinterpreted teaching of the Wisdom-Religion of antiquity; but such misinterpretations are usually far more dangerous, because distorted and unreal, than are obviously untrue and clearly fallacious philosophical or religious speculations.

But after such brief allusion to the cases of the Buddhas of Compassion, let us take the not infrequent case of the ordinary man who yearns to do good to his fellows. He can always search out ways and means of helping those he loves, as well as those who have not yet evoked his love but who may be equally in need of his compassionate aid. He can do so without touching upon or in any wise infringing upon their free will as individuals. We have no right spiritually, intellectually, psychically or physically, to attempt to control the free will or free action of another. Imagine for a moment that it is possible to take over the burden of another, perhaps by affecting the direction his own will takes or perhaps not: in such attempt — which actually is impossible of achievement — we deliberately interfere with the self-choice or free will of that other, and thus, instead of doing a service to him, we are in actual fact doing him a dis-service, because we are weakening his character throughout, instead of acting impersonally and indirectly in the manner before explained, which latter both aids him in his trouble and strengthens his character and prepares it more easily to carry his own karmic burden as a man should.

As has been on numerous occasions already stated, it is precisely because the heart of Nature is Harmony that it is also what the ancient Greek philosopher Empedocles called 'love,' but which the more sophisticated generation of our own day might prefer to call Compassion. Compassion is Nature's fundamental law. It is, because of this fact, the natural bounden duty of every human being to help Nature and to work with her, which is but another way of saying that it is our duty to help all Individuals who compose Nature and to do so to the extent of our ability. As H. P. Blavatsky says in *The Voice of the Silence:*

Help Nature and work on with her; and Nature will regard thee as one of her creators and make obeisance.[230]

Gentleness, kindness, pity, compassion, love, mercy: in fact, all the fine and ennobling attributes of the fully developed human being, belong distinctly in their action to this line of co-operation with Nature's fundamental essence and being. The man who would stand idly by when another is in trouble, listening with stony-hearted indifference to the cries of misery or to the wailings of pain without stirring a finger to assuage the suffering or to relieve the distress, is acting directly contrary to Nature's fundamental law, and is thus taking upon himself a very heavy burden of karmic responsibility, which Nature, in its re-establishment of harmony, will infallibly visit upon him to the uttermost of his fault.

It is futile argument and an entire distortion of the sense of the doctrine of Karman, to think that because some human being is undergoing disaster, or is in a situation of distress and suffering, he therefore should be left unhelped and uncomforted on the fallacious and heartless ground that he is 'merely working out his karmic deserts.' This idea is simply monstrous both ethically and naturally and runs directly counter to all the teachings of all the great Seers and Sages of all the ages.

Also in *The Voice of the Silence,* one of the most beautiful devotional works of any time, we find a very significant teaching which points directly towards and against this monstrous and mistaken

---

230. Fragment I, p. 14 (orig. ed.).

conclusion, and does so in the following highly significant words:

Inaction in a deed of mercy becomes an action in a deadly sin.[231]

It is doubtful if stronger words could be found to describe the indubitable fact that deliberate and wilful inaction, when action in a deed of mercy is humanly called for, becomes a direct and positive action of the most fundamental kind, which the great author of *The Voice of the Silence* speaks of as a 'deadly sin.' Here in such case although the man be totally inactive, making no motion either of mind or heart, this very fact runs so directly counter to Nature's own structural and fundamental operations, that he thereby makes of himself a temporary point of opposition to Nature's forces, and in doing so inaugurates for himself a stream of karmic consequences which will react upon him as powerfully and as positively as if he had with his own will and deliberate choice done some strong deed of evil.

The Buddha, the Christ, and such other Great Ones, have left behind them in no uncertain words the doctrine of our ethical responsibility to all others, and their teaching calls upon us to be up and doing in fulfilling our whole duty towards others, whomsoever they may be. Outside of other considerations which occur readily enough to the mind, one must be exceedingly dense of understanding not to realize that there is no evolving or developing power in life which is so strong and certain and so quick in its consequences as self-forgetful action in compassionate service to others. Such service teaches us how speedily to find the resources of our own hearts and minds and to see the wondrous mysteries lying latent in them; it also teaches us how most quickly and surely to develop the finer parts of our spiritual and intellectual faculty. Benevolence running to beneficent action in service to others may truly be described as the royal road of discipleship; and, indeed, only a strong-hearted man or woman can follow this path consistently, and to its end.[232]

---

231. *Op. cit.*, Fragment II, 'The Two Paths,' p. 31 (orig. ed.).

232. Note again in *The Voice of the Silence*, a book prepared *for the daily use of disciples*, the following:

"Let thy Soul lend its ear to every cry of pain like as the lotus bares its heart to drink the morning sun.

"Let not the fierce Sun dry one tear of pain before thyself hast wiped it from the sufferer's eye.

"But let each burning human tear drop on thy heart and there remain, nor ever brush it off, until the pain that caused it is removed."
— Fragment I, pp. 12-13 (orig. ed.).

It is easy enough to go through life involved in one's own personal and purely selfish affairs, but the effects or consequences of such a course of living are bitter in the extreme, and turn to the ashes of death in the mouth. Such a course of life shrivels the character and bemeans it, simply because the sphere of action becomes more and more restricted and localized; whereas benevolence eventuating in beneficent action towards all, irrespective of individuals, is the quickest and most certain cure for all the various pettinesses of mind and heart to which we as human beings are, alas! so sensitively alive when we see them in the characters of those who surround us.

Why do people follow the pathway of the lower self? Because they imagine that it is the easier way, and that it advantages them to do so. But in very truth there is a way of striking even a selfish man's mind, of firing his nobler imagination, eventually showing him that the spiritual solidarity of all beings and creatures is the fundamental basis of Nature herself. A man simply cannot live unto himself alone, strive as he may to do so; when he does try to do so, he begins thereupon and immediately to run foul not only of Nature's laws but of the merely human laws made by his fellow-men. Fire such a man's imagination, and in a little while he begins to think for himself along the lines suggested to him, and, slowly or rapidly as the case may be, he comes to see that genuine spiritual and intellectual and even social co-operation in a common effort, for the common good, is man's great Work; and that a man is great precisely in so far as he succeeds in doing this, and weak and ignoble exactly in proportion as he tries to separate himself from the great multitude of his fellow-men. It is simply lack of spiritual imagination which makes men selfish and which causes them in their blindness and ignorance to follow the 'left-hand' path, the path of individual getting, almost always meaning a getting for the individual at the cost of others' welfare.

A man simply cannot, by Nature's own laws, long live unto himself alone; and it is because so many millions of unwise and ignorant men try to live so, that there is so much misery and unhappiness in the world. History shows us that men have been great precisely in proportion as they have forgotten themselves, and lived for the world. This is obvious because the great men have a great field of view and rest never content until they enter upon these greater fields of vision. The man who lives for himself alone has an extremely limited and restricted vision, and all too soon finds that most other men have the same limited and restricted field of vision, and thus there arise constant jarrings and conflicts and the pathetic entanglements of destiny which often so wring the heart. It is the great men who embark upon great courses because their vision is great, and it is the small men, because of their ignorance and foolishness and restricted vision, who try to separate themselves off into a little corner of selfhood there to live for themselves in ignoble isolation. Nature will not long tolerate it.

Man's imagination can be fired with a great and glorious vision. Consider the universe around us. Is there a single sun, is there a single atom, that can live unto itself alone? Nowhere. And when any individual element tries to follow its own selfish path, all the other elements in the universe range themselves against it, and little by little it is forced by the immense cosmic pressure to come back into the order and harmony of the Universe. A man who works with Nature, who works for harmony, who works for love, who works for compassion and pity, who works for brotherhood and kindliness, has all Nature's evolutionary stream with him and working for him; and the man who works for hate, who works for personal gain, who swims *in adversum flumen*, who sets his puny will against Nature's evolving River of Lives, has all Nature's incalculable weight pressing against him.

There is nothing so intellectually crippling and so spiritually blinding to a human being as a dwelling upon and a dwelling in his own limited personal powers. Therein lie neither happiness, nor peace, nor again wisdom; and besides, when men follow this Path of the Cripples, it spells conflict, it spells distress, it spells pain and suffering. Yet — wonderful and compassionate paradox of Nature's operations — it is mainly through pain and suffering and distress, and the weariness of conflict and strife, that men learn better, and seek the sunlighted ways of Wisdom and Peace. Pain and suffering and distress are therefore really angels in disguise; they are the growing-pains of future achievement, the birth-pangs of coming success. They are lovely underneath their sordid garments; they are our very best friends because they awaken us to know the spiritual powers and faculties lying latent and dormant within our souls. Sorrow and pain strengthen the moral fiber in us. They stimulate our intellect, arouse our sleeping and often cold hearts, and thus teach us sympathy with and for others. They make real Men out of us. The soft sloth of luxury and self-indulgence never does this. It is self-indulgence which leads to the downward path, to spiritual and intellectual blindness, to consequent loss of wisdom and vision.

III

One of the main purposes of this and the preceding chapter will have failed in attaining its objective if the reader has not already grasped one of the essential ideas contained in the elaboration of this theme of the weaving of the Webs of Destiny: to wit, that although every individual is engaged throughout eternity in weaving its own Web of Destiny, which in very fact and truth is that Individual's self at any moment in time, nevertheless no such individual Web of Destiny stands alone, but is most intricately and indeed inseparably interwoven with all other environing Webs of Destiny, because each Individual contributes its part or quota to the weaving of the Web of the Cosmic Whole. Each Individual, furthermore, precisely because it is inseparable from the Universe, is itself therefore an agent of Kosmic destiny, contributing its portion of the Great Work of the Universe, because it imbodies within itself every substance, force, quality, attribute, that the Universe itself contains.

The deduction to be drawn from this great truth is one of immense import: it is that our destinies as individuals are constantly and forever crossing and recrossing each other; our pathways constantly crisscross each other. Thus it is that we, throughout the entire course of the Cosmic Manvantara, are acting upon and reacting against each other: one upon all and all upon one, and each upon each. This is why our karman as individuals is so complicate and often so difficult to understand in its deeper reaches, so that it is small wonder that even highly intelligent and conscientious and devoted students of the Esoteric Philosophy stumble at times in their understanding of the mysteries of karmic action, and thus often misinterpret side-lines and minor aspects and operations of the inscrutable Karmic Law.

We see in the above reasoning likewise the philosophical and scientific as well as religious *rationale* of the iterated and reiterated moral injunction of all the great Sages and Seers of all ages, who tell us with no single dissentient voice that no man can live unto himself alone. In consequence it is not only that whatever an individual does, he himself is responsible for it, but also that other individuals are strongly affected thereby, and often in such profound and mysterious ways that the original karmic cause leading such affected individuals into a sphere of contact with the original actor is extremely difficult to uncover or discover and to make plain. Often these originating causes of the crisscrossing of any strands of the different webs of two individuals lie in the far past karmic history of both, whether it be in the last life, or, what is much more likely, in another preceding life in the distant past.

It is by reasoning along these lines, which comprise the whole inner meaning or purport of the doctrine of Karman, that we come to realize how great and how far-reaching, as well as inseparable, are the actions which we perform upon each other for each other's weal or woe, for their happiness or for their suffering, for their bliss or for their pain. Incognisant as the great masses of our fellow-men are of the often distant causes of the tribulations, the accidents and grief, that fall upon them, they are all too prone to ascribe it to the decrees of an inexorable Cosmic Divinity, or to the fortuitous mischances of a soulless Universe, dead throughout, but which in some mysterious manner works out its inscrutable fate upon them.

Neither view is correct, because either view ignores the fundamental meaning of the doctrine of Karman which is that of rigid and utterly inflexible justice combined with cosmic compassion, otherwise cosmic harmony, which are operative everywhere and throughout endless time. How sublime an idea it is that each Individual is an Agent, whether he recognises it or not, whether he wills it or not, of the Cosmic Harmony and consequent Destiny! We live in a Universe of the strictest order and regularity, which means that Cosmic Law operates everywhere, and which therefore signifies that any man who throws into disharmony even his tiniest portion of the environment in which he finds himself, by the fact becomes proportionately out of tune with the Cosmic Whole, which will react upon him with power and effectual consequences exactly and mathematically apportioned to the originating cause of his act.

Thus also we bring joy to others by our thoughts and feelings and their outflowing consequences as acts, and in an exactly identical way we bring upon them pain and grief, for which they are only indirectly and inactively responsible, and thus bring 'unmerited suffering'[233] upon them — for which 'unmerited suffering' the Karmic Law will hold us strictly accountable, aye, to the uttermost; but

---

233. This phrase may startle some people, particularly those, perhaps, whose studies of Karman and of other branches of the Esoteric Philosophy have not been of long duration. Yet the phrase is a true one; in its way it is as true a statement of the facts as is the other equally true statement that suffering, whether 'merited' or 'unmerited' and however brought about, can in all instances, by reason of the nature of Karman as described in the text above, be causally brought back to the originator who is the unfortunate individual whom we may perhaps graphically describe with some truth as the 'victim.'

There is indeed such a thing as 'unmerited suffering' in human life, but this

proportioned with infinite Wisdom to the magnitude of our fault or evil doing.

It would be quite erroneous to suppose that Karman or karmic consequences are outside of us and different in any wise from the fundamental essence within us. The precise contrary of this is the fact. Nothing whatsoever can touch us, speaking absolutely, unless

---

phrase must in no circumstances be construed to mean injustice or 'unjust suffering,' or, on the other hand, that such 'unmerited suffering' has no Karmic cause in the actor and his victim.

Not much has been written about the matter of unmerited suffering in Theosophical books, not even by our greatest exponent of the Esoteric Philosophy up to the present, H. P. Blavatsky, because the whole attempt hitherto has been to elucidate and elaborate the greater, fundamental teaching regarding Karman, i. e., that it is essentially infinite justice, and that whatever happens to us at whatever time and in whatever manner, whether it bring us suffering or joy, can ultimately be traced back to causes set in motion, karmically speaking, by ourselves either in this or in another life. This statement is all-inclusive, and comprises everything that takes place in our lives — as H. P. B. so nobly says: ". . . not an accident in our lives, not a misshapen day, or a misfortune, that could not be traced back to our own doings in this or in another life."

The truth of the matter is that what we human beings, with our weak and imperfectly developed intelligence and lack of vision, call, and in a manner very truly, 'unmerited suffering' is but a minor aspect or operation of the more fundamental law briefly sketched and elaborated in the text above: inflexible cosmic justice guided by cosmic wisdom and active throughout eternity. It would be therefore both wrong in substance, and philosophically inaccurate, were we ever to suppose that a man's 'present' karman could either in nature or in theory be distinct from or ungeared from or independent of his past — which is equivalent to saying his past karman; and intimately connected with this philosophically fundamental idea is the other idea that the future, though to us human beings apparently based on the past and the present, is really in the Kosmic view identic with the eternal NOW. (The reader is referred to a passage in a previous paragraph in the text above, in a citation from one of the Master's letters.)

However, in order to avoid any needless argument because of lack of elaboration of the idea of 'unmerited suffering,' and because no fair statement of the case could be made by citing brief extracts from H. P. Blavatsky which might corroborate our position, which no fair-minded man would ever do, the following citations of the most important passages written by H. P. Blavatsky on the subject of 'unmerited suffering' are given hereinunder with a few extracts teaching the larger or fundamental nature of Karman from others of her writings. As far as the present writer can recollect, all that H. P. Blavatsky has said, at least of any importance, about so-called 'unmerited suffering' is found in *The Key to Theosophy*. Let us then first quote these passages and follow them with

we ourselves in some manner, somewhen, somewhere, have so acted as to arouse the sleeping or active forces of Nature, which thereupon sooner or later react upon us in ratio and proportion exactly and wonderfully balanced or equilibrated with the cause originating in ourselves. Karman, therefore, and traced back to its origin, is the consequence of the action of our own free will. The free-willing

---

a few giving the larger or general teaching, of which the passages about 'unmerited suffering' are referrible to one of its secondary or minor meanings:

"Our philosophy teaches that Karmic punishment reaches the Ego only in its next incarnation. After death it receives only the reward for the unmerited sufferings endured during its past incarnation. [Here is appended a footnote as follows: "Some Theosophists have taken exception to this phrase, but the words are those of Master, and the meaning attached to the word 'unmerited' is that given above. . . . the essential idea was that men often suffer from the effects of the actions done by others, effects which thus do not strictly belong to their own Karma — and for these sufferings they of course deserve compensation."] The whole punishment after death, even for the materialist, consists, therefore, in the absence of any reward, and the utter loss of the consciousness of one's bliss and rest. Karma is the child of the terrestrial Ego, the fruit of the actions of the tree which is the objective personality visible to all, as much as the fruit of all the thoughts and even motives of the spiritual 'I'; but Karma is also the tender mother, who heals the wounds inflicted by her during the preceding life, before she will begin to torture this Ego by inflicting upon him new ones. *If it may be said that there is not a mental or physical suffering in the life of a mortal which is not the direct fruit and consequence of some sin in a preceding existence; on the other hand, since he does not preserve the slightest recollection of it in his actual life, and feels himself not deserving of such punishment, and therefore thinks he suffers for no guilt of his own, this alone is sufficient to entitle the human soul to the fullest consolation, rest, and bliss in his post-mortem existence.* Death comes to our spiritual selves ever as a deliverer and friend.

". . . At the solemn moment of death every man, even when death is sudden, sees the whole of his past life marshalled before him, in its minutest details. . . . But this instant is enough to show to him the whole chain of causes which have been at work during his life. He sees and now understands himself as he is, unadorned by flattery or self-deception. He reads his life, remaining as a spectator looking down into the arena he is quitting; he feels and knows the *justice of all the suffering that has overtaken him.*" — *The Key to Theosophy,* pp. 161-2 (orig. ed.). The italics are the present writer's.

"We say that man suffers so much unmerited misery during his life, through the fault of others with whom he is associated, or because of his environment, that he is surely entitled to perfect rest and quiet, if not bliss, before taking up again the burden of life." — *Op. cit.,* p. 35

". . . Devachan is the idealized continuation of the terrestrial life just left behind, a period of retributive adjustment, and a reward for unmerited wrongs and sufferings undergone in that special life." — *Op. cit.,* p. 133

". . . Reincarnation will gather around him all those other Egos who have suffered, whether directly or indirectly, at the hands, or even through the unconscious instrumentality, of the past *personality.* They will be thrown by Nemesis in the way of the new man, concealing the *old.* . . ." — *Op. cit.,* p. 141

"ENQ. But, surely, all these evils which seem to fall upon the masses somewhat indiscriminately are not actual merited and INDIVIDUAL Karma?

"THEO. No, they cannot be so strictly defined in their effects as to show that each individual environment, and the particular conditions of life in which each person finds himself, are nothing more than the retributive Karma which the individual generated in a previous life. We must not lose sight of the fact that every atom is subject to the general law governing the whole body to which it belongs, and here we come upon the wider track of the Karmic law. Do you not perceive that the aggregate of

entity thinks, or feels, or acts, or thinks and feels and therefore acts, setting in motion thereby an inescapable train of results or consequences; and these results, precisely because we are essentially one with the Universe, some day flow back upon us as karmic con-

---

individual Karma becomes that of the nation to which those individuals belong, and further, that the sum total of National Karma is that of the World? . . . it is upon this broad line of Human interdependence that the law of Karma finds its legitimate and equable issue." — *Op. cit.*, p. 202

The preceding citations from *The Key to Theosophy* are the most important statements as regards the matter of 'unmerited suffering' that the Great Theosophist wrote. Turning now to *The Mahatma Letters to A. P. Sinnett*, p. 310, we find the following brief allusion to the same matter:

". . . 'the adept *becomes*, he is not *made*' is true to the letter. Since every one of us is the *creator* and producer of the *causes* that lead to such or some other *results*, we have to reap but what we have sown. *Our chelas are helped but when they are innocent of the causes that lead them into trouble;* when such causes are generated by foreign, outside influences. Life and the struggle for adeptship would be too easy, had we all scavengers behind us to sweep away the *effects* we have generated through our own rashness and presumption."

To suppose that this extract from the Mahâtman's letter teaches 'unmerited' suffering or equivalently 'unmerited' help, as meaning distinct from originating karmic causes, is absurd and arises only from a superficial and hasty perusal and analysis of the Master's words. The entire citation says nothing *except* that Karman is the cause of all that happens to us, as is evident in the first two sentences and their concluding unequivocal and inclusive affirmation "we have to reap but what we have sown." This is all-inclusive, and says not a word about 'unmerited' in the sense of unjustified or uncaused karmic consequences.

The teacher immediately in the next sentence goes on to point out that in the case of chelas, who are here particularly specified — as indeed throughout the whole paragraph they are alluded to — even the chelas, although chelas because of preceding karmic causes, are helped when they are 'innocent' of the originating causes leading to trouble and these causes are generated by foreign outside influences. This is because chelas are as it were entrants into a new world, into a new sphere of forces, all of them dangerous and some of them terrible, wherein these chelas are like little children only lately born, and in a sense also like little children are unable successfully to meet and repel 'foreign outside influences' which impinge upon them. Precisely so is it with a little child. It is born into a new world almost helpless, needing guidance and succor and aid, which it receives from its parents who watch over it and protect it and help it; yet if the little child pokes its finger into the fire the finger is burned and the child's innocence is no protection to it. To prevent such catastrophes the parents watch over the child.

The parallel is exact where chelas are concerned. Born into a new world, of which the forces and influences are 'foreign' and 'outside,' they are almost helpless, unable to protect themselves adequately, and in consequence are carefully watched over, guided, helped, until they grow accustomed to the new world; yet if the chela ignores the Master's warnings and deliberately 'pokes his finger'

sequences. They could never have touched us unless we as entities, having free will, set those natural forces in action. For example, I put my hand into the fire; my hand is burned, but I by my own free will voluntarily or involuntarily caused my hand to be burned. The

---

into the fire, or wilfully experiments with the dread forces and denizens of the new world, he must reap the consequences.

To suppose then that the Master here teaches 'unmerited' suffering as signifying non-karmic results, causelessly impinging on the sufferer, is preposterous nonsense, for nothing of the kind is here taught; but the doctrine of Karman as H. P. Blavatsky taught it, as for instance in her *The Key to Theosophy*, is unqualifiedly stated in the first two sentences of this extract and in inclusively general terms.

Of course there is 'unmerited' suffering in the sense here and elsewhere explained, of the imperfect *personal* man's suffering in the set of circumstances in one life what that particular 'person,' the 'new man' of the present life, is not self-consciously conscious of having caused, who therefore suffers keenly from the apparently uncaused but nevertheless karmic events which befall him.

The above covers the case so far as the minor operation or 'track' of karmic law is concerned. Turning now to the general statements of the law which is all-inclusive and therefore comprises likewise the minor track called 'unmerited sufferings,' it could not be better stated than in H. P. Blavatsky's own words in her great work, *The Secret Doctrine*. An example will here suffice, and the reader is referred to her writings and to previous citations from her, setting forth the general law of Karman, to be found in the pages of the present work, as for instance, in the text of the preceding chapter, on pages 473-4.

". . . Karma-Nemesis, or the Law of Retribution. This Law — whether Conscious or Unconscious — predestines nothing and no one. It exists from and in Eternity, truly, for it is ETERNITY itself; and as such, since no act can be co-equal with eternity, it cannot be said to act, for it is ACTION itself. It is not the Wave which drowns a man, but the *personal* action of the wretch, who goes deliberately and places himself under the *impersonal* action of the laws that govern the Ocean's motion. Karma creates nothing, nor does it design. It is man who plans and creates causes, and Karmic law adjusts the effects; which adjustment is not an act, but universal harmony, tending ever to resume its original position, like a bough, which, bent down too forcibly, rebounds with corresponding vigour. If it happen to dislocate the arm that tried to bend it out of its natural position, shall we say that it is the bough which broke our arm, or that our own folly has brought us to grief? . . . KARMA is an Absolute and Eternal law in the World of manifestation; . . . for Karma is one with the Unknowable, of which it is an aspect in its effects in the phenomenal world."— Vol. II, pp. 304-6

The reader who is interested in this matter may find some interesting comments and ideas in *The Theosophical Forum*, issues of March 15, May 15, 1933; and in the issue of August 15, 1933, of *The English Theosophical Forum*.

The whole difficulty, if indeed there be any to reasonable people of philosophical bent, lies in the perhaps unconscious idea that great minds like those of the Masters and their Messenger H. P. Blavatsky, were guilty, consciously or otherwise, of 'contradictions.' This is not so; there are no contradictions, but we have here real paradoxes. Everything that happens to an Individual is karmic, but as this Individual is constantly evolving, thus changing its character,

fact that very likely my hand's entering the fire was the result of negligence or stupidity on my part in no wise sets aside the laws of Nature which act and react inevitably whenever they are invoked, consciously or unconsciously. I deliberately drink poison and I die. This is what men call self-murder — suicide. I used my relatively free will to do this crime upon myself, and part of the consequences — the physical death — immediately or soon thereafter results; but there are other consequences bound up with this, because, choosing to commit suicide, I commit a crime upon myself which is contrary to Nature's intention, and therefore there are ethical principles involved in the situation as well as physical, spiritual, and intellectual causes which have been set in motion by my impulse and by my act. I have weakened my character by being thus a coward and by being afraid to face life and to face the things which I myself have put myself into; and consequently because I am one with the Universe, sooner or later the ripples or vibrations as resulting effects will search me out and find me again and I shall then feel as consequences, as a part of my future karman, those results of this my act, which did not find immediate exhaustion when the act was committed.

One of the results is obvious: by giving way to the evil impulse to be cowardly and to commit suicide, I thereby weaken my will — and this is one of the ethical and psychical consequences. Instead of facing the difficulties which caused me to commit suicide, I turn my back upon them. I am a coward, and I kill myself. My mind would have been strengthened and my moral fiber thus increased had I lived and courageously faced the difficulties like a true man.

IV

Karman is not something outside of ourselves, in the sense of

---

therefore its destiny, if the karmic retribution be not immediate — as it rarely is — its effects, light or heavy, fall upon the 'later man' or 'new man,' who thus in very truth, being a larger incarnation or imbodiment of the soul-forces of the higher nature, can be said with justice to undergo 'unmerited suffering'; but it is karmic retribution just the same.

In conclusion of this long note, it becomes necessary at least to state that Karman often is exhausted through its mysterious and inscrutable works by bringing about through the instrumentality of the Reincarnating Ego a purging of the latter, which the hapless 'new man' — a ray-child of the Reincarnating Ego — has to suffer however as 'unmerited' pain. His compensation and reward is the long, even though illusory, unstained bliss and felicitous readjustment in the Devachan. Keep in mind therefore always the unity of all being — and you have the explanation on your thumb-nail, if you can understand it!

being different from, distinct from, ungeared from, or apart from our inner essence. The cosmic karmic law, so far as the individual is concerned, is always quiescent unless aroused into action or evoked by the thoughts and feelings and consequent acts of the individual himself. Every man is weaving the fabric of his own being throughout the ages, throughout unending time. He himself is therefore his own Web of destiny; and whatever he does or has done, or does in the future, it is the law of his own being as well as the law of Nature, that he must abide by the consequences thereof, because among other things he has made it all to become a part of himself, because his character has been proportionately changed, his mind has been correspondingly altered, his ethical principles have been in due ratio affected, and even his physical body is proportionately affected thereby. Thus it is in very truth that a man is his own karman.

If a man work evil, evil returns to him in this life or in some future life; because he has thereby biased or distorted the structure of his character, and this distortion or bias will eventuate in biased or distorted understanding and consequent action, producing corresponding evil upon himself. Equally so, if he work good, good comes back to him in this life or in some future life, because the working of good is the building of harmony into himself, a straightening of the tangles of character, and an enlarging of intellectual and psychical faculty, and a consequently beneficial effect even upon his physical body: the constant doing of good results in the making of the interior structure of man a more harmoniously co-operative agent with all the other great and guiding spiritual forces of the Universe surrounding him, and in which he lives for ever.

We have lived lives innumerable before the present one; and in no one single past life has any human being been able to exhaust all the causes set in motion therein — to bring to fruition all the karmic seeds that were then sown; and it is just because of this stored-up karmic treasure that we have to live life after life after life after life in order to work these causes out.[234]

---

234. Karman generally may be divided into two main classes: karman which has not yet been worked out or exhausted, and karman which is now in the making. Another way of phrasing the matter is: karman which is now beginning to exhaust itself arising in the past, and karman which is being accumulated or which will not begin to exhaust itself until the future. That class of karman which is now beginning to exhaust itself we may call 'ripe,' and the technical Sanskrit word for it is प्रारब्ध (prârabdha), i. e., that which is beginning; and that class of karman which is in the making and will exhaust itself in the future we may call 'unripe' and the technical Sanskrit word for this is सञ्चित (sañchita).

Before the Reincarnating Ego reimbodies itself anew, guided by the divine-spiritual Monad within it, because of its inherent and native attribute or faculty of relatively free will, i. e., the power of choice, it has in consequence the quality or capacity of selecting those particular and confluent, congruent, karmic causes which in the life then opening it can best work out — as karmic effects. This is simply the same power of selection at the beginning of a new birth on earth that every normal man invokes and uses his whole incarnated life long. In such life he selects from moment to moment, or from day to day, or from year to year, the pathway or course of action which seems to him to be preferred; and there are possibly a thousand million by-roads or pathways — i. e., different choices — that he might have taken at each such moment of selection. We have an infinite number of karmic experiences behind us; and when each new life opens, when we appear on the stage to play our new rôle, we do so strictly according to the karmic part that we have selected or chosen from the Book of our then awakened vision and memory. Those karmic causes not then selected by us, we shall have to chose or imbody in a subsequent selection, when in some future new life we shall begin a new career on earth. But as regards any one earth-life, there are invariably certain conditions, involving a certain selection and consequent path of action, lying before us, bringing us to certain civilizations, certain families — and the watching and waiting Higher Self oversees this general field of our choice: this path, and this other path, and that path, pretty much as a man exercises the faculty when in driving his motor-car he reaches bifurcating roads or a crossing of several routes. When such a man comes to bifurcating roads which are new to him, he obviously knows not the pathway, but he says: "I will take *this* path in preference to the other two or three or four, branching from this point." He might have taken another, or one of several others; but in any case he makes his choice. The only difference between the man making his choice and the Higher Self, is that the Higher Self has a vision and a forevision, and a hind-vision, which by comparison with the discrimination of the incarnated man, are incomparably stronger and more certain-sure.[235]

---

235. The writer has often been asked whether karman influences the insane, mentally deficient, or idiots, and whether the insane, the mentally deficient, and the idiots can cause new karman. In answer to this interesting question it may be observed that karman has no hold upon these three classes of humans, except a merely physical karman; as when an idiot, etc., puts his finger into the

The thoughts we think, the emotions we allow to sway us, and the consequent acts we do, all bear their fruitage in this life or in some succeeding life when their chance for manifestation occurs: then out they come, a rushing tide of energies — these latent forces which we have built into ourselves and which in the aggregate we call our character. When the appropriate time comes and the environment is ready, our character then manifests correspondingly for our own weal or woe — or, what comes to the same thing, the karmic seeds we now sow will bring forth their fruitage either then or at a later date along lines of least resistance as all other energies of Nature do. Indeed, it is thus that we atone finally for our misdeeds towards others, and indeed to ourselves; and the resultant of all this, in the grand sweep of time and destiny, eventuates in a strengthening and developing evolution of the substance of our character towards a grander and ever-expanding destiny.

Karman, therefore, essentially is natural harmony, involving the concordance and symmetry of the Universe as a Whole; and any action by any entity on any plane running counter to this concord-

---

fire he is bound to be physically burned. But all other kinds of karman take no hold on individuals who in such cases have not the usual spiritual and mental power of choice and action. Where the individual will is inoperative and has no power of intelligent discrimination and selection, it is obvious that in such cases there is no future truly karmic result; nevertheless, of course former unworked-out karman brought these idiots, etc., into physical being, and a certain amount of consequent physical karman is bound to be exhausted in such incarnations. It is all the result or consequence of the mistakes and evil-doing of a former life or of former lives.

When, for example, an idiot-incarnation is ended, the waiting Monad —for the Monad during such an incarnation may truly be described as waiting — will then have worked out this particular aspect or part of its accumulated karmic fruitage, results, consequences; and the next incarnation of the Monad will very probably be a more or less normal one, although equally probably low in the human scale. Karman brought the idiot-state about, but karman will have no other effect on the idiot himself than an ordinary physical one. The idiot-state resembles that of a beast. The beast makes no truly spiritual or intellectual or ethical or psychical karman worth speaking of, because it exercises no especial, or human, strong faculty of will, of judgment, of discrimination, of choice; and consequently the beast is relatively irresponsible. An idiot, etc., is likewise relatively irresponsible, if not wholly so. Nevertheless, as said above, just as karman brings about the birth even of a beast, so karman brings about the birth also of an idiot, or of one mentally deficient, or of one insane. For karman to take a grip on one's destiny, one must exercise the faculties of free will, choice, bringing about continued positive action in a determinate direction.

ance or this symmetry of structure, runs directly counter to the natural harmony of things, in other words 'against' Nature, which immediately is aroused into action and becomes there and then, or at a later time, operative by reaction.

In *The Secret Doctrine* there is a passage which contains such a wealth of Wisdom as regards the nature and consequences of karmic action, written with such singular lucidity of expression, that, although this passage has already been cited two or three times, it is felt that there is no need to offer any apology for repeating it here. H. P. Blavatsky says:

> But verily there is not an accident in our lives, not a misshapen day, or a misfortune, that could not be traced back to our own doings in this or in another life. If one breaks the laws of Harmony, or, as a theosophical writer expresses it, "the laws of life," one must be prepared to fall into the chaos one has oneself produced.[236]

To which, as said before, one may add that there is not a joy or a happiness or a stroke of 'good luck' as the saying runs, of which we ourselves, somewhere, somewhen, in the present or in the near or distant past, have not prepared the causes of its coming.

Nevertheless, as already explained and elaborated at some length in previous paragraphs of this chapter, because of the extremely complicate and intricate nature of the Webs of Destiny in which we are all involved, causing us to act and react upon others, weakly or strongly as the case may be, we often suffer dumbly and as it were unfairly, because our eyes are blinded, and we have no cognitional memory of the originating causes of our suffering. Because our characters have improved and grown better by the coming into us of new streams of spiritual energy, however feeble these may be, we have the strong feeling that the suffering and pain which we undergo are 'unmerited' — and so in very truth they are for the 'new man' which in the later incarnation we have become. It was not this 'new man' which committed the faults, did the evil deeds, lived the selfish and perhaps ignoble life of the 'old man': and consequently to the 'new man' of the present life, with his changed character and more noble spiritual impulses and larger intellectual vision, the suffering that comes upon him is not strictly in the 'new man's' karman — although it is strict karmic justice following upon the causal actions of the 'old man' who was, but now no longer is because he has become the 'new man.'

---

236. *The Secret Doctrine*, Vol. I, pp. 643-4.

Consider the following illustration: An average young man commits a crime, let us say, when he is twenty years old. He is successful in hiding it. As he grows to maturity and passes through the stages of thirty years, forty years, fifty years, sixty years, the Reincarnating Ego of him by a steady infusion into his brain-mind of a larger flow of its own monadic wisdom and intelligence, gradually changes his life greatly for the better, so that in his sixtieth year, he has already become known in his community as not only a good man, but an honorable citizen, an affectionate and faithful father and friend, and in general an example of upright manhood. This is because the 'soul' of him is more largely incarnated.

In his sixtieth year, due to some karmic cause, his crime becomes known. He sees crashing around him all that he held dear. His reputation is at stake. His friends and his family are seriously affected, and he himself suffers the tortures of the damned. (One is reminded here of the case of Jean Valjean, in Victor Hugo's *Les Misérables*). Question: Is this man of sixty, with the newly incarnated spirit of morality and his larger heart-life and his sense of fellow-feeling for others, responsible for the crime of the wayward, wilful, and quasi-ignorant lad of twenty? Human law says Yes. The Esoteric Tradition says No, not entirely, for here the 'new man' is undergoing 'unmerited suffering' for the sin of the hapless and thoughtless 'old man' of twenty.

Pause a moment in reflexion. Even human justice, vacillating and feeble as it is — even man-made laws recognise something at least of the same fact, and few even average juries would visit the statutory legal punishment upon the man of sixty that would have been appropriate and, according to human law, just for the man of twenty. The point here is that the man of sixty is *not* the same as the man of twenty, albeit from birth until death the Reincarnating Ego is the same; and it is the Reincarnating Ego which thus undergoes retribution, karmically speaking, through the sufferings brought about by the man of twenty.

Transfer the illustration to the Reincarnating Ego in its passage through several births. In each new earth-life or reincarnation, the 'new man' although the karmic child of the 'old man' of the past life, nevertheless is the 'new' entity because imbodying, in however small measure, a larger inflow of the wisdom and light of the Monad. In one of its preceding lives, some dire crime was committed by the 'man' of that life; its karmic causes endure and, let us say at the fourth reincarnation thereafter, the 'new man' of this fourth rebirth finds himself suffering unaccountably from others' acts, and can see no causal justice in it all. His sufferings in this fourth life are indeed 'unmerited' by this 'new man'; but the reincarnating ego is the seat of the original causes of the 'old man'; and thus although the 'new man,' the human being, suffers with unmerited trouble and grief, we see that the causes on the large scale were made several lives before.

The *rationale* of this subtil thought should be sufficiently clear if we take the picture of a man now become a human demigod, a true Mahâtman, who is the karmic fruitage of the 'old man' of far past lives. Should this noble 'new man' undergo any suffering of any kind in his present life, due to the karmic consequences or fruitage of the evil-doing of the 'old man' now long past? Shall we and can we say that the Mahâtman has 'merited' such portion of karmic retribution as now in Nature's infinite justice he is working out? Certainly not; yet karmic indeed it is, and no one knows it better than this grand 'new man'; but nevertheless the Mahâtman did not commit the follies and wickednesses of his long-past karmic parent, the 'old man' who was.[237]

---

237. The illustration given in the text is exaggerated, and intentionally so, in order to bring out clearly and in graphic outline the gist of the subtil thought. The distinction is so obvious between the Mahâtman as he now is as the 'new man' and as he was in far past incarnations as the 'old man,' that even the most cursory or rapid reader can hardly fail in having his attention caught. Exaggerated, yes, truly, so far as the Mahâtman's undergoing as 'unmerited suffering' those lower reactions of karmic destiny which are so common to the ordinary man; but not exaggerated, and even understated, when we take into consideration the unmerited and immense load of karmic responsibility which the entire Hierarchy of Compassion, headed by the Buddhas of Compassion, deliberately take upon themselves for the benefit of the world.

Of course, with the relentless logic of the Esoteric Philosophy and in its profound metaphysic, we are bound even here to ascribe this sublime Choice to the spiritual and intellectual training of these Great Ones, extending over many past lives, and due, so to speak, to the accumulated karmic 'merit' of many small choices made in those past lives to ally oneself with the light-side of Nature or the Hierarchy of Compassion. Thus, in another sense from that ordinarily meant when we speak of 'unmerited suffering' and almost the converse of the latter, nevertheless this binding of a Great Soul unto the karmic responsibility, perhaps for many lives of repeated incarnations for the benefit of humanity, is karmic in its origin. Yet it is 'unmerited' in the sense that the loss of all individual progress by the Mahâtman for the benefit of mankind is due to no fault or defection of character in him, but solely to the sublime instincts of infinite compassion. Here we see clearly the difference between the Pratyeka-Buddhas and the Buddhas of Compassion. The difference should be clearly and carefully noted.

V

There is then no such thing as unmerited suffering except in the sense that has already been set forth. Nothing that happens to us is unjust in the sense of never having been causally originated. The word 'unmerited' here cannot be used in the old-fashioned sense as being something put upon someone by an outside force, whether this outside force be 'God,' acting in co-operation with his ministrant angels, or whether it be what the materialists call 'Nature,' or again the wholly erroneous idea of the fatalists that chance or fortuity exists. Nothing is 'unmerited' in any of the three foregoing senses — all signifying that there was no originating cause inhering in the man himself; because if this idea were true, then a man could never at any instant of his existence feel sure lest he might at the next moment be in some terribly unjust, inharmonious, and wicked state of circumstances, which he had never at any time in the past brought upon himself, thus being involved in an inscrutable destiny that an outside power whipped him into with the cruel scourges of what to him is fate.

Moreover, we must always remember that there are different kinds of Karman to which all beings and entities and things throughout Universal Nature are more or less subject. For instance, there is our own individual or personal karman; there is our family karman; there is our national karman; there is the karman of our Globe; there is the karman affecting our planet as one of the family of the Solar System. The Solar System again is a component part of our Home-Universe, called the Galaxy, and so on *ad infinitum*: all a marvelous working of action and reaction, of action and interaction, between and among all beings and all entities and all things, inextricably interconnected with the laws and operations and structure of the Universe, these all interworking and interwoven and interacting — a truly marvelous picture indeed!

Now, as said, any man of course has his own individual karman; he is subject likewise to the karman of his nation, and here is at least in part the key to what is meant by 'partly unmerited Karman.' A man's individual karman draws him to incarnate in a particular nation at a particular time, and he is thereby subjected to all the intricate conditions and incidental happenings of the nation of which he composes so small a part, and by which he is swept into a larger course of destiny and action than perhaps would have been his karman or destiny had his individual karman been different, leading him to some other national sphere. He thus is swept on by the current of circumstances — although in the last analysis due to his own past sowing of karmic causes — along with the karman of the nation of which he now forms a part. A flood or a famine sweeps over his home or the country in which he lives. A tidal wave comes in upon the land and sweeps twenty thousand beings into the waters. Or again, an earthquake shakes down a city, and scores of thousands of human bodies perish in the disaster.[238] How does it happen that a man, or a man and his family, or a community, in cases like these, suffer, losing not only property, but it may be life? In every case the man who finds himself in such surroundings has put himself there as the karmic effect or consequences of previous karmic action in this or in another life — such action comprising thoughts, desires, instincts, emotions, yearnings.

If the reader remember the teachings and the reflexions and deductions derivative from them, which have been elaborated in the present and preceding chapters, he will realize that the Universe, precisely because it is an aggregate of literally innumerable Webs of Destiny, is composite of vast interacting, interrelated, intermingling Hierarchies both great and small, each one an individual by itself, but all karmically involved in and encompassed by the Over-Soul of the Universe — our own Home-Universe in the present instance — and all finally therefore in the last analysis karmically subservient and obedient to this Over-Soul's fundamental swabhâva or characteristic cosmic 'law' or web of 'laws.'

Consequently, as each one of us is *in his inmost essence* identic with the Over-Soul of the Universe, therefore the fundamental essence of our being is the same as the fundamental essence of the Universe. Its origin is ours, and its destiny is ours, and its 'laws' are ours.

---

238. The loss of life involved in some of these earthquakes and in tidal waves accompanied or unaccompanied with seismic action, is often frightful. The list below consists of estimates, official and otherwise, of notable earthquakes that have occurred within the last three hundred years or so, and the loss of life was in each instance apparently due not only to the quake itself but to the accompanying dangers of tidal wave and fire:

Mt. Etna, Sicily	Sept.	1693 : 60,000	Assam	June 12, 1897 :	1,542
Japan	Feb. 2, 1703 : 200,000		India	1905 :	20,000
Lisbon, Portugal	Nov. 1, 1755 : 50,000		Valparaiso, Chile	Aug. 16, 1906 :	1,500
Calabria, Italy	Feb. 4, 1783 : 60,000		Kingston, Jamaica	Jan. 14, 1907 :	1,400
Quito, Ecuador	Feb. 4, 1797 : 40,000		Messina, Sicily	Dec. 28, 1908 :	77,000
Naples	Dec. 16, 1857 : 12,300		Cartago, Costa Rica	1910 :	1,500
Ecuador & Peru	Aug. 13-5, 1868 : 24,000		Central Italy	Jan. 13, 1915 :	30,000
Java	Aug. 25-9, 1883 : 35,000		Yokohama & Tokyo	Sept. 1, 1923 : 100,000
Japan	1891 : 9,960		Managua, Nicaragua	Mar. 31, 1931 : 1,000
Japan	1896 : 29,000		Kansu Prov., China	Dec. 26, 1932 : 70,000

Therefore, what happens in any part of the Universe affects favorably or adversely, to use human language here, every other part without exception, in exactly the same way, to employ a homely simile, as a diseased heart or liver or brain or even a burnt finger or a callus on the foot will affect adversely the entire body until the disease or affection is healed.   We are thus, whether we will it or nill it, conscious or unconscious collaborators with the Universe, each one of us enjoying his own measure of free will, and yet all of us subject to the grand sweep of its harmony and its cosmical impulses arising from the great fundamental tone and essence of our common being.

It should be evident, therefore, to any thoughtful mind that what we humans call the exterior or Nature-aspect of Karman is the always supreme and usually over-riding functioning or activity of the Over-Soul as working both through all things, or from within, and, as it were, upon us also from the outside, because of our eternal and intimate union and contact with all other beings and things whatsoever.   Thus it will be seen that what is called 'unmerited Karman,' outside of that portion of it which has been alluded to in previous paragraphs, is that which we suffer from the impact upon us of the forces and beings of the world in which we live, and on a larger scale from the impact of forces and beings of the surrounding Universe in which we move and live and have our being, and whose fundamental essence and tone are our fundamental essence and tone.

Strictly on the hierarchical scheme before described, we live within the vital and ethereal as well as psychical, intellectual, and spiritual life-being of Entities greater and indeed far greater than we; and, to a certain extent because of this fact, we must slavishly follow them in their own wide-sweeping cosmic thoughts and acts, exactly as the life-atoms composing my body must, will they, nill they, follow the dictates and mandates of my personal will, and hence must go with me when I go to another part of the world, say to Berlin or to California or to London, or to Stockholm, or wherever it may be.   The life-atoms in my body have no choice in the matter.   Yet this is in no wise fatalism as already described.

Yet, while the above is so, and while this often brings about a great deal of 'unmerited suffering' on a large and diffuse scale for an ego in the life in which it may be incarnated, that same individual ego infallibly shall receive due karmic recompense in the Devachan for the trials and sufferings, such as they may be, which it has experienced in the life just closed; and furthermore is entitled to and should receive every possible help and all-supporting sympathy, in his woes and troubles, from his fellow-men, who in-

stinctively proffer it from a spirit of intuitive compassion and because of a conscious or unconscious and instinctive recognition of
our common brotherhood and spiritual quasi-identity.

Moreover, because of man's own intricate constitution, comprising as it does divine, spiritual, intellectual, psychical, astral, and
physical parts, and just because he is a composite entity, the bundle
of forces and substances which compose him and form his constitution, often work as it were in temporarily inharmonious manners,
and these inharmonious manners produce what in many cases can
properly be called unmerited pain or suffering, because all arising
at former times which are thus not strictly the karman of the now
imbodied entity, or Kshetrajña. Nevertheless, when the last analysis
of causes and effects is properly made, we are logically brought back
to find that it is the man himself, or the entity itself, i. e., the complex
constitution, which brings these sufferings about, because the karman of a man is the man himself, the karman of an entity is the entity itself, at any moment throughout infinity — past, present, or
future, which three periods of time resolve themselves into an eternal NOW.

This same idea, so philosophically subtil, yet so logically perfect,
was in the mind of the writer of the statement found in the Christian
teaching (given here in effect): "I do not the things that I should
do, but I do the things that I should not do. Lord, give Thou me
health."[239] These words contain the substance of the idea, when they
are properly understood, and likewise contain the substance of the
Christ-mystery. The point is indeed very subtil, and one must try to
subtilize one's thought and not take mere words or teachings too literally. Perhaps another illustration may aid in elucidating the concept: There is in man a spiritual entity, call it the inner Buddha or
the immanent Christ. There is in man likewise a human entity, call
it the human soul. Now, this Christ-entity which works through
the human entity will actually sometimes bring the human entity
into situations of pain and suffering (so that the human entity may
learn thereby) which the mere human entity nevertheless, partly
consciously, partly unconsciously, helped to bring about by its own
attitude of selfless devotion and impersonal yearning to grow, but
which nevertheless it did not itself self-consciously choose. The
consequences are, in many cases, and strictly speaking, unmerited
by the merely *human* entity; nevertheless it is for the human entity's
ultimate best, and it could not have occurred to this human entity

---

239. *Romans*, chs. vii-viii.

even by the immanent Christ's or inner Buddha's working through it unless the human entity had, as it were blindly, like a child groping in the night, put itself into the place of a vehicle or mediator or transmitter of the spiritual and impersonal impulses arousing the action of the ever watchful and unerring Karmic Law. It is, on both sides of the matter, Karman. Some people, seeing only one side of this equation, will say 'unmerited' since the human entity suffers because of the god's working through it. Other people seeing only the other side, will say, no, fully 'merited' because the human entity itself acted. Each group of people is in part wrong and in part right. The solution of the subtil problem is by combining the two views — and discovering that they are but two sides of the one picture.

Now, reverse the illustration, which is on the foundation of the Christian theological scheme which has been so frightfully misunderstood dating almost from the time of the death of the Avatâra Jesus, to wit: The man, the human being, by reason of his imperfections, his weaknesses, his deliberate choosings of evil and of imperfect good, makes the immanent Christ or the inner Buddha within himself suffer continually, and undergo thereby what some people would call 'unmerited' suffering and pain; and yet the inner Buddha or the immanent Christ in its unspeakable beauty and desire for the greater good of the man, deliberately so acts as a plank of salvation for the best good of the imperfect human instrument which it oversees and through which it is working.

These two very mysterious and wonderful processes or operations are going on within us all the time; and here again we see one reason why our karman is so intricate and so complicated, and why the philosopher of one School, catching a gleam of light, but only one gleam where there are numbers of rays, says Fatalism; and the philosopher of another School, catching only one gleam of light where there are numbers of rays, says utter Free Will, and an almost inactive Cosmic Law. Both are wrong in some degree, yet both are right in some degree. Man is more than his single imperfect human will and human intelligence, because he is a compound being. Through him, as the very core of his being, works the unfettered and majestic power of the Brâhmic Âtman, involving relatively utter free will, relatively utter wisdom, and both of cosmic character; and it is this Âtmic power which gives to man such free will as he has as yet imperfectly unfolded, such developed and relatively unfettered understanding as he now has, and such range of judgment and reach or vision of genius as may work through him, hindered and crippled in all cases, however, by the imperfectly evolved lower being of the man, comprising his brain, emotions, astral body, etc.

The words 'unmerited' and 'merited,' therefore, in all these different questions, must not be taken too literally. Our Masters and H. P. Blavatsky taught the doctrine of Karman from the Buddhist standpoint, because it is there perhaps best elaborated and most easily comprehensible to Western minds, difficult as it is; and one must understand what this Buddhist standpoint is, if one desire to understand their words. The Buddhist teaching is that every human being at any instant of his existence, is but the karmic fruitage of the preceding instant and of all preceding instants; is but the result, the karmic consequences, of the preceding instant and of all preceding instants. Furthermore, that every instant, and *a fortiori* every new earth-life, produces a 'new man,' with 'new' increments of intelligence and of will and of judgment, and of discrimination and of conscience, as well as of consciousness, so that each new earth-life is a 'new man' who is different from the 'old man' of the last preceding earth-life, and yet is the karmic child or product of that last earth-life and of the preceding earth-lives. Thus it is that a man at any moment during the long series of imbodiments is very strictly the karman of all preceding imbodiments, and in consequence the man at any moment in his long pilgrimage is his own karman.

In the words of the Lord Buddha, as imbodied in the old Buddhist Scripture called the *Dhammapada:*

All that we are is the result of what we have thought: it is founded on our thoughts, it is made up of our thoughts. If a man speaks or acts with an evil thought, pain follows him, as the wheel follows the foot of the ox that draws the carriage.

All that we are is the result of what we have thought: it is founded on our thoughts, it is made up of our thoughts. If a man speaks or acts with a pure thought, happiness follows him, like a shadow that never leaves him.[240]

These are the recorded words of the noblest Sage and Seer of historic times; and in these few pregnant sentences, if one is clever enough to unveil it, lies the revelation of what Karman is in all its majestic and mysterious complexity.

When an avalanche buries and kills a man who happens to be walking under its fall, the ignorant cry at once: Why, what a sad and what an unmerited death! True enough from the standpoint of that body, because the body did not bring it about. But the Ego, the Reincarnating Ego, as a chain of inescapable karmic cause and

---

240. Chapter i, verses 1-2.

effect, running through and from all preceding lives, brought that body to be walking at that spot at that identical time; and the Ego in its own sphere is quasi-omnipotent so far as this physical sphere of manifestation is concerned, and thus karmically brought about the death of its own body.

This illustration, however, should not be misunderstood to mean, as some light-minded nitwit might be supposed to imagine, that the Reincarnating Ego joys in destroying a body through which it works, for such a misconception would not only be ludicrous, but what is far worse, it would be immoral; the spiritual Monad working through the Reincarnating Ego is a Servant of the Cosmic Law, and an Agent of its mysterious and intricate workings, and acts strictly according to what is the ultimate best for anything within the sphere of its own operative action. In like manner even an ordinary man may find it necessary of his own choice to have a limb amputated.

VI

Karman is not Fatalism, because in each instant whatever happens to a man is the strict karmic result of the Reincarnating Ego's own choice in this or some other life or lives, although the 'man' or the human entity may not know and realize this, and therefore to this 'man' an occurrence may justly be called 'unmerited.' Nor is Karman something working outside of us and upon us, while we, creatures of an unfettered and absolute free will, according to this wrong conception, continually bruise our heads against the surrounding Universe somewhat after the fashion of a fly banging its nose against a window, trying to go out. This conception is entirely erroneous, and it is not the meaning of Karman. Of course we suffer from the faults of others, and often in an 'unmerited' way, but in the sense hereinbefore explained; however, we should not be in the position to suffer from others' faults at any time or in any place unless we ourselves had causally brought it about. Karmic attraction drew us to the milieu. We can truly, in the sense before explained, call the sufferings 'unmerited,' because the present incarnation, the present body, the present *astral Monad* itself did not bring them about; but the Reincarnating Ego did originally initiate the causes, bringing the ego into this new milieu of birth on earth; and therefore, whatever we suffer in our present life, in the last analysis is karmic because it is ourselves. It comes to us and affects us, as pain or pleasure, because we ourselves experience this pain or pleasure. If it were not our karman we could not experience this pain or pleasure.

The events or circumstances would flow past us, unrecognised, unfelt, unknown, just as a man may stride over an ant running to its nest. The ant is utterly incognisant of the demigod walking over it; but the man strides over the ant-hill just the same.

Take into consideration the fact that man is an inseparable part of the Universe, with Infinity as his own core of being, and with great imperfection on several planes as his vehicle; and the great problems of Karman will then largely solve themselves, and we shall see that this question of so-called 'unmerited' or 'merited' suffering or joy is really a battle of words, an unfortunate logomachy arising out of a misunderstanding of the teaching.

A beginner in Theosophy cannot understand Karman in all its extremely profound, indeed cosmically vast, ranges, but it is the general doctrine in its broad sweep that man must learn to understand: we are weaving the fabric of our own being inner and outer, and by so doing we entangle ourselves in our own individual Web of Destiny — which is our future self. No one, in the absolute sense, is to blame for our sorrows, and no one, in the same sense, is responsible for our joys, except we ourselves. This means that every acting being or entity, every will, every intelligent will that is, every Monad, is one of the builders of the Universe itself, and therefore one of the makers of this harmonious concordance of things therein, which in its vast aggregate is the structure of Universal Nature, or, in other words, the nature of *things as they are.*

When we shall have evolved forth from within ourselves our own inner spiritual faculties and powers so that they become operative in our lives and become our self-conscious will, then we shall have reached the noblest part of the destiny before us — at least for this Manvantara; for we shall have become then at one with the Universe in which we move, and live, and have our being.

But do we stop for ever there? Nay, there are ever other fields of destiny beyond, veiled in the magic light of the future, hiding still more splendors than the highest we here and now can conceive of. Life is endless; evolution is unending because without beginning; and we, as evolving and revolving and ever developing Monads go ever higher and higher along the marvelous Pathways of Destiny.

The Webs of Destiny in their vast aggregate are the Universe itself, and the individual Webs form that Universe, and thus in all senses of the word are in origin the same, and in destiny identic and essentially one with it. They give to the Universe, itself expanding through evolution, the indescribable beauty of the ever-unfolding Mystery in variety which we may call the Cosmic Life.

CHAPTER XVII

HEAVENS AND HELLS — I

THE Theosophical Philosophy is in no sense of the word a philosophy of pessimism, nor does it teach anything whatsoever which brings fear to the human heart or despair to the human soul. On the contrary, it explains the nature of the Universe and all in it, and in consequence, it throws a dazzling light not only upon the nature of man himself, his origin and destiny, but lays bare much of his far-past history, involving as this history does the story of the products of man's activity both in the nature of civilizations and in those functions of his higher nature which have produced the great world-religions and world-philosophies of olden times.

Among others of the fruitful results that accrue to the student of its doctrines, it enables him to discern that back of the body of main teachings in every one of the great world-religions or world-philosophies there is a Fundamental Truth common to them all, springing forth from which Fundamental Truth — the Esoteric Tradition forming the theme of study in the present work — a noble seed of thought was taken and was implanted in this or in that or in some other philosophical or religious system by its respective founder — some Great Sage and Seer.

The student of the Esoteric Philosophy likewise soon discovers, in his examination of these old-world religious and philosophical systems, that as time passed, these originally faithful echoes of the archaic Wisdom of the Gods became more or less perverted and diverted from their pristine significance, thus exemplifying a fact which is discernible everywhere else in human history: that whatever has a human origin, however grand in its inception, is subject, because of weakness of human understanding and will, to senescence, decay, and final decrepitude.

The story is almost invariably the same: When the Sage and Seer who brought the new-old, old-new Message of spiritual liberation to any particular people passed, men inferior in spiritual and in intellectual capacity succeeded in authority. These successors were 'new' men in interpretation and authority, less taught than their Predecessors, or even untaught, and therefore less strongly guided by the Ancient Wisdom and by the Spirit of Knowledge. The result was in each and every case a degeneration or falling away from the ancient and original Truth, until the religion or philosophy — which includes them all — finally became what every observing eye may now see that most if not all of the great religions and philosophies have become — to wit, largely a set of recognised and commonly accepted or rejected formulae: religious, quasi-philosophical perhaps, but which yet in very large part have lost their former immense appeal to the human heart and the human mind, and the powerful moral influence and sway which once they exercised.

As a natural consequence of such degeneration, involving a growing misunderstanding of the fundamental postulates of the systems in question, the inner or esoteric and highly significant meanings of most of the original teachings or doctrines of these systems have been forgotten; so that what was once understood and recognised to be a truth of Nature has now all too often come to be a theological doctrine or teaching, not merely out of tune with the events of human life, but shorn of its former appeal to the intellectual and ethical nature of man.

Chief among such teachings of the archaic religions and philosophies was that portion of the respective theologies outlining man's composite nature and his destiny after the dissolution of the physical body. It was precisely because of the inevitable tendency of such systems to degenerate and to lose their appeal over human minds and hearts, that in far distant ages of the past, there were established those secret and carefully guarded Schools of teaching, later known as the Mysteries, wherein in every land, and among every people, were taught the secrets of human life and man's destiny to those who were found well qualified and worthy to be the recipients of its communication: worthy and well-qualified not alone because of intellectual capacity, but equally strongly because of a highly developed moral sense. One could write a fascinating and indeed thrilling tale about the origin and conduct and final closing in each land of these Mystery-Schools; and it is one of the dreams of the present writer some day, if time and strength permit, to undertake a study of these things and thus to offer an initial contribution to what it is hoped Theosophical writers in the future, who may be worthy and qualified to do so, will finally give to the world as a consistent and reasoned history of this very difficult subject. H. P. Blavatsky had in mind to do this, to form Volumes III and IV of her great work, *The Secret Doctrine;* but for various reasons her intention was unfulfilled, and these two volumes never appeared.

I

Every nation on earth, from the most highly civilized to the most savage and uncultured, and both of the present and of the past, has or has had a collection of doctrines or beliefs regarding the post-mortem destiny of what is popularly called the human 'soul.' These beliefs take two general forms: post-mortem reward or recompense or retributive compensation for a good and highly moral life lived on earth, and, conversely, punishment or vengeance or retributive justice for an evil life lived on earth. These two states or conditions of the 'soul,' so called, after death, have been with virtual universality supposed to be passed in some equivalently characteristic or corresponding dwelling-place or locality, called 'heaven' for the one class of excarnate souls, and 'hell' for the second class of disimbodied humans. The ideas respecting the post-mortem destiny of these two classes of excarnate humans vary largely both with regard to the types of retributive compensation or retributive punishment, and in the length of duration ascribed to these two kinds of post-mortem existence; and the ideas concerning the situations or localities where the so-called 'heavens' or 'hells' are supposed to be, likewise vary in the different religious and philosophical systems. Nevertheless, there are certain very striking and strong similarities among all these differing ideas, and in many instances these similarities merge into identities, or nearly so.

As shown above, the many and various ideas or teachings regarding the so-called heavens and hells have suffered the sad fate of degeneration in all the various religions and in most if not all of the various philosophies. They have become almost without exception highly embroidered misinterpretations of the original doctrine which was first delivered, and in part at least elaborated, by the great founder of each system in an attempt to explain to the multitudes the infallible results of evil living on the one hand, and of a good and moral life on the other hand. As time passed, all these later evolutions or developments of the original teachings came to be accepted literally instead of symbolically and figuratively, and in the cases of a few of these religions, such literal misinterpretations have brought almost untold suffering and misery to human hearts.

On the other hand, it was the original root-meanings behind the misinterpretations which inspired and stirred the world in the past. All we have to do, therefore, is to search for these original truths; for they not only guide men into paths of rectitude, but they do away with superstition, eradicate fear from the human heart, dissipate the obscurities of the human mind, and in the place of these plant knowledge and hope. These verities are limitless because based on Nature herself, and therefore are as wide and profound and ageless as is Nature. Moreover, they aid in bringing light and comfort, and in doing away with bewilderment and religious indecision.

Coincidently with the benefits that the study of these truths brings, there ensues to the student himself a broadening and deepening of his understanding which comes from a realization — or a conviction, if the term be preferred — that there are indeed vast ranges of discoverable truth in the laws and functions of the Universe, which man with even his imperfectly developed mind may unveil. It may be added that these ranges of natural verities may be found and explored to the limits of his capacity and his intelligence by the searcher possessing an inquiring and indefatigable intellect and an indomitable and impersonal will.

If it were only for the freeing of the human mind and soul from ancient and modern superstitions, often paralysing human effort because of unreasoning fear, or stultifying men's hearts and minds because of the dread feeling of the injustice and notions of caprice that these fearful or erratic superstitions instill, the enunciation of Nature's truths in regard to the post-mortem states becomes a highly important and praiseworthy labor of love and justice.

The farther the student goes back in time in his search for the real and original meaning and significance of these strange and yet fascinatingly interesting teachings concerning 'heavens' and 'hells,' the nearer he approaches to the original formulation of the verities of Nature in these respects, as that formulation was delivered by its Promulgator; and, conversely, the nearer we come down to our own modern times, the more clearly do we see the degeneration spoken of, and the deplorable effects that it has had on men: the farther does the researcher find himself wandering from the original primal truth.

It is probably only the different forms of the accepted Western religion — because it is one of the two latest, considered as world-movements, relatively speaking — which teach an eternal hell in which men who have lived their one life on earth evilly are destined to pass eternity in everlasting torment;[241] although indeed for a

---

241. With due apologies to the modern sensitive mind which turns with properly merited disgust from the exoteric religious description of the tortures and torments of the supposititious 'damned,' it may nevertheless be suggestively interesting to make the following few citations from what has been for a dozen

long time during the Dark Ages and a certain portion of the earliest
'modern' period, before the idea became unpopular, Western Chris-
tianism likewise had rather vague and inchoate notions that hell
was but a generalizing term, as indeed it truly is, and that there were
different hells more or less appropriate to and fit for the different
kinds and grades of human souls steeped with different tinctures
of evil-doing. Even as late as the time of the great Dante who lived
and wrote in the thirteenth and fourteenth centuries, such ideas

---

centuries or more the orthodox conception of the nature of the torments of
those whose evil ways during earth-life have brought them unto eternal damnation in 'endless fire.' The following three quotations are selected from the
author's reading as being typical of such views.

The first is the view of a quite orthodox English Baptist clergyman, the
famous Spurgeon:

"When thou diest thy soul will be tormented alone; that will be hell
for it; but at the Day of Judgment thy body will join thy soul and thou wilt
have twin hells; thy soul *sweating drops of blood,* and thy body suffused
with agony. In fierce fire, exactly like that we have on earth, thy body will
be, asbestos-like, forever unconsumed, all thy veins roads for the feet of
pain to travel on; every nerve a string on which the devil shall for ever
play his diabolical tune of hell's unutterable lament."

Or again the following from an author whose name unfortunately the present
writer has mislaid:

"The world will probably be converted into a great lake or liquid globe
of fire, in which the wicked shall be overwhelmed, which shall always be in
tempest, in which they shall be tossed to and fro, having no rest day nor
night . . . their heads, their eyes, their tongues, their hands, their feet, their
loins and their vitals shall for ever be full of a glowing, melting fire, fierce
enough to melt the very rocks and elements; also they shall eternally be full
of the most quick and lively sense to feel the torments; not for one minute,
nor for one day, nor for one age, nor two ages, nor for ten thousand millions
of ages, one after another, but for ever and ever."

And finally, the following is from a Roman Catholic book for children written
by the Reverend Father Furniss:

"The fourth dungeon is the boiling kettle. Listen: there is a sound like
that of a kettle boiling. The blood is boiling in the scalded brains of that
boy; the brain is boiling and bubbling in his head; the marrow is boiling
in his bones. The fifth dungeon is the red-hot oven, in which is a little
child. Hear how it screams to come out; see how it turns and twists itself
about in the fire; it beats its head against the roof of the oven; it stamps
its feet upon the floor of the oven."

Compare the foregoing superstitious nightmares — for such they truly are —
of nevertheless earnest men, with the teaching as to the unsubstantial nature

were more or less prevalent and commonly accepted, as is shown by Dante himself in his masterpiece, *La Divina Commedia*, 'The Divine Comedy.'

Equivalently there seem to have been during the same periods of the Christian era, widely prevalent notions and even teachings that 'heaven' was but a generalizing term which actually signified different spheres or realms of felicity or bliss, in which human souls who had lived good lives on earth found their respective post-mortem habitats in carefully graded series. This is likewise exemplified in Dante's great work.

On the other hand, Western religion in its post-mediaeval period and also Mohammedanism, the latter in its more orthodox forms, seem to be the only two great religious systems which teach the existence of but one general heaven, and that those who live a more or less virtuous and noble life on earth and who are more or less given to high thinking, will, after death, pass endless eternity in some kind of indescribable bliss, but nevertheless apparently totally oblivious of those who are suffering the pains of eternal torment in hell.[242]

If we accept the views of many early Christian Fathers, such as Tertullian, the 'bliss' of the 'saints' is actually increased by the sight of the unspeakable torments of the 'damned'![243] How can there be a 'heaven' under such conditions for any truly compassionate soul, if consciousness and knowledge of the dreadful fate of their unfortunate fellows accompany their own supposititious bliss? In such cases there must be the full knowledge and perhaps even the vision of the others who are suffering eternal torment. This monstrous

---

of all manifested existences of the sole reality, the divine Foundation and Background of Cosmic Life, which all the great archaic philosophical and religious systems held, and which fact of unsubstantiality even so late a writer as Shakespeare shows in the following passage from *The Tempest*, Act IV, Sc. 1:

"   .   .   .   . These our actors,
As I foretold you, were all spirits and
Are melted into air, into thin air:
And, like the baseless fabric of this vision,
The cloud-capp'd towers, the gorgeous palaces,
The solemn temples, the great globe itself,
Yea, all which it inherit, shall dissolve
And, like this insubstantial pageant faded,
Leave not a rack behind. We are such stuff
As dreams are made on, and our little life
Is rounded with a sleep. . . ."

242. *Luke*, xvi, 19-26.   243. Tertullian, *De spectaculis*, par. 30.

teaching is a lie because it is sheer superstition. What is a super-stition? A superstition is something 'added on' to an original truth, thereby distorting the latter. This can be illustrated, perhaps by a very simple instance.

We may take a book which contains some grand teaching. We may revere the teaching in that book and the noble mind or minds which formulated it; but from the minute when our reverence de-generates into any one of the many forms of fear or of blind credulity in imagining that if even by accident or chance we happen to mis-handle or ill-treat that book some secret force will emanate from it or from somewhere else and strike us dead or inflict disease upon us or subject us to the dangers of eternal torment: from this minute we suffer under a superstition which is based upon blind credulity and empty fear without any instinct of the nature of divine pity or compassion; and in consequence the original and proper reverence for noble thought vanishes.

The Latin word *superstitio* in its original sense meant something added upon or to another thing. It is not indeed a superstition to believe in any truth, no matter how strange it may seem to us in the first instance — and many truths are very strange indeed. The records of European religious and philosophical and scientific history are simply replete with instances where a natural fact or a philo-sophical and religious truth has at first been called a 'superstition' and later on quietly accepted as a fact in Nature.

Now, all great religions — particularly those of archaic origin — Brâhmanism; Buddhism; the teachings of the great Chinese Sage, Lao-Tse; the best philosophical teachings of the Greek and Roman civilizations; the original religion of the Germanic peoples of north-ern Europe; and even many of the hoary doctrines of so-called barbarian and savage peoples — who are not young races at all, but really degenerate descendants of once mighty sires, who lived in times of great civilizations, all traces of which have vanished from the earth — all have or had sublime teachings based solely on the discovery and understanding of some of the most recondite of the mysteries of Nature. It is only decent, as well as being common sense, to understand these mysteries before we permit ourselves to criticize what we do not comprehend. This is simply an obvious rule which all fair-minded and sensible people follow — or should follow! It is rank stupidity to criticize, as is so often done, without under-standing even the elements of what lies before us. We proud and haughtily self-satisfied Occidentals have been stupid in this sense for too long a time, and the currents of the stream of new knowledge and discovered facts are now running strongly against us, both to our confusion and to our embarrassing bewilderment.

As an instance, Brâhmanism, in its doctrines concerning the post-mortem adventures of what is popularly in the West called the human 'soul,' has many teachings which approximate closely to, if they are not identic with, the verities of the Esoteric Philosophy. The same, and in the same respects, may be said of Buddhism, another of the great World-Religions, and perhaps the least degenerated at the present time from the original ideas of its Great Founder. Indeed, the same may be said of Taoism, and of Confucianism; and without any exception that the present writer can at the moment recall to mind, this identic comment may be made with regard to all the archaic religious and philosophic systems of the past, wherever their remnants or present-day relics may be found on the globe.

It is true that some of the teachings of these ancient religions or philosophies which by many ages preceded the respective eras of Mohammedanism and Christianity, are more or less degenerate as we find them today; and in addition to this inner degeneration they have been grossly misunderstood and therefore grossly misinter-preted as individual systems by Occidental scholars. Yet these archaic religions and philosophies are in general faithful, each one to its own original source.

Jesus the Syrian Sage and Avatâra taught at least his immediate circle of disciples the same basic truths of Nature that are found in other great systems. He, being one of the Great Seers or Sages who appear from time to time on earth as Avatâras, of necessity learned, first through initiation and then by means of the strait and intimate union with the divinity which inspired him, and then passed on, as much as he could make comprehensible of the teaching of that same Ancient Wisdom, variously called the Esoteric Philo-sophy, or the Esoteric Tradition, or by other names, which has been throughout millions of years the same everywhere, all over the earth and in all ages; for his system, equally with all previous systems, originally emanated from this great Brotherhood of the Seers and Sages mentioned before.

But Christianity in its doctrines — and especial reference at the present moment is to those of its teachings concerning its heaven and its hell — has wandered very widely indeed from the original spirit-ual and intellectual thought of its great Founder, Jesus the Christ, and for the reason that inferior and weaker men became its under-standers and propagandists after the time of the great Sage Jesus: men who were untaught, unguided by the Ancient Wisdom; and while many of them undoubtedly were thoroughly sincere, some of them very probably were intellectually insincere in the sense of attempting to impart as universal truths of Nature what were the more or less vagrant ideas of their own minds — misunderstood and misinterpreted hints and flashes which they had received from the Great Source. It was briefly thus that the original teachings of Jesus the Avatâra were either lost or became degenerate from the form in which he had first imparted them.

II

Lest there arise a misunderstanding in the mind of the reader as to what the Esoteric Tradition, the Esoteric Philosophy, has to say with regard to that portion of its doctrines which deals with the matter of the 'heavens' and 'hells,' it may be as well to state here, before going farther, and to state with emphasis, that the Theosophical Philosophy, the modern-day exponent to the world of the Archaic Wisdom of the Gods, utterly rejects as being entirely incompetent and insufficient, and most often irrelevant, the popular and exoteric ideas held by all the great world-religions or world-philosophies about these matters. This applies with particular force to the ideas of the two latest and therefore youngest great religions in their teachings concerning 'heaven' and 'hell.' This is not saying that the Theosophical Philosophy rejects these as being entirely unfounded, or baseless, or as having no inner or esoteric significance. The exact opposite of this is true; but it is the exoteric or public, and highly embroidered or ornamented, misinterpretations thereof which the Esoteric Philosophy says to be unfounded on Nature's own facts and to be misunderstandings of the esoteric stream of the Secret Teachings.

The Theosophical Philosophy has as wide and varied a scheme of spheres of bliss on the one hand, and of purgation on the other hand, as would satisfy — were it only understood — the most exacting exotericist; but its teachings show clearly that these different spheres are not at all or in any sense merely the habitats or worlds of dead men or of their 'souls,' but rather, strictly and in utmost truth, actual and integral and therefore component parts of the structure of Universal Nature herself. It will be remembered by the reader, if he have carefully read the foregoing chapters, that Universal Nature or the Universal Kosmos is structurally a complete and highly differentiated organism — and let us take as an instance in point our own Home Universe, the Galaxy, all that is included within the vast and far-flung zone of the Milky Way. Furthermore, this structure of Universal Nature is continuous throughout and permeated and inspired and guided by an all-dominant hierarchic intelligence of kosmic magnitude, one of an infinity of others like it which infill the spaces of Boundless Space; the greatest part of Universal Nature being thus almost innumerable interlocking and interwoven Hierarchies which compose and indeed *are* all the vast realms of the Invisible, thus comprising all ranges of the Kosmic Structure from super-divine through all intermediate stages down to our own physical sphere which is but the shell or outmost integument of all. By far the most important part, therefore, of the Kosmos is these vast realms or worlds or spheres which are unseen and intangible to us humans; and therefore it is these invisible worlds which comprise in their respective and different hierarchies, and in their inhabitants, those spheres of habitation and karmic consequences which the Esoteric Philosophy speaks of as 'heavens' and 'hells.'

From the foregoing it is instantly obvious that neither 'heavens' nor 'hells' when thus understood as integral realms of Nature, are localities 'formed' by any cosmic creator, but actually are part and parcel of the life and substance of the invisible, incomprehensible, and super-divine Divinity whose all-permeant Life and Intelligence and Will and Substance not only infill the Universe, but in fact are it. This last thought was in the mind of the Christian Paul, himself an Initiate in at least some of the lower degrees of the ancient Mysteries, when he stated: "in It we live, and move, and have our being,"[244] quoting the Greek poet Aratus (third century 'B. C.').

What an immensely changed viewpoint this cosmic picture gives to us as men! Instead of being the hapless and helpless creatures of an inscrutable 'Creator' who 'made' us with such portions of intelligence and will as we have, either to enter a foolish heaven of bliss, or to suffer eternal torment in a hell of the damned — both nightmares of a monkish imagination — we see a vision before us of literally innumerable Spheres, Worlds, Realms, composing the Infinite Cosmic Life and being of the substance of that life itself, and which thus are the wonderful Houses or Mansions of experience through which the peregrinating Monads are continuously evolving and revolving.

Thus it is that the majestic archaic Wisdom-Religion of the Gods envisages these divisions or Worlds of the Universe as Man-

---

244. *Acts*, xvii, 28.

sions of Experience, and postulates a continuous progress throughout the Kosmic Manvantara of each Individual of the innumerable evolving Hosts of beings. The 'heavens,' therefore, are seen in the brilliant light of this wonderful teaching to be those spiritual realms of experience through which all Monads whatsoever shall and indeed must at some time in their ages-long peregrinations pass, and in which they dwell for periods proportionate with the karmic merit attained or won; and the so-called 'hells' are those spheres or realms of purgation, to which all Monads whatsoever during certain periods of their ages-long peregrinations must pass, therein washing the matter-laden, and therefore heavily laden, souls; so that once cleansed they may rise again along the ascending arc of Cosmic Experience.

It was to these almost innumerable Worlds or Houses of cosmic experience that the great Avatâra Jesus alluded in his well-known and so grossly misunderstood statement: "In my Father's house are many mansions."[245]

Modern Theosophy, adopting the technical terms of ancient Brâhmanism, because they are convenient and expressive, groups these almost innumerable hierarchical Worlds or Realms of the Cosmic Structure under the terms Lokas and Talas, and once the esoteric philosophical teaching concerning these Lokas and Talas is properly understood, the reader will have a dazzling light thrown on the inner significance of the archaic verities which have grown through long ages of misunderstanding and misinterpretation into the exoteric theological notions of 'heavens' and 'hells.'

The following from a previous work by the present writer, gives the outline of the teaching concerning Lokas and Talas:

Tala (*Sanskrit*). A word which is largely used in the metaphysical systems of India, both in contrast and at the same time in conjunction with *loka* (q. v.). As the general meaning of *loka* is "place" or rather "world," so the general meaning of *tala* is "inferior world." Every *loka* has as its twin or counterpart a corresponding *tala*. Wherever there is a *loka* there is an exactly correspondential *tala*, and in fact, the *tala* is the nether pole of its corresponding *loka*. *Lokas* and *talas*, therefore, in a way of speaking, may be considered to be the spiritual and the material aspects or substance-principles of the different worlds which compose and in fact are the Kosmic Universe. It is impossible to separate a *tala* from its corresponding *loka* — quite as impossible as it would be to separate the two poles of electricity.

The number of talas as generally outlined in the exoteric philosophies of Hindûsthân is usually given as seven, there being thus seven lokas and seven talas; but, as a matter of fact, this number varies. If we may speak of a loka

---

245. *John*, xiv, 2.

as the spiritual pole, we may likewise call it the "Principle" of any world; and correspondentially when we speak of the tala as being the negative or inferior pole, it is quite proper also to refer to it as the "Element" of its corresponding loka or principle. Hence, the lokas of a hierarchy may be called the "Principles" of a hierarchy, and the talas, in exactly the same way, may be called the "Elements" or substantial or material aspects of the hierarchy. It should likewise be remembered that all the seven lokas and all the seven talas are continuously and inextricably interblended and interworking; and that the lokas and the talas working together form the Universe and its various subordinate hierarchies that encompass us around. The higher lokas with the higher talas are the forces or energies and substantial parts of the spiritual and ethereal worlds; and the lowest lokas and their corresponding talas form the forces or energies and substantial parts of the physical world surrounding us; and the intermediate lokas with their corresponding talas form the respective energies and substantial parts of the intermediate or ethereal realms.

Briefly, therefore, we may speak of a tala as the material aspect of the world where it predominates, just as when speaking of a loka we may consider it to be the spiritual aspect of the world where it predominates. Every loka, it should be always remembered, is coexistent with and cannot be separated from its corresponding tala on the same plane.

As an important deduction from the preceding observations, be it carefully noted that man's own constitution as an individual from the highest to the lowest is a hierarchy of its own kind, and therefore man himself as such a subordinate hierarchy is a composite entity formed of lokas and talas inextricably interworking and intermingled. In this subordinate hierarchy called man live and evolve vast armies, hosts, multitudes, of living entities, monads in this inferior stage of their long evolutionary peregrination, and which for convenience and brevity of expression we may class under the general term of Life-Atoms.[246]

The foregoing citation contains the gist of the real and occult meaning not only of the original Brâhmanical teaching concerning the lokas and talas, but also that of the Esoteric Tradition; and the essential point of thought therein briefly set forth, the reader is earnestly requested to study with some care, as it has a direct bearing on the theme of the present chapter.[247]

It will be seen from the above that the true meaning and significance of these widely extended inner Worlds and Realms, which exoteric devotion and religious fanaticism have wrongly turned into spheres of felicity for dead men, on the one hand, and into spheres of purgation and torment, on the other hand, are neither the one nor the other, but are indeed the structural and component parts of the Universe itself. The point is so important and of such wide philo-

---

246. *Occult Glossary*, pp. 173-5.
247. Consult also *Occult Glossary*, p. 65, under the heading 'Heaven and Hell.'

sophical and religious significance, that it is difficult to stress it sufficiently. Wash then your minds clean of all moldy superstitions connected with these wholly exoteric and therefore distorted and inaccurate ideas.

It is, however, perfectly true that, in a very general way of
speaking, the Spiritual Worlds are Realms or Houses or Mansions
or Globes of real felicity or bliss, as contrasted with the matter-
laden or matter-sunken Worlds or Realms or Houses, or Globes like
the grossly material spheres such as our own planet Terra and the
other planets and spheres of the solar system existing on the same
Cosmic Plane on which our own Globe Earth is. The reason of
this is that in the Spiritual Worlds all things are of a spiritual character: that is to say, incomparably more ethereal, luminous, and
by their very nature closer to the Spiritual Heart of the Universe;
whereas all the material worlds or spheres or planes or globes are,
to adopt the language of the mystics of all countries, farther removed or at a greater distance from the Spiritual Heart of Being.

It is through all these different Worlds, whether spiritual or of
a material or of an intermediate character between the two, that the
peregrinating Monads pass and repass, go and return, on their marvelous cyclical journeys, thus gaining experience and a sense of at-
one-ment with the Universe itself as an Organism or Organic Entity
quivering throughout with Life and Intelligence. It is during the
course of these peregrinations, these great and wonderful adventures,
that the Monads weave their Webs of Destiny; so that these Webs
— which in very truth are the individual Monads themselves — not
only extend through these almost innumerable worlds, visible and
invisible, but are actually interwoven with the substance and fabric
of these structural worlds themselves.

Nevertheless, it should likewise be remembered that so far as
the matter of compensatory rewards and retributive punitions is
concerned, these likewise have a very real existence; for it should
be sufficiently obvious to every reflective mind that all beings and
entities whatsoever not only enjoy compensatory bliss for lives well
lived, because such bliss is correspondential with and answers to
their own characters and natures, but likewise must by the same rule
of logic and universal symmetry enter upon spheres of purgation
or punitional experience when the life last lived has made them so
heavy with material stain and passional complex that they are unable to 'rise' into the spiritual and more ethereal spheres where
they would be out of place and where they could not enter *simply
because their psycho-magnetic natures do not draw them thither.*

Just here, in these last words italicized, lies the key to the secret why certain excarnate 'souls' enter their devachanic rest wherein they enjoy unspeakable compensatory bliss for the tribulations of earth-life; and why, contrariwise, other 'souls,' usually few in number fortunately, sink into less spiritual conditions. It is a matter of attractions both in the general and in the particular; or, what comes to the same thing, it is all a case of individuals finding their respective proper and fit habitats in precisely the surroundings and conditions and states for which their inner unfoldment fits them.

III

It should be clearly understood that whereas modern Theosophy has conveniently grouped the worlds of post-mortem spiritual felicity under the single Tibetan term *Devachan*, nevertheless Devachan is, strictly speaking, not a locality or 'place' but is a state or condition — or, to speak more accurately, states or conditions, ranging all the way from the lower or quasi-material devachanic condition through all the intermediate degrees upwards to the realms of relatively pure spirit where the highest or most ethereal devachanic conditions or states are. Similarly, in the other direction, there are conditions or grades or states which are precisely appropriate to, and form fit habitats for, 'souls' in whom the matter-attraction has been predominant during the earth-life just ended; and necessarily, therefore, it is to these more material and less ethereal spheres that such 'sin-laden' and stained 'souls' naturally gravitate.

The lowest parts of these latter states or conditions form aggregatively what is called the *Avîchi*, itself a generalizing term for the different ranges of these states and conditions in which such souls find themselves. Be it carefully noted, therefore, that neither the Devachan in all its serial degrees, nor the Kâma-loka or intermediate realms, nor the Avîchi beneath it, is a place or locality, but each is a series of states or conditions into which entities are drawn on account of the causes originated in the earth-life just ended. It is of course perfectly true that there can be no state or condition of an entity or being apart from a locality or place. This is obvious; but neither the Devachan in all its ranges, nor the Kâma-loka in all its ranges, nor the Avîchi in all its ranges is a place in itself: all are states or conditions experienced usually post mortem by excarnate beings — the reference here being to excarnate human souls. These states correspond to 'Heaven,' 'Purgatory,' and 'Hell.'

We have thus, then, superior states or conditions grouped under the general term Devachan; then intermediate states or conditions grouped under the generalizing term Kâma-loka; and finally we have the lowest post-mortem states or conditions grouped under the generalizing term Avîchi.[248]   Naturally, these states or conditions must not be looked upon or thought of as 'water-tight' or separated series; but each one of the three serial groups of states or conditions melts imperceptibly into, or blends by imperceptible degrees with, the one next adjoining it; so that, following the quite correct picture before us, we must consider the devachanic states as ranging from the highest or quasi-spiritual through many intermediate ranges or states or conditions down to the lowest or quasi-ethereal of the Devachan, where imperceptibly the state or condition becomes the highest of the Kâma-loka.   The kâma-lokic states themselves pass from the more ethereal downwards through the intermediate stages to the grossest or most material of the kâma-lokic series, where they blend imperceptibly or pass imperceptibly into the highest or least material of the Avîchi conditions, which in their turn pass downwards into constantly increasing materiality, until we reach the lowest Avîchi condition which is not far from what has been described in modern Theosophical literature as the realm of 'absolute matter,' which merely means the grossest material substance that our own general Cosmic Hierarchy contains.

Yet this is not all: higher than the Devachan in the one direction and lower than the Avîchi in the other direction there are other Worlds or Planes or Spheres, in the endless Cosmic Continuum; and in each direction there is a border land or frontier before the structural framework passes, in the case of the right-hand, into the cosmic hierarchy above it, and in the case of the left-hand, into the cosmic hierarchy below our own.   Here we enter upon or at least range the beginning of forbidden territory; and in consequence the author speaks of necessity with great reserve and no small reluctance.   Yet this much may be said: Above the Devachan, superior to its highest

---

248. Hence, as deduced from the text, the only 'hell' that the Theosophist recognises is the range of conditions or states of the consciousness experiencing them which are grouped under the term *Avîchi*.   Be it noted also that just because the Avîchi is a certain series or range of states of consciousness of entities experiencing them, there can be, and in fact there are, Avîchis even for human beings in earth-life, before death.

What is said about the Avîchi in the preceding paragraph, refers in generalizing fashion to the Avîchi at its worst and in its most intense form, as belonging to nearly 'absolute matter' and the very unfortunate beings dwelling therein.

conditions or states, and with no wide-ranging frontier or dividing line, begin the steadily rising and ineffable ranges or series of spiritual conditions or states of being which are grouped under the generalizing term Nirvâna; and in the other direction beneath the lowest Avîchi, and without wide or greatly extended division-line, are those certain ranges of absolute matter which are the dread and fearful destiny of what in modern Theosophy are technically called 'lost souls.' Here these unfortunate and 'lost' entities are dissipated into their component life-atoms: are, to employ the words frequently used, "ground over in Nature's laboratory." This last and lowest range of being of our own cosmic Hierarchy is what the Esoteric Philosophy points out as being the 'Eighth Sphere,' or, otherwise, the 'Planet of Death.'[249]

No exoteric heaven ever imagined by the most fecund dreaming

---

249. As written to one of his two lay-chelas, Mr. A. P. Sinnett, in a letter in the late autumn of 1882, the Master K. H. refers to this matter in the following solemn and warning words:

"Bad, irretrievably bad must be that *Ego* that yields no mite from its fifth Principle, and *has* to be annihilated, to disappear in the *Eighth Sphere.* A mite, as I say, collected from the Personal Ego suffices to save him from the dreary Fate. Not so after the completion of the great cycle: either a long Nirvana of Bliss (unconscious though it be in the, and according to, your crude conceptions); after which — life as a Dhyan Chohan for a whole Manvantara, or else *'Avitchi Nirvana'* and a Manvantara of misery and Horror as a ———— you *must not* hear the word nor I — pronounce or write it. But 'those' have nought to do with the mortals who pass through the seven spheres. The *collective* Karma of a future Planetary is as lovely as the collective Karma of a ———— is terrible. Enough. I have said too much already." — *The Mahatma Letters to A. P. Sinnett*, p. 171

The reader's careful attention is directed in the citation just given to the expression *'Avîchi-Nirvâna.'* In these two words lies one of Nature's dread secrets, or mysteries, if the student is intuitive enough to understand it, or if he have received the blessing of initiation. It may be pointed out here that, just as said above in the text, both Avîchi and Nirvâna are states or conditions of consciousness of a being which experiences these states or conditions, or is in them; so that Nirvâna, with all its mystical implications as a word, is as appropriate to the term Avîchi in certain cases or instances — happily exceedingly rare — as it is to signify the upper or spiritual pole of consciousness. The reference here is to certain exceedingly rare types of beings whose consciousness is both spiritual and wicked, and who in consequence find their only fit habitat in a condition or state which is at once Avîchi and a Nirvâna in Avîchi; which condition or state lasts for an entire Manvantara. Yet even this is not a 'hell' in the Christian meaning of the word, but really something still more awful and dread.

of monkish recluse can equal the ineffable bliss entered into by truly spiritual excarnate souls because they have earned this compensatory bliss in the last life, and also because their relatively high spiritual unfoldment of character and inner forces entitles them to it; and, contrariwise, no monkish imagination has ever reached beyond a conception of 'torments' more or less appropriate to physical sensation, whether experienced in an ethereal body, or in an 'asbestos-like' body such as that which Christian theology was once so fond of preaching. Therefore no such exoteric 'hell' is in any wise an approximation to the states of consciousness experienced by those fortunately exceedingly rare beings or entities who drop into the Eighth Sphere. These last are not 'tormented,' whether by grotesque devils with hooves or not, but endure through ages an agony of consciousness which is the exact and infinitely graded karmic retribution of causes which these beings or entities themselves threw into the scales of karmic retribution when in the spheres of causation.

A sharp and clear distinction twixt fact and fancy is thus made by the Esoteric Philosophy, the Esoteric Tradition: between the exoteric 'heavens' and 'hells' on the one hand, which are largely imaginary and which certainly are no places or localities, and, on the other hand, the actual states and conditions of compensatory bliss and retributive punitional karmic retribution. It is in the hierarchical Worlds or Planes, or Spheres, or Globes, that these various states and conditions of the consciousness of the respective peregrinating Monads are found, both after death and before birth on Earth. Our own globe Earth, in fact, is technically a 'hell,' to use the popular word, as envisaged by the relentless logic and metaphysic of the Esoteric Philosophy; and this is because our Earth is a relatively dense material sphere and the conditions and states of consciousness of the beings inhabiting it are relatively heavily involved in the magical webs of Mâyâ — illusion. It is just for this reason that H. P. Blavatsky, in *The Voice of the Silence,* speaks of "Men of Myalba" — *Myalba* being a Tibetan term which is used for one of the hells in the Esoteric Philosophy of Northern Buddhism, and Myalba is our Earth.

Indeed, for human beings during the period of their manvantaric existence on and in the different globes of the planetary chain, of which our own globe Earth is the fourth and most material, it is just these globes of our Earth-chain which provide the 'places' or 'localities' in which our Human Hierarchy finds both its 'heavens' and its 'hells,' i. e., its places of retributive justice, either by way of compensatory bliss in the Devachan or of retributive punition in

the lower Kâma-loka and the Avîchi. Conditions of life and existence on the higher globes of our Earth-chain are extremely beautiful
and felicitous when compared with the highly illusory and often
terrible conditions in which human consciousness is involved here
on earth; and for the sake of emphasis the author repeats the statement that for the reimbodying human soul, its devachanic bliss and
its punitional retribution are found in the states and conditions provided by the different globes of our own Earth's planetary chain.
It is to be carefully noted that this last statement applies to the
'human soul.' What the post-mortem destiny of the spiritual soul
of a man is belongs to another wondrous story, which is touched upon
elsewhere in this work, but about which much cannot be said because
the teachings are distinctly of an esoteric character and cannot be
given in a published work.

IV

Before leaving this portion of our study, it is perhaps advisable
to advert briefly to the matter of the lokas and talas,[250] for purposes
of rounding out the thought. Seven interblending lokas and talas
are actually the hierarchical conditions or states of each and of every
one of the Worlds, Spheres, Planes, Houses, or Mansions, hereinbefore alluded to. In other words, these various Worlds, etc., are
based on substances or matters existing in those particular phases of
substantiality or ethereality which are described by the different
names of these lokas and talas. Lokas, speaking generally, are the
spiritual and less illusory conditions or states in any one such world
or sphere or globe, while talas are those particular states or conditions appropriate to substances and matters of a grosser and more
material character. Yet the lokas and talas are inseparable; each
loka has its inseparable and corresponding twin tala, throughout the
series: the highest loka having as its nether pole or *alter ego*, the most
spiritual or ethereal of the talas, and thus down the series until the
lowest or least spiritual of each pair is reached.

Now as Nature's structure is repetitive throughout, as several
times before explained, every subordinate hierarchy or indeed world
repeats faithfully in its structural framework what the higher hierarchies and worlds are and contain; so that each such subordinate
hierarchy or world is itself composed of, builded of, and actually *is*,

---

250. The reader is referred for a fairly elaborated description of the nature
of the lokas and talas to the author's *Fundamentals of the Esoteric Philosophy.*

its own series of lokas and talas, corresponding faithfully each to each in the manner just stated.

The lokas and talas are enumerated in the *Padma-Purâṇa* in the following fashion, and they are given in two columns here and with the names which seem to be most commonly ascribed to each series, although it should be stated that the names of the talas as mere names vary in lists given in different writings:[251]

LOKAS	TALAS
1. Satya-loka	1. Atala
2. Tapar-loka	2. Vitala
3. Janar-loka	3. Sutala
4. Mahar-loka	4. Talâtala
5. Swar-loka	5. Mahâtala
6. Bhuvar-loka	6. Rasâtala
7. Bhûr-loka	7. Pâtâla

Be it noted that these talas are not 'hells,' as before stated, for they are *conditions*. Indeed, far from these twins being actual hells in any sense, or indeed 'heaven' in another sense, a quaint story imbodying a profound truth concerning this matter is told about one of the great sages, Nârada. It is stated of him that once he visited 'these regions,' and on his return to Earth gave an 'enthusiastic account' of them, stating that in some respects, though not in all, they were more full of delights than is the heaven of Indra, and that they abounded with luxuries and sense-gratifications of all kinds. This quaint yarn shows us clearly that these talas and their corresponding lokas each to each are merely the material spheres or quasi-ethereal spheres which infill Cosmic Space; whereas of course the highest lokas and talas are purely spiritual; and whereas the former or material belong to the rûpa- or 'formed' worlds, the latter or spiritual are the arûpa- or 'non-form' spheres.

The Esoteric Philosophy, in this being at one with the ideas of its many philosophical and religious 'children' on the same topic, envisages all these hierarchical lokas and talas, inextricably and from manvantaric 'eternity' interwoven as they are, not in any sense as

---

251. The Talas as given in the text above are found in this order as stated in the *Padma-Purâṇa*, likewise in the *Bhâgavata-* and in the *Skanda-Purâṇa*. In the *Vishṇu-Purâṇa*, Bk. II, ch. v, their names vary considerably from those in the three Purâṇas just mentioned, although they are likewise seven in number.

The student should remember that it is not the talas and their various attributes or qualities which vary, but the names often vary which are given to them.

being 'created'; nor as the product of fortuity, in any sense of this foolish word; nor again as being limited in manvantaric form or space — except in so far as they are most emphatically aggregated or collected together into different Universes or aggregate hierarchical cosmic bodies. They are not separate and distinct from each other, but throughout the Cosmic Manvantara are all interwoven, and of course are encompassed with surrounding infinitude. This infinitude is not 'emptiness,' nor 'empty space,' nor void of life and intelligence, all of which notions run strictly counter and contrary to the teachings of the Esoteric Philosophy, but each such aggregated Universe is one of a numberless and indeed infinite host of Universes, comprising the unbounded universal ALL.[252]

---

252. It would seem needful to point out here that the above passage, and others similar to it, that may be found in the present work, because they are distinctly pantheistic in character and significance, must not be misunderstood or misinterpreted to mean 'pantheism' as this word is generally understood in modern Occidental philosophical thought. Such passages as the above, where allusion is strongly made to encompassing Infinitude, or to the all-comprising and all-permeant DIVINE, do not mean that the Divine is the aggregate of manifested Universes alone, and that it is not transcendent therein and above.

The Esoteric Philosophy which is distinctly and radically pantheistic in type or character, is so in its own sense and according to its own interpretation of this word, as meaning not only that the Divine, cosmically speaking, permeates and interpenetrates in and through all, throughout boundless duration, but likewise in addition it transcends all the manifested aggregates of Universes, and is consequently therefore superior to them all, being the Ineffable Source and Originant of all beings and entities and things whatsoever, and the ultimate goal to which all shall return.

The thought, although in minor and microcosmic manner, is well expressed by Kṛishṇa in the famous Hindû philosophical treatise, the *Bhagavad-Gîtâ*, where this manifestation of the Cosmic Logos speaks of the divinity of which he is an avatâric. exemplar in substantially the following words: "I establish all this boundless Universe with portions of myself, and yet remain separate and above them all." (ch. x, śl. 42)

The pantheistic significance, therefore, is not that every stock and stone is 'God,' which is a ludicrous distortion of the esoteric meaning, but that nothing in boundless space and in endless duration is essentially different from the eternally Divine, and that this eternally Divine encompasses and is the essential Fount of the minutest of the minute, as well as the Greatest of the Great, and yet transcends them all. The student of truly philosophical mind with a grasp of even simple metaphysical subtilties of expression, will understand the profound significance of the distinctions here made, which are simple enough, but perhaps because of their very simplicity frequently escape attention and elude observation.

Furthermore, and this thought is of the first magnitude in importance, these many hierarchies of lokas and talas, or equivalently of Worlds, Planes, etc., are taught as coming into existence by a process of emanational evolution, which, briefly stated, may be described as the highest unfolding the higher, and the higher unfolding the inferior, and the inferior in their turn, and on precisely identic lines of procedure, unfolding the lowest, until in such fashion a sample Universe, or rather a typical Universal Hierarchy, is emanationally evolved forth in being for the Cosmic Manvantara in which it then and thus expresses itself. The two terms 'highest' and 'lowest' in the preceding sentence are thus seen not to be absolute superlatives, but referable only to the Hierarchy in question, and thus to any of the numberless multitudes of such Universal Kosmical Hierarchies.

This process is identical with that postulated and taught by virtually all the greatest philosophical and religious systems of the globe, being a fundamental part of the teaching of the great religions and philosophies of the Indian Peninsula, of China, Babylon, Persia, Egypt, and of several at least of the great philosophical Schools of ancient Greece and Rome, such as the Stoics and even the Platonic and Neo-Platonic and Pythagorean and Neo-Pythagorean Systems. All these different systems in whatever part of the world and whenever they flourished were, as said before, 'children' of the once universally diffused Wisdom-Religion of antiquity which we call the Esoteric Philosophy, or the Esoteric Tradition.

Furthermore — and it seems necessary to state here once again what has already previously been stated in the course of the writing of this work — the Theosophical Philosophy is strictly evolutionist in character when dealing with the origin, unfolding growth, course, and destiny of the Cosmos and all in it; although this word 'evolution' must never be misunderstood or misinterpreted to mean 'evolutionism' as the word is used in modern European science, for such 'evolutionism' is little more than materialistic transformism, and this the Esoteric Philosophy emphatically and unqualifiedly repudiates, and trusts to time and the advancing knowledge slowly being accumulated in the annals of modern science to prove its case as being the only possible and thoroughly satisfactory explanation of the coming into being, existence, and destiny of all things.

The Theosophist is as much, if not more, an emanationist as he is an evolutionist; in fact so much is this the case that he could be best described, so far as this matter goes, as being an emanational evolutionist. The Darwinian or quasi-Darwinian or neo-Darwinian idea of epigenesis, or the supposed intrusion of novelties — biological and otherwise — into the evolutionary process, is likewise diametrically contrary to the whole spirit of the esoteric teaching. Such intrusion, no one knows how or whence, of novelties or absolute affections or attributes or qualities, arising no one knows how or whence into the evolutionary process, is rejected as being fundamentally fortuitous and therefore mere erratic action, and also on the grounds that it is simply a new phase of the ancient materialistic hypothesis. Unquestionably the evolutionary process consists in unfolding in progressive measure and series of 'new' attributes and qualities in the life of an organism or organic entity, whether such be a Universe or a denizen of such Universe: such as a god, or a demi-god, or a daemon, or a man, or a beast, or a plant, or a mineral, or an elemental, or what not. Such 'new' appearances, however, are only 'new' in the sense that they make their appearances where they were not precedaneously evident, but in all cases arise from within the evolving entity itself, as relatively necessary products of the emanational expressions of the spiritual and quasi-spiritual forces and substances which are the causal or driving or intelligently guided and invisible parts of such evolving entity. In simpler words, therefore, such new appearances are merely expressions of what already lies latent or unexpressed in the constitution or substance of the evolving entity, and which appear when the time is ripe for their appearance and when the urge of inner self-expression thus brings them forth.

Thus, then, and when properly understood, it is seen that the various 'heavens' and 'hells' of the ancients, and of less ancient religious systems, are really popular forms of stating that the Universe is composite of spheres or worlds or globes of spirit, and spheres or worlds or globes of more or less dense matter; and because the ancient religions and philosophies, even in their degenerate days, still held as lingering memories of their original esoteric teaching some recognition of the fact that there are states or conditions of bliss and other states or conditions of punitional retribution, for excarnate human beings, such as the Devachan and the Avîchi have already been described to be, these states or conditions have for ages been confused with the broader and more fundamental fact of the hierarchical structure of the spiritual and material Worlds, Planes, Spheres, and Globes, as before described. In studying this subject, therefore, one must clearly distinguish between the states or conditions of beings peregrinating in and through these Worlds, etc., and these Worlds and Planes and Spheres themselves.

V

During the last fifteen or sixteen centuries, strange ideas have from time to time arisen and for a time prevailed in Occidental lands concerning the nature of the one heaven commonly accepted, which was considered to be of everlasting duration, and concerning the one hell also considered to endure throughout everlasting time. For instance, the ideas of a century ago, or one hundred and fifty years ago, were more or less to the effect that before the universe was created by the divine fiat, by 'Almighty God,' there existed nothing whatsoever except Infinite God. 'He' was not matter; 'He' was a Spirit. Nobody knew exactly what a spirit was; but the teaching set forth that 'God is a Spirit'; and it was commonly thought that Heaven was the dwelling of God and his ministrant or quiescent angels. Indeed, the angels also had been created by God.

Then, at some indefinite time — presumably after God had made the Earth and all in it — 'Hell' was created, which became the habitat of the rebellious angel whom human beings in the West later called Satan, and also of the angels who then or who later rebelled with their chief, and who accompanied him in his fall from Heaven, entering this receptacle existing in space somewhere — supposedly a 'spiritual' receptacle or chamber of Nature — called Hell; and there the devil and his angels abode; and this likewise was the destiny of all evil human souls who had not been saved from this fate in the manner which the popular theology taught.

Theologians of that period had very definite ideas indeed about all these matters. It had all been worked out to their own satisfaction, partly from the Jewish and Christian Testaments, and partly from what previously living theologians had conceived and taught. They even knew, some of them at least, just when the universe, which to them was Heaven, and Hell, and the Earth, as well as the crystalline spheres surrounding the Earth and dotted with the celestial luminaries placed there for human delectation and edification by Almighty God — yes, these old theologians even knew when it was all created: the year, the month, the day, and the hour! Witness the finding on this point of Dr. John Lightfoot, a famous English biblical scholar and Hebraist, who lived in the first half of the seventeenth century. This erudite and reverend gentleman had worked out to his own perfect mental and emotional satisfaction the exact year, month, day, and hour, when God created the Universe by his divine fiat, as aforesaid. Dr. Lightfoot wrote:

Heaven and earth, centre and circumference, were made in the same instance of time, and clouds full of water, and man was created by the Trinity on the 25th of October 4004 B. C. at 9 o'clock in the morning.

It is to be supposed that the particular time of day when Almighty God saw fit to create the world was chosen as the morning-time, at the hour of 9 o'clock, by our own earth-reckoning!

We Westerners have been so psychologized through hundreds of years past by ideas coming to us from so many directions and impinging upon our respective consciousnesses, that, unconsciously to ourselves, when we hear these words 'heavens' and 'hells' or 'heaven' and 'hell' used, we picture to ourselves some kind of places or localities — the heaven or heavens as existing 'above,' and the hell or hells as existing 'below,' the Earth — in some to us unknown and indefinable regions of space, perhaps: places where evil and unregenerate human souls in the one case pass eternity in unspeakable torment, and in the other case, where regenerate and 'saved' human souls pass eternity in unspeakable bliss — 'in the bosom of Abraham,' to use one form of the favorite old phraseology of the Occidental world.

The mere fact that most men in the Occident today no longer accept or believe in these superstitions is in itself a good thing; but, on the other hand, the fact that Occidentals have swung too far in the contrary direction involving an almost universal denial of retributive justice of any kind — except in the imperfect human sphere — is emphatically a mistake; for it is contrary to what exists in Nature itself and, furthermore, violates, just as the superstitions did, the intuitions of the human spirit and the moral instinct of the human heart, as well as the undying sense and perceptions of sound reason inherent in man's intellect. For everywhere the seeing and understanding eye observes corresponding effects following swiftly or more slowly, as the case may be, on causes which have been set in motion; and retribution is naught but this: the meticulously just and unerringly exact working out of causes, that is, forces or energies, once set in motion. If the energies thus working originated in moral thought and consequent action, the respective results follow correspondingly; if in evil and restricted thought and action, the respective results follow with equal and ineluctable pressure on the actor — sooner or later, in this life or in a later life on Earth; but their consequences also are the devachanic condition in the former case, and in the worst instances, the Avîchi in the latter case.

The oldest religions known, and likewise others which are younger, but which are still of ancient origin, do not speak of one 'heaven' only. The 'heavens' are many in the teachings of these old reli-

gions — usually enumerated as nine, sometimes as seven, or even
of other numbers. The same observation applies to those states of
punitional retribution likewise recognised by the old religions; which
states or conditions of 'dead people' humanly speaking, Occidentals
have translated as the 'hells' of these old systems, forgetting that we
moderns give to these words 'heavens' and 'hells' — because we do
not understand the original meanings or full sense of these older
religions — the Occidental significances popular in the West and
therefore well-known to ourselves.

Furthermore, the 'heavens' and 'hells' of these older and oldest
religions and philosophies were in all cases anciently, and still are,
considered to be states or conditions of temporary character, places
of temporary bliss or purgation; and those who were supposed to
dwell in these 'heavens' and 'hells' did so for a time whose length
was supposed to depend upon the original energy in the causative
thoughts and acts of those who found themselves either in the one
condition or in the other.

Moreover, these 'heavens' and 'hells,' in addition to being temporary abiding-places, were in no cases considered to be the seats
or localities where excarnate souls found themselves by reason of a
divine mandate, in which they themselves had no part except as
helpless, non-choosing victims, and where in consequence they reaped
a judicial reward on the one hand for good living on Earth, or on the
other hand suffered a judicial punishment for an evil life in the last
incarnation on Earth. No outside deity said to the excarnate ego:
"Soul, thou hast lived a life of good and spiritual and high-minded
doing during thy sojourn on Earth. Come hither to heaven, and
rest here in peace and everlasting bliss." Nor, equivalently, on the
other hand: "Soul, thou hast during thy sojourn on Earth lived a
life of wilful degradation and perverse sin. Go yonder to hell, and
dwell there in eternal torment." Such supposititious mandates of
an extra-cosmic deity are the mere dreamings of uninitiated minds
of theological bent which, realizing, however faultily, the actual existence of states of bliss and of states of punitional purgation, have
misunderstood or misinterpreted these intuitions, and have distorted
them in the varying forms of the exoteric teachings of the 'heavens'
and of the 'hells' belonging to the various formal and largely man-
invented theologies of the different systems.

In the archaic religions, the excarnate 'souls' were in all cases
considered to have attained the heavens on the one hand, or the hells
on the other hand, because of merit or demerit for which they themselves were responsible when last in earth-life. They thus received

the exact proportionate retributive justice for what they had thought, felt, and done, when in earth-life.

As said, the 'heavens' among the ancient peoples were not places of bliss eternal, nor were the 'hells' places of everlasting torment. In every case the beings entered them for a while, as a necessary stage in the wonderful post-mortem journey of what is popularly called in the West the 'soul.' Our life on Earth, those wise old philosophers taught, is but one such temporary or cyclical stage. In their view it was like putting up at an inn for a day and a night, as the poets have so often sung. We come to this Earth from the invisible worlds; we live here for a little while, and then pass on to other stages in the invisible spheres, following the courses of our peregrinations — all a part of life's wonderful Adventure.

Likewise, the 'heavens' and 'hells' being considered temporary only, they were therefore destined to pass away and vanish when the universe in which they were contained had completed its course of evolutionary manifestation, and all things re-entered into the substance of the Divine from which they had in the beginning of things emanationally evolved forth.[253]

Much of what has been said above, Theosophy also teaches: for instance, the Earth is not the only dwelling-place of thinking and sentient beings, nor is it the sole standard by which thinking beings should attempt in religious and philosophical speculations to regulate or gage the Universe; it is but one Cosmic 'inn' so to say, in a journey lasting throughout endless time — one event in an everlasting Adventure — 'everlasting,' that is to say, as long as the manifestation-period of the Universe in which we at present live, endures, in its present cycle or period of manvantaric manifestation.

When that manifestation-period of the Universe has reached its end, then the Universe likewise (just as a human being does when

---

253. "So in the larger process of the world the primal causes descend into the elements, and the elements into bodies, then bodies are resolved into the elements again, and the elements into the primal causes."—Erigena, *The Division of Nature*, 866, 696 B; (trans. by Bett, p. 85: *Johannes Scotus Erigena*)

Thus even in the writings of a mediaeval Neo-Platonist Christian theologian-philosopher may be found a clear echo of the archaic Wisdom-Religion and its teachings of the serial evolution or unfolding of the Universe, and its final return to its primordial divine source.

Yet it must be remembered that Erigena's work was formally condemned by the official church and put on the *Index* in the thirteenth century, though it had dominated all mediaeval Christian thought for more than two centuries.

death overtakes the physical body) enters into its period of rest and recuperative repose until the time comes for it to begin a new cycle of emanational evolution in manifestation, when everything within it and all of it reappears anew, but on a somewhat higher plane, in somewhat higher worlds, in somewhat higher stages of self-expression or life, thus moving in its new course to a higher destiny than the one which had preceded it, higher because the Universe itself is more emanationally evolved, i. e., more fully 'grown.' Thus the 'heavens' and 'hells' themselves were rightly considered to be merely temporary and temporal dwelling-places or mansions, as conceived by these archaic religions and philosophies — dwelling-places which, with the Universe in which they belong, finally pass away or dissolve into super-spirit or Divinity, re-enter the substance of Brahmâ, as the Hindû would doubtless phrase it, there to repose until Brahman again breathes forth the Universe and all of it and all in it.

CHAPTER XVIII

HEAVENS AND HELLS — II

THE student of the Esoteric Philosophy, the Esoteric Tradition, very soon learns not to take at their literal or face value the statements about 'heavens' and 'hells' which he will find in the various great literatures of the world, as well as in the folk-lore or mythological stories of ancient peoples — civilized, barbarian, or savage. It may perhaps be alleged in a general way that all such statements or allusions, wherever found, have some basis in natural fact, but in virtually all cases time and human imagination have wrought their work of degeneration and consequent misunderstanding upon the original verities or truths, such as they were, which were first delivered to the various peoples of earth by the great Sages of the Past.

Some of the ideas connected with the 'heavens' and the 'hells' of the different peoples of the earth, are often rather quaint. The Guaycurus, who are Indians of northern South America, placed their heaven in the moon; and it was to the moon that their great heroes and sages went for a time after physical death, until they again returned to earth. The Saliva Indians, also of northern South America, thought that heaven was a place where there would be no mosquitos at all!

Other more civilized peoples likewise have had curious ideas of their own. One or more have placed hell in the sun, for instance, which was a rather favorite locality for 'hell' as outlined in the imagination of some English writers of not so long ago — doubtless due to the then new astronomical ideas about the sun's being a sphere in fierce combustion. Others placed their 'hell' in the moon, like the untutored South American savage. It happened also that 'heaven' in the mind of certain people was located in the sun; commonly, however, it was located in some unknown portion of the blue empyrean.

Moreover, all the 'hells' of legend and story are not places or localities of suffering or pain or torment; some of them are even described as places of pleasure or relative beauty, such as our earth is to us. 'Hell' — or the 'hells' — has sometimes been placed at the center of our earth. This was a common teaching in mediaeval European times; and it was also the literary theme of Dante, as outlined in his *La Divina Commedia*. Dante took this conception over from a very much misunderstood old Greek and also Latin teaching; for the Romans in former ages had borrowed very much from the Greeks in religious and philosophic matters, as well as in jurisprudence and laws. Dante, writing of the geographical character, so to say, of his *Inferno*, divides it into nine stages, or rather nine degrees, of increasingly terrible torment. These 'Circles' of 'hell' he locates towards the center of the earth or about it. Above his *Inferno* he describes seven stages of his Purgatory which, with the Ascent out of Purgatory and the Terrestrial Paradise which follows the highest of the purgatorial regions so called, make nine more stages or intermediate spheres, or superior hells if you like. Then still more ethereal and still farther removed from his *infernal* regions, come the nine spheres or worlds of 'heaven'. These are capped, or topped, by the Empyrean, where dwell God and his ministrant angels with the numerous company of the Blest. This hierarchical system comprising the hells, the regions of Purgatory, and the regions of Heaven, is again based upon old but much misunderstood Greek teachings coming from the Neo-Platonic School into Christian theological speculation, mainly through the writings of the pseudo-Dionysius the Areopagite.

According to the *Iliad* of Homer, which represented in a mystical sense what we may call the Bible of the Greeks, and to which they referred for the true meaning of their mythological teachings—much as Christians used to refer to the New Testament and to the Old Testament for the real significance of Christian theological doctrines —we find four basic stages of the kosmic hierarchy: Olympus or Heaven; Earth; Hades, or the Underworld, often supposed to be at the center of the Earth; and gloomy Tartarus, the lowest of all.[254] Tartarus is supposed to have been the region, according to this mythology, whither the Titans who had rebelled against Zeus, Father of Gods and Men, were cast and who were there imprisoned, bound in chains, until a future time came for their loosening and freedom.

Tartarus evidently in this mythology represents the Elemental Worlds, where the titanic forces of unfolded Nature are held in the rigid bonds of what it is popular in the West to call 'law.' Loosened, these terrible natural forces wreak devastation on earth; and thus indeed did the Greek mythographers understand the secret meaning

---

254. For further information see *Fundamentals of the Esoteric Philosophy*, p. 148.

of this part of their mythology, and therefore they referred to the imprisoned Titans as producing by their movements in Tartarus the earthquakes and the tidal waves and other phenomena that Nature shows, when the terrible forces of Nature seem temporarily to be unloosened and unchained.

I

It is to the 'heaven-worlds' or to the 'hell-worlds' respectively that refer so many passages in the ancient literatures regarding the 'paths' to the 'gods' or to the 'demons,' for naturally the literatures imbodying the teachings or tenets of these old religions or philosophies use the terms or phrases which were popular when such literatures were composed; for even their great authors had to take account of the lack of spiritual capacity and the intellectual prejudices of the peoples among whom they came: in other words, they had to speak a familiar tongue in order to be understood.

Thus in the *Mahâbhârata,* there is the following expression:

Two paths are known: one leads to the gods, and one leads to the fathers.[255]

And also in the same work, there occurs the following:

The sun is said to be the gate of the paths which lead to the gods; and the moon is said to be the gate of the paths which lead to the fathers.[256]

In these two citations, the expressions 'gods' and 'fathers' are technical terms, and belong to the religion of ancient Hindûsthân. 'Fathers' signifies what the Christian has much less clearly called 'departed spirits,' while 'gods' refers to the same thing that the ancient Greeks and Romans meant when they spoke of the divinities, many of whom were 'men made perfect' — in other words, divine beings who have long since passed through the human stage and now have gained divinity, that is to say, become at one with their own inner god.

The higher worlds or the 'heaven-worlds' are thus the regions of the gods; while the lower or material worlds are the domains or regions of the 'demons' so called — in other words, of entities whose karman or destiny has led them into spheres and planes more grossly material than even our Earth is, and in the manner which has been set forth in preceding pages of the present work.

The Ancient Mysteries, such as those of Greece, of course con-

---

255. XII, śl. 525.   256. XIII, śl. 1082.

tained teachings identical with what has been outlined above. The whole attempt in the ancient initiatory rites and ceremonies of archaic Greece was the bringing of the human consciousness into a recognition of its inseparable oneness with Universal Nature, and of man's essential kinship with the gods.

"The purpose and objective of all initiation," said Sallust, the Neo-Platonic philosopher, "is to bring man into conscious realization of his inseparable unity with the order of the Universe and with the gods";[257] and Proclus, another famous Neo-Platonic philosopher of somewhat late date, says practically the same thing. He writes in substance:

> Who does not know that the Mysteries, and all initiations, have for their sole object the withdrawing of our souls from material and mortal life, in order to unite us with the gods, and to dissipate the darkness in the soul by spreading the divine light of Truth therein?[258]

These ancient Greek teachings and initiatory methods were identical in substance with the doctrines taught and the systems practised in the Far East — necessarily so because all were originally derived from the Wisdom-Religion of far-past antiquity. The phraseology of course differed in different countries, but the root-thoughts were universally the same. The pathway to the 'gods' on the one hand, or the pathway to the 'fathers' on the other hand, of which the Hindû speaks, are but a manner of phrasing the activities of the evolving and revolving human souls, throwing them on the one hand into the pathway leading to the gods or the superior spheres, and, on the other hand, into the pathway leading to the inferior realms. These pathways are the same as the 'Circulations of the Universe,' which are dealt with in other parts of the present work.

One is strongly reminded at the present point of thought of a beautiful passage left to us by the famous Neo-Platonist philosopher, Plotinus, whom his contemporaries called *Theiotatos*, meaning 'divinest.' The substance and the ideas, if not the words themselves, given in the subjoined extract, are the great Neo-Platonist's own:

> There are vast and greatly diversified regions open to the departing soul. The law of the Divinity is inescapable, and no one can possibly ever evade the pain and anguish brought about by the doing of evil deeds. . . . The stained soul is swept forwards towards its doom, as it were unconsciously to itself, driven always by the inherent impulses of past ill doing, and so it continues until the

---

257. *On the Gods and the World*, ch. iv.
258. Commentary on the *Timaeus* of Plato.

soul which thus is worn and harried, finds its fit place and reaches the destiny which it never knowingly sought, but which it receives through the impetuosity of its own self-will. Nature thus prepares the length and the intensity of the pain, and likewise regulates the ending of the punishments and gives to the soul the ability to rise again from the places of suffering which it may reach; and this is through the divine harmony that permeates the Universal Plan. Souls which are attracted to body are drawn to body for punishment, while nobler souls which are cleaner and having little if any attraction towards body are by this fact outside of the attractions of the material spheres; and there where the divine essence is, the divine of the divine and truth itself, there such a liberated soul finds itself.[259]

These words are remarkably faithful, at least in the substance of their thought, to the essential and indeed esoteric meaning of the doctrines of the Esoteric Tradition dealing with the same teachings regarding the different Worlds, and Spheres, etc., which are in discussion in the present chapter; and the reader's attention is invited to the many points of thought in this extract from Plotinus on which he should fasten his attention.[260]

II

It is not necessary to spend more time in mere descriptions of the various 'hells' and 'heavens' as they have been given in the different

---

259. *Enneads,* 'On the Soul,' IV, iii, 24.

260. It is an exceedingly pleasing thing to notice the manner in which Neo-Platonic thought, which in many ways is really the cream of the teachings of Plato, is returning to its own in the minds of modern mystical as well as metaphysical thinkers. The 'return' is meeting with no small number of difficulties, due to the unfortunate and indeed foolish prejudices against ancient mystical thought, a prejudice arising from religious and scientific miseducation and misinstruction. Nevertheless there are courageous and thoughtful men today who have no hesitation in acknowledging their spiritual and intellectual debt to it, and in particular, it would seem, to Plotinus, one of its latest representatives during the time of the Roman Empire. Thus the famous English cleric and philosopher, Dean Inge, writes of Plotinus as follows:

"No other guide even approaches Plotinus in power and insight and profound spiritual penetration. I have steeped myself in his writings and I have tried not only to understand them as one might understand any other intellectual system, but to take them as a guide to right living and right thinking. . . . he insists that spiritual goods alone are real; he demonetises the world's currency as completely as the Gospels themselves. . . . I have lived with him for nearly thirty years and I have not sought him in vain in prosperity or adversity."

religious and philosophical systems of the past. Such descriptions may be found under their proper heads in the more comprehensive of the various encyclopaedias. The aim of the present chapter is no mere disquisition, descriptive or otherwise, on the particularities of teaching of the exoteric theories concerning the 'heavens' and 'hells.' The Theosophist does not use these words 'heavens' and 'hells' except perhaps in a purely figurative way, or in the historic literary sense.

The fundamental idea behind or within the subject of the 'heavens' and the 'hells' may be expressed somewhat as follows: The Universe, filled full with entities in all the evolutionary grades of its hierarchical structure, exists on many Cosmic planes: in other words contains vast numbers of Worlds and Spheres, each one filled, *de facto*, full of life, or, equally accurately, filled full with lives, which the modern scientist, untaught and unguided by the Ancient Wisdom, calls 'energy' or nowadays less often force, or energies or forces.

As it has been so often said before in the present work, there are no absolute frontiers or division-lines between World and World, or Sphere and Sphere; indeed, no 'absolutes' of any kind in Universal Nature; hence no jumping-off places, so to say, or no utter beginnings and utter endings of the interpenetrating and interwoven divisions of the cosmos. Relative and indeed important beginnings and endings of course exist; but they relate to the cosmic divisions mentioned, and hence are relative to the evolving and revolving entities who conceive these points or stages of juncture as 'beginnings' and 'endings'; and hence it is that we are naturally barred, and with all the justification of the Universe behind us, from separating off from the All any such entity as a Globe, a Sphere, a World, a Hierarchy, or what not.[261]

The Universe being thus a composite Organism, formed at the

---

261. Leibniz (1646 — 1716), the great and widely influential German-Slavic philosopher and mathematician — who contemporaneously with the great Isaac Newton perfected the philosophy and mechanism of the Differential Calculus — states fairly closely the same conception of an organic Nature as a living Organism, and as manifest in interrelated and interwoven Hierarchies, thus forming an endless continuum of Being, in the following words, chosen as an example of his teaching on this point:

"All the natural divisions [or classes] of the World show one sole concatenation of beings, in which all the various classes [orders] of living creatures, like so many links, are entwined so perfectly that it is impossible

one pole, so to say, of Cosmic Spirit, and at the other pole, so to say, of concreted or crystallized spirit, which we men call matter, and of all the intermediate grades or stages between these twain: the highest of the Planes or Worlds or hierarchies provides the substance of the original archaic thought behind the teachings regarding the 'heavens,' which in the old world-religions and world-philosophies were usually enumerated as seven or nine or ten or even twelve sometimes; and, equivalently, the 'hells,' so called, were those Spheres or Worlds of denser or grosser matter, but which were likewise full of life, and therefore of lives; and therefore equally with the Worlds of spirit were the theaters or scenes for the play and interplay of the forces and substances which compose them. It is these inner and invisible Worlds which Nature in her many-chambered constitution contains, and which in very fact compose the structure of Nature herself, and that are the 'spheres' through which the human entity, and equivalently entities on other planets — self-conscious beings equivalent to men — pass post mortem, after death, taking the direction 'up' or 'down,' as we human beings usually say, because following the course of the causal effects set in motion during the last life or imbodiment. We men live here on this our physical globe. Here we pass our physical existence. Then our physical body dies in its proper time. Immediately the best part of man vanishes from this sphere — yet it is not annihilated; that is not the meaning; but it vanishes from this physical plane, because the instrument or vehicle or body which held it here and enabled it to function on this plane of matter is broken off from the constitution and is finally dissipated into its component chemical elements. It is somewhat as if one broke a telegraphic instrument: no longer can the messages come through from the other end: the receiver is destroyed.

The body then dies, of course; because the body is a highly composite and semi-sentient entity, and is indeed but a vitalized and in one sense mechanically constructed instrument; but the bundle of invisible forces which ensouls it, commonly the 'life' which ensouls a body, has its own marvelous course of destiny, and of necessity

---

to state, either by imagination or by observation, where any one either begins or ends."

And again and similarly:

"Everything in Nature progresses by stages [degrees], and this law of advancement, which applies to each individual, forms part of my theory of unbroken succession [continuity]."

therefore follows its own path, and begins its amazing peregrinations through the spheres; and being in its essence pure spirit, this essence is not a composite in the sense that a body is.

At death the physical body is laid aside like an old and worn-out garment — and reference is not here made to cases of accidental death in adult life, nor to suicide, because, here, although the same general rule prevails in time, the rupturing of the golden cord of vitality brings about an intermediate series of conditions which necessitate treatment by themselves. The vital-astral body likewise, which is a little more ethereal than the physical body, is dropped at death. It decays away or dissolves and thus vanishes in due time, lasting but a trifle longer than does the physical cadaver. But the finest part of the man that was, after the death of the body supervenes, i. e., the splendor of the spiritual part of him, and the grandeur of the intellectual essence which he is: all this bundle of finer forces and substances leaves the physical vehicle at the instant when the 'golden cord of life,' so called, is snapped; it is released; it now re-enters by degrees the spiritual Monad, which is the spiritual core or heart, the spiritual-intellectual essence, of the man-being that was on earth; and in the bosom of the Monad, all this noblest portion of the essential man abides on and in the higher planes of the inner and invisible Cosmos in the peace and unspeakable bliss of the devachanic condition until the time comes anew when Nature shall re-call it forth to a new reappearance on Earth through reincarnation.

But what about that other part of the human constitution, man being, as so often said, a composite entity, compounded of heaven and earth, of spirit and matter: what becomes of that *intermediate* part which men call the human soul, the part which manifests merely human love, merely human affections, also human hates, human attractions and repulsions, and the ordinary psychical and mental and emotional phenomena of the average human being? What becomes of this?

When death supervenes after the withdrawal of man's finest part, as above outlined, this human intermediate nature falls instantly asleep, so to say, and sleeps a dreamless sleep for a period of shorter or longer duration. Then because the higher part of this intermediate nature or human soul is the radiance reflected upon it from the Monadic Spirit, which has now gone to its own and which is the noblest and best part of the man that was, this radiance in consequence is attracted ever more strongly, as time passes, back to its own source, the spirit which sent it forth; and finally rejoins it.

This radiance of the spirit is what the Theosophist calls the reincarnating ego; and following upon its post-mortem junction with its spirit, it enters upon its devachanic period. Devachan is a word adopted from the Tibetan, and it is the state or condition of indescriptible bliss and recuperative rest and felicitous imagination which this intermediate nature enjoys until the time comes for the next earth-incarnation.

But before this junction with the spirit takes place, which happens because this higher part of the intermediate nature is a *radiance* of the spirit and not the spirit itself: and because this radiance has elements of mere humanity in it instead of being purely divine or godlike as is its parent the Monadic Spirit, it needs purgation or cleansing of these lower or merely human attributes before it can enter into the unqualified and unadulterate devachanic bliss, wherein no merely human element, involving imperfection, can obviously find entrance.

How is it purged or cleansed? It ascends through the spheres, that is to say through other worlds of the inner and invisible parts of Nature. If the past life on Earth has been a noble and a good one, the spheres to which the excarnate ego is attracted are the highly ethereal ones, and hence are places in which it experiences relative happiness and peace and bliss, and it is in these ethereal realms that it enters into the devachanic condition. But before it can enter the devachanic condition, it necessarily has to pass through the various stages of the Kâma-loka, where in each one of the ascending stages or steps, as it rises towards the devachanic condition, it casts aside or is purged of those particular and imperfect human attributes which are appropriate to and correspond to these respective kâma-lokic serial degrees in the 'ascent.' Finally, after passing through the various and rising stages of the Kâma-loka, which in the case of a good man the excarnate ego quickly does, it merges into the state of consciousness which is the lowest of the series of the devachanic degrees, and finds its proper resting-point, or stage of longest devachanic duration, in the particular devachanic condition or stage to which it is karmically entitled.

Here then is the real meaning of the original thought which gave rise to the later doctrine of the 'heavens' as above described. In each one of these spheres or worlds this better portion of the human soul, the excarnate ego, remains for a time, and then leaves that stage or degree or sphere or world for a still higher one, attraction of greater or less strength being the cause of the greater or less time spent in each such invisible degree or degrees of the different worlds.

Finally, it achieves reunion — albeit quite unconscious — with its monadic essence, the Monad or spiritual soul, as has already been stated, and there it abides for centuries until its innate natural proclivities and attractions impel it or draw it towards a descent through the same spheres to a new incarnation on earth.

But if, on the contrary, its life on earth had been lived evilly, if the man's thoughts and emotions, and consequent actions, were so full of selfishness and evil desire that he gave way to them wilfully, and thus lived a gross and densely material life, then, whither do his attractions lead him? The question answers itself. Is the excarnate ego in such circumstances fit for the spheres of spiritual bliss and felicitous consciousness just last depicted? Obviously not.

What then happens? Its attractions of more or less material character begin immediately to pull it or direct it towards spheres less ethereal and of grosser and more material type than those which would have attracted it had its proclivities and instincts and the forces motivating its past life been of a more spiritual type. It enters these lower and more material spheres, one after another, and in them passes a greater or less time, depending upon the force of the attractions which brought it there, until the energies originally set in motion work themselves out. Then, whatever remains after this process of purgation or cleansing becomes fit, like gold cleansed in the fire, to resume its journey towards rejoining its golden sun, its spiritual Self. Here, then, is the original meaning very condensed behind the later-developed doctrines of the so-called 'hells'; for these 'hells,' as the ancient teachings explained them, are simply spheres more or less grossly material, into which the reimbodying ego is drawn by its own innate and as yet unappeased hunger or thirst for them and for the experiences to which they give rise. Equivalently, the 'heavens' are the ethereal and spiritual spheres or worlds, certain ranges of cosmic space invisible to us, towards which the reimbodying entity feels itself attracted by its own innate aspiration towards them.

It is, however, well to insist once again here that these particular spheres or worlds to which the reimbodying ego is drawn in the one and in the other case are most emphatically not 'heavens' or 'hells' in themselves and as these words have been commonly misunderstood, but they are, as said before, integral portions of the hierarchical structure of the Universe, which, because of their spiritual and ethereal character on the one hand, and of their material or grossly material character on the other hand, by Nature's own structure, provide the place and the scenery and environment towards which the reimbodying although excarnate ego[262] is drawn because of its preponderance or bias to the one or to the other type of existence.

Our Earth, technically speaking, was always considered in ancient times to be one of the 'hells' because it is a globe of more or less dense and coarse matter. Indeed, when a human being is awakened to see things as they are, and the compassionate heart perceives and feels all the various workings of human selfishness and passion, and notices the misery, degradation, and suffering, mental as well as physical, that are so observable on every side, as well as the dreadful diseases, both physical and mental, and the sanguinary wars in which many millions are maimed, tortured, and die, and the earthquakes, tidal waves, cyclones and hurricanes, which devastate and lay waste man's noblest works and the untiring labor of his everbusy hands — then indeed do his heart and mind stand aghast at individual as well as general destruction and suffering and loss, and he exclaims: Despite all its natural beauty and consistency in law and evolution, our Earth is in truth all too often an example of a veritable hell!

Yet at the same time our planet Earth is by no means the most material habitat of human conscious beings that the solar system contains; for there are many planets or planetary worlds within our solar system, most of them invisible to us, which are far more dense and coarse and gross than our Earth is.

The foregoing two paragraphs must not be misunderstood to imply that there is no beauty to be seen in our common Mother, the Earth, and that it is to be considered the 'worst of all possible worlds'; this idea would be entirely erroneous. It is neither the worst of all possible worlds nor the best of all possible worlds, but a goodly fair instance of a world of an intermediate character, for in its evolution both good and evil have been pretty fairly mingled in the Craters of Destiny. In fact, it is man himself, with his wilful and imperfect intelligence who makes most of the hellish misery that surrounds him; and it is indeed the teaching of Esotericism that even the physical Earth and its products and fruits would be far finer than they are, and its devastating forces of occasional destruction less terrible than they are, were man so to live in sympathy with the divinity

---

262. 'Reimbodying ego' is here used as a generalizing term, signifying what elsewhere has been called the 'peregrinating ego,' or 'peregrinating monad.' Immediately after death of the physical body, we may speak of it as the 'excarnate ego,' but it is likewise the 'reimbodying ego' because of its peregrinating character.

within his own heart that even surrounding Earth-life would feel its influence, and would itself be correspondingly raised and partially harmonized.

III

With reference to what has been said in foregoing parts of the present pages concerning the structural framework of the Universe, and by analogy any subordinate part thereof, as being builded and composed of different lokas and talas, these two lines constantly interacting because for ever interwoven, each loka having its corresponding tala with which it is inseparably and throughout eternity blended: it may be of interest to the inquisitive reader and thoughtful student to show hereunder a series of 'correspondences,' as they are called by mystics, both Esotericists and not, between these inseparably interwoven lokas and talas, and what is called in the quasi-esoteric philosophy of Hindûsthân, the hierarchical range of the Tattwas.

Now तत्त्व (tattwa) is a Sanskrit word, of which various etymologies have at different times been given, all of them more or less accurate, at least mystically speaking; and one of these etymologies is here offered because perhaps the most easily comprehensible. *Tattwa* is really a compound, then, formed of तत् (*tat*), a pronominal particle signifying 'that,' with the suffix त्व (*twa*), which gives it the value of a substantive or a noun — thus corresponding to the suffix *tas* in Latin, as in *unitas*, 'unity,' *veritas*, 'verity.' Thus the word can be closely translated as 'thatness,' or it corresponds exactly to the late Latin or mediaeval scholastic *quidditas*. Hence the actual significance of this term *tattwa* is the energic-substantial basis of all derivatives from it, in the course of Nature's evolutionary unfoldment, and thus it corresponds with relatively accurate precision to the term Principle or Element.

In the relation which the tattwas bear to the Cosmos or Universe, they are therefore the Cosmical or Universal Principles or Elements out of which the Universe is builded or formed, or which compose it, and therefore are the Cosmic Elements composing the universal Scale of existence — or rather of existences.

It is thus seen that the tattwas and the corresponding lokas and talas are radically or in essence virtual identities, the three different series being the same substantial cosmical and elemental realities viewed from different aspects; and also it may be said with perfect truth that the lokas and the talas are the respective manifestations of their corresponding tattwas, when the tattwas are considered in an evolved or hierarchical development. The tattwas originate the others.

There are seven cosmical tattwas which repetitively reproduce themselves in all subordinate ranges of the cosmic hierarchies as these latter unfold or evolve during the process of world-building; and these hierarchies considered as structurally arranged worlds or spheres or planes are in fact the inseparably conjoined and interwoven lokas and talas. Hence because there are seven cosmical *tattwas* or cosmical Principle-Elements, there are likewise the seven corresponding and forever interacting and interwoven hierarchical lokas and talas, each such pair of lokas and talas corresponding to the cosmical tattwa from which they originally sprang and which is the dominant cosmical Principle or Element in them. The three series are now given below numbered to correspond with each other and in the order of their cosmical unfolding or evolution:

1. Âdi-tattwa — proceeding from First Logos
2. Anupapâdaka-tattwa ”   ”   Second Logos
3. Âkâśa-tattwa   ”   ”   Third Logos
4. Vâyu-tattwa
5. Taijasa-tattwa
6. Âpas-tattwa
7. Pṛithivî-tattwa

1. Satya-loka	1. Atala
2. Tapar-loka	2. Vitala
3. Janar-loka	3. Sutala
4. Mahar-loka	4. Talâtala
5. Swar-loka	5. Mahâtala
6. Bhuvar-loka	6. Rasâtala
7. Bhûr-loka	7. Pâtâla

One exceedingly important point for the proper understanding of the manner in which these cosmical tattwas unfold, i. e., evolve, and thus produce the hierarchies formed by the corresponding lokas and talas, is that, beginning with the first or Âdi-tattwa, the second or Anupapâdaka-tattwa emanates or flows forth from it the while retaining, although the second in order, a certain portion of the first tattwa in its own substance and aggregate of forces; from the second tattwa emanates or unfolds or evolves the third tattwa in serial order which contains not only its own swabhâva or characteristic forces and substances, but likewise contains its portion of its parent, the second cosmic tattwa and its grandparent cosmic tattwa; then the fourth cosmic tattwa similarly is emanated or unfolded from the third cosmic tattwa, and although it contains as dominants its own swâbhâvic forces and substances, nevertheless likewise it manifests forth, because it contains, a portion of its parent, of its grandparent, and its great-grandparent; and thus down to the seventh and last. It might likewise be added that once this course of hierarchical emanation or evolution is completed, the Universe thus emanated and evolved or unfolded exists for ages in the plenitude of its incomprehensibly great activities; and when the time of the Cosmic Pralaya, or period of Cosmic Rest, approaches, the whole process which took place in unfolding the Universe, now enters upon the reverse procedure of infolding or involving itself, beginning with the lowest, so that the seventh or lowest is first 'radiated' away into the next higher tattwa which thus gathers the lowest up into itself. The process is then repeated, with the next succeeding higher cosmic tattwa, into which enter the 'seeds' or sleeping 'germs' of the cosmic tattwa already infolded, and thus the entire process of infolding continues until all the lower tattwas, each infolded or involved into the next higher, are drawn up into or withdrawn into the highest or originating cosmic tattwa; and then the Manvantara of the Universe is ended, and the long period of Cosmic Rest ensues until the time of the succeeding Cosmic Manvantara arrives, when everything is emanated or evolved or unfolded anew just as before it took place, but now on a somewhat higher series of Planes of the greater and encompassing Universe.

The above was likewise the teaching of the Stoics of ancient Greece and Rome, and was a faithful re-echo as far as it went — which was not very far — of the secret teaching of the Esoteric Philosophy, the Esoteric Tradition. The same teaching is found likewise in certain passages of the Jewish Christian Bible where this cosmic drama of the dissolution of the Universe is referred to. For instance:

And all the hosts of heaven shall be dissolved, and the heavens shall be rolled together as a scroll.[263]

Or again,

And the heaven departed as a scrowl when it is rolled together.[264]

IV

There is another teaching of the Ancient Wisdom, very wonderful, very mysterious, which reaches into the most recondite and secret parts of our esoteric philosophy, and which is difficult to understand unless one has first examined the elements or the founda-

263. *Isaiah*, xxxiv, iv.   264. *Revelation*, vi, 14.

tions of the Mystery-Teachings. The doctrine to which reference is here made is that of Nirvâna, and possibly there has been no one teaching of the great religious philosophies of the Orient imbodying this doctrine in their systems which has been so wholly misunderstood and therefore so wholly misinterpreted. The Nirvâna is not a 'heaven'; it is not a Cosmic Sphere; it is not a Cosmic World; it is not a Cosmic Plane; it is wholly and absolutely a condition, a state, of the consciousness experiencing it; it is the state of consciousness of the Spiritual Soul when all sense of limiting personality, or even of imperfect egoic individuality, has wholly vanished: when it has clean gone, so that naught remains but the unfettered consciousness of the Spiritual Essential Self, which is the indivisible and ineffable *essence* of the human being — the divine-spiritual Individuality; it is pure monadic consciousness.

It is, in a manner of expression, an alliance of the godlike nature within man with the evolving Spiritual Soul, so that this Spiritual Soul becomes identified and at-one with its Inner God; its consciousness then becomes cosmic in the, hierarchically speaking, unlimited reaches of that particular Cosmic Hierarchy.

As concerns the problem, so difficult for Western minds, of the identity or non-identity of the individual spirit, say of a man, with the Cosmic Spirit, and of the relation it bears to the Cosmic Spirit when the individual spirit is considered a Monad, it should be carefully noted by the reader that the Esoteric Tradition does teach indeed the identity of all 'souls' with the Oversoul, or of all Monads with the Cosmic Monad; but this identity at the same time does not signify a loss of the individuality of any such subordinate 'soul' or monad. The very name, 'Monad,' signifies a unit, i. e., a unitary individuality, which endures throughout the entire Cosmic Manvantara, or Cosmic World-Period. The beautiful words in which Sir Edwin Arnold in his *Light of Asia* imbodies the ancient Buddhist teaching, "The Dewdrop slips into the shining Sea," when properly understood, give exactly the correct idea. To the Western mind, it would seem that the dewdrop slipping into the sea suffers an entire extinction of its individuality or individual being, and this is because the Western mind is accustomed to think in terms of mechanics and of material substance. Actually, the 'slipping into the shining sea' of the 'dewdrop,' or Monad, means that it sinks into the Cosmic Vast in order to regain in this fashion its own inmost cosmic reach or sphere of virtually unlimited consciousness, the meanwhile retaining, as it were in the form of a seed for the future, its own monadic individuality. In due and proper time, when it reissues forth again into manifestation, it will do so as a reappearance or renascence of the monadic individuality that it formerly was, plus all the accumulated awakenings of consciousness, called 'experience,' which it had ingathered during its former evolving, i. e., unfolding, peregrinations.[264a]

Plotinus has the following interesting exposition of the same thought, which proves the spiritual power of the great Greek Neo-Platonist's mind and intuition — faithful echoer as he was, albeit somewhat feebly, of the archaic East. Plotinus is referring to the reunion of the Individual with the Cosmic Divine:

Of matters of earth it will then recollect nothing, for the reason that memory, which signifies a passage of thought from thing to thing, has there sunken into abeyance, and consequently there can be no such limited memory in the Spiritual World. Indeed, there will not even remain a recollection of the individual as individual, i. e., no thought where the individual self is contemplator, for this implies limitation. . . . When the spirit is in the Spiritual World, of necessity it enters into complete oneness for the time being with the Mind of the Divinity, and this by the fact itself of its union therewith, for this union brings about the abolition of all intervals of consciousness which men call the functions and working of memory. The individual spirit is taken into complete harmonic unison with the Divine, and in this union becomes temporarily one with the Divine — yet not at all to its own annihilation, because the two are essentially one; and yet, because they are two, they remain two.[265]

Lest the words of Plotinus be construed too strictly in their present collocation with other teachings of the Esoteric Philosophy, it should be pointed out that while all that Plotinus remarks in the above extract is perfectly true and quite in accordance with the teachings of the Esoteric Tradition, nevertheless Plotinus, with all his remarkable spiritual and intellectual capacity of understanding and grasp of subject, was an Echoer of the Ancient Wisdom, and of necessity spoke to the men of his time in a philosophical language which they could understand. The point is this: when the individual human being attains, in the above words, "complete harmonic unison with the Divine," this does not signify that he transcends entirely outside of the sphere of his own constitution and enters into an exterior consciousness in no wise different from his own highest, except perhaps in the sense of larger and deeper intensity, but the true meaning is that his own 'highest' is already, and has been from eternity, and will be unto eternity, identic in essence with the Divine; the significant reach of which thought is simply that the highest part of man is already nirvânic in state. It is the Dhyâni-Buddha in him.

264a. *The Secret Doctrine*, Vol. II, p. 80.
265. *Enneads*, 'On the Problem of the Soul,' IV, iv, 1, 2.

The point is of the utmost importance for it so clearly emphasizes the inseparable unity of man's fundamental or highest consciousness with the Consciousness of the Universe — or the Divine.
On the other hand, the lower portions of man's composite or complex
constitution are, obviously enough, 'sunken' into materiality, which
is precisely the reason why man can have contact with material
worlds and can live in them and experience in and of them and thus
learn from them.   He is a component and integral part of these
material worlds in his lowest parts, as he is of the Divine in his
highest parts.   His highest parts are grouped under the term 'the
inner god,' or the Divine-Spiritual Monad; whereas his lower or
most material parts are grouped under the generalizing term 'the
personality,' a word taken from the Latin *persona* signifying a mask
through which the Actor — the real Man — works and expresses
himself.   The intermediate portions of man's constitution compose
the 'higher human' or Human Monad.   Thus the personality means
the human mask in which we express ourselves and which is a web of
thought and feeling woven by our desires and our appetites and our
emotions and our commonplace thoughts.   This personality thus
builds up around itself a Web of Destiny, as has been described
in previous chapters.   Hence, when personality is completely sur-
mounted, or in other words, when the fundamental consciousness of
the human being rises above this concreted web of illusion, and passes
through and transcends the intermediate portion of the human constitution, it reaches the state of pure Spiritual Monadic Consciousness, and this state or condition is the Nirvâna.   In it all personality
has vanished into pure spiritual individuality, in which consciousness becomes relatively universal — i. e., universal throughout the
Cosmic Hierarchy in which the Monad moves and lives and has its
being — and therefore perceives and learns and deals with fundamental causes.   This state or condition therefore implies sheer, unadulterate knowledge, ineffable wisdom, undiluted bliss, and hence,
unspeakable peace — states of consciousness of which the ordinary
man has no conception, and which therefore, because of the ratiocinative characteristics of his ordinary consciousness, he looks upon
as being different kinds of consciousness, instead of being, as they
truly are, aspects or facets of his spiritual consciousness which is
the 'Gem' or 'Jewel' alluded to in the well-known Tibetan invocation:
"Om mani padme hum," signifying in verbal translation, "Verily,
the Jewel in the Lotus!", *lotus* here meaning the human constitution
in which the spiritual 'Gem' reposes or lives or is.
    In the Nirvâna, the Monadic Essence of the human being then

virtually becomes allied in unity with the Cosmic or Universal Over-soul of our Cosmos.[266]

Another point of importance: the difference between the bliss and wisdom and peace which the nirvânî has, and the bliss and peace and comparative rest which the devachanî has, is this: the nirvânî is completely and wholly *Self*-conscious, while the devachanî is in a state which it is difficult to describe in ordinary words, but which actually is by comparison with the spiritual reality of the Nirvâna, a condition of highly felicitous dreaming. The term 'dreaming' is somewhat inaccurate, nor does it convey actually the idea that the devachanî's condition is more or less lacking in self-conscious realization of its own felicity, but merely that, however 'spiritual' the devachanic condition is, by comparison with the nirvânic, it is illusory enough.

Nirvâna, as should be clear enough from what has just been said, is a state which may be attained by human beings of rare and exceptional spiritual power and development even when in the flesh. Buddha is an example of this, as all human or Mânushya-Buddhas also are. Sankarâchârya, a great avatâric sage of India, was another instance of one who had attained Nirvâna while alive on Earth; and men of even smaller spiritual capacity than the two just named can experience Nirvâna in relatively minor degree. Obviously, therefore, such a state of supreme spiritual grandeur is in every respect

---

266. Plotinus again says very truly, regarding the portion of the man which modern Theosophy calls the personality as being sunken in materiality:

"Nor has the soul of man sunken entirely into the realm of matter, because something of it is unceasingly and for ever in the Spiritual World, although that portion of our soul which is sunken into the realms of sense is partially controlled here, and finds itself intoxicated therewith, thus becoming blind to what its own higher part holds in contemplation of the Divine." — *Enneads*, 'The Descent of the Soul into Imbodiment,' IV, viii, 8.

The great Greek Neo-Platonist in these few lines makes the exactly proper distinction between the 'highest' part of man, which he says "is unceasingly and for ever in the Spiritual World," and that portion of our soul "which is sunken into the realms of sense," and thus here again faithfully re-echoes the teaching of the archaic Wisdom-Religion in the latter's illuminating explication of the nature of the Nirvâna on the one hand, and the ordinary human characteristics as we know them on the other hand.

Thus man's divine consciousness, as said in the text above, is for ever nirvânic in character; and in this wondrous fact lies the key to the esoteric mystery involved in the attaining of Buddhahood by the Bodhisattvas and the continuance none the less of the Buddha in human life as a complete and perfect man.

far superior, both in intensity of evolved consciousness and in lofty quality of illuminated spirituality, to the highest and noblest spiritual state that is experienced by any being in even the highest of the 'heavens.'

In the opposite direction, so to say, of the Nirvâna, and forming its nether pole, if one may so phrase it, there is the Avîchi, popularly but improperly called a 'hell.' It is, however, exactly enough described, at least figuratively, when we call it the nether pole of the Nirvâna. Certain states or conditions of beings in the Avîchi, because of an accompanying 'spirituality of wickedness' have been properly and truly named Nirvâna-Avîchi. There is, nevertheless, one point to carry in mind in this connexion, and it is that Avîchi is both a state and a world or sphere, which the Nirvâna is not; for Nirvâna is a state or condition only; although it is equally true that since the Nirvâna is the state of consciousness of certain beings, and as these beings must have position in abstract space, or locality, therefore, as explained before, such nirvânîs are or exist in the spiritual realms.

If a human being has passed through a long series of lives very evilly, and consciously so, with a continuously increasing 'absorption' of the soul in material things, this leads to a coarsening and materializing of that human being's consciousness; and the final result of the tremendous material attractions or impulses thus inbuilded into the fabric of his consciousness is that such a being is drawn or sinks into the Avîchi; and it is quite possible for a human being of the character just described to experience such an Avîchi-state even while living in the body on Earth.

When the consciousness of material personality in the man on Earth becomes thus accentuated, grossly material and strong in the human being: when nearly all sense or intuition of the divine has withdrawn from both heart and mind, and in consequence thereof the man becomes an incarnate expression of sheer selfishness: when there remains not even a spark of the Divine Fire consciously vibrant in the intellectual fabric of his being: then already, though perhaps living on Earth, the unfortunate man is in the Avîchi-state.

Furthermore, if the downward impulses of the human being already in an Avîchi-state of consciousness, as just described, so continue to grow stronger that even the last feeble link with his Monadic Sun is ruptured, he then in due course of time passes over the frontier of even the Avîchi, and enters into the fatal karmic current which carries him swiftly to a final and irretrievable disintegration of his psychical composition. In such case the wretched entity fades out and is 'lost.' The particles of his thus disintegrated psychical nature are then drawn down with the rapidity of lightning and join the element-atoms in that particular mother-fount of elemental matter to which his swabhâva has attracted him. Here then is the case which the Esoteric Philosophy speaks of as a 'lost soul.' Such instances of 'lost souls' are, fortunately, as rare at the one pole as the cases of nirvânic attainment are rare at the other or divine-spiritual pole of human consciousness. In the latter case the man becomes an incarnate god on Earth, a nirvânî; and in the former case the being passes even out of the Avîchi-state into elemental matter, where what remains of his psychical constitution is dissipated into its component life-atoms, which are there ground over and over in Nature's elemental alchemical laboratories.

The Avîchi itself is, in fact, on the lower frontiers of 'absolute matter,' i. e., elemental matter. It is perhaps the nearest to the mediaeval idea of a 'hell' that Nature provides. But for all that, it is not a judicial punishment meted out upon some unfortunate and hapless and helpless soul by an overlording Deity; because the unfortunate entity which takes this 'left-hand path,' often called the 'lunar path,' does so originally of its own volition entirely, acting from the impulses of its relatively free will. It attains its fearful fate as the unerringly just consequence of karmic causes, induced and set in motion by evil thoughts, by low and selfish desires, and unchastened and unbridled passions and appetites of a materially evil character.

Yet even such an unfortunate being has still a chance to escape its dreadful fate, indeed many chances, before it reaches final dissolution. It is said, and truly said, that even one single pure and soul-impressing thought, if experienced in time, will save the descending being from the karmic consequences of many lifetimes of evil living; for actually the existence of such a thought would imply that the link with his own inner god has not yet been finally broken. Further, while we may truly say that the entity descending the path into the Avîchi, and perhaps beyond, experiences no pain in the ordinary sense, and no grotesque or terrible torments inflicted upon him by outside forces such as the 'hell' of the Occidental religion is supposed to imply, nevertheless, a sense of a constantly, continuously, and increasingly progressive diminution of spiritual and intellectual consciousness is always present, combined with a fiery intensity of concentrated evil impulses bereft of all aspiration and love and hope. These last at least are said to surround the fading consciousness of such an unfortunate being with a suffering which can hardly be described in ordinary words. One may truly say that it is one of the most horrifying experiences that human imagination can conceive, for there is a more or less conscious realization, however 'fading' it may be, of the withdrawal of the spiritual light and life, and a growing realization of the impending dissolution of all self-conscious life. One may well suppose that the grotesque pains of the supposed Earth-hells can nothing equal the psychical and mental and emotional torture that the realization of this fact must bring to the weakening and fading consciousness. Nor could any theatrical torments of a mediaeval 'hell' equal the torture of heart and mind which such an entity must experience in realizing that his condition has been brought about by his own perverse will and his consequent acts. Hence, as said, if such an entity goes from worse to the worst, then it returns to the mother-fountain of material Nature from which its life-atoms were originally drawn, much as a rain-drop vanishes in a flame.

In such a case, the Monad, which long before this event takes place has already ruptured its links of union with the unfortunate and dissolving entity, immediately begins to evolve a new psycho-spiritual emanation from itself, a new human Ego-to-be, which thus appears as a 'god-spark' beginning its long evolutionary journey through time and space from its Parent-Monad, and destined in time to turn in its peregrinations back towards the Parent-Monad again. It is true that this new emanational ray contains all the best — such as that best may be — that was in the entity which now is gone or 'lost'; yet the intermediate vehicle for expressing such garnered spiritual experience is gone or 'lost,' and hence no human experiences can as yet be gained or 'accumulated' until another intermediate nature or human ego has been evolved or builded to form the new link between the Monadic ray and the worlds of materiality. Nearly a whole manvantara may thus be lost so far as time is concerned.

It is indeed a dreadful fate, this which overtakes a human ego too weak to resist the temptations and strong attractions downwards into matter; but fortunately the cases of 'lost souls' are exceedingly rare, so that their number is insignificant when compared with the thousands of millions of average human entities. The matter is one which, as is clear enough, imbodies a deal of mysterious and very difficult teaching, so that in a published work such as the present it is not only wise but useful to draw the veil over it all except in so far as to point out the possibility of a soul's becoming 'lost' through its own evil choice and lives, and briefly to describe its ultimate destiny in the succinct manner which has just been done.

One might add, however, that the Monad itself, thus freed from its perverse and wayward vehicle, is relatively unaffected thereby except in the sense of what is after all a really frightful waste of time which in some instances may, as said above, mean a whole manvantara more or less. By the time that the Monad shall have again and anew evolved forth from itself a properly fit and appropriate human vehicle through which it may work and express itself in the material worlds, the host of evolving entities with which it had previously been a unit is now far in advance on the aeons' long evolutionary journey. Nevertheless, it is all karmic, even so far as the Monad itself is concerned; but this again is 'another story' as the saying goes.

Much more indeed could be said about this mysterious teaching, one of the most secret and carefully guarded of the Ancient Wisdom. Teachings dealing with such matters, and even those which explain in their fulness the different kinds of post-mortem destiny of the reimbodying egos, are indeed both wonderful and true mysteries; but 'mysteries' only because men, as a rule, have not proved themselves worthy to be taught their meaning, and where to look for the proper solutions of them — nor indeed do most men even know that these fascinating mysteries exist, all of which is perhaps just as well! Nevertheless, all are hinted at with more or less clearness in the great philosophies and religions of far bygone ages, and in certain cases even openly, although briefly and usually allegorically, mentioned in the ancient religious and philosophical literatures, if one know where to look for them. But even when one has found them and may be puzzling over their significance one must have a key by which to open them, and the Esoteric Tradition alone gives us that key.

V

Everywhere in Nature we find causal and effectual or consequential relations inseparably bound together in an unbroken chain of causation. Every force or energy is an originating cause; being a causal activity it produces consequential fruits which are its effects; and these fruits or effects are likewise in their turn energic, and therefore instantly become new causes, in their turn producing other consequential effects or fruits, and so forth for ever — which means throughout the long, long, course of the Cosmic Manvantara. Thus every evil life, or series of evil lives, is followed by a corresponding retribution; and every good and aspiring life likewise receives its exactly corresponding compensatory retribution. This retributive justice in either direction works out partly by effects corresponding to preceding causes perhaps generated aeons ago, and manifesting themselves in some succeeding reincarnation on earth, and also partly by the peregrinating Monad's going higher or going lower: that is, either into a more spiritual World or Plane or into a more material World or Plane, in the post-mortem adventures of the Monad. In either case, the Monad produces or evolves forth all the necessary faculties and powers of perception from within itself by which the reimbodying Ego, its child, contacts, and lives for the time in, such a higher or lower World or Sphere or Plane; then when the effects in either case have worked themselves out, the Ego returns in due course of time to incarnation on this earth for a new earth-life.

A most important and suggestive teaching in this connexion states that man receives in life, and in the states of being post mortem, *precisely what he had previously longed for;* for his longings and yearnings not only indicate the directions which his consciousness takes post mortem, but likewise are the energic impulses building for him the new vehicles enabling him to experience in and through them the destiny which he has builded for himself. If during his earth-life his mind be full of aspirations and his heart with yearnings for an unfettered spiritual consciousness, i. e., for the things of the spirit, for the divine splendor of the spirit, and for the grandeur of spiritual intellections, these aspirations and yearnings function as extremely powerful attractions guiding him to Spheres of type similar to what he has aspired towards or yearned for — to the so-called 'heavens' if one like to use the word. But if he yearn or long for the things of dense and gross matter, by precisely the same rule and from the same causes, he is attracted or drawn strongly to them, and thus goes to them after his death on earth. But in neither case is the dwelling or residing in the one class of worlds or in the other class of worlds eternal.

It is the sublime and luminous doctrine of Karman as taught in all its mysterious reaches by the Esoteric Philosophy which gives to us the true facts and the true explanations based on Nature herself concerning all these matters. According to this wonderful teaching, which is at once so consoling to the human heart and so illuminating to the human mind, man gets or receives in compensatory reward or in retributive purgation the precise consequences or effects flowing forth from the causes that previously he himself had called into action; which simply means that he receives retributive justice by means of the *fruit or effects of what he had previously sown.* If he have sown evil, it is suffering and pain that he will reap in the next life or in succeeding lives partly, and partly during the course of the post-mortem journey or Adventure of the Monadic soul or Reimbodying Ego; unless, indeed, the karmic consequences, or the fruits of the working of the so-called law of cause and effect, appear during the same earth-life in which the causal thoughts and acts were had or done.

In very truth man reaps exactly what he himself has sown. He is therefore the maker of his own destiny; he carves his own future career; he is the pioneer of his own wonderful pilgrimage; he is "the captain of his soul." He himself is the mysterious pathway which, when the ego is following the upward direction, leads ever more inwards and inwards into the glories of the invisible realms and spaces of spiritual consciousness; or, conversely, he himself makes himself to be the pathway in his journey downward towards the dread regions or realms of the Underworld.

The splendor of our spiritual intuitions, the grandeur of our intellectual conceptions, the widespread sympathetic understanding of the better part of our intermediate or psychic or human nature — all come from or flow forth from the inmost part of us, our own inner god. When death overtakes the physical body at any time, all this higher and grander part then returns to the fountain-head of us, our inmost Spiritual Self, whence we originally issued forth in the beginning of this Manvantara as an emanation or ray, only to reissue again after a long period of rest and spiritual bliss, to pick up the threads of earth-life again.

What thoughtful man of compassionate heart, with mind lightened from the Divine Ray within, would not accept the teachings of the Esoteric Philosophy, the Esoteric Tradition, as briefly outlined in the preceding pages, in preference to the one-sided and obviously unjust exoteric 'heavens' and 'hells' of the different popular religious systems, signifying places or localities of indefinite character: of peace and bliss on the one hand, where the righteous shall dwell through eternity with a recognition of the glory of God Almighty upon their souls, and bathing in the spiritual feeling that they are one with Him and in His holy favor; or, on the other hand, signifying places or localities where weak and imperfect souls are condemned or damned for a greater or less length of time, to endure unspeakable and theatrical torments. How narrow and unsatisfactory both these notions are, and how our souls turn in instinctive revolt from the manifest injustices in either case! As regards the heavens, would not the very angels themselves, according to the Christian system, turn in horror from such spiritual selfishness? Think of the millions and millions who have not attained such or any other heaven, and who, according to the Christian theory, the orthodox Western theory, are even now either in the vague and dimly illuminated regions of Purgatory or are undergoing the pangs and torments of inextinguishable fire, burning in unspeakable torture unto time without ending! How can there be in Eternal Justice an eternal heaven of the blissful, when such hellish conditions prevail, according to the abominable theory, elsewhere in the Universe? One can only feel that the self-isolated saint in his holy heaven lives in a very paradise of fools — and one is in truth bound to say, of very selfish fools!

There are indeed 'hells' innumerable and 'heavens' innumerable, but they are mere conditions or states of temporary spiritual compensation on the one hand, and of temporary purgation on the other hand; and, when compared with eternity, they are all but like fugitive and evanescent wisps of cloud upon the mountain-side. They come, they endure but a moment when compared with eternity, and they pass. Far greater than any such 'heaven,' than any such sphere or loka of bliss and felicity, is the grandiose vision of endless growth in faculty and power, and endless opportunity to work for the world; and every Buddhalike or Christlike man knows it.

ドイ